YELLOWSTONE & GRAND TETON

DON PITCHER

GRAND TETON NATIONAL PARK

To West Thumb and Yellowstone National Park

To Togwotee Pass and Dubois

26 / 287

BUFFALO VALLEY RD

Buffalo River

Snake River

Moran Junction

Pacific Creek

Two Ocean Lake

Emma Matilda Lake

Oxbow Bend

Signal Mountain 7,593ft

JACKSON LAKE LODGE

JACKSON LAKE DAM

SIGNAL MOUNTAIN LODGE

SIGNAL MOUNTAIN

POTHOLES TURNOUT

LEEKS MARINA

COLTER BAY

COLTER BAY VISITOR CENTER

Jackson Lake

Elk Island

FLAGG RANCH

89 191 287

Snake River

GRASSY LAKE

John D Rockefeller Jr Memorial Parkway

LIZARD CREEK

Colter Canyon

Webb Canyon

Ranger Peak 11,355ft

Waterfalls Canyon

Eagles Rest Peak 11,258ft

Bivouac Peak 10,825ft

Moose Basin

Traverse Peak 11,051ft

Mt Moran 12,605ft

Leigh Lake

Thor Peak 12,028 ft

Survey Peak 9,277ft

Moose Mtn 10,054 ft

Winegar Hole Wilderness

Caribou-Targhee National Forest

Jedediah Smith Wilderness

Bridger-Teton National Forest

GREATER YELLOWSTONE AREA

To Billings

Columbus
Joliet
Boyd
Absarokee
Cooney State Park
Fishtail
Roberts
Washoe
Red Lodge
Belfry

To Powell
Heart Mtn 8,123ft
CODY
Buffalo Bill State Park
To Thermopolis

MONTANA
WYOMING

RED LODGE MOUNTAIN

Custer National Forest

Granite Peak 12,799ft

CHIEF JOSEPH SCENIC HWY

Trout Pk 12,244ft

Shoshone National Forest

Wapiti

Valley

Nye

Cooke City
Silver Gate City

Fortress Mtn 12,085ft

North Fork Shoshone River

SLEEPING GIANT

Absaroka

Range

Yellowstone National Park

Colter Pk 10,683ft

Yellowstone Lake

Livingston
Pine Creek
Chico Hot Springs
Jardine
Corwin Springs
Miner

Gallatin National Forest

River

Tower Junction

Canyon Village

Lake Village

West Thumb

Mt Hancock 10,214ft

Bozeman
Gallatin Gateway

Emigrant

GARDINER
Mammoth Hot Springs

Norris

Madison Junction

Lewis Lake

Shoshone Lake

To Butte

Mt Holmes 10,336ft

Old Faithful

Continental Divide

Anceney

BIG SKY
Big Sky

Grayling

WEST YELLOWSTONE

Island Park

Caribou-Targhee National Forest

Gallatin Range

Madison Range

Hebgen Lake

Henrys Lake

Island Park Reservoir

McAllister
Norris
Ennis
Cameron

Ennis Lake

Madison River

Red Rock Lakes National Wildlife Refuge

Beaverhead National Forest

Gravelly Range

Contents

Discover Yellowstone & Grand Teton

If ever a place deserved the term "Wonderland," it would have to be the northwest corner of Wyoming. In this spectacularly scenic region lies the world's oldest national park – Yellowstone – along with one of the most stunning mountainscapes on the planet – Grand Teton National Park. Jackson Hole is a prosperous and bustling center for recreation and commerce; it's one of the most popular vacation destinations in North America. Beyond these three renowned areas are a wealth of attractions to please those who love the great outdoors and the West, including a world-class museum complex in Cody, gorgeous badlands topography near the Old West town of Dubois, and several delightful mountain settlements surrounding Yellowstone National Park. The region attracts more than three million visitors each year from around the globe.

The Greater Yellowstone Ecosystem is a mountainous region bisected by the Continental Divide. Several peaks – including Grand Teton – top 13,000 feet. Powerful geological forces crafted this landscape – their energy especially visible in Yellowstone. The park sits atop a geologic hotspot that caused three stupendous volcanic eruptions in the last two million years, covering thousands of square miles with ash and affecting the global climate for years thereafter.

There's no evidence that it will erupt anytime soon, but the heat from this seething cauldron creates the geysers, hot springs, and fumaroles for which Yellowstone is famous. Despite all this heat, ice and water have also played important roles. Glaciers carved out valleys such as Jackson Hole and rivers eroded the colorful Grand Canyon of the Yellowstone.

The Teton Range provides an incredible skyline that rises abruptly above Jackson Hole, a relatively flat basin through which the Snake River flows. In summer the sagebrush flats are a garden of flowers set against the mountain backdrop. Autumn turns the cottonwoods and aspens into swaths of yellow and orange, and winter transforms everything a glorious, sparkling white, set against a fluorescent blue sky.

With all the activities – from mountain biking to river rafting to gourmet dining – it's impossible to be bored here. The country is so beautiful that you may just want to kick back, tip up your new cowboy hat, and sip a Teton Ale while taking it all in. Welcome to one of the world's great wonderlands. You may never want to go home.

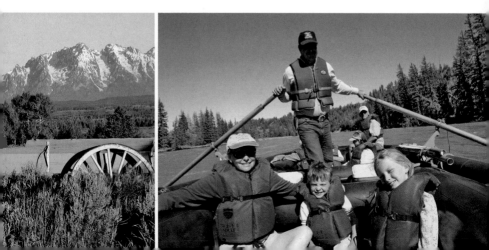

Planning Your Trip

When planning a trip to the Yellowstone area always err on the side of too much time if at all possible. Although the distances are not great, this isn't freeway driving and you'll want sufficient time to savor the sights and soak up the beauty of this magical place. If you have only a few days, pick one place and explore it well rather than trying to see all the sights. A week is sufficient time to see many regional highlights, but set aside more if you plan to visit Cody and Jackson or take a backcountry trek. Those with the time (and money) should consider booking a week at a Jackson Hole or Wapiti Valley guest ranch.

Begin planning your travels by contacting Yellowstone (307/344-7381, www.nps.gov/yell), Grand Teton (307/739-3600, www.nps.gov/grte), and the Jackson Hole Chamber of Commerce (307/733-3316, www.jacksonholechamber.com) to request publications, including park newspapers and the helpful *Yellowstone National Park Trip Planner*.

▶ WHERE TO GO

Yellowstone National Park

Yellowstone's famed Old Faithful has predictable eruptions that delight crowds every 90 minutes or so, while Mammoth Hot Springs features an ever-changing palette of softly colored springs. Bucolic Lamar Valley in the northeast corner is the best place to see wolves and other wildlife. Grand Canyon of the Yellowstone may be the park's most spectacular feature, with the river plummeting

Old Faithful Geyser

IF YOU HAVE...

- **ONE DAY:** Visit Yellowstone National Park.
- **TWO DAYS:** Add Grand Teton National Park.
- **THREE DAYS:** Add Jackson.
- **ONE WEEK:** Add Cody.
- **TWO WEEKS:** Add West Yellowstone, Cooke City, or Dubois.

308 feet over Lower Falls. South of here is Yellowstone Lake—the largest high-elevation lake in North America.

Grand Teton National Park

Capped by 13,772-foot Grand Teton, the Teton Range rises abruptly from the valley floor, with the Snake River winding sinuously beneath ragged peaks. Craig Thomas Discovery and Visitor Center provides a great introduction to the park. Two of the most picturesque areas are Jenny Lake and the old barns of Mormon Row. The Colter Bay Indian Arts Museum on the northern end of the park houses an extraordinary collection,

while Jackson Lake is popular for fishing and boating.

Jackson Hole

Wyoming's preeminent tourist town, trendy Jackson occupies the southern end of the valley called Jackson Hole. Four arches created from hundreds of elk antlers frame Town Square, host to faux shoot-outs and farmers' markets all summer. Jackson is crowded with dozens of galleries, and the National Museum of Wildlife Art is just north of town. Winter sleigh rides draw visitors to the National Elk Refuge, while skiers challenge the slopes of Jackson Hole Mountain Resort. All sorts of summer fun fill the calendar, from river rafting to classical music.

Gateways To Yellowstone

The Montana towns of West Yellowstone, Gardiner, Cooke City, and Silver Gate border Yellowstone, and visitors use them as bases for park explorations. The Wyoming towns of Cody and Dubois, east and southeast respectively, from Yellowstone, are close enough for a long day trip into the park. Cody is home to both the Buffalo Bill Historical Center and the Cody Nite Rodeo, with scenic Wapiti Valley to the west.

Buffalo Bill Historical Center

▶ WHEN TO GO

The Yellowstone region is accessible at all times of the year, but because much of this country lies above 6,000 feet in elevation, summers start late (June) and are relatively short. The vast majority of visitors to Yellowstone and Grand Teton arrive in the hectic months of July and August when the snows are gone, temperatures are warm, skies are often clear, local businesses and attractions are all open, and wildlife are readily visible.

Summer is also when many regional festivals take place, including rodeos and all sorts of other fun in the surrounding towns. But if you come in the summer you'll need to share this wonderland with other wanderers. Despite these crowds, it's surprisingly easy to find a quiet spot to escape into the wild places where few others tread.

Fall is a favorite time to visit the parks. The crowds have diminished, most businesses and campgrounds are still open, and on crisp mornings the air is filled with the bugling of elk. Autumn also means brilliant yellow and orange aspens and cottonwoods in Grand Teton and parts of Yellowstone, with the peak of color in early October. The Jackson Hole Fall Arts Festival is a major September event. Temperatures drop as fall progresses and the snow gradually moves down the mountains; most Yellowstone National Park roads are closed by early November.

Yellowstone winters are cold, snowy, and starkly beautiful. Park access is by snowcoach or guided snowmobile. Jackson Hole is a major winter destination, with three ski resorts and a wide range of winter activities.

bison and the Grand Tetons

cabin used in the film *Shane*, Grand Teton National Park

▶ BEFORE YOU GO

The vast majority of visitors arrive by car, though there are daily flights into Jackson from many major cities. You can also fly into a regional airport such as Salt Lake City, Utah or Billings, Montana and rent a car. Bus service is very limited. Most national chains offer car rentals in Jackson, with fewer options in the towns of Cody and West Yellowstone. Public transportation within the parks is virtually nonexistent.

Lodging reservations are highly recommended for midsummer travel throughout the region, especially over holiday weekends. Reserve well ahead of your trip for the best options. Winters can also be busy, particularly in Jackson over the Christmas–New Year's holiday period. Some of the most in-demand lodges fill months ahead of time.

What To Take

When you visit dictates what you need to bring. Summers in the mountains are mild (often in the 70s and 80s °F, and often gloriously sunny (with afternoon thunderstorms). Shorts and Tevas are ubiquitous, but bring pants and long-sleeved shirts for cooler evenings. Carry a light Gore-Tex jacket for rainy days or on-the-water trips. For other seasons, bring several layers of noncotton clothing to adjust to varying temperatures. If you plan to spend time in Yellowstone in midwinter, come prepared; the thermometer at Old Faithful once hit -66°F!

As a general rule, keep it casual. A few of the fanciest restaurants in Jackson Hole and Grand Teton require a sports jacket or tie, and you may feel like Michael Moore at a Republican fund-raiser if you show up wearing shorts and a tie-dyed T-shirt when others are dressed for a night out. For summer travel, pack comfortable walking shoes, sunglasses, a hat, sunscreen, insect repellent, and prescription medications. Be sure to bring a bathing suit even if you don't plan to swim in local lakes or pools—many hotels and B&Bs have hot tubs.

Explore Yellowstone & Grand Teton

▶ BEST OF YELLOWSTONE & GRAND TETON

This summertime trip provides a wonderful introduction to the region, following a circular loop that begins in Cody and takes in the Yellowstone sights before heading south into Grand Teton National Park and Jackson, over to the Wind River Valley town of Dubois, and then north through Bighorn Basin back to your starting point. Cody is accessible by non-stop flights from Denver and Salt Lake City, and car rentals are available at the airport.

Day 1

Cody provides an excellent base for travelers en route to Yellowstone, with good lodging and restaurants, plenty to do, and lots of warm, sunny weather. Settle into a hotel or bed-and-breakfast (Cody Lodging Company rents guest houses that are perfect for families) and take a look around the downtown shops. You may want to book a raft trip down the Shoshone River or watch the evening gunfight in front of Buffalo Bill's famous Irma Hotel, but be sure to get seats for Cody Nite Rodeo, one of the finest rodeos in the region. Nearby is Trail Town, a fascinating collection of historic log structures—including one used by Butch Cassidy and the Sundance Kid.

Day 2

Cody's acclaimed Buffalo Bill Historical Center could easily take several days to fully explore. This massive building actually houses five separate collections: the Buffalo Bill Museum, the Whitney Gallery of Western Art, the Plains Indian Museum, the Cody Firearms Museum, and the Draper Museum of Natural History. It may be a bit overwhelming, but the ticket lets you return a second day at no extra charge. Enjoy lunch or dinner at one of the better local restaurants such as Mayor's Inn or Wyoming Rib and Chop House.

Day 3

Saddle up and head northwest to Yellowstone via Chief Joseph Scenic Highway, which climbs over Dead Indian Pass before dropping through national forest lands to the rustic Montana towns of Cooke City and Silver Gate. If you have the time, drive spectacular Beartooth Highway to the top of 10,947-foot Beartooth Pass for an alpine walk. Back on the main route, continue into Yellowstone National Park, stopping for the night at Pebble Creek Campground in

Trail Town, Cody

the northeast corner, a great spot for wildlife watching. Both Silver Gate and Cooke City also have comfortable motel and cabin options.

An alternate, and quicker, way into Yellowstone from Cody is to head due west through lush Wapiti Valley, along the Shoshone River. Travel through the bizarre rock formations and forested slopes within Shoshone National Forest, past Buffalo Bill's old summer home at Pahaska Tepee, and over Sylvan Pass to the Yellowstone Lake area.

Day 4

Today is a full day of seeing Yellowstone's sights. Drive west to Mammoth Hot Springs (two hours including a short stop to watch wildlife in Lamar Valley). Stroll the boardwalks at the colorful terraces, check out historical photos in the visitor center, and get lunch before turning south to Norris Geyser Basin. Take in the Back Basin loop to see if Echinus Geyser is active, or head down Porcelain Basin to take in the ever-changing colors. In the afternoon, drive the dozen miles to Grand Canyon of the Yellowstone, with its spectacular waterfalls and multihued canyon walls. An evening hike along one of the rim trails makes a great way to end the day. Lodging and campsites are in Canyon Village.

Day 5

Continue exploring Yellowstone by driving south through lush Hayden Valley (pull out your binoculars to glass for bears or wolves) to Yellowstone Lake, where you can take a one-hour boat cruise and enjoy lunch at historic Lake Yellowstone Hotel. The road continues another 21 miles southwest along the lake shore to West Thumb, where you may want to stop for a brief look at the hot springs and other features before turning west to explore famous Old Faithful Geyser and Upper Geyser Basin area (including Old Faithful Inn). It will probably be midafternoon by this point. There's no camping at Old Faithful, but excellent lodging options are available nearby, or you could backtrack to West Thumb and south to the campground at Lewis Lake.

Comfortable Flagg Ranch Resort has cabins a few miles outside the southern edge of Yellowstone.

Day 6

Drive south into Grand Teton National Park to take in the spectacular mountain vistas and explore a few of the sights. Stop first at the Craig Thomas Discovery and Visitor Center for an orientation to the park and its history. Several local companies offer Snake River float trips for an on-the-water introduction, or you can rent a bike and head up the paved bike path to Jenny Lake, a wonderful jumping-off point for hikes. Overnight at a park campground (Jenny Lake is especially notable) or lodge.

Day 7

Another day in Grand Teton, this time with a focus on the less-traveled east side of the park, including the photo-perfect barns of Mormon Row, before heading out of the park into remote Gros Ventre Valley, and down to bustling Jackson where you bed down for the night. There are innumerable lodging and

ONE DAY IN YELLOWSTONE

The three most popular attractions in Yellowstone are Old Faithful, Mammoth Hot Springs and the Grand Canyon of the Yellowstone. One could easily spend a full day in each of these areas, but it is possible to make quick visits to all three while circling through the park. The following itinerary assumes you are coming in from West Yellowstone. Get an early start on the day since you'll need to cover a lot of ground and the park speed limit is only 35 miles an hour.

Old Faithful: Your first stop will be the world's best-known geyser which erupts approximately every 90 minutes. Drop by the visitor center to see the next predicted eruption and explore the area in the interim. Paved paths lead to nearby geysers, hot springs, and other features. Several interesting buildings are in the area, most notably **Old Faithful Inn,** built more than a century ago and still one of the largest log structures in the world.

Mammoth Hot Springs: Drive north from Old Faithful Geyser, stopping briefly to see the colorful bubbling mud and active small geysers at **Fountain Paint Pot.** You might also have time for fascinating **Norris Geyser Basin,** the hottest such basin in North America. When you reach Mammoth Hot Springs, take a quick tour of Albright Visitor Center, then turn your car east for the drive to **Tower Fall,** where a steep trail leads 0.5 mile downhill to the base of this pretty waterfall.

Grand Canyon of the Yellowstone: The road south from Tower Fall crosses 8,859-foot Dunraven Pass before dropping to this spectacular canyon. The most famous vista point (don't miss this one) is **Artist Point** on the south side, but others on both sides provide more options, including a steep trail that leads to the top of Lower Falls (twice the height of Niagara Falls).

Now it's time to circle back to your starting point. If it's already late in the day, drive directly back to West Yellowstone via Norris and Madison, but if there are still a couple of hours of daylight, continue south to **Lake Yellowstone** for a big dinner or sunset drink at historic **Lake Yellowstone Hotel** before continuing on to the town of West Yellowstone.

Town Square shootout in Jackson

dining choices in Jackson. Bubba's Bar-B-Que has great family fare; Cadillac Grille or Snake River Grill are fine upscale choices.

Day 8

Take this day to appreciate Jackson Hole. Explore the downtown shops and galleries, take in an evening rodeo, visit the National Wildlife Museum, ride the tram up Mt. Rendezvous at Jackson Hole Resort, laugh at the corny shoot-out, and get your photo taken in front of the famed elk antler arches surrounding Town Square. You'll quickly see why Jackson is such a destination.

Day 9

Take the main highway (U.S. Hwy. 26/89/191) north to Moran Junction before heading east over scenic Togwotee Pass (9,658 feet) and down to the quaint cowboy town of Dubois, where you've reserved one of the classic 1930s cabins at Twin Pines Lodge. Savor a creekside dinner at Sundance Café.

Day 10

This day takes us out of the Yellowstone area and through the badlands and green pastures of the Wind River Reservation, stopping at the town of Lander for lunch before turning north through Shoshoni (great malts at Yellowstone Drug Store) and Thermopolis (Wyoming's best hot springs), before finally rolling back to Cody. This is an all-day 235-mile drive, and if you have the time, be sure to add a night in Thermopolis at the beautiful Plaza Hotel.

▶ CAMPING AND HIKING IN THE TETONS

This five-day car tour is perfect for families and those who prefer to camp in the great outdoors. Some of the activities described below are a bit pricey, and it's easy to spend a small (or large) fortune visiting Jackson Hole, but it is also possible to have a wonderful time without breaking the bank if you cook your own meals and keep costly activities to a minimum. Even if you're on a tight budget, do try to choose at least one splurge.

Day 1

Choose from five campgrounds within Grand Teton National Park or several others on nearby Bridger-Teton National Forest. A quiet out-of-the-way choice is Gros Ventre Campground in the park, but many visitors prefer Jenny Lake Campground for its central location and wonderfully scenic setting. Once you're set up, drive to the park's Craig Thomas Discovery and Visitor Center for details on the park, maps, brochures, and guidebooks. The $25 per vehicle entrance fee covers both Yellowstone and Grand Teton for seven days. Just across the river in Moose are several Dornan's shops, with groceries, a great wine shop, inexpensive meals, and outdoor gear—including bike and canoe rentals. A nice evening drive is the winding road to the 7,593-foot summit of Signal Mountain, where the panorama encompasses the majestic Teton Range, Jackson Lake, Snake River, and the long valley called Jackson Hole.

Day 2

This is a day to explore Grand Teton. Starting from Jenny Lake, take the park road north to Jackson Lake. If you like to fish or boat, stop at one of the marinas; the largest is Colter Bay Marina, which offers scenic cruises, boat and kayak rentals, and guided fishing on this large reservoir. Not far away is the very impressive Colter Bay Indian Arts Museum and the grandiose Jackson Lake Lodge, built at the behest of John D. Rockefeller (who also played a big role in establishing Grand Teton National Park). A couple of loop trails near Colter Bay provide an escape from the summertime crowds and the chance to look for moose and trumpeter swans. Pull off for the view at Oxbow Bend before continuing south on U.S. Hwy. 26/89/191 to the old Cunningham homesteader cabin and a couple of spectacular turnouts facing the Tetons, including Snake River Overlook, where Ansel Adams took his famous photo. A side road down to Schwabacher Landing is equally popular with photographers at dawn and dusk. Turn east onto Antelope Flats Road for another photo op, this time of the picturesque barns along Mormon Row. Next stop is pretty Chapel of the Transfiguration near the Craig Thomas Discovery and Visitor Center, and our final stop is Jenny Lake, where you began the day.

Day 3

The booming town of Jackson is today's destination. Stop by the sod-roofed Jackson Hole and Greater Yellowstone Visitor Center for a plethora of brochures and a helpful staff to answer your questions. You can't miss shady Town Square with its four elk-antler arches, but you may need to park in the big lot a couple of blocks to the north. Evening shoot-outs are a summer favorite here, and several dozen art galleries (and many other businesses) fill nearby

horses near Jackson

Million Dollar Cowboy Bar and elk antler arch in downtown Jackson

JACKSON HOLE FOR KIDS

Those traveling with children will find an abundance of kid-friendly options in Jackson Hole. A few noteworthy examples include:

- the hands-on **Children's Discovery Gallery** at the **National Museum of Wildlife Art**
- playgrounds at **Mike Yokel Jr. Park** (Kelly and Hall streets), **Miller Park** (Powderhorn Lane and Maple Way), and **Baux Park** (base of Snow King Mountain)
- the excellent swimming pool and corkscrew water slide at the **Teton County Recreation Center**
- the fine children's section of the library
- chuckwagon dinners at **Bar-T-Five** or **Bar J**
- pizzas at the **Calico** (where the lawn is great for kids)
- comedies and melodramas at **Jackson Hole Playhouse** or **Off-Square Theatre Company**
- the **Alpine Slide** at **Snow King Resort**
- the chairlifts at **Jackson Hole Resort**
- the evening shoot-outs at **Town Square**

- horseback or wagon rides
- a trip to the fish hatchery
- a night at the rodeo (including the kids-only calf chase)
- a boat ride and hike at **Jenny Lake** inside Grand Teton National Park
- day camp at the recreation center (grades 1-6)

young cowpoke in Jackson

shops. Just north of town is the outstanding National Museum of Wildlife Art. For a great half-day adventure, book an easy float or rollicking whitewater raft trip down the Snake River; there are a dozen local companies to choose from. Back in town, travelers will find an amazing variety of dining choices, including an outstanding brewpub, hip espresso joints, natural-food lunches, some of the best steaks you've ever tasted, and even a couple of Thai eateries. Don't miss the Million Dollar Cowboy Bar with its saddle barstools and nightly country-and-western bands. Directly behind town is Snow King Resort, with a summertime lift (great for hikers and mountain bikers), plus a kids-love-it alpine slide. Twice-weekly rodeos are another favorite family activity. Take the scenic route back to Jenny Lake by driving to Teton Village to check out

the activities, including hourly horseback rides, an all-summer classical music series, a climbing wall, and chairlift rides to the alpine. Narrow and winding Moose-Wilson Road continues north from here into the park, providing potential hikes along the way.

Day 4

After you see the local sights, it is a good time to get out on foot. The Craig Thomas Discovery and Visitor Center has details on many short—and long—park hikes, including one of the most popular, to Inspiration Point. This one begins with a shuttle boat ride across Jenny Lake. It's a 0.5 mile hike to Hidden Falls, and another steep 0.5 mile to the top of a 400-foot hill overlooking the lake. Beyond this, other trails continue to nearby lakes or high into the Tetons.

Day 5

Four days in Jackson Hole have barely scratched the surface of this fascinating and scenic place. You may want to return to a spot you missed, or check out something different such as remote Gros Ventre River Valley, Teton Pass for some high-country hiking, or back into Jackson for a day of shopping and play.

▶ WHERE THE BUFFALO ROAM

Yellowstone and Grand Teton provide world-class opportunities to see wildlife, and many visitors consider the chance to see bison, elk, wolves, bears, moose, and other large mammals the highlight of their trips. Early morning and early evening usually provide the best wildlife-viewing opportunities in the summer. At other times of the year they tend to be equally visible in the middle of the day. Bring a pair of binoculars and telephoto lenses for a close-up view, but make sure your behavior isn't disturbing the animal or causing it to move away. Always stay at least 25 yards from wildlife and 100 yards from bears. Do not block traffic if you are stopping to see an animal. Check with Yellowstone and Grand Teton visitor centers for details on recent wildlife sightings and handouts showing where you're most likely to find them. Below are a few of the best spots.

A number of regional companies offer wildlife-viewing tours in Yellowstone and Grand Teton national parks. One of the best is Wildlife Expeditions, operated by the nonprofit Teton Science School. Another nonprofit group, Yellowstone Association Institute, leads private wildlife tours in Yellowstone plus very popular three-day wolf-discovery adventures.

bighorn sheep, Yellowstone National Park

Yellowstone National Park
NORTHEAST CORNER

In the remote northeast corner of Yellowstone, Lamar Valley is a great place to look for wildlife of all types, from the ubiquitous ground squirrels to an occasional grizzly. Elk, pronghorn antelope, and large herds of bison are commonly seen, and coyotes are often sighted, but the main attraction is wolves. Several wolf packs occupy this area, including the often-seen Druid Peak Pack, and wolf aficionados hang out on nearby slopes for a glimpse of the wolves. You can rent a spotting scope in Silver Gate, just outside the park's northeast boundary.

MAMMOTH AREA

Despite the crowds of people at this popular

YELLOWSTONE
WILDLIFE VIEWING AREA

Old Faithful and in other parts of the Upper Geyser Basin, and the slow-moving bison often create traffic jams when they decide to use the main roads as trails. In the winter this is a great place to watch bison plowing snow with their massive heads to get at the vegetation beneath. Both elk and bison spend considerable time along the Firehole River and in the hot springs areas to stay warm when temperatures plummet.

Grand Teton National Park
OXBOW BEND AND WILLOW FLATS

Near Moran Junction, this slow-moving loop off the Snake River is a great place to watch for swimming beavers, muskrats, and river otters, or for moose browsing on willows along the shore. Also keep your eyes open for birds—bald eagles, white pelicans, ospreys, and others. The best times to see animals are in the early morning or at dusk. Rent a canoe from Dornan's in Moose to paddle around Oxbow Bend. Another excellent place to scan for moose and elk is Willow Flats, a marshy area just up from Jackson Lake Dam.

corner of the park, Mammoth is also a good place to find wild animals. Elk are almost always somewhere in the area, particularly in the fall when the males' bugling keeps hotel guests awake at night. Pronghorn antelope are fairly common, particularly along the one-way Old Gardiner Road, and bighorn sheep are often seen on steep hillsides between Mammoth and Gardiner. Look for moose in the Willow Park area 10 miles south of Mammoth, especially in the fall.

HAYDEN VALLEY

This lovely open valley south of Canyon is a mix of grasses and sage, with occasional lodgepole pines. It's a great place to see grazing bison and elk, plus the occasional grizzly, especially on the east side of the valley. Waterfowl, including Canada geese, trumpeter swans, pelicans, and many kinds of ducks are plentiful in marshes and along the Yellowstone River. Stop at LeHardys Rapids in June and July to see spawning cutthroat trout.

UPPER GEYSER BASIN

Elk and bison are almost always visible near

GRAND TETON
WILDLIFE VIEWING AREA

MORMON ROW

This part of the park is best known for the photo-friendly barns backdropped by the Tetons, but you will often find a herd of bison in the open country nearby. The back roads connecting Mormon Row with Kelly are excellent places to find pronghorn antelope.

TETON PARK ROAD

This scenic road follows a beautiful sage-brush-covered plateau with stands of lodge-pole pines and aspens. Pronghorn antelope and Uinta ground squirrels are here, along with elk (especially in the fall), and some bison. Southwest of the visitor center is the narrow and winding Moose-Wilson Road (not for RVs), where you may encounter moose, mule deer, or an occasional black bear.

NATIONAL ELK REFUGE

In the summer this is a good place to see trumpeter swans, particularly near the Jackson Hole Visitor Center. You may see elk and other animals in the summer here, but winter is the main attraction, with horse-drawn sleighs carrying visitors among thousands of elk on the feeding grounds here.

SAY CHEESE: TOP 10 PHOTO OPS

Okay, this one's rather subjective, but the following are good starting points for your photo safari.

- **Grand Canyon of the Yellowstone** from Artist Point
- **Old Faithful** at sunset
- Colorful **Palette Springs** at Mammoth Hot Springs
- **Bugling elk** in the fall within Grand Teton National Park
- Early morning at **Schwabacher Landing** along the Snake River
- **Moulton Barn** on Mormon Row
- **Snake River Overlook**
- **Oxbow Bend** and **Mt. Moran** with fall colors
- Horses at **Triangle X Ranch**
- **Elk antler arches** at Jackson Hole (with your kids, of course)

photographers at Schwabacher Landing along the Snake River

YELLOWSTONE NATIONAL PARK

The words "national park" seem to stimulate an almost Pavlovian response: Yellowstone. The geysers, canyons, and bears of Yellowstone National Park are so intertwined in our collective consciousness that even 1960s American cartoons used the park as a model: Jellystone Park, where Yogi Bear and Boo Boo were constantly out to thwart the rangers. One source estimated that nearly one-third of the U.S. population has visited the park, and each year three million people roll through its gates.

There is something about Yellowstone National Park that calls people back again and again, something more than simply the chance to see the curiosities of the natural world. Generations of parents have brought their children to see the place that they recall from their own childhood visits. Other cultures have the Ganges River, Rome, or Mecca as places with deep spiritual meaning. In America, our national parks have become places for similar renewal, and as the nation's first national park, Yellowstone remains one of our most valued treasures.

So, into the park we come in our cars with our crying babies in the back—babies who suddenly quiet down at the sight of a bison or elk. I recall bringing relatives to Yellowstone after I had worked in the vicinity all summer and had become a bit jaded. Their emotional reaction surprised me, and more than a decade later they still tell stories of the bison calves, the astounding geysers, the rush of the waterfalls, and the night they spent at Old Faithful Inn. Yellowstone is a collective religious experience that sends us back to our roots in the

© DON PITCHER

HIGHLIGHTS

◖ Norris Geyser Basin: Yellowstone's hottest and oldest geyser basin is home to the world's tallest geyser (but don't wait for an eruption, or you may be here for years). Echinus Geyer is the real crowd-pleaser (page 45).

◖ Mammoth Hot Springs: Ever-changing, with water trickling over multihued terraces, Mammoth is a moving watercolor painting. Albright Visitor Center houses an interesting museum (page 47).

◖ Wildlife-Viewing: Peaceful and away from the big Yellowstone sights, the Northeast Corner is not only a good place to see bison and elk, but wolves as well (page 54).

◖ Tower Fall: Located in the northern end of the park, this very accessible 132-foot waterfall is a short walk from the parking lot (page 55).

◖ Grand Canyon of the Yellowstone: No adjectives can really describe the power and beauty of this painted canyon where the Yellowstone River drops over two high waterfalls. Lots of viewpoints from all angles, but acrophobics should avoid the Brink of the Lower Falls (page 55).

◖ Mud Volcano Area: Think of this as a bad case of geological heartburn. The names tell all: Dragon's Mouth Spring, Churning Caldron, and Sulphur Caldron (page 58).

◖ Yellowstone Lake: America's largest high-elevation lake occupies an ancient volcanic caldera. Boat tours and fishing are popular, or just relax with a drink inside historic Lake Yellowstone Hotel's Sunset Room (page 59).

◖ Old Faithful: This is the big enchilada. The eruptions are more-or-less predictable, always crowded, and always fun. But don't

miss the many other sights in the area, particularly Riverside Geyser and Morning Glory Pool (page 65).

◖ Old Faithful Inn: This massive log structure is Yellowstone's most majestic lodge and a delightful place to soak up the ambience. Don't miss it (page 67).

◖ Midway Geyser Basin: The featured attractions are spectacular Great Fountain Geyser and brilliantly colored Grand Prismatic Spring, Yellowstone's largest at 370 feet across (page 73).

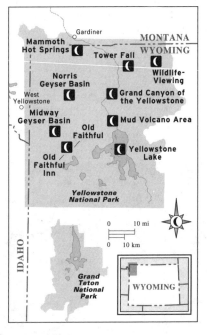

LOOK FOR ◖ TO FIND RECOMMENDED SIGHTS, ACTIVITIES, DINING, AND LODGING.

natural world. The smell of wood smoke from a campfire, the picnic lunch on the shore of Yellowstone Lake, the backcountry horseback ride, the hike down to the lip of Lower Falls, the quick strike of a trout on the line, the gasp of the crowd as the first spurt of Old Faithful jets upward, the herds of bison wading Firehole River, the evening piano tunes drifting through the air at Lake Yellowstone Hotel, the howl of a distant wolf, and even the cheesy Yellowstone trinkets—all of these things combine to leave an indelible mark on visitors to Yellowstone National Park.

PLANNING YOUR TIME

America's first and most famous national park, Yellowstone is the primary regional destination. Travelers often take a cursory tour of the park in a single day, but try to set aside a minimum of three days to discover this diverse and geologically fascinating place. If you have only a day or two, pick a couple of spots and see them right. Don't just check out the views everyone else sees; find a nearby trail and do a

little exploring on your own. It would be easy to spend a full week in Yellowstone, plus another week in nearby Grand Teton National Park and Jackson Hole. Before visiting, contact Yellowstone (307/344-7381, www.nps.gov/yell) for a copy of the park newspaper and other information.

For geyser action, check out the **Norris Geyser Basin,** home to Steamboat Geyser, which blasts 300 feet into the air on its extremely rare eruptions. **Old Faithful** is the most famous of dozens of geysers, hot springs, and other geothermal features that fill Upper Geyser Basin, the largest concentration of geysers in the world. The equally acclaimed **Old Faithful Inn** is a delightful century-old log structure. Stay for a meal or a night, or just step inside to soak up the ambience. Five miles north of Old Faithful, take time to visit **Midway Geyser Basin** with its massive Grand Prismatic Spring, the park's largest hot spring.

Mammoth Hot Springs, home to park headquarters and a small, interesting museum,

© DON PITCHER

Liberty Cap at Mammoth Hot Springs

YELLOWSTONE

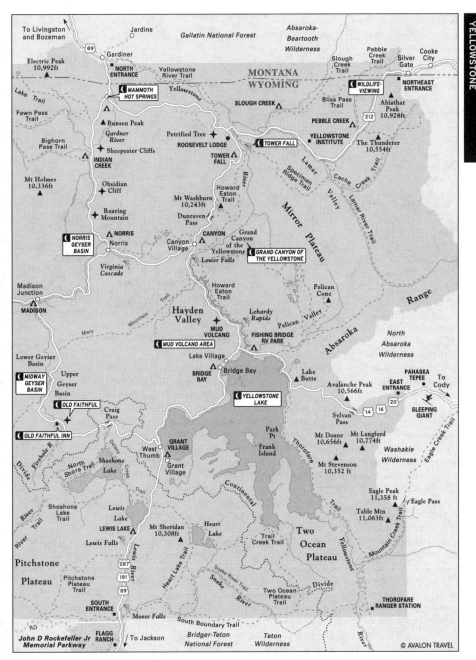

To Livingston and Bozeman
Jardine
Gallatin National Forest
Absaroka-Beartooth Wilderness
89
Gardiner
NORTH ENTRANCE
Electric Peak 10,992ft
Lake Trail
Fawn Pass Trail
Yellowstone River Trail
MONTANA
WYOMING
Pebble Creek Trail
Silver Gate
Cooke City
Slough Creek Trail
WILDLIFE-VIEWING
NORTHEAST ENTRANCE
212
Abiathar Peak 10,928ft
MAMMOTH HOT SPRINGS
Yellowstone
Bunsen Peak
Gardner River
Sheepeater Cliffs
INDIAN CREEK
Bighorn Pass Trail
Petrified Tree
ROOSEVELT LODGE
TOWER FALL
SLOUGH CREEK
PEBBLE CREEK
Bliss Pass Trail
YELLOWSTONE INSTITUTE
The Thunderer 10,554ft
Mt Holmes 10,336ft
Obsidian Cliff
TOWER FALL
Howard Eaton Trail
River
Specimen Ridge Trail
Lamar
Cache Creek Trail
Lamar River Trail
Roaring Mountain
Mt Washburn 10,243ft
Dunraven Pass
NORRIS GEYSER BASIN
NORRIS
Norris
Virginia Cascade
CANYON
Canyon Village
Grand Canyon of the Yellowstone
Lower Falls
GRAND CANYON OF THE YELLOWSTONE
Mirror Plateau
Lamar Valley
Range
Madison Junction
MADISON
Mary
Mountain
Trail
Hayden Valley
Howard Eaton Trail
Lehardy Rapids
MUD VOLCANO
MUD VOLCANO AREA
Pelican Valley
Pelican Cone
North Absaroka Wilderness
Absaroka
FISHING BRIDGE RV PARK
Lower Geyser Basin
MIDWAY GEYSER BASIN
Upper Geyser Basin
OLD FAITHFUL
Craig Pass
OLD FAITHFUL INN
Firehole R.
Divide
Lake Village
BRIDGE BAY
Bridge Bay
Lake Butte
YELLOWSTONE LAKE
Avalanche Peak 10,566ft
PAHASKA TEPEE
EAST ENTRANCE
14 16 20
SLEEPING GIANT
To Cody
North Shore Trail
Delacy Creek
Shoshone Lake
Trail
WEST THUMB
GRANT VILLAGE
Grant Village
Park Pt
Frank Island
Thorofare
Sylvan Pass
Mt Doane 10,656ft
Mt Langford 10,774ft
Washakie Wilderness
Shoshone Lake Trail
Lewis Lake
LEWIS LAKE
Mt Sheridan 10,308ft
Heart Lake
Continental
Mt Stevenson 10,352 ft
Eagle Peak 11,358 ft
Eagle Pass
Eagle Creek Trail
River Trail
Lewis Falls
Lewis River
Heart Lake Trail
Trail Creek Trail
Two Ocean Plateau
Yellowstone
Table Mtn 11,063ft
Mountain Creek Trail
Pitchstone Plateau
Pitchstone Plateau Trail
287 191 89
Snake River Trail
Snake River
Two Ocean Plateau Trail
Divide
THOROFARE RANGER STATION
SOUTH ENTRANCE
Moose Falls
South Boundary Trail
Bridger-Teton National Forest
Teton Wilderness
River
John D Rockefeller Jr Memorial Parkway
FLAGG RANCH
RD
To Jackson
© AVALON TRAVEL

is famous for its ever-changing palette of softly colored springs. The bucolic **northeast corner** is a good place to see bison, elk, and wolves, and nearby **Tower Fall** provides a great photo op.

The park's most spectacular feature may be the **Grand Canyon of the Yellowstone** with the river plummeting 308 feet over Lower Falls. South of here is Hayden Valley (look for bison, elk, and occasional bears), along with the belching geysers and hot springs of **Mud Volcano,** and **Yellowstone Lake,** the largest high-elevation lake in North America. On its north shore is the picturesque and graceful Lake Yellowstone Hotel.

THE SETTING

On a map, Yellowstone appears as a gigantic box wedged so tightly against the northwest corner of Wyoming that it squeezes over into Montana and Idaho. The park measures 63 by 54 miles and covers 2.2 million acres, making it one of the largest national parks in the Lower 48 (although it is dwarfed by Alaska's Wrangell-St. Elias National Park and Preserve, which covers almost six times as much land). The United Nations has declared Yellowstone both a World Biosphere Reserve and a World Heritage Site.

The park is accessible from all four sides, and a loop road provides easy access to all of the best-known sights. Because of its popularity as a destination, tourist towns surround Yellowstone: Jackson to the south, Cody to the east, Gardiner and Cooke City on the northern margin, and West Yellowstone on its western border. Also because so many people visit the park, there is a well-developed network of facilities inside the park, including visitor centers, campgrounds, hotels, restaurants, a hospital, gift shops, ATMs, one-hour photo shops, espresso stands, and other supposed necessities of modern life. Although less than 2 percent of the park is developed, Yellowstone contains more than 2,000 buildings of various types. In some spots (most egregiously around Old Faithful), these developments have grown to the point that the natural world seems simply

Three million people roll through Yellowstone's gates each year.

© DON PITCHER

a backdrop for the human world that pulls visitors in to buy T-shirts or to watch park slide shows on wildlife or geysers while missing the real thing just outside the door.

More than any other national park, Yellowstone seems to provide the oddities of nature, creating, as historian Aubrey L. Haines noted, "a false impression that the park is only a colossal, steam-operated freak show." Yellowstone is a mix of the real and the unreal, a place where our fantasies of what nature should be blend with the reality of crowds of fellow travelers and the impact we have on the place we love so much. In midsummer, a trip into Yellowstone can be something less than a natural experience. Long lines of cars back up behind RVs creeping up the narrow roads, and throngs of visitors crowd the benches around Old Faithful Geyser waiting for an eruption, while dozens of others cluster around bewildered elk to get photos to email their friends. Despite this crowding—or perhaps because most folks prefer to stay on paved paths—many parts of the park remain virtually uninhabited. In the Yellowstone backcountry, one can still walk for days without seeing more than a handful of other hardy hikers.

A PLACE OF CONTROVERSY

Yellowstone National Park evokes a torrent of emotions in anyone with a knowledge of and concern for the natural world. Perhaps more than any other wild place in America, the park seems to be in a perpetual state of controversy, be it over fire policies, bison and wolf management, snowmobile use, or some other issue; there's always something getting folks stirred up. Perhaps it is because so many Americans have visited the park that we feel a vested interest in what it means to us. Writer Paul Schullery in his wonderful book *Searching for Yellowstone* put it best when he noted, "Caring for Yellowstone National Park brings to mind all the metaphors of growth and change; it is a process more organic than political; a crucible of ideas, ambitions, dreams, and belief systems; a cultural, intellectual, and spiritual crossroads at which we are forever debating which way to turn." As visitation has risen in recent decades, more and more folks have begun to suggest some sort of limit on numbers to preserve the experience and protect the park. Don't-tread-on-me Westerners consider the idea of limits an example of environmental extremism for the elite, but as visitation increases conflicts and controversies are natural outcomes.

Geology

Yellowstone is, without a doubt, the most geologically fascinating place on this planet. Here the forces that elsewhere lie deep within the earth seem close enough to touch. They're palpable not only in the geysers and hot springs but also in the lake that fills part of an enormous caldera, the earthquakes that shake this land, the evidence of massive glaciations, and the deeply eroded Grand Canyon of the Yellowstone.

FIRE AND ICE
The Yellowstone Hotspot

When geologists began to study the Yellowstone area in depth, they found a surprising pattern. Extending far to the southwest was a chain of volcanic fields, the most ancient of which—16 million years old—lay in northern Nevada. In addition, geologic fault lines created a 100-mile-wide semicircle around the Yellowstone area, as if some deep-seated force were pushing the land outward and upward the way a ripple moves across a pond.

Both the volcanic activity and the wavelike pattern of faults are caused by the same source: a plume of superheated material moving up from the core of the planet through a narrow tube, creating a hot spot beneath the earth's crust. As the North American continent slid to the southwest through the eons, this plume traced a line of volcanoes across the West, and as the land continues to move, the plume causes massive deformations in the crust that show up as mountain ranges, fault lines, and earthquakes. It's a little like somebody tugging a piece of cloth across a candle. Approximately 40 such hot spots are known to exist around the globe, but most are beneath the seas. Other than Yellowstone, the best-known example is the chain of Hawaiian Islands. The earth has been moving over the Yellowstone hot spot at the rate of 15 miles per million years for the last 10 million years, and on the present track, the spot might eventually end up in Hudson Bay in 100 million years or so. Don't hold your breath.

Tambora on Steroids

The volcanic activity revealed by Yellowstone's geysers, hot springs, and fumaroles is not always benign. Within the last two million years there have been three stupendous volcanic eruptions in the area, the most recent taking place 640,000 years ago. The largest of these eruptions took place two million years ago and created an event beyond the realm of imagination: 600 cubic miles of ash were blasted into the atmosphere! This eruption—probably one of the largest to ever occur on earth—ejected 17 times more material than the massive Tambora eruption of 1815, an explosion that was heard 1,600 miles away. Compared to an explosion that is better known to Americans, the 1980 eruption of Mt. St. Helens, the first Yellowstone event was 2,400 times as large. Ash from this first Yellowstone eruption carried east to Iowa, north to Saskatchewan, south to the Gulf of Mexico, and west to California. This titanic infusion of ash into the atmosphere undoubtedly affected the global climate for years to follow.

The process that creates these explosions starts when molten rock pushes up from the center of the earth, bulging the land upward into an enormous dome. Eventually the pressure becomes too great and fractures develop around the dome's margins, sending hot gases, ash, and rock blasting into the atmosphere. After the most recent eruption (640,000 years ago), the magma chamber collapsed into a gigantic, smoldering pit reaching 28 by 47 miles in surface area and perhaps several thousand feet deep. Through time, additional molten rock pushed up from underneath and flowed as thick lava over the land. The most recent of these lava flows was 70,000 years ago.

Two resurgent domes—one near Old Faithful and the other just north of Yellowstone Lake near LeHardys Rapids—have been discovered by geologists. Measurements at LeHardys Rapids showed that the land rose almost three feet from 1923 to 1985, before subsiding again until 2004, when the land began to rise rapidly—as much as 17 cm (6.7 inches) in just three years. This upsurge is raising the outlet of Yellowstone Lake, creating new beaches on the north shore while flooding forests along the lake's southern margins. Obviously, Yellowstone's volcanism is far from dead, and scientists believe another eruption is

possible or even likely, although nobody knows when it might occur.

The **Yellowstone Volcano Observatory** (http://volcanoes.usgs.gov/yvo)—a partnership of the USGS, Park Service, and University of Utah—monitors Yellowstone's ever-changing volcanic system and produces an excellent small publication about the park's geologic origins; find it in visitor centers.

Glaciation

Not everything in Yellowstone is the result of volcanic activity. The entire Yellowstone region has undergone a series of at least eight major glaciations during the last million years, the last of which—the Pinedale Glaciation—began about 70,000 years ago. At its peak, the Pinedale Glaciation covered almost all of Yellowstone and reached southward into Jackson Hole and north much of the way to Livingston, Montana. Over Yellowstone Lake

FIREHOLE RIVER AREA, 1839

At this place there is also large numbers of hot Springs some of which have formed cones of limestone 20 feet high of a Snowy whiteness which make a splendid appearance standing among the ever green pines Some of the lower peaks are very serviceable to the hunter in preparing his dinner when hungry for here his kettle is always ready and boiling his meat being suspended in the water by a string is soon prepared for his meal without further trouble...Standing upon an eminence and superficially viewing these natural monuments one is half inclined to believe himself in the neighborhood of the ruins of some ancients City whose temples had been constructed of the whitest marble.

Mountain man Osborne Russell

the ice field was 4,000 feet thick and covered 10,000-foot mountains. This period of glaciation ended about 15,000 years ago, but trees did not appear in the Yellowstone area until 11,500 years ago, and it wasn't until about 5,000 years ago that the landscape began to appear as it does today.

GEYSERS

Yellowstone is famous for geysers, and geyser-gazers will not be disappointed. At least 60 percent of the world's geysers are in the park, making this easily the largest and most diverse collection in existence. Yellowstone's more than 300 geysers are spread through nine different basins, with half of these in Upper Geyser Basin, the home of Old Faithful.

Geysers need three essentials to exist: water, heat, and fractured rock. The water comes from snow and rain falling on this high plateau, while the heat comes from molten rock close to the earth's surface. Massive pressures from below have created a ring of fractures around the edge of Yellowstone's caldera. This is one of the hottest places on the planet, with heat flows more than 60 times the global average.

How They Work

Geysers operate because cold water is dense and sinks, while hot water is less dense and rises. The periodic eruption of geysers is caused by constrictions in the underground channels that prevent an adequate heat exchange with the surface. Precipitation slowly moves into the earth, eventually contacting the molten rock. Because of high pressures at these depths, water can reach extreme temperatures without vaporizing (as in a pressure cooker). As this super-heated water rises back toward the surface, it emerges in hot springs, fumaroles, mud pots, and geysers. The most spectacular of these phenomena are geysers. Two general types of geysers exist in Yellowstone. Fountain geysers (such as Great Fountain Geyser) explode from pools of water and tend to spray water more widely, whereas cone-type geysers (such as Old Faithful) jet out of nozzlelike formations.

In a geyser, steam bubbles upward from the superheated source of water and expands as it rises. These bubbles block the plumbing system, keeping hot water from reaching the surface. Eventually, however, pressure from the bubbles begins to force the cooler water above out of the vent. This initial release triggers a more violent reaction as the sudden lessening of pressure allows the entire column to begin boiling, explosively expelling steam and water to produce a geyser. Once the eruption has emptied the plumbing system, water gradually seeps back into the chambers to begin the process anew. Some of Yellowstone's geysers have enormous underground caverns that fill with water; in its rare eruptions, massive Steamboat Geyser can blast a million gallons of water into the air!

As an aside, the term "geyser" is one of the few Icelandic terms in the English language; it means to "gush forth." There are probably 30 active geysers in Iceland, many more on Russia's Kamchatka Peninsula, and a few in New Zealand, where geothermal development has greatly lessened geyser activity.

A fine online source with details about Yellowstone's geysers—and others around the globe—is maintained by the nonprofit **Geyser Observation and Study Association** (www .geyserstudy.org). The GOSA website has frequent postings of geyser activity, and volunteer observers are often present in the park during the summer, particularly at Grand Geyser in Upper Geyser Basin.

Protecting the Geysers

Unfortunately, some of Yellowstone's geysers have been lost because of human stupidity or vandalism. At one time, it was considered great sport to stuff logs, rocks, and even chairs into the geysers for a little added show. Others poured chemicals into them to make them play. As a result of such actions, some geysers have been severely damaged or destroyed, and some hot springs have become collection points for coins, rocks, sticks, and trash. It shouldn't be necessary to point out that such actions ruin these thermal areas for everyone and destroy something that may have been going on for hundreds of years.

Grand Geyser, Upper Geyser Basin

OTHER GEOTHERMAL ACTIVITY

Although geysers are Yellowstone's best-known features, they make up only a tiny fraction of perhaps 10,000 thermal features in the park. **Hot springs** appear where water can reach the ground surface relatively easily, allowing the heat that builds up in the chambers of geysers to dissipate. When less groundwater is present, you may find **fumaroles,** vents that shoot steam, carbon dioxide, and even hydrogen sulfide gas. **Mud pots** (also called paint pots) are essentially wet fumaroles. Hydrogen sulfide gas combines with water to produce hydrosulfuric acid. This acid breaks down surrounding rocks to form clay, and the clay combines with water to create mud. As gas passes through the mud, it creates the bubbling mud pots. Probably the best examples of these different forms are at Fountain Paint Pot in Lower Geyser Basin, where geysers and hot springs are found in the wetter areas below, while mud pots and fumaroles sit atop a small hill. Hydrogen sulfide is,

of course, poisonous, and toxic fumes sometimes kill bison and elk that cluster around the geothermal areas in the winter. Scientists joke that Norris Geyser Basin would be considered an EPA Superfund site if it weren't within a national park!

The colors in Yellowstone's hot springs come from a variety of sources, including algae and bacteria as well as various minerals, particularly sulfur, iron oxides, and arsenic sulfide. The algae and bacteria are highly temperature-specific and help create the distinct bands of colors around many hot springs. Interestingly, many of these algal species are found only in hot springs, although they exist around the world. The bacteria have proven of considerable interest to science because of their ability to survive such high temperatures. One such organism, *Thermus aquaticus,* was discovered in a Yellowstone hot spring in 1967, and scientists extracted an enzyme that was later used to develop the increasingly important technique of DNA fingerprinting. Above 190°F, even these hot-water bacteria and algae cannot survive, so the hottest springs may appear a deep blue because of the water's ability to absorb all wavelengths of light except blue, which is reflected back into our eyes.

A couple of other terms are worth learning before heading out to see the sights of Yellowstone. **Sinter** (also called "geyserite") is a deposit composed primarily of silica. The silica is dissolved by hot water deep underground and brought to the surface in geysers or hot springs. At the surface the water evaporates, leaving behind the light gray sinter, which can create large mounds (up to 30 feet high) around the older geysers. The rate of accumulation is very slow, and some of the park's geysers have obviously been active for many thousands of years. The other precipitate that is sometimes deposited around Yellowstone's hot springs and geysers is **travertine,** consisting of calcium carbonate that has been dissolved underground.

A Note of Warning

The surface around many of the hot springs and geysers is surprisingly thin, and people have been killed or seriously injured by falling through into the boiling water. Stay on the boardwalks in developed areas, and use extreme caution around backcountry thermal features. If in doubt, stay away!

Exploring Yellowstone

Yellowstone is perhaps the most accessible large national park in America. Nearly all of the famous sights are within a couple of hundred feet of the Grand Loop Road, a 142-mile figure-eight through the middle of the park. Whatever you do, *don't* see Yellowstone at 45 miles per hour; that's like seeing the Louvre from a passing train.

For all too many visitors, Yellowstone becomes a checklist of places to visit, geysers to watch, and animals to see. This tends to inspire an attitude that treats this great national treasure as a drive-through theme park, where the animals come out to perform and the geyser eruptions are predicted so everyone can be there on time. If you're one of this crowd, give yourself a giant kick in the rear and take a walk, even if it is just around Upper Geyser Basin where you see something beyond Old Faithful.

PARK ACCESS

Entrance to Yellowstone (307/344-7381, www .nps.gov/yell) costs $25 per vehicle, or $12 for individuals entering by bicycle, foot, skis, or as a bus passenger. Motorcycles or snowmobiles are $20. The pass covers entrance to both Yellowstone and Grand Teton national parks and is good for seven days. If you're planning to be here longer or to make additional visits, get an annual pass covering both parks for $50, or the America the Beautiful Pass—good for all national parks—for $80 per year. An Interagency Senior Pass for all national parks is available to anyone older than 62 for a one-time fee of $10, and people with disabilities can get a free Interagency Access Pass. Both of these latter passes also give you 50 percent reductions in most camping fees.

Upon entering the park, you'll receive a Yellowstone map and a copy of *Yellowstone Today,* a quarterly newspaper that describes facilities and services and provides camping, fishing, and backcountry information. This is the best source for up-to-date park information. It's also packed with enough warnings to scare off a platoon of Marines. Examples include cautions against falling trees, bathing in thermal pools (hydrogen sulfide and meningitis), unpredictable wildlife, improper food storage, health problems from the altitude, narrow roads, theft, imitating wolf howls, and scalding water. And, oh yes, "swim at your own risk." **Pets are prohibited on trails or boardwalks anywhere in Yellowstone.** Kennel facilities are not available in the park but can be found in Jackson and Cody.

If you are planning a trip to Yellowstone, request a copy of the annual *Yellowstone National Park Trip Planner* booklet for an overview of sights, visitor centers, what to do, services, camping, and more. It's also available as a PDF on the park website, www.nps.gov/yell/plan yourvisit/index.htm. Call 307/344-2113 for a recorded **park weather** forecast.

VISITOR CENTERS

The Park Service maintains visitor centers at Mammoth Hot Springs, Norris Geyser Basin, Old Faithful, Canyon Village, Fishing Bridge, and Grant Village. All of these sell maps and natural-history books covering the park and surrounding areas. In addition, you'll find smaller information stations at Madison and West Thumb and a Park Service ranger at the West Yellowstone Visitor Center.

Open daily, the **Albright Visitor Center** (307/344-2263) at Mammoth is the only year-round visitor facility in Yellowstone.

A brand new 26,000-square-foot **Old Faithful Visitor Education Center** (307/545-2750) opens in 2010 or 2011, providing a massive improvement over the temporary structure that serves as a visitor center until then. The visitor center is open daily mid-April–early November and mid-December–mid-March.

Recently built **Canyon Visitor Education Center** (307/242-2550) is a must-see, with fascinating exhibits detailing park geology; open daily May–mid-October.

Grant Visitor Center (307/242-2650, daily late May–Sept.) houses informative exhibits and a film on the role of fires in the park. **Fishing Bridge Visitor Center** (307/242-2450, daily late May–Sept.) contains decrepit exhibits of birds, animals, and geology.

TOURS

During summer, most people come into Yellowstone in private cars or RVs, but there *are* other ways of getting around. An interpretive bus tour provides a quick overview of the park while leaving the driving to an expert. This is especially true for RVers who can

park at Fishing Bridge RV Park or Bridge Bay Campground and then don't need to worry about traveling on narrow park roads.

In-Park Tours

From mid-May–late September, Xanterra Parks and Resorts (307/344-7311 or 866/439-7375, www.travelyellowstone .com) guides full-day bus tours from Canyon Lodge, Lake Yellowstone Hotel, Old Faithful Inn, Fishing Bridge RV Park, Bridge Bay Campground, and Grant Village. Tours of the lower loop road are $63 adults or $32 ages 8–15 (free for younger kids). A longer "Yellowstone in a Day" tour (not recommended unless you're into sensory overload and more than nine hours of riding around) costs $75 adults or $35 kids. The in-a-day tour is available only from Mammoth or Gardiner. Also available are professionally taught four-hour **Photo Safaris** ($71 adults, $36 kids) several mornings a week out of Old Faithful Inn, and all-day **Lamar Valley wildlife excursions** ($39–46 adults, $20–23 kids) to search for wolves.

The most distinctive park tour offerings are classic **Historic Yellow Bus tours.** Built in the 1930s, these lovingly refurbished vehicles get almost as much attention as the scenery. Tours head in various directions on different days. All-day trips over Beartooth Pass, into Grand Teton National Park, or to the town of Cody are $72–92 adults or $36–46 kids.

Other Park Tours

Upper or lower loop tours are available out of West Yellowstone from **Buffalo Bus Touring Co.** (406/646-9564 or 800/426-7669, www .yellowstonevacations.com, $111 adults or $90 kids under 17). Park entrance fees are extra.

Additional Yellowstone tours leave out of Jackson ($106) aboard **Alltrans/Gray Line of Jackson Hole** (307/733-3135 or 800/443-6133, www.graylinejh.com). Those without vehicles can use Gray Line tours for access to Yellowstone from Jackson; the bus can pick you up at many places along the road system, though you'll need to schedule this in advance.

Karst Stage (406/388-2293 or 800/287-4759,

RETURN OF THE OLD YELLOW BUSES

After a 50-year hiatus, Yellowstone visitors can again step onboard a vintage yellow bus to tour the park. Built in the 1930s by the White Motor Company, these photogenic low-slung 13-passenger buses were used by the Yellowstone Park Transportation Company until the 1950s. The buses traveled to train depots, providing the primary means of transport as visitors stopped in a different park hotel each night. At their peak in 1940, some 98 yellow buses were in the Yellowstone fleet, but as private vehicle usage increased the old buses fell out of favor and were sold and dispersed across the country.

The buses ended up in private collections, most notably by the Skagway Streetcar Company in Alaska, where eight of them were used for tours until 2001. In that year – some 50 years after the buses left the park – Xanterra bought these buses for $38,000 apiece,

spending another $1.9 million to totally refurbish them. The buses were painstakingly rebuilt using retro-style instruments, reupholstered seats, yellow and black paint and decals to match the originals, new convertible tops, and a Ford E-450 chassis with automatic transmissions and modern 5.4-liter engines.

Xanterra began offering park tours in the yellow buses in 2007, and travelers can now choose from several different options led by knowledgeable drivers, including half-day photo safaris, morning wildlife adventures, and all-day trips into the Beartooth Mountains. The buses are always an attention-grabber, and the open roof is great for watching wildlife and taking in Yellowstone's sights. They're a delightful step back in time to a simpler era. Contact **Xanterra Parks & Resorts** (307/344-7311 or 866/439-7375, www.travelyellowstone.com) for details on yellow bus tours.

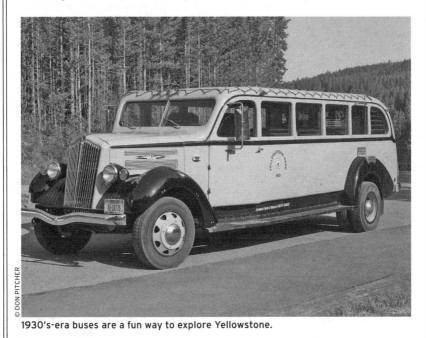

© DON PITCHER

1930's-era buses are a fun way to explore Yellowstone.

www.karststage.com) has Wednesday-only summertime tours departing Livingston, Montana and continuing to Bozeman, Big Sky, Old Faithful, Lake Hotel, Canyon Village, Mammoth, Gardiner, and Emigrant, before returning to Livingston. The cost is $85 per person, with a four-person minimum. Call at least three days ahead of your travel date.

Natural-History Tours

In addition to traditional classes, the **Yellowstone Association Institute** (307/344-2294, www.yellowstoneassociation .org) leads a popular series of **Lodging and Learning** packages. These two- to five-day programs blend education, recreation, and comfortable lodging. Naturalist-guides from the association lead excursions, and participants are provided accommodations in park hotels, plus breakfasts and lunches. The programs include special ones for families, winter ski treks, winter wildlife, and hiking. For the private touch, the institute has **Yellowstone Ed-Ventures,** where a wildlife biologist travels along in your own vehicle. It's sort of like having a personal trainer for Yellowstone.

For a listing of licens ed tour operators offering wildlife, natural-history, and photography tours in the park, contact the Park Service (307/344-7381, www.nps.gov/yell). Operated by the highly respected Teton Science School, **Wildlife Expeditions** (307/733-2623 or 888/945-3567, www.wildlifeexpeditions .org) leads a variety of wildlife-viewing safaris throughout the region, including multi-day wildlife tours into Yellowstone. Also highly recommended are naturalist Carl Swoboda's **Safari Yellowstone** (800/723-2747, www .safariyellowstone.com), geologist Dr. Keith Watts of **Earth Tours** (307/733-4261, www .earth-tours.com), and **Tory and Meredith Taylor** (307/455-2161), who lead personalized wolf-viewing tours in the winter.

Other companies with guided van tours into Yellowstone include **Brushbuck Guide Services** (888/282-5868, www.brushbuck phototours.com), **Callowishus Park Touring Company** (307/413-5483, www.callowishus

.com), **EcoTour Adventures** (307/690-9533, www.jhecotouradventures.com), **Jackson's Hole Adventure** (307/654-7849, www.jackson holeadventure.com), **Upstream Anglers and Outdoor Adventures** (307/739-9443 or 800/642-8979, www.upstreamanglers .com), **Wilderness Wildlife Explorations** (307/413-1687, www.wwexplorations.com), **The Hole Hiking Experience** (307/690-4453 or 866/733-4453, www.holehike.com), **Yellowstone Safari Co.** (406/586-1155 or 866/586-1155, www.yellowstonesafari .com), **Yellowstone Yearround Adventures** (406/223-2601, www.yellowstoneyearround .com), **Yellowstone Country Adventures** (406/994-0422, www.yellowstonecountry-adventures.com), and **Phidippides** (307/527-6789 or 866/527-6789, www.codyshuttle.com).

ROADS

The speed limit on all park roads is a vigilantly enforced 45 mph (or less); exceed this and you're likely to get a ticket! Be especially cautious on the south side of the park, where rangers seem to wait most evenings and the relatively straight road makes it easy to speed. During summer

© DON PITCHER

Yellowstone traffic jam

YELLOWSTONE

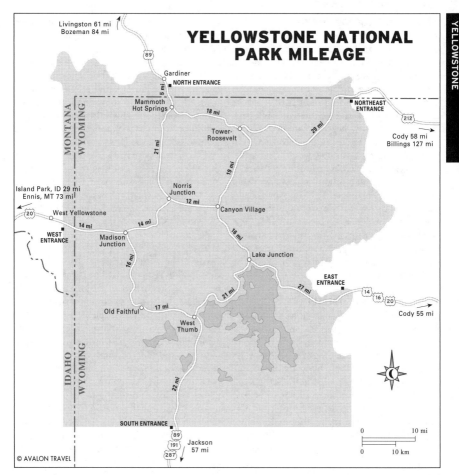

YELLOWSTONE NATIONAL PARK MILEAGE

Livingston 61 mi
Bozeman 84 mi

89

Gardiner
NORTH ENTRANCE

Mammoth
Hot Springs

NORTHEAST ENTRANCE

212

Cody 58 mi
Billings 127 mi

18 mi

Tower-
Roosevelt

29 mi

MONTANA
WYOMING

21 mi

19 mi

Island Park, ID 29 mi
Ennis, MT 73 mi

Norris
Junction

12 mi

Canyon Village

20

West Yellowstone

14 mi   14 mi

**WEST
ENTRANCE**

Madison
Junction

16 mi

16 mi

Lake Junction

**EAST
ENTRANCE**

27 mi

14 16 20

Cody 55 mi

21 mi

Old Faithful   17 mi

West
Thumb

IDAHO
WYOMING

22 mi

SOUTH ENTRANCE

89
191   Jackson
287   57 mi

0   10 mi

0   10 km

© AVALON TRAVEL

you're not likely to approach the speed limit because long lines of traffic form behind monstrous RVs or when wildlife is visible.

Gas stations are at Old Faithful, Canyon Village, Mammoth Hot Springs, Fishing Bridge, Grant Village, and Tower Junction, while repair services are available at all of these except Mammoth Hot Springs and Tower Junction. Additional service stations are in towns surrounding the park.

Seasonal Road Closures

Most roads in Yellowstone close on the Monday after the first Sunday in November and usually open again by mid-May. Only the road between Mammoth and Cooke City is kept plowed all winter; other roads are groomed for snowmobiles and snowcoaches (snow conditions permitting) by mid-December. Plowing begins in early March, and the roads reopen in sections. The roads connecting Mammoth to West Yellowstone open first, while Dunraven Pass is plowed last. Spring storms may cause closures or restrictions on some park roads, so get current road conditions at entrance stations and visitor centers, or by calling 307/344-7381.

The Construction Maze

Yellowstone's roads have long been a source of irritation. Much of the roadbed was built at the turn of the 20th century, when horses and carriages were the primary means of travel. Increasing traffic and larger vehicles contributed to deterioration of park roads, as did stretched-thin park maintenance budgets. Yellowstone is now nearing completion on a massive 20-year, $300-million reconstruction program, and each summer you'll find a different section undergoing rebuilding. Be ready for delays up to 30 minutes somewhere during your journey. Fortunately, all this work means that the roads are vastly better than they were a decade ago. Contact the park (307/344-7381, www.nps.gov/yell/planyourvisit/roadclosures .htm) for the latest on the road situation and this year's construction delays, or check the park newspaper.

WILDLIFE-VIEWING

Yellowstone provides a marvelous natural setting in which to view bison, elk, moose, wolves, coyotes, pronghorn antelope, bighorn sheep, and other wild animals. One of the easiest ways to find wildlife is simply by watching for the brake lights, the cars pulled half off the road, and the cameras all pointed in one direction. Inevitably, you'll find an elk or a bison placidly munching away, trying to remain oblivious to the chaos that surrounds it. Be sure to bring binoculars for your trip to Yellowstone. A spotting scope is also helpful in searching for distant bears and wolves.

Because of the constant parade of visitors and the lack of hunting, many of Yellowstone's animals appear to almost ignore the presence of people, and it isn't uncommon to see visitors approach an animal without respecting its need for space. Although they may appear tame, Yellowstone's animals really are wild, and attacks are not uncommon. Those quiet bison can suddenly erupt with an enormous ferocity if provoked by photographers who come too close. Between 1983 and 1994, four people were killed by bison in Yellowstone and

Grand Teton national parks. **Stay at least 25 yards away from bison and elk and at least 100 yards away from bears.** Do not under any circumstances feed the park's animals. This creates an unnatural dependency, is unhealthy for the animal, and may even lead to its death. You'll find some entertaining (and simultaneously scary) wildlife safety videos of wildlife encounters with foolish tourists on the Yellowstone website (www.nps.gov/yell).

The Park Service has a free pamphlet showing where you're most likely to see wildlife in Yellowstone. Pick one up at any visitor center. During summer, the best wildlife-viewing hours are early in the morning and in the late afternoon to early evening.

Bears

Both black and grizzly bears are found throughout Yellowstone, but the days of bear jams along the park roads are long past because rangers actively work to prevent bears from becoming habituated to people. Most bears have returned to their more natural ways of living, although problems still crop up with individuals wandering through campgrounds in search of food. You're more likely to encounter a bear in the backcountry areas, and some places are closed to hiking for extended periods each year for this reason. The best places to watch for grizzlies along the road system are in the Hayden and Lamar valleys, near Mt. Washburn, and in the Antelope Creek drainage (just south of Tower Fall).

Safety in grizzly country is always a concern, but statistically you are considerably more likely to be hurt in a traffic accident than to be mauled by a bear. There were just 22 bear-caused injuries in the park between 1980 and 1997—one injury for every 2.1 million visitors! Most of these injuries took place in backcountry areas and involved female bears with cubs or yearlings, and nearly all attacks took place after a surprise encounter with a bear. Three people were killed by Yellowstone bears in the last three decades of the 20th century, the most recent being a 1986 fatality caused when a photographer approached an adult female grizzly too closely.

Bighorn Sheep

About 250 bighorns live within Yellowstone National Park, with much larger populations in the surrounding national forests. Look for bighorn sheep on cliffs in the Gardner River Canyon between Mammoth Hot Springs and the town of Gardiner. Ewes and lambs also frequently appear just off the road on Dunraven Pass north of Canyon, and day-hikers commonly encounter rams up close on the slopes of Mt. Washburn. Another place to see bighorns is along Specimen Ridge.

Birds

Trumpeter swans—beautiful white birds with seven-foot wingspans—are a fairly common sight in Yellowstone, particularly on the Madison and Yellowstone rivers and on Yellowstone Lake. Many trumpeter swans winter in hot-spring areas. These are some of the largest birds in America, weighing 20–30 pounds. Another large white bird here is the ungainly-looking and bulbous-billed **white pelican,** a common sight on Yellowstone Lake and near Fishing Bridge. More than 350 pairs of pelicans nest on the Molly Islands in Yellowstone Lake; this is one of the largest white-pelican breeding colonies in the Rockies. **Bald eagles**—America's national bird—and **ospreys** have managed comebacks in recent years and are frequently seen along the Yellowstone River and above Yellowstone Lake. Look for **golden eagles** flying over the open grasslands of Lamar Valley or Hayden Valley.

Bison

Bison are found in open country throughout Yellowstone, including Hayden, Lamar, and Pelican Valleys, along with the Firehole River Basin (including Old Faithful). A favorite time to see bison in Yellowstone is late May, just after the new calves have been born. The calves' antics are always good for laughs. Be sure to use caution around bison; many people

© DON PITCHER

bighorn sheep near East Entrance

have been gored when they've come too close. Always stay at least 25 yards away, preferably farther.

Coyotes

Although wolves get the media attention, visitors to Yellowstone are probably more likely to see another native of the dog family: the coyote. Keep your eyes open for coyotes anywhere in Yellowstone but especially in open grassy areas, where they are more easily spotted. During summer, you'll often see them in small packs or alone as they hunt small mammals such as mice, voles, and pocket gophers. At other times of the year they prey on larger animals, including the calves of elk and pronghorn antelope, and scavenge carrion. Good places to look for coyotes are in the Blacktail Plateau area and Lamar Valley, along with the Upper and Lower Geyser basins near Old Faithful.

Deer

Mule deer (also known as black-tailed deer) are common in many parts of Yellowstone during summer, but most migrate to lower elevations when winter comes. They are typically found in open areas containing sagebrush or grass. Mule deer are named for their long mulelike ears. They also have black-tipped tails and a peculiar way of pogoing away when frightened.

The smaller **white-tailed deer** are far less common in Yellowstone. You are most likely to find them along rivers or in brushy areas at low elevations, such as around Mammoth Hot Springs or in Lamar Valley. Other places to watch for them are along Yellowstone Lake and in the Upper Geyser Basin.

Elk

One animal virtually every visitor to Yellowstone sees is elk. About 30,000 of these regal animals summer in the park, and approximately 15,000 remain through the winter, primarily on the north end of Yellowstone. In summer, look for elk in Mammoth Hot Springs, Elk Park, and Gibbon Meadows, but you're certain to also see them elsewhere in Yellowstone. The bugling of bull elk is a common autumn sound in Yellowstone, as anyone who visits Mammoth at that time of year can

Elk relax on the terraces at Mammoth Hot Springs.

attest. Winter snows push the elk to lower elevations on the north side of Yellowstone or out of the park into surrounding areas.

Moose

The largest members of the deer family, moose are typically seen eating willow bushes in riparian areas inside Yellowstone National Park. The best places to look for moose are Hayden Valley, around Yellowstone Lake, the Willow Park area north of Norris, the southwestern corner along the Bechler and Falls rivers, and along the Gallatin, Lamar, and Lewis river drainages.

Pronghorn Antelope

These speedy and colorful ungulates (hoofed mammals) are common sights on the plains of Wyoming, but most of Yellowstone doesn't provide adequate habitat. Pronghorn antelope are found only in sagebrush and grassy areas on the northern end of the park from Lamar Valley to the Gardiner area.

Wolves

The best place to look for wolves is the open terrain of **Lamar Valley,** where the Druid pack are visible at many times of the year. Another excellent spot is **Hayden Valley,** where members of Mollie's pack are commonly seen. Visit early in the morning or near dusk to increase your odds of seeing them. You may well hear their plaintive cry from your campground late at night, particularly at Slough Creek or Pebble Creek campgrounds. Binoculars or spotting scopes are helpful for roadside wolf-watching. Rent quality scopes ($25 per day) from **Silver Gate General Store** (406/838-2371, www .pineedgecabins.com) in Silver Gate, Montana, just outside the park's northeast corner.

Wolf-watchers should follow the advice listed in the park newspaper. Noise can be a problem, especially in popular wolf-viewing areas, so avoid slamming car doors and keep other sounds to a minimum. And yes, it is illegal to imitate a wolf howl in the park. Do not follow the wolves around because this may disturb them and affect their survival. Denning activity typically takes place early April–early May, with active denning areas closed to humans; check with the Park Service for closed areas.

Sights

The following tour of Yellowstone sights begins on the west side of the park (the most popular entrance is via West Yellowstone) and traces a more-or-less clockwise path around the Grand Loop, ending at the geyser basins north of Old Faithful.

MADISON

The tourist town of **West Yellowstone, Montana** is right outside the park's western boundary. **West Entrance** is the busiest of all the park entry stations, handling more than one-third of the nearly three million people who enter Yellowstone each year. A 14-mile road heads east to Madison Junction, closely paralleling the scenic Madison River (a major tributary of the Missouri River) in which geese,

ducks, and trumpeter swans are common. Bison and elk are other critters to watch for in the open meadows. The Madison River is open only to fly-fishing and is considered one of the finest places in the nation to catch trout (although they can be a real challenge to fool). On warm summer evenings you're likely to see dozens of anglers casting for wily rainbow and brown trout and mountain whitefish.

At Madison Junction, the road splits, heading south to Old Faithful and north to Mammoth. This is where the Gibbon and Firehole rivers join to form the Madison River. The 406,359-acre North Fork Fire of 1988 ripped through most of the Madison River country, but the land is recovering well in most places, and wildflowers are abundant in midsummer.

Madison Canyon is flanked by mountains named for two photographers who had a marked influence on Yellowstone. To the north is 8,257-foot **Mt. Jackson**—as in William H. Jackson, whose photos helped bring the area to national attention—and to the south is distinctive, 8,235-foot **Mt. Haynes,** named for the man who held the park photo concession for nearly four decades. These mountains and the surrounding slopes were created by rhyolite lava flows.

The Northwest Corner

From West Yellowstone, Montana, U.S. Hwy. 191 heads north to Bozeman, passing through a small corner of Yellowstone National Park en route. There are no entrance stations or developed facilities here, but the area provides backcountry access for hikers and horsepackers from several trailheads. The drive itself is scenic, and the road is wide and smooth. The road enters the park approximately 10 miles north of West Yellowstone and gradually climbs through stretches that were burned in the fires of 1988 before emerging into unburned alpine meadows near tiny Divide Lake. North of here, U.S. Hwy. 191 follows the growing Gallatin River downhill through a pretty mix of meadows, sagebrush, rocky outcrops, and forested hillsides with grassy carpets beneath. Approximately 31 miles north of West Yellowstone, the road exits Yellowstone and enters Gallatin National Forest. It's another 17 miles from here to the turnoff for Big Sky Resort or 60 miles from the park boundary to Bozeman.

Madison Junction to Norris

The **Madison Information Station** (307/344-2821) near Madison Junction is open daily 9 A.M.–5 P.M. late May–September and closed the rest of the year. A small bookstore is also here. Directly behind Madison Campground is 7,500-foot **National Park Mountain,** named in honor of a fabled incident in 1870. Three explorers were gathered around the campfire, discussing the wonders that they had found in this area, when one suggested that rather than letting all of these wonders pass into private hands, they should be set aside as a national park. Thus was born the concept that led to the world's first national park. The tale was passed on as the gospel truth for so long that the mountain was named in honor of this evening. Unfortunately, the story was a complete fabrication. Cynics may read something into the fact that National Park Mountain was torched by the fires of 1988.

North of Madison Junction, the road follows the Gibbon River nearly all of the 14 miles to Norris. It crosses the river five times and hangs right on the edge through Gibbon Canyon. The pretty, 84-foot-high **Gibbon Falls** is approximately five miles up the road and situated right at the edge of the enormous caldera that fills the center of Yellowstone. The 1988 fires consumed most of the trees around the falls, but the new lodgepoles are now topping 20 feet. Another five miles beyond this point, the road emerges from the canyon into grassy **Gibbon Meadows,** where elk and bison are commonly seen. The prominent peak visible to the north is 10,336-foot **Mt. Holmes.** On the west end of Gibbon Meadows is a barren area that contains **Sylvan Springs Geyser Basin.** No maintained trail leads to this small collection of pools and springs, but hikers sometimes head across the north end of the meadows at the Gibbon River Picnic Area. The path is wet most of the summer.

An easy half-mile trail leads to **Artist Paint Pots,** filled with colorful plopping and steaming mud pots and hot springs. Although it's a short hike, the paint pots see far fewer visitors than roadside sites, making it a nice place to escape the crowds. The forest was burned in the North Fork Fire, so it's also a good place to see how the lodgepole pines are regenerating. Just south of the parking area for Artist Paint Pots is a trail to **Monument Geyser Basin,** where there isn't much activity, but the tall sinter cones form all sorts of bizarre shapes, including Thermos Bottle Geyser. The mile-long hike climbs 500 feet and provides views of the surrounding country. Another attraction is **Chocolate Pots,** found along the highway just north of Gibbon Meadows. The reddish-brown color comes from iron, aluminum, and manganese oxides. Just before you reach Norris, the road crosses through the appropriately named **Elk Park.**

◖ NORRIS GEYSER BASIN

Although Old Faithful and the Upper Geyser Basin are more famous, many visitors to Yellowstone find Norris Geyser Basin equally interesting. Norris sits atop the junction of several major fault lines, providing conduits for heat from the molten lava below. Because of this, it is apparently the hottest geyser basin in North America, if not the world; a scientific team found temperatures of 459°F at 1,087 feet underground and was forced to quit drilling when the pressure threatened to destroy the drilling rig! Because of considerable sulfur (and hence sulfuric acid) in the springs and geysers, the water at Norris is acidic; most of the world's acid geysers are here. The acidic water kills lodgepole trees in the basin, creating an open, nearly barren place. Norris Basin has been around at least 115,000 years, making it

the oldest of any of Yellowstone's active geyser basins. It is a constantly changing place, with small geysers seeming to come and go on an almost daily basis.

The paved trail from the often crowded parking area leads to **Norris Geyser Basin Museum and Information Station** (307/344-2812, daily late May–Sept. 9 A.M.–5 P.M.), built of stone in 1929–1930. The small museum houses exhibit panels on hot springs and geothermal activity. Be sure to pick up the detailed brochure ($0.50) describing the various features at Norris. Ranger-led walks are given several times a day in the summer, and there's usually one in the area ready to answer your questions. A little bookstore is housed in a nearby building. From the museum, the Norris Basin spreads both north and south, with two rather different trails to hike. Take the time to walk along both. The Norris Campground is only a quarter-mile from the geyser basin.

Porcelain Basin

Just behind the museum is an overlook that provides an impressive view across the always-

NORRIS GEYSER BASIN

To Norris Campground

To ◖ MAMMOTH HOT SPRINGS

Whirligig Geyser

Porcelain Basin

Nuphar Lake

NORRIS MUSEUM

BOOKSTORE

Emerald Spring

P

NORRIS JUNCTION

To Canyon Village

Steamboat Geyser

Back Basin

Porkchop Geyser

Cistern Spring

Echinus Geyser

To Madison Junction

0   250 yds

0   250 m

© AVALON TRAVEL

changing Porcelain Basin. The path descends into the basin, passing hissing steam vents, bubbling hot pools, and small geysers, including **Constant Geyser,** with frequent and sudden bursts to 20 feet or more. **Whirligig Geyser** is another one that is often active, spraying a noisy fan of water. (Watch your glasses and camera lenses in the steam; silica deposits can be difficult to remove.) For an enjoyable short walk, follow the boardwalk around the mile-long loop through Porcelain Basin. Stop to admire the bright colors in the steaming water, indicators of iron, arsenic, and other elements, along with algae and cyanobacteria.

Back Basin

A mile-long loop trail takes you to the sights within the Back Basin south of the museum. Before heading out, check at the museum for the latest on geyser activity. Most people follow the path in a clockwise direction, coming first to **Emerald Spring,** a gorgeous green pool with acidic water just below boiling. A little way farther down the path is **Steamboat Geyser.** Wait a few minutes and you're likely to see one of its minor eruptions, which may reach 40 feet. On rare occasions, Steamboat erupts with a fury that is hard to believe, blasting more than 300 feet into the air—more than twice the height of Old Faithful—making this the world's tallest geyser. Eruptions can last up to 20 minutes or more, enough time to pour out a million gallons of water, and the explosions have been heard up to 14 miles away. Steamboat's unforgettable eruptions cannot be predicted; a 50-year span once passed between eruptions, while several eruptions may occur in one year. If you ever see this one erupt, consider yourself incredibly lucky!

The path splits just below Steamboat; on the right is **Cistern Spring,** whose deep blue waters are constantly building deposits of sinter and have flooded the nearby lodgepole-pine forests, killing the trees. If you turn left where the trail splits, you come to **Echinus Geyser** (pronounced e-KI-nus). The name—Greek for "spiny"—comes from the pebbles that lie

around the geyser; resembling sea urchins, they are a result of sinter accumulation. Sometimes Echinus settles into a regular pattern with frequent eruptions, but in the last few years they decreased and it may stay dormant for weeks or months. When Echinus does erupt, the geyser sends explosions of acidic steam and water (pH 3.5) 40–60 feet. These generally last 3–5 minutes but sometimes continue for much longer. Unlike Old Faithful, this is one geyser where you can get up close and personal. Bench-sitters may get splashed, although the water is not hot enough to burn.

Continue along this trail beyond Echinus to see many more hot springs and steam vents. **Porkchop Geyser** was in continuous eruption for several years, but in 1989 it self-destructed in an explosion that threw rocks more than 200 feet, leaving behind a bubbling hot spring.

Norris Junction to Canyon

From Norris Geyser Basin to Canyon, the road cuts across the center of the park on the high Solfatara Plateau, an area scorched in the 1988 North Fork Fire. The lodgepole pines had been uprooted in a wild 1984 windstorm, and four years later the wind-whipped fires arrived, creating a holocaust. Now, more than two decades later, lodgepoles are a lush thicket of green.

Virginia Cascades Road is a 2.5-mile-long, one-way road that circles around this blow-down area and provides a view of the 60-foot-tall Virginia Cascade of the Gibbon River. Stop at the shady picnic area for lunch or to head across the meadow to fly-fish. Back on the main highway heading east, keep your eyes open for elk and bison as the road approaches Canyon. Also note the dense forest of lodgepole pines that was established after a fire burned through in 1955.

Norris Junction to Mammoth

The park road between Norris and Mammoth Hot Springs provides some interesting sights, although much of this country burned in the 1988 North Fork Fire. Just beyond the highway junction is the **Norris Soldier Station.** Built by the army in 1897 and modified in 1908, it is one of just three stations still standing in the park. The attractive log building now houses the small **Museum of the National Park Ranger** (307/344-7353, daily late May–late Sept. 9 A.M.–5 P.M.) with displays and a video on the history of park rangers.

Just up the road is **Frying Pan Spring** (named for its shape), where the water is actually not that hot. The bubbles are from pungent-smelling hydrogen-sulfide gas. **Roaring Mountain** is a bleak, steaming mountainside four miles north of Norris. In 1902, the mountain erupted into activity with fumaroles that made a roar audible at great distances. It is far less active today and is best seen in winter, when the temperature difference results in much more steam.

Obsidian Cliff

Stop at Obsidian Cliff to see the black glassy rocks formed when lava cooled rapidly. One mountain man (not, as many sources claim, Jim Bridger) told tall tales of "Glass Mountain," where his shots at an elk kept missing. When he got closer, he found he had actually been firing at a clear mountain of glass. The elk was 25 miles away, but the mountain was acting as a telescope to make the animal appear close. Obsidian Cliff was an important source of rock for Indians in making fine arrowheads and other tools. Obsidian from here was of such value that Indians traded it extensively; obsidian points made from this rock have even been found in Ohio and Ontario. (It is illegal to remove obsidian; leave it for future generations to enjoy.) North of here the countryside opens up along Obsidian Creek at **Willow Park,** one of the best places to see moose, especially in the fall.

Sheepeater Cliff and Golden Gate

Approximately 13 miles north of Norris, the road passes Indian Creek Campground (one of the quietest in the park) and the basalt columns of Sheepeater Cliff, named for the Indian inhabitants of these mountains. North of this point, the country opens into Swan Lake Flats, where you get a fine gander

at 10,992-foot Electric Peak nine miles to the northwest.

At Golden Gate the road suddenly enters a narrow defile, through which flows Glen Creek. Stop to look over the edge of **Rustic Falls** and to note how the road is cantilevered over the cliff edge. Acrophobics should *not* stop here. Instead, have someone else drive, close your eyes, and say three Hail Marys.

Bunsen Peak and the Hoodoos

Just south of Mammoth is Bunsen Peak, an 8,564-foot inactive volcanic cone. Any chemistry student will recognize the name because Robert Wilhelm Eberhard von Bunsen not only first explained the action of geysers but also invented the Bunsen burner. Parts of Bunsen Peak look like a chemistry experiment run amok. The North Fork Fire of 1988 swept through this area in a patchy mosaic, leaving long strips of unburned trees next to those that are now just blackened telephone poles.

North of Golden Gate, the main road soon passes the Hoodoos, a fascinating jumble of travertine boulders leaning in all directions. The rocks were created by hot springs thousands of years ago and toppled from the east face of Terrace Mountain. Just before Mammoth, turn left onto Upper Terrace Drive, a half-mile loop road providing access to the upper end of Mammoth Hot Springs. (No trailers or large RVs.)

◖ MAMMOTH HOT SPRINGS

Mammoth Hot Springs lies at an elevation of 6,239 feet near the northern border of Yellowstone, just five miles from the town of Gardiner, Montana. Here you'll find park headquarters, a variety of other facilities, and delightfully colorful hot springs. The Mammoth area is an important wintering spot for elk, pronghorn antelope, deer, and bison. During the fall, at least one bull elk and his harem can be seen wandering across the green lawns, while lesser males bugle challenges from behind the buildings or over the hill. The bugling may even keep you awake at night if you're staying in the Mammoth Hotel.

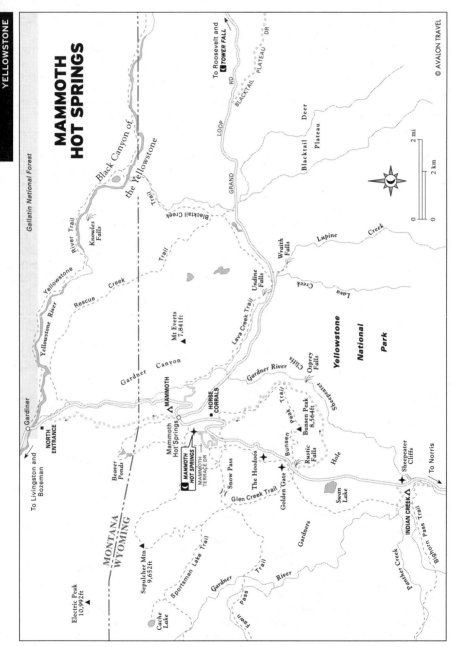

MAMMOTH HOT SPRINGS

© AVALON TRAVEL

Origins

Mammoth Hot Springs consists of a series of multihued terraces down which hot, mineral-laden water trickles. This water originates as snow and rain that falls on the surrounding country, although some is believed to come from the Norris area, 20 miles to the south. As it passes through the earth, the water comes into contact with volcanic magma containing massive amounts of carbon dioxide, creating carbonic acid. The now-acidic water passes through and dissolves the region's sedimentary limestone, and the calcium carbonate remains in solution until it reaches the surface at Mammoth. Once at the surface, the carbon dioxide begins to escape into the atmosphere, reducing the acidity and causing the lime to precipitate out, forming the travertine terraces that are so prominent here. As the water flows over small obstructions, more carbon dioxide is released, causing accumulations that eventually grow into the lips that surround the terrace pools. The rate of accumulation

of travertine (calcium carbonate) is astounding: more than two tons a day at Mammoth Hot Springs. Some terraces grow by eight inches per year. The first explorers were fascinated by these terraces; mountain man Jim Bridger noted that they made for delightful baths. A later operation—long since ended—coated knickknacks by dipping them in the hot springs!

The springs are constantly changing as underground passages are blocked by limestone deposits, forcing the water in new directions. As a result, old dried-out terraces stand on all sides, while new ones grow each day. Areas that were active just a few years ago may now be simply gray masses of crumbling travertine rock, and new areas may appear and spread in a matter of days. Mammoth is guaranteed to be different every time you visit. One of the most interesting aspects of the hot springs here is the variety of colors, results of the many different species of algae and bacteria that live in the water. Various factors, including temperature

© DON PITCHER

travertine terraces at Canary Spring

and acidity, affect the survival of different species; bright yellow algae live in the hottest areas, whereas cooler waters are colored orange and brown by other algae.

Visiting the Springs

Mammoth Hot Springs covers a steep hillside and consists of a series of colorful springs in various stages of accretion or decay. The area is accessible by road from below or above (Upper Terrace Drive), and a boardwalk staircase connects the two. At the bottom of Mammoth Hot Springs and off to the right is a 37-foot-tall mass of travertine known as **Liberty Cap** for its faint similarity to the caps worn in the French Revolution. The spring that created this formation no longer flows. (You may well think Liberty Cap shows a striking similarity to something else a bit more—shall we say—masculine.)

The springs at Mammoth change continuously, and every visit brings something new. For details on currently active areas, pick up the Park Service's informative brochure ($0.50)

from the box at the parking area. The most interesting areas in the last few years have been **Palate Spring** near the base and **Canary Spring** in the vicinity of the overlook. Along Upper Terrace Drive, both **Angel Terrace** and **Orange Spring Mound** have been active.

All of the water flowing out of Mammoth terraces quickly disappears into underground caverns. In front of the Mammoth Hotel are two sinkholes from which steam often rises. Caverns above the terraces were once open to the public but later were closed when it became apparent that they contained poisonous gases. Dead birds are sometimes found around one of the small pools in this area appropriately named Poison Spring.

Historic Buildings

Mammoth contains several other historic structures built during the army's tenure at **Fort Yellowstone.** The most distinctive are the six buildings (all in a row) constructed between 1891 and 1909 as quarters for the officers and captains. Most of the grunt soldiers

historic buildings at Mammoth Hot Springs

lived just behind here in barracks, one of which is now the park administration building. The U.S. Engineers Department was housed in an odd stone building with obvious Asian influences; it's right across from the visitor center. The visitor center has an informative pamphlet ($0.50) that describes the Fort Yellowstone Historic District in detail. Displays around the grounds provide additional details.

Although one wing survives from a hotel built in 1911, most of the **Mammoth Hot Springs Hotel** was constructed in 1937. Step inside to view the large map of the United States built from 15 different types of wood. Mammoth also features a Yellowstone General Store, post office, gas station, restaurant, fast-food eatery, and medical clinic. Mammoth Campground is a short distance down the road. Just up the hill—less than a mile from the hotel—is the Mammoth corral, where horseback rides are offered. Also here is a small **cemetery** populated mostly by infants and a few civilians who died here in the early 1900s.

Albright Visitor Center

Spread over the two floors of the Albright Visitor Center are exhibits on park wildlife and history, but the real treats are the works of two artists who helped bring Yellowstone's magnificent scenery to public attention. Twenty-three of painter Thomas Moran's famous Yellowstone watercolors line the walls (but they're hard to see in the dim lighting), and his studio has been re-created in one corner. Equally impressive are 26 classic photographs—including one of Thomas Moran at Mammoth Hot Springs—taken by William H. Jackson during the 1871 Hayden Survey. The paintings and photos are must-sees for anyone with an artistic bent. The center also has an information desk, videos about the park and Moran every half-hour, and racks of books. Check at the information desk for schedules of wildlife talks and frequent ranger-led walks to surrounding sights in the summer. (A major remodeling of the visitor center is expected in 2010.)

Named for Horace Albright—Yellowstone's first National Park Service superintendent—this

© DON PITCHER

Albright Visitor Center, Mammoth Hot Springs

year-round visitor center is housed in the army's old bachelor officers' quarters. It's open daily 8 A.M.–7 P.M. late May–early September, daily 8 A.M.–6 P.M. the rest of September, and daily 9 A.M.–5 P.M. the remainder of the year.

North Entrance Road
The main road north from Mammoth Hot Springs follows the Gardner River, dropping nearly 1,000 feet in elevation before reaching the town of Gardiner, Montana. (Both the river and the misspelled town are named for Johnson Gardner, a ruthless trapper from the 1820s.) The river is a favorite of fly-fishing enthusiasts. A turnout near the Wyoming-Montana border notes the "boiling river" section of the Gardner River; it's always worth a stop, and the half-mile hike has a big reward at the end. Sometimes during the winter you can spot bighorn sheep on the mountain slopes just north of the river as you head down to Gardiner.

The "back way" to Gardiner is the **Old Gardiner Road,** a five-mile gravel road (great for mountain bikes, but not for RVs or trailers) that starts behind Mammoth Hot Springs Hotel. Traffic is downhill only, so you'll need to take the main road for your return into the park; mountain bikes can go in both directions. This is one of the best places to spot pronghorn antelope in the park, and it also provides a fine escape from the crowds at Mammoth.

To Tower Junction
The 18-mile drive from Mammoth to Tower Junction takes visitors through some of the driest and most open country in Yellowstone. Two waterfalls provide stopping places along the way. Beautiful **Undine Falls** is a 60-foot-high double falls immediately north of the road. Just up the road is a gentle half-mile path to the base of **Wraith Falls,** where Lupine Creek cascades 90 feet. Look for ducks and trumpeter swans in **Blacktail Pond,** a couple of miles farther east.

Blacktail Plateau Drive, approximately nine miles east of Mammoth, turns off from the main road. The rough seven-mile dirt road is a one-way route that loosely follows the Bannock Trail, a path used by the Bannock tribe on their way to buffalo-hunting grounds east of here. Their travois trails are still visible. The Bannocks used this route from 1838 to 1878, but it was probably used for hundreds or thousands of years by various tribes crossing the high plateau. Much of Blacktail Plateau Drive is through open sagebrush, grass, and aspen country, where you're likely to see deer and pronghorn antelope. The trees are very pretty in the fall. On the east end, the road drops back into a forest burned by a severe crown fire in 1988 but now containing young aspen and lodgepole pines and abundant summertime flowers.

A two-thirds-mile boardwalk, **Forces of the Northern Range Self-Guiding Trail** is six miles east of Mammoth Hot Springs. Half a mile beyond where Blacktail Plateau Drive rejoins the main road is the turnoff to the **petrified tree.** The 20-foot-tall stump of an ancient redwood tree (50 million years old) stands behind iron bars; a second petrified tree that used to stand nearby was stolen piece by piece through the years by thoughtless tourists. The **Tower Ranger Station,** originally occupied by the U.S. Army, is just before Tower Junction where the road splits, leading to either Northeast Entrance Road or Canyon.

THE NORTHEAST CORNER
Of the five primary entryways into Yellowstone, the Northeast Entrance is the least traveled, making this a great place to escape the hordes in midsummer. It is also one of the few places to see tall mountains in Yellowstone. The road heads east from Tower Junction and immediately enters **Lamar Valley,** an area of grass and sage along the sinuous Lamar River. Osborne Russell, who trapped this country in the 1830s, described it with affection:

We descended the stream about 15 mls thro. the dense forest and at length came to a beautiful valley about 8 Mls. long and 3 or 4 wide surrounded by dark and lofty mountains. The stream after running thro. the center in a NW direction rushed down a tremendous canyon of basaltic rock apparently just wide enough to admit its waters. The banks of the stream in the valley were low and skirted in many places with beautiful Cotton wood groves. Here we found a few Snake indians comprising 6 men 7 women and 8 or 10 children who were the only Inhabitants of this lonely and secluded spot. They were all neatly clothed in dressed deer and Sheep skins of the best quality and seemed to be perfectly contented and happy.... We stopped at this place and for my own part I almost wished I could spend the remainder of my days in a place like this where happiness and contentment seemed to rein in wild romantic splendor surrounded by majestic battlements which seemed to support the heavens and shut out all hostile intruders.... There is something in the wild romantic scenery of this valley which I cannot...describe; but the impressions made upon my mind while gazing from a high eminence on the surrounding landscape one evening as the sun was gently gliding behind the western mountain and casting its gigantic shadows across the vale were such as time can never efface from my memory.

Yellowstone River Picnic Area

Picnic areas don't generally merit a mention, but this one—1.5 miles east of Tower Junction on the Northeast Entrance Road—is an exception because of its proximity to a grand view. A two-mile trail takes off from here for Grand Canyon of the Yellowstone River. The hike is easy and provides a good chance to see bighorn sheep, but be careful to stay away from the canyon rim. For a loop hike (four miles round-trip), continue to the Specimen Ridge Trail, where you turn left and follow it back to your starting point.

Yellowstone Association Institute

The nonprofit Yellowstone Association Institute (307/344-2294, www.yellowstoneassociation .org) offers many classes out of Lamar Valley's historic Buffalo Ranch, approximately 10 miles east of Tower Junction. To augment the park's small wild herd, bison were brought here in 1902 from private ranches. The bison stayed in pens at night and were herded during the day. After 1915, they were allowed to roam freely in summer, although all of the park's bison were rounded up and driven here for winter. After

THE NORTHEAST CORNER

© AVALON TRAVEL

1938, the roundups ended, but the bison were fed hay every winter in Lamar Valley. Finally in 1952, even this practice was halted and the bison were allowed to roam throughout the park. The historic buildings are worth a look, or better still, take one of the institute's excellent classes.

Specimen Ridge

Just east of the historic Buffalo Ranch is a turnout across from Specimen Ridge, where explorers discovered the standing trunks of petrified trees that had been buried in volcanic ash and mudflows 50 million years ago. Through the centuries, the trunks literally turned to stone as silica entered the wood. The process was repeated through the centuries as new forests gradually developed atop the volcanic deposits, only to be buried by later flows. Scientists have found 27 different forests on top of each other, containing walnut, magnolia, oak, redwood, and maple—evidence that the climate was once more like that of today's midwestern states. Erosion eventually revealed the trees, many of which are still standing. It's one of the largest areas of petrified trees known to exist.

There is no trail to the petrified forest, but during summer rangers lead hikes into the area. Check with the Albright Visitor Center for upcoming treks. Mark Marschall's *Yellowstone Trails* provides a description of the 1.5-mile route if you want to try it on your own. A lesser-known petrified forest in the northwest corner of Yellowstone is accessible via U.S. Hwy. 191.

◖ Wildlife-Viewing

The Northeast Corner is still one of the best places in Yellowstone to view bison, with a gorgeous backdrop of open country and wooded mountains. Elk and mule deer are also commonly seen, and the reintroduction of wolves has added another dimension to wildlife-viewing. The valley contains several small ponds created when the retreating glaciers left large blocks of ice that formed "kettles." Erratic glacial boulders are scattered

along the way. There are campgrounds at Slough Creek and Pebble Creek and very good fishing in Slough Creek, too. But look out for one other critter: the ubiquitous ground squirrels that dart into the road, playing chicken with your tires.

Between the Slough Creek and Pebble Creek campgrounds, wolf aficionados fill roadside turnouts each morning and evening, waiting patiently for members of the Druid Peak Pack (and other packs) to appear. Bring your binoculars and spotting scope! During the wolf denning season, the Park Service prohibits parking or walking along certain stretches of the road, but two turnouts are available.

Northeast Entrance

At the east end of Lamar Valley, the road continues northeast up Soda Butte Creek and between the steep rocky cliffs of **Barronette Peak** (10,404 feet) and **Abiathar Peak** (10,928 feet). Stop at **Soda Butte,** where you'll find a substantial travertine mound similar to those at Mammoth. Although the springs are no longer very active, the air still reeks of hydrogen sulfide, the "rotten egg" gas. South of Soda Butte and several miles up a backcountry trail is **Wahb Springs,** found within Death Gulch. Here poisonous gases are emitted from the ground, killing animals in the vicinity. Early explorers reported finding dead bears that had been overcome by the fumes. Less than one mile north of Soda Butte is a pullout where a half-mile trail leads to pretty **Trout Lake.** It's a nice afternoon break from the crowds elsewhere in Yellowstone.

North of Pebble Creek Campground, the road squeezes through beautiful **Icebox Canyon,** past Barronette Peak, and into the (unburned) lodgepole pine forests. It follows the creek all the way to the edge of the park, crossing into Montana two miles before the park border. The **Northeast Entrance Station** is a classic log building built in 1935 and now designated a National Historic Landmark. The twin towns of Silver Gate and Cooke City are just up the road.

TOWER FALL/ROOSEVELT
Roosevelt Lodge

Lying at the junction of the roads to Canyon, Mammoth, and Lamar Valley, Roosevelt Lodge was built in 1920 and named for President Theodore Roosevelt, who camped a few miles to the south during his 1903 visit. A lifelong supporter of Yellowstone, Roosevelt helped push through legislation that clamped down on the rampant destruction of park wildlife early in the 20th century.

The Roosevelt area is a favorite of families, wolf-watchers, and anglers, many of whom return year after year. The main building has the rough-edged flavor of a hunting lodge and a peacefulness that you won't find at Old Faithful, Canyon, or Mammoth. Inside are two large stone fireplaces, and the porch out front has comfortable rocking chairs that fill each evening. Folks plop their feet on the rail, nurse a beer, and watch the evening roll in. Heavenly. Rustic cabins—most built in the 1920s—provide simple accommodations, and Roosevelt has a restaurant and little gift shop/general store, along with horseback rides. It's also the only place in Yellowstone to offer wagon rides and Old West cookouts; call well ahead for reservations.

Stop at the overlook to **Calcite Springs,** two miles southeast of the junction, where a walkway provides dramatic views into the canyon of the Yellowstone River, with steaming geothermal activity far below. The cliff faces contain a wide strip of columnar basalt, some of which overhangs the highway just to the south.

◖ Tower Fall

On summer afternoons the parking lot at Tower Fall overflows with cars as folks stop to see Tower Creek plummeting 132 feet before joining the Yellowstone River. The tower-like black rocks of the area are volcanic basalt. Nearby are a campground and a Yellowstone General Store. Tower Fall overlook is just a couple of hundred paved feet from the parking area, or you can follow the path a half-mile down the switchbacks to the canyon bottom. Unfortunately, the Park Service has closed the fascinating side trail to the base of the falls, but you do get a good view of the river from the bottom of this path. A ford of the Yellowstone River—used by Bannock Indians in the 19th century—is just a quarter-mile away. For more than 100 years, a huge boulder stood atop Tower Fall; the water and gravity finally won in 1986.

Dunraven Pass and Mt. Washburn

Continuing southward, the road climbs along Antelope Creek and eventually switchbacks up the aptly named Mae West Curve. The North Fork Fire swept through this country in 1988, but the area is now verdant with new trees, grasses, and flowers. Ten miles south of Tower Junction, the old Chittenden Road turns off and leads a mile uphill to a large parking area and trailhead for popular day hikes up **Mt. Washburn,** the 10,243-foot peak that dominates this part of Yellowstone.

South of this is **Dunraven Pass** (8,859 feet), named for the Earl of Dunraven, who visited the park in 1874 and whose widely read book *The Great Divide* brought Yellowstone to the attention of wealthy European travelers. This is the highest point along any park road, even higher than the three other places where the road crosses the Continental Divide! Look for whitebark pines near the road, and be sure to stop just south of here for a view across to the distant Grand Canyon of the Yellowstone.

◖ GRAND CANYON OF THE YELLOWSTONE

Yellowstone is best known for its geysers and animals, but for many visitors the Grand Canyon is the park's most memorable feature. This 20-mile-long canyon ranges 1,500–4,000 feet across and has colorful yellow, pink, orange, and buff cliffs that drop as much as 1,200 feet on either side. The river itself tumbles abruptly over two massive waterfalls, sending up a roar that's audible for miles along the rims. Grand Canyon is accessible by road from both the north and south sides, with equally amazing views. The lodgepole pine forests around here escaped the 1988 fires.

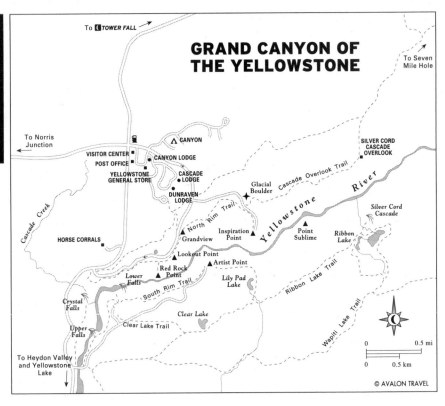

Carving a Canyon

After a massive volcanic eruption 650,000 years ago, rhyolite lava flows came through what is now the Grand Canyon. The flows eventually cooled, but geothermal activity within the rhyolite weakened the rock with hot steam and gasses, making it susceptible to erosion. Through the centuries, a series of glaciers blocked water upstream, each time creating a lake. As each glacier retreated it undammed the stream, allowing the water in the lake to empty suddenly. The weakened rhyolite was easily eroded by these periodic floods of water and glacial debris, thus revealing pastel yellow and red canyon walls colored by the thermal activities. The **Lower Falls** are at the edge of the thermal basin, above rock that was not weakened by geothermal activity. The **Upper Falls** are at a contact point

between hard rhyolite that does not erode easily and a band of rhyolite that contains more easily eroded volcanic glass. Today the canyon is eroding more slowly, having increased in depth just 50 feet during the last 10,000 years.

North Rim Vistas

A one-way road takes visitors to a series of extremely popular overlooks along the north rim of Grand Canyon of the Yellowstone. Farthest east is **Inspiration Point,** where the views of the canyon and Lower Falls are, well, inspirational. A wheelchair-accessible canyon view is available from the edge of the parking lot. **North Rim Trail** leads along the rim from Inspiration Point up to Chittenden Bridge, three miles away, and some sections of this scenic and nearly level path are paved. Just a couple of hundred feet up from Inspiration Point, be sure to look for a 500-ton boulder deposited by a glacier during the glaciation that ended 15,000 years ago. The glacial erratic (as such rocks are called) originated in the Beartooth Mountains at least 30 miles north of here and was carried south atop a moving river of ice.

The one-way road continues westward to overlooks at **Grandview Point** and **Lookout Point.** From Lookout Point, a half-mile trail drops 500 hundred feet to **Red Rock Point** for a closer view of Lower Falls—you can feel the spray. Farthest west along the one-way North Rim Road is the trail to the **Brink of the Lower Falls.** The trail is a half-mile long and paved, descending 600 feet to a viewing area where you can peer over the edge as the water plummets in a thunderous roar over the 308-foot precipice (twice the height of Niagara Falls). This is probably the most breathtaking sight in Yellowstone, but if you suffer from vertigo don't even think about peering over the brink! Just south of where the one-way road rejoins the main highway is a turnoff to the **Brink of the Upper Falls,** where a short walk

© DON PITCHER

Upper Falls of the Yellowstone River

leads to a less dramatic but still beautiful view of the 109-foot-high Upper Falls.

A party of prospectors wandered north into this country in 1867, following the Yellowstone River downstream without suspecting the canyon below. A. Bart Henderson wrote in his diary of strolling down the river and being:

> very much surprised to see the water disappear from my sight. I walked out on a rock & made two steps at the same time, one forward, the other backward, for I had unawares as it were, looked down into the depth or bowels of the earth, into which the Yellow plunged as if to cool the infernal region that lay under all this wonderful country of lava and boiling springs.

Canyon Village

Canyon Village on the north rim is a forgettable shopping mall in the wilderness, complete with various stores and eating places, a post office, gas station, cabins, lodges, and a campground. It's a good place to come on a rainy summer afternoon when the kids are starting to scream for ice cream. Horseback rides are available less than one mile south of here.

The real attraction at Canyon Village is the recently opened **Canyon Visitor Education Center** (307/242-2550). This must-see stop has fascinating exhibits detailing park geology, from geysers and hot springs to the supervolcano that powers everything. A room-size relief model illuminates the park's volcanic eruptions, ashfall, lava flows, and glaciers. Kids can turn the 9,000-pound rotating globe to find volcanic hotspots, and a giant lava lamp illustrates how magma rises in the earth. Upstairs, check out the exhibits on earthquakes, including a seismograph showing today's temblors. There are all sorts of other high-tech exhibits, plus exhibits on lodgepole pine forests and grassland habitats. You could easily spend an hour here and will certainly come away with a better understanding of Yellowstone's inner workings.

The visitor center is open daily May–mid-October. Hours are 8 A.M.–7 P.M. late

May–early September, with reduced hours for most of May and September–mid-October. It's closed in winter.

South Rim Vistas

The south rim is lined with additional dramatic views into Grand Canyon. Cross the Chittenden Bridge over the Yellowstone River (otters are sometimes seen playing in the river below) and continue 0.5 mile to Uncle Tom's parking area, where a short trail leads to views of the Upper Falls and Crystal Falls. More unusual is **Uncle Tom's Trail,** which descends 500 feet to Lower Falls. The trail is partly paved, but it's steep and includes 328 metal steps before you get to the bottom—good exercise if you're in shape. It was named for "Uncle" Tom Richardson who, with the help of wooden ladders and ropes, led paying tourists to the base of the falls around the turn of the 20th century. Because there was no bridge, Uncle Tom also rowed his guests across the river near the present Chittenden Bridge. After his permit was revoked in 1903, visitors had to make do on their own.

One mile beyond Uncle Tom's parking area,

© DON PITCHER

Lower Falls of the Yellowstone River from Artist Point

the road ends at the parking area for **Artist Point,** the most famous—and crowded—of all Grand Canyon viewpoints. A short paved path leads to an astoundingly beautiful spot where one can look upriver to the Lower Falls or down the opposite direction into the canyon. Look for thermal activity far below. The point is apparently where artist Thomas Moran painted some of his famous watercolors. Avoid the crowds and afternoon thunderstorms by getting here early in the morning; it's almost always deserted at sunrise.

HAYDEN VALLEY

Just a few miles south of Canyon, the country abruptly opens into beautiful Hayden Valley, named for Ferdinand V. Hayden, leader of the 1871 expedition into Yellowstone. Reaching eight miles across, this relatively level part of the park was once occupied by an arm of Yellowstone Lake. The sediments left behind by the lake, along with glacial till, do not hold sufficient water to support trees. As a result, the area is occupied primarily by grasses, forbs, and sage. This is one of the best areas in the park to see wildlife, especially bison and elk. The Yellowstone River wanders across Hayden Valley, and streams enter from various sides. These waterways are excellent places to look for **Canada geese,** trumpeter swans, pelicans, and many kinds of ducks. **Wolves** are also frequently sighted; just look for the line of cars and the crowds with binoculars and spotting scopes. Although they are less common, **grizzly bears** can sometimes be found feeding at the eastern end of the valley. Because of the bears, hikers need to be especially cautious when tramping through the grasses and shrubs, where it is easy to surprise a bear or to be likewise surprised. On the north end of Hayden Valley, the road crosses **Alum Creek,** named for its highly alkaline water, which could make anything shrink. In the horse-and-buggy days, Yellowstone wags claimed that a man had forded the creek with a team of horses and a wagon but came out the other side with four Shetland ponies pulling a basket!

◖ Mud Volcano Area

Shortly after the road climbs south out of

Hayden Valley, it passes one of the most interesting of Yellowstone's many thermal basins. On the east side of the road, a turnout overlooks **Sulphur Caldron,** where a highly acidic pool is filled with sulfur-tinted waters and the air is filled with the odor of hydrogen-sulfide gas. Directly across the road is the Mud Volcano area, where a two-thirds-mile loop trail provides what could be a tour through a bad case of heartburn. Pick up a Park Service brochure ($0.50) from the box for descriptions of all the bizarre features here. The area is in a constant state of flux as springs dry up or begin overflowing, killing trees in their path. **Churning Caldron** is a frothing pool where periodic jets send superheated water into the air. Just up the trail is one of the most interesting features, **Black Dragons Caldron,** where an explosive spring blasts constantly through a mass of boiling black mud. The wildest place at Mud Volcano is **Dragon's Mouth Spring,** which the Park Service notes is named for "the rhythmic belching of steam and water shooting from the cavernous opening." It's easy to imagine the fires of hell not far below this spring. The waters are 180°F. During winter (and often in summer), the Mud Volcano area is a good place to see elk or bison.

Along the Yellowstone

South of Mud Volcano, the road parallels the Yellowstone River. At **LeHardys Rapids** a boardwalk provides an overlook where early-summer visitors see blush-red spawning cut-throats. In late summer, this part of the Yellowstone River is a very popular fly-fishing spot—some call it the finest stream for cutthroat fishing in the world—and a good place to view ducks and swans. Earlier in the year, it's open only to the bears that gorge on the cutthroats. By the way, the Yellowstone River, which begins at Yellowstone Lake, is the longest free-flowing (undammed) river in the Lower 48.

◖ YELLOWSTONE LAKE

When first-time visitors see Yellowstone Lake, they are stunned by its magnitude. The statistics are impressive: 110 miles of shoreline, 20 miles

© DON PITCHER

Yellowstone Lake

north to south and 14 miles east to west, with an average depth of 139 feet and a maximum depth of 390 feet. This is the largest high-elevation (over 7,000 feet) lake in North America; Lake Tahoe is bigger, but lower. Yellowstone Lake can seem like a sheet of glass laid to the horizon at one moment and just a half hour later be a roiling ocean of whitecaps and wind-whipped waves. These changeable waters can be dangerous to those in canoes or small boats; several people have drowned, including experienced park rangers. The water is covered by ice at least half of the year, and breakup does not come until late May or early June. Even in summer, water temperatures are often only in the 40s. David Folsom, who was part of an exploration party traveling through the area in 1869, described Yellowstone Lake as an:

inland sea, its crystal waves dancing and sparkling in the sunlight as if laughing with joy for their wild freedom. It is a scene of transcendent beauty which has been viewed by few white men, and we felt glad to have looked upon it before its primeval solitude should be broken by the crowds of pleasure seekers which at no distant day will throng its shores.

Fishing Bridge

The area around famous Fishing Bridge (built in 1937) was for many years a favorite place to catch cutthroat trout. These same fish are a major food source for grizzlies, and this area is considered some of the most important bear habitat in Yellowstone. Conflicts between bears

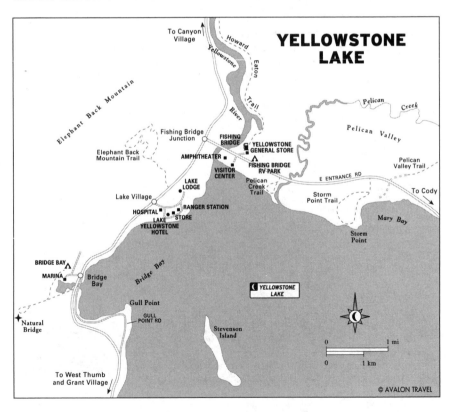

and humans led to the death of 16 grizzlies here. To help restore trout populations and to provide food for the grizzlies, the Park Service banned fishing from Fishing Bridge in 1973 and tried to move the developments to the Grant Village area. Lobbying by folks from Cody (worried lest they lose some of the tourist traffic) kept some of the facilities at Fishing Bridge from closing. Remaining facilities include an RV park, Yellowstone General Store (gifts, groceries, and a snack bar), visitor center, amphitheater, and gas station. The bridge itself is still a popular stopping point and a good place to see large cutthroat trout in the shallows.

Fishing Bridge Visitor Center (307/242-2450, daily late May–early Sept. 8 A.M.–7 P.M., and daily 9 A.M.–6 P.M. for the rest of Sept.) houses a few ancient bird displays and an information desk. Be sure to head out the back door for bucolic views across Lake Yellowstone.

Lake Yellowstone Hotel

Lake Yellowstone Hotel, the oldest extant park hostelry, was built in 1889–1891 by the Northern Pacific Railroad and originally consisted of a simple boxlike structure facing Yellowstone Lake. The hotel was sold to Harry Child in 1901, and two years later Robert Reamer—the architect who designed Old Faithful Inn—was given free rein to transform this into a more attractive place. Hard to believe that the same architect could create a grand log masterpiece and a sprawling Southern colonial mansion with distinctive ionic columns in the same park! Lake Yellowstone Hotel is the second-largest wood-framed building in North America and requires 500 gallons of paint each year to keep it in shape. During the 1960s and 1970s the hotel fell into disrepair under the management of General Host Corporation, and in disgust, the Park Service bought out the concession and leased it to another company. Major renovations in the 1980s transformed the dowdy old structure into a luxurious grand hotel with much of the charm it had when President Calvin Coolidge stayed here in the 1920s.

Today, Lake Yellowstone Hotel is one of the nicest places to stay in the park, with fine vistas out over the lake and comfortable quarters. Relax with a drink in the sunlit **Sun Room** while a pianist or a string quartet provides the atmosphere. Free 45-minute historic **tours of Lake Yellowstone Hotel** are given at 5:30 P.M. Monday–Friday early June–late September. The hotel also houses a restaurant, gift shop, and snack bar.

Be sure to take a walk along the lakeshore out in front of the hotel, where the Absaroka Range forms a backdrop far to the east. The highest mountain is Avalanche Peak (10,566 feet). Almost due south is the 10,308-foot summit of Mt. Sheridan, named for General Philip Sheridan, a longtime supporter of expanding the park to include the Tetons. Watch for the big white pelicans catching fish on the lake.

Just east of Lake Yellowstone Hotel is the **Lake Ranger Station,** built in 1922–1923 and now on the National Register of Historic Places. Inside the octagonal main room you will find a massive central fireplace, exposed log rafters, and rustic light fixtures. A short walk away is **Lake Lodge,** another rustic log structure that houses a reasonably priced cafeteria with grand windows fronting the lake. A Yellowstone General Store stands nearby, and dozens of plain cabins are behind it.

To West Thumb

The highway south from Lake Junction to West Thumb follows the lakeshore nearly the entire distance. A campground and boat harbor are at **Bridge Bay,** along with a ranger station, marina, and store. Stop here for hour-long boat tours of Yellowstone Lake, offered several times a day throughout the summer, or for guided fishing trips and boat rentals.

Back on the main road, keep your eyes open for Canada geese and trumpeter swans as you drive south. **Gull Point Drive,** a two-mile-long side road, offers views of **Stevenson Island** just offshore; farther south, **Frank Island** and tiny **Dot Island** become visible. The small **Potts Hot Springs Basin,** just north of West Thumb, is named for fur trapper Daniel T. Potts, one of the first white men to explore the Yellowstone country. His travels here in

1826 were described the following year in a Philadelphia newspaper article. It was perhaps the first published mention of Yellowstone Lake and the hot springs.

East Entrance Road

Heading east from Fishing Bridge, the road follows the shore of Yellowstone Lake past country that escaped the 1988 fires. Three miles east of the bridge are Indian Pond—popular with birders—and the trailhead for Storm Point Trail. North of here, Pelican Valley is considered important grizzly habitat and is closed to all overnight camping year-round. Even daytime use is not allowed until July 4, and then only between 9 A.M. and 7 P.M. Before venturing out on the Storm Point Trail or into Pelican Valley, check at the Lake Ranger Station for current bear information. The half-mile **Pelican Creek Nature Trail** starts one mile east of Fishing Bridge and provides an easy hike to a beach along Yellowstone Lake. Much of the way is on boardwalk over a marshy area.

At **Steamboat Point** the road swings out along the shore, providing excellent views across the lake and of a noisy fumarole. For an even better view (don't miss this one!), take the **Lake Butte Overlook** road, which continues one mile to a small parking area 1,000 feet above the lake. This is a fine place to watch sunsets and to get a feeling for the enormous size of Yellowstone Lake. Back on the main highway and heading east, you soon leave Yellowstone Lake behind and it is visible in only a few spots as the road climbs gradually, passing scenic **Sylvan Lake,** a nice place for picnics. Just up the road is tiny Eleanor Lake (little more than a puddle) and a steep trail to 10,566-foot **Avalanche Peak.**

Immediately east of Eleanor Lake, the main road climbs to 8,530-foot **Sylvan Pass,** flanked by Hoyt Peak on the north and Top Notch Peak to the south. Steep scree slopes drop down both sides. East of Sylvan Pass, the road descends quickly along Middle Creek (a tributary of the Shoshone River), providing good views to the south of Mt. Langford and Mt. Doane. **East Entrance Ranger Station**

was built by the army in 1904. For many years, the road leading up to Sylvan Pass from the east took drivers across Corkscrew Bridge, a bridge that literally looped over itself as the road climbed steeply up the narrow valley. The road continues eastward to Cody through beautiful Wapiti Valley.

WEST THUMB AND GRANT VILLAGE

The South Entrance Station consists of several log structures right along the Snake River. Just 1.5 miles beyond the entrance is an easily missed turnout where you can walk down to 30-foot-high **Moose Falls.** Beyond this point, the road climbs a long, gentle ramp to Pitchstone Plateau, passing green forests of lodgepole pine. Stop at a turnout to look back at the majestic Tetons. Abruptly, this gentle country is broken by the edge of **Lewis River Canyon,** with rhyolite walls that rise to 600 feet. The fires of 1988 burned hot throughout much of this area, and dead trees line both sides of the canyon in all directions. Young trees are now carpeting many areas, but some remain almost barren more than two decades later.

The road parallels the river for the next seven miles. Nearly everyone stops for a look at 29-foot-high **Lewis Falls.** Camping is available at the south end of **Lewis Lake,** which—like the lake, falls, river, and canyon—was named for the Lewis and Clark expedition's Meriwether Lewis. Lewis Lake is the park's third-largest body of water (after Yellowstone Lake and Shoshone Lake) and is popular with canoeists, kayakers, and anglers. The clear waters contain brown trout and Mackinaw (lake trout). Approximately four miles north of Lewis Lake, the highway tops the Continental Divide, 7,988 feet above sea level. This is one of three such crossings that roads make within Yellowstone.

Grant Village

This odd scattering of buildings is named for President Ulysses S. Grant, who signed the act establishing Yellowstone and whose terms in office were marked by massive corruption scandals. Grant Village was built in the 1980s to replace facilities at Fishing Bridge, an area of important grizzly habitat. Unfortunately, instead of one bad development, Yellowstone now has two because some of the buildings at Fishing Bridge still stand. Unlike some of the more historic places in Yellowstone where a natural rusticity prevailed, Grant Village has less charm than most Wal-Marts. An ugly steakhouse restaurant and waterside cafeteria face Yellowstone Lake, but the marina that was once here is closed. Also sprawled around Grant Village are a campground, rows of chintzy condos, a Yellowstone General Store, a visitor center, a gas station, and post offices. Much of the area around here was consumed in the 1988 Snake River Fire; unfortunately, the fire missed this scar on the Yellowstone landscape.

Grant Visitor Center (307/242-2650, daily late May–early Sept. 8 A.M.–7 P.M. and daily 9 A.M.–6 P.M. for the rest of Sept.) houses an informative exhibit and film on the role of fires in the park, particularly the massive 1988 fires. These provide a good background for understanding the changes taking place as the burned areas recover.

West Thumb

If you look at a map of Yellowstone Lake, it's possible to imagine the lake as a giant hand with three mangled fingers heading south and a gnarled thumb hitching west. Hence the name West Thumb. This section of Yellowstone Lake is the deepest (to 390 feet) and is actually a caldera that filled with water after erupting 150,000 years ago. Considerable heat is still just below the surface, as revealed by **West Thumb Geyser Basin.** Get a Park Service booklet ($0.50) from the box for details on the area's geothermal origins and attractions.

A short loop trail leads past steaming hot springs and pools at West Thumb. Right on the shore is **Fishing Cone,** where tourists once caught fish and then plopped them in the cone to be cooked; after several clowning tourists were injured, the Park Service put a stop to this stunt. The **West Thumb Information Station** (daily late May–mid-Sept. 9 A.M.–5 P.M.)

houses a small bookstore, and in winter the station is used as a warming hut.

West Thumb to Upper Geyser Basin

Heading west from West Thumb, the highway climbs over the Continental Divide twice. Most of these forests escaped the 1988 fires. A few miles beyond the eastern crossing of the divide is a turnout at **Shoshone Point,** where you catch glimpses of Shoshone Lake and the Tetons. In 1914, highwayman Ed Trafton (his real name was Ed Harrington) held up 15 stagecoaches as they passed by this point carrying tourists. He got away with $915.35 in cash and $130 in jewelry but made the rather obvious blunder of posing for photos. He was captured the following year and spent five years in Leavenworth. When he died, a letter in his pocket claimed that he had been author Owen Wister's model for the Virginian. Others suspected that he was more likely to have been Wister's model for the villain, Trampas.

Approximately 14 miles beyond West Thumb, pull off to see the Firehole River as it drops over **Kepler Cascades.** The western crossing of the Continental Divide is at **Craig Pass,** where a tiny pond (Isa Lake) empties into both the Atlantic and Pacific oceans through its two outlet streams.

OLD FAITHFUL AND UPPER GEYSER BASIN

As you approach Old Faithful from either direction, the two-lane road suddenly widens into four, and a cloverleaf exit takes you to Yellowstone's most fabulous sight. Welcome to Upper Geyser Basin, home of Old Faithful, about 400 buildings of all sizes, and a small town's worth of people. For many folks, this is the heart of Yellowstone, and a visit to the park without seeing Old Faithful is like a baseball game without the national anthem. If you came to Yellowstone to see the wonders of nature, you're going to see more than your share here, but you'll probably have to share your share with hundreds of other folks. On busy summer days more than 25,000 visitors come

OLD FAITHFUL AND UPPER GEYSER BASIN

To Madison Junction

Biscuit Basin

To Mystic Falls

Mustard Spring

Avoca Spring

Sapphire Pool

Shell Geyser

Jewel Geyser

Little Firehole River

Mirror Pool

Firehole

Gem Pool

Atomizer Geyser

Artemisia Geyser

River

Morning Glory Pool

Far, Mortar, and Spiteful Geysers

Riverside Geyser

Grotto Geyser

Comet Geyser

Daisy Geyser

Giant Geyser

Splendid Geyser

Punch Bowl Spring

Round Spring

Chromatic Spring

Beauty Pool

Black Sand Pool

Firehole

Grand Geyser

Solitary Geyser

OBSERVATION POINT

River

Crested Pool

Castle Geyser

Lion Geyser

Geyser Hill

Giantess Geyser

Sunset Lake

Opalescent Pool

Rainbow Pool

Cliff Geyser

Beehive Geyser

Chinese Spring

Black Sand Basin

Emerald Pool

STORE

OLD FAITHFUL

OLD FAITHFUL LODGE

Iron

Spring

OLD FAITHFUL INN

VISITOR CENTER

RANGER STATION/CLINIC

SNOW LODGE

STORE

POST OFFICE

Creek

To Fern Cascades

To Lone Star Geyser

To West Thumb

	PAVED TRAIL
	UNPAVED TRAIL
	BOARDWALK

0   0.5 mi

0   0.5 km

© AVALON TRAVEL

through the Old Faithful area! Fortunately, the Upper Geyser Basin contains the largest concentration of geysers in the world, and the adventurous will even discover places almost nobody ever visits. But be very careful: The crust can be dangerously thin around some of the hot springs and geysers, and people have been badly scalded and even killed by missteps. Stay on the boardwalks and trails.

◖ Old Faithful

The one sight seen by virtually everyone who comes to Yellowstone is Old Faithful Geyser, easily the most visited geyser in the world. Old Faithful is neither the tallest nor the most frequently erupting geyser in Yellowstone, but it always provides a great show and is both highly accessible and fairly predictable. Contrary to the rumors, Old Faithful never erupted "every hour on the hour," but for many years its period was a little more than an hour. It has slowed in recent years and is now averaging around 90 minutes per cycle, but varies from 45 to 120 minutes. In general, the longer the length of the eruption,

the longer the interval until the next eruption. Check at the visitor center for the latest prognostications on this and other geysers in the basin.

An almost level paved path circles Old Faithful, providing many different angles from which to view the eruptions, although none of these is particularly close to the geyser because of the danger from hot water. Along the north side is **Chinese Spring,** named in 1885 for a short-lived laundry operation. Apparently, the washman had filled the spring with clothes and soap, not knowing that soap can cause geysers to erupt. One newspaper correspondent claimed—although the tale obviously suffered from embellishment and racism—that:

> The soap awakened the imprisoned giant; with a roar that made the earth tremble, and a shriek of a steam whistle, a cloud of steam and a column of boiling water shot up into the air a hundred feet, carrying soap, raiment, tent and Chinaman along with the rush, and dropping them at various intervals along the way.

© DON PITCHER

Old Faithful Geyser

Old Faithful provides a textbook example of geyser activity. The first signs of life are when water begins to splash out of the vent in what is called preplay. This splashing can last up to 20 minutes, but it's generally only a few minutes before the real thing. The water quickly spears into the sky, reaching 100–180 feet for 1.5–5 minutes before rapidly dropping. During a typical eruption, between 3,700 and 8,400 gallons of water are sent skyward.

On any given summer day, the scene at Old Faithful is almost comical. Just before the predicted eruption time, the benches encircling the south and east sides are jammed with hundreds of people waiting expectantly for the geyser to erupt, and with each tentative spray the camera shutters begin to click. Listen closely and you'll hear half the languages of Europe and Asia. Once the action is over, there's a mad rush back into the visitor center, the stores, and Old Faithful Inn, and within a few minutes the benches are virtually empty. A tale is told of two concessioner employees who once decided to have fun at Old Faithful by placing a large crank atop a box and putting the contraption near the geyser. When they knew it was ready to erupt, they ran out and turned the crank just as Old Faithful shot into the air. Their employer failed to find humor in the prank, and both were fired, or so the story claims.

Visitor Center

As of 2008 the ugly and much-maligned Old Faithful Visitor Center had been torn down and all services relocated to temporary buildings. A new center is being built, but at typical Park Service speed, meaning it gets done years later than planned, or shortly before the end of the universe, whichever comes first. The new two-story 26,000-square-foot **Old Faithful Visitor Education Center** (307/545-2750) will house state-of-the-art exhibits on hydrothermal features in Yellowstone, an auditorium, research library, and bookstore—plus all sorts of earth-friendly aspects to make it a "green" building. I'm certain the new $27-million facility will be worth the wait, but don't expect to see it until 2010 or 2011.

Inside the visitor center (whatever its incarnation), you can watch various films about Yellowstone or peruse the books, maps, and other park publications. In summer, be sure to check the board for the **predicted eruptions** of six major geysers in the area: Old Faithful, Grand, Daisy, Riverside, Great Fountain, and Castle. Rangers can provide all sorts of other information, from where to see bighorn sheep to where to find the restrooms.

The Old Faithful visitor center is open mid-April–early November and mid-December–mid-March. Hours are daily 8 A.M.–7 P.M. (information window till 8 P.M.) late May–early September, and daily 8 A.M.–6 P.M. the

YELLOWSTONE'S FIRST "TOURIST"

From the surface of a rocky plain or table, burst forth columns of water of various dimensions, projected high in the air, accompanied by loud explosions, and sulphurous vapors, which were highly disagreeable to the smell.... The largest of these wonderful fountains, projects a column of boiling water several feet in diameter, to the height of more than one hundred and fifty feet.... After having witnessed three of them, I ventured near enough to put my hand into the water of its basin, but withdrew it instantly, for the heat of the water in this immense couldron, was altogether to great for comfort, and the agitation of the water, disagreeable effluvium continually exuding, and the hollow unearthly rumbling under the rock on which I stood, so ill accorded with my notions of personal safety, that I retreated back precipitately to a respectful distance.

Angus Ferris in 1833

rest of September. During the fall, winter, and spring when park gates are open, the visitor center operates daily 9 A.M.–5 P.M.

If you're not in the park, but want to see the current situation at Old Faithful, check out the **live webcam** at www.nps.gov/archive/yell/oldfaithfulcam.htm.

◖ Old Faithful Inn

Matching one of the great sights of the natural world is one of America's most majestic hotels, Old Faithful Inn. Now more than a century old, the building was designed by Robert Reamer and built in the winter of 1903–1904. One of the largest log structures in existence, the inn has delighted generations of visitors and continues to enthrall all who enter. Its steeply angled roofline reaches seven stories high, with gables jutting from the sides and flags flying from the roof. Surprisingly, the hotel does not face the geyser. Instead, it was built facing sideways to allow newly arriving visitors the opportunity to view the geyser as they stepped from carriages. As you open the rustic split-log front doors with their hand-wrought hardware, you enter a world of the past. The central lobby towers more than 75 feet overhead and is dominated by a massive four-sided stone fireplace that required 500 tons of stone from a nearby quarry. Four overhanging balconies extend above, each bordered by posts made from gnarled lodgepole burls found within the park. Above the fireplace is an enormous clock designed by Reamer and built on the site by a blacksmith. Reamer also designed the two side wings that were added in 1913 and 1928.

On warm summer evenings, visitors stand out on the porch where they can watch Old Faithful erupting, or sit inside at the hand-crafted tables to write letters as music spills from the grand piano. It's enough to warm the heart of even the most cynical curmudgeon. A good restaurant is on the premises, along with a rustic but comfortable bar, a gift shop, fast-food eatery, ice-cream shop, and ATM. Free 45-minute **tours** of Old Faithful Inn are given several times daily during the summer; check the activity desk for times. Old Faithful

© DON PITCHER

Old Faithful Inn

© DON PITCHER

interior of Old Faithful Inn

Inn closes during the winter; it would be hard to imagine trying to heat such a cavern when it's 30°F below zero outside! The building underwent a major renovation in the last few years, with structural upgrades to protect the building from earthquakes and a variety of other improvements. Today, it is open early May–mid-October.

Another nearby building of interest is **Old Faithful Lodge.** Built in 1928, this is the large stone-and-log building just south of the geyser of the same name. The giant fireplace inside is a joy on frosty evenings, and cafeteria windows face the geyser—unlike those at the inn.

Much newer, but an instant classic, is the award-winning **Old Faithful Snow Lodge,** which opened in 1999. This large building offers a sense of rustic elegance, with heavy timbers, a window-lined main entrance, a large stone fireplace, overstuffed couches, and handmade wrought-iron light fixtures and accents. It is one of just two Yellowstone lodges (the other being Mammoth Hot Springs Hotel) open in winter.

Old Faithful Inn has a gift shop, restaurant,

snack bar, ice-cream parlor, lounge, and ATM. Cafeteria meals, espresso, and baked goods are available at Old Faithful Lodge, and Old Faithful Snow Lodge houses a restaurant and snack bar. Both of these also have gift shops. In addition, the Old Faithful area has two gas stations, a post office, and medical clinic.

Geyser Hill Area

Upper Geyser Basin is laced with paved trails that lead to dozens of nearby geysers and hot springs. The easiest path loops around Geyser Hill, just across the Firehole River from Old Faithful. Here are more than 40 different geysers. Check at the visitor center to get an idea of current activity and predicted eruptions, and while you're there pick up the excellent Upper Geyser Basin map ($0.50), which describes some of them. Several geysers are particularly noteworthy. When it plays, **Beehive Geyser** (it has a tall, beehive-shaped cone) vents water as high as 180 feet into the air. These spectacular eruptions vary in frequency; one time you visit they may be 10 days apart, while the next time you come they may be happening twice daily. **Lion Geyser Group** consists of four different interconnected geysers with varying periods of activity and eruptions up to 80 feet. Listen for the roar when Lion is ready to erupt. **Giantess Geyser** may not be active for years at a time—or may erupt several times a year—but the eruptions are sensationally powerful, sending water 100–200 feet skyward. **Doublet Pool** is a beautiful deep-blue pool that is a favorite of photographers. Not far away is **Sponge Geyser,** which rockets water an astounding 2.29 billion angstroms into the air (that's nine inches for the nonscientific crowd). It's considered the smallest named geyser in Yellowstone and gets its title by sending up a spurt of water big enough to be mopped up with a sponge.

Observation Point Loop Trail splits off shortly after you cross the bridge on the way to Geyser Hill and climbs to an excellent overlook where you can watch eruptions of Old Faithful. This is also a good place to view the effects of, and recovery from, the 1988 North Fork Fire. It's two miles round-trip to Observation Point from the visitor center. Another easy trail splits off from this path to **Solitary Geyser,** which is actually just a pool that periodically burps four-foot splashes of hot water. This is not a natural geyser. In 1915, the hot spring here was tapped to provide water for Old Faithful Geyser Bath, a concession that lasted until 1948. The lowering of the water level in the pool completely changed the plumbing system of the hot springs and turned it into a geyser that at one time shot 25 feet in the air. The system still hasn't recovered, although water levels have been restored for many decades.

Firehole River Loop

Another easy, paved path follows the Firehole River downstream from Old Faithful, looping back along the other side for a total distance of three miles. Other trails head off from this loop to the Fairy Falls Trailhead, Biscuit Basin, and Black Sand Basin. The loop is a very popular wintertime ski path, and sections are open to bikes in the summer. Twelve-foot-high **Castle Geyser** does indeed resemble a ruined old castle. Because of its size and the slow accretion of sinter (silica) to form this cone, it is believed to be somewhere between 5,000 and 50,000 years old. Castle sends up a column of water and steam 75 feet into the air and usually erupts every 11–13 hours. Check at the visitor center for a guess at the next eruption.

Daisy Geyser is farther down the path and off to the left. It is usually one of the most predictable of the geysers, erupting to 75 feet approximately every 120–150 minutes. The water shoots out at a sharp angle and is visible all over the basin, making this a real crowd-pleaser.

Just east of Daisy is **Radiator Geyser,** which isn't much to look at—eruptions to two feet—but was named when this area was a parking lot and the sudden eruption under a car led people to think its radiator was overheating. A personal favorite, **Grotto Geyser** is certainly the weirdest of all the geysers, having formed around a tangle of long-petrified tree stumps. It is in eruption one-third of the time, but most eruptions reach only 10 feet.

Look for **Riverside Geyser** across the Firehole from the path and not far downstream from Grotto. This picturesque geyser arches spray 75 feet over the river and is one of the most predictable, with 20-minute-long eruptions approximately every six hours. The paved trail crosses the river and ends at famous **Morning Glory Pool.** For many years, the main road passed this colorful pool, which became something of a wishing well for not just coins but also trash, rocks, logs, and other debris. Because of this junk, the pool began to cool, and the beautiful blue color is now tinged by brown and green algae, despite efforts to remove the debris.

Turning back at Morning Glory, recross the bridge and head left where the path splits at Grotto Geyser. **Giant Geyser** is on the left along the river. Years may pass between eruptions of Giant (or it might erupt every week or so), but when it does go, the name rings true because the water can reach 250 feet. Cross the river again and pass **Beauty Pool** and **Chromatic Pool,** which are connected below the ground so that one declines as the other rises. Very pretty.

Grand Geyser is one of Yellowstone's most dramatic geysers.

© DON PITCHER

Grand Geyser is a wonderful sight. The water column explodes in 1–4 towering bursts lasting 9–12 minutes and sometimes reaching 200 feet. It's the tallest predictable geyser on the planet; see the visitor center for the next eruption or wait with the crowds if the pool looks full. When Grand isn't playing, watch for smaller eruptions from nearby **Turban Geyser.** Hang around long enough in the summer and you'll almost certainly meet one or more of the "geyser-gazers," generally a retiree with plenty of time to watch and make notes. Some of them spend their entire summer watching geysers, relaying geyser activity by radio back to the Old Faithful Visitor Center. Grand Geyser is a favorite because its behavior has been studied and follows a predictable pattern.

Two little fun geysers are a short distance to the south: **Sawmill Geyser** and **Tardy Geyser.** The latter is just 10 feet or so from the trail, providing an up-close look at a small but active geyser. Cross the river again just beyond these two geysers and pass **Crested Pool** on your way back to Castle Geyser. The pool contains deep-blue water that is constantly boiling, preventing the survival of algae.

Black Sand Basin

Just one mile west of Old Faithful is Black Sand Basin, a small cluster of geysers and hot springs. Most enjoyable is unpredictable **Cliff Geyser,** which often sends a spray of hot water 25–30 feet over Iron Spring Creek. Three colorful pools are quite interesting in the basin: **Emerald Pool, Rainbow Pool,** and **Sunset Lake. Handkerchief Pool** is now just a small spouter but was famous for many years as a place where visitors could drop a handkerchief in one end and then recover it later at another vent. In 1929, vandals jammed logs into the pool, destroying this little game. The pool was covered with gravel in subsequent eruptions of Rainbow Pool.

Biscuit Basin

Three miles north of Old Faithful, this basin is named for biscuitlike formations that were found in one of the pools; they were destroyed in an eruption following the 1959 Hebgen Lake earthquake. From the parking lot, the trail leads across the Firehole River to pretty **Sapphire Pool** and then past **Jewel Geyser,** which typically erupts every 7–10 minutes to a height of 15–20 feet. The boardwalk follows a short loop through the other sights of Biscuit Basin. From the west end of the boardwalk, a one-mile trail leads to **Mystic Falls.**

MIDWAY AND LOWER GEYSER BASINS

Heading north from Upper Geyser Basin, the road follows the Firehole River past Midway and Lower Geyser basins, both of which are quite interesting. This stretch of the river is popular with fly-fishing enthusiasts, and several side roads provide access to a variety of hot springs and other sights.

GRAND PRISMATIC SPRING, 1839

At length we came to a boiling Lake about 300 ft in diameter forming nearly a complete circle as we approached on the south side The steam which arose from it was of three distinct Colors from the west side for one third of the diameter it was white, in the middle it was pale red, and the remaining third on the east light sky blue Whether it was something peculiar in the state of the atmosphere the day being cloudy or whether it was some Chemical properties contained in the water which produced this phenom-

enon I am unable to say and shall leave the explanation to some scientific tourist who may have the Curiosity to visit this place at some future period – The water was of deep indigo blue boiling like an imense caldron running over the white rock which had formed the edges to the height of 4 or 5 feet from the surface of the earth sloping gradually for 60 or 70 feet. What a field of speculation this presents for chemist and geologist.

Mountain man Osborne Russell

© DON PITCHER

Grand Prismatic Spring

YELLOWSTONE

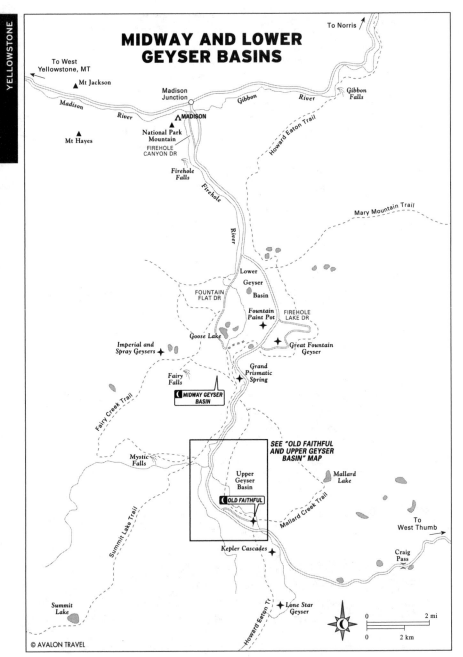

MIDWAY AND LOWER GEYSER BASINS

To Norris

To West
Yellowstone, MT

▲ Mt Jackson

Madison
Junction

Madison River

Gibbon River

Gibbon Falls

Howard Eaton Trail

▲ MADISON

▲ Mt Hayes

National Park
Mountain

FIREHOLE
CANYON DR

Firehole
Falls

Firehole River

Mary Mountain Trail

Lower
Geyser
Basin

FOUNTAIN
FLAT DR

Fountain
Paint Pot

FIREHOLE
LAKE DR

Goose Lake

Imperial and
Spray Geysers ✦

✦ Great Fountain
Geyser

Grand
Prismatic
Spring

Fairy
Falls

Fairy Creek Trail

☾ **MIDWAY GEYSER
BASIN**

SEE "OLD FAITHFUL
AND UPPER GEYSER
BASIN" MAP

Mystic
Falls

Mallard
Lake

Upper
Geyser
Basin

☾ **OLD FAITHFUL**

✦

Mallard Creek Trail

To
West Thumb

Summit Lake Trail

Kepler Cascades ✦

Craig
Pass

Summit
Lake

Howard Eaton Tr

Lone Star
Geyser

0   2 mi

0   2 km

© AVALON TRAVEL

◪ Midway Geyser Basin

Midway is a large and readily accessible geyser basin with a loop path leading to most of the sights. **Excelsior Geyser** is actually an enormous hot spring that pours 4,000 gallons per minute of steaming water into the Firehole River. The water is a deep turquoise. During the 1880s, this geyser was truly stupendous, with explosions that reached 380 feet in the air and almost as wide. These violent eruptions apparently damaged the plumbing system that fed them, and the geyser was dormant for nearly a century until smaller eruptions took place in 1985.

At 370 feet across, **Grand Prismatic Spring** is Yellowstone's largest hot spring. The brilliant reds and yellows around the edges of the blue pool are from algae and bacteria that can tolerate temperatures of 170°F. It's difficult to get a good perspective on this spring from the ground; see aerial photos to really appreciate its beauty.

Firehole Lake Drive

This road (one-way heading north) goes three miles through Lower Geyser Basin, the park's most extensive geyser basin. **Great Fountain Geyser** is truly one of the most spectacular geysers in Yellowstone. Charles Cook, of the 1869 Cook-Folsom-Peterson Expedition, recalled his impression of the geyser: "We could not contain our enthusiasm; with one accord we all took off our hats and yelled with all our might." Modern-day visitors would not be faulted for reacting similarly.

Great Fountain erupts every 9–12 hours (although it can be irregular) and usually reaches 100 feet, but it has been known to blast more than 200 feet. Eruptions begin 70–100 minutes after water starts to overflow from the crater and last for 45–60 minutes in a series of decreasingly active eruptive cycles; but don't leave too early or you may miss the real show! Eruption predictions are posted at the geyser and in the Old Faithful Visitor Center. While you're waiting, watch the periodic eruptions of **White Dome Geyser** just 100 yards down the road. Because of

its massive 30-foot cone, this is believed to be one of the oldest geysers in the park. Eruptions occur every 10 minutes to three hours and spray 30 feet into the air.

Another mile ahead, the road literally cuts into the mound of **Pink Cone Geyser,** which now erupts every 6–20 hours and reaches a height of 30 feet. The pink color comes from manganese oxide. Just up from here at the bend in the road is **Firehole Lake,** which discharges 3,500 gallons of water per minute into Tangled Creek, which in turn drains across the road into **Hot Lake. Steady Geyser** is unusual in that it forms both sinter (silica) and travertine (calcium carbonate) deposits. The geyser is along the edge of Hot Lake and, true to its name, erupts almost continuously, although the height is only five feet. Firehole Lake Drive continues another mile to its junction with the main road right across from the parking area for Fountain Paint Pot. In the winter, Firehole Lake Drive is popular with skiers but is closed to snowmobiles.

Fountain Paint Pot

Always a favorite of visitors, Fountain Paint Pot seems to have a playfulness about it that belies the immense power just below the surface. Pick up a trail guide ($0.50) as you head up the walkway for the full story. **Silex Spring,** off to the right as you walk up the small hill, is colored by different kinds of algae and bacteria. The spring has been known to erupt as a geyser (to 20 feet) but is currently dormant.

Fountain Paint Pot is a few steps up the boardwalk and consists of colorful mud that changes in consistency throughout the season depending on soil moisture. The pressure from steam and gases under the Paint Pot can throw gobs of mud up to 20 feet into the air. Just north of here are fumaroles that spray steam, carbon dioxide, and hydrogen sulfide into the air.

Continuing down the boardwalk, you come upon an impressive overlook above a multitude of geysers that change constantly in activity, including **Morning Geyser,** which has been known to erupt more than 200 feet. The most active is **Clepsydra Geyser,** which is in eruption much of the time. **Fountain Geyser** explodes in a stunning display that can last 30 minutes and reach up to 50 feet. Eruptions are unpredictable but impressive, particularly at sunset. The rest of the loop trail passes dead lodgepole pines that are being petrified as the silica is absorbed, creating a bobby-socks appearance.

Fountain Flat

Fountain Flat Drive provides access to meadows along the Firehole River and is a good place to see bison and elk. The paved road ends after one mile at a parking area, but hikers and cyclists (or skiers in winter) can continue another four miles on Old Fountain Freight Road to its junction with the main road again near Midway Geyser Basin. The road ends in a parking area near **Ojo Caliente**—a small hot springs with a big odor—right along the river. This is one of the most popular fly-fishing spots in the area. Several more hot springs are upstream from here, and the **Fairy Falls Trail** starts three miles south of the parking area.

Firehole Canyon Drive

This one-way road (south only) curves for two miles through Firehole Canyon, where dark rhyolite cliffs rise hundreds of feet above the river. The road begins just south of Madison Junction and was intensely burned in the 1988 North Fork Fire, giving the canyon's name a dual meaning. **Firehole Falls,** a 40-foot drop, is worth stopping to see, as is **Firehole Cascades** a bit farther up. Kids of all ages enjoy the popular hot springs–warmed **swimming hole** a short distance up the road. It's one of the few places along the Yellowstone road system where swimming is openly allowed (albeit not encouraged). No lifeguard, of course.

© DON PITCHER

swimming at Firehole Cascades in the Firehole River

Hiking

Short nature trails (a half-mile or less) are briefly described above in the *Sights* section, but Yellowstone also has a wonderful diversity of day hikes that are perfect for all levels of ability. Park visitor centers distribute free handouts for trails covering Mammoth, Old Faithful, Grant Village, Canyon, and Lake Yellowstone areas. You can also purchase a day-hike sampler pamphlet or various hiking books. Good ones are *Yellowstone Trails* by Mark C. Marschall and *A Ranger's Guide to Yellowstone Day Hikes* by Roger Anderson and Carol Shively Anderson.

The Park Service offers free naturalist-led programs and interpretive walks, along with half-day **Ranger Adventure Hikes** ($15 adults, $5 kids) most days. See your copy of *Yellowstone Today* for the current schedule.

MAMMOTH AREA
Bunsen Peak
- Distance: 4.2 miles round-trip
- Rating: moderately strenuous
- Elevation: 7,250 feet with a 1,300-foot climb
- Trailhead: Five miles south of Mammoth on the Mammoth-Norris Road, across from the Glen Creek Trailhead

This trail begins a short way up the Bunsen Peak Road (closed to motor vehicles) from the Golden Gate entrance and climbs through forest and meadow to the top of Bunsen Peak, where you'll find panoramic vistas of the entire region. Return via the same path.

Osprey Falls
- Distance: 8 miles round-trip
- Rating: strenuous
- Elevation: 7,250 feet
- Trailhead: Five miles south of Mammoth on the Mammoth-Norris Road, across from the Glen Creek Trailhead

This dirt track is open to hikers and mountain-bikers but closed to cars. Follow it 2.5 miles to the Osprey Falls Trail, where a steep path (no bikes allowed) drops 700 feet in less than a mile to the base of this 150-foot waterfall. You'll need to climb back out the same way, so don't get too late a start.

Beaver Ponds Loop
- Distance: 5 miles round-trip
- Rating: moderate
- Elevation: 6,240 feet
- Trailhead: Between Liberty Cap and the stone house next to Mammoth Terraces

This trail begins with a 350-foot climb up and above Clematis Gulch. Turn right at the junction with Sepulcher Mountain Trail, and the trail soon levels out and rambles through meadows and aspen to a series of beaver ponds. Past here, the route loops back to Mammoth through forests and grassland. This trail provides a good opportunity to see mule deer, elk, pronghorn antelope, and moose, but it is best hiked in the spring or fall when temperatures are lower. Black and grizzly bears are sometimes seen along the way, so be sure to make noise while you walk.

Sepulcher Mountain Trail
- Distance: 11 miles round-trip
- Rating: strenuous
- Elevation: 6,240 feet with a 3,400-foot elevation gain
- Trailhead: Between Liberty Cap and the stone house next to Mammoth Terraces

Follow the Beaver Ponds Trail to the Sepulcher Mountain Trail junction and then climb sharply (you'll be sweating) through forest and meadows to the top of this 9,652-foot peak just northwest of Mammoth. Return the same way or via a loop trail that continues along the opposite side of the mountain through an open slope to the junction of Snow Pass Trail, which descends to the Howard Eaton Trail, and then back to Mammoth. You'll find abundant late-summer flowers in the expansive meadows on the south side of Sepulcher Mountain (named for several strange rocks at its summit). Before heading out, check at the visitor center to see if there are any major bear problems in the area and to get a topographic map and hiking tips.

NORTHEAST CORNER
Slough Creek Trail
- Distance: 4 miles round-trip
- Rating: moderate
- Elevation: 6,250 feet
- Trailhead: On the dirt road toward Slough Creek Campground, where the road turns left

This trail—actually a wagon road—makes for a delightful day hike through Douglas fir forests and open meadows. The first mile gains 400 feet in elevation, but it's mostly downhill on the way back. The road continues all the way to the park boundary, 11 miles north of the campground, and is used for access to Silver Tip Ranch. This is the only way into the ranch, and because no motor vehicles are allowed you may meet folks on a horse-drawn wagon during your hike. Day-hikers often go up the road as far as the first meadow, but more adventurous hikers continue to the second meadow (10 miles round-trip).

Pebble Creek Trail
- Distance: 4 miles round-trip
- Rating: strenuous
- Elevation: 7,300 feet
- Trailhead: Warm Creek Picnic Area, 1.5 miles west of the Northeast Entrance station

This remote area is far from the crowds around Old Faithful or Canyon. The trail climbs 1,000 feet in 1.5 miles before dropping into flower-filled mountain meadows along Pebble Creek. A second trailhead at Pebble Creek Campground anchors the other end of

this trail, but at 12 miles it's too long for most day-hikers. Backpackers use this route for longer trips into the area.

TOWER-ROOSEVELT AREA
Lost Lake Trail
- Distance: 4 miles round-trip
- Rating: moderate
- Elevation: 6,300 feet
- Trailhead: Behind Roosevelt Lodge

This trail climbs through forested hills to Lost Lake, where you can either return via the Roosevelt Horse Trail or contour along the hillside to the Petrified Tree parking area, where another path loops back to the lodge. Black bears are often seen in the area, so stay alert.

Mt. Washburn
- Distance: 6 miles round-trip
- Rating: moderately strenuous
- Elevation: 8,850 feet with a 1,400-foot elevation gain
- Trailheads: Dunraven Pass parking area (14 miles south of Tower Junction on the Tower-Canyon Road) or Chittenden Road parking area (9 miles south of Tower Junction)

This outstanding and extremely popular day hike is accessible from two different trailheads along the Tower-Canyon Road, both of which are equal in length and in elevation gained. Either route ascends 10,243-foot Mt. Washburn on a wide path, and the north end is open to mountain bikes. The summit provides commanding vistas in all directions, with a shelter at the base of the fire lookout (which has telescopes, water, and toilets). Many wildflowers bloom in midsummer, and bighorn sheep are frequently seen right along the trail. Bring warm clothes and rain gear because conditions on top may be much cooler and windier than below. Mornings are better times to climb Mt. Washburn since afternoon thunderstorms often roll in during the summer. The Dunraven Pass parking area is often full, but space is generally available at the north trailhead.

GRAND CANYON OF THE YELLOWSTONE
Seven Mile Hole Trail

- Distance: 11 miles round-trip
- Rating: strenuous
- Elevation: 8,000 feet
- Trailhead: Glacial Boulder pullout on the road to Inspiration Point

This trail provides fantastic views for the first mile or so, minus the crowds at nearby Inspiration Point. Look for **Silver Cord Cascade,** a thin ribbon of water dropping over the opposite wall of the canyon, but be careful not to go too close to the very loose edge. It's a very long way down! The trail switchbacks steeply to the Yellowstone River, passing odoriferous thermal areas en route. Many anglers come to Seven Mile Hole (it's seven miles downriver from Lower Falls) while other folks come to relax along the river. Save your energy for the strenuous 1,400-foot climb back up, and bring lots of drinking water. Three campsites are available near the base of the trail for those who want to make this an overnight hike (backcountry permit required).

South Rim Trail

- Distance: 6 miles round-trip
- Rating: easy
- Elevation: 7,700 feet
- Trailhead: East end of Chittenden Bridge across from Wapiti Lake Picnic Area

This hike follows the almost-level and partly paved South Rim Trail two miles to Artist Point, providing many viewpoints en route, including an optional hike down Uncle Tom's Trail, a steep 500-foot drop to Lower Falls. The least-traveled part of the trail (it's called **Ribbon Lake Trail**) continues eastward along the top, providing an abrupt escape from the mob scene at Artist Point, as well as a chance to see the kaleidoscopically colored canyon, hear the roar of the river from far below, and watch for squirrels and birds. But be careful to stay away from the edge where the rocks are loose. It's doubtful that anyone could survive such a fall, and I once

came perilously close to testing that postulate. The trail continues to Lily Pad Lake, where a spur path leads uphill for a wonderful view of the canyon and **Silver Cord Cascade.** With a drop of 1,200 feet, Silver Cord is the highest falls in Yellowstone. You can return the same way or via a number of loop hikes in the area; get the park's *Canyon Area Trail Guide* for details. (As an aside, the old trail to Point Sublime has been closed because of unsafe conditions along the canyon rim.)

YELLOWSTONE LAKE AREA
Natural Bridge

- Distance: 3 miles round-trip
- Rating: easy
- Elevation: 7,750 feet
- Trailhead: Bridge Bay Marina parking lot near the campground entrance road

This natural bridge is a 51-foot-high span of rock that was carved by the waters of Bridge Creek. The trail meanders through the forest for 0.25 mile and then follows a paved road the rest of the way. A short, but steep, switchback trail to the top of the bridge starts in front of the interpretive exhibit. Above the bridge, the trail crosses the creek and continues along the cliff before rejoining the road. Cyclists can ride bikes to Natural Bridge on a separate trail that begins south of the marina. The Natural Bridge area is closed in spring and early summer when bears are feeding on spawning trout in the creek.

Storm Point Trail

- Distance: 2.3 miles round-trip
- Rating: easy
- Elevation: 7,800 feet
- Trailhead: Indian Pond pullout, 3 miles east of Fishing Bridge Visitor Center

This pleasant loop trail is essentially level and goes past a large colony of yellow-bellied marmots before reaching windswept Storm Point, where waves often pound against the rocks. Following the shoreline to the west, the trail eventually loops back through the lodgepole forest to Indian Pond. The trail may be closed in spring and early summer because of grizzlies, and mosquitoes may make a June or July trip less enjoyable.

Elephant Back Mountain Trail
- Distance: 3.6 miles round-trip
- Rating: moderate
- Elevation: 7,800 feet
- Trailhead: Pullout 1 mile south of Fishing Bridge Junction

This nice hike climbs 800 feet in elevation through dense lodgepole forests to panoramic views across Yellowstone Lake and into Pelican Valley. After 1 mile the trail splits into a loop, both sides of which join at the overlook.

Avalanche Peak Trail
- Distance: 4 miles round-trip
- Rating: very strenuous
- Elevation: 8,500 feet with a 2,100-foot elevation gain
- Trailhead: Across the road from the pullout at the west end of Eleanor Lake (8 miles west of East Entrance)

This trail begins on the east side of Middle Creek and climbs very steeply. It emerges from the forest halfway up at the base of a large bowl, and then it continues to the left and switchbacks over talus slopes to an open area below the summit. Follow the trail up the narrow ridgeline and cross it with extreme caution. At the summit, you can see most of the peaks in the Absarokas and Tetons, but snow is present on top until mid-July. Hiking isn't recommended here in September and October because of the presence of grizzly bears feeding on whitebark pinenuts.

WEST THUMB AND GRANT VILLAGE
Lewis River Channel and Dogshead Loop
- Distance: 11 miles round-trip
- Rating: moderate
- Elevation: 7,780 feet

- Trailhead: Dogshead Trailhead just north of Lewis Lake on west side of road (5 miles south of Grant Village)

Choose between two trails—or combine them into a loop hike—to Shoshone Lake. The 4-mile-long Dogshead Trail is more direct, while the 7-mile Lewis Channel Trail takes a much more scenic trek via the channel connecting Shoshone and Lewis lakes. This slow-flowing creek is popular with anglers who come to fish for brown and cutthroat trout during the fall spawning season, and it's also used by canoeists and kayakers heading into Shoshone Lake. Much of the Lewis Lake area was burned in the 1988 fires.

Yellowstone Lake Overlook
- Distance: 2 miles round-trip
- Rating: moderate
- Elevation: 7,750 feet
- Trailhead: On the right as you enter West Thumb Geyser Basin parking area

This fine day hike gains 400 feet in elevation in 1 mile, enough for a commanding vista across the lake, with the Absaroka Mountains behind.

DeLacy Creek Trail
- Distance: 6 miles round-trip
- Rating: easy
- Elevation: 7,950 feet
- Trailhead: DeLacy Creek Trailhead (9 miles west of West Thumb Junction)

This trail provides access to Shoshone Lake—Yellowstone's largest backcountry lake—which is circled by more trails. Keep your eyes open for moose, sandhill cranes, and other animals in the meadows along the way.

OLD FAITHFUL AREA
Lone Star Geyser Trail
- Distance: 5 miles round-trip
- Rating: easy
- Elevation: 7,600 feet
- Trailhead: Lone Star Geyser Trailhead 3.5 miles south of Old Faithful Junction (just east of Kepler Cascades)

A wide paved trail (actually an old road) leads to this popular geyser. It's a favorite of bicyclists in the summer and skiers in the winter. Lone Star Geyser erupts every three hours from a distinctive nine-foot-high cone, with eruptions generally reaching 45 feet and lasting for 30 minutes. Bikes are not allowed beyond the geyser. Hikers can also get to Lone Star via the Howard Eaton Trail out of Old Faithful (6 miles round-trip). For a longer hike, you can continue south from Lone Star on **Shoshone Lake Trail** to Shoshone Lake, 8 fairly easy miles from the main road.

Mystic Falls Trail

- Distance: 2.5 miles round-trip
- Rating: moderate
- Elevation: 7,100 feet
- Trailhead: At the back of the Biscuit Basin boardwalk (2 miles north of Old Faithful Junction)

This path follows a pretty creek to where the Little Firehole River cascades 70 feet over **Mystic Falls.** You can switchback farther up the trail to the top of the falls and then connect with another trail for the loop back to Biscuit Basin (3 miles round-trip). This is a very nice short hike and can be lengthened into a trip to **Little Firehole Meadows** (10 miles round-trip), where bison are often seen in the summer.

Fountain Freight Road/Fairy Falls

- Distance: 5 miles round-trip to Fairy Falls
- Rating: easy
- Elevation: 7,250 feet
- Trailhead: 1 mile south of Midway Geyser Basin (4.5 miles north of the Old Faithful Interchange)

The 4-mile-long Fountain Freight Road is closed to cars, but it's a great place for mountain bikers and those out for a relatively level walk. A steel bridge crosses the Firehole River at the southern trailhead, and the road soon passes the west side of Grand Prismatic Spring; rough trails lead up the hillside for a better view. One mile up from the trailhead you'll come to **Fairy Falls Trail** on your left. It's an easy walk to the falls, a 200-foot ribbon of water cascading into a large pool. The hike to Fairy Falls can be combined with longer treks to Little Firehole Meadow and Mystic Falls or to a pair of small peaks called Twin Buttes. Half a mile beyond Fairy Falls is **Imperial Geyser,** with periodic small eruptions. Nearby **Spray Geyser** erupts frequently, sending water six feet in the air. For a longer version of the hike to Fairy Falls (10 miles round-trip), start from the north end, where Fountain Flat Drive ends.

BACKCOUNTRY HIKING

Most Yellowstone visitors act as though they were chained to their cars with a 100-yard tether—as if by getting away from their vehicles they might miss some other sight down the road. For the 2 percent or so who *do* abandon their cars, Yellowstone has much to offer beyond the spectacular geysers and canyons for which it is famous. Although many parts of the Yellowstone backcountry are heavily visited, regulations keep the sense of wildness intact by separating campsites and limiting the number of hikers. If you head out early or late in the season, you'll discover solitude just a few miles from the traffic jams.

Much of Yellowstone consists of lodgepole (or burned lodgepole) forests on rolling terrain. With a few exceptions, anyone looking for dramatic alpine scenery would probably be better off heading to Grand Teton National Park, the Beartooth Mountains, or the Wind River Mountains. The Yellowstone backcountry is still enjoyable to walk through, however, and many trails lead past waterfalls, geysers, and hot springs. Besides, this is one of the finest places in America to view wildlife—including bison, elk, grizzlies, and wolves—in a setting other than a zoo.

Before August, when they start to die down, you should be ready for the ubiquitous mosquitoes. Ticks are a nuisance mid-March–mid-July in lower-elevation parts of Yellowstone. The fires of 1988 created some problems for backcountry hikers but also offer a good opportunity to see how the land is recovering two decades later.

A few two- to four-day backcountry hikes covering various parts of Yellowstone are described below. The park has more than 1,000 miles of trails, so this is obviously a tiny sampling of the various hiking options.

Before you head out you will probably want to look over your hiking options. Two excellent source books are *Yellowstone Trails* by Mark Marschall and *Hiking Yellowstone National Park* by Bill Schneider. Get them from park gift shops or visitor centers, which also sell topographic park maps. The best maps are those produced by Trails Illustrated; these feature all of the major trails and show the severity of burn from the 1988 fires—a considerable help when planning hiking trips.

If you need a trailhead drop-off or pickup, contact **Back Country Sports** (208/652-3385) out of Ashton, Idaho.

Rules and Regulations

The Park Service maintains more than 300 campsites in the Yellowstone backcountry, most of which have pit toilets and fire rings, along with storage poles to keep food from bears. Hikers may stay only at designated campsites. Wood fires are not allowed in many areas and are discouraged elsewhere, so be sure to have a gas stove for cooking. Bear-management areas have special regulations; they may be for day-use only, include seasonal restrictions, or specify minimum group sizes (larger groups are safer). Pets are not allowed on the trails within Yellowstone, and special rules apply for those coming in with horses, mules, burros, and llamas. Because of wet conditions and the lack of forage, no stock animals are permitted before July.

A free **backcountry use permit** is required of each overnight party and is available in person from various Yellowstone ranger stations and visitor centers within 48 hours of your hike. Because of the popularity of backcountry trips, you should make reservations before your arrival in the park. Unfortunately, the Park Service has taken a lesson from the

IRS and makes the process as complex as bureaucratically possible. Try to follow me here. Backcountry campsite reservations (not the same thing as a backcountry use permit) cost $20 per trip, and the reservation forms are available from the Backcountry Office, P.O. Box 168, Yellowstone National Park, WY 82190, 307/344-2160. You can also download them at www.nps.gov/yell, or request one by sending an email to YELL_Backcountry_Office@nps.gov. Campsite reservation requests must be mailed in, using these forms; reservations are not accepted by phone, fax, or over the Internet. You'll receive a confirmation notice by return mail and will exchange the notice for a permit when you get to the park; the permit must be obtained in person at a ranger station within 48 hours of your first camping date. Before receiving your permit, you will be given a lengthy rundown on what to expect and what precautions to take, and will be shown a bear-safety video. The ranger stations are generally open 8 A.M.–4:30 P.M. seven days a week June–August.

For backcountry rules, bear-safety tips, and suggestions for hiking and horsepacking, pick up Yellowstone's detailed *Backcountry Trip Planner,* which shows locations of campsites throughout the park and provides complete information on wilderness access and precautions. You should also pick up or request the free park pamphlet *Beyond Road's End.* Downloadable PDF versions of both these are available online at www.nps.gov/yell/planyour visit/publications.htm.

Those interested in horsepacking or llama trips should contact the park (307/344-7381, www.nps.gov/yell) for a list of outfitters authorized to operate in Yellowstone. The outfitters offer everything from day trips to weeklong adventures deep into the backcountry.

Sportsman Lake Trail and Electric Peak

The land west of Mammoth is some of the most rugged in Yellowstone, with several peaks topping 10,000 feet. Several trails cut westward across this country, one of the most interesting being the 24-mile-long Sportsman Lake Trail. The route begins at Glen Creek Trailhead five miles south of Mammoth and follows Glen Creek (a good place to see elk in autumn) for four miles before crossing into the Gardner River drainage. Along the way, a short spur trail leads to pretty Cache Lake. Considerably more challenging is a second side trip, the climb up 10,992-foot Electric Peak, the tallest mountain in this corner of Yellowstone. Many folks camp near Electric Peak and spend a day climbing. It's eight miles round-trip and you gain 3,000 feet on the way up, but the trail becomes harder to follow the higher you climb. See a park trail guidebook for details and precautions on this hike. It is possible to day hike to the top of Electric Peak from the Glen Creek Trailhead, but it's not recommended unless you have a masochistic streak, have done a lot of hiking, and are in great shape.

Beyond the side trail to Electric Peak, Sportsman Lake Trail crosses the Gardner River twice, and there are no bridges. The water can be dangerously deep early in the summer, so this hike is generally done in August or September. After you ford the river, the trail climbs to Electric Divide (watch for bighorn sheep) and then drops steeply to Sportsman Lake and down along pretty Fan Creek to the Fawn Pass Trailhead on U.S. Hwy. 191. Because this is a one-way hike you will need to set up some sort of vehicle shuttle. Another problem is bears. This country overflows with grizzly activity, and a party size of four or more is recommended for travel here. Off-trail travel is prohibited in some areas; see the Park Service for details.

Black Canyon of the Yellowstone
For an early-summer backpacking trip, it's hard to beat this 19-mile trek along the northern edge of Yellowstone. Start at the Hellroaring Trailhead, 3.5 miles west of Tower, and follow the Yellowstone River Trail in a steep descent to the river, 600 feet below. A suspension bridge crosses the river, and from here on you remain on the north side all the way to Gardiner. One ford at Hellroaring Creek

can be dangerous before August, but it can be avoided if you hike a mile or so upstream to a stock bridge crossing. After this point, the hike alternates between high ridges overlooking Black Canyon of the Yellowstone and quieter stretches where the trail drops down along the edge of the water. Dramatic Knowles Falls is a highlight. The trail is in good condition, but you may find it hot and dry in midsummer.

Pebble Creek and Bliss Pass Trails
Pebble Creek Trail cuts through a section of Yellowstone that is far away from the geysers and canyons for which the park is famous. The crowds don't come here, but the country is some of the nicest mountain scenery to be found. The trail connects with the Northeast Entrance road at both ends, making access easy. You can start from either end, but if you begin at Warm Creek Picnic Area (1.5 miles west of the entrance station), you get to the high meadows more quickly. From the picnic area the trail climbs 1,100 feet in the first 1.5 miles, but beyond this it's all downhill. The best time to hike this trail is in late summer, when the water levels are lower (there are four fords) and the mosquitoes have abated. Hikers are treated to abundant alpine flowers and grand mountain scenery along the way, with the chance to see moose or elk in the meadows.

For a longer alternative hike, follow Pebble Creek Trail 5.5 miles from the picnic area and then turn west onto Bliss Pass Trail. The path crosses Pebble Creek (quite deep until late summer) before climbing 1,400 feet over Bliss Pass and then dropping 2,700 feet to Slough Creek Trail. From here it is an easy walk to Slough Creek Campground. Total distance from the Warm Creek Picnic Area to Slough Creek Campground is 20 miles.

Shoshone Lake
The largest lake in the Lower 48 without direct road access, Shoshone Lake is probably the most visited part of Yellowstone's backcountry. Its shoreline is dotted with more

than two dozen campsites, but most of these fill on midsummer nights with hikers, canoeists, and kayakers. Because of the lake's popularity, reserve well ahead for a summertime campsite. On-water access is via Lewis Lake and the Lewis River Channel. Anglers come to fish in the channel or lakes; Shoshone Lake has good numbers of brown, lake, and brook trout, all of which were planted here. Hikers reach Shoshone Lake primarily from the DeLacy Creek Trailhead on the north side between West Thumb and Old Faithful, or from the east side via Dogshead Trailhead. A 22-mile trail circles Shoshone Lake, although it is away from the shoreline much of the distance. You may see moose or elk and are certain to meet clouds of mosquitoes before August. The finest lake vistas come from the east side, where the trail follows the lakeshore for four miles. On the west end of the lake, hikers will find Shoshone Geyser Basin, an area filled with small geysers, beautiful pools, and bubbling mud pots. Most of the lake escaped the 1988 fires, but trails from the east side (via Dogshead Trailhead) traverse burned stands of lodgepole.

Heart Lake

The Heart Lake area is another extremely popular backcountry and day-hiking area, offering easy access, a pretty lake, hot springs, and impressive mountain vistas. Heart Lake Trail begins just north of Lewis Lake (six miles south of Grant Village). The trail is fairly easy, climbing slowly through unburned forests for the first five miles and then following Witch Creek down past burned forests to Heart Lake, eight miles from the trailhead. Witch Creek is fed almost entirely by the hot springs and geysers scattered along it.

Near the Heart Lake patrol cabin the trail splits. Continue straight ahead another 26 miles to eventually reach the isolated and challenging Thorofare Trail on the southeast end of Yellowstone Lake; getting there requires fording the Yellowstone River, which may be waist deep even in late summer. For something

a bit less remote, turn right and hike 0.5 mile to the Mt. Sheridan Trail, which heads west and climbs 2,800 vertical feet in three miles. Reaching the 10,308-foot summit will certainly leave you winded. A fire lookout at the top provides views across Yellowstone Lake and south to the Tetons.

At the base of Mt. Sheridan and just to the north is a small thermal area that contains Rustic Geyser (eruptions to 50 feet, but irregular) and Columbia Pool, among other attractions. Be very careful when walking here because of the overhanging rim at the pool edge.

Although many people simply hike to Heart Lake for an overnight trip, one could take many longer hikes out of here, including into the remote Thorofare. A complete loop around the lake is approximately 34 miles round-trip but requires two Snake River fords that are at least to your knees in late July; check with the rangers for flow levels. The Heart Lake area is prime grizzly habitat and is closed until the first of July. Do not take chances in this country!

Bechler River

The southwest section of Yellowstone is known as Cascade Corner, a reference to its many tall waterfalls; more than half of the park's falls are here. This scenic and wild country escaped the fires of 1988 and is popular with anglers. Primary access is from either the Bechler Ranger Station (pronounced BECK-ler) or the Cave Falls Trailhead, both of which are well off the beaten path and must be reached via Cave Falls Road from the Idaho side. It's 22 miles in from Ashton, Idaho, the last 10 on a gravel road. As an alternative, Grassy Lake Road provides a narrow and rough gravel connection to Cave Falls Road. Grassy Lake Road begins at Flagg Ranch Resort near Yellowstone's South Entrance; see a good map for the exact route.

All hikers must register at the Bechler Ranger Station, even if they are heading out from Cave Falls Trailhead, three miles farther down the road. Cave Falls is a wide but not particularly tall drop along the Falls River. It's named for a cave on the west end of the waterfall. The Forest Service's **Cave Falls Campground** ($10) is open mid-May–August.

A spiderweb of trails cuts across the Bechler country, leading to many waterfalls and past several hot springs. One popular hike goes from Bechler Ranger Station to the Old Faithful area, a distance of 30 miles; it's downhill much of the way if you do this in reverse by starting at Old Faithful. From Bechler Ranger Station the trail cuts across expansive Bechler Meadows and then up narrow Bechler Canyon, passing Colonnade, Ouzel, and Iris falls along the way. Many people stop overnight at Three River Junction to enjoy the hot springs–warmed water. Beyond this point, the trail punches over the Continental Divide and then runs west of Shoshone Lake to Lone Star Geyser and the trailhead at Kepler Cascades. It's best to hike this route in August or September after the Bechler River drops enough to be more safely forded. This also allows time for the meadows to dry out a bit (watch out for leeches) and for the mosquitoes to quiet to a dull roar. For the long trek between Bechler Ranger Station and Old Faithful you will need to set up some sort of vehicle shuttle, but shorter in-and-out loop trips could be created by reading the various Yellowstone hiking guides and studying topographic maps.

The Thorofare

If any part of Yellowstone deserves the title untamed wilderness, it has to be the Thorofare. Situated along Two Ocean Plateau and cut through by the upper Yellowstone River, this broad expanse of roadless country reaches from Yellowstone Lake into the Teton Wilderness south of the park. This is *the* most remote country anywhere in the Lower 48; at its heart you'd need to hike 30 miles in any direction to reach a road. Because of the distances involved, many people choose to traverse the Thorofare via horseback. There is considerable grizzly activity in this area, so

various restrictions are in place. In addition, some major river crossings are impassable until late summer. Access to the Thorofare is via Heart Lake Trail, the Thorofare Trail, or through Teton Wilderness within Bridger-Teton National Forest.

The Thorofare Trail begins at Nine Mile Trailhead on the East Entrance Road and hugs the shore of Yellowstone Lake for the first 17 miles. This stretch was spared from the fires of 1988 and provides some incredible opportunities to watch sunsets over the lake, particularly from campsites near Park Point. The trail continues along Southeast Arm and then follows the broad Thorofare Valley upstream beside the Yellowstone River (great fishing). There are several difficult creek and river crossings before you reach the Thorofare Ranger Station at mile 32, but this is not even the halfway point! Civilization is another 36 miles away. To get there, follow the often muddy South Boundary Trail, which heads west over the Continental Divide, through four difficult creek or river fords, through forests burned in the 1988 fires, and past Snake Hot Springs before finally ending at the South Entrance Station.

Needless to say, trips into the Thorofare are only for those with a lot of stamina and extensive backcountry experience. Shorter variations are possible, of course, but most involve hiking in and out the same way. Check at the Lake Ranger Station for conditions in the Thorofare and study Yellowstone hiking guides before even considering a big trip here. It's spectacular and remote country, but that means you're on your own much of the time.

One way to cut nine miles off your hike into the Thorofare is by a boat ride across Yellowstone Lake. The folks at Bridge Bay Marina (307/344-5217) can drop you off at a few campsites on the east side, but this is a pricey option: $152 each way. Contact the Park Service's Backcountry Office (307/344-2160) to find out which campsites are accessible by motorboat. These sites tend to fill up fast, so you'll need to reserve well ahead.

Summer Recreation

Summer is the busy time for Yellowstone. Anyone who loves the outdoors will find all sorts of options, from fishing and hiking (described above) to wildlife watching and horseback rides.

FISHING

In the early years of the park, fish from Yellowstone Lake were a specialty at the various hotels, and because there was no limit on the take, up to 7,500 pounds of fish were caught each year. After commercial fishing was halted, park policy shifted to planting nonnative species. But by the 1970s, Yellowstone Lake had been devastated by overfishing, and new regulations were needed. Beginning in 1973, bait fishing was banned, Fishing Bridge was closed to anglers, and catch-and-release rules were put into place. Increased fish populations have been a boon for wildlife, especially grizzlies, bald eagles, and osprey. Because of these regulations, Yellowstone National Park has achieved an almost mythical status when it comes to fishing. Each year 75,000 visitors spend time fishing in the park. The most commonly caught fish in Yellowstone are cutthroat, rainbow, brown, lake, and brook trout, along with mountain whitefish. Montana grayling are found at only a few small lakes within the park, most notably Grebe Lake.

The Yellowstone River is still considered one of the best places in the world to catch cutthroat trout, and the Madison River is a justifiably famous fly-fishing river with a wide range of conditions. Yellowstone Lake is where the lure anglers go to catch cutthroats and lake trout. Beginners may have luck in the Gallatin River, but they're less likely to do well in the Firehole River, where the fish are smart and wary. Peaceful Slough Creek in the northeast

fly-fishing along the Firehole River

© DON PITCHER

corner of Yellowstone is filled with fat rainbows and cutthroats, attracting fly-fishers from around the globe.

Several good books—available in local stores and visitor centers—provide tips on fishing Yellowstone waters. Try one of the following: *Bud Lilly's Guide to Fly Fishing the New West,* by Bud Lilly and Paul Schullery (Frank Amato Publications), *Yellowstone Fishes: Ecology, History, and Angling in the Park,* by John Varley and Paul Schullery (www.stackpolebooks. com), or *Fishing Yellowstone,* by Richard Parks (www.globepequot.com).

Trouble in Paradise

The last 15 years or so were not at all kind to aquatic ecosystems in Yellowstone as a series of diseases and nonnative threats appeared. Perhaps the greatest threat comes from **lake trout** (Mackinaw), a species that had been illegally planted either accidentally or intentionally in the 1980s or earlier. Lake trout were first discovered in Yellowstone Lake in 1994, and studies have since revealed that many thousands of them now inhabit the lake. A highly aggressive and long-lived species, lake trout feed on and compete with the prized native cutthroat, threatening to devastate the population. (The average lake trout eats 80–90 cutthroat trout per year in Yellowstone.) Cutthroat spawn in the shallow waters of the lake's tributary streams, where they are caught by grizzly bears, bald eagles, and other animals. Lake trout spawn in deeper waters that are inaccessible to predators, so fewer cutthroat and more lake trout could have an impact on grizzlies and eagles. Eradication of the lake trout is virtually impossible, but the Park Service has used gill nets to catch many thousands of them. There are no size or possession limits on lake trout caught in Yellowstone Lake, its tributaries, and the Yellowstone River, but any lake trout you catch in these lakes must be killed and reported.

Another problem is threatening trout, especially rainbow trout, throughout the Rockies. **Whirling disease,** a devastating parasite-caused disease, has seriously hurt populations of rainbow trout in parts of the Madison River outside Yellowstone. The disease was discovered in Yellowstone Lake cutthroats in 1998, and there are fears that it could spread to other lakes and rivers in the park. It is spread in part when mud or water is brought in from contaminated areas on waders, boats, and boots. Be sure to clean up thoroughly with a bleach solution before entering or leaving an area. Get details on whirling disease at www.whirlingdisease.org.

As if the other problems weren't enough, **New Zealand mud snails** were discovered in park waters in 1995. These miniscule snails (natives of New Zealand) are now in the Firehole and Madison Rivers, where they can form dense colonies on aquatic plants and streambed rocks, crowding out native aquatic insects that are a food source for fish.

Fishing Regulations

In most parts of Yellowstone, the fishing season extends from the Saturday of Memorial Day weekend in late May to the first Sunday of November, but Lake Yellowstone opens June 15, and the Yellowstone River above the falls opens July 15. Hayden Valley and some other areas are entirely closed to fishing, and only artificial lures and flies are allowed in the park. Lead cannot be used. All native species in the park—Montana grayling, cutthroat trout, and mountain whitefish—are catch-and-release only. Barbless hooks are preferable for catch-and-release fishing because they cause less damage and are easier to remove. Some rivers, including the Madison River, the Firehole River, and the Gibbon River (downstream from Gibbon Falls) are open only to fly-fishing. For complete details, request the park's fishing regulations brochure, or find it online at www.nps.gov/yell/planyourvisit/ publications.htm.

Anglers don't need a state fishing license but must obtain a special Yellowstone National Park permit, available from visitor centers, ranger stations, Yellowstone General Stores, and fishing shops in surrounding towns. The adult **fishing fee** is $15 for a three-day permit, $20 for a seven-day permit, or $35 for a season permit. Kids under age 15 can get a free permit, or can fish without a permit under the supervision of an adult who has one. Park visitor centers and ranger stations have copies of current fishing regulations.

BOATING

Bridge Bay Marina runs hour-long **Scenicruiser boat tours** of Yellowstone Lake ($14.25 adults, $9 ages 2–11) several times a day in the summer, providing a fine introduction to the area. Also available at the marina are **guided fishing charters** (starting at $192 for two hours for up to six people) and **boat rentals** ($9.50 per hour for a 16-foot rowboat; $47 per hour for an 18-foot motorboat with a 40-horsepower outboard). **Fly-fishing guides** are also available; $410 for two people per day.

The best Yellowstone Lake fishing is from boats rather than from the shoreline. If you're bringing your own boat or canoe to Yellowstone, pick up a park boat permit—and check out the regulations—at the Lake Ranger Station or Grant Village Visitor Center. Boat slips are available at Bridge Bay Marina. All streams are closed to watercraft, with the exception of the Lewis River Channel between Shoshone and Lewis lakes. Motorboats are allowed only on Lewis Lake and parts of Yellowstone Lake.

Sea Kayaking

Several companies offer guided sea kayak trips in the park. **Snake River Kayak and Canoe School** (307/733-9999 or 800/529-2501, www .snakeriverkayak.com) leads a variety of trips in Yellowstone, starting with three-hour sunset paddles ($105) on Yellowstone Lake and half-day paddles in the West Thumb area ($185), all the way up to six-day trips that leave the crowds behind as you explore the lake; these cost $1,300 per person, all-inclusive. The company also guides sea kayaking tours of Lewis and Shoshone lakes and has a full range of kayaking classes in Jackson and Grand Teton National Park.

Jackson Hole Kayak School (307/733-2471, www.jacksonholekayak.com) has day tours of

Scenicruiser boat tour on Yellowstone Lake

© DON PITCHER

Yellowstone Lake or Lewis Lake for $160–250 per person (rate depends upon the number of fellow kayakers). They also offer multi-day treks, including three-day tours of Yellowstone Lake or Lewis and Shoshone lakes for $440–720 per person. Multi-night trip prices include transportation from Jackson, kayaking and camping gear, supplies, and all meals.

O.A.R.S. (209/736-4677 or 800/346-6277, www.oars.com) offers half-day sea kayak trips from Grant Village for $88 adults or $68 kids. These can typically be booked the day before. In addition, they guide multi-day trips in the Yellowstone-Grand Teton region, all the way up to a six-day paddle, float, and hike adventure for $1,540 adults or $1,385 kids. Tents are included, and sleeping bags are available for rent if you lack one.

BICYCLING

Cycling provides a unique way to see Yellowstone up close. Unfortunately, park roads have narrow shoulders and traffic is heavy, making for dangerous conditions. These problems are exacerbated early in the year by high snowbanks, so bikes are not allowed on

certain roads. Call 307/344-7381 for current road conditions. The Park Service produces a helpful "Bicycling in Yellowstone National Park" handout with details on bicycle routes and safety, plus a map showing road conditions; get it from visitor centers or online at www.nps.gov/yell.

If you're planning a cycling trip through Yellowstone, be sure to wear a helmet and high-visibility clothing. A bike mirror also helps. If you want to avoid some of the hassles and don't mind spring conditions, visit the park between late March and the third Friday in April, when motorized vehicles are usually prohibited from entering the park (except for park administrative vehicles). During this period, cyclists are allowed to ride only on the stretch between the West Entrance and Mammoth Hot Springs; other roads are closed to cycling because they're being plowed. Fall is also a good time to ride because traffic is much lighter than in summer. The best times to ride in summer are in the morning before traffic thickens or late in the afternoon before the light begins to fade and you become less visible to motorists.

© DON PITCHER

cyclists near Mammoth Hot Springs

YELLOWSTONE

Where to Ride

The best main park roads to ride (less traffic or better visibility and shoulders) are the following sections: Mammoth to Tower, Tower to Cooke City, Canyon to Lake, and Lake to Grant Village. Bikes are not allowed on backcountry trails or boardwalks inside Yellowstone. Several relatively short but fun mountain-bike rides are available around the park, including the paved trail from Old Faithful to Morning Glory Pool (two miles), the partly paved trail to Lone Star Geyser in the Old Faithful area (two miles), Fountain Flat Drive to the vicinity of Midway Geyser Basin (six miles), the old Chittenden Road up Mt. Washburn (three miles each way, but gaining 1,400 feet on the way up), Bunsen Peak Road near Mammoth (six miles and steep in places), the Old Gardiner Road from Mammoth to Gardiner (five miles), and Blacktail Plateau Drive (seven miles) east of Mammoth. Of these routes, cars are allowed only on the Old Gardiner Road and Blacktail Plateau Drive, but traffic is light on these two.

Bike Rentals and Tours

Rent bikes inside Yellowstone at Old Faithful Snow Lodge ($8 per hour or $35 for 24 hours) and in the surrounding towns of West Yellowstone, Jackson, and Cody. **Backroads** (800/462-2848, www.backroads.com) has six-day multi-sport trips into Yellowstone and Grand Teton that include biking, hiking, rafting, and kayaking. These are offered as either camping trips ($4,200 for two people including meals) or trips on which you stay at local inns ($5,900 for two people including meals). Contact the Park Service for a list of other permitted bicycle-tour operators.

TRAIL RIDES

Summertime trail rides are available from the corrals at Mammoth Hot Springs, Canyon Village, and Roosevelt Lodge. These cost $35 for one hour or $54 for a two-hour ride. Kids must be at least eight years old and 48 inches tall, and there is a 250-pound weight limit, much to the relief of the horses. Roosevelt also has **stagecoach rides** ($9.50 adults, $7.65 ages 2–11) several times a day in the summer.

trail rides near Mammoth Hot Springs

© DON PITCHER

In addition, **Old West dinner cookouts** at Roosevelt combine a horseback or wagon ride with a filling steak dinner.

For details on trail rides, contact Xanterra Parks and Resorts (307/344-7311 or 866/439-7375, www.travelyellowstone.com). Several outfitters provide backcountry pack trips inside Yellowstone; get a list from Park Service visitor centers (307/344-7381, www .nps.gov/yell).

HOT SPRINGS

Many people are disappointed to discover that there are no places in Yellowstone where you can soak in the hot springs. Not only is "hotpotting" illegal, but it can also be dangerous because temperatures often approach boiling and bathers can cause severe damage to these surprisingly fragile natural wonders.

Legal bathing pools are found in cold-water streams that have hot springs feeding into them. You're not allowed to enter the source pool or stream itself. Families often stop for a swim in the Firehole River along Firehole Canyon Drive near Madison. The Park Service doesn't encourage this, and there are no lifeguards, so parents need to watch children closely.

Thirty miles north of Yellowstone in the little burg of Pray, Montana, is **Chico Hot Springs** (406/333-4933 or 800/468-9232, www.chicohotsprings.com). If you're staying in the Mammoth Hot Springs area of Yellowstone, a side trip to Chico may be worthwhile. The large outdoor pool is a great place to relax, the gourmet restaurant serves some of the best dinners anywhere around, and the classic old hotel is a favorite.

Winter Recreation

Winter transforms Yellowstone into an extraordinarily beautiful place where the fires and brimstone of hell meet the bitter cold and snow of winter. The snow often averages four feet in depth but can exceed 10 feet on mountain passes. The snow is usually quite dry, although late in the season conditions deteriorate as temperatures rise. Early in the winter or after major storms, backcountry skiing can be difficult because of the deep powder. Temperatures are generally in the 10–25°F range during the day, while nights frequently dip below zero. (The record is -66°F, recorded on February 9, 1933.) Winds can make these temperatures feel even lower, so visitors should come prepared for extreme conditions.

The thermal basins are a real wintertime treat. Hot springs that are simply colorful pools in summer send up billows of steam in the winter, coating nearby trees with thick layers of ice and turning them into "ghost trees." The geysers put on astounding displays as boiling water meets frigid air; steam from Old Faithful can tower 1,000 feet into the air! Bison and

elk gather around the hot springs, soaking up the heat and searching for dried grasses, and bald eagles are often seen flying over the heated waters of Firehole River. The bison are perhaps the most interesting to watch as they swing their enormous heads from side to side to shovel snow off the grass. Grand Canyon of the Yellowstone is another place transformed by the snow and cold. Although the water still flows, the falls are surrounded by tall cones of ice, and the canyon walls lie under deep snow.

The **Winter in Wonderland website**— www.winterinwonderland.com—provides a portal to all sorts of winter activities, lodging, tours, ranger led programs, field seminars, and information. It's jointly maintained by the National Park Service, Yellowstone Association, and Xanterra.

SNOWMOBILING
Historical Winter Use

During Yellowstone's first 75 years as a park, winter visitation was almost unknown. The only people in the park were caretakers who spent months at a time with no contact with the world outside. This began to change in 1949, when snow-plane tours were first offered from the West Entrance. The planes skimmed over the surface and could hold only two people—the driver and a passenger—so visitation barely topped 30 people that winter. In 1955, snowcoaches were permitted to come into Yellowstone, and more than 500 people visited, although few stayed overnight.

Snowmobiling Changes Everything

The first snowmobilers arrived in 1963, when the machines were still a novelty. As snowmobiling became increasingly more popular, communities around Yellowstone benefited economically and began promoting the park as a winter wonderland. In the winter of 1971–1972 the Park Service began encouraging snowmobile use by grooming the roads and opening Old Faithful Snow Lodge. By the end of that winter, more than 25,000 people had visited, and by the early 1990s it had rocketed to more than 140,000 people, with the park admitting more snowmobiles than all other national parks combined. Noise and air pollution from the two-cycle engines became a serious problem from the 1,600 snowmobiles that flooded into Yellowstone on busy days.

In the heavy-snow winter of 1996–1997 large numbers of bison moved out of Yellowstone, some of them along the groomed snowmobile road out the west side of the park. Nearly 1,100 bison were killed that year as part of Montana's effort to protect cattle from brucellosis. The slaughter precipitated a lawsuit by the Fund for Animals that forced the Park Service to rethink its winter-use policies. To address the effects of snowmobiles and other uses, the Park Service under President Clinton attempted to ban snowmobiles from the park. Industry groups and others successfully fought the closure, with support from the snowmobile-friendly Bush administration.

Snowmobiling Today

After a decade of heated debate, the Park Service adopted a new winter use plan in 2007

that allows a maximum of 540 snowmobiles and 83 snowcoaches per day. All snowmobiles must be commercially guided and meet best-available emission and noise requirements (i.e., four-stroke engines). The new rules have significantly reduced snowmobile trips into the park.

Snowmobiles are available for rent from all four sides of the park and inside Yellowstone at Mammoth and Old Faithful, with the majority of snowmobilers—all guided of course—coming in from West Yellowstone, where prices are usually a bit lower and access is quicker. Contact chamber of commerce offices in West Yellowstone, Jackson, or Cody for a listing of companies offering snowmobile tours.

SNOWCOACHES

The easiest and most enjoyable way to get into Yellowstone in the winter is on the ungainly snowcoaches—machines that look like something the Norwegian Army might have used during World War II. Most were actually built by a Canadian company, Bombardier. They can be noisy, and the windows fog up (hence the spray bottles of antifreeze). But despite their ancient condition and spartan interiors, these beasts still work well and can carry 10 passengers, gear (two suitcases per person), and skis. You will also see (or ride in) several other over-snow vehicles, including vans on tracks.

Snowcoach Tours

A variety of snowcoach tours are provided by Xanterra Parks and Resorts (307/344-7311 or 866/439-7375, www.travelyellowstone.com). All snowcoach tours and transportation are half price for kids ages 2–11 and free for toddlers. Adult per-person rates to Old Faithful are $128 round-trip from Flagg Ranch (where the plowing ends just south of Yellowstone), $102 round-trip from West Yellowstone, and $128 round-trip from Mammoth. Xanterra also provides all-day tours most days of the week from Mammoth to Canyon for $113 round-trip and Old Faithful to Canyon for $118 round-trip. Half-day tours from Mammoth to Norris Geyser Basin cost $53.

Shorter snowcoach tours depart two or three times a week from Old Faithful for the Firehole River/Fountain Flats area (three hours; $29 round-trip). Three-hour winter wildlife bus tours to the Lamar Valley ($27) depart from Mammoth on Wednesdays, providing a good opportunity to see wolves. Also available from Mammoth is a daybreak bus tour (3.5 hours; $29 with a box breakfast). For any of these trips, be sure to make reservations well in advance.

During the winter, **Alltrans/Gray Line** (307/733-3135 or 800/443-6133, www.jacksonholealltrans.com) has daily bus runs from Jackson to Flagg Ranch for $106 round-trip, arriving in time to meet the snowcoach departures for Yellowstone. Reservations required.

Yellowstone Alpen Guides (406/646-9591 or 800/858-3502, www.yellowstoneguides.com) leads snowcoach tours from West Yellowstone. All-day trips are $110 adults, $100 seniors, $90 kids to either Grand Canyon of the Yellowstone or Old Faithful. Guests on the latter run have an option of getting dropped at Biscuit Basin, where they can ski to Old Faithful and meet the rest of the group for the return trip. Ski or snowshoe rentals are available. The company's eight classic Bombardier snowcoaches (one built in 1953) have been modernized but are still a charming anachronism.

Buffalo Bus Touring Co. (406/646-9564 or 800/426-7669, www.yellowstonevacations.com) operates modern snowcoach vans, with all-day tours from West Yellowstone to Old Faithful ($104 adults, $84 kids) or Canyon ($114 adults, $94 kids). Park entrance fees are additional.

Triangle C Ranch (307/455-2225 or 800/661-4928, www.trianglec.com) also provides all-day snowcoach trips in a converted Ford Excursion from either Jackson or Dubois into Yellowstone, with pickups directly from your hotel. These head to either Old Faithful or Canyon for the day, departing at 7 A.M. and returning by 6 P.M. The cost is $250 per person including breakfast and lunch.

For a truly unique experience, book a trip with **Yellowstone Expeditions** (406/646-9333 or 800/728-9333, www.yellowstoneexpeditions.com). The company has day tours from West Yellowstone using converted vans, but is best known for a remote base camp near Canyon that's perfect for those who want to really explore Yellowstone in winter. Guests stay in eight heated tent cabins, with two yurts providing a central kitchen and dining/social area. These trips start at $1,900 for two people for three nights and four days, up to $3,000 for two people for seven nights and eight days. The price includes lodging, food, bedding, round-trip transportation from West Yellowstone to the base camp near Canyon, and backcountry ski guides. Ski and snowshoe rentals are extra. Days are spent skiing or snowshoeing in the Canyon area or along trails around Hayden Valley, Norris, or Mt. Washburn. The cedar sauna is perfect after a long day in the backcountry. This is the only overnight accommodation at the Canyon area during the winter.

SKIING AND SNOWSHOEING

Cross-country skis and snowshoes provide the finest ways to see Yellowstone in the winter. Rent them from Old Faithful Snow Lodge or Mammoth Hot Springs Hotel. Both places also provide lessons and guided tours for groups or individuals. The towns surrounding Yellowstone also have shops that rent skis ($16/day) and snowshoes ($12/day). The Old Faithful area is the center for skiing within Yellowstone, with trails circling the Upper Geyser Basin and leading to nearby sights. You'll find similar ski trails (not always groomed) in the Tower Fall, Canyon, and Mammoth areas. Get free ski-trail maps at park visitor centers. Old Faithful Snow Lodge is open in winter, providing an excellent base for day trips into nearby areas or for a snowcoach tour of the park.

Skiers and snowshoers sometimes assume that they can't possibly cause problems for Yellowstone's wildlife, but studies show that elk and bison often move away from skiers, which forces the animals to expend energy they need to survive through the bitterly cold winters. It's best to stay on the trails and to keep from skiing into areas where elk or bison may be disturbed

YELLOWSTONE

by your presence. For more on skiing and winter visitation in the park, see Jeff Henry's *Yellowstone Winter Guide* (www.roberts-rinehart.com), or *Winter Tales and Trails: Skiing, Snowshoeing and Snowboarding in Idaho, the Grand Tetons and Yellowstone National Park* by Ron Watters (Great Rift Press).

Skier Shuttles and Tours

Xanterra Parks and Resorts (307/344-7311 or 866/439-7375, www.travelyellowstone.com) operates **skier snowcoach shuttles** ($14 round-trip) from Mammoth southward to Golden Gate and Indian Creek where you can ski downhill to Mammoth. Snowcoaches also shuttle skiers from Old Faithful to Fairy Falls Trailhead or the Continental Divide area for $13 and you can ski back on your own to Snow Lodge. The Continental Divide run is eight miles long and primarily downhill.

From Mammoth, Xanterra has weekly **Cooke City See and Ski Tours** ($68) by van, with the opportunity to ski gentle trails in the Absaroka Mountains.

In addition, Xanterra provides all-day Grand Canyon snowcoach-and-guided-ski tours ($125 round-trip) twice a week from Old Faithful and once weekly from Mammoth. **Afternoon ski-daddles** are guided five-hour ski tours from Old Faithful to Fairy Falls or DeLacey Creek. They're offered twice a week and cost $42.

Guided three-hour **snowshoe tours** ($27 with snowshoes) are offered twice weekly from Old Faithful. They're a great way to explore the country. Besides these concessioner-run tours, park naturalists sometimes lead ski trips from Old Faithful to nearby sights. Stop by the visitor center for details.

Safety on Skis

Before your trip, call Yellowstone (307/344-7381) to request the informative *Winter Backcountry Trip Planner,* with details on trails, equipment, weather, and avalanche safety. Online at www.nps.gov/yell/planyourvisit/backcountrytrip-planner.htm, find an 11-minute winter backcountry video. Yellowstone's roads are traveled by snowmobiles and snowcoaches, making for

potential conflicts with skiers. Be sure to keep to the right while skiing. Most trails are identified by orange metal markers on the trees. If you're planning a backcountry trip, pick up a use permit from one of the ranger stations. A thorough understanding of winter camping and survival is imperative before you head out on any overnight trip, and avalanche safety classes are a wise investment.

Get avalanche-safety information from the **Gallatin National Forest Avalanche Center** (406/587-6981, www.mtavalanche.com) in Bozeman. The recording does not cover the entire park, but it does include the Washburn Range and areas near Cooke City and West Yellowstone. It's updated daily in the winter. Call 307/344-2113 for a recording of the latest park weather forecast.

WINTER PRACTICALITIES
Accommodations

Only two places offer wintertime lodging inside Yellowstone. **Mammoth Hot Springs Hotel,** on the north end of the park, is the only accommodation accessible by road and has ski and snowshoe trails nearby, while the modern **Old Faithful Snow Lodge and Cabins** puts you close to the geysers and many miles of ski trails. Each has a restaurant, lounge, gift shop, and rentals of skis and snowshoes. Mammoth has a couple of advantages over Old Faithful: far fewer snowmobiles so it's much more quiet, and road access to the Lamar Valley where wolves, bison, and elk are major attractions. You might even see a pack of wolves take down an elk. (See the *Accommodations* section for lodging prices and seasons.)

A wide variety of two-night **Winter Getaway** package trips are available out of Mammoth or Old Faithful. In addition, the Yellowstone Association Institute has excellent **Lodging and Learning** packages throughout the winter, notably a three-night winter "Trail of the Wolf" trip ($778 d) that includes two nights at Mammoth Hotel and one night at Old Faithful Snow Lodge, plus breakfasts and lunches, a snowmobile or snowcoach tour, and a naturalist-led trek to Lamar Valley. Get details on various winter lodging, learning, and play options from Xanterra Parks and Resorts (307/344-7311 or 866/439-7375, www.travel yellowstone.com).

The only wintertime camping place is Mammoth Campground, where temperatures are milder and the snow lighter.

During winter, the most popular (and crowded) times to visit Yellowstone are around Christmas and New Year's and the Presidents' Day weekend in February. If you plan to arrive at these times, make lodging reservations six months in advance. The rest of the winter, you should probably reserve at least three months ahead.

Services

Only the Mammoth and Old Faithful visitor centers are open during winter. Free ranger-led activities include evening programs at Mammoth and Old Faithful. Check the winter edition of *Yellowstone Today* for details, or find it on the web at www.nps.gov/yell.

Xanterra Parks and Resorts (307/344-7311 or 866/439-7375, www.travelyellowstone.com) offers a variety of guided ski and snowmobile tours and provides wildlife bus or van tours. In addition, the **Yellowstone Association Institute** (307/344-2294, www.yellowstone association.org) has outstanding winter classes.

The **Mammoth Clinic** (307/344-7965) is open daily 8:30 A.M.–5 P.M. June–August, and weekdays—except Wednesdays—in the winter for medical emergencies.

The Yellowstone General Store at Mammoth is open for groceries and supplies year-round, but only meals and gas are available at Old Faithful. Warming huts are at Old Faithful, Madison Junction, Canyon, West Thumb, Fishing Bridge, and Indian Creek (south of Mammoth Hot Springs). They contain restrooms and snack machines (except Indian Creek and West Thumb), and all are open 24 hours (except for Old Faithful, where other facilities are available). The huts at Madison and Canyon also have snack bars selling hot chili or soup. Park rangers are often at the warming huts during the middle of the day.

Roads

Most of Yellowstone's roads officially close to cars on the Monday after the first Sunday in November and remain shut down all over except for the 56 miles between Mammoth and Cooke City. Roads don't open for cars again until sometime between mid-May and early June. The roads are groomed for snowmobiles and snowcoaches mid-December–mid-March. The rest of the winter you'll find only skiers and park personnel on the roads.

Accommodations

Yellowstone accommodations vary from extremely basic cabins with four thin walls starting at $67 up to luxury suites that will set you back $593. Following a fine old Park Service tradition, the rooms do not have TVs, and most lack phones. Web access is limited to slow phone connections (where available). What they do offer is the chance to relax in comfortable accommodations and explore the magical world outside. Most are open early June–mid-September, with additional winter lodging at Mammoth Hot Springs Hotel and the Old Faithful Snow Lodge. Several

hundred more motels and other places to stay operate outside park boundaries in the towns of Jackson, Cody, West Yellowstone, Gardiner, and Cooke City.

Xanterra Parks and Resorts (307/344-7311 or 866/439-7375, www.travelyellowstone.com) is Yellowstone's lodging concessioner. **Make Yellowstone lodging reservations six months ahead** for the park's prime hotels, or you may find that the only rooms available are in Grant Village, the laughingstock of park lodges. Those traveling with small children should also request cribs when making reservations. Wheelchair-accessible (ADA-compliant) rooms are available at most of the park's cabins and hotels. (As an aside, several Web-based companies purport to make reservations for hotels and lodges inside Yellowstone, but all of these charge a service fee. Save yourself money and hassles by just going directly to Xanterra.)

At the turn of the 20th century, most visitors to Yellowstone stayed in park hotels rather than roughing it on the ground. Three of these wonderful old lodging places remain: Old Faithful Inn, Lake Yellowstone Hotel, and Mammoth Hot Springs Hotel. Standard motel rooms can be found at Grant Village. In addition, three nicer places opened in the 1990s: the Old Faithful Snow Lodge and two small lodges at Canyon Village. All told, more than 2,200 rooms and cabins provide overnight accommodations in Yellowstone.

Not all lodging options inside the park are nearly as pleasant, however. Hundreds of simple boxes are clustered in the Lake, Mammoth, Old Faithful, and Roosevelt areas. Most of these cabins offer a roof over your head, simple furnishings, and communal showers, but the more expensive cabins are considerably nicer, and four of them even include private hot tubs. Fortunately, prices are fairly reasonable for all of the cabins, and the park concessioner is gradually renovating the oldest units.

Lodging rates are listed for two people; children under age 12 stay free. Add $11 per person for additional older kids or adults in the hotel rooms or cabins. Prices at some park lodging places are lower in May when snow still covers much of the park, but you need to book before April 1. Also available are a variety of winter and summer package deals that include lodging, tours, hikes, and more. Especially noteworthy are the four-day **Lodging and Learning** packages that combine tours, educational activities, and hikes led by naturalist-guides from the **Yellowstone Association Institute** (307/344-2294, www.yellowstone association.org) with accommodations in park hotels, plus breakfasts and lunches.

Rates listed are without tax, which is 6 percent on the south half of the park (inside

Teton County—including Old Faithful, Grant Village, and Lake Village) and 8 percent on the north half (inside Park County—including Roosevelt, Mammoth Hot Springs, and Canyon Village).

MAMMOTH HOT SPRINGS

The rambling **Mammoth Hot Springs Hotel** sits in the northwest corner of Yellowstone near park headquarters in the settlement of Mammoth. Built in 1937 (one wing was constructed in 1911 and the original hotel was built even earlier), the hotel has 211 rooms in a variety of configurations. Elk are a common sight on the grounds, and in the fall the bulls' bugling may wake you in the morning. There's live piano music downstairs in the **Map Room** most summer evenings as a counterpoint to the elk songs. (The room is named for a distinctive map of the United States crafted from 16 types of wood; it's on the northern wall.) Also just off the lobby is a gift shop. Just steps away are Park Service headquarters, the fine Albright Visitor Center and other historical buildings, along with places to eat and buy groceries, gas, and trinkets.

Mammoth Hotel rooms are comfortable but modest. Walls are not entirely soundproof, furnishings show some wear, and the hallway floors squeak, but baths are large and the hotel exudes a graceful aura that fits the setting well. Several rooms on each floor provide low-cost accommodations ($89 d) with communal baths down the hall, but most have two beds and private baths ($121 d); ask for a corner room if available. The hotel also houses two luxury suites ($448 d). It is open early May–mid-October and mid-December–mid-March.

Early-season discounts are available, and winter rates are below those in summer. In the winter, "Frosty Fun" packages are a better bet, including one that provides two nights' lodging, two breakfasts, hot tub access, and ice skates, at $250 for two people. Hot tubs are available ($15 per hour) during winter, offering a great way to relax after a day of cross-country skiing. Mammoth Hotel and Old Faithful Snow Lodge offer the only wintertime hotels inside the park.

Behind the hotel are 116 **⟨** **Mammoth**

Cabins, including **Budget Cabins** ($79 d) with a shared bathhouse, and delightful **Frontier Cottages** ($112 d) with small porches and private baths. Most of these accommodations were built in 1938, and all contain two double beds. Some are duplex units that can be joined for families or friends traveling together. Dozens of ground squirrels populate the grounds, providing endless entertainment for the kids. Four units also have private outdoor **hot tubs** and are the finest cabins in Yellowstone ($222 d). The Mammoth cabins are open early May–early October.

ROOSEVELT LODGE

At the junction of the roads to Canyon, Mammoth, and Lamar Valley, **❲ Roosevelt Lodge** is *the* place to escape the crowds and return to a quieter and simpler era. The lodge is decidedly off the beaten path to the major Yellowstone sights, and that suits folks who stay here just fine. Named for President Theodore Roosevelt—perhaps the most conservation-minded president ever—the lodge has the well-worn feeling of an old dude ranch, and many families treat it as such. More than a few folks book cabins for several weeks at a stretch, enjoying the wolf-watching, fly-fishing, horseback and wagon rides, and barbecue cookout dinners. (Cookouts book up six months ahead, so reserve your space when you make a Roosevelt Lodge reservation.)

The main lodge features two large stone fireplaces, a family-style restaurant with notable meals, a lounge, a gift shop, a little general store, and a big front porch with old-fashioned rocking chairs. Surrounding it are 82 utilitarian cabins, most of which were built in the 1920s. Most basic—and just a step up from camping—are the **Roughrider Cabins** with one, two, or three beds, a writing table, and a woodstove (the only ones in any Yellowstone lodging). These cabins share a communal bathhouse, cost $67 for up to six guests, and fill up quickly. Call far ahead to reserve one of these classics! The same price will also get you larger cabins without the woodstove (but still no private bath). Nicer **Frontier Cabins** with hardwood floors, one or two double beds, and

private baths go for $112 d. All of these cabins can get stuffy in midsummer, and some windows lack screens. Two of the Roosevelt cabins are wheelchair-accessible. The Roosevelt Lodge and cabins are open mid-June–early September.

CANYON VILLAGE

Centrally situated **Canyon Lodge** is just a half-mile from Grand Canyon of the Yellowstone, one of the park's premier attractions. The main lodge is part of a late-1950s complex of ugly structures built around a large parking lot. The area has all the charm of an aging shopping mall from an era when bigger meant better. The lodge itself covers the space of a football field and houses a dining room, cafeteria, lounge, and snack shop, but no guest rooms.

Behind the lodge in the trees (at least the setting is peaceful), the road circles past three sprawling clusters of cabins, all with private baths and double beds. You'll find 480 cabins here. The most basic "pioneer" units cost $74 d and aren't much to look at outside but are actually fairly roomy and comfortable inside. Two newer types of cabins are available at Canyon: the **Frontier Cabins** for $101 d and the **Western Cabins** for $156 d. The western cabins are being renovated over several summers; ask for an updated one if available.

Providing far better accommodations are two 1990s additions: **Dunraven Lodge** and **Cascade Lodge.** Rooms at both of these attractive log- and rock-trimmed structures are furnished with rustic lodgepole pieces and have two double beds and private baths. Rooms in the lodges cost $172 d. The cabins and lodges at Canyon are open June–mid-September.

LAKE VILLAGE

The Lake Village area has a full range of lodging options for travelers, with a central location and good services.

Lake Yellowstone Hotel

The fascinating Southern colonial-style **❲ Lake Yellowstone Hotel** delivers a magnificent view across Yellowstone Lake. Begun in 1889, the

YELLOWSTONE

building expanded and changed through the decades to yield its current configuration of 158 guest rooms. The hotel has been lovingly restored and exudes a grandeur and charm rarely found today. It's the sort of place where Fred Astaire and Ginger Rogers would feel comfortable dancing—if they were still alive.

The Lake Yellowstone's inviting hotel rooms all contain updated furnishings, private baths, and in-room phones. Standard units cost $216 d on the backside or $227 d facing the lake, and a delightfully spacious two-bedroom suite is the most elaborate (and most expensive) accommodation in the park at $593 for up to six people. For the best vistas, ask for a third-floor room on the lake side when making your reservations.

Downstairs is a good restaurant (reservations required for dinner), along with a fast-food eatery; the cafeteria at Lake Lodge is only a short walk away. The real treat at Lake Yellowstone Hotel is the **Sun Room,** where rows of windows front the lake. The room's ambience is further enhanced by period wicker furnishings and evening chamber music or classical piano. It's a great place to sip a martini or write a postcard. The hotel is open mid-May–mid-October.

Annex and Frontier Cabins

Out back is the **Lake Yellowstone Hotel Annex,** where the recently refurbished rooms cost $150 d. No view, but each room has two double beds, phones, a bath, and pleasant furnishings. Some of these are wheelchair-accessible.

Also behind Lake Yellowstone Hotel are more than 100 units originally built in the 1950s, jammed together in row after identical row to create the **Frontier Cabins.** Fortunately, they were nicely restored a few years back and are surprisingly comfortable, clean, and cheap: $134 for up to four. Units are small, with just enough space for two double beds and a private bath. Cabin guests can pretend they're traveling on a more ample budget by spending time in the adjacent Lake Yellowstone Hotel dining room and the Sun Room. Lake Yellowstone Hotel Cabins are open mid-May–September.

Lake Lodge Cabins

A short distance east of Lake Yellowstone Hotel is **Lake Lodge.** Built in the 1920s, this archetypal log building has a gracious lobby containing two stone fireplaces, comfortably rustic furnishings, an open ceiling where the supporting log trusses

© DON PITCHER

Frontier Cabins at Lake Yellowstone Hotel

and beams are visible, and a delightful front porch. One end of the building houses a large and reasonably priced cafeteria with picture windows framing Lake Yellowstone, and the other end contains a recreation hall for employees. Lodging options at Lake Lodge are not nearly as gracious, consisting of plain-vanilla **Pioneer Cabins** from the 1920s and 1930s, each with a double bed and private bath for $74 d, and more comfortable **Western Cabins** built in the 1950s and 1960s that include two double beds and private baths with showers. The latter cabins cost $145 for basic, older units or $156 for nicely remodeled ones. The 186 cabins at Lake Lodge are open mid-June–late September. Guests here often walk over to the nearby Lake Yellowstone Hotel for fine dining and the chance to relax in the Sun Room.

GRANT VILLAGE

Southernmost lodging in Yellowstone, **Grant Village** has condo-type units from the 1980s, each with exceptional parking-lot vistas. These buildings would be completely out of place in *any* national park, especially Yellowstone. Six hideously ugly lodge buildings contain motel-type units for $145–150 d; make sure to request a remodeled room. All of these have two double beds and private baths, and several wheelchair-accessible rooms are available. A park visitor center and campground are in the area, along with a variety of concessioner facilities, including a restaurant, waterside café, general store, lounge, snack shop, and gift shop. Grant Village is open late May–September and has 300 units.

OLD FAITHFUL

The Old Faithful area contains a plethora of lodging options, including two large hotels and several dozen cabins.

Old Faithful Inn

Built in 1903–1904, timeless **❰ Old Faithful Inn** is easily the most delightful place to stay inside Yellowstone—if not in all of America. I wouldn't trade it for a thousand Hiltons. If you're able to get a room at OFI during your

visit to the park, do so; you certainly won't regret it! The inn's 329 rooms are located in three parts of the building: Old House rooms from the original structure, plus the East and West Wings, added in the teens and twenties. Each section has its own character, but even those staying in the simplest budget rooms here will enjoy the five-star lobby with its towering stone fireplace, the old-fashioned writing tables, cushy overstuffed chairs, a classy bar and restaurant, and evening piano music. Old Faithful Inn is open early May–mid-October.

Most rooms in the **Old House** section of the hotel are cramped spaces with a brass double bed, dresser, log walls, robes, an in-room sink, and communal baths down the hall; these go for $93 d. Of the cheap rooms, the best ones (these are often reserved a year ahead) are the dormer rooms on the second floor—particularly room 229—but those who stay there must walk past folks in the lobby to take a shower! Mid-range rooms in the Old House contain private baths and one or two queen beds: $125 d; request numbers 46, 148, 154, or 240.

Many other types of rooms are available throughout this sprawling hotel. The **West Wing's** rooms (also called "high-range rooms") are comfortable, with one queen or two double beds and private baths: $167 d. Note, however that some of these lack even a parking lot view. Attractively appointed rooms in the **East Wing** (also called "premium rooms") are very comfortable, containing two double beds, phones, and tub baths with colorful tiles. Premium rooms vary in price from $212 to 239 d, with higher rates for those facing the geyser. Good choices include numbers 1002, 2002, 3002, 1004, 2004, 3004, 1024, 2024, and 3024; all have notable Old Faithful vistas, but 2024 and 3024 have the best dead-on views. If you have the cash, rent a six-person suite for $417–527; ask for suite numbers 1002, 2002, or 3002.

Old Faithful Lodge

Although it is an attractively rustic building that would be a major focal point almost anywhere else, **Old Faithful Lodge** is overshadowed by its grand neighbor, Old Faithful Inn. The lodge does not contain guest rooms but houses a large cafeteria (open for lunch and dinner only), recreation hall, gift shop, bake shop, ice-cream stand, espresso cart, and showers. Unlike the inn, the lodge has enormous windows that face the geyser, providing those eating in the cafeteria with dramatic views of the eruptions. The lodge's massive fir logs and stone pillars add to a feeling of permanence. Behind and beside Old Faithful Lodge are approximately 130 moderately priced but cramped cabins. These contain older (but functional) furnishings, and most have two beds. The simplest **Budget Cabins** share communal bathhouses and cost just $68 d; they're some of the cheapest rooms in Yellowstone and just a few steps from Old Faithful. Slightly nicer (but still small) **Frontier Cabins** have one or two beds and private baths and cost $112 d. There is even a pair of handicapped-accessible cabins here. The cabins at Old Faithful Lodge are open mid-May–mid-October.

Snow Lodge

Completed in 1999, the 100-room **Old**

Faithful Snow Lodge provides accommodations in both summer and winter (Mammoth Hot Springs Hotel is Yellowstone's only other wintertime hotel). Both inside and out, Snow Lodge evokes the spirit of "parkitecture" from the early 1900s. The building blends the past and present, with timbers (recycled from old buildings), hardwood floors, a central stone fireplace, custom-designed overstuffed couches, and wrought-iron accents, along with all the modern conveniences you expect from a fine hotel—unless you're expecting TVs, which no park hotels contain. Rooms are beautifully appointed and comfortable, and all have private baths. The hotel also houses a restaurant, snack shop, lounge, and gift shop, along with a ski shop and snowmobile rentals in winter. Rates are $201 d.

In addition to the hotel, 34 four-plex Snow Lodge Cabins are available behind the building, costing $147 d. Built in 1989, these **Western Cabins** have standard motel furnishings, with two double beds and a full bath. Duplex **Frontier Cabins** provide simple accommodations with bath for $99 d. The Snow Lodge and

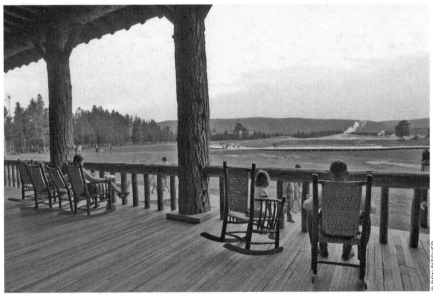

Old Faithful Snow Lodge

© DON PITCHER

Cabins are open early May–late October and mid-December–mid-March. Rates are the same in summer and winter, but early-season discounts are available in May. "Winter Getaway" packages are a better bet, including one that provides two nights' lodging, two breakfasts, and a round-trip snowcoach transport to Old Faithful at $538 for two people.

Camping

Tent camping in Yellowstone's early days left a bit to be desired. One 1884 tourist noted that during the height of summer, "the principle upon which the beds are populated is said to be the addition of visitors so long as they may arrive, or until the occupants 'go for their guns.' The plan is simple, and relieves the authorities of responsibility." It's still crowded in the park, but at least guns are prohibited today!

Camping is available at a dozen sites scattered along the Yellowstone road network. Most of these campsites are open from at least Memorial Day–mid-September, but only Mammoth Campground remains open throughout the year. Generators are allowed in more than half of the campgrounds but can be used only between 8 A.M. and 8 P.M. Roadside or parking-lot camping is prohibited, and rangers vigorously enforce this rule.

Reservations are available—and advised— for five concessioner-managed campgrounds: Bridge Bay Campground, Canyon Campground, Grant Village Campground, Madison Campground, and Fishing Bridge RV Park. Contact Xanterra Parks and Resorts (307/344-7311 or 866/439-7375, www.travel yellowstone.com) for reservations (no extra charge). The other seven (Park Service-managed) campgrounds inside Yellowstone are available on a first-come, first-camped basis with no reservations. You can pay with cash, checks, or credit cards.

During July and August, virtually all campsites in Yellowstone fill *before noon,* so get there early or reserve a space! The busiest weekends are—not surprisingly—around July 4 and Labor Day, but Yellowstone's most popular campgrounds fill up even in late fall and early summer. Call the Park Service at 307/344-2114 for a recording noting which campgrounds are full.

MADISON
Madison Campground
Sixteen miles north of Old Faithful, this is the closest campground to Yellowstone's most famous attraction. West Yellowstone is 14 miles to the west. The campground is near the confluence of the Gibbon, Madison, and Firehole rivers and makes a fine base for exploring all the park's main attractions. All 277 campsites at Madison fill early in the day throughout the summer. Generators are allowed, and the campground has flush toilets and a dump station, but no showers. It's open May–October and costs $19. Contact Xanterra Parks and Resorts (307/344-7311 or 866/439-7375, www.travelyellowstone.com) for reservations (highly recommended). Group sites are available.

NORRIS GEYSER BASIN
Norris Campground
One of Yellowstone's most dramatic geyser basins is just a quarter-mile from Norris Campground. The campsites fill early most days, and the campground has flush toilets. Food and supplies are available at Canyon Village, 12 miles east of Norris. Generators are permitted, and the campground is open mid-May–late September. The 116 sites cost $14. No reservations.

MAMMOTH HOT SPRINGS
Mammoth Campground
This very popular campground is near a residential area and along the busy park road, but just a short walk from the hot springs, visitor

center/museum, shops, horseback rides, and eating places in Mammoth. Generators are permitted 8 A.M.–8 P.M., and road traffic can be noisy, so this isn't the most peaceful spot. It has flush toilets and is the only park campground that remains open year-round. The 85 sites (all pull-through) cost $14. No reservations.

Indian Creek Campground

This quiet campground generally fills late in the day, but it is just eight miles south of Mammoth, where you'll find food and other services. No generators, and it has vault toilets. It sits alongside pretty Indian Creek and is open mid-June–mid-September. The 75 sites go for $12 each. No reservations.

TOWER-ROOSEVELT AREA
Pebble Creek Campground

This campground makes a good base for wildlife-watching in Lamar Valley and for exploring the scenic Icebox Canyon area. It's in a quiet corner of the park, seven miles from the Northeast Entrance. Food and limited supplies are available at Tower Fall and Roosevelt. Pebble Creek Campground has vault toilets and is open mid-May–September. The 32 campsites are $12. No reservations.

Slough Creek Campground

This fairly small 29-site campground is especially popular with anglers who come here to fly-fish for cutthroat trout and with wildlife enthusiasts who watch the bison, elk, and wolves of Lamar Valley. Good local hiking is nearby, too. Food and limited supplies are available at Tower Fall and Roosevelt. The campground is open late May–October and has vault toilets. Campsites are $12. No reservations.

Tower Fall Campground

Close to this dramatic waterfall on Tower Creek, this campground has 32 sites and vault toilets. Limited groceries and supplies are available at the nearby general store, with meals at Roosevelt Lodge. The campground is open

© DON PITCHER

campground at Mammoth Hot Springs

mid-May–September. Campsites cost $12. No reservations.

CANYON VILLAGE
Canyon Campground

This exceptionally popular camping area is close to the dramatic overlooks at Grand Canyon of the Yellowstone. A park visitor center, Yellowstone General Store, restaurant, cafeteria, post office, gas station, and other lodging are a short walk away. Not surprisingly, the campground fills early most summer days. It has coin-operated washers and dryers, coin-operated showers, flush toilets, and a dump station. Generators are permitted. Canyon Campground is open early June–early September and costs $19. Contact Xanterra Parks and Resorts (307/344-7311 or 866/439-7375, www.travelyellowstone.com) for reservations—highly recommended.

LAKE VILLAGE
Bridge Bay Campground

This camping area is adjacent to the Bridge Bay Marina on the north side of Lake Yellowstone and also near a ranger station and store. Meals are available at Lake Yellowstone Hotel and Lake Lodge, just a few miles from here. This 432-site campground (largest in Yellowstone) fills quickly most summer days. Generators are permitted, and it has flush toilets and a dump station, but no showers or laundry. The campground is open late May–mid-September and costs $19. Contact Xanterra Parks and Resorts (307/344-7311 or 866/439-7375, www.travelyellowstone.com) for reservations—highly recommended. Group sites are also available.

Fishing Bridge RV Park

On the north end of Yellowstone Lake, this very crowded 346-site campground is open only to hard-sided RVs, with a 40-foot maximum length. No tents, pop-ups, or other campers that bears might break into easily are allowed. Sites with full hookups cost $36 for up to four people, and generators are permitted.

Bathhouses have coin-op showers, flush toilets, washers, and dryers. Dining is available a few miles away at Lake Yellowstone Hotel and Lake Lodge. The RV Park is open mid-May–September and fills early most days. Contact Xanterra Parks and Resorts (307/344-7311 or 866/439-7375, www.travelyellowstone.com) for reservations—highly recommended.

GRANT VILLAGE
Grant Village Campground

Near the south end of Yellowstone Lake and 19 miles southeast of Old Faithful, this campground fills early and offers 425 woodsy sites. It has coin-op showers nearby, flush toilets, washers and dryers, and a dump station. Generators are permitted. Nearby are restaurants, a park visitor center, and a general store. The campground is open late June–late September and costs $19. Contact Xanterra Parks and Resorts (307/344-7311 or 866/439-7375, www.travel yellowstone.com) for reservations—highly recommended. Group sites are available.

Lewis Lake Campground

On the southeast end of Lewis Lake, this 85-site campground is the southernmost in the park. It fills early and is open mid-June–early November. It has vault toilets, and a boat ramp is nearby. Campsites are $12. Food and other services are available at Grant Village to the north or Flagg Ranch to the south. No reservations.

CAMPING OPTIONS

When everything else is packed, folks head to campgrounds on surrounding Forest Service and Grand Teton National Park lands or to private campgrounds and motels in the gateway towns. The farther you get from Yellowstone, the more likely you are to find space. If you reach Nebraska, you should have no trouble at all. Campers can take showers ($4) at Old Faithful Lodge, Mammoth Hotel, Grant Village, Fishing Bridge RV Park, and Canyon Village Campground.

Food

Yellowstone's dining options are surprisingly varied. The cafeterias and fast food joints cater to families and others looking for something predictable, but you can also do something more distinctive such as the Old West cookouts at Roosevelt Lodge. Both Old Faithful Inn and Lake Yellowstone Hotel have memorable dining rooms where the setting is half the experience. All restaurants, cafeterias, and lounges in Yellowstone are entirely nonsmoking.

RESTAURANTS

You'll find restaurants at Mammoth Hot Springs, Lake Yellowstone Hotel, Old Faithful Inn, Old Faithful Snow Lodge, Grant Village, Roosevelt Lodge, and Canyon Lodge. All of these are open for three meals a day throughout the summer, typically early May–early October. Dining is available at the Snow Lodge mid-April–October and for the winter season mid-December–early March. Call 307/344-7311 or 866/439-7375 for dining reservations at any of the park restaurants.

The enormous ◖ **Old Faithful Inn Dining Room** (daily in summer 6:30–10 A.M., 11:30 A.M.–2:30 P.M., and 5–10 P.M.) is a wonderful option, with impressive all-you-can-eat buffets for breakfast ($11 adults, $5 kids) and lunch ($13 adults, $7 kids), plus a dinner menu that stars bison rib eye steaks, grilled chicken breast, boar tenderloin, and wild Alaska salmon ($16–33 entrees). The cozy lounge serves single-malt scotches, tequilas, and cognacs.

Yellowstone's fine-dining choice is the ◖ **Lake Yellowstone Hotel Dining Room** (307/242-3899, daily mid-May–early Oct. 6:30–10 A.M., 11:30 A.M.–2:30 P.M., and 5–10 P.M.), with breakfast buffets ($13 adults, $5 kids), plus upscale lunches and dinners that emphasize seasonal and organic foods such as Montana rack of lamb, antelope medallions with lobster tail, and seafood cioppino. Dinner entrées cost $17–38.

© DON PITCHER

cafeteria inside Old Faithful Lodge

Meals in other restaurants throughout the park are also reasonably priced ($16–29), but the quality can vary from so-so to quite good. Typical menus include steaks, burgers, seafood, pasta, chicken, salads, and limited vegetarian dishes. Park restaurants are open for three meals daily throughout the summer. Hours vary a bit, but are typically 6:30–10 A.M. for breakfast, 11:30 A.M.–2:30 P.M. for lunch, and 5–10 P.M. for dinner. In winter, only the Mammoth and the Snow Lodge restaurants are open 6:30–10 A.M. for breakfast, and 5:30–8 P.M. for dinner. Mammoth is also open 11:30 A.M.–2:30 P.M. for lunch in the winter months.

The filling breakfasts (buffet also available) and decadent sundaes at **Mammoth Hot Springs Dining Room** are noteworthy, while **Roosevelt Lodge Dining Room** emphasizes down-home cowboy fare such as barbecue ribs, beef brisket, rib eye steaks, and crispy fried chicken. The dinner menu at **Grant Village Dining Room** includes portabella mushroom cannelloni, bison meatloaf, prime rib, and wild Alaska salmon. It also has a substantial breakfast buffet. The building's tall windows face Lake Yellowstone, although trees obscure the view. **Lake House at Grant** has a filling breakfast buffet ($10 adults, $5 kids), along with create-your-own pizzas and a pasta bar.

Obsidian Dining Room at the Snow Lodge has a fun Western flair. In addition to an extensive breakfast menu, the restaurant serves specialty burgers, steaks, and seafood. Unfortunately, the quality isn't stellar.

Dinner reservations are _required_ in the summer at Old Faithful Inn Dining Room (307/545-4999), Lake Yellowstone Hotel Dining Room (307/242-3899), and Grant Village Dining Room (307/242-3499), and they should be made before your arrival. For a dinner table at Old Faithful Inn, reserve a week ahead if you want a choice of seating times.

CAFETERIAS AND FAST FOOD

Yellowstone has always catered to families, and several park cafeterias provide reasonably priced meals. Hours vary a bit, but are typically 6:30–10 A.M. for breakfast, 11:30 A.M.–2:30 P.M.

for lunch, and 5–10 P.M. for dinner. Your kids' noise will almost certainly be drowned out by racket from the rest of the hoi polloi (I'm speaking from experience here). You shouldn't, however, come here expecting a memorable meal; sometimes they're downright awful. **Lake Lodge Cafeteria** is notable, with tall windows facing the Lake Yellowstone. Similarly impressive is **Old Faithful Lodge Cafeteria,** housed in a grand stone-and-timber building. Head to the side porch for delightful Old Faithful Geyser views from the big rocking chairs. Less distinguished is **Canyon Lodge Cafeteria,** with a 1960s design that hasn't aged well. In Mammoth, **Terrace Grill** is a family favorite for burgers, veggie burgers, sandwiches, espresso, and ice cream. You'll find snack shops or delis selling similar fare at Old Faithful, Lake, and Canyon. All these places can also put together picnic lunches.

Many of the park's **Yellowstone General Stores** have food services of the burger, fries, and milkshake variety, and can put together box lunches for a to-go meal.

COOKOUTS

The ◖ **Old West Wagon Cookouts** at Roosevelt Lodge are a longtime family favorite and so popular that you'll need to make reservations at least six months ahead. Cookouts take place nightly mid-June–early September, and you either hop on board the horse-drawn wagons or astride a horse for a saunter into history. They take place in Pleasant Valley, three miles from the lodge, and include cowboy music, a campfire, and a big buffet with charbroiled steak and all the trimmings: baked beans, coleslaw, potato salad, corn, corn muffins, watermelon, apple cobbler, and beverages. Top it off with a cup of cowboy coffee. No discounts are given for vegetarians, but the staff can make substitutions if you notify them in advance. Covered seating is available in case of rain.

Wagon rides with dinner last 90 minutes round-trip and cost $55 adults, $45 ages 5–11, or free for younger kids. Horseback riders can choose either a one-hour trail ride and meal at $66 adults, $56 ages 8–11, or a two-hour trail ride at $80 adults or $70 kids. Make reservations at 307/344-7311 or 866/439-7375, www.travelyellowstone.com. If you're in the area and don't have a reservation, ask to get on the waiting list. You might get lucky and find a last-minute cancellation.

LOUNGES

Just because you're in a national park doesn't mean you can't tip back a gin and tonic. **Old Faithful Tavern** inside Old Faithful Inn is a fine place for a drink in the evening. Beverage service is also available on the upstairs mezzanine and the outside deck facing Old Faithful. Another good place for a drink is **Firehole Lounge** at nearby Old Faithful Snow Lodge.

Lake Yellowstone Hotel's aptly named **Sun Room** fills a large wing of the lobby and is surrounded on three sides by picture windows. It exudes a casual elegance, making this a wonderful spot to while away the hours reading a book, writing postcards, or just listening to chamber music with a drink in your hand.

Smaller bars are off the dining rooms at Mammoth Hot Springs, Roosevelt Lodge, Lake Lodge, Grant Village, and Canyon Lodge. The little corner bar at Mammoth has the only public TV inside Yellowstone; none of the in-park hotel rooms have televisions. Smoking is prohibited in Yellowstone lounges.

GROCERIES AND SUPPLIES

The park's 12 Yellowstone General Stores are at Mammoth, Canyon Village, Old Faithful, Fishing Bridge, Grant Village, Lake, Tower Fall, Bridge Bay, and Roosevelt. Each outlet has its own personality, and several of these—most notably the Lower Basin store at Old Faithful and the ones at Lake and Fishing Bridge—are grand old log structures. The Mammoth general store is another historic structure, here for nearly a century.

In addition to groceries, beer, and liquor, these stores sell a variety of merchandise, clothing, souvenirs, film and photo supplies, T-shirts, and accessories. The larger ones also have popular soda fountains with burgers, shakes, and other fast food. General stores at Canyon and Old Faithful deliver the best selection, and the Mammoth store is open year-round. The others are generally open mid-May–September and keep normal business hours. Yellowstone General Stores are managed by Delaware North Park Service (www.yellowstonegeneralstores.com).

Information and Services

RANGER PROGRAMS

Park naturalists lead slide shows, films, guided walks, kids' programs, campfire talks, and other activities at the campgrounds and visitor centers. These are always favorites of visitors, and on summer days you can choose from a multitude of Yellowstone activities, all of which are half-day. **Ranger Adventure Hikes** are offered most summer days for a $15 fee ($5 for kids). Get a complete listing of ranger programs in the *Yellowstone Today* paper you receive upon entering the park or online at www.nps.gov/yell. Evening slide programs are also offered in winter at Mammoth and Old Faithful. For a more in-depth look at the park, take a class through the Yellowstone Association Institute (www.yellowstoneassociation.org) or join one of its popular Lodging and Learning packages.

SUPPORTING THE PARK

The **Yellowstone Association** (307/344-2289, www.yellowstoneassociation.org) is a nonprofit organization that assists with education, research, publishing, and book sales inside the park. The organization also teaches dozens of classes through the acclaimed Yellowstone Association Institute.

The **Yellowstone Park Foundation** (406/586-6303, www.ypf.org) is another

YELLOWSTONE ASSOCIATION

Founded in 1933, the nonprofit Yellowstone Association (307/344-2293, www.yellowstoneassociation.org) assists in educational, historical, and scientific programs. The organization publishes several natural-history publications and provides funds to produce trail leaflets and park newspapers, along with the excellent *Yellowstone Science* magazine. In addition, the association manages book sales at visitor centers, funds park exhibits and research, and otherwise assists the park in educating the public. The organization is best known for the **Yellowstone Association Institute,** operating out of the historic Buffalo Ranch in Lamar Valley.

Instructors at the institute lead more than 100 different natural-history and humanities classes in the summer, along with several others in winter. Most of these last 2–5 days and typically cost around $90 per day – a real bargain. Courses cover the spectrum from wolf ecology to fly-fishing and provide a great way to learn about this wonderful wild place. Class size is small; most classes contain 10–15 students. Participants typically stay at the Buffalo Ranch in comfortable log cabins ($25 per person per night) and cook meals in the shared kitchen.

In addition to these classes, the Yellowstone Association Institute also offers **Lodging and Learning** programs, 2–5-day packages that blend education, recreation, and lodging. Naturalist-guides from the association lead small-group excursions (13 people maximum), and participants are provided with accommodations in park hotels, plus breakfasts and box lunches. Its **Yellowstone for Families** program ($1,230 for two adults plus $380 per child) is especially popular, with a mix of activities for both kids and parents over four days: animal tracking, wildlife-watching, photography, painting, hiking, and more.

For folks who really want the personalized touch (and can afford it), the institute offers **Yellowstone Ed-Ventures,** private tours in which a wildlife biologist travels with you in your vehicle for 6–8 hours, providing an introduction to park wildlife and ecology. The charge is $495 for up to six people.

Membership in the Yellowstone Association starts at $10 per year and is tax-deductible. Members get discounts on classes taught by the Yellowstone Association Institute and can sign up early. They also receive quarterly newsletters and discounts for purchases of items sold by the association.

© DON PITCHER

Yellowstone Association Institute at historic Buffalo Ranch in Lamar Valley

nonprofit group that works with the National Park Service by providing funds for projects and programs that would not be otherwise supported. Its biggest project was helping to raise $15 million for the new visitor center at Old Faithful. All funding comes from individuals and corporations, not from the government.

The primary environmental group involved with protecting Yellowstone and the surrounding public lands is the **Greater Yellowstone Coalition** (406/586-1593, www.greateryellowstone.org), based in Bozeman, Montana. This private nonprofit organization is involved in all sorts of environmental issues within the 10-million-acre Greater Yellowstone Ecosystem, including such hot-button issues as logging, gas development, winter use, and bison management. It represents more than 8,500 members and publishes a quarterly newsletter detailing various issues. Annual membership costs $35.

SERVICES

For a complete directory of the many Yellowstone visitor services, see *Yellowstone Today,* which you receive upon entering the park. You can also download a PDF copy off the Web from the Yellowstone site, www.nps.gov/yell.

A year-round **post office** is in a 1930s-era stone building at Mammoth Hot Springs, with seasonal post offices at Old Faithful, Lake Village, Canyon Village, and Grant Village.

Check the visitor centers for a schedule of church services. **Cell phone** users will find spotty service in many parts of Yellowstone—and nonexistent in much of the backcountry—but your phone will probably work in the country around Old Faithful, Lake, and Mammoth (and possibly elsewhere).

Internet access is even more limited. Hotel guests can use hotel phones—where they exist—for dial-up service from your laptop. If you're trying to find wireless Internet, your best bet is in surrounding towns. Wi-Fi is not readily available anywhere in the park, though you might come across a hot-spot around concessioner employee housing areas.

Shopping

Nearly every road junction in Yellowstone has some sort of general store, gas station, or gift shop. **Yellowstone General Stores** (www.yellowstonegeneralstores.com) are especially interesting because they tend to be in rustic old log structures and staffed by friendly retired folks and fresh college kids. The stores are being modernized but still retain the historic charm from past eras. Here you'll find all of the standard tourist supplies and gifts, plus groceries, snack bars, booze, camping equipment, books, fishing supplies, and locally made arts and crafts. The largest general stores are at Old Faithful and Canyon.

The **Old Faithful Inn Gift Shop** is well worth a visit, with a good selection of items from apparel to artwork. It often has book signings and guest presentations during summer. **Old Faithful Lodge Gift Shop** features artists in residence creating paintings or pottery (for sale, of course). Additional gift shops can be found in the other hotel complexes at Old Faithful Snow Lodge, Lake Yellowstone Hotel, Lake Lodge, Mammoth Hot Springs, Roosevelt Lodge, Canyon Lodge, and Grant Village. Park gift shops are managed by Xanterra Parks and Resorts, which has further info on their website, www.travelyellowstone.com.

Banking

You'll discover **ATMs** at most of the settled areas, including Old Faithful Inn, Old Faithful Snow Lodge, Fishing Bridge, Lake Yellowstone Hotel, Mammoth Hot Springs Hotel, Mammoth General Store, Canyon General Store, Canyon Lodge, and Grant Village. Park lodges and hotels are able to provide a limited **currency exchange** for international travelers Monday–Friday 8 A.M.–5 P.M.

Publications

If you're planning a trip to Yellowstone, call the park at 307/344-7381 to request a copy of the *Yellowstone National Park Trip Planner.* It provides detailed up-to-date information on hiking and camping, fishing, services, road construction, safety issues, park highlights, and lots more. The same information (and much more) is available online at www.nps.gov/yell/planyourvisit/publications.htm. Also be sure to request the latest version of the park paper, *Yellowstone Today;* it's issued quarterly.

Several print and online sources provide unofficial information on Yellowstone. One of the better private sources is the Lander-based *Yellowstone Journal* (307/332-2323 or 800/656-8762, www.yellowstonepark.com). The publication comes out several times a year and is sold in stores inside and around the park. A good freebie publication called simply *Yellowstone Park* is published annually by the *Billings Gazette* and is available online at www.billingsgazette.com. Find it in regional visitor centers outside the park. Also check out the Web-only *Yellowstone Traveler* (www.yellowstoneparktraveler.com), maintained by Circumerro Publishing.

Bookstores

The nonprofit **Yellowstone Association** (www.yellowstoneassociation.org) operates bookstores within most park visitor centers, including those at Canyon Village, West Thumb, Mammoth, Norris, Old Faithful, and Madison. Concessioner stores also carry a limited selection of regional titles, and the surrounding towns have shops selling books.

Laundry and Showers

In summer, find coin-operated washers and dryers at Fishing Bridge RV Park, Canyon Village Campground, and Grant Village Campground. Public showers ($4) are at Fishing Bridge RV Park, Old Faithful Lodge, Mammoth Hotel, Grant Village, Roosevelt Lodge, and Canyon Village Campground.

Medical

For medical emergencies 24 hours a day, the park manages **Lake Hospital** (307/242-7241), a 10-bed acute-care facility. It's open mid-May–September; also here are a clinic and pharmacy. Outpatient services are available both here and at the **Old Faithful Clinic** (307/545-7325), open mid-May–mid-October. Open weekdays year-round and daily in the summer, the **Mammoth Hot Springs Clinic** (307/344-7965) has a physician available. Call 911 for emergencies anywhere in the park.

GRAND TETON NATIONAL PARK

Grand Teton National Park remains one of the preeminent symbols of American wilderness. The Tetons rise abruptly from the valley floor, their bare triangular ridges looking like broken shards of glass from some cosmic accident of creation. With six different summits topping 12,000 feet, plus some of the finest climbing and hiking in Wyoming, the Tetons are a paradise for lovers of the outdoors. They have long been a favorite of photographers and sightseers and once even appeared in an ad promoting Colorado tourism! The Tetons change character with the seasons. In summer the sagebrush flats are a garden of flowers set against the mountain backdrop. When autumn arrives, the cottonwoods and aspens become swaths of yellow and orange. Winter turns everything a glorious, sparkling white, set against the fluorescent blue sky.

Grand Teton National Park isn't only about mountains, of course. Boat rides on Jackson Lake and raft trips down the Snake River, along with photo-perfect Jenny Lake, the barns of Mormon Row, and the winding road up Signal Mountain are all accessible to anyone with a vehicle. Two brand-new visitor centers—Craig Thomas Discovery and Visitor Center and the Laurance S. Rockefeller Preserve Interpretive Center—provide exceptional introductions to the park. Bring your bike or hiking shoes to explore a multitude of trails and country roads, and keep your eyes open for bison and other wild creatures along the way.

© DON PITCHER

HIGHLIGHTS

◖ Craig Thomas Discovery and Visitor Center: This recently opened center has tall windows facing the Tetons and state-of-the-art exhibits on the natural world (page 117).

◖ Chapel of the Transfiguration: Built in 1925, this quaint log church has a back window that frames the Tetons. No one makes better wedding chapels than this (page 117)!

◖ Jenny Lake: You won't be the first – or last – person to discover this idyllic lake in the heart of Grand Teton National Park (page 119).

◖ Signal Mountain: Too narrow for RVs, but the road up Signal Mountain provides panoramic vistas of the Tetons; it's best at sunrise or sunset (page 120).

◖ Colter Bay Indian Arts Museum: Tucked away in a nondescript visitor center, this amazing collection includes quality Indian artistry; open summers only (page 121).

◖ Teton Viewpoints: Ansel Adams wannabes take note: This is where that famous photo of the Tetons was taken (page 125).

◖ Blacktail Butte and Mormon Row: The historic farm buildings provide a picture-perfect setting and a good spot to view bison (page 126).

LOOK FOR ◖ TO FIND RECOMMENDED SIGHTS, ACTIVITIES, DINING, AND LODGING.

◖ Inspiration Point and Hidden Falls: Getting there is half the fun with a shuttle boat trip across Jenny Lake followed by a 0.5-mile hike to this scenic point. Expect a queue in midsummer, or just hike around the lake to avoid the crowds (page 129).

GRAND TETON

PLANNING YOUR TIME

Travelers to Grand Teton National Park typically see it at the same time they're visiting Yellowstone National Park and the town of Jackson. Backcountry hikers are attracted to the scenic canyons and alpine areas within the park, and the 13,772-foot Grand Teton is a goal of mountain climbers. Photographers can't resist the mountain-and-river **Teton Viewpoints** that captivated millions of earlier visitors, including Ansel Adams. A couple of days are sufficient to see park sights.

Jenny Lake is one of the most scenic areas

in the park. Here a boat transports hikers to **Inspiration Point,** a base for longer explorations into the Tetons. Historic Jenny Lake Lodge has upscale accommodations and gourmet meals; it's one of several good choices in the park.

Enjoy the view from the summit of **Signal Mountain,** and scan for moose in the sloughs at Oxbow Bend. Bison roam the flats near **Mormon Row,** which has some of the most photographed barns in America with a Teton Range backdrop to die for. Jackson Lake is popular for fishing and boating and the **Colter**

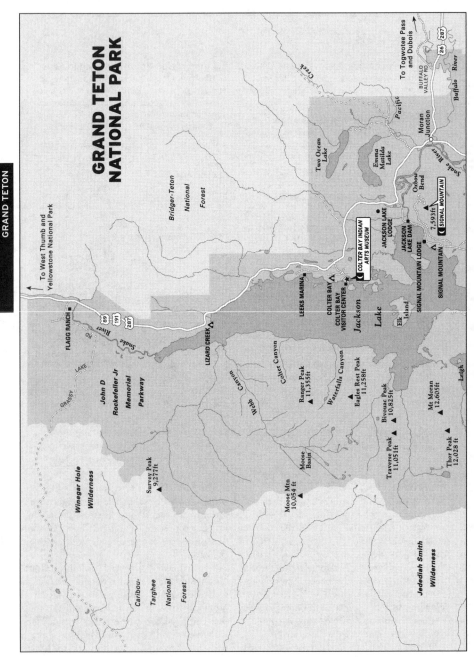

GRAND TETON NATIONAL PARK

To West Thumb and Yellowstone National Park

Bridger-Teton National Forest

Two Ocean Lake

Pacific Creek

To Togwotee Pass and Dubois

26 287

BUFFALO VALLEY RD

Buffalo River

Emma Matilda Lake

Moran Junction

Oxbow Bend

Snake River

7,593ft ▲ SIGNAL MOUNTAIN

JACKSON LAKE LODGE

COLTER BAY INDIAN ARTS MUSEUM

JACKSON LAKE DAM

SIGNAL MOUNTAIN LODGE

SIGNAL MOUNTAIN

LEEKS MARINA

COLTER BAY
COLTER BAY VISITOR CENTER

Jackson Lake

Elk Island

Leigh

89 191 287

FLAGG RANCH

Snake River

John D Rockefeller Jr Memorial Parkway

GRASSY LAKE RD

LIZARD CREEK

Webb Canyon

Colter Canyon

Ranger Peak 11,355ft ▲

Waterfalls Canyon

Eagles Rest Peak 11,258ft ▲

Bivouac Peak 10,825ft ▲

Mt Moran 12,605ft ▲

Thor Peak 12,028ft ▲

Traverse Peak 11,051ft ▲

Survey Peak ▲ 9,277ft

Moose Basin

Moose Mtn 10,054ft ▲

Winegar Hole Wilderness

Caribou-Targhee National Forest

Jedediah Smith Wilderness

© AVALON TRAVEL

Bay Indian Arts Museum houses an extraordinary collection of Native American pieces.

The little settlement of **Moose,** on the south end of Grand Teton National Park, is home to park headquarters and the striking **Craig Thomas Discovery and Visitor Center.** Nearby is **Chapel of the Transfiguration,** a rustic log church with a dramatic backdrop. The narrow and winding Moose-Wilson Road heads south to Teton Village and Wilson.

Before your visit, contact Grand Teton National Park (307/739-3600, www.nps.gov/grte) for publications and maps, or use its website to learn more about the area.

GEOLOGY
Building a Mountain Range

The precipitous Teton Range has perhaps the most complex geologic history in North America. Although the Tetons are ancient by any human scale, they are the youngest mountains in the Rockies, less than 10 million years old (versus 60 million years for the nearby Wind River Mountains). The Tetons are a fault-block range, formed when the earth's crust cracked along an angled fault. Forces within the earth have pushed the western side (the Tetons) up, while the eastern part (Jackson Hole) dropped down like a trapdoor. Geologists believe the fault could slip up to 10 feet at a time, producing a violent earthquake. All this shifting has created one of the most dramatic and asymmetric mountain faces on earth.

Unlike in typical mountain ranges, the highest parts are not at the center of the range but along the eastern edge, where uplifting continues. The western slope, which drops gently into Idaho, is much less dramatic, although the views are still impressive. This tilting-and-subsidence process is still going on today, pushed by the movement of a plume of magma beneath Yellowstone as the continental plate slides over the top. Because of this subsidence, the town of Wilson in Jackson Hole now lies 10 feet below the level of the nearby Snake River; only riverside dikes protect the town from flooding.

As the mountains rose along this fault, millennia of overlying deposits were stripped

Bison graze below the Grand Teton range.

© DON PITCHER

away by erosion, leaving three-million-year-old Precambrian rock jutting into the air above the more recent sedimentary deposits in the valley. Because of this shifting and erosion, sandstone deposits atop Mt. Moran match those 24,000 feet below Jackson Hole. Although the most recent major earthquake on the Teton Fault was at least 2,000 years ago, geologists are convinced that Jackson Hole could experience a major temblor at any time.

Rivers of Ice

In counterpoint to the uplifting actions that created the general outline of the Tetons, erosional forces have been wearing them down again. Glaciers, which are created when more snow falls than melts off, have proven to be one of the most important of these erosional processes. After a period of several years and under the weight of additional snow, the accumulated snow crystals change into ice. Gravity pulls this ice slowly downhill, creating essentially a frozen river that grinds against whatever lies in the way, plucking loose rocks and soil and polishing hard bedrock. This debris moves slowly down the glacier as if on a conveyer belt, eventually reaching the glacier's terminus.

When a glacier remains the same size for a long period, large piles of glacial debris accumulate at its end, creating what glaciologists call a terminal moraine. One of these created Jackson Lake, when a huge glacier dumped tons of rock at its snout. After the glacier melted back, this terminal moraine became a natural dam for the waters of the Snake River. Similar mounds of glacial debris dammed the creeks that formed Jenny, Leigh, Bradley, Taggart, and Phelps lakes within Grand Teton National Park.

The earth has experienced cyclical periods of glaciation for hundreds of thousands of years, probably because of changes in the earth's orbit around the sun. During the colder parts of these cycles, glaciers appear and advance. The entire Yellowstone region has undergone a series of massive glaciations, the last of which is called the Pinedale Glaciation. It began around 70,000 years ago and had essentially

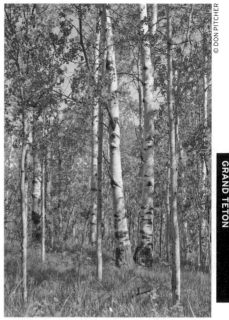

© DON PITCHER

Quaking aspens are common in Grand Teton.

GRAND TETON

disappeared by 15,000 years ago. At its peak, the Pinedale Glaciation covered all of Yellowstone and reached well into Jackson Hole.

Streams flowed from the ends of these glaciers, carrying along gravel, sand, silt, and clay. The cobbles and sands from these streams were dropped on the flat valley below, while the finer silts and clays continued downstream, leaving behind soils too rocky and nutrient-poor to support trees. Only sagebrush grows on this plain today, while the surrounding hills and mountain slopes (which were spared this rocky deposition) are covered with lodgepole and subalpine fir forests. Trees can also be found covering the silty terminal moraines that ring the lakes.

Other reminders of the glacial past are the "potholes" (more accurately termed "kettles") that dot the plain south of Signal Mountain. These depressions were created when large blocks of ice were buried under glacial outwash. When the ice melted, it left a kettle-shaped pond surrounded by glacial debris. Only a dozen or so small glaciers remain in the Tetons; the largest is the 3,500-foot-long Teton Glacier, visible on the northeastern face of Grand Teton. For a far more detailed picture of Teton geology, read *Interpreting the Landscape: Recent and Ongoing Geology of Grand Teton and Yellowstone National Parks,* by John Good and Kenneth Pierce (Moose, WY: Grand Teton Association).

Exploring Grand Teton

Grand Teton National Park has fewer "attractions" than Yellowstone—its big sister to the north—and an easy day's drive takes you past the road-accessible parts of the park. The real attractions are the mountains and the incomparable views one gets of them from Jackson Hole. This is one backdrop you will never tire of seeing.

PARK ACCESS
Entrance Stations
Grand Teton National Park (307/739-3600, www.nps.gov/grte) has two entrance stations. One is just north of the Craig Thomas Discovery and Visitor Center on Teton Park Road, and the second is on U.S. Hwy. 89/191/287 at Moran Junction. Entrance to the park is $25 per vehicle or $12 for individuals entering by bicycle, foot, or as a bus passenger. Motorcycles and snowmobiles are $20. *The pass covers entrance to both Yellowstone and Grand Teton national parks and is good for seven days.* If you're planning to be here longer or to make additional visits, get an annual pass covering both parks for $50, or the **America the Beautiful Pass**—good for all national parks—for $80 per year. An **Interagency Senior Pass** for all national parks is available to anyone older than 62 for a one-time fee of $10, and people with disabilities can get a free Interagency Access Pass. Both of these latter passes also give you 50 percent reductions in most camping fees.

At the entrance stations, park visitors receive a copy of *Teewinot,* the park newspaper. It lists park facilities and services, along with interpretive programs, nature walks, and other activities. Family favorites for generations are the evening campfire programs held at campground amphitheaters throughout the summer. The park also produces a helpful accessibility handout with details on wheelchair-accessible visitor centers, trails, sights, picnic areas, activities, campsites, and accommodations.

Visitor Centers
Grand Teton National Park headquarters is in the settlement of Moose near the southern end of the park. The striking new **Craig Thomas Discovery and Visitor Center** (307/739-3399, daily year-round) in Moose provides an outstanding introduction to the park. Also brand new is the **Laurance S. Rockefeller Preserve Interpretive Center** (307/739-3654, daily May–mid-October) halfway between Moose and Teton Village on the Moose-Wilson Road.

Jenny Lake Visitor Center (307/739-3392) is open daily late May–late September; closed the remainder of the year.

On the east side of Jackson Lake, **Colter Bay Visitor Center** (307/739-3594) is open daily mid-May–mid-October; closed the rest of the year. Also here is the Indian Arts Museum, notable for its extraordinary collection of historic Native arts.

Just north of Grand Teton inside John D. Rockefeller Jr. Memorial Parkway is **Flagg Ranch Information Station** (307/543-2861), open daily early June–early September.

Ranger-Led Programs
Check your copy of the *Teewinot* for details on several dozen options for talks, hikes, junior ranger classes, boat cruises, campfire programs, and historical lectures. You might learn

© DON PITCHER

Laurance S. Rockefeller Preserve Interpretive Center

about the legacy of Laurance Rockefeller at one talk, or learn how teepees were used at another. There's always something of interest, and many of these free programs are geared to families.

Tours

Grand Teton Lodge Company (307/543-3100 or 800/628-9988, www.gtlc.com) has three-hour bus tours of Grand Teton National Park on Mondays, Wednesdays, and Fridays for $35 ($18 kids under 12), along with eight-hour tours of Yellowstone National Park on Tuesdays, Thursdays, and Saturdays for $65 ($40 kids). Tours depart Jackson Lake Lodge at 8:30 A.M.

Summertime bus tours of Grand Teton and Yellowstone national parks are available several times a week from **Alltrans/ Gray Line of Jackson Hole** (307/733-3135 or 800/443-6133, www.jacksonholealltrans .com). Yellowstone tours last 11 hours and cost $106 plus park entrance fees. Eight-hour Grand Teton tours are $90 plus the park entrance. Those without vehicles can use Gray

Line tours for access to the parks; reserve to schedule a pickup in Jackson, Grand Teton, or Yellowstone. In Yellowstone, travelers can connect with other buses to West Yellowstone or Gardiner, Montana.

In winter, Alltrans provides daily bus runs between Jackson and Flagg Ranch Resort for $58 one-way or $106 round-trip, arriving in time to meet the snowcoach departures for Yellowstone. Reservations are required. Taxi companies in Jackson can also provide shuttles to Flagg Ranch in the winter, including **Buckboard Transportation** (307/733-1112 or 877/791-0211, www.buckboardtrans.com); $100 for up to four people one-way.

Operated by Teton Science School, **Wildlife Expeditions** (307/733-2623 or 888/945-3567, www.wildlifeexpeditions.org) leads an array of wildlife-viewing safaris throughout the region, from four-hour sunset trips for $125 to four-day tours through Yellowstone and Grand Teton for $1,895. Their trips change seasonally—depending upon which animals are visible—and are offered in customized

GRAND TETON

vehicles with multiple roof hatches for better wildlife-viewing. Also highly recommended is naturalist Carl Swoboda's **Safari Yellowstone** (800/723-2747, www.safariyellowstone.com).

Other companies offering guided van tours of the park include **Brushbuck Guide Services** (888/282-5868, www.brushbuck phototours.com), **Callowishus Park Touring Company** (307/415-5483, www.callowishus .com), **EcoTour Adventures** (307/690-9533, www.jhecotouradventures.com), **Jackson's Hole Adventure** (307/654-7849 or 800/392-3165, www.jacksonholeadventure .com), **Upstream Anglers and Outdoor Adventures** (307/739-9443, www.upstream anglers.com), **Grand Teton Adventure Company** (307/734-4454 or 800/700-1558, www.grandtetonadventures.com), **Wilderness Wildlife Explorations** (307/413-1687, www .wwexplorations.com), and **Wyoming Photo Experience** (307/413-3777, www.wyoming photoexperience.com).

Roads

Grand Teton National Park is bisected by the main north-south highway (U.S. Hwy. 26/89/191) and by the road heading east over Togwotee Pass (U.S. Hwy. 26/287). Both of these routes are kept open year-round, although wintertime plowing ends at Flagg Ranch Resort, just south of the Yellowstone boundary. In addition, a paved park road cuts south from Jackson Lake Dam to Jenny Lake and Moose. Only the southern end of this road is plowed in winter; the remainder becomes a snowmobile and cross-country ski route. South of Moose, a narrow, winding road (the Moose-Wilson Road) connects the park to Teton Village, nine miles away. It is rough dirt in places—no trailers or RVs—and is closed in winter.

WILDLIFE-VIEWING

Grand Teton National Park is an excellent place to look for wildlife, especially in the early morning or at dusk. Moose are often seen at Willow Flats along Jackson Lake just north of the dam, at Oxbow Bend, south of

the settlement of Moose, and along the Snake River. Look for bison along Antelope Flats Road, Teton Park Road, and near Moran Junction. Herds of pronghorn antelope are common on the sagebrush flats near Kelly. Elk are frequent sights in fall as they migrate down from the high country to the elk refuge near Jackson, but smaller numbers are in the park during summer. (Grand Teton is the only national park outside of Alaska that allows hunting. The rules are pretty strange, however, requiring elk hunters to become temporarily deputized park rangers before they head out!) Grizzlies are found only on the park's northern margins, but black bears are present in wooded canyons and riverbeds, so be careful when hiking or camping in the park. Other animals to look for are bald eagles and ospreys along the Snake River and trumpeter swans and Canada geese in ponds and lakes. Look for mule deer in meadows and at forest edges, such as those near Colter Bay.

Bison

Herds of bison (buffalo) are commonly seen in the Moran Junction area and in the Mormon Row area. They were present historically (hence the name Buffalo River) but had been extinct for perhaps a century when eight bison were released into Grand Teton National Park in 1969. The population grew slowly for the first decade until they discovered the free alfalfa handout at the elk refuge north of Jackson. Partly because of this winter feeding, the population has grown to almost 600 animals—much to the chagrin of the elk-refuge managers. A few bison are hunted outside the park to control their numbers.

Wolves

Wolves were reintroduced to Yellowstone National Park starting in 1995 and have continued to expand into surrounding areas, including Grand Teton National Park. They're most easily seen in winter, particularly on the adjacent National Elk Refuge where they prey on elk, but they may sometimes be seen during summer inside the park.

Sights

The following tour takes you past points of interest along the main roads. The route follows a general clockwise direction beginning in Moose and continuing to Jenny Lake, Signal Mountain, Jackson Lake, Colter Bay, and the eastern half of the park past Mormon Row and Blacktail Butte.

MOOSE
◀ Craig Thomas Discovery and Visitor Center

Begin your visit inside the dramatic new **Craig Thomas Discovery and Visitor Center** (307/739-3300, www.nps.gov/grte), where 30-foot-high windows pull your eyes outward for a spectacular Teton Range panorama. Inside, you'll find state-of-the-art exhibits showcasing the natural world, a large three-dimensional map revealing the lay of the land, mountaineering displays, interactive child-friendly activities, an auditorium with films on the park and its wildlife, and a Grand Teton Association bookstore. The visitor center is open daily 8 A.M.–7 P.M. late May–early September, and daily 8 A.M.–5 P.M. (except Christmas) the rest of the year.

The commercial center at Moose is across the Snake River bridge and just east of the visitor center. Here you'll find a plethora of operations run by **Dornan's** (307/733-2415, www.dornans.com): a general store, gift shop, lodging, fishing shop, restaurant and bar, wine shop, bike shop (with rentals), canoe and kayak rentals, and a chuck wagon eatery. Also here the sporting-goods store **Moosely Seconds** (307/739-1801) and fishing shop, **Snake River Angler** (307/733-3699, www.snakeriverangler.com). Moose has pretty much everything you might need for a day in the park.

◀ Chapel of the Transfiguration

Just inside the South Entrance to Grand Teton National Park, a side road leads to Chapel of the Transfiguration and Menor's Ferry. The rustic log church (built in 1925) is most notable for its dramatic setting. Episcopal services are held on summer Sundays, with Eucharist at 8 and 10 A.M.

The back window faces directly toward the Tetons, providing ample distractions for worshippers (or wedding guests). The bell out front was cast in 1842. Nearby **Menor's Ferry** is named for William D. Menor, who first homesteaded here in 1894 and later built a cable ferry to make it easier to cross the river. His old whitewashed store still stands. You can cross the river in a reconstructed version of the old ferry when the water level is low enough; check out the ingenious propulsion mechanism that uses the current to pull it across. For many years, Menor's Ferry served as the primary means of crossing the river in the central part of Jackson Hole. Wagons were charged $0.50, while those on horseback paid $0.25. (William Menor's brother, Holiday, lived on the opposite side of the river, but the two often feuded, yelling insults across the water at each other and refusing to acknowledge one another for years at a time.)

Also here is the half-mile **Menor's Ferry Trail;** a brochure describes historic points of interest along the path. Bill Menor's cabin houses a small country store that sells the old-fashioned supplies he stocked at the turn of the 20th century. It is open daily 9 A.M.–4:30 P.M. late May–September; closed the rest of the year.

Menor sold out to Maude Noble in 1918, and she ran the ferry until 1927, when a bridge was built near the present one in Moose. Her cabin now houses an excellent collection of historical photos from Jackson Hole. Maude Noble gained a measure of fame in 1923 when she hosted the gathering of residents to save Jackson Hole from development.

Heading northwest beyond the Menor's Ferry area, the main road climbs up an old river bench, created by flooding from the rapid melting of the glaciers, and passes the trailhead to the turquoise waters of **Taggart Lake.** The land around here was burned in the 1,028-acre Beaver Creek lightning fire of 1985, and summers find a riot of wildflowers.

The **River Road** (a.k.a. RKO Road) is a rugged 15-mile dirt-and-boulders route through open sagebrush country along the Snake River. It's a fine place to watch for bugling elk in the fall. Access the road off Teton Park Road from the south end near the Cottonwood Creek picnic area, and from the north end near Signal Mountain Road. The road is closed in early summer due to active wolf denning, and is virtually impassable for most rental cars; you'll need a high-clearance 4WD vehicle (or mountain bike) in the rocky draws. By the way, the road's alter-ego name, RKO, came when several RKO movies were filmed here in the 1940s and early 1950s. A highlight along the River Road is historic **Bar BC Ranch,** with its weathered log buildings and dramatic riverside setting. The ranch—second dude ranch in the valley—was owned by Struthers Burt, who was instrumental in establishing the park.

Murie Ranch

Down a quiet dirt road just south of the visitor center is the home of Olaus and Mardy Murie, two giants of the environmental movement. Olaus was a pioneering biologist in Alaska's Arctic regions, and founder of the Wilderness Society. In 1945, the Muries bought the old STS Dude Ranch in Moose, Wyoming, and made it their home. Together they worked to protect the Arctic National Wildlife Refuge, pushed for protection of wilderness areas, and wrote the classic book, *Wapiti Wilderness.* Olaus died in 1963, shortly before the Wilderness Act was passed, but Mardy—first woman to graduate from the University of Alaska—lived till 2003 (age 101) at her little log cabin in Moose. She wrote several books, played an important role in passing the Alaska National Interest Lands Conservation Act, and received the Presidential Medal of Freedom for her conservation work in both Alaska and Wyoming.

Today, the historic ranch's 17 structures (built in 1927) are part of a National Historic District. Befitting the Muries' love of nature,

they are now managed as the **Murie Center** (307/739-2246, www.muriecenter.org), which puts on a variety of conservation seminars and events throughout the year. Also here are the Murie archive and library. Park rangers lead historical tours of the Murie ranch in the summer.

MOOSE-WILSON ROAD

This narrow and winding road heads south from park headquarters in Moose, continuing nine miles to Teton Village. It is paved most of the way, but a 1.5-mile section is dirt. Keep your speed down to reduce the amount of dust in the air and to keep the backseat passengers from getting ill from all the curves. No trailers or RVs are allowed, and the road is not plowed in the winter. It is especially pretty in autumn when the aspens are turning. This is also a good place to watch for moose and other animals in summer or for easy cross-country ski adventures on a sunny winter day.

Two backcountry trailheads—Death Canyon Trailhead and Granite Canyon Trailhead—are accessible from the Moose-Wilson Road.

Laurance S. Rockefeller Preserve

The Rockefeller family played a pivotal role in establishing Grand Teton National Park, but for many decades they continued to own the JY Ranch, an inholding in the heart of the park. Laurance S. Rockefeller (1910–2004; grandson of John D. Rockefeller) donated the land to Grand Teton in 2001, and today this preserve is a wonderful place to relax and explore. The preserve's distinctive **Interpretive Center** (307/739-3654, daily 8 A.M.–5 P.M. May–mid-Oct.) is down a side road off the Moose-Wilson Road halfway between Moose and Teton Village. Eight miles of trails lead from here through the preserve, across sagebrush meadows, through forests, and along the shores of Phelps Lake.

The visitor center itself is unlike any you've ever seen, with a minimalist feeling that reflects Laurance S. Rockefeller's Buddhist and emotional connections to nature. Instead of the usual array of things to see and gizmos to show you the inner workings of the planet, you'll find dramatic mountain views, large, high-ceiled rooms with a few memorable exhibits, including an amazing photo mosaic and a surround-sound space where you can sit and listen to a parade of nature noises—from frogs to thunderclaps. The resource room contains classic natural history books and a fireplace. The building itself was built using recycled materials (including old blue jeans for insulation), uses composting toilets, and is heated and cooled from deep geothermal wells. The visitor center evokes different emotions from visitors. Some love its clean esthetics and eco-friendly design; others find it sterile and bizarre. Love it or hate it, this is a must-see, and the extraordinary preserve itself is well worth exploring.

◖ JENNY LAKE

The most loved of all Grand Teton lakes is Jenny Lake, nestled at the foot of Cascade Canyon and surrounded by a luxuriant forest of Engelmann spruce, subalpine fir, and lodgepole pine. Jenny Lake is named for Jenny Leigh, the Shoshone wife of Beaver Dick Leigh.

GRAND TETON

GRAND TETON

Jenny Lake rests at the foot of
Cascade Canyon.

A one-way loop road leads south past Jenny and String lakes, providing excellent views of the **Cathedral Group:** Teewinot, Grand Teton, and Mt. Owen. This is the most popular part of the park, and day-hikers will find a plethora of trails to sample, along with crowds of fellow hikers. Paths lead around both Jenny and String lakes, while another nearly level trail follows the east shore of **Leigh Lake** to several pleasant sandy beaches. **String Lake** is narrow but very pretty and makes a fine place for canoeing or swimming. Get supplies from the small store at Jenny Lake and information or guidebooks from the **Jenny Lake Visitor Center,** (307/739-3392, daily 8 A.M.–7 P.M. early June–early Sept., and daily 8 A.M.–4:30 P.M. mid-May–Memorial Day and Labor Day–Sept.). Coin-operated storage lockers are next to the store. **Jenny Lake Ranger Station,** (307/739-3343) is open daily 8 A.M.–5 P.M. late May–late-September.

Frequent **shuttle boats** (307/734-9227, www.jennylakeboating.com, $9.50 round-trip for adults) provide access to hiking trails to the Inspiration Point and Cascade Canyon

areas. One-hour scenic boat cruises are offered nightly at 6:30 P.M. in the summer; $15 adults, $8 kids. You can also rent canoes and tandem kayaks here.

Beautiful **Jenny Lake Lodge** sits on the northeast end of the lake and provides the finest lodging in the park, and the gourmet meals are legendary.

JACKSON LAKE
◖ Signal Mountain

As the road approaches Jackson Lake, a paved but narrow side road (no RVs or trailers) turns east and leads to the summit of Signal Mountain, 800 feet above Jackson Hole. On top are panoramic views of the Tetons, Jackson Lake, the Snake River, and the long valley below. To the south lies **The Potholes,** a hummocky area created when retreating glaciers left behind huge blocks of ice. The melting ice created depressions, some of which are still filled with water. Signal Mountain was burned by a massive 1879 fire and offers a good opportunity to see how Yellowstone may look in a century.

Hugging the southeast shore of Jackson Lake, **Signal Mountain Lodge** (307/543-2831, www .signalmountainlodge.com) includes cabins and campsites, plus a gift shop, convenience store, gas station, marina with boat rentals, restaurant, and bar. Just east of the lodge is **Chapel of the Sacred Heart,** a small Roman Catholic church that has summer services at 5:30 P.M. on Saturdays and at 5 P.M. Sundays. The road then crosses **Jackson Lake Dam,** which raises the water level by 39 feet, alters the river's natural flow, and inundates a large area upstream. Many conservationists fought to have Jackson Lake excluded from the park, concerned that it would establish a bad precedent for allowing reservoirs in other parks. Nevertheless, once you get away from the dam, the lake appears relatively natural today (except in drought years when it gets the "bathtub ring" effect).

Along Jackson Lake

A turnout near Jackson Lake Junction provides views over **Willow Flats,** where moose are frequently seen, especially in the

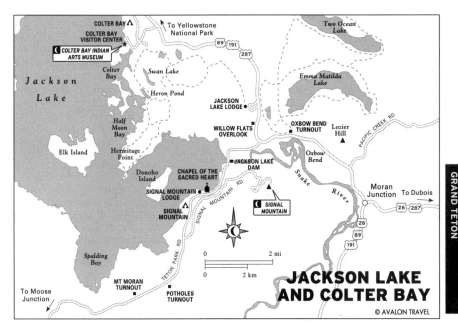

JACKSON LAKE AND COLTER BAY

GRAND TETON

morning. Topping a bluff overlooking the flats is **Jackson Lake Lodge,** built in the 1950s with the $5 million financial backing of John D. Rockefeller Jr. Architects are not thrilled about the design (one author termed it "the ugliest building in western Wyoming"), but the 60-foot-tall back windows frame an unbelievable view of the Tetons and Jackson Lake. Immediately across from the lodge is a trail leading to **Emma Matilda** and **Two Ocean** lakes. It is 14 miles round-trip around both lakes, with lots of wildlife along the way, including moose, trumpeter swans, pelicans, and ducks. You may have to contend with large groups on horseback.

COLTER BAY
Colter Bay Indian Arts Museum
Colter Bay Village is one of the most developed parts of Grand Teton National Park, with a full marina, stores, a gas station, cabins, a campground, restaurants, and acres of parking. The main attraction here is the Colter Bay Indian Arts Museum (307/739-3594, daily

8 A.M.–7 P.M. early June–Labor Day, and daily 8 A.M.–5 P.M. mid-May–Memorial Day and Labor Day–Sept., free) housed in the visitor center. Inside you will find the extraordinary David T. Vernon collection of Indian arts, the finest of its kind in any national park and one of the best in Wyoming. The collection spreads through several rooms on two floors and includes exquisitely beaded buckskin dresses, moccasins, kachina dolls, ceremonial pipes, war clubs, shields, bows, baskets, headdresses, and a remarkable grizzly bear claw necklace. Stop to chat with Native artisans as they work on paintings, beaded items, wood carvings, pottery, and weaving. They're at the museum daily Memorial Day–Labor Day. This museum should not be missed! Step out back to join the shoreside fun or to rent a canoe or boat from the nearby marina.

ROCKEFELLER MEMORIAL PARKWAY
North of Colter Bay, the highway cruises along the shore of Jackson Lake for the next

nine miles, providing some fine vantage points of the Tetons. The burned area on the opposite shore was ignited by lightning in the 1974 Waterfalls Canyon Fire, which consumed 3,700 acres. By late fall each year, Idaho spud farmers have drawn down water in the lake, leaving a long, barren shoreline at the upper end.

Shortly after the road leaves the upper end of Jackson Lake, a signboard announces your entrance into John D. Rockefeller Jr. Memorial Parkway. This 24,000-acre parcel of land was transferred to the National Park Service in 1972 in commemoration of Rockefeller's unstinting work in establishing Grand Teton National Park. The land forms a connection between Grand Teton and Yellowstone and is managed by Grand Teton National Park. Much of this area was severely burned by the 1988 Huck Fire, which began when strong winds blew a tree into power lines. Despite

BEAVER DICK LEIGH

Around 1863, Richard "Beaver Dick" Leigh became the first white man to attempt a permanent life in Jackson Hole. An Englishman by birth, Beaver Dick lived in a log cabin with his Shoshone wife, Jenny, and their four children, scraping out the barest existence by hunting, trapping, and guiding. As guide for the 1872 Hayden Survey of the Jackson Hole area, Beaver Dick gained the respect of the surveyors, who named Leigh Lake for him and Jenny Lake for his wife. Today a local bar denigrates this remarkable man by calling itself Beaver Dick's and using a cartoonish image of him in its ads. The real man was nothing like this, and reading his diaries and letters is a lesson in how difficult life was for early Wyoming settlers. On one terrible Christmas in 1876, Beaver Dick watched his entire family – Jenny, their newborn baby, and the four other children – all slowly die from smallpox. Their deaths left him badly shaken, as he related in a letter to a friend:

i got Dick in the house and to bed and Tom went over to get Mr. Anes. Wile Tom and Anes was sounding the ice to see if a horse could cross my wife was struck with Death. she rased up and looked me streaght in the face and then she got excited...and she sade she was going to die and all our childron wold die and maby i wold die...she was laying very quiet now for about 2 hours when she asked for a drink of water. i was laying downe with one of my daughters on eatch arme keeping them quiet because of the fevor. i told Anes what she wanted and he gave

hur a drink and 10 minuts more she was ded...i can not wright one hundreth part that pased thrue my mind at this time as i thaught deth was on me. i sade Jinny i will sone be with you and fell asleep. Tom sade i ad beene a sleep a half hour when i woke up everything was wet with presperation i was very weak. i lade for 10 or 15 minuts and saw William and Anne Jane had to be taken up to ease themselves every 5 minuts and Dick Juner very restlas...Anne Jane died about 8 o clock about the time every year i used to give them a candy puling and thay menchond about the candy puling many times wile sick...William died on the 25 about 9 or 10 o clock in the evening...on the 26th Dick Juner died...Elizabeth was over all danger but this, and she caught cold and sweled up agane and died on the 28 of Dec about 2 o clock in the morning. this was the hardist blow of all...i shall improve the place and live and die near my famley but i shall not be able to do enything for a few months for my mind is disturbed at the sights that i see around me and [the] work that my famley as done wile thay were liveing.

But the human spirit is remarkably resilient. Beaver Dick later married a Bannock girl, raised another family, and guided for others, even meeting Theodore Roosevelt on one of his hunting trips. Beaver Dick Leigh died in 1899 and was buried on a ridge overlooking Idaho's Teton Basin.

immediate efforts to control the blaze, it consumed 4,000 acres in the first two hours and later grew to cover nearly 200,000 acres, primarily within the Forest Service's Teton Wilderness. Dense young lodgepole pines now carpet much of the land.

On the northern end of Rockefeller Parkway is **Flagg Ranch Resort** (307/543-2861 or 800/443-2311, www.flaggranch.com), where the modern facilities include a gas station, convenience store, gift shop, cabins, restaurant, and campground with RV hookups. The park service operates the **Flagg Ranch Information Station** (307/543-2861, daily 9 A.M.–4 P.M. early June–Labor Day). During the winter, Flagg Ranch is the jumping-off point for snowcoach and guided snowmobile trips into Yellowstone.

Two nearby trails provide easy day hikes. The nearly level **Polecat Creek Loop Trail** is 2.3 miles round-trip and follows a ridge overlooking a marsh and through conifer forests. **Flagg Canyon Trail** is five miles round-trip and provides views of a rocky canyon cut through by the Snake River.

Grassy Lake Road

Grassy Lake Road takes off just north of Flagg Ranch Resort and continues 52 miles to Ashton, Idaho. It's a scenic drive, but don't attempt this narrow and rough dirt road with a trailer or an RV. This route provides a shortcut to the Bechler River area of Yellowstone and is a popular wintertime snowmobile route. Huckleberry Hot Springs, a short hike north from the Grassy Lake Road bridge over the Snake River, was the site of a public swimming pool until 1983, when it was razed by the Park Service. The hot springs are accessible via an unmaintained trail, but you'll need to wade Polecat Creek to reach them. Although they remain popular with hikers and cross-country skiers, it's worth noting that the springs may pose a risk from dangerously high radiation levels.

A few miles east of the Idaho-Wyoming border on Grassy Lake Road is **Squirrel Meadows Guard Station** (208/652-7442, www.fs.fed.us/r4/caribou-targhee) a two-room Forest Service

cabin with bunk beds, a hand pump for water, and an outhouse. The cabin sleeps up to six for $35. Wintertime access is via snowmobile or skis for the last 12 miles to the cabin from the Idaho side. Cabins are also available just across the Idaho border at **Squirrel Creek Guest Ranch** (208/652-3972, www.idahoranch.com, $75–105 d).

JACKSON LAKE TO MORAN JUNCTION
Oxbow Bend

Heading east and south from Jackson Lake, the road immediately passes Oxbow Bend, where the turnout is almost always filled with folks looking for geese, ducks, moose, and other animals. The oxbow was formed when the meandering river cut off an old loop. The calm water here is a delightful place for canoes, although the mosquitoes can be a major annoyance in midsummer. Come fall, photographers line the shoulder of the road for classic shots of flaming aspen trees with Grand Teton and **Mt. Moran** in the background. Mt. Moran is the massive peak with a flattened summit, a skillet-shaped glacier across its front, and a distinctive black vertical diabase dike that looks like a scar from some ancient battle. It rises 12,605 feet above sea level and is named for Thomas Moran, whose beautiful paintings of Yellowstone helped persuade Congress to set aside that area as the world's first national park.

Moran Junction

At Moran Junction you pass the park's Buffalo Entrance Station and meet the road to Togwotee Pass and Dubois. A post office and school are the only developments remaining here. The epic Western *The Big Trail* was filmed nearby in 1930, starring an actor named John Wayne in his first speaking role. (Wayne had never ridden a horse before this.) An interesting side trip is to head east from Moran on U.S. Hwy. 26/287 for three miles to **Buffalo Valley Road.** This narrow and scenic road leads to Turpin Meadow, a major entryway into the Teton Wilderness. It is very pretty, especially in early summer when

GRAND TETON

flowers carpet the fields. Buck-and-rail fences line the road, and the pastures are filled with horses and cattle. Beyond Turpin Meadow, the road turns to gravel and climbs sharply uphill, rejoining the main highway a couple of miles below Togwotee Mountain Lodge. The Blackrock Ranger Station of Bridger-Teton National Forest is eight miles east of Moran Junction on U.S. Hwy. 26/287. Nearby is historic **Rosie's Cabin,** built early in the 20th century by Rudolph Rosencrans, an Austrian emigrant who was the first forest ranger in this part of the Tetons.

MORAN JUNCTION TO MOOSE

Heading south from Moran, U.S. Hwy. 26/89/191 immediately crosses the Buffalo River (a.k.a. Buffalo Fork of the Snake River), where bison were once abundant. With a little help from humans, bison have been reestablished and are now often seen just south of here along the road.

The turnoff to the **Cunningham Cabin** is six miles south of Moran Junction. The structure actually consists of two sod-roofed log cabins connected by a covered walkway called a "dogtrot." Built around 1890, it served first as living quarters and later as a barn and smithy. A park brochure describes the locations of other structures on the property.

Pierce Cunningham came here as a homesteader and, with his wife, Margaret, settled to raise cattle. Although this was some of the better land in this part of the valley, the soil was still so rocky that they had a hard time digging fencepost holes. Instead, they opted to build the buck-and-rail fences that have become a hallmark of Jackson Hole ranches. Cunningham Ranch gained notoriety in 1893 when a posse surrounded two suspected horse thieves who were wintering at Cunningham's place while he was away. Vigilantes shot and killed George Spencer and Mike Burnett in an example of "mountain justice." Later, however, suspicions arose that hired killers working for wealthy cattle barons had led the posse and that the murdered men may have been innocent. **Spread Creek** is just north of the

THE MAGIC OF THE TETONS

Somewhere at the eastern base of the Tetons did those hoofprints disappear into a mountain sanctuary where many crooked paths have led. He that took another man's possession, or he that took another man's life, could always run here if the law or popular justice were too hot at his heels. Steep ranges and forests walled him in from the world on all four sides, almost without a break; and every entrance lay through intricate solitudes. Snake River came into the place through canyons and mournful pines and marshes, to the north, and went out at the south between formidable chasms. Every tributary to this stream rose among high peaks and ridges, and descended into the valley by well-nigh impenetrable courses.... Down in the bottom was a spread of level land, broad, and beautiful, with the blue and silver Tetons rising from its chain of lakes to the west and other heights residing over its other sides.

From Owen Wister's The Virginian

Cunningham cabin; it gained its name by having two mouths, separated by a distance of three miles.

The highway next rolls past **Triangle X Ranch,** one of the most famous dude ranches in Jackson Hole. Although it's on park land, the Turner family has managed Triangle X for more than 60 years. (One of the owners, John Turner, was director of the U.S. Fish and Wildlife Service under the first President Bush.) Stop by just after sunup to watch wranglers driving 120 head of horses to the corrals. It's a scene straight out of an old Marlboro ad.

Southwest from Triangle X, the road climbs along an ancient river terrace and passes **Hedrick Pond,** where the 1963 Henry

Fonda movie *Spencer's Mountain* was filmed. Although the book on which the movie was based was set in Virginia, the producers found the Tetons a considerably more impressive location. Trumpeter swans are often seen on the pond. Hedrick Pond isn't really visible from the road and there are no signs pointing it out, but you can get there by parking near the S-curve road sign 1.4 miles south of Triangle X. The pond is a good example of a kettle pond, created when retreating glaciers left behind a block of ice covered with gravel and other deposits. The ice melted, leaving behind a depression that filled to become Hedrick Pond.

C Teton Viewpoints

Several turnouts provide popular photo-opportunity spots, the most famous being **Snake River Overlook.** Ansel Adams's famous shot of the Tetons was taken here and has been repeated with less success by generations of photographers. Throughout the summer, a progression of different flowers blooms in the open sagebrush flats along the road, adding brilliant slashes of color. They're prettiest in late June; in the high country, the peak comes a month or more later than elsewhere.

Just north of Snake River Overlook is the turnoff to **Deadman's Bar.** A steep partially dirt road (not for RVs) drops to one of the primary river-access points used by river rafters. The river bar received its name from an incident in 1886. Four German prospectors entered the area, but only one—John Tonnar—emerged. Bodies of the other three were found along the Snake River, and Tonnar was charged with murder. The jury in Evanston believed his claim of self-defense and he was set free, an act that so angered locals that they vowed to take care of future Jackson Hole criminals with a shotgun. A skull from one of the victims is on display in the Jackson Hole Museum.

Schwabacher Landing sits at the end of a one-mile gravel road that splits off just north of the Glacier View Turnout. It's a pleasant place for riverside picnics and some of the most famous Teton Range photos—the ones you see in local galleries—were taken just a few hundred yards upstream from the parking area. Schwabacher Landing was formerly a common

© DON PITCHER

Schwabacher Landing along the Snake River

starting point for rafting trips, but the river channel has shifted westward, making access difficult. Most floaters now put in at Pacific Creek or Deadman's Bar.

◖ Blacktail Butte and Mormon Row

One mile north of the turnoff to Moose, Antelope Flats Road heads east along Ditch Creek. Just south of here lies Blacktail Butte, a timbered knoll rising over the surrounding sagebrush plains. It's a favorite of rock climbers and has a hiking trail up the back (east) side. You will want to stop at the much-photographed old farm buildings known as Mormon Row. The farmland here was homesteaded by predominantly Mormon settlers in the early 1900s but was later purchased by Rockefeller's Snake River Land Company and transferred to the Park Service. Only one set of buildings—an acre of the Moulton Ranch—is still in private hands. The other buildings were allowed to decay until the 1990s, when the Park Service recognized their value and stepped in to preserve the structures. Herds of bison often wander past the old farmsteads in summer, providing one of

the best places to view them. Also keep your eyes open for small groups of pronghorn antelope in the vicinity.

Shadow Mountain Area

North from the Teton Science Schools turn-off, the paved road splits. Turn left (west) on Antelope Flats Road to head back to Mormon Row and the main highway, or continue straight to climb Shadow Mountain (8,252 feet). The name comes from the shadows of the Tetons that fall across the mountain's face each evening. The road (officially it's Forest Road 30340) is paved for the first mile or so, but it turns to gravel as it snakes rather steeply up the mountain. The road is definitely not recommended for RVs or trailers, or for any vehicles after rains, when some sections turn to slippery mud. The views from the top of Shadow Mountain are truly amazing, with the Tetons in all their glory. Several dispersed campsites can be found along this route on Forest Service land.

Teton Science Schools

Hidden away in a valley along upper Ditch Creek is Teton Science Schools (TSS,

Snake River and the Teton Range

© DON PITCHER

307/733-4765, www.tetonscience.org), a fine hands-on school for both young and old. Founded in 1967 as a summer field-biology program for high-school kids, it has grown into a year-round program with classes that run the gamut from elementary-school level all the way up to intensive college courses and a graduate program. Summertime visitors will enjoy their one- to seven-day adventure getaways for adults and families on such diverse subjects as Teton geology, bird-banding, canoeing, sunset hikes, and wildlife expeditions. These classes fill up fast, so make reservations early to be sure of a spot. The school's excellent month-long wilderness emergency medical technician (EMT) course in early winter is one of the few programs of its kind in the nation.

Based at the old Elbo dude ranch (started in 1932), TSS includes two dormitories, a central kitchen, a dining area, and other log structures. Visitors to the school should visit the **Murie Natural History Museum,** which displays thousands of specimens of birds, mammals, and plants. Included are casts of animal tracks used by famed wildlife biologist Olaus Murie in producing his *Peterson's Guide to Animal Tracks.* It's open to the public, but call ahead to arrange an appointment.

Separately, the **Jackson Campus** of TSS occupies an 860-acre parcel west of town along Hwy. 22. This eco-friendly facility provides room for additional programs (including a great elderhostel) and lodging for guests. In addition, the school operates very popular **Wildlife Expeditions** (307/733-2623 or 888/945-3567, www.wildlifeexpeditions.org) with safaris throughout the Grand Teton and Yellowstone area.

KELLY AND VICINITY

The small settlement of Kelly borders on the southeastern end of Grand Teton National Park and has log homes and a cluster of Mongolian-style yurts—certainly the most unusual dwellings in Wyoming. Folks living in the yurts share a common bathhouse and rent the land. The town has a shoebox-size post office and a couple of rental cabins, along with a real treat, **Kelly**

on the Gros Ventre (307/732-9837, Mon.–Sat. 7 A.M.–3 P.M. and Sun. 9 A.M.–2 P.M.), serving sandwiches, bagels, and Jackson Hole's best espresso. The shop also has ice, beer, pop, and firewood—all the staples for camping! The Park Service's **Gros Ventre Campground** is three miles west of here.

Gros Ventre Road leads east from the Kelly area, passing **Kelly Warm Spring** on the right. Its shallow and warm waters are a favorite place for local kayakers to practice their rolls or for families to wade and hunt for frogs on a summer afternoon. A short distance up the road and off to the north (left) are the collapsing remains of the *Shane cabin,* where a scene from the classic 1951 Western was filmed. Beyond this point, the road enters Bridger-Teton National Forest and the Slide Lake area, where there is a Forest Service campground.

Gros Ventre Slide

One of the most extraordinary geologic events in recent Wyoming history took place in the Gros Ventre (pronounced GROW-vont, "Big Belly" in French trapper lingo) Canyon, named for the Gros Ventre Indians of this area. Sheep Mountain, on the south side of the canyon, consists of sandstone underlain by a layer of shale that becomes slippery when wet. Melting snow and heavy rains in the spring of 1925 lubricated this layer of shale, and on June 23 the entire north end of the mountain—a section 2,000 feet wide and one mile long—suddenly slid 1.5 miles downslope, instantly damming the river below and creating Slide Lake. A rancher in the valley, Guil Huff, watched in amazement as the mountain began to move, but he managed to gallop his horse out of the way as the slide roared within 30 feet. Huff's ranch floated away on the new lake several days later.

For two years folks kept a wary eye on the makeshift dam of rock and mud. Then, on May 18, 1927, the dam suddenly gave way, pushing an enormous wall of water through the downstream town of Kelly. Six people perished in the flood, and when the water reached Snake River Canyon nine hours later it filled the canyon to the rim with boiling water, trees, houses,

GRAND TETON

and debris. Today a smaller Slide Lake still exists, and the massive landslide that created it more than 75 years ago remains an exposed gouge visible for miles around. Geologists say that, under the right conditions, more of Sheep Mountain could slide. Dead trees still stand in the upper end of Slide Lake. The Forest Service has a **Gros Ventre Geological Trail** 10 miles up Gros Ventre Road. This 0.25-mile path leads to an incredible viewpoint overlooking the slide and is marked with interpretive signs.

Gros Ventre Valley

Above Slide Lake (six miles up), the road turns to gravel, becoming quite rutted in places. Surprising scenery makes the sometimes bone-jarring route easier to take. The landscape here is far different from that of the Tetons, with brilliant red-orange badland hills rising sharply above the Gros Ventre River. Two more Forest Service campgrounds (Red

Hills and Crystal Creek) are four miles above Slide Lake, or you can camp in dispersed sites off the road. **Grizzly Lake Trail** starts at the Red Hills Campground and continues for 3.5 miles to this small mountain lake. There are wonderful vistas of the Red Hills and Gros Ventre River valley below.

The road continues another 15 beautiful miles along the river above the lake, getting rougher at the upper end. Several remote guest ranches are up here. Beyond Cow Creek Trailhead (29 miles from Kelly) the route is virtually impassable unless you have a high-clearance 4WD and are ready to get stuck. Hard-core mountain bikers sometimes continue up this road/trail and then drop into the Green River watershed north of Pinedale. Cow Creek Trail and other paths lead into the Gros Ventre Wilderness, which borders the south side of the road. On the drive back down the Gros Ventre River valley you will discover some fine views across to the Tetons.

Hiking

The precipitous Tetons that look so dramatic from the roads are even more impressive up close and personal. Grand Teton National Park is laced with 200 miles of trails, and hikers can choose anything from simple day treks to week-long trips along the crest of the range. Unlike nearby Yellowstone, where most of the country is forested, the Tetons contain extensive alpine scenery. This means, however, that many of the high passes won't be free of snow until late July and may require ice axes before then. Check at the visitor centers or Jenny Lake Ranger Station for current trail conditions. In addition, this high country can be dangerous when frequent thunderstorms roll through in summer. Several people have been killed by lightning strikes in the Tetons. Most storms hit in the afternoon, so it's good to get an early start to avoid them if possible. Besides, trailhead parking spots fill early, especially on warm summer weekends.

Get the helpful *Grand Teton Day Hikes* pamphlet from park visitor centers or online

at www.nps.gov/grte. For the guided version, get a schedule of free ranger walks and hikes (including special ones for kids) from visitor centers or in the park newspaper. These are offered daily throughout the summer.

MOOSE-WILSON ROAD AREA
Phelps Lake

- Distance: 4 miles round-trip to the lake
- Rating: moderate to strenuous
- Elevation: 6,800 feet
- Trailhead: Death Canyon Trailhead (3 miles south of Moose off the Moose-Wilson Road)

This trailhead is a popular access point for backpackers heading into the wilderness, but shorter hikes are possible. It's 1.8 miles round-trip to **Phelps Lake Overlook,** where you get a view across this beautiful mountain lake 600 feet below. From Phelps Lake Overlook you can hike steeply down for a lakeside picnic on the sandy beach, and then back the same way.

Death Canyon Patrol Cabin

- Distance: 8 miles round-trip
- Rating: strenuous
- Elevation: 6,800 feet
- Trailhead: Death Canyon Trailhead (3 miles south of Moose off the Moose-Wilson Road)

This challenging hike covers some of the same country as the Phelps Lake hike, but it continues beyond Phelps Lake Overlook to Death Canyon Patrol Cabin at the junction of Death Canyon Trail and Static Peak Trail. Getting to the cabin requires climbing 420 feet to the overlook, losing 400 feet in elevation, and then climbing 1,000 feet higher. And you've got to go back the same way. The small log cabin was built by the Civilian Conservation Corps in the 1930s and is still used by trail maintenance crews. Continue 0.5 mile beyond the cabin up Death Canyon Trail for a dramatic vista into Death Canyon.

JENNY LAKE AREA
◖ Inspiration Point and Hidden Falls

- Distance: 2.2 miles round-trip with boat shuttle; 5.8 miles round-trip by trail
- Rating: moderate
- Elevation: 6,800 feet
- Trailhead: East Boat Dock on Jenny Lake

The fun trek to Inspiration Point is one of the most popular day hikes in Grand Teton National Park. The trail starts on the west side of Jenny Lake. It's 2.4 miles by foot from the Jenny Lake Ranger Station on the east side, or you can ride one of the summertime Jenny Lake Boating **shuttle boats** (307/734-9227, www.jennylakeboating.com, daily mid-May–Sept., $9.50 adults round-trip, $5 ages 2–11, free for tots and anyone over age 80) that cross the lake every 15 minutes or so. Hours vary, but in peak season (July to mid-Aug.) it's 7 A.M.–7 P.M. Shuttle boat lines lengthen around 11 A.M., so get here early in the morning to avoid the crush and to better your odds at finding a parking spot. Boat tickets are not available in advance. Afternoon thunderstorms

frequently build up over the Tetons, which is another good reason to start your hike early.

From the boat dock on the west side, the trail climbs 0.5 mile to picturesque Hidden Falls, and then continues steeply another 0.5 mile to Inspiration Point, which overlooks Jackson Hole from 400 feet above Jenny Lake. Avoid the crowds on the way down from Inspiration Point by following a second trail back to Jenny Lake. If you miss the last boat at 6 P.M., it's a 2.4-mile hike around the lake to the parking area.

Cascade Canyon

- Distance: 14–19 miles round-trip
- Rating: strenuous to very strenuous
- Elevation: 6,800 feet
- Trailhead: East Boat Dock on Jenny Lake

Many day-hikers continue at least part of the way up Cascade Canyon beyond Inspiration Point. The trail climbs gradually, gaining 640 feet in the next 3.6 miles, and provides a good chance to fish for trout or watch for moose and other animals along Cascade Creek. Those with strong legs can make a *very* long day hike all the way up to Lake Solitude (14 miles round-trip with shuttle boat) or even Hurricane Pass (19 miles round-trip with shuttle boat, and gaining almost 3,600 feet on the way up). If you're into hiking that far, it probably makes more sense to reserve a backcountry campsite and take things a bit more leisurely.

Taggart and Bradley Lakes

- Distance: 6 miles round-trip to both lakes
- Rating: moderate
- Elevation: 6,900 feet
- Trailhead: Taggart Lake Trailhead at Taggart Creek parking lot (2 miles north of Moose)

A very popular day hike follows **Taggart Lake Trail** to the lake and then back via the **Beaver Creek Trail,** a distance of 4.4 miles round-trip. A side loop to Bradley Lake adds about 2 miles to this journey. These trails provide a fine way to explore the damlike glacial

GRAND TETON

© DON PITCHER

Watch for moose along the Snake River.

moraines that created the lakes. You can also continue beyond Bradley Lake on a trail that climbs to beautiful Amphitheater Lake, the primary access point for climbs up Grand Teton. (Climbers generally begin from Jenny Lake, however.)

Amphitheater Lake

• Distance: 10 miles round-trip
• Rating: very strenuous
• Elevation: 6,750 feet
• Trailhead: Lupine Meadows Trailhead, accessible off Teton Park Road just south of Jenny Lake

Looking for a fast climb into the mountains? Amphitheater Lake is only 5 miles up the trail but is 3,000 feet higher, making this the quickest climb to the Teton tree line. Many folks day-hike the Amphitheater Lake Trail to savor the wonderful vistas across Jackson Hole along the way. Camping is available at Surprise Lake, 0.5 mile below Amphitheater Lake, but you'll need a backcountry permit. The mountain behind this alpine cirque is 11,618-foot **Disappointment Peak,** directly in front of Grand Teton. It was named in 1925 by a group

of climbers who mistakenly thought they were on the east face of the Grand.

COLTER BAY AREA
Colter Bay Trails

• Distance: 9 miles round-trip
• Rating: easy
• Elevation: 6,800 feet
• Trailhead: Hermitage Point Trailhead at the south end of Colter Bay Visitor Center parking lot

A spiderweb of mostly level trails heads south from this trailhead, passing beaver ponds and willow patches where trumpeter swans, moose, and ducks are commonly seen. The longest destination is **Hermitage Point,** on the tip of a peninsula jutting into Jackson Lake. Get a map of Colter Bay trails from park visitor centers to see the various options. Shorter loop paths include the 2-mile **Lakeshore Trail** and the 3-mile **Swan Lake-Heron Pond Trail.**

BACKCOUNTRY HIKING

The most popular backcountry hiking area centers on the crest of the Tetons and the lakes that lie at its feet, most notably Jenny Lake.

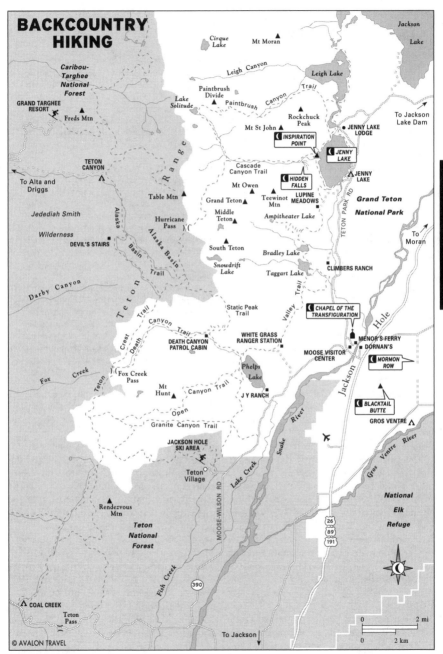

BACKCOUNTRY HIKING

Jackson Lake

Cirque Lake

Mt Moran

Caribou-Targhee National Forest

GRAND TARGHEE RESORT

Freds Mtn

Leigh Canyon

Leigh Lake

Leigh Canyon Trail

Paintbrush Divide

Lake Solitude

Paintbrush Canyon

Rockchuck Peak

To Jackson Lake Dam

Mt St John

JENNY LAKE LODGE

INSPIRATION POINT

JENNY LAKE

Teton Range

TETON CANYON

To Alta and Driggs

Cascade Canyon Trail

JENNY LAKE

Mt Owen

HIDDEN FALLS

Table Mtn

Grand Teton

Teewinot Mtn

LUPINE MEADOWS

Grand Teton National Park

Jedediah Smith Wilderness

Hurricane Pass

Middle Teton

Ampitheater Lake

DEVIL'S STAIRS

South Teton

Bradley Lake

To Moran

Alaska Basin Trail

Snowdrift Lake

Taggart Lake

CLIMBERS RANCH

Darby Canyon

Teton Crest Trail

Static Peak Trail

Valley Trail

CHAPEL OF THE TRANSFIGURATION

Jackson Hole

Death Canyon Trail

DEATH CANYON PATROL CABIN

WHITE GRASS RANGER STATION

MENOR'S FERRY

DORNAN'S

MOOSE VISITOR CENTER

MORMON ROW

Fox Creek

Fox Creek Pass

Mt Hunt

Phelps Lake

J Y RANCH

Canyon Trail

Jackson Hole

Snake River

BLACKTAIL BUTTE

GROS VENTRE

Open

Granite Canyon Trail

JACKSON HOLE SKI AREA

Teton Village

MOOSE-WILSON RD

Lake Creek

Gros Ventre River

National Elk Refuge

Rendezvous Mtn

Teton National Forest

26
89
191

COAL CREEK

Teton Pass

Fish Creek

390

To Jackson

0   2 mi
0   2 km

GRAND TETON

© AVALON TRAVEL

GRAND TETON

LIGHTNING SAFETY

Lightning is a significant hazard for travelers on foot or horseback in Wyoming, particularly in the high mountains such as the Tetons, Wind River Range, Snowy Range, or the Big Horns. Three people were killed by lightning strikes in 1998 and 1999 in the Snowy Range west of Laramie, and others are hit almost every year around the state. Perhaps the most famous incident came in the 1990s, when acclaimed writer Gretel Ehrlich was struck while riding a horse on her ranch at the foot of the Big Horns. Her long and excruciating recovery is detailed in *A Match to the Heart* (Random House, www.randomhouse.com).

CREATING A THUNDERHEAD

Thunderstorms are created by a combination of convective forces, moisture, and unstable air. On sunny days as the ground warms, heat begins to rise convectively. When the air above is unstable (much cooler at higher altitudes than closer to the ground), the warm air rises rapidly. As it rises, the air cools enough that tiny droplets of moisture precipitate out, forming clouds that may grow into thunderheads if there is enough moisture and atmospheric instability. This rapid development of

thunderheads generates enormous amounts of energy that is released as lightning, wind, hail, and rain. During a lightning strike, an electrical charge reaches toward the ground and is met by an opposite charge rising from the earth. They connect in a brilliant flash of light, heat, and noise as 35,000 amperes of charge are released.

PROTECTING YOURSELF

Nearly 100 people die each year from lightning strikes in the United States, and hundreds of others are injured. Statistically speaking, golfers are the most likely to get zapped because they are often in open areas carrying metal golf clubs when a storm rolls in. Others at risk include softball and soccer players, mountain climbers, horseback riders, swimmers, and hikers.

Several factors are important in protecting yourself from lightning. One is to pay attention to building storms, even distant ones, and especially those that build quickly. Mountain thunderstorms − created when winds push air masses upslope against a mountain range − are five times more likely to occur than storms over adjacent valleys. The color

---

Teton Crest Trail stretches from Teton Pass north all the way to Cascade Canyon, with numerous connecting paths from both sides of the range. Three relatively short (two- to three-day) loop hikes are described below. For more complete descriptions of park trails, see *Jackson Hole Hikes* by Rebecca Woods (Jackson: White Willow Publishing) or *Teton Trails* by Katy Duffy and Darwin Wile (Grand Teton Association, www.grandtetonpark.org). Get topographic maps at **Teton Mountaineering** in Jackson. Best is the waterproof version produced by Trails Illustrated.

Permits

The backcountry trails of Grand Teton National Park are some of the most heavily used paths in Wyoming, and strict regulations are enforced. Backcountry-use permits are required of all overnight hikers, and you'll need to specify a particular camping zone or site for each night of your trip. Get permits and detailed backcountry brochures from the visitor centers in Moose or Colter Bay or the Jenny Lake Ranger Station. Get there early in the morning during summer for permits to popular trails. A limited number of backcountry permits can be reserved in advance January 1–May 15 online at www.nps.gov/grte/plan yourvisit/bcres.htm, or by writing the Permits Office, Grand Teton National Park, P.O. Drawer 170, Moose, WY 83012. You can also request permits by faxing 307/739-3438. You'll need to pick the permit up in person and pay a $25 service fee for reservations. No charge for permits if you get them the of thunderheads is another factor to watch; black bases mean significant amounts of moisture and may portend a more violent thunderstorm.

The most dangerous times are – surprisingly – before a thunderstorm comes directly overhead. Strikes can hit up to five miles in front of a fast-moving thunderstorm. In 1999, a Boy Scout was struck in the Tetons while watching a distant thunderstorm; overhead it was mostly blue sky! To determine your distance from an approaching storm, count the number of seconds between a lightning strike and the subsequent thunderclap, then divide by five to get the approximate distance in miles. If thunder arrives within five seconds, the storm is dangerously close, just one mile away.

If you see a storm approaching, get off ridgetops and other high places, move out of open fields, away from trees or other tall objects, and away from water. Lightning follows the path of least resistance, which usually means taller objects or those containing metal. Safer places are inside a car or house. If those options aren't possible, stay as low as possible and stand on an insulated pad or a four-foot square of polyethelene. Put your ankles and knees together and crouch down, or drop to your knees and bend forward, putting your hands on your knees. Do not lie flat on the ground. Move away from others in your group and avoid rocks and boulders if possible. Horseback riders should dismount and move away from the horse. Metallic and electronic objects attract lightning, so stay away from power lines, fence posts, golf clubs, cell phones, climbing gear, or metal objects in your backpack. Even a metal cap rivet can attract lightning. Don't stand in a group of people. If you're indoors when a storm hits, move away from windows, doors, appliances, pipes, and telephones.

Lightning strikes are sometimes preceded by a tingling sensation, and your hair may stand on end. If this happens, move immediately into the crouching position. If someone near you is struck by lightning, get immediate help by calling 911 and be ready to perform CPR. Injured people do not carry an electrical charge and can be handled safely. For additional lightning safety information, contact the nonprofit **Lightning Protection Institute** (800/488-6864, www.lightning.org).

GRAND TETON

day of your trip. Get additional information on permits and reservations by calling 307/739-3309. Be sure to also request the park's *Backcountry Camping* handout (also available online at www.nps.gov/grte) with details on regulations, snow conditions, minimizing impacts, and bear safety. On the back is a trail map that shows camping zones and access.

Safety in the Backcountry

Grizzlies are primarily found in the northern end of Grand Teton National Park, but black bears roam throughout the park, particularly in the forested areas along the lakes. Special boxes are provided for food storage at backcountry campsites along Jackson, Leigh, and Phelps Lakes. Backcountry campers at other sites are required to use a hard-sided food storage canister provided by the Park Service at no charge. Hanging of food is no longer allowed in the backcountry, and bikes are not allowed on trails anywhere inside the park. Campfires are not permitted at higher elevations, so be sure to bring a cooking stove.

Backcountry hikers (and day-hikers for that matter) need to be aware of the dangers from summertime **thunderstorms** in the Tetons. A common weather pattern is for clear mornings to build to blustery thunderstorms in late afternoon, followed by gradual clearing as evening arrives. Lightning is a major threat in the park's exposed alpine country, and rain showers can be surprisingly heavy at times. Make sure all of your gear is wrapped in plastic (garbage bags work well), and carry a rain poncho or other rainwear. Many hikers carry cell phones for emergencies, but coverage is spotty in the mountains. Unfortunately, the phones can also create a false sense of security for those who are not familiar with backcountry travel. Don't head unprepared into the mountains thinking you can always call for a rescue if you sprain your ankle.

Cascade Canyon to Paintbrush Canyon

One of the most popular hikes in Grand Teton National Park is this 19-mile loop trip up Cascade Canyon, over Paintbrush Divide, and down Paintbrush Canyon (or vice versa). The trip offers a little of everything: dense forests, alpine lakes, flower-covered meadows, and magnificent views of the Tetons. This trip is best done in late summer because a cornice of snow typically blocks Paintbrush Divide until the latter part of July. Most folks do it as an overnight trip, but it's possible to do the entire loop in a single very long day if you're in good shape and have a masochistic streak. Be sure to bring plenty of water along.

Begin at the String Lake Trailhead and head south around Jenny Lake, stopping to enjoy the views (and crowds) at Inspiration Point before heading up along Cascade Creek. The trail splits at the upper end of this canyon; turning left takes you to Hurricane Pass and the Teton Crest Trail, where you'll discover wonderful views of the back side of Grand Teton. Instead, turn right (north) and head up to beautiful Lake Solitude. Behind you, Teewinot, Mt. Owen, and Grand Teton are framed by the glacially carved valley walls. Above Lake Solitude, the trail climbs sharply to Paintbrush Divide and then switchbacks even more quickly down into Paintbrush Canyon. The trail eventually leads back to String Lake. Be sure to stop at beautiful Holly Lake on the way down.

Death Canyon Loop

Another fine loop trip departs from the Death Canyon Trailhead, approximately three miles

south of park headquarters on the Moose-Wilson Road. Many hiking options are available here, with trails leading to Phelps Lake, up Open Canyon, or into Death Canyon. (The name came about when a survey party was in the area in 1899 and one of the men disappeared. He was never seen again.) Despite the name, Death Canyon provides a wonderful 26-mile loop hike that takes you over three high passes and into spectacular alpine country. From the trailhead, hike to Phelps Lake Overlook before dropping to a junction, where you turn right to hike up Death Canyon. Bear left at a patrol cabin built in the 1930s, and continue climbing all the way to Fox Creek Pass (9,520 feet). After this the going is fairly easy for the next three miles along Death Canyon Shelf to Mt. Meek Pass, where you drop into famous Alaska Basin. Return to your starting point by climbing east from Alaska Basin over Static Peak Divide (10,800 feet) and then switchbacking downhill to the CCC cabin and the trailhead. This is a late-season trek because snow often blocks the passes until July; get snow conditions at the Jenny Lake Ranger Station.

Rendezvous Mountain to Death Canyon

This 23-mile-long loop hike is different in that much of the way is downhill. Begin at the new Jackson Hole tram in Teton Village, where a $25 ticket takes you to the top of Rendezvous Mountain. From the summit, the trail leads down to a saddle, across the South Fork of Granite Creek, and up to Teton Crest Trail. Head north on this trail to Marion Lake—a popular camping site—and then over Fox Creek Pass. The trail splits, and the right fork drops sharply down into scenic Death Canyon. At the lower end of Death Canyon, cliffs rise nearly 3,000 feet on both sides. The trail forks at Phelps Lake, and from here you can either hike back to Teton Village via the Valley Trail or head to the trailhead at White Grass Ranger Station, 1.5 miles northeast of Phelps Lake.

Recreation

Summers in Grand Teton are ideal for outdoor play. The weather is typically warm and sunny, but with just enough variety to keep things interesting. For high adventure (literally), you could climb Grand Teton with a guide, or for something less challenging, sit back and watch the scenery float past from a river raft or ride horseback through the sagebrush.

CLIMBING

The Tetons are considered some of the premier mountaineering country in the nation, with solid rock, good access, and a wide range of climbing conditions. Hundreds of climbing routes have been described for the main peaks, but the goal of many climbers is Grand Teton, better known as "the Grand." At 13,772 feet, this is Wyoming's second-highest summit, exceeded only by 13,804-foot Gannett Peak in the Wind River Mountains.

First to the Top

In the climbing trade, first ascents always rate highly, but the identity of the first climbers to have scaled Grand Teton has long been a matter of debate. The official record belongs to the party of William Owen (as in nearby Mt. Owen), Bishop Spalding (as in nearby Spalding Peak), John Shive, and Frank Petersen, who reached the summit in 1898. Today, however, it appears that they were preceded by two members of the 1872 Hayden Expedition: Nathaniel P. Langford (first superintendent of Yellowstone National Park) and John Stevenson. In addition, another party apparently made it to the top in 1893. Owen made a big deal out of his climb and spent 30 years trying to work himself into the record books by claiming the Langford party never reached the top. The whole thing got quite nasty, with Owen even accusing Langford of bribing the author of a history book to gain top honors. In 1929, Owen convinced the Wyoming Legislature to declare his group the first on top. Few people believe it today, and the whole thing looks pretty foolish because even seven-year-old kids have made it up the Grand.

Several thousand people climb the mountain each summer, many with no previous climbing experience (but with excellent guides and a couple of days of training). The record time is an unbelievable three hours, six minutes, and 25 seconds for Bryce Thatcher in 1983. This time includes starting from—and returning to—the parking lot at the foot of the mountain! And just to prove that it could be done, in 1971 one fanatic actually skied the Grand (he's the ski-school director at Snow King Resort), followed in 1989 by a snowboarder. Both lived to tell the tale.

Getting There

Most climbing takes place after the snow has melted back (mid-July) and before conditions again deteriorate (late Sept.). Overnight mountain climbing or off-trail hiking requires a special permit available from the **Jenny Lake Ranger Station,** (307/739-3343, daily 8 A.M.–5 P.M. late May–late-Sept.). There's no need to register if you're climbing or doing off-trail hiking for the day only, just for overnight trips. (Still, it's a good idea to leave a detailed trip itinerary with a responsible person in case of an emergency.) Winter climbers should register at the **Craig Thomas Discovery and Visitor Center.** The climbing rangers—one of the most prestigious and hazardous jobs in the park—are all highly experienced mountaineers and can provide specific route information for the various summits. Call 307/739-3604 for recorded climbing information, or talk to staff at the ranger station for weather conditions, route information, and permits.

Many climbers who scale Grand Teton follow the Amphitheater Lake Trail from Lupine Meadows to its junction with the Garnet Canyon Trail. This leads to the **Lower Saddle,** which separates Grand Teton and Middle Teton. Exum and the Park Service have base-camp huts and steel storage boxes here. No

GRAND TETON

outhouses at Lower Saddle, and climbers are required to use high-tech carry-out bags for human waste—complete with a system that breaks down feces (www.whennaturecalls .com).

Other folks pitch tents behind boulders in the extraordinarily windy mountain gap at Lower Saddle. See Park Service handouts for camping restrictions and recommendations in this fragile alpine area, where heavy use by 4,000 climbers each year has caused considerable damage. The final assault on the summit of Grand Teton requires technical equipment and expertise. No motorized drills are allowed for placing climbing bolts.

Mountaineers who have registered to climb the Grand can stay at **Climbers' Ranch,** near Taggart Lake, for $16 per night. Lodging is in small log cabins with 4–8 bunks; hot showers and a cooking shelter are close by, but you'll need to bring your own sleeping bag and food. The ranch is open June–September. Call 307/733-7271 after June 1 for reservation information, or visit the American Alpine Club's website (www.americanalpineclub.org) for details. Reservations can be made online. The ranch has space for 65, but 45 of these are kept open for walk-ins. It's a good idea to reserve in April for July and August.

Climbing Schools

Jackson Hole is blessed with two of the finest climbing schools in North America: **Jackson Hole Mountain Guides** (165 N. Glenwood, 307/733-4979 or 800/239-7642, www.jhmg.com) and **Exum Mountain Guides** (307/733-2297, www.exumguides.com) with a summertime office at the south end of Jenny Lake near the boat dock. Both are authorized concessions of the National Park Service and the U.S. Forest Service and offer a wide range of classes, snow training, and climbs in the Tetons and elsewhere—even as far away as Alaska and the Himalayas. Exum has been around since 1931, when Glenn Exum pioneered the first solo climb of what has become the most popular route to the top of the Grand, the Exum Route. It's the only company

permitted to guide all Teton peaks and routes throughout the year. Exum's base camp is in the busy Lower Saddle area, while Jackson Hole Mountain Guides' base camp is 450 feet lower in elevation in a more secluded location (it takes an extra hour of climbing on the day of your ascent). Exum has some of the most experienced guides in the world, but they take up to four clients in a group, while Jackson Hole limits its Grand Teton ascent parties to three clients.

During midsummer, you'll pay around $850–1,250 per person (depending on the number of people in the group) for an ascent of Grand Teton; this includes two days of basic and intermediate training followed by a two-day climb up the Grand and back. Food, gear, and shelter are also included. If you're planning to climb the Grand during the peak summer season, be sure to make reservations several months in advance to be assured of a spot. For July and August, make Grand Teton climbing reservations before the end of March.

Reservations generally are not needed for the companies' one-day basic ($140) and intermediate ($160) climbing schools. Also available are climbs of other faces, such as Baxter's Pinnacle, Symmetry Spire, and Cube Point, along with more advanced classes and climbs in the Wind River Mountains and up Devils Tower and other precipices throughout the western states. In addition, both companies offer a multitude of **winter classes and expeditions,** such as avalanche safety, ski mountaineering, and ice climbing. Jackson Hole Mountain Guides has additional climbing operations in Cody, Lander, Red Rocks, and Moab. Exum also operates from City of Rocks, Devils Tower, and the Wind River Mountains.

On Your Own

If you already have the experience and want to do your own climbing, the most accessible local spot is **Blacktail Butte,** just north of Moose near Ditch Creek. The parking lot here fills on warm summer afternoons as hang-dogging enthusiasts try their moves on the rock face. Get climbing supplies at **Moosely Seconds**

© DON PITCHER

climbers trying their moves on Blacktail Butte

Mountaineering (307/739-1801) in Moose, or in Jackson at **Teton Mountaineering** (170 N. Cache Dr., 307/733-3595 or 800/850-3595, www.tetonmtn.com). Both stores rent climbing shoes and other gear. **Enclosure Indoor Climbing Center** (670 Deer Lane, 307/734-9590, www.enclosureclimbing.com) has challenging indoor climbing walls where you can practice your moves.

For complete details on local climbing, see Reynold Jackson's *A Climber's Guide to the Teton Range* (The Mountaineers Books, www .mountaineersbooks.org), the smaller *Teton Classics: 50 Selected Climbs in Grand Teton National Park,* by Richard Rossiter (Globe Pequot Press), or *Teton Rock Climbs* by Aaron Gams (www.tetonrockclimbs.com), a digital CD-ROM guidebook of routes. Mountain climbing is inherently dangerous, and even the best climbers have accidents on The Grand. Over the years, many people have died in the Tetons, and in 2008, George Gardner—an Exum guide with 28 years of experience—died in a fall while solo climbing.

RAFTING

Several rafting companies lead scenic half-day 10-mile float trips (around $50–60 adults, $35–45 kids) down the Snake River inside the park, putting in at Deadman's Bar and taking out in Moose. For full details on guided Snake River whitewater and float trips—including those within Grand Teton—see *River Rafting* in the *Jackson Hole* chapter.

Float It Yourself

The Park Service (307/739-3602, www.nps .gov/grte) has useful information on running the sections of the river inside Grand Teton; ask for a copy of *Floating the Snake River.* Note that life jackets, boat permits ($20 for a seven-day permit), and registration are required to run the river through the park, and that inner tubes and air mattresses are prohibited. Floating the gentler parts (from Jackson Lake Dam to just above Pacific Creek) is generally easy for even novice boaters and canoeists, but below that point things get dicier. The water averages 2–3 feet deep, but it sometimes exceeds 10 feet and flow rates are often more than 8,000 cubic feet per second, creating log-jams, braided channels, strong currents, and dangerous sweepers. Peak flows are between mid-June and early July. Inexperienced rafters or anglers die nearly every year in the river. Flow-rate signs are posted at most river landings, the Craig Thomas Discovery and Visitor Center, and the Buffalo Ranger Station in Moran. If you're planning to raft or kayak on the whitewater parts of the Snake River, be sure to contact the Bridger-Teton National Forest office in Jackson (307/739-5500, www.fs.fed .us.btnf) for additional information, including its *Snake River Canyon Floater's Guide.*

Excellent waterproof maps of the Grand Canyon of the Snake River are sold at the visitor center. In addition to showing the rapids, these maps describe local geology and other features.

Rent rafts from **Snake River Kayak and Canoe School** (307/733-9999 or 800/529-2501, www.snakeriverkayak.com), **Leisure Sports** (1075 S. U.S. Hwy. 89 in Jackson, 307/733-3040, www.leisuresportsadventure.com), **Riding**

floating the Snake River

and Rafts (307/654-9900, www.riding andrafts.com), 35 miles southwest of Jackson in Alpine, or **Rent-a-Raft** (307/733-2728 or 800/321-7328) in Hoback Junction 12 miles south of Jackson. You can also rent whitewater kayaks from Leisure Sports, Snake River Kayak and Canoe School, Rent-a-Raft, or **Rendezvous River Sports/Jackson Hole Kayak School** (307/733-2471, www.jackson holekayak.com). **Teton Taxi** (307/733-1506, www.tetontaxi.com) provides a shuttle to transport your car from the put-in point to your take-out spot.

BOATING

Canoeists will discover several excellent places to paddle within Grand Teton, particularly the Snake River Oxbow Bend, String Lake, and Leigh Lake. Canoes are available for rent both in the park at Colter Bay Marina and Signal Mountain Lodge, and in Jackson.

Boaters within Grand Teton will need to buy a permit; seven-day permits cost $20 for motor-boats, $10 for nonmotorized craft. Motorboats are allowed only on Jackson Lake, Jenny Lake (10-horsepower max), and Phelps Lake. Sailboarding, water-skiing, jet skis, and sailing are permitted on Jackson Lake, but no personal watercraft are allowed anywhere in the park. See the park boating brochure for details.

Jenny Lake Boating (307/734-9227, www .jennylakeboating.com) has a variety of services on the south end of this gorgeous, mountain-rimmed lake, including shuttle boats ($9.50 adults, $5 kids) to Inspiration Point, one-hour scenic boat cruises ($15 adults, $8 kids), and rentals of canoes and tandem kayaks ($13 per hour or $60 per day).

Marinas

Jackson Lake has three marinas, all of which are generally open sometime in May–late September. **Signal Mountain Lodge Marina** (307/543-2831, www.signalmountainlodge .com) rents a range of floating objects, including sea kayaks, canoes, motorboats, runabouts, pontoon boats, and deck cruisers. Join a four-hour **guided sailboat tour** for $299.

Colter Bay Marina (307/543-3100 or 800/628-9988, www.gtlc.com) is near a Park Service campground, cabins, and the Colter Bay Indian Arts Museum. It's an exceptionally busy place in the summer, with motorboat, kayak, and canoe rentals, along with guides to take you to the hot fly-fishing spots. Scenic **Jackson Lake cruises** ($23 adults, $12 kids under 12) are also available from Colter Bay Marina, as are breakfast or evening cruise-and-dine trips ($36 for breakfast; $60 for dinner).

A short distance north of Colter Bay is **Leek's Marina** (307/543-2494, www.signalmountain lodge.com), a simple place with a couple of docks, a pizza restaurant, and gas pumps.

Kayaks and Canoes

O.A.R.S. (209/736-4677 or 800/346-6277, www.oars.com) offers multi-day sea kayaking trips around Jackson Lake—perfect for beginning kayakers and families. You don't need any paddling experience for these trips, which are supported by a motorized skiff. Overnight trips cost $259 adults or $210 youths; two-night kayak trips are $412 adults or $330 kids. O.A.R.S. also has combination trips that include kayaking on the lake and rafting down the Snake River. A three-day multi-sport trips cost $644 adults or $541 youths; four-day trips run $620 adults or $521 kids. For the whole enchilada, check out their six-night combo trips that include kayaking on Yellowstone and Jackson Lakes, park tours, camping, and a raft trip down the Snake River for $1,540 adults, $1,385 youths. The company supplies kayaks, a guide, tents, and dry bags, with sleeping bags available for rent. These popular trips fill quickly, so reserve several months ahead.

Jenny Lake Boating (307/734-9227, www.jennylakeboating.com) rents canoes and tandem kayaks for $13 per hour or $60 per day. Canoes are also available at the Signal Mountain and Colter Bay marinas.

FISHING

Grand Teton National Park rivers and lakes contain cutthroat, lake, and brown trout, along with whitefish. Park anglers must have a valid Wyoming state fishing license, available for $14 for one day if you aren't a resident. Kids younger than 14 don't need a license if they're with an adult who has a valid fishing license. Pick up a helpful handout describing fishing regulations and seasons from park visitor centers. Fishing licenses and supplies are available at park marinas and stores.

Yellowstone and Grand Teton have different fishing regulations and license requirements. If you're heading into Yellowstone to fish, you'll need to purchase a special Yellowstone National Park fishing license. Both parks prohibit the use of non-native baitfish.

Located in Moose, **Snake River Angler** (307/733-3699, www.snakeriverangler.com) sells and rents fishing supplies. Their guides offer learn-to-fly-fish lessons for beginners ($125 for two people), along with boat-based guided fishing ($440–475 for two). Fishing guides are also available from **Signal Mountain Lodge Marina** (307/543-2831, www.signal mountainlodge.com) and **Colter Bay Marina** (307/543-3100 or 800/628-9988, www.gtlc .com), along with a number of Jackson-based operations.

In Jackson, drop by Jack Dennis' Outdoor Shop (50 E. Broadway, 307/733-3270 or 800/570-3270, www.jackdennis.com) to pick up a free copy of *Western Fishing Newsletter,* with descriptions of regional fishing areas and advice on which lures to try.

BIRDING

The diversity of habitat types within Grand Teton National Park means that bird-watchers can find everything from trumpeter swans to calliope hummingbirds. The park produces a free *Bird-Finding Guide* with descriptions of birding hot spots. A couple of the best places are Willow Flats and Blacktail Ponds. A checklist of park birds is also available from visitor centers.

BIKING

Great news for cyclists: Grand Teton has completed a new eight-mile paved pathway between

GRAND TETON

© DON PITCHER

bison and bicyclists on the road near Mormon Row

Moose and Jenny Lake, paralleling Teton Park Road and providing a much-safer alternative for bike riders. Future additions will extend the path north to Colter Bay and south to Jackson, but don't expect to see these until 2011 at best. The bike paths (also open to runners, roller-bladers, and strollers) are part of a long-term transportation plan that will eventually total 41 miles of pathways.

Pick up the park's bicycling pamphlet for details on cycling options. Bikes are not allowed on any trails within Grand Teton National Park, but you *can* ride mountain bikes on several wonderful dirt roads, including Two Ocean Lake Road (three miles), Grassy Lake Road (52 miles from Flagg Ranch to Ashton, Idaho), and the River Road (15 delightfully remote miles in the heart of the park). In addition, the paved secondary roads in the Antelope Flats-Mormon Row-Kelly area see less traffic and provide the opportunity to see bison and spectacular mountain vistas. Shadow Mountain Road is an off-the-beaten-path dirt road that takes off from the Antelope Flats area and climbs through Forest Service land to splendid vistas. The primary north-south

highway through the park—US 26/89/191—is heavily trafficked, and cars often top the speed limit. Cyclist should avoid this route.

Teton Park Road is closed to cars and other motorized traffic until May, and during April it is plowed and open to cyclists, walkers, and inline skaters. When the weather warms up, this is a wonderful traffic-free way to see the park.

Rentals and Tours

Rent bikes from **Adventure Sports** (307/733-3307, www.dornans.com) at Dornan's in Moose; $22 for a half-day or $32 for all day. They'll provide a map showing good mountain biking roads in the park. **Teton Mountain Bike Tours** (307/733-0712 or 800/733-0788, www.wybike.com) leads scenic half- or all-day bike trips through Grand Teton for all levels of ability, with prices starting at $60 for a four-hour ride in the Antelope Flats area.

HORSEBACK RIDING

Grand Teton Lodge Company (307/543-3100 or 800/628-9988, www.gtlc.com) has horseback rides at **Jackson Lake Lodge Corral** and **Colter Bay Village Corral;** $36 for one hour or $53 for two hours. Located in Rockefeller Parkway between Grand Teton and Yellowstone, **Flagg Ranch Resort** (307/543-2861 or 800/443-2311, www.flagg ranch.com) offers hour-long horseback trail rides in the summer for $35. Additional rides are available in Buffalo Valley, just east of the park; see the *Jackson Hole* chapter for details on these.

SWIMMING

Swimming is allowed in all park lakes, but they can be quite cold. Jenny, String, and Leigh lakes all have delightful spots for swimming on the east side, including some sandy or gravelly beaches. The Snake River is dangerous and swimming isn't recommended. Jackson Lake Lodge has a large heated outdoor pool, but it's open only for guests at the lodge or nearby Colter Bay Village. In addition, the town of Jackson has a wonderful recreation center with pools, and the shallow pond at Kelly Warm Spring is a fun spot to splash around.

WINTER RECREATION

The snow-covered landscape of Grand Teton National Park draws cross-country skiers, snowshoers, and snowmobilers throughout the winter.

Skiing

Cross-country skiing is popular on park roads and trails in the winter. The main thoroughfare—Teton Park Road—provides stellar views of the Teton Range and is groomed weekly for both parallel and skate skiing (with sections for hikers and snowshoers) from Taggart Lake to Signal Mountain, a distance of 14 miles. Park three miles northwest of Moose at the Taggart Lake Trailhead, where plowing ends. More adventurous skiers will enjoy side trails to Jenny Lake (eight miles round-trip) or the more challenging Taggart Lake-Beaver Creek loop (three miles with an elevation change of almost 400 feet). Another fun area is the Moose-Wilson

Road, an easy four-mile round-trip ski from the Granite Canyon Trailhead (where plowing stops). A good optional side route is the trail to Phelps Lake overlook (five miles round-trip with an elevation change of 520 feet). Other enjoyable places to ski include Antelope Flats Road and trails at Taggart Lake, Flagg Ranch, and Colter Bay.

Most park ski routes (other than Teton Road) are not machine-groomed but are often well packed by other skiers. After a new snowfall you'll need to break trail as you follow the orange markers. Pick up a brochure describing ski trails from the Craig Thomas Discovery and Visitor Center, or find the information on the park website (www.nps.gov/grte). If you're planning to camp overnight in the park, you'll need to get a free permit from the visitor center.

Snowshoeing

Park naturalists lead two-hour snowshoe hikes late December–March and provide snowshoes ($5 donation). No experience is necessary. The hikes generally depart from the **Craig Thomas Discovery and Visitor Center** at 2 P.M. several times a week. Reservations are required, and no kids under age eight. Call 307/739-3399 for reservations and details on other winter activities in the park.

Snowmobiling

Snowmobiles are allowed on the **Continental Divide Snowmobile Trail,** which cuts through Grand Teton National Park and provides a link between the Wind River Mountains and Yellowstone National Park. Within Grand Teton the trail is generally open early January–mid-March and parallels U.S. Hwy. 26/287 from the east park boundary to Moran Junction and then along U.S. Hwy. 89 north to Yellowstone. Restrictions on snowmobile access within Yellowstone have greatly reduced the number of snowmobilers heading through Grand Teton National Park in the last few years. For the latest, pick up the snowmobiling handout at the visitor center.

GRAND TETON

Accommodations

Several places provide concessioner lodging inside Grand Teton National Park. As in most national parks, none of the lodge rooms contains TVs, radios, or air conditioning. Some rooms contain phones and Wi-Fi access is available in Jackson Lake Lodge. Reserve at least nine months ahead to be sure of getting a room in the peak summer season. Dozens of additional accommodations are south of the park in Jackson. **Grand Teton Lodge Company** (owned by Vail Resorts Hospitality, www.gtlc.com) is the primary concessioner in the park, managing Jackson Lake Lodge, Jenny Lake Lodge, Colter Bay Village, and a variety of park services.

MOOSE

Near park headquarters in Moose, **Dornan's Spur Ranch Cabins** (307/733-2522, www .dornans.com) has a dozen modern log cabins filled with handcrafted lodgepole pine furniture. One-bedroom cabins are $175 d or $205 for up to four people, and two-bedroom cabins cost $250 for up to six people. There's a three-

night minimum stay in the summer. All cabins include full kitchens and are open most of the year (closed Nov. and Apr.). Off-season rates are 30 percent lower.

JENNY LAKE

For four-star accommodations a stone's throw from the Tetons, stay at (**Jenny Lake Lodge** (307/733-4647 or 800/628-9988, www.gtlc .com, late May–early Oct.), where 37 comfortably appointed cabins surround a cozy Old West main lodge. This is a marvelous honeymoon or big-splurge place, and the $500 s or $585 d price includes horseback rides, bikes, breakfast, and a six-course dinner. (Note, however, that the meals are served only at specific times, so you'll need to adjust your schedule accordingly.) For the ultimate in extravagance, choose the lodge's luxurious suites; $728–785 d.

JACKSON LAKE

Built on a grand scale, the 385-room **Jackson Lake Lodge** (307/543-3100 or 800/628-9988,

cabin at Jenny Lake Lodge

© DON PITCHER

www.gtlc.com, late May–early Oct.) occupies a bluff above Willow Flats on the southeast side of Jackson Lake. Sixty-foot-high windows look across to the Tetons, and fireplaces flank the spacious central hall where Wi-Fi and guest computers are available. Outside is a large swimming pool and kiddie pool (major attractions for families), and inside you'll find restaurants, a lounge, gift shop, newsstand, clothing shop, and ATM. All rooms contain two double beds and phones; some also have small fridges. Most guests stay in 348 cottage units surrounding the main building, but 37 guest rooms are available inside the lodge itself. Rooms in the lodge without a view (unless you count the parking lot) are $219 d, while those with big windows fronting the Tetons are $319 d. Cottages cost $219–239, or $289 d for ones with mountain vistas. A separate modern structure facing Moose Pond houses some of the nicest rooms and suites: $319–550 d, and a single luxury suite in the lodge costs $750 d. Extra guests (beyond two) in any of these rooms are $10 per adult. Pets can stay in the cottages for $15 extra.

On the south shore of Jackson Lake, **Signal Mountain Lodge** (307/543-2831 or 800/672-6012, www.signalmountainlodge .com, early May–mid-Oct.) offers a variety of lodging options. Simple and rustic log cabins start at $124 d, up to $181 for a two-room unit that sleeps six. Motel-style rooms with fridges and microwaves are $160 for up to four people or $212 for a nicer room with a fireplace and king bed. The lodge's finest options include lakefront suites for $237–255, cozy bungalows with kitchens and private decks for $170–248 d, and a three-room cabin with fireplace in the living room, full kitchen, and laundry for $302.

COLTER BAY

Family-oriented **Colter Bay Village** (307/543-3100, ext. 1080, or 800/628-9988, www.gtlc.com) has 166 rustic cabins of varying sizes and types, some of which sleep six people. There are no phones or cooking facilities in any of these cabins. The most basic are canvas-and-log structures with outdoor grills and picnic tables, indoor woodstoves, and bring-your-own-

linen bunk beds. Restrooms are nearby, and the showers are coin-operated. These tent cabins cost just $43 d ($6 for each additional person up to six). Sleeping bags and other camping supplies are available for rent. The tent cabins are open late May–late September.

Slightly nicer are little one-room cabins that share a bath for $49 d. Cabins with a private bath start at $89 d for those with a double bed, up to $135 d for those with two double beds and a twin bed. Two-room cabins with a bath are $149 d or $179 for up to four. Additional guests are $6 each in all of these, and the cabins are open late May–September. Guests at Colter Bay Village can use the big swimming pool at nearby Jackson Lake Lodge.

ROCKEFELLER MEMORIAL PARKWAY

In Rockefeller Parkway just three miles south of Yellowstone, **Flagg Ranch Resort** (307/543-2861 or 800/443-2311, www.flagg ranch.com) has modern four-plex log cabins with patios and two queen beds or a king bed. Rates are $172–182 d, plus $10 for additional adults. The main lodge houses a convenience store, restaurant, gift shop, and central area with couches and a large fireplace. Flagg Ranch is open late May–late September and early December–early March, but lodging is available only in summer.

BUFFALO VALLEY

Several lodging places are in beautiful Buffalo Valley, east of Moran Junction on U.S. Hwy. 26/287.

Hatchet Resort

Eight miles east of Moran Junction, Hatchet Resort (307/543-2413 or 877/543-2413, www .hatchetresort.com) has clean year-round accommodations and a friendly staff in a delightful country setting. Well-maintained log-walled motel rooms with newly added kitchens and fireplaces go for $199 d, while modern log suites featuring vaulted ceilings, fridges, microwaves, and hot tubs are $265 d. Hatchet also has five simple budget rooms with shared baths for $99 d. All guests have access to the large outside hot tub, and the small resort also has free Wi-Fi, a restaurant (surprisingly good breakfasts and burgers), bar/pizzeria, general store, and gas station on the premises. (Hatchet Resort is not a park concessioner.)

Buffalo Valley Ranch

Buffalo Valley Ranch (307/543-2062 or 888/543-2477, www.buffalovalleyranch.com) is adjacent to Heart Six Ranch (same owners) and is 12 miles east of Moran Junction. A triplex log building houses a pair of one-bedroom units ($159 d), along with a spacious two-bedroom unit ($259 for up to eight guests), all with kitchenettes, private baths, washers, and dryers. Also here is a small seasonal café serving three meals daily. The ranch affords fine views across Buffalo Valley to the Tetons, but book early since the cabins fill in the summer. Also here is **Buffalo Valley Café,** serving tasty meals three times daily all summer.

Luton's Teton Cabins

You'll discover spectacular views of the Tetons from **Luton's Teton Cabins** (307/543-2489, www.tetoncabins.com), 36 miles northeast of Jackson (five miles east of Moran Junction). The modern duplex cabins have full kitchens, private baths, and front porches facing the mountains. One-bedroom units cost $225 d, two-bedroom units are $348 for up to six people, while deluxe cabins sleep six for $386. Cabins are open May–October. No phones, but free Wi-Fi. Horse lovers can use the corrals at no charge.

KELLY AREA
Anne Kent Cabins

For rustic accommodations with an unbeatable Teton view from the front deck, stay at Anne Kent Cabins (307/733-4773, www.annekent cabins.com, June–Sept.) in the quiet village of Kelly a dozen miles northeast of Jackson. These cabins are perfect for those who want a real taste of Wyoming from a family with a long local history. Two rental options are available. Your best bet is to request the very comfortable log house, which has bedrooms in the loft and basement, two baths, a complete kitchen, washer, and dryer (but no phone). Wi-Fi may be available. The home could sleep

old wagons in Kelly

© DON PITCHER

14 adults and kids in a pinch and goes for $250 per night (plus $25 per person for more than four guests). Next door are two cabins that rent together and sleep five guests for $200. The front one (built in 1939) includes a bedroom and kitchen, while the back cabin contains a second bedroom plus bath. The Anne Kent Cabins feature handmade lodgepole furniture created by co-owner Ron Davler, who crafts them at the adjacent Jackson Hole Log and Rawhide Furniture.

Moulton Ranch

Moulton Ranch on Historic Mormon Row (307/733-3749, www.moultonranchcabins .com, late May–Sept.) rents several cabins in one of Jackson Hole's most majestic locations. This is the only private property on Mormon Row inside Grand Teton National Park, and the much-photographed Moulton Barn—one of the prototypical Wyoming images—is just a few hundred feet away. The six cabins are cozy and not at all elaborate, but where else might you awake to a spectacular Teton vista with bison grazing outside your window? Rates start at $80 d for a tiny cottage with a separate bathhouse, up to $220 for a modern cabin with space for six. The latter is especially popular and features a kitchenette, deck, and picture window facing the Tetons. No phones (your cell phone probably works here), but Wi-Fi is available in some cabins.

Budges' Slide Lake Cabins

Budges' Slide Lake Cabins (307/733-9061, www.jacksonholecabins.com, open year-round) are five secluded but modern cabins along Slide Lake, six miles east of Kelly. Each has a woodstove, full kitchen, patio, and phone (but no TVs). Rates are $245 d, plus $30 each for each additional adult guest (maximum of eight). Weekly rates are $1,650 d. A small cabin in nearby Kelly sleeps two for $100, including a kitchen and bath, but no TV or phone.

GUEST RANCHES

Within Grand Teton National Park, 25 miles north of Jackson, **(Triangle X Ranch** (307/733-2183 or 888/860-0005, www.trianglex .com, May–Oct. and late Dec.–mid-Mar.) is a classic family-oriented ranch with unmatched

© DON PITCHER

Triangle X Ranch

GRAND TETON

GRAND TETON

© DON PITCHER

horses at Triangle X Ranch

Teton views. The ranch has been in the Turner family for more than 75 years, and the acclaimed author Barry Lopez once worked as a wrangler here. Horseback riding is the main focus, but it also offers kids' programs and nightly events such as Dutch-oven cookouts, naturalist presentations, square dancing, and campfire sing-alongs. All-inclusive weekly rates are $3,510 for two adults. In winter Triangle X goes upscale, with fewer guests (maximum of 35 versus 80 in the summer), a hot tub, and three gourmet meals a day. The nightly winter rate is $240 d, including lodging, meals, and use of cross-country skis and snowshoes. There's a two-night minimum stay in winter and a one-week minimum stay in summer (four nights in spring and fall). No credit cards accepted in the summer.

Wyoming's most elaborate—and expensive—guest ranch, **Lost Creek Ranch** (307/733-3435, www.lostcreek.com, late May–Sept.), is 21 miles north of Jackson. This showplace resort emphasizes fitness, with a spa facility that includes exercise classes, a weight room, steam room, sauna, and hot tub, along with massage and facials (extra charge). Guests stay in modern duplex log cabins and enjoy gourmet meals in the main lodge's patio overlooking the Tetons. Amenities include such nontraditional items as a heated swimming pool, tennis courts, and a skeet range, in addition to more standard horseback riding, kid programs, float trips, hiking, Yellowstone tours, and fly-fishing. It's all a bit too Disneyesque for my tastes, and the prices are too Madison Avenue. Weekly all-inclusive rates run $6,500 for two people in a duplex cabin or an astounding $15,000 for up to four people in a luxurious two-bedroom, two-bath cabin with a living room and fireplace. Some consider this a small price to pay for such pampering. The ranch hosts a maximum of 45 guests at a time. There is a one-week minimum stay.

You might get lucky and find a space at historic (**Moose Head Ranch** (26 miles north of Jackson, 307/733-3141 in summer or 850/877-1431 Oct. –May, www.ranchweb. com/moose-head-ranch). This family ranch has space for 44 guests and receives so many repeat customers that it's almost always booked up. New guests should call for reservations in October for the following summer, but cancellations occasionally occur, even in midsummer. The 120-acre ranch is entirely surrounded by Grand Teton National Park and features modern log cabins, horseback riding, private trout ponds, fly-fishing lessons, and gourmet meals. There's a five-night minimum stay, and all-inclusive rates are $5,110 per week for two people. The ranch is open June–mid-August.

Buffalo Valley Ranches

A longtime favorite—it began taking guests in the 1920s—is **Turpin Meadow Ranch** (307/543-2496 or 800/743-2496, www.turpinmeadowranch.com). The ranch's Buffalo Valley location provides impressive Teton vistas, along with all of the traditional ranch activities: horseback riding, cookouts, fly-fishing, day trips to Yellowstone, and pack trips. Guests stay in modern cabins and have access to an indoor hot tub. Summertime all-inclusive rates are $3,790 for two people for a six-night stay. The ranch is open year-round and is a favorite snowmobile spot in winter.

A classic family summer destination, **Heart Six Ranch** (307/543-2477 or 888/543-2477, www.heartsix.com) is in the heart of Buffalo Valley, 12 miles east of Moran Junction and 43 miles northeast of Jackson. Horseback rides are a star attraction, along with kids' programs, day trips to Yellowstone National Park and the Jackson Hole rodeo, and a range of evening activities including cookouts, nature programs, and western music. Or, you can just relax in the hot tub while kids play in the outdoor pool. All-inclusive weekly rates are $3,990 for two people. The ranch takes in up to 50 guests at a time and is open year-round. Only weekly stays are available June–August, but at other times of the year the ranch offers nightly lodging ($75–250 d). This is a favorite base for snowmobilers mid-December–March.

Gros Ventre Ranches

Looking for a peaceful place to really relax? Twenty miles up a dirt road in undeveloped Gros Ventre Valley (30 miles northeast of Jackson), **Goosewing Ranch** (307/733-5251 or 888/733-5251, www.goosewingranch.com) is one of the most remote guest ranches in Jackson Hole. The well-appointed modern log cabins have fireplaces, private baths, and decks. Guests can use the outdoor hot tub all year and the outdoor heated pool in the summer. Popular summertime activities include horseback excursions, fly-fishing, mountain-biking, hiking, and children's programs. All-inclusive weekly mid-summer rates cost $3,780 for two people. There's a three-night minimum stay, and the ranch accommodates a maximum of 30 guests. When winter arrives, the ranch becomes a favorite destination for snowmobiling, with a variety of packages available.

Situated up undiscovered Gros Ventre River Valley (15 miles northeast of Jackson near Slide Lake), **Gros Ventre River Ranch** (307/733-4138, www.grosventreriverranch.com, May–Oct.) is a small ranch with accommodations for up to 45 guests in modern log cabins and a homestead house and is known for its delicious meals. The main activities are horseback riding, world-class fly-fishing, cookouts, canoeing, and mountain-biking. The lodge has a pool table, table tennis, and large-screen television. Weekly all-inclusive rates are $3,370 for two people.

Situated along the rolling Gros Ventre River, **Red Rock Ranch** (307/733-6288, www.theredrockranch.com, June–mid-Sept.) faces spectacular orange-red badlands. The ranch is 32 miles northeast of Jackson, and the quiet location and drop-dead-gorgeous scenery are reason enough to stay here. Guests settle into comfortable log cabins with woodstoves, and take part in horseback riding, cookouts, and other activities. The ranch also features kids' programs, stocked fishing ponds, a large swimming pool, and hot tub. There's space for a maximum of 30 guests, and a six-night minimum stay is required. All-inclusive rates are $3,700 for two adults for six nights.

Camping

Grand Teton National Park has five camp-grounds; $17–19 (half-price if you have a **Senior Pass** or **Access Pass**). These are available on a first-come, first-served basis with no reservations, and by mid-afternoon in the peak summer season all park campgrounds sometimes fill up. The maximum stay is seven days at Jenny Lake or 14 days at other camp-grounds. Camping (or overnight parking) is not allowed along roadsides, overlooks, or parking areas within the park. Off-the-road camping is restricted to specific sites and re-quires a special permit.

Grand Teton rangers lead popular evening **campfire programs** at all five campgrounds throughout the summer. All campgrounds have running water but no utility hookups. Showers and a coin laundry are available at Colter Bay Village. Several special hiker/biker sites are at Jenny Lake and Colter Bay for $7. Group sites can be found at Colter Bay and Gros Ventre camp-grounds, but reservations are required. All Grand Teton National Park campgrounds are closed in winter, but limited tent camping and RV park-ing ($7; restrooms and water but no hookups) are available near the Colter Bay Visitor Center. Get recorded park campground and lodging informa-tion at 307/739-3603, or find additional details on the Web at www.nps.gov/grte.

Jenny Lake Campground

First to fill is always Jenny Lake Campground, with 50 tent sites (no RVs) near this wonder-fully scenic lake in the heart of the park. The campground is open mid-May–late September and usually fills by 8 A.M. in midsummer. Not far away is a little general store, plus Jenny Lake Lodge with gourmet meals.

Signal Mountain Campground

On the south shore of Jackson Lake, Signal Mountain Campground has 81 sites, a trailer dumping station, and room for RVs up to 30 feet long. It frequently fills by 10 A.M. in mid-summer and is open early May–mid-October.

The campground is close to Signal Mountain Lodge, which has a restaurant and general store. It's 32 miles from Jackson.

Colter Bay Campground

On the east side of Jackson Lake, Colter Bay Campground is one of the largest in the park, with 350 sites, a dump station, and nearby coin-operated showers and laundry facilities. Also close by are the Indian Arts Museum, a general store, a pair of eateries, and rustic cab-ins for rent. Leeks Marina, with a popular piz-zeria, and Jackson Lake Lodge are just a few miles down the road. Colter Bay Campground is open late May–late September and typically fills by mid-afternoon in midsummer.

Lizard Creek Campground

This campground has 60 quiet campsites on the north end of Jackson Lake and is open early June–early September. These sites usually fill by late afternoon in the peak season, and RVs must be less than 30 feet. The nearest food and supplies are in Flagg Ranch or Colter Bay, both approximately eight miles away.

Gros Ventre Campground

With over 350 sites, Gros Ventre Campground is both the largest campground in the park and the last to fill (if at all). The campground is on the southern edge of the park along the Gros Ventre River near Kelly and is 10 miles from Jackson. It's open early May–mid-September and has a dump station and five group sites. There's a great little espresso-and-sandwiches shop in nearby Kelly, but the nearest stores or restaurants are in Jackson or Moose.

CAMPING OPTIONS

In addition to the five NPS campgrounds, park concessioners maintain two seasonal RV parks with full hookups, showers, washers, and driers. **Flagg Ranch Resort** (307/543-2861 or 800/443-2311, www.flaggranch.com, late May–late Sept.) in Rockefeller Parkway has

100 pull-through RV sites with full hookups for $50, and 75 tent sites for $25. Reservations are highly recommended.

On the south shore of Jackson Lake is **Colter Bay RV Park** (307/543-3100 or 800/628-9988, www.gtlc.com, $54 RVs, late May–late Sept.). No tent spaces are available here, but evening nature programs are offered in the summer.

Grand Teton Park RV Resort (307/733-1980 or 800/563-6469, www.yellowstonerv.com, open year-round) is six miles east of the park along Hwy. 26/287. There are fine views of the Tetons, and facilities include a heated seasonal pool and hot tub, recreation room, and grocery store. The cost is $53 d for RVs with hookups, $40 d for tents. Simple camping cabins go for $72–78 d.

The Forest Service has quite a few campgrounds in the surrounding country (described in the *Jackson Hole* chapter), and several private RV parks are available in Jackson.

Food

Though more limited than your choices in nearby Jackson, Grand Teton National Park has a good variety of dining options, from the all-you-can-eat outdoor affairs at Dornan's to memorable Jenny Lake Lodge meals. Most places do not require reservations, though you may need to wait for a table on a busy summer evening.

RESTAURANTS AND BARS
Several dining options exist at **Jackson Lake Lodge** (307/543-3100 or 800/628-9988, www.gtlc.com), including the Mural Room (daily 7–9:30 A.M., 11:30 A.M.–1:30 P.M., and 5:30–9 P.M. mid-May–Sept.) with its 60-foot windows fronting the Tetons. The restaurant serves three meals a day, while the nearby **Blue Heron Lounge** (daily 11 A.M.–midnight) offers equally impressive views and musicians provide accompaniment for your cocktails most evenings. Dinner reservations are preferred; call 307/543-3463. Casual meals are available at **Pioneer Grill** (daily 6 A.M.–10:30 P.M.), also inside Jackson Lake Lodge, or the very popular **Pool Snack Bar,** next to the big outdoor swimming pool. The latter has an all-you-can-eat dinner buffet ($22 adults, $12 kids) with hamburgers, brisket, barbecue chicken, and other Western grub June–August.

Marvelous old **Jenny Lake Lodge** (307/543-3300, www.gtlc.com, daily 7:30–9 A.M., noon–1:30 P.M., and 6–8:45 P.M. late May–early Oct.) has impeccable service, windows that face the mountains, and a cozy setting. Five-course dinners are the featured attractions, and the wine list is extensive. Lunch is à la carte ($9–11), but breakfast and dinner are fixed price (and pricey: $69 for a five-course dinner, $21 for breakfast). This is a dress-up place, so a jacket and slacks are recommended for dinner. Reservations should be made a day or more in advance since lodge guests have priority.

Colter Bay Village has two dining choices: the **Chuckwagon** (6:30–10:30 A.M., 11:30 A.M.–1:30 P.M., and 5:30–9 P.M.) for steaks and pasta and the **John Colter Café Court** (daily 11 A.M.–10 P.M.) for chicken, pizza, deli sandwiches, salads, and snacks.

An old favorite with an egalitarian setting—look for the tepees—is **Dornan's Chuck Wagon Restaurant** (307/733-2415, www.dornans.com, mid-June–mid-Sept.), offering reasonable meals every summer since 1948. The all-you-can-eat breakfasts ($9; daily 7–11 A.M.) include pancakes, ham, bacon, biscuits, and eggs. Sandwiches are the main lunch attraction (daily noon–3 P.M., $8–10), and dinners (daily 5–9 P.M., $16–19) include grilled-to-order barbecue ribs, chicken, steaks, salmon, or trout, plus a big outdoor salad bar. Sunday dinners ($23) include prime rib or New York steak.

Across the street—and open all year—is Dornan's **Dornan's Pizza and Pasta Co.** (307/733-2415, daily 11:30 A.M.–9:30 P.M. mid-June–mid-Sept., reduced winter hours, closed Apr. and Nov.), offering a wide range of homemade pizzas ($16), sandwiches, calzones, salads, and pastas. Dining is available on a big outside deck where you can watch the rafts float by topped by can't-beat-the-view Teton vistas. The bar (A.K.A. Spur Bar) has beer on draught and mixed drinks, along with monthly wine tastings ($10) the first Sunday of each month. Monday-evening Hootenannies are a fun addition in winter; these move outside to the adjacent Chuck Wagon Restaurant when summer arrives. Folk musicians perform once or twice a month, and there's free Wi-Fi. Check out the board on the wall next to the bathrooms. In 1944, local resident Farney Cole used the board to defend himself from a bear attack. He survived, as did the bear.

Signal Mountain Lodge (307/543-2831, www.signalmountainlodge.com) houses Trapper Grill (daily 9 A.M.–10 P.M., $8–15), with casual fare three meals daily in summer and a popular deck for al fresco dining. Also here is **Peaks Restaurant** (daily 5:30–10 P.M., $19–36), with an upscale menu and spectacular vistas of the Tetons. Known for it's blackberry margaritas, Deadman's Bar at Signal Mountain serves a pub menu.

Leek's Marina (307/543-2494, www

.signalmountainlodge.com, $13–22, daily 11 A.M.–10 P.M.) is home to a very popular pizzeria that also serves calzones, sandwiches, salads, and beer on tap. Musicians drop by every other Wednesday evening for an open mike session. Open summers only.

The main lodge at **Flagg Ranch Resort** (307/543-2861 or 800/443-2311, www.flaggranch.com) houses Bear's Den Restaurant, serving three meals a day. Also here are a saloon and grocery store.

Buffalo Valley Café (307/543-2062 or 888/543-2477, www.buffalovalleyranch.com, daily 7 A.M.–9 P.M. mid-May–Labor Day) is outside the park in this quaint valley three miles east of Moran Junction. The seasonal café serves breakfast, lunch, and dinner and is popular with campers, folks staying in nearby cabins, and locals who drive up from Jackson. Steaks are on the menu, but the buffalo burgers ($9) are the real attraction. Sit on the screened deck for Teton backdrops with your meal.

GROCERIES AND SUPPLIES

The best in-the-park store is **Dornan's Trading Post** (307/733-2415, www.dornans.com, open year-round), near park headquarters in Moose. The store is stocked with groceries, tasty deli sandwiches, fresh baked goods, and camping supplies. The cart out front has espresso, and next door is **Dornan's Wine Shoppe,** with one of the biggest selections of fine wine and beer in Jackson Hole, including more than 1,700 different wines. Wine tastings take place here on the first Sunday of the month October–June. Other nearby Dornan's operations include Moose Pizza and Pasta Co. and the Chuck Wagon, and a gift shop. In winter, the gift shop rents cross-country skis, snowshoes, and pull-behind sleds. It also has computers for Internet access.

Colter Bay General Store (307/543-3100) has a good choice of groceries and supplies, while convenience stores operate at Signal Mountain, Flagg Ranch Resort, and Jenny Lake. The store at Flagg Ranch Resort is open in both summer and winter seasons (mid-May–mid-Oct. and mid-Dec.–mid-Mar.). All of the others are open only in summer.

© DON PITCHER

U.S. 20/287 heading west to the Tetons

Information and Services

SUPPORT ORGANIZATIONS

The **Grand Teton Association** (307/739-3403, www.grandtetonpark.org) operates bookstores in park visitor centers and the store at Menor's Ferry. It also has an online service for Grand Teton books and other publications. All profits finance new publications or assist the Park Service in its research and interpretive programs.

The nonprofit **Grand Teton National Park Foundation** (307/739-0629, www.gtnpf.org) provides support for park projects (including the new visitor center at Moose) that would not otherwise be funded, and all contributions are tax-deductible.

KIDS IN THE PARK

It's hard to imagine a more kid-friendly park than Grand Teton. Two marvelous new visitor centers—Craig Thomas Discovery and Visitor Center and Laurance S. Rockefeller Preserve Interpretive Center—have a variety of fascinating exhibits, including the yes-you-can-touch variety. River rafting trips, and horseback rides are fun for older kids, and everyone loves the boat rides across Jenny Lake to Inspiration Point. Park restaurants all have kid-friendly meals and Jackson Lake Lodge offers the perfect combo: a fun outdoor pool with a popular snack bar. If you have older kids (and a bike trailer), rent a bike and head out the back roads around Mormon Row and Kelly.

All sorts of ranger-led programs are listed in the park paper, including many family options. Grand Teton's **Junior Ranger** program is filled with educational activities for kids. It takes an hour or so, and is a great way to introduce children to the natural world. The "graduation" ceremonies are fun too. One of the joys of Grand Teton is its proximity to Jackson, providing all sorts of in-town options if your kids are getting bored, from the speedy alpine slide at Snow King to the noisy shootout on Town Square.

SERVICES

Gas is available year-round at Dornan's in Moose, summer and winter at Flagg Ranch Resort, and summers only at Colter Bay Village, Signal Mountain Lodge, and Jackson Lake Lodge. You'll find gift shops at Signal Mountain, Flagg Ranch Resort, Jackson Lake Lodge, Moose, and Colter Bay. Year-round post offices are in Moran, Moose, and Kelly. Get cash from ATMs at Dornan's in Moose, Jackson Lake Lodge, Colter Bay Village, Flagg Ranch Resort, and Signal Mountain Lodge.

Outdoor Gear

The little settlement of Moose has several businesses in addition to the Dornan's shops and eateries. **Adventure Sports** (307/733-3307, www.dornans.com) rents mountain bikes, canoes, and kayaks. Next door is **Moosely Seconds** (307/739-1801, www.skinnyskis.com, daily late May–Sept.), with good deals on outdoor clothing and climbing gear. The shop also rents ice axes, crampons, rock shoes, trekking poles, approach shoes, plastic boots, and snowshoes. **Snake River Angler** (307/733-3699, www.snakeriverangler.com) sells and rents fishing supplies and camping equipment.

Medical

Get emergency medical assistance at the **Grand Teton Medical Clinic** (307/543-2514, daily 10 A.M.–6 P.M. late May–early Oct.) near the Chevron station at Jackson Lake Lodge. The nearest hospital is **St. John's Medical Center** in Jackson.

JACKSON HOLE

One of the most-visited slices of wild country in North America, Jackson Hole attracts well more than three million travelers each year. They come here for a multitude of reasons: to camp under the stars in Grand Teton National Park, to play and shop in the New West town of Jackson, to hike flower-bedecked trails up forested valleys, to ride sleighs among thousands of elk, to raft down the Snake River, to ski or snowboard at one of three local resorts, or to simply stand in wonderment as the sun colors the sky behind the mountains. Many continue north to Yellowstone National Park, another place on everyone's must-see list. Drive north from Jackson toward Yellowstone and you'll quickly discover the biggest reason so many people are attracted to this place—its beauty. The Tetons act as a magnet, drawing your eyes away from the road and forcing you to stop and absorb some of their majesty. Welcome to one of the world's great wonderlands.

In the lingo of the mountain men, a "hole" was a large valley ringed by mountain ranges, and each was named for the trapper who based himself there. Jackson Hole, on Wyoming's far western border, is justifiably the most famous of all these intermountain valleys. Although Jackson Hole reaches an impressive 50 miles north to south and up to 16 miles across, the magnificent range of mountains to the west is what defines this valley. Shoshone Indians who wandered through this country called the peaks Teewinot (Many Pinnacles); later explorers would use such labels as Shark's Teeth or Pilot Knobs. But lonely French-Canadian trappers arriving in the early 1800s provided the

HIGHLIGHTS

◖ **Visitor Center:** Officially called the Jackson Hole & Greater Yellowstone Visitor Center, this large facility provides a one-stop introduction to the region, with information on the town, national forests, and the Elk Refuge (page 160).

◖ **Town Square:** Where else could you mix three million tourists, hundreds of elk antlers arranged in arches, and a faux shoot-out on summer evenings (page 160)?

◖ **National Museum of Wildlife Art:** One of Wyoming's top museums, with works by all the American masters, from Alfred Jacob Miller to Robert Bateman (page 163).

◖ **National Elk Refuge:** Winter is the peak season, with thousands of elk and horse-drawn sleighs in a scene straight out of Currier and Ives (page 164).

◖ **River Rafting:** Running the Snake River is a major summertime attraction, with many companies providing the raft and guide for a whitewater rock-and-roll or a gentle float trip past the Tetons (page 169).

◖ **Jackson Hole Mountain Resort:** This famous ski area keeps on trucking with all sorts of winter and summer activities – including an all-summer classical music festival and brand new tram up Rendezvous Mountain (page 179).

LOOK FOR ◖ TO FIND RECOMMENDED SIGHTS, ACTIVITIES, DINING, AND LODGING.

◖ **Alaska Basin:** This one's for backpackers, with access from Driggs, Idaho, to the heart of the Teton Range. It's a gorgeous alpine valley, where high trails lead into Grand Teton National Park (page 227).

name that stuck: les Trois Tetons (literally, the Three Breasts).

The valley—originally called Jackson's Hole—was named for likable trapper David E. Jackson, one of the men who helped establish the Rocky Mountain Fur Company. When Jackson and his partners sold out in 1830, they realized a profit of more than $50,000. Jackson's presence remains in the names of both Jackson Hole and Jackson Lake. Eventually, more polite folks began calling the valley Jackson Hole

in an attempt to end the ribald stories associated with the name Jackson's Hole. (It's easy to imagine the jokes with both Jackson's Hole and the Tetons in the same place.) By the way, in 1991, a group calling itself the Committee to Restore Decency to Our National Parks created quite a stir by suggesting that Grand Teton National Park be renamed. A letter sent to the Park Service and various members of Congress noted: "Though a great many Americans may be oblivious to this vulgarity, hundreds of millions of French people around the world are not! How embarrassing that these spectacular, majestic mountains are reduced to a dirty joke overseas." After a flurry of letters in response, the hoax was revealed; it was a prank by staff members of *Spy* magazine.

PLANNING YOUR TIME

Wyoming's preeminent tourist town, Jackson is both an important access point for Yellowstone and Grand Teton national parks

and a destination in its own right. Visitors should probably plan on at least two days, but you could easily spend a couple of weeks just having fun in Jackson Hole (if your credit card doesn't get maxed out). Jackson has two peak seasons, in summer when families and international travelers stay here as part of a Yellowstone trip, and winter, when skiing and snowboarding are the big draws.

Prior to your trip, contact the Jackson Hole Chamber of Commerce (307/733-3316,

© DON PITCHER

Town Square shoot-out, Jackson

JACKSON HOLE

www.jacksonholechamber.com) for brochures, or browse their website for links to hundreds of local businesses. Once in town, be sure to drop by the **Jackson Hole & Greater Yellowstone Visitor Center** for publications, maps, and detailed area information.

Town Square in the heart of Jackson is shady and set with picturesque elk antler arches on the corners, and a nearby street corner closes for entertaining shoot-outs most summer evenings. Acclaimed as one of the top artistic centers in the nation, Jackson has more than 30 **art galleries,** and the impressive **National Museum of Wildlife Art** perches along a hillside just north of town.

Visitors are drawn to the **National Elk Refuge** for its wintertime sleigh rides among the elk. Skiers and snowboarders enjoy the slopes at famous **Jackson Hole Mountain Resort,** smaller **Snow King Resort,** or on the deep powder of **Grand Targhee Resort,** a morning bus ride away on the west side of the Tetons. Jackson's restaurants are easily the finest (and most expensive) in Wyoming, and lodging varies from cozy old log units to ultra

luxurious hotels. In summer, the **Snake River** is a major center for whitewater rafting and fly-fishing, while mountain bikers and hikers head out on miles of paths. Horseback rides and chuck wagon cookouts are other summertime favorites, as are the twice-weekly Jackson Hole rodeos. At Teton Village, visitors enjoy classical music performances during the Grand Teton Music Festival in July and August. More adventurous visitors head out on extended backcountry trips into Grand Teton National Park and national forest lands, including beautiful **Alaska Basin** on the west side of the Tetons.

HISTORY

The first people to cross the mountain passes into Jackson Hole probably arrived while the last massive glaciers were still retreating. Clovis stone arrowheads—a style used 12,000 years ago—have been found along the edges of the valley. These early peoples were replaced in the 16th and 17th centuries by the Shoshone, Bannock, Blackfeet, Crow, and Gros Ventre tribes, who hunted bison from horseback. When the first fur trappers tramped into Jackson Hole, they found Indian trails throughout the valley.

John Colter

Transport yourself back to the early 19th century, a time when people from the new nation called America saw the world west of the Mississippi River as just a blank spot on the map. In 1803, Thomas Jefferson bought the Louisiana Territory from France, and to learn more about this gigantic piece of real estate he sent Meriwether Lewis and William Clark on a military expedition to the Pacific coast, a trip that took nearly 2.5 years. Although the expedition skirted around Wyoming—heading across Montana instead— it proved the opening wedge for the settlement of the West and, indirectly, the discovery of Jackson Hole. On the return trip, the party met two fur

trappers en route to the upper Missouri River. One of Lewis and Clark's respected scouts, John Colter, was allowed to join the trappers, "provided no one of the party would ask or expect a similar permission."

After a winter of trapping with his partners, Colter headed alone down the Platte River, but before he could get back to civilization he met a company of trappers led by Manuel Lisa. They were on their way to the Rockies, determined to cash in on the huge demand for beaver furs by trapping the rich beaver streams that Lewis and Clark had described. Wealth beckoned, and John Colter gladly turned around again, guiding Lisa's men up to the mouth of the Big Horn River, where they built a small fort. From there Colter was sent on a mission: Contact Indians throughout the region, trading beads and other items for beaver furs.

His wanderings in the winter of 1807–1808 were the first white exploration of this region. A map produced by William Clark in 1814 and based on Colter's recollections shows an incredible midwinter journey around Yellowstone and Jackson lakes, across the Tetons twice, and up through Jackson Hole. He did not get back to the fort until the following spring, telling tales of huge mountain ranges and a spectacular geothermal area that others quickly laughed off as "Colter's Hell."

Colter went on to become one of the most famous of all mountain men, and his later harrowing escape from the Blackfeet in Montana has become the stuff of legend. After being captured and stripped naked, he was forced to literally run for his life. Somehow he managed to outdistance his pursuers for six miles before hiding in a pile of logs until dark. He walked barefoot the 300 miles back to Manuel Lisa's fort, surviving on roots and tree bark. Shortly thereafter, Colter was reported to have thrown his hat on the ground, declaring, "I'll be damned if I ever come into [this country] again." He returned to St. Louis, married, and established a farm near that of fellow explorer Daniel Boone. Colter lived long enough to give William Clark a description of the country he had visited, but he died from jaundice just three years later, in 1813.

JACKSON HOLE IN 1835

This Valley is called "Jackson Hole" it is generally from 5 to 15 mls wide: the southern part where the river enters the mountain is hilly and uneven but the Northern portion is wide smooth and comparatively even the whole being covered with wild sage and Surrounded by high and rugged mountains upon whose summits the snow remains during the hottest months in Summer. The alluvial bottoms along the river and streams inter sect it thro. the valley produce a luxuriant groth of vegetation among which wild flax and a species of onion are abundant. The great altitude of this place however connected with the cold descending from the mountains at night I think would be a serious obstruction to growth of most Kinds of cultivated grains. This valley like all other parts of the country abounds with game.

From *Journal of a Trapper 1834-1843*, by Osborne Russell

JACKSON HOLE

THE WHITE SHOSHONE

The little Jackson Hole town of Wilson is named for one of Wyoming's most fascinating characters, "Uncle Nick" Wilson. Born in 1842, Wilson grew up in Utah, where he made friends with a fellow sheepherder, an Indian boy, and learned to speak his language. Then, suddenly, Nick's life took a strange twist. The mother of Chief Washakie (from Wyoming's Wind River Reservation) had recently lost a son, and in a dream she was told that a white boy would come to take his place. Unable to convince her otherwise, Washakie sent his men out to find the new son. They came across Nick and offered him a pinto pony and the chance to fish, hunt, and ride horses all he wanted. It didn't take much persuading, and for the next two years he lived as a Shoshone, learning to hunt buffalo, to use a bow and arrow, and to answer to his new name, Yagaiki. He became a favorite of Chief Washakie, but when word came (falsely) that

Nick's father was threatening to attack the Shoshones with an army of men to retrieve his son, the chief reluctantly helped Nick return home.

At age 18, Nick Wilson became one of the first Pony Express riders, a job that nearly killed him when he was struck in the head during a Paiute Indian attack. A doctor managed to remove the arrow point, but Wilson remained in a coma for nearly two weeks. Thereafter, Wilson always wore a hat to cover the scar, even inside buildings. He went on to become an army scout and a driver for the Overland Stage before returning to a more sedate life as a farmer. Many years later, in 1889, Nick Wilson led a party of five Mormon families over steep Teton Pass and down to the rich grazing lands in Jackson Hole. The town that grew up around him became Wilson. In later years, "Uncle Nick" recounted his adventures in *The White Indian Boy*.

Because of the abundance of beavers along tributaries of the Snake River, Jackson Hole became an important crossroads for the Rocky Mountain fur trade. Although no rendezvous was ever held in the valley, many of the most famous mountain men spent time here. They first trapped beavers in Jackson Hole in 1811, but it was not until the 1820s that fur trapping really came into its own as mountain men fanned throughout the wilderness in search of the "soft gold." This quest continued for the next two decades, finally dying out when overtrapping made beavers harder to find and silk hats replaced fur hats. After the last rendezvous in 1840, most of the old trappers headed on to new adventures, the best becoming guides for those en route to Oregon and California. Because Jackson Hole was not near the Oregon Trail or other routes west, the area remained virtually deserted until the late 19th century.

Settlers

The first Jackson Hole homesteaders arrived in 1884, followed quickly by a handful of others fleeing the law. The settlers survived by grazing cattle, harvesting hay, and acting as guides for rich hunters from Europe and eastern states. Gradually they filled the richest parts of the valley with homesteads. Conflicts soon arose between the Bannock Indians, who had been hunting in Jackson Hole for more than 100 years, and the new settlers who made money guiding wealthy sportsmen.

By 1895, Wyoming had enacted game laws prohibiting hunting during 10 months of the year. Claiming that the Indians were taking elk out of season, Constable William Manning and 26 settlers arrested a group of 28 Indians (mostly women and children) who had been hunting in Hoback Canyon. When the Bannocks attempted to flee, an elderly Indian was shot four times in the back and died. Most of the others escaped. Settlers in Jackson Hole feared revenge and called in the cavalry, but the Indians who had been hunting in the area all returned peaceably to their Idaho reservation. Astoundingly, *The New York Times* headlined its report of the incident, "Settlers Massacred—Indians Kill Every One at Jackson's Hole—Courier Brings the

JACKSON HOLE

News—Red Men Apply the Torch to All the Houses in the Valley." Absolutely none of this was true, but the attack by whites succeeded in forcing the Indians off their traditional hunting grounds, an action eventually upheld in a landmark U.S. Supreme Court case.

Jackson Hole Comes of Age

By the turn of the 20th century, the Jackson Hole settlements of Jackson, Wilson, Kelly, and Moran had all been established. The towns grew slowly; people survived by ranching, guiding, and engaging in the strange new business of tending to wealthy "dudes" from back East. Eventually, tourism would vastly eclipse raising cattle in importance, but even today Teton County has nearly as many cattle as people.

Jackson, Jackson Hole's primary settlement, was named by Maggie Simpson, who opened a post office here in 1894. Three years later Grace Miller—wife of a local banker known derisively as "Old Twelve Percent"—bought a large plot of land and planned a townsite, but the town wasn't officially incorporated until 1914. In an event that should come as no surprise in "The Equality State," Jackson later became the first town in America to be entirely governed by women. The year was 1920, and not only was the mayor a woman (Grace Miller), but so were all four council members, the city clerk, the treasurer, and even the town marshal. They remained in office until 1923.

Through the years Jackson has grown, spurred on by the creation of Grand Teton National Park and the development of Jackson Hole Mountain Resort. In the last 25 years, Jackson Hole has seen almost continuous growth; tourists have flooded the region to play, investors have built golf courses and ostentatious hotels, and wealthy families have snatched up their own parcels of paradise. Today, Teton County has the highest per capita income of any county in America (around $70,000), and locals quip that the billionaires are buying land so fast that they're driving the millionaires out of Jackson Hole.

Although much of the area is public land and will remain undeveloped, rapid growth on private land is transforming Jackson Hole into the Wyoming version of Vail or Santa Fe. Even the formerly quiet town of Wilson failed to fight off the development onslaught, with a massive new grade school and a collection of modest new homes that locals call Whoville (after those in the Dr. Seuss book). As a former resident of Wilson, I can appreciate the joke going the rounds: How many Wilsonites does it take to change a light bulb? Seven. One to screw it in, and the other six to talk about how good the old one used to be.

Growth in Jackson Hole has forced land values sky-high, and affordable housing has become an oxymoron, unless you consider $1.1 million—the median single-family home price—affordable. Despite all of the problems brought on by growth, the area is still remarkably beautiful, and the surrounding public lands will remain wild. Locals like to point out that this is more than a place to visit; for them it is a place to live surrounded by the best of the old (and new) West.

Jackson

The town of Jackson (pop. 9,000) lies near the southern end of Jackson Hole, hemmed in on three sides by Snow King Mountain, the Gros Ventre Range, and East Gros Ventre Butte. At 6,200 feet in elevation, Jackson experiences cold snowy winters, wet springs, delightfully warm and sunny summers, and crisp but color-filled falls. Jackson is unlike any other place in Wyoming; on a typical summer day more than 35,000 tourists flood the town. Sit on a bench in Town Square on a summer day and you're likely to see cars from every state in the Union. Tourists dart in and out of the many gift shops, art galleries, fine restaurants, Western-style saloons, and trendy boutiques. The cowboy hats all look as if the price tags just came off.

JACKSON

JACKSON HOLE

© AVALON TRAVEL

0.5 mi

0.5 km

NATIONAL ELK REFUGE

SEE "DOWNTOWN JACKSON" MAP

To National Wildlife Museum and Grand Teton National Park

To Spring Creek Resort

To Teton Village, Wilson, and Teton Pass

To Cache Creek Canyon

To Hoback Junction

West Gros Ventre Butte

East Gros Ventre Butte

SPRING GULCH RD

SADDLE BUTTE DR

ELK REFUGE RD

RANCHER

ELK REFUGE INN

FLAT CREEK MOTEL

NATIONAL ELK REFUGE HEADQUARTERS

ST JOHN'S MEDICAL CENTER

Mike Yokel Jr Park

SNOW KING RESORT

Ropetow

Rafferty   Chairlift

COTTAGES AT SNOW KING

Baux Park

ICE RINK

BUCKRAIL LODGE

Cougar   Triple   Chairlift

Summit   Chairlift

43 NORTH

Bridger - Teton

National

Forest

ALPINE MOTEL

MOOSE ST

TETON ST

JEAN ST

GLENWOOD ST

PEARL AVE

GILL AVE

DELONEY AVE

BROADWAY

JACKSON ST

KELLY AVE

CLISSOLD ST

KARNS AVE

REDMOND ST

MILLWARD ST

CACHE ST

KING ST

WILLOW ST

SIMPSON AVE

HANSEN AVE

KELLY AVE

KARNS AVE

CACHE CREEK DR

PINE DR

FLAT CREEK DR

SNOW KING AVE

Flat Creek

PAINTED BUFFALO INN

BUBBA'S BBQ

JACKSON HOLE LODGE

ELK COUNTRY INN

COWBOY VILLAGE

VIRGINIAN LODGE

VIRGINIAN RV PARK

TETON CO FAIRGROUNDS/ JACKSON RODEO

THE LODGE AT JACKSON HOLE

WYOMING INN

JACKSON WHOLE GROCERY

JACKSON HOLE KAYAK SCHOOL

LIBRARY

Powderhorn Park

POST OFFICE

TETON ROCK GYM

VIRGINIAN LN

SCOTT LN

ALPINE LN

MAPLE WAY

POWDERHORN LN

PONY EXPRESS MOTEL

TETON GABLES MOTEL

ALBERTSON'S

DAYS INN

KMART

MOTEL 6

SUPER 8 MOTEL

MOVIEWORKS CINEMA

LEISURE SPORTS

JACKSON HOLE BUFFALO MEAT PRODUCTS

SMITH'S

GREGORY LN

HIGH SCHOOL RD

SOUTH PARK LOOP RD

JACKSON HIGH SCHOOL

Bike Path

Bike Path

BAR T-5

26 89 191

22

26 89 191

26 89 191

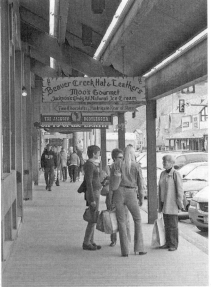

© DON PITCHER

shopping in Jackson

JACKSON HOLE

In other parts of Wyoming, Jackson is viewed with a mixture of awe and disdain—awe over its gorgeous scenery, but disdain that Jackson is not a "real" town, just a false front put up to sell things to outsiders. Yes, Jackson is almost wholly dependent on the almighty tourist dollar, but as a result it enjoys a cultural richness lacking in other parts of the state. Besides, if you don't like all the commercial foolishness, it's easy to escape to a campsite or remote trail in the wonderful countryside of nearby Grand Teton National Park or Bridger-Teton National Forest.

Keep your eyes open around Jackson and you're likely to see well-known residents such as Hollywood stars Harrison Ford and his girlfriend Calista Flockhart, Danny DeVito and his wife Rhea Perlman, Connie Stevens, and Sandra Bullock, along with former Secretary of the Interior James Watt (who resigned in disgrace in 1983), attorney Gerald Spence (of Karen Silkwood and Imelda Marcos notoriety), Yvon Chouinard (mountaineer and founder of Patagonia), industrial heir Charles DuPont,

and members of the extended Rockefeller family. Former Vice President Dick Cheney has a luxury home in Teton Pines and is a frequent visitor, which explains all of the Blackhawk helicopters, Secret Service agents, and Suburbans with dark-tinted windows.

◖ VISITOR CENTER

Anyone new to Jackson Hole should be sure to visit the spacious **Jackson Hole and Greater Yellowstone Visitor Center** (532 N. Cache Dr., 307/733-3316, www.jacksonholechamber.com, daily 8 A.M.–7 P.M. Memorial Day–Labor Day, and daily 9 A.M.–5 P.M. the rest of the year) on the north side of town. (The phone is answered only on weekdays, but on weekends you can leave a message and you'll be mailed an information packet.)

The information center is a two-level, sod-roofed wooden building—jokingly called the "little prairie on the house"—with natural-history displays, a blizzard of free leaflets extolling the merits of local businesses, a gift shop selling books and maps, and an covered upstairs deck overlooking the National Elk Refuge. Ducks and trumpeter swans are visible on the marsh in the summer, and elk can be seen in the winter. Downstairs, the "bear cave" is a big kid draw. The information center is staffed by the Jackson Hole Chamber of Commerce, along with Fish and Wildlife Service, Forest Service, and other agency personnel in the summer. Free nature and history talks are generally given several times a week during the summer, or you can watch a video about the refuge.

In addition to the main information center, you'll find brochure racks at the airport, the stagecoach stop on Town Square, next to the public restrooms at Cache and Gill, and the Mangy Moose in Teton Village.

◖ TOWN SQUARE

In 1932, the local Rotary Club planted trees in the center of Jackson, adding four picturesque arches made from hundreds of elk antlers in the 1950s and 1960s. Today the trees offer summertime shade, and at any time of day or night you'll find visitors admiring or posing

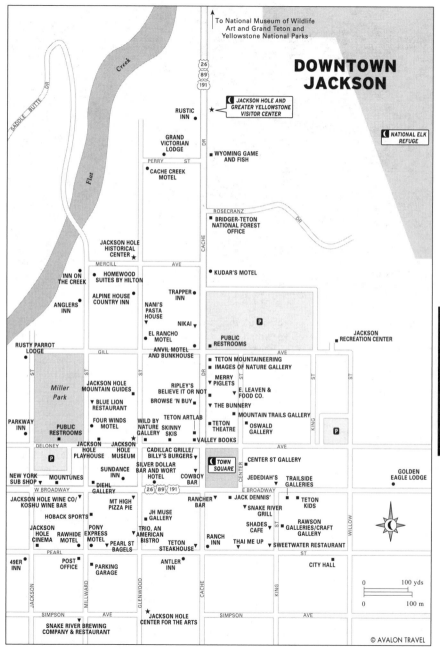

To National Museum of Wildlife
Art and Grand Teton and
Yellowstone National Parks

26
89
191

DOWNTOWN JACKSON

**JACKSON HOLE AND
GREATER YELLOWSTONE
VISITOR CENTER**

**NATIONAL ELK
REFUGE**

RUSTIC
INN

GRAND
VICTORIAN
LODGE

PERRY ST

WYOMING GAME
AND FISH

CACHE CREEK
MOTEL

ROSECRANZ

BRIDGER-TETON
NATIONAL FOREST
OFFICE

JACKSON HOLE
HISTORICAL
CENTER

MERCILL AVE

CACHE

KUDAR'S MOTEL

INN ON
THE CREEK

HOMEWOOD
SUITES BY HILTON

TRAPPER
INN

ALPINE HOUSE
COUNTRY INN

NANI'S
PASTA
HOUSE

ANGLERS
INN

NIKAI

EL RANCHO
MOTEL

JACKSON
RECREATION CENTER

RUSTY PARROT
LODGE

ANVIL MOTEL
AND BUNKHOUSE

GILL

PUBLIC
RESTROOMS

AVE

Miller
Park

JACKSON HOLE
MOUNTAIN GUIDES

TETON MOUNTAINEERING

IMAGES OF NATURE GALLERY

MERRY
PIGLETS

RIPLEY'S
BELIEVE IT OR NOT

BLUE LION
RESTAURANT

BROWSE 'N BUY

E. LEAVEN &
FOOD CO.

THE BUNNERY

FOUR WINDS
MOTEL

WILD BY
NATURE
GALLERY

TETON ARTLAB

MOUNTAIN TRAILS GALLERY

PARKWAY
INN

SKINNY
SKIS

TETON
THEATRE

OSWALD
GALLERY

PUBLIC
RESTROOMS

JACKSON
HOLE
PLAYHOUSE

JACKSON
HOLE
MUSEUM

VALLEY BOOKS

DELONEY

CADILLAC GRILLE/
BILLY'S BURGERS

CENTER ST GALLERY

SILVER DOLLAR
BAR AND WORT
HOTEL

NEW YORK
SUB SHOP

MOUNTUNES

SUNDANCE
INN

TOWN
SQUARE

JEDEDIAH'S

TRAILSIDE
GALLERIES

GOLDEN
EAGLE LODGE

W BROADWAY

DIEHL
GALLERY

COWBOY
BAR

26 89 191

E BROADWAY

JACKSON HOLE WINE CO/
KOSHU WINE BAR

MT HIGH
PIZZA PIE

RANCHER
BAR

JACK DENNIS'

TETON
KIDS

HOBACK SPORTS

JH MUSE
GALLERY

SNAKE RIVER
GRILL

RAWSON
GALLERIES/CRAFT
GALLERY

JACKSON
HOLE
CINEMA

PONY
EXPRESS
MOTEL

TRIO, AN
AMERICAN
BISTRO

SHADES
CAFE

RAWHIDE
MOTEL

PEARL ST
BAGELS

TETON
STEAKHOUSE

RANCH
INN

THAI ME UP

SWEETWATER RESTAURANT

PEARL

ST

49ER
INN

POST
OFFICE

PARKING
GARAGE

ANTLER
INN

CITY HALL

0   100 yds

0   100 m

JACKSON

MILLWARD

GLENWOOD

CACHE

KING

WILLOW

SIMPSON AVE

SIMPSON AVE

SNAKE RIVER BREWING
COMPANY & RESTAURANT

JACKSON HOLE
CENTER FOR THE ARTS

© AVALON TRAVEL

SADDLE BUTTE DR

Flat

Creek

JACKSON HOLE

JACKSON HOLE

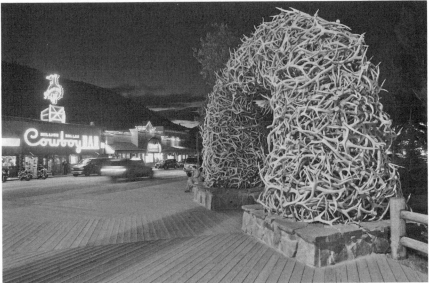

© DON PITCHER

antler arch in Town Square at night

for photos in front of the arches that mark the corners of Town Square. During winter, the snow-covered arches and trees are draped with lights, giving the square a festive atmosphere. Surrounded by dozens of boardwalk-fronted galleries, bars, restaurants, factory outlets, and gift shops, the square is the focal point of tourist activity in Jackson.

During summer, **stagecoaches** wait to transport you on a leisurely ride around town, and each evening "cowboys" put on a free **shoot-out** for throngs of camera-happy tourists. The shoot-out starts at 6:15 P.M. Monday–Saturday nights all summer. They've been killing each other like this since 1957. With stereotypical players and questionable acting, the "mountain law" system seems in dire need of reform. Most folks love the sham; Canon and Olympus love it even more. Warning: The sound of blanks is surprisingly loud and can be frightening for small children.

ART

Artists have long been attracted by the beauty of Jackson Hole and the Tetons. Mount Moran, the 12,605-foot summit behind Jackson Lake, is named for Thomas Moran, whose watercolors helped persuade Congress to set aside Yellowstone as the first national park. The late Conrad Schwiering's paintings of the Tetons have attained international fame; one was even used on the Postal Service's Wyoming Centennial stamp in 1990. Ansel Adams's photograph of the Tetons remains etched in the American consciousness as one of the archetypal wilderness images. A copy of the image was included in the payload of the *Voyager II* spacecraft en route out of our solar system. Today many artists live or work in Jackson Hole, and locals proclaim it "Art Center of the Rockies," ranking it with New York, San Francisco, Santa Fe, and Scottsdale. See the callout *Jackson Hole Art Galleries* for a more complete picture.

Jackson Hole Center for the Arts

If you have any doubts that Jackson Hole is an arts mecca, look no further than the sparkling new Jackson Hole Center for the Arts (240 S. Glenwood, 307/734-8956, www

.jhcenterforthearts.org). This 41,000-square-foot masterpiece has space for 15 different non-profit arts organizations under one roof, with an amazing array of classes and workshops. Drop by to pick up a schedule of classes. Newly added in 2007, the 525-seat **Performing Arts Pavilion** is a lovely performance space. Call the box office for tickets, 307/733-4900, or find the online calendar of upcoming performances.

One of the primary tenants is the **Art Association** (307/733-6379, www.artassociation.org), offering dozens of classes and workshops year-round in everything from photography and ceramics to stained glass and woodworking. **ArtSpace Gallery** displays changing exhibitions by regional and national artists, and is open all year Monday–Friday 8:30 A.M.–5:30 P.M.

Dancer's Workshop (307/733-6398, www.dwjh.org) occupies much of the second floor, with 60 classes per week in modern, ballet, pointe, hip hop, ballroom, jazz, country-and-western, and other forms. The facilities also house Contemporary Dance Wyoming, the state's only professional dance company.

Also at the Center for the Arts, **Off Square Theatre Company** (307/733-3670, www.offsquare.org) is a professional repertory company with comedies in the summer, and a variety of productions and workshops throughout the winter.

◖ NATIONAL MUSEUM OF WILDLIFE ART

Jackson is home to the magnificent National Museum of Wildlife Art (307/733-5771 or 800/313-9553, www.wildlifeart.org,), two miles north of town along U.S. Hwy. 26/89 and directly across from the National Elk Refuge. A monumental sculpture of five elk greets visitors at the base of the hill, and the building's Arizona sandstone exterior blends in with nearby rock outcroppings. Step inside the doors of this 51,000-square-foot museum to discover a marvelous interior. As visitors enter the main gallery, a larger-than-life bronze mountain lion crouches above, ready to pounce. Kids will have fun in the hands-on Children's Discovery Gallery, and can join hands-in-the-paint activities on Monday mornings. Adults

© DON PITCHER

the elk sculpture at the National Museum of Wildlife Art

will appreciate the artwork spread throughout a dozen galleries, along with the video theater, Rising Sage Café (tasty lunches), 200-seat auditorium, and gift shop.

The museum collection features pieces by Carl Rungius, George Catlin, Albert Bierstadt, Karl Bodmer, Alfred Jacob Miller, N. C. Wyeth, Conrad Schwiering, John Clymer, Charles Russell, Robert Bateman, and many others. Of particular interest are the reconstructed studio of John Clymer and the spacious Carl Rungius Gallery, where you'll find the most complete collection of his paintings in the nation. Also of note is the exhibit on American bison, which documents these once vastly abundant animals and their slaughter; the museum's bison collection is the largest in the world. Six galleries showcase photography, painting, and other art that changes throughout the year. Spotting scopes in the cozy members' lounge (open to the public) are useful for watching residents of the adjacent National Elk Refuge.

Museum admission costs $10 adults or $8 seniors, but it's always free for kids 18 and under. Hours are daily 9 A.M.–5 P.M. in summer, and Sunday 1–5 P.M., Monday–Saturday 9 A.M.–5 P.M. mid-October–April. Free audio tours detail works in the permanent collection, and you can watch films on wildlife and artists on Sundays and Thursdays in the summer.

Wildlife films, slide lectures, talks, concerts, kids' programs, and other activities take place throughout the year in the auditorium and galleries; pick up a schedule of upcoming events at the entrance desk or visit the museum website. One of the most popular events comes in mid-September. Called **Western Visions**, it includes jewelry, photography, furniture, and the Miniature Show & Sale, with small works by 100 of the country's leading artists. A winter highlight is **Art After Hours/Tapas Tuesdays** (Tues. 5–9 P.M.), when the museum opens for après-ski programs combined with tapas served by Rising Sage Café.

HISTORICAL MUSEUMS

The small **Jackson Hole Museum** (105 N. Glenwood, 307/733-2414, www.jacksonhole

history.org, Mon.–Sat. 9:30 A.M.–6 P.M. and Sun. 10 A.M.–5 P.M. late May–Sept., closed the rest of the year) has a surprising homespun charm. Inside are displays and collections illustrating the days when Indians, trappers, cattlemen, and dude ranchers called this magnificent valley home. Check out the rock-encrusted flintlock musket, the old postcards, and a replica of the "Colter stone." Admission costs $3 adults, $2 seniors, $1 ages 3–18, and $6 families. In the summer, the museum sponsors free hour-long **historical walking tours** of Jackson's downtown on Tuesdays and Thursdays at 10:30 A.M.

Also managed by the local historical society, the **Jackson Hole Historical Center** (105 Mercill Ave., 307/733-9605, Tues.–Fri. 10 A.M.–5 P.M. year-round, free) is a small research facility housing photo archives, a library of classic regional books, and rotating exhibits throughout the year.

◖ NATIONAL ELK REFUGE

Immediately north of Jackson is the National Elk Refuge (307/733-9212, www.fws.gov/nationalelkrefuge), winter home for thousands of these majestic animals. During summer, the elk range up to 65 miles away to feed on grasses, shrubs, and forbs in alpine meadows. But as the snows descend each fall, the elk move downslope, wintering in Jackson Hole and the surrounding country. The chance to view elk up close from a horse-drawn sleigh makes a trip to the National Elk Refuge one of the most popular wintertime activities for Jackson Hole visitors.

History

When the first ranchers arrived in Jackson Hole in the late 19th century, they moved onto land that had long been an elk migration route and wintering ground. The ranchers soon found elk raiding their haystacks and competing with cattle for forage, particularly during severe winters. The conflicts peaked early in the 20th century when three consecutive severe winters killed thousands of elk, leading one settler to claim that he had "walked for a mile on dead elk lying from one to four deep." Following a national outcry, the federal government began buying land in 1911 for a permanent winter elk refuge that would eventually cover nearly 25,000 acres.

Today more than 7,000 elk (two-thirds of the local population) typically spend November–May on the refuge, administered by the U.S. Fish and Wildlife Service. Because development has reduced elk habitat in the valley to one-quarter of its original size, refuge managers try to improve the remaining land through seeding, irrigation, and prescribed burning. In addition, during the most difficult foraging period, the elk are fed alfalfa pellets paid for in part by sales of elk antlers collected on the

ART GALLERIES

More than 30 galleries crowd the center of Jackson. Over the last decade as Jackson has grown, local galleries have also changed. You can still find places selling romanticized cowboy oil paintings and campy prints of sexy Indian maidens with windblown hair and strategically torn garments, but the town is increasingly filled with galleries where the emphasis is far more contemporary.

The **Jackson Hole Gallery Association** (www.jacksonholegalleries.com) produces a helpful gallery guide; pick up one from local galleries or the visitor center. **Third Thursday Art Walks** are a monthly staple, when many galleries open for extended evening hours June–October.

Three excellent galleries with changing exhibits of modern art are **Diehl Gallery** (155 W. Broadway, 307/733-0905, www.diehlgallery.com), **Muse Gallery** (62 S. Glenwood St, 307/733-0555, www.jhmusegallery.com), and **Teton Artlab** (307/699-0836, 135 N. Cache St., www.tetonartlab.com). All three are well worth a visit, as is **Wild Hands** (265 W. Pearl Ave., 307/733-4619, www.wildhands.com), with functional and playful art and pottery.

In a quiet spot just a block off Town Square, the two-level **Trailside Galleries** (130 E. Broadway, 307/733-3186, www.trailsidegalleries.com) displays everything from grandiose Western works to impressionist and wildlife art. Other traditionalist galleries worth a look are **Mountain Trails Gallery** (150 N. Center St., 307/734-8150, www.mtntrails.net), **Legacy Gallery** (75 N. Cache, 307/733-2353, www.legacygallery.com), **Hennes Gallery** (5850 N. Larkspur Dr., 307/733-2593, www.joannehennes.com), and **Wilcox Gallery** (165 Center St., 307/733-3950, www.wilcoxgallery.com).

Rawson Galleries (50 King St., 307/733-7306) features traditional watercolors, displayed in a crowded space; open July-October. The same building also houses **Craft Gallery** (307/413-4205, www.craftfineart.com), where the emphasis is local, with an eclectic mix of contemporary glass, wood, metal, and ceramic pieces.

Photo Galleries

Many nationally known photographers live or work in Jackson Hole. Tom Mangelsen displays his outstanding wildlife and landscape photos at **Images of Nature Gallery** (170 N. Cache Dr., 307/733-9752 or 888/238-0177, www.mangelsen.com) and has galleries at 15 other locations around the country.

Inside **Wild by Nature Gallery** (95 W. Deloney, 307/733-8877 or 888/494-5329, www.wildbynature.com), photographer Henry H. Holdsworth shows strikingly beautiful wildlife and nature imagery.

In Gaslight Alley at 125 North Cache, **Brookover Gallery** (307/733-3988, www.brookovergallery.com) exhibits grandiose landscapes by photographer David Brookover. **Wild Exposures Gallery** (60 E. Broadway Ave., 307/739-1777, www.wildexposuresgallery.com) has large-format and panoramic works from three local photographers: Jeff Hogan, Andrew Weller, and Scott McKinley.

At **Oswald Gallery** (165 N. Center St., 888/898-0077, www.oswaldgallery.com) the emphasis is on contemporary fine art photography. There's always something visually challenging; this isn't the place to look for pretty nature scenes.

horse-drawn sleigh at the National Elk Refuge

refuge. During this time, each elk eats more than seven pounds of supplemental alfalfa per day, or 30 tons per day for the entire herd. Elk head back into the mountains with the melting of snow each April and May; during summer you'll see few (if any) on the refuge.

Visiting the Refuge

The National Elk Refuge is primarily a winter attraction, although it's also an excellent place to watch birds and other wildlife—including nesting trumpeter swans—in summer. Refuge staff are on duty year-round in the Jackson Hole & Greater Yellowstone Visitor Center, leading nature talks, summertime wildlife viewing from the back deck, and theater programs. Visit the picturesque and historic (built in 1898) **Miller Ranch** on the east side of the refuge, 0.75 mile out Elk Refuge Road. It's open daily 10 A.M.–4 P.M. Memorial Day–Labor Day, with a naturalist available to answer questions about the refuge.

The main winter attraction here is the chance to see thousands of elk up close from one of the **horse-drawn sleighs** that take visitors through the refuge. The elk are accustomed to these sleighs and pay little heed, but people on foot would scare them. A tour of the National Elk Refuge is always a highlight for wintertime visitors to Jackson Hole. In December and January the bulls have impressive antlers that they start to shed by the end of February. The months of January and February are good times to see sparring matches. You might also catch a glimpse of a wolf or two because a pack now lives in the area year-round and hunts elk in winter. Morning is the best time to look for wolves.

Begin your wintertime visit to the refuge at the Jackson Hole & Greater Yellowstone Visitor Center (532 N. Cache Dr.), where you can buy sleigh-ride tickets ($16 adults, $12 ages 6–12, free for kids under age six). Rides are on a first-come basis through Bar-T-Five (307/733-5386 or 800/772-5386, www.bart5.com), the folks who run the sleighs. The visitor center shows an interpretive slide show about the refuge while you're waiting for a shuttle bus to take you to the boarding area. Sleighs run daily 10 A.M.–4 P.M. mid-December–March (closed Christmas), heading out as soon as enough folks show up for a ride—generally just long enough for the early-comers to finish watching the slide show. The rides last 45–60 minutes. Be sure to wear warm clothes or bring extra layers because the wind can get bitterly cold.

Hatchery

Four miles north of town and next to the elk refuge is the **Jackson National Fish Hatchery** (307/733-2510, http://jackson.fws.gov, daily 8 A.M.–4 P.M. year-round), which rears a half million cutthroat and lake trout annually. There's also a small pond open for fishing on the grounds, a great spot for kids and novice anglers.

KITSCH

If you're a fan of the *National Enquirer,* check out the weird and wacky collection at **Ripley's Believe It or Not** (140 N. Cache, 307/734-0000, www.ripleysbelieveitornotjh.com, daily 9 A.M.–10 P.M. in summer and daily 10 A.M.–6 P.M. the rest of the year). Here you'll discover a shrunken head, six-legged buffalo calf, six-foot-long cigar, antique bedpan collection, and even art created from dryer lint. Who says art is only for the elite? Entrance costs a steep $11 adults, $9 ages 5–12, free for kids under five. The family rate is $42, a bargain price for families of 10 from Salt Lake City.

For more foolishness, have the kids drag you to the **Teton Maze** (307/734-0455 or 877/629-3786) across from the Snow King chairlift. As the ads proclaim, it's a-Maze-ing.

Summer Recreation

Summer visitors to Jackson Hole can choose from an overwhelming array of outdoor options. Top favorites include float trips and whitewater rafting on the Snake River, mountain biking, hiking, and horseback rides, but kids love the alpine slide at Snow King, the fun pool at the rec center, and the tram rides at Jackson Hole Resort, not to mention the Town Square shoot-outs and evening rodeos that fill the summer calendar. If you've only booked a few days, you'll wish for more time to explore this fascinating place.

HIKING

The country around Jackson abounds with hundreds of miles of hiking trails, providing recreation opportunities for all levels of ability. Many of the most popular local trails are within nearby **Grand Teton National Park.** Notable in-the-park hikes are found in the Taggart Lake and Jenny Lake areas, at Colter Bay, and off the Moose-Wilson Road. The Information Center in Jackson has a brochure detailing these hikes, and a local outdoors shop, Skinny Skis (65 W. Deloney Ave., 307/733-6094 or 888/733-7205,

www.skinnyskis.com) produces an excellent free summertime guide to hiking in the area called **Trailhead.**

For a fast trip to the alpine, take the new **Jackson Hole Ski Resort tram** to the summit of Rendezvous Mountain ($25), where trails fan out in various directions and the bird's-eye view is hard to beat. Visitors can also ride the **Bridger gondola** ($19 adults, free for kids under age 13) to the 9,095-foot level, with access to additional hiking trails, along with Headwall Deli for casual meals or Couloir Restaurant for fine dining. (See *Alpine Rides* in this chapter for specifics.)

Snow King

Closest to town are the trails at Snow King, where you can either hike up the mountain or ride the chairlift ($12) to the summit and hike back down. Once on top, you'll find a half-mile nature trail and wonderful across-the-valley views of the Tetons. Nearby is the **Cache Creek Trail,** which follows this pretty creek uphill for six miles along an old road that's closed to motor vehicles. It's a great family hike or mountain-bike ride. For an alternate loop back (four miles round-trip), turn onto the **Putt-Putt Trail** two miles up. Cyclists often use Cache Creek Trail to connect with Game Creek Trail for a loop around Snow King Mountain. All of the trails in the Snow King area are open to mountain bikes, and you can transport bikes on the chairlift.

Teton Pass

Ski Lake is a more challenging hike or bike ride, with spectacular views awaiting. It starts west of Wilson on Hwy. 22 at Phillips Canyon. Walk up the dirt road 0.5 mile and take the left fork in the road to the start of the trail. It side-slopes around to a viewpoint and then climbs through the forest to Ski Lake, nestled high in the alpine and three miles from your starting point. The **Black Canyon Overlook Trail** starts from the parking area at the top of Teton Pass, 10 miles west of Jackson. It follows Pass Ridge for two miles, with an abundance of wildflower meadows and forest along the way. You can continue from here down Black Canyon to the end of Trail Creek Road at the base of the pass for a longer hike, but you will need a shuttle ride back up the pass.

Snake River Canyon

The Snake River Canyon south of Jackson is best known as a river-rafting destination, but a couple of good hikes are a landlubber's option. The **Cabin Creek Trail** begins 0.5 mile up a dirt road behind Cabin Creek Campground (17 miles from Jackson). The trail follows the creek uphill to a pass that is filled with late-summer wildflowers, and from here you'll be treated to delightful views of the Snake River drainage. Return the same way, or head back downhill along the **Dog Creek Trail** that ends near the junction of Wilson-Fall Creek Road with U.S. Hwy. 89/26. Either way, it's about six miles of hiking, but if you head back via Dog Creek Trail you'll need a shuttle back to your car.

Granite Creek

This beautiful valley has good hiking, a quiet

out-of-the-way location, and the added bonus of a hot spring. Get here by driving south from Jackson 12 miles to Hoback Junction and then another 12 miles east on U.S. Hwy. 189 to the turnoff for Granite Hot Springs. The **Granite Creek Falls Trail** starts at the junction of Swift Creek and Granite Creek, eight miles up the road. It follows the creek upstream to impressive Granite Falls and then on to **Granite Hot Springs,** where you can soak in the wonderful mineral pool for $6. Towel and swimsuit rentals are available. The trail is two miles long and quite easy, and camping is available in the area.

For a more challenging hike, try the **Shoal Falls Trail,** which starts from the same trailhead eight miles up Granite Creek Road and leads five miles to an overlook near Shoal Falls. Get trail details from the Forest Service.

Guided Hikes

The **Teton County Parks and Recreation Department,** inside the Recreation Center (155 E. Gill St., 307/739-9025, www.teton wyo.org/parks), sponsors a wide range of outdoor activities throughout the summer. Adult hikes ($15–18) take place every Tuesday May–October, plus on Thursdays late May–mid-July. Longer hikes (including an overnighter) are offered several times a summer. For a break from the young'uns (1st–6th grade), take them to the summer day camp at the rec center, available weekdays for $30 per day. You don't need to be a local resident to take part in any of these activities, but reserve ahead because some fill up. The Parks and Rec office also rents out volleyball, horseshoe, bocce ball, and croquet sets.

Educational nature walks into the mountains around Jackson are led by **The Hole Hiking Experience** (307/690-4453 or 866/733-4453, www.holehike.com). Rates start at $95 adults, $75 for kids for a four-hour hike. Longer trips, including multi-night backpacking, are also available. For a free version, Grand Teton National Park offers guided walks and nature talks throughout the year.

For a different sort of guided hike, check

out the excellent and free **historical walking tours** offered by the Jackson Hole Museum.

◖ RIVER RAFTING

Jackson Hole's most popular summertime recreational activity is running Wyoming's largest river, the Snake. Each year more than 150,000 people climb aboard rafts, canoes, and kayaks to float down placid reaches of the Snake or to blast through the boiling rapids of Snake River Canyon. (As an aside, the name "Snake" comes from the Shoshone Indians, who used serpentine hand movements as sign language for their tribal name—a motion trappers misinterpreted as a snake and applied to the river flowing through Shoshone land.)

Almost 20 different rafting companies offer dozens of raft trips each day of the summer. Although you may be able to walk up and get a raft trip the same day, it's a good idea to reserve ahead for any river trip in July and August. In general, try to book a trip three or four days in advance if possible and at least one week ahead if you need a specific time, prefer an overnight float trip, or are traveling with a larger group. One or two people are more likely to get on-board at the last minute.

You may want to ask around to determine the advantages of each company. Some are cheaper but require you to drive a good distance from town; others offer more experienced crews; still others provide various perks such as fancy meals, U-paddle trips, overnight camps along the river, interpretive trips, or boats with fewer (or more) people. Several operators also lead seven-hour combination trips that include a lazy float followed by a meal break and a wild whitewater run.

The rafting companies generally operate mid-May–late September, and river conditions change throughout the season. Highest flows—and the wildest rides—are generally in May and June. Get a complete list of floating and boating outfits, along with descriptive brochures, from the visitor center in Jackson.

For full details on **do-it-yourself floats** see *River Rafting* in the *Grand Teton* chapter.

Float Trips

The gentlest way to see the Snake is by taking one of the many commercial float trips. Along the way, you'll be treated to stunning views of the Tetons and glimpses of eagles, ospreys, beavers, and perhaps moose or other wildlife along the riverbanks. Several companies—Barker-Ewing Float Trips, Will Dornan's Snake River Float Trips, Grand Teton Lodge Co., Heart Six, Sands, Signal Mountain, Solitude, and Triangle X—offer 10-mile scenic float trips along the quiet stretch **within Grand Teton National Park,** putting in at Deadman's Bar and taking out at Moose ($50–60 adults, $35–45 kids). (Grand Teton Lodge Company and Heart Six often put in at Pacific Creek.)

Several other rafting operations offer 13-mile **South Park float trips outside the park,** putting in at the bridge near Wilson and taking out above Hoback Junction ($50 adults, $40 kids, lunch included). Companies offering this trip include Barker-Ewing Whitewater & Scenic, Lewis and Clark; Sands, Will Dornan's Snake River Float Trips, Snake River Kayak and Canoe School, and Teton Expeditions. The in-the-park trips are considerably more scenic, so know what you're getting before you sign up since the differences are not emphasized by the rafting companies (at least not by those who don't operate inside the park). Given the choice, I would always choose the trip that passes below the Tetons over the one that skirts suburban Jackson. Some companies add options such as breakfast cookouts or overnight trips with camping along the way.

Age limits vary, but kids must generally be at least eight to float the river. Raft companies usually have folks meet up in either Jackson or Moose, but Heart Six departs from its ranch in Buffalo Valley, 45 miles northeast of Jackson. A wide variety of special voyages are also available from the various companies, including overnight camping and fish-and-float trips.

Call one of the following rafting outfits for details or pick up their slick brochures at the visitor center or from their offices scattered around town: **Barker-Ewing Float Trips** (307/733-1800 or 800/365-1800, www.barkerewing.com), **Barker-Ewing Whitewater & Scenic** (307/733-1000 or 800/448-4202, www.barker-ewing.com), **Dave Hansen Scenic Float Trips** (307/733-6295 or 800/732-6295, www.davehansenscenicfloat trips.com), **Grand Teton Lodge Company** (307/543-3100 or 800/628-9988, www.gtlc .com), **Will Dornan's Snake River Float Trips** (307/733-3699 or 888/998-7688, www.jackson holefloattrips.com), **Grand Teton Lodge Float Trips** (307/543-2811 or 800/628-9988, www .gtlc.com), **Heart Six Ranch** (307/543-2477 or 888/543-2477, www.heartsix.com), **Lewis and Clark Expeditions** (307/733-4022 or 800/824-5375, www.lewisandclarkexpeds .com), **Sands Wild Water** (307/733-4410 or 800/358-8184, www.sandswhitewater .com), **Signal Mountain Lodge and Marina** (307/543-2831 or 307/543-2831, www.signal mountainlodge.com), **Mad River Boat Trips** (307/733-6203 or 800/458-7238, www.mad-river.com), **Snake River Kayak and Canoe School** (307/733-9999 or 800/529-2501, www .snakeriverkayak.com), **Solitude Scenic Float Trips** (307/733-2871 or 888/704-2800, www .solitudefloattrips.com), **Teton Expeditions** (307/733-1007 or 888/700-7238, www.teton expeditions.com), and **Triangle X Float Trips** (a.k.a. National Park Float Trips, 307/733-5500 or 888/860-0005, www.trianglex.com). Snake River Kayak and Canoe School also has "rubber duckie" inflatable kayaks for a unique whitewater adventure.

As an aside, one of the oldest names in the business, **Barker-Ewing,** is actually two different operations with rather different agendas. Barker-Ewing originated in 1963 when Dick Barker and Frank Ewing started guiding clients down the Snake River. They went their separate ways in 1984, and today, the Barker family operates Grand Teton National Park float trips under the name Barker-Ewing Float Trips, while the Ewing family runs Snake River whitewater trips and South Park floats under the name Barker-Ewing Whitewater & Scenic. Both companies splash "Barker-Ewing" across the top of their brochures, adding to the confusion for many travelers. Despite any tension

between the two companies, both are first-rate operations with some of the most experienced guides anywhere.

You can also float the river with any of the local fishing outfitters and combine angling with drifting downriver. One good company—it gives a really personalized tour—is **Wooden Boat River Tours** (307/732-2628, www.wood boattours.com, $100 per person), which has classic wooden dories.

Note that a few of the raft operators are regarded as "training grounds" for other companies; recommended outfits with good records include Barker-Ewing Float Trips, Solitude, Dave Hanson, and Triangle X. Grand Teton Lodge Float Trips often use massive 15-person rafts with two oarsmen. Unfortunately, three people died in a 2006 accident when one of their rafts hit a tree that had been uprooted by high water, throwing all the passengers into the river. Use caution before booking a river trip when the river is running high following a heavy snowpack year.

Whitewater Trips

Below Jackson, the Snake enters the wild Snake River Canyon, a stretch early explorers labeled "the accursed mad river." The usual put-in point for whitewater "rapid-transit" trips is West Table Creek Campground, 26 miles south of Jackson. The take-out point is Sheep Gulch, eight miles downstream. In between, the river rocks and rolls through the narrow canyon, pumping past waterfalls and eagle nests and then over the two biggest rapids, Big Kahuna and Lunch Counter, followed by the smaller Rope and Champagne rapids. For a look at the action from the highway, stop at the paved turnout at milepost 124, where a trail leads down to Lunch Counter. The river changes greatly throughout the season, with the highest water and wildest rides in June. By August the water has warmed enough for a quick dip. Be sure to ask your river guide about the Jeep that sits in 60 feet of water below Lunch Counter!

Whitewater trips last around 3.5 hours (including transportation from Jackson) and cost around $60 adults, $50 children (age limits vary). Seven-hour combination trips covering 16 miles include a float trip, meal, and whitewater run for around $85 adults, $75 kids. You'll find discounted rates early or late in the summer. The U-paddle versions are more fun than letting the guide do all the work in an oar raft, and the smaller eight-person rafts provide the most challenging (and wettest) runs. Most companies include round-trip transportation from Jackson. (Prices are a bit lower from Snake River Park Whitewater, but you'll need to drive to their office at Hoback Junction, 13 miles south of town.) Many companies also offer trips that combine a 13-mile scenic float trip through South Park with an eight-mile whitewater trip for around $95 adults or $75 kids.

Rafting companies provide wetsuits and booties, but expect to get wet, so wear lightweight clothes and bring a jacket for the return ride. Note that this is not exactly a wilderness experience, especially in mid-July, when stretches of the river look like a Los Angeles freeway with traffic jams of rafts, kayaks, inner tubes, and other flotsam and jetsam. The river isn't as crowded on weekdays and early in the morning; take an 8 A.M. run for the fewest people. Early in the season when the river is high and fast your trip can be quite short, sometimes just 45 minutes on the water.

Don't take your own camera along unless it's waterproof; bankside float-tographers are positioned along the biggest rapids to shoot both commercial and private rafters. Stop by **Float-O-Graphs** (130 W. Broadway, 307/733-6453 or 888/478-7427, www.floatographs.com) for a photo from your run. Another company with a similar service is **Snake River Whitewater Photos and Video** (140 N. Cache Dr., 307/733-7015 or 800/948-3426, www.snakeriverphotos.net). Both companies also post photos online.

For details on whitewater raft trips, contact one of the following companies: **Barker-Ewing Whitewater & Scenic** (307/733-1000 or 800/448-4202, www.barker-ewing.com), **Dave Hansen Whitewater** (307/733-6295 or 800/732-6295,

www.davehansenwhitewater.com), **Jackson Hole Whitewater** (307/733-1007 or 800/700-7238, www.jhww.com), **Lewis and Clark Expeditions** (307/733-4022 or 800/824-5375, www.lewisandclarkexpeds.com), **Mad River Boat Trips** (307/733-6203 or 800/458-7238, www.mad-river.com), **Sands Wild Water** (307/733-4410 or 800/358-8184, www.sandswhitewater.com), **Snake River Kayak and Canoe School** (307/733-9999 or 800/529-2501, www.snakeriverkayak.com), **Snake River Park Whitewater** (307/733-7078 or 800/562-1878, www.snakeriverwhitewater.com), or **Teton Whitewater** (307/733-2285 or 866/716-7238, www.tetonwhitewater.com).

Recommended companies with good safety records and well-trained staff include Barker-Ewing, Dave Hansen, and Sands. The largest local rafting company, Mad River, has a reputation as a proving ground for novice guides (but its prices are typically lower than those of other operators).

FISHING

Jackson Hole has some of the finest angling in Wyoming, with native Snake River cutthroat (a distinct subspecies) and brook trout in the river, along with Mackinaw (lake trout), cutthroat, and brown trout in the lakes. The Snake is a particular favorite of beginning fly-fishing enthusiasts; popular shoreside fishing spots are just below Jackson Lake Dam and near the Wilson Bridge. Jackson Lake may provide higher odds for catching a fish, but you'll need to rent a boat from one of the marinas. This is the place parents take kids. Another very popular fishing hole is just below the dam on Jackson Lake. Flat Creek on the National Elk Refuge is an acclaimed spot for fly-fishing. Note that Wyoming fishing licenses are valid within Grand Teton National Park but not in Yellowstone, where you'll need a separate permit.

Fishing Guides

Many local companies guide fly-fishing float trips down the Snake River and other area waterways. Two people (same price for one person) should expect to pay $425–475 per day for a guide, rods and reels, lunch, and boat. Your fishing license and flies are extra. The visitor center has a listing of local fishing guides and outfitters, and its racks are filled with their brochures. You'll also find links to many of these at www.jacksonholechamber.com.

On Your Own

If you'd rather do it yourself, pick up a copy of the fat and free *Western Fishing Newsletter,* which offers descriptions of regional fishing areas and advice on which lures to try. Find it at **Jack Dennis' Outdoor Shop** (50 E. Broadway, 307/733-3270 or 800/570-3270, www.jackdennis.com). While there, you may want to buy a regional guide to fishing such as *Flyfisher's Guide to Wyoming* by Ken Retallic (Wilderness Adventures Press; www.wildav .com) or *Fishing Wyoming* by Kenneth Lee Graham (Globe Pequot Press; www.globe pequot.com).

Jackson has several excellent fly-fishing shops, including the aforementioned Jack Dennis' Outdoor Shop. **Westbank Anglers** (3670 Teton Village Rd., 307/733-6483 or 800/922-3474, www.westbank.com) is a nationally known fly-fishing dealer with a slick mail-order catalog, excellent fishing clinics, and float trips. **High Country Flies** (185 N. Center St., 307/733-7210 or 866/733-7210, www .highcountryflies.com), **Orvis Jackson Hole** (485 W. Broadway, 307/733-5407, www.orvis .com), and **Will Dornan's Snake River Angler** (in Moose, 307/733-3699 or 888/998-7688, www.snakeriverangler.com) all offer fly-fishing classes and sell quality gear. Rent fishing rods, fly rods, float tubes, and waders from Jack Dennis, High Country Flies, or **Leisure Sports** (1075 S. U.S. Hwy. 89, 307/733-3040, www.leisuresportsadventure.com).

BOATING
Kayaking and Canoeing

In business for more than 30 years, **Snake River Kayak and Canoe School** (365 N. Cache, 307/733-9999 or 800/529-2501, www .snakeriverkayak.com) offers a wide variety of river kayaking and canoeing classes for all levels of ability, plus fishing trips and raft trips. Full-day private lessons—including transportation, boats, paddles, wet suit, rubber booties, and life jackets—cost $360 for two students (lower rates if you have more people). Beginners may want to start out with one of the three-hour "rubber duckie" inflatable kayak river trips for $70. In addition, the school has sea kayak tours of all lengths in Yellowstone National Park. It rents practically anything that floats: canoes, sea kayaks, whitewater kayaks, inflatable kayaks, drift boats, and rafts, all with paddles and roof racks included. Also available are dry bags and life jackets.

The folks at **Rendezvous River Sports/ Jackson Hole Kayak School** (945 W. Broadway, 307/733-2471, www.jacksonhole kayak.com) teach a wide range of kayaking courses from the absolute beginner level to advanced "hairboating" for experts. Classes include kayak roll clinics, river rescue, special women's clinics, and kids' classes, plus multi-day tours in Yellowstone. Private lessons are available, and the company rents sea kayaks and whitewater kayaks, plus inflatable kayaks.

Leisure Sports (1075 S. U.S. Hwy. 89, 307/733-3040, www.leisuresportsadventure .com) rents rafts, canoes, inflatable kayaks, water skis, wet suits, dry bags, life vests, and all sorts of other outdoor equipment (including personal watercraft). Next to Dornan's in Moose, **Adventure Sports** (307/733-3307, www.dornans.com) also rents canoes and kayaks.

HORSEBACK RIDING
Trail Rides

Think of the Wild West and one animal always comes to mind—the horse. A ride on Old Paint gives city slickers a chance to saunter back in time to a simpler era and to simultaneously learn how ornery and opinionated horses can be. If it rains, you'll also learn why cowboys are so enthralled with cowboy hats. In Jackson Hole you can choose from brief half-day trail rides in Grand Teton National Park all the way up to weeklong pack trips into the rugged Teton Wilderness. The visitor center has a brochure listing local outfitters and stables that provide trail rides and pack trips.

For rides by the hour or day ($35 for a one-hour ride, $45 for two hours, or $75–140 for a half-day), try **Teton Village Trail Rides** (in Teton Village, 307/733-2674), **Snow King Stables** (behind Snow King Resort, 307/733-5781, www.snowking.com), **Spring Creek Ranch** (atop Gros Ventre Butte off Spring Gulch Road, 307/733-8833 or 800/443-6139, www.springcreekranch .com), **A/OK Corral** (in Hoback Junction, 307/733-6556, www.horsecreekranch.com), **Mill Iron Ranch** (10 miles south of Jackson, 307/733-6390 or 888/808-6390, www .millironranch.net), or **Goosewing Ranch** (25 miles east of Kelly near the Gros Ventre Wilderness, 307/733-5251 or 888/733-5251, www.goosewingranch.com).

Of these, Teton Village Trail Rides, Spring Creek Ranch, and Mill Iron Ranch are the most popular, but you probably won't go wrong with any of these companies. Mill Iron Ranch, Spring Creek Ranch, and A/OK Corral also offer rides that include breakfast or dinner cookouts. Farther afield are several companies offering trail rides, including four that operate out of Buffalo Valley (45 miles northeast of Jackson): **Buffalo Valley Ranch** (307/543-2062 or 888/543-2477, www.buffalo valleyranch.com), **Castagno Outfitters** (307/543-2407, www.castagnooutfitters .com), **Turpin Meadow Ranch** (307/543-2496 or 800/743-2496, www.turpinmeadow ranch.com), and **Yellowstone Outfitters** (307/543-2418 or 800/447-4711, www.yellow stoneoutfitters.com). (Yellowstone Outfitters also operates Teton Village Trail Rides.) More trail rides are offered at **Togwotee Mountain Lodge** (307/543-2847 or 800/543-2847, www .togwoteelodge.com), 48 miles northeast of Jackson on the way to Togwotee Pass. The minimum age for horseback riding is typically 5–6; young children ride while the horse is being led around by a parent.

Trail rides are also available in Grand

© DON PITCHER

Teton Village Trail Rides

JACKSON HOLE

Teton National Park at **Jackson Lake Lodge** and **Colter Bay Corral**; get specifics at 307/543-2811 or 800/628-9988, www.gtlc.com. In Alpine (35 miles southwest of Jackson), **Riding and Rafts** (307/654-9900, www.ridingandrafts.com) offers unguided horse rentals for $45 for a half-day ride; it's the only place for do-it-yourselfers in the area.

Jackson Hole Llamas (307/739-9582 or 800/830-7316, www.jhllamas.com) leads backcountry treks with these fascinating and gentle animals.

Chuck wagon cookouts are a very popular family option in Jackson Hole during the summer. Guests travel in horse-drawn wagons (or by horseback) and are treated to a delicious all-you-can-eat meal and entertainment.

Wagon Trains

Two local companies lead overnight wagon-train rides (in wagons with rubber tires) into the country around Jackson Hole. Guests split their time between riding in the wagons and riding on horseback. **Wagons West** (307/543-2418 or 800/447-4711, www.wagonswestwyo.com) heads up into the Mt. Leidy Highlands for 2–6 days. The shortest trips (two days and one night) are $445 adults, $395 kids under 14. Four-day, three-night trips are $775 adults, $695 kids; and six-day, five-night trips run $995 adults, $895 kids. **Teton Wagon Train/Double H Bar** (307/734-6101 or 888/734-6101, www.tetonwagontrain.com) charges $895 adults, $815 ages 9–14, and $765 ages 4–8 for a three-night package that includes horseback and wagon riding, meals, and camping gear.

MOUNTAIN BIKING

Jackson Hole offers all sorts of adventures for cyclists, particularly those with mountain bikes. Most local bike shops provide maps of local mountain-bike routes, or you can buy a waterproof Jackson Hole mountain-biking map. Note that mountain bikes are not allowed on hiking trails in Grand Teton National Park or in Forest Service wilderness areas. The main road in Grand Teton National Park is plowed but closed to cars and other motorized traffic during April. It's great for an easy and scenic ride.

Bike Paths

The Jackson area is a great place for bikes, and is fast becoming a destination for cycling enthusiasts, thanks in part to the **Jackson Hole Community Pathways** (307/732-8573, www.tetonwyo.org/pathways). This expanding network of paved paths covers 33 miles now, with more coming in the next few years. Eventually these trails will all be linked, providing paved continuous bike paths from Hoback Junction north through Grand Teton National Park and west into Teton Valley, Idaho. Visit the Community Pathways website for details, or get additional details from Friends of Pathways (www.friendsofpathways.org), a nonprofit advocacy group. Local bike shops sell a plasticized map showing paths and trails open to bikes.

A seven-mile paved trail heads south of town, paralleling the highway to the Snake River bridge. A fun loop ride is to use this path for a connection to the very popular Game Creek Trail, which meets the Cache Creek Trail, circling back to Jackson behind Snow King. (Some of this route is not paved.) The longest continuous paved bike path goes from Wilson westward to the summit of Teton Pass (a gain of 2,000 feet in 3.5 miles), with a second arm continuing from Wilson to Teton Village and then north into Grand Teton National Park parallel to the Moose-Wilson Road. The gap between Jackson and the Snake River should be completed by 2010, and long-term plans will connect Jackson bike paths north into the park along U.S. Hwy 26/89. Meanwhile, the park is creating paved paths of its own for cyclists and others, including the section from Moose to Jenny Lake, finished in 2009.

A four-mile path starts behind the main post office on Maple Way, crosses U.S. Hwy 89, and continues past the high school before turning north to meet the road to Wilson (Hwy. 22). This road has wide shoulders but gets lots of traffic.

The trails at Snow King Resort are open to mountain bikers, and you can either pedal uphill or ride the chairlift with your bike ($12). Jackson Hole Mountain Resort has seven miles of bike trails on the lower sections of the mountain for all levels of ability. Access is via the Teewinot chairlift ($10).

Bike Rentals and Tours

Rent mountain bikes from **Hoback Sports** (520 W. Broadway Ave., 307/733-5335, www .hobacksports.com), **The Edge Sports** (490 W. Broadway, 307/734-3916, www.jackson holeedgesports.com), **Grand Targhee Ski Resort** (307/353-2300 or 800/827-4433, www .grandtarghee.com), **Wilson Backcountry Sports** (307/733-5228, www.wilsonback country.com), **Adventure Sports** (307/733-3307) in Moose, **Fitzgerald's Bicycles** (245 W. Hansen St., 307/734-6886, www.fitzgeraldsbicycles.com), **Jackson Hole Sports** (307/739-2687, www.jacksonhole .com) in Teton Village, **Teton Village Sports** (307/733-2181, www.tetonvillagesports .com) in Teton Village, **Wildernest Sports** (307/733-4297, www.wildernestsports.com) in Teton Village, and **Boardroom of Jackson Hole** (225 W. Broadway Ave., 307/733-8327, www.boardroomjacksonhole.com). All of these places rent bikes and helmets for around $40 per day, $25 per half day, and some also rent bike trailers, road bikes, hybrid bikes, child bikes, and car racks. Boardroom also rents skateboards and wakeboards.

Half-day mountain-bike tours are available from **Fat Tire Tours/Hoback Sports** (307/734-4425, www.hobacksports.com). Options include an easy National Elk Refuge ride ($45) and a more adventurous one ($65) that includes a chairlift ride to the top of Snow King leading into nearby trails. **Teton Mountain Bike Tours** (307/733-0712 or 800/733-0788, www.wybike.com) has scenic half- or all-day bike trips through Grand Teton National Park, Bridger-Teton National Forest, and the National Elk Refuge. These trips are for all levels of ability, starting at $60 for a four-hour ride in the Antelope Flats area.

ALPINE RIDES
Jackson Hole Resort

Take a fast and scenic ride to the top of Rendezvous Mountain (10,450 feet) aboard the newly rebuilt **aerial tram** (307/733-2292 or 888/333-7766, www.jacksonhole.com) at Teton Village. The tram ride takes nine minutes, gains more than 4,000 feet in elevation, and costs $25, with discounted rates for kids and seniors. Open daily Memorial Day–September, this is a sensational way to reach the alpine. On top is a small snack shop, but you should bring a lunch since the choices are limited and pricey. Several trails provide enjoyable hikes from the summit. Be sure to pack drinking water and a warm jacket. Dogs and bikes aren't allowed on the tram.

Rendezvous Mountain is a favorite place for paragliders to launch. Tandem paragliding flights ($225) are available from **Jackson Hole Paragliding,** 307/739-2626, www .jhparagliding.com. No experience is needed for these half-hour flights, with access via the tram.

Summer visitors can also ride the **Bridger gondola** ($19 adults, free for kids under 13) to the 9,095-foot level. It doesn't reach the top of the mountain, but affords panoramic vistas over Jackson Hole and access to hiking trails, along with Headwall Deli for casual meals or Couloir Restaurant for fine dining. Take mountain bikes up the **Teewinot chairlift** (free with your gondola ticket or $10 separately).

In addition to alpine rides, Teton Village is home to a number of other activities all summer, including a bungee trampoline, 25-foot outdoor climbing wall, and a kid-only fishing pond. The resort sells $12 tickets for each of these (though the fishing is free if kids already have a pole), or $50 for five tickets.

Snow King

At Snow King Mountain right on the edge of Jackson, the resort's main **chairlift** operates late May–early September, taking folks for a 20-minute ride to the summit of the 7,751-foot mountain ($12 adults, $8 kids round-trip). The

JACKSON HOLE

TRAM I AM

For four decades, the main attraction at Jackson Hole Resort was the 52-passenger aerial tram that climbed the summit of Rendezvous Mountain, providing jaw-dropping views across Jackson Hole. But all things must pass. In 2005, Jackson Hole Resort stunned local residents – and skiers around the country – by announcing that the aerial tram would be retired at the end of summer 2006. In operation since 1966, the tram had simply become too worn out to repair. The old one was demolished the following year, and work began on a new, and much-improved tram. Opening day for the new $30-million tram came in 2008, much to the relief of skiers, boarders, and Jackson Hole businesses.

Manufactured in Switzerland and powered by 1,970-horsepower engines, the new fire-engine red tram holds 100 people – almost twice the capacity of the old one – and takes 10 minutes to get to the summit (versus 12 minutes for the old tram). It can carry 600 passengers per hour, more than twice as many as before.

chairlift runs daily 9 A.M.–8 P.M. in midsummer. On top you'll find a short nature trail and panoramic views of the Tetons.

Also at Snow King is the 2,500-foot-long **Alpine Slide** (307/733-7680 or 800/522-5464, www.snowking.com), a summertime favorite of kids. For anyone older than six, the cost is $15 for one ride or $65 for five rides (lower prices after 4 P.M.). For children ages 2–6 riding with an adult it's an additional $2 per ride.

Grand Targhee Ski Resort

On the other side of the Tetons at Grand Targhee Ski Resort (307/353-2300 or 800/827-4433, www.grandtarghee.com), you can ride the **chairlift** ($13 adults, $6 kids) to the 10,200-foot summit of Fred's Mountain, where Grand Teton stands just seven miles away. The lift operates daily late June–mid-

September. Mountain bikers can bring a bike (or rent one) to ride the trails high up the slopes for $21.

SWIMMING AND GYMS

Jackson is home to **Teton County/Jackson Recreation Center** (155 E. Gill St., 307/739-9025, www.tetonwyo.org/parks, Mon.–Fri. 6 A.M.–9 P.M., Sat. noon–9 P.M., and Sun. noon–7 P.M.), which includes an indoor aquatics complex with a lap pool, 185-foot corkscrew water slide, and hot tub, plus a wading pool featuring a waterfall, slide, and water geyser. Basketball and volleyball courts are also inside the rec center, and after your workout, relax in the sauna and steam room. Nonresident prices are $6.25 adults, $5 ages 13–17, $4 seniors and ages 3–12, and $20 families; free for tots under three. The rec center also offers a variety of courses and activities, including yoga, toddler swimming, basketball, volleyball, and aerobics.

Out of the way is the wonderful hot mineral pool at **Granite Hot Springs** (307/734-7400, $6), 35 miles southeast of Jackson. The springs are open daily summers and winters (see the *Bridger-Teton National Forest* section).

Take exercise and yoga classes at **Jackson Hole Athletic Club** (838 W. Broadway, 307/733-8830, www.jacksonholeathleticclub.org), which also houses a full gymnasium with all of the usual workout equipment, weights, and a steam room. Day passes are $15.

Teton Sports Club (4030 W. Lake Creek Dr., 307/733-7004, www.tetonsportsclub.com) is near the Aspens south of Teton Village and offers aerobic classes, cardio machines, free weights, hot tubs, a sauna, and a summer-only outdoor pool. Day passes are $15. Massage therapists and personal trainers are available. The health club at **Amangani** (307/734-7333 or 877/734-7333, www.amangani.com) is also open to the public on a limited basis for massage and other services.

SPAS

Jackson is a wonderful place to pamper yourself. Most of the top-end hotels provide spa facilities open to both guests and the general public, including Amangani, Rusty Parrot, Snow King Resort, Spring Creek Ranch, Snake River Lodge, Teton Mountain Lodge, Four Seasons Resort, and Hotel Terra. The visitor center has brochures from additional spas, acupuncture clinics, and yoga studios to center your soul. There's even a **Teton Wellness Festival** in early October to get in touch with your inner self (and outer self at the same time). Visit www.tetonwellness.org for links to local centers, from homeopaths to Pilates classes.

ROCK CLIMBING

Jackson Hole is home for two highly regarded climbing schools: **Jackson Hole Mountain Guides** (165 N. Glenwood, 307/733-4979 or 800/239-7642, www.jhmg.com) and **Exum Mountain Guides** (307/733-2297, www .exumguides.com), with a summertime office at the south end of Jenny Lake. Both offer a wide range of classes—including those for kids and families—plus guided climbs up Grand Teton and wintertime courses in avalanche safety and ice climbing.

Largest indoor rock gym in the Rockies, **Enclosure Indoor Climbing Center** (670 Deer Lane, 307/734-9590, www.enclosureclimbing .com) has a huge diversity of climbing terrain, roped climbing areas, and bouldering, plus a fitness center and even child care. There's also an **outdoor climbing wall** (307/739-2753, $12) in the heart of Teton Village next to the pond. See the *Grand Teton National Park* chapter for additional rock-climbing options, including **Blacktail Butte,** a popular place to practice your moves.

UP IN THE AIR

Two local companies offer early morning hot-air balloon rides in the summer. **Wyoming Balloon Co.** (307/739-0900, www.wyoming balloon.com) takes off from the Jackson Hole side of the mountains. An hour-long flight is $295 adults, $245 kids (six and older). If you're heading over the mountains, **Teton Balloon Flights** (208/787-5500 or 866/533-6404, www.tetonballooning.com) has one-hour hot-

air balloon flights over Teton Valley (on the Idaho side) for $250 per person.

The top of the Jackson Hole Resort tram is a favorite place for paragliders to launch. Tandem paragliding flights ($225) are available from **Jackson Hole Paragliding** (307/690-8726, www.jhparagliding.com). No experience is needed for these 15-minute flights.

Cowboy Up Hang Gliding (307/413-4164, www.cuhanggliding.com) has tandem flights from Alpine (35 miles southwest of Jackson), using an ultralight to gain altitude for flights over the Salt River Range. These cost $169 for a flight that lasts at least 20 minutes.

Over the pass in Driggs, Idaho, **Teton Aviation Center** (208/354-3100 or 800/472-6382, www.tetonaviation.com) has glider flights; $250 for a one-hour flight, a great way to come eye-to-eye with Grand Teton.

GOLF AND TENNIS

Like many resort areas, Jackson Hole has an abundance of tony golf courses, including five in the valley plus another six over the pass in Teton Valley. **Jackson Hole Golf and Tennis Club** (307/733-3111, www.ghgtc.com), one mile north of town, has a public 18-hole golf course designed by Robert Trent Jones Jr. and rated one of the 10 best in America. Also here are a private swimming pool, tennis courts, fitness center, and North Grille for summertime patio dining.

Teton Pines Country Club (on Teton Village Rd., 307/733-1773 or 800/238-2223, www.tetonpines.com) is Jackson Hole's other golf spot open to the public. Its Arnold Palmer–designed 18-hole championship course is very challenging; 14 of the holes require over-water shots. The club also features a grand clubhouse, tennis courts, a large (and private) outdoor pool, along with fine dining at The Pines restaurant. Both Teton Pines and Jackson Hole Golf and Tennis Club have rentals and lessons for golfers and tennis aficionados.

A new Tom Fazio-designed 18-hole course—**Shooting Star Golf Course**—opened in 2009 next to Teton Village. Two private golf courses (Snake River Sporting Club and 3 Creek

Ranch) are open only to members willing to fork over $30,000 or more.

For the dedicated golfer, **Alpine Miniature Golf** (307/733-5200 or 800/522-5464, www .snowking.com, daily in summer, $8) has a Lilliputian 18-hole hillside course next to the Alpine Slide at Snow King Resort.

Public tennis courts are on the east end of the rodeo grounds along Snow King Drive, and within Miller Park at Deloney and Gill streets.

TOWN PARKS

Eight parks are scattered around Jackson, including the famous Town Square. Several others are of note, particularly if you have children in tow. The largest, **Miller Park,** covers a grassy city block at Deloney and Gill streets and includes basketball and tennis courts, a picnic shelter, restrooms, and a delightful playground. **Powderhorn Park,** on the west side of town near Powderhorn Lane and Alpine Lane, has additional playground equipment, a picnic shelter, and restrooms. **Mike Yokel Jr. Park,** on East Kelly Avenue near Snow King, features a sand volleyball court, horseshoe pits, a playground, a picnic shelter, and restrooms. **Baux Park** at the base of Snow King Mountain is similar, with a playground, horseshoe pits, and picnic tables. **Home Ranch Park** is next to the parking lot at Cache and Gill and has picnic tables and restrooms. **Owen Bircher Park** in Wilson includes a summertime roping arena (a good place to watch budding cowboys and cowgirls on summer afternoons) that becomes a wintertime ice rink. The park also has a sand volleyball court, a softball/soccer field, picnic tables, and restrooms.

In addition to those mentioned in the town parks, public restrooms can also be found half a block south of Town Square on Cache Drive.

Winter Recreation

Jackson Hole has an international reputation as a winter destination. As access has become easier and the facilities more developed, many people have discovered the wonders of a Jackson Hole winter, especially one centered on a week of skiing or snowboarding. Three very different ski resorts attract the crowds: Grand Targhee for down-home, powder-to-the-butt conditions; Snow King for steep, inexpensive, edge-of-town slopes; and Jackson Hole for flashy, world-class skiing. All three places have rental equipment, ski schools, and special programs for kids. Snowboarders and telemarkers are welcome on the slopes. These resorts combine with an incredible abundance of developed and wild places to ski cross-country to make Jackson Hole one of the premier ski and snowboard destinations in America.

See your travel agent for package trips to any of the Jackson-area resorts. For daily ski reports, including information on both downhill and Nordic areas and the backcountry, listen to KMTN (FM 96.9) in the morning.

DOWNHILL SKIING AND SNOWBOARDING

If you plan to spend more than a couple of days in the area, it is probably worth your while to join the **Jackson Hole Ski and Snowboard Club** (307/733-6433, www.jhskiclub.com). In return for a $30 membership, you receive an impressive number of premiums, including reduced rates for lift tickets and season passes, plus discounted lodging, meals, drinks, snowmobile trips, and shopping at local stores. Join up at any local ski shop or the office inside Snow King Resort.

Grand Targhee Ski Resort (307/353-2300 or 800/827-4433, www.grandtarghee.com)—just five miles above Alta, Wyoming—is the main attraction for the Teton Valley area. The resort offers excellent skiing and snowboarding in winter, along with a wide range of summer activities. (Get the complete scoop, including details for on-mountain lodging and meals, in the *Alta, Wyoming* section later in this chapter.)

Ski and Snowboard Rentals

Rent or buy downhill skis and snowboards from **Hoback Sports** (520 W. Broadway Ave., 307/733-5335, www.hobacksports .com), **Boardroom of Jackson Hole** (225 W. Broadway Ave., 307/733-8327, www.board roomjacksonhole.com), **The Edge Sports** (490 W. Broadway, 307/734-3916, www.jackson holeedgesports.com), **Gart Sports** (485 W. Broadway, 307/733-4449, www.gartsports .com), **Jack Dennis' Outdoor Shop** (50 E. Broadway, 307/733-3270 or 800/570-3270, www.jackdennis.com) and in Teton Village (307/733-6838), **Jackson Hole Sports** (in Teton Village, 307/739-2687, www.jackson hole.com), **Pepi Stiegler Sports** (in Teton Village, 307/733-4505, www.jackdennis.com/ pepis), **Wildernest Sports** (in Teton Village, 307/733-4297, www.wildernestsports.com), or **Teton Village Sports** (307/733-2181 or 800/874-4224, www.tetonvillagesports.com). Rentals are also available at all three ski areas.

C Jackson Hole Mountain Resort

Just 12 miles northwest of Jackson is Jackson Hole Mountain Resort (307/733-2292 or 888/333-7766, www.jacksonhole.com), the largest and best-known Wyoming ski area. A true skiers' and snowboarders' mountain, Jackson Hole is considered the most varied and challenging of any American ski area. The powder is usually deep (average snowfall is 38 feet), lift lines are short, the slopes are relatively uncrowded, and the vistas are unbelievable. First opened in 1965, Jackson Hole Mountain Resort has become one of the nation's favorite ski areas. The resort has invested many millions of dollars in the last decade or so, upgrading facilities, adding lifts, expanding snowmaking, completing a spacious children's center, and building an ice rink and snowboarding half-pipe. These improvements have enhanced the resort's reputation as an expert's

paradise to also include facilities that are more friendly to families and intermediate skiers. Jackson Hole Mountain Resort is owned by the Kemmerer family, whose ancestors founded the town of Kemmerer, Wyoming, and is one of the few major American ski resorts that is still independently owned.

The mountain has one unusual feature that occurs in midwinter: A temperature inversion frequently develops over the valley, meaning that when it's bitterly cold at the base of the mountain, the top is 15–20°F warmer. Skiers often remain on the upper slopes all day to enjoy these warmer temperatures.

With an unsurpassed 4,139-foot vertical drop (longest in the United States), 2,500 acres of terrain spread over two adjacent mountains, runs that exceed four miles in length, and 24 miles of groomed trails, Jackson Hole Mountain Resort is truly a place of superlatives. Half of the resort's 60 runs are in the advanced category—including several of the notorious double-diamonds—but it is so large that even rank beginners will find plenty of bunny slopes on which to practice. (As a trivial aside, Montana's Big Sky Resort also claims the longest vertical drop of any American mountain—4,300 feet—but this involves taking three lifts and ending your run below where you start.)

The only way to the summit of 10,450-foot **Rendezvous Mountain** is aboard one of the brand-new 100-passenger aerial tram cars. Powered by 1,970-horsepower engines, they climb nearly two and a half miles in 10 minutes, offering jaw-dropping views across Jackson Hole. Rendezvous Mountain is where experts strut their stuff on these steep and fast slopes, and if you're not at least close to the expert status you'll find your blood pressure rising as the tram heads up the mountain. More than a few skiers and boarders have taken the tram back down after seeing what lies below. Yes, those death-defying cliff-jumping shots are real; check out infamous **Corbet's Couloir,** a rocky gully that requires a leap of faith and suicidal urges. Fortunately, intermediate skiers and boarders are not given short shrift at

Jackson Hole Mountain Resort, particularly on the friendlier slopes of 8,481-foot **Apres Vous Mountain.** Intermediate (and advanced) down-hillers could spend all day playing on these slopes, and a high-speed quad here means that riders can blast to the summit of Apres Vous in just five minutes. Because of the speed of this and other lifts, the wait at the base is usually just a few minutes.

In addition to these lifts, you can ride a gon-dola, three other quad chairs, two triple chairs, a double chair, and Poma lift. Snowboarders will appreciate the half-pipe and boarders' ter-rain trail. The resort's **Kids Ranch** provides supervised day care ($95 per day), including a spacious play area; it's the only drop-off day-care center in Jackson Hole, and it's open seven days a week in winter. Not far away is a spe-cial "magic carpet" (a conveyer belt of sorts) for children learning to ski or snowboard.

Summer visitors to Jackson Hole Mountain Resort find an amazing variety of activities in-cluding horseback rides, music festivals, rock-climbing, paragliding, bike rentals, disc golf, fishing in the stocked kids-only pond, the bun-gee trampoline, shopping, or just soaking up the view while nursing a beer. There's even a **via ferrata** rock climbing course on the upper mountain based on similar ones in the Alps. It features cables, iron ladders, and metal rungs anchored into cliffs, and is accessible atop Bridger gondola. This is one of just four such routes in the United States.

Rates and Services: Get to Teton Village from the town of Jackson by hopping on the START bus ($3 each way; 307/733-4521, www.startbus.com). This is the only inex-pensive part of a visit to Jackson Hole Resort, where prices for lift tickets approach the strato-sphere. Regular season single-day tickets are $87 adults, $51 ages 6–14, and $55 seniors. Afternoon-only rates are $70 adults, $41 kids, and $44 seniors. Multi-day tickets—the most common kind bought—are $375 per week (five days of skiing) for adults, and $220 for kids 5–14 and seniors. Lifts are open 9 A.M.–4 P.M. daily Thanksgiving–early April.

Skis and snowboards can be rented at shops in Jackson or Teton Village. The ski school of-fers a special Kinderschule program for chil-dren, and beginning snowboarders can learn from the pros. Jackson Hole Resort even has special steep snowboarding and skiing camps, where you learn from extreme downhill fanat-ics. Tommy Moe—gold and silver medalist at the 1994 Winter Olympics—teaches a "Steep and Deep" ski camp and is a ski ambassador for the resort.

Ski hosts are scattered around the mountain, ready to provide information and free hourly tours of the slopes from the top of Rendezvous Mountain. Racers and spectators will enjoy NASTAR events, along with various other competitions throughout the winter.

Get recorded snow conditions by calling 307/733-2291; the messages are changed each morning before 5 A.M. The resort's website is packed with additional details, including the current weather and snow conditions.

Into the Backcountry

If you're looking for untracked powder, the Jackson Hole Mountain Resort can set up pri-vate lessons for access to parts of the mountain that are off-limits to mere mortals.

In lower Rock Springs Canyon, two miles south of the resort, **Rock Springs Yurt** has a backcountry location that's accessible by cross-country skis or snowshoes. It's a two-mile trek, but you gain 1,000 feet along the way, making this a challenging trip. The fully equipped yurt is available for guided day trips and overnight stays. It sleeps eight for $400, including din-ner and breakfast cooked by the "yurt meister." Contact Jackson Hole Resort (307/739-2663 or 800/450-0477, www.jacksonhole.com) for details. The yurt is also open to hikers in the summer.

Powderhound skiers with a ton of cash will find unparalleled outback conditions accessible via **High Mountain Heli-Skiing** (307/733-3274, www.heliskijackson.com). Operating from Togwotee Mountain Lodge (307/543-2847 or 800/543-2847, www.togwo teelodge.com) 48 miles northeast of Jackson, **Togwotee Snowcat Skiing** takes skiers and snowboarders into a wide variety of terrain with spectacular vistas of the Tetons en route.

Teton Village

At the base of Rendezvous Mountain is the Swiss-style Teton Village—alias "the Vill." Everything skiers and boarders need is crowded together here: lodges, condominiums, espresso stands, restaurants, après-ski bars, gift shops, groceries, ski, snowboard, and snowshoe rentals and lessons, storage lockers, car rentals, a skating pond, child care, personal trainers, dogsled tours, and even a travel agency for escapes to Hawaii. Tune your radio to FM 100.1 "Teton Village Radio" for parking and transportation information.

On-the-mountain facilities include a fine-dining establishment at the top of Bridger gondola, Casper Restaurant at the bottom of Casper Bowl, and snack bars at the base of Thunder chairlift, and the top of Apres Vous chairlift. Casper Restaurant serves a barbecue picnic most days and is a popular place to join friends for lunch.

Snow King Resort

Snow King Resort (307/733-5200 or 800/522-5464, www.snowking.com) has three things that other local ski areas lack: location, location, and location. The resort sits directly behind town and just seven blocks from Town Square. This is the locals' place, Jackson's "town hill," but it also offers surprisingly challenging runs. It may not be the largest or fanciest place around, but the King's ski runs make up in difficulty what they lack in size. From below, the mountain (7,808 feet at the summit) looks impossibly steep and narrow. High atop the big chairlift, the vista provides a panoramic tour of Jackson Hole and the Tetons.

Snow King was the first ski area in Wyoming—it opened in 1939—and one of the first in North America. The original chapter of the National Ski Patrol was established here in 1941. The mountain has a 1,571-foot vertical drop. You'll find more than 400 acres of skiable terrain at Snow King, with the longest run stretching nearly a mile. A triple chair, two

double chairs, and a Poma lift climb the mountainside. Other features include snowmaking, a tubing park, and a very popular terrain park for snowboarders. It's the only local resort with lighted runs.

Rates and Services: Prices for lift tickets at Snow King are well below those at other Jackson Hole resorts: $41 per day ($31 per half day) for adults and $31 per day ($21 per half day) for kids under 13 and seniors. Hours of operation are 10 A.M.–4 P.M., with **night skiing** (Tues.–Sat. 4–8 P.M.) available on the lower sections of Snow King for an additional $20 adults or $15 kids and seniors. In addition, the King has special two-hour rates for lift tickets ($22 adults, $17 kids and seniors); these are perfect for skiers and boarders who arrive late in the afternoon and want to hit the slopes for a bit. With some of the best snowmaking in Wyoming, the resort usually opens by Thanksgiving and remains in operation through March.

At the base of Snow King you'll discover a lodge with reasonable ski-and-stay packages. Also at Snow King are two restaurants, a lounge (called, not surprisingly, The Lounge), ski and snowboard rentals and lessons, plus a variety of other facilities, including an indoor ice rink and mountaintop snack shack. Jackson's START buses (307/733-4521, www.startbus.com) provide frequent service to town (free) or Teton Village ($3).

CROSS-COUNTRY SKIING

For many Jackson Hole residents the word "skiing" means heading across frozen Jenny Lake or telemarking down the bowls of Teton Pass rather than sliding down the slopes of the local resorts. Jackson Hole has become a center for cross-country enthusiasts and offers an impressive range of conditions—from flat-tracking along summertime golf courses where a gourmet restaurant awaits to remote wilderness settings where a complete knowledge of snowpack structure, avalanche hazards, and winter survival techniques is essential. Beginners will probably want to start out at a Nordic center, progressing to local paths and the more gentle lift-serviced ski runs with experience. More advanced skiers will quickly discover incredible snow in the surrounding mountains.

Ski Rentals

Rent or buy cross-country skis from **Skinny Skis** (65 W. Deloney Ave., 307/733-6094 or 888/733-7205, www.skinnyskis.com), **Teton Mountaineering** (170 N. Cache Dr., 307/733-3595 or 800/850-3595, www.teton mtn.com), or **Wilson Backcountry Sports** (Wilson, 307/733-5228, www.wilsonback country.com). Local Nordic centers also rent equipment. Most places rent both classical cross-country skis and skate skis (much faster and a better workout), along with telemark and alpine touring skis.

Nordic Centers

Nordic skiing enthusiasts will find two different developed facilities near Jackson and a third at Grand Targhee in Alta, Wyoming. The largest is **Jackson Hole Nordic Center** (307/739-2629, www.jacksonhole.com) in Teton Village, with 17 kilometers of groomed trails—both set track and skating lanes—that cover a wide range of conditions. Call 307/733-2291 for the snow report. This is the best place to learn cross-country skiing. Daily trail passes are $13 per day. Traditional cross-country skis, skate skis, and telemarking equipment are available for rent, and the center offers a wide spectrum of lessons and tours. Hours are daily 8:30 A.M.–4:30 P.M. You can exchange your alpine lift ticket at Jackson Hole Mountain Resort for one at the Nordic center (but, hey, it had better be for no extra charge since you've already dropped $87!).

Along Teton Village Road, **Teton Pines** (307/733-1005 or 800/238-2223, www.teton pines.com) features 13 kilometers of groomed track (both classical and skating) on a summertime golf course. Daily trail passes cost $10 adults or $5 children and seniors, and ski rentals and lessons are available. Hours are daily 9 A.M.–5 P.M. The clubhouse here has a restaurant for gourmet après-ski lunches and dinners.

On the west side of the Tetons 42 miles out

of Jackson, **Grand Targhee Nordic Center** (307/353-2300 or 800/827-4433, www.grand targhee.com) has 20 kilometers of groomed cross-country ski trails (classical and skating) covering rolling terrain. Trail passes are $10 adults and $6 seniors and kids. Lessons and ski rentals are also available. Hours are daily 9:30 A.M.–4 P.M. Guests with Targhee lodging packages can ski free on the cross-country tracks.

On Your Own

Nordic skiers who would rather explore Jackson Hole and the mountains that surround it on their own will discover an extraordinary range of options, from beginner-level treks along old roads to places where only the most advanced skiers dare venture. Because Jackson has so many cross-country fanatics (and visiting enthusiasts), tracks are quickly broken along the more popular routes, making it easier for those who follow. For complete coverage of all these options, pick up a copy of the helpful free winter outdoors guide *Trailhead* at Skinny Skis (65 W. Deloney Ave., 307/733-6094 or 888/733-7205, www.skinnyskis.com). If you're heading out on your own, be prepared for deep snow (four feet in the valley) and temperatures that often plummet below zero at night.

The **Teton County Parks and Recreation Department** (155 E. Gill, 307/739-9025, www.tetonwyo.org/parks) leads all-day cross-country ski outings most Tuesdays mid-December–mid-March. Bring your own skis and a lunch; they provide the guide and transportation. The department also grooms 17 miles of local pathways for cross-country and skate skiing in the winter; call 307/739-6789 for the grooming hotline with daily updates. **Friends of Pathways** produces a free map of local Nordic trails (including the grooming schedule), and has a downloadable PDF version on the web at www.friendsofpathways.org.

Jackson Area: Even rank beginners will enjoy exploring several local spots. The closest place to Jackson for on-your-own cross-country skiing is **Cache Creek Canyon.** The trailhead is at the east end of Cache Creek Drive, where the plowing ends at a parking lot. The trail is groomed by the parks and rec department a couple of times per week. For a longer trip, take the Rafferty ski lift at Snow King and then ski west through the trees and down to Cache Creek, returning via the road. Ask at Snow King Resort for specifics and safety precautions. Another popular local place is along the **Snake River dikes,** where Hwy. 22 crosses the river one mile east of Wilson. The dikes extend along both sides of the river for several miles, making for easy skiing. This is also a good place to watch ducks, moose, and other critters or to listen to the river rolling over the rocks. The northeast side gets groomed for skate and touring skis on a regular basis.

Grand Teton National Park: Cross-country skiing is popular on park roads and trails in the winter. The main thoroughfare—Teton Park Road—provides stellar views of the Teton Range and is regularly groomed for both parallel and skate skiing from Taggart Lake to Signal Mountain, a distance of 14 miles. Park three miles northwest of Moose at the Taggart Lake Trailhead. More adventurous skiers will enjoy side trails to Jenny Lake (eight miles round-trip).

Get to **Moose-Wilson Road** by heading one mile north of Teton Village to where the plowing ends at the Granite Canyon Trailhead. The nearly level road continues for two scenic miles across a creek and through groves of aspen. For more adventure, head up Granite Canyon Trail along the moraine, which offers a range of skiing conditions. Just don't ski into the canyon since avalanches are a hazard.

For unsurpassed vistas of the Tetons, try skiing to the top of 8,252-foot **Shadow Mountain,** 14 miles northeast of Jackson. From the town of Kelly, drive another five miles north to a parking area (the road isn't plowed beyond this point), and then ski up the nearby Forest Service road that snakes up the mountain. It's fairly steep in places and seven miles round-trip. Snowmobilers also use this road, so be ready to move out of the way quickly.

Granite Hot Springs: One of the most popular ski- and snowmobile-in sites is Granite Hot Springs (307/734-7400), a delightful hot spring–fed pool on Forest Service land. Get there by driving 25 miles southeast of Jackson into Hoback Canyon and then skiing 10 miles in from the signed parking area. The route is not difficult, but because of the distance it isn't recommended for beginners unless they're prepared for a 20-mile round-trip trek. The pool costs $6 adults, $4 ages 3–12, and is free for infants. It's open daily 11 A.M.–5 P.M. in winter. Bring your swimsuit or rent a suit and towel here. Ask the attendant about places to snow camp nearby.

Teton Pass: Locals head to 8,429-foot Teton Pass when they really want to test their abilities. The summit parking area fills with cars on fresh-snow mornings as everyone from advanced beginners to world-class ski mountaineers heads out for a day in the powder or a week of wilderness trekking in the Tetons. Snow depths of eight feet or more are not uncommon in midwinter. (The snow once became so deep on the pass that it took plows two weeks to clear the road!) The slopes around Teton Pass cover the full spectrum, but be sure you know your own ability and how to avoid avalanches. Check the previously mentioned Skinny Skis *Trailhead* winter guide for specifics on Teton Pass, or talk to folks at Skinny Skis or Teton Mountaineering. This is the backcountry, so you won't see any signs at the various bowls; ask other skiers if you aren't sure which is which. Avalanches do occur in some of these bowls, and it's possible to get lost up here during a storm, so come prepared.

Those without backcountry experience should contact **Rendezvous Backcountry Tours** (307/353-2900 or 877/754-4887, www .skithetetons.com), **Jackson Hole Mountain Guides** (307/733-4979 or 800/239-7642, www.jhmg.com), or **Jackson Hole Nordic Center** (307/739-2629, www.jacksonhole .com), for guided ski tours at Teton Pass and elsewhere.

Ski Tours
Jackson Hole Mountain Guides (307/733-4979 or 800/239-7642, www.jhmg .com) runs winter ascents of Grand Teton, plus

safety and avalanche courses and ski mountaineering trips. Longer winter trips, including a five-day Teton Crest tour, are also available.

Over on the western slopes of the Tetons, **Rendezvous Backcountry Tours** (307/353-2900 or 877/754-4887, www .skithetetons.com) maintains three Mongolian-style yurts in the Jedediah Smith Wilderness, each situated several hours of skiing (or hiking) from the next. These immensely popular huts can sleep up to eight and have kitchens, bunks, sleeping bags, and woodstoves; $300–350 per night plus $150 for a guide to take you in on the first day. You'll need to be experienced in backcountry skiing and have the necessary safety equipment and avalanche training. If you don't quite measure up, the company provides guided ski tours to the huts. A three-day, two-night catered trip is $1,230 per person including guide, meals, lodging, sleeping bags, and avalanche equipment. The backcountry yurts are available December–April, but call far ahead for reservations. The most popular one (Baldy Knoll) fills a year in advance! Rendezvous also has a close-in family yurt with space for six; $85 d or $110 for three or more guests (including children). It's open year-round, with drive-up access in summer and a half-mile walk in winter. The family hut has running water, a kitchen, and bath, while the backcountry yurts have outhouses.

Jackson Hole Nordic Center at Teton Village has guided ski tours into Grand Teton National Park; a half-day for two people costs $200.

ICE-SKATING

Each winter, the town of Wilson floods a hockey rink–size part of the town park for skating, hockey, and broomball. A warming hut stands next to the rink. Jackson maintains two ice rinks at Snow King for figure skaters and general playing around. All three of these are free and lighted most winter evenings. Contact Teton County Parks & Recreation (307/733-5056, www.tetonwyo.org/parks) for details.

All three local ski resorts have ice-skating and skate rentals. You'll find skating ponds in Teton Village at the base of **Jackson Hole Mountain**

Resort and over in Alta at **Grand Targhee Ski Resort.** For the out-of-the-elements version, skate over to **Snow King Resort,** where the indoor ice-skating rink is open in the winter and offers skate rentals and lessons.

SNOWSHOEING

Snowshoeing began as a way to get around in the winter, but the old-fashioned wood-and-rawhide snowshoes were bulky and heavy. In recent years snowshoeing has become a popular form of recreation, as new technology created lightweight and easily maneuverable snowshoes. Snowshoeing requires no real training: Just strap them on, grab a pair of poles, and start walking. But be careful where you walk (see the sidebar *Avalanche Safety* in the *Essentials* chapter for tips).

Rent snowshoes from **Skinny Skis** (65 W. Deloney Ave., 307/733-6094 or 888/733-7205, www.skinnyskis.com), **Teton Mountaineering** (170 N. Cache Dr., 307/733-3595 or 800/850-3595, www.tetonmtn.com), **Wilson Backcountry Sports** (Wilson, 307/733-5228, www.wilsonbackcountry.com), and **Grand Targhee Ski Resort** (in Alta, 307/353-2300 or 800/827-4433, www.grandtarghee.com).

Guided Trips

Teton County Parks and Recreation Department (155 E. Gill, 307/739-9025, www.tetonwyo.org/parks) leads all-day snowshoe tours most Thursdays mid-December–mid-March for $15. Bring your own skis and a lunch; it provides the guide and transportation.

Snowshoe walks into the mountains around Jackson are also offered by **The Hole Hiking Experience** (307/690-4453 or 866/733-4453, www.holehike.com), the only company permitted to guide snowshoeing trips in nearby national forests. Their most popular trips go to Shadow Mountain north of Kelly. Rates start at $95 adults, $75 kids for a four-hour snowshoe trek.

The Saddlehorn Activity Center at **Jackson Hole Mountain Resort** (307/733-2292 or 888/333-7766, www.jacksonhole.com) has snowshoe rentals and guided snowshoe tours.

In addition, a snowshoe trail parallels Nordic Center ski tracks, and Forest Service naturalists lead snowshoe hikes in the area on Wednesdays and Fridays.

Free naturalist-led snowshoe tours are offered at **Grand Targhee Ski Resort** (307/353-2300 or 800/827-4433, www.grandtarghee.com). Additionally, naturalist-led snowshoe hikes are available in Grand Teton National Park. (See *Snowshoeing* in the *Grand Teton* chapter for details.)

SLEIGH RIDES

Several companies offer romantic dinner and horse-drawn sleigh rides in the Jackson Hole area mid-December–March. Make reservations well in advance for these popular trips. If you don't have the cash for one of these, take a day-time sleigh ride at the National Elk Refuge.

Jackson Hole Mountain Resort (307/739-2603, www.jacksonhole.com) picks up Teton Village guests for a romantic 30-minute ride to rustic Solitude cabin, where they are served a four-course beef tenderloin or roasted tiger prawn dinner (vegetarian options available) with nightly entertainment. Prices are $75 adults, $40 children under 11, and free for infants. There are two seatings nightly, and reservations are required.

Spring Creek Ranch (307/733-8833 or 800/443-6139, www.springcreekranch.com) has 45-minute afternoon sleigh rides at the top of Gros Ventre Butte for $32 per person. It also has packages ($77 per person) that combine a sleigh ride with a meal at the Granary Restaurant. This is one of Jackson's finer restaurants, so bring your dress clothes.

Mill Iron Ranch (307/733-6390 or 888/808-6390, www.millironranch.net) is a friendly family-run operation with evening sleigh rides in a down-home setting 10 miles south of Jackson in Horse Creek Canyon. Guests get a 45-minute ride that takes you past an elk herd to the lodge for a big T-bone steak dinner; $75 adults, $55 kids. In scenic Horse Creek Canyon, this is the most authentic of the local sleigh rides. Call for reservations.

Dinner sleigh rides are also offered at **Grand Targhee Ski Resort** (307/353-2300 or 800/827-4433, www.grandtarghee.com), where a horse-drawn sleigh transports you to a remote yurt for a Western-style meal; $35 adults, $15 kids.

Spotted Horse Ranch (307/733-2097 or 800/528-2084, www.spottedhorseranch.com) offers 45-minute sleigh rides in conjunction with nearby Camp Creek Inn; a ride and candlelit dinner is $45 for adults or $25 for kids under 13. Rides take place Thursday–Sunday evenings, and the ranch is 16 miles south of Jackson along the Hoback River.

TUBING

Two local ski areas have sliding parks with customized inner tubes and rope tows. At Snow King Resort it's called **King Tubes** (307/734-8823 or 800/522-5464, www.snowking.com) and is available on weekday evenings and weekends after noon. Rates are $14 for one hour or $21 for two hours for adults, $10 for one hour or $16 for two hours for kids. The **Grand Targhee tube park** (307/353-2300 or 800/827-4433, www.grandtarghee.com) is open for après-ski fun only (after 5 P.M.) and costs $8 per hour.

DOGSLEDDING

Founded by eight-time Iditarod musher Frank Teasley, **Jackson Hole Iditarod Sled Dog Tours** (307/733-7388 or 800/554-7388, www.jhsleddog.com) has excellent half-day trips ($210 per person including lunch) and all-day trips ($285 per person including a big steak or trout dinner). The main destination is wonderful Granite Hot Springs (only accessible on all-day rides), but when snow conditions are right, the teams may run in the Cliff Creek, Grays River, Shadow Mountain, and Gros Ventre areas. All trips include round-trip transportation from Jackson to his base on the Hoback River.

Another Iditarod veteran, Billy Snodgrass, operates **Continental Divide Dogsled Adventures** (307/739-0165 or 800/531-6874, www.dogsledadventures.com), with dog teams at Togwotee Mountain Lodge (48 miles north of Jackson). Prices start at $100 per person for a 90-minute dogsled ride at Teton Village. Full-day tours in the gorgeous country around Brooks Lake cost $259 (including transportation from Jackson). Longer trips are also available, including a two-day adventure on which you stay overnight in a surprisingly comfortable yurt; $840 per person, all-inclusive.

SNOWMOBILING

Snowmobiling is one of Jackson Hole's most popular wintertime activities. Hundreds of miles of packed and groomed snowmobile trails head into Bridger-Teton National Forest. Some of the most popular places include the Togwotee Pass area 48 miles north of Jackson, Cache Creek Road east of town, and Granite Hot Springs Road 25 miles southeast. Only guided snowmobile groups are allowed into Yellowstone, with all-day tours around $250–270 for one rider or $350–370 for two riders. Tours to other areas are usually less expensive, and some motels offer package deals. The visitor center has brochures and a complete listing of local snowmobile-rental companies, plus maps of snowmobile trails.

Entertainment and Events

Although there are no anti-smoking ordinances, virtually all Jackson Hole restaurants and bars are now **entirely smoke-free.** The only exception is the smoky Virginian Bar on the south end of town at 750 W. Broadway. Jackson Hole Mountain Resort, Grand Targhee Resort, and Snow King Resort all prohibit smoking everywhere except in designated areas.

At the gorgeous new 525-seat theatre at **Jackson Hole Center for the Arts** (307/733-4900, www.jhcenterforthearts.org) you might see everyone from Leo Kottke and Keb Mo to the Preservation Hall Jazz Band and Willie Nelson.

NIGHTLIFE

Barflies will keep buzzing in Jackson, especially during midsummer and midwinter, when visitors pack local saloons every night of the week. At least one nightclub always seems to have live tunes; check Jackson's free newspapers to see what's where. Cover charges are generally $5 on the weekends, and most other times you'll get in free. Check out the free weekly, *Planet Jackson Hole* (307/732-0299, www.planetjh .com) for upcoming music and entertainment.

The famous **Million Dollar Cowboy Bar** (on the west side of Town Square, 307/733-2207, www.milliondollarcowboybar.com) is a favorite of real cowboys and their wannabe cousins. Inside the Cowboy you'll discover burled lodgepole pine beams, four pool tables (nearly always in use), display cases with stuffed dead bears and other cuddly critters, bars inlaid with old silver dollars, and barstools made from old saddles. Until the 1950s, the Cowboy was Jackson's center for illegal gambling. Bartenders kept a close eye on Teton Pass, where messengers used mirrors to deliver warnings of coming federal revenuers, giving folks at the bar time to hide the gaming tables in a back room. Today the dance floor fills with honky-tonking couples as the bands croon lonesome cowboy tunes six nights a week. Looking to learn swing and two-step dancing? You can join an excellent free beginners' class at 7:30 P.M. every Thursday, and then dance up a storm when the band comes on at 9.

Silver Dollar Bar & Grill (50 N. Glenwood St., 307/733-2190, www.worthotel.com) inside the Wort Hotel offers a setting that might seem more fitting in Las Vegas: Gaudy pink neon lights curve around a bar inlaid with 2,032 (count 'em!) silver dollars. It tends to attract an older crowd with nightly drink specials (best martinis in Jackson), but Tuesday nights are the notable exception, when rock bands and no cover attract a packed house of partying 20-somethings.

a packed house at Silver Dollar Bar & Grill

In Teton Village is **Mangy Moose Restaurant & Saloon** (307/733-4913, www.mangymoose.net) Jackson Hole's jumpingest pickup spot and *the* place to rock out. The Moose attracts a hip skier/outdoorsy crowd with rock, blues, or world beat bands Wednesday–Saturday both summer and winter. This is also where you'll hear nationally known acts. Call their music hotline at 307/733-9779 or find upcoming acts on the Mangy Moose website.

On the way to Teton Village, and next door to Calico Restaurant, **Q Roadhouse** (2550 Moose-Wilson Rd., 307/739-0700, www.qjacksonhole.com, daily 5–10 P.M.) is a cavernous, indestructible pub (concrete floors and an industrial décor), where the menu includes blackened catfish, shrimp jambalaya, and jerked Jamaican pork ($17–28). Throw your peanut shells on the floor and join the happy crowds of locals listening to rock tunes and putting back the beers.

Jammed against the hill on the west end of town, **Sidewinders Tavern and Sports Grill** (802 W. Broadway, 307/734-5766, www.sidewinderstavern.com, daily 11:30 A.M.–12:30 A.M.) is a bar/restaurant with pub grub (including buffalo wings, burgers, pizzas, and chicken-fried steak), 28 beers on tap, and 27 flat-screen TVs for sports enthusiasts. Look for the giant American flag out front.

Close to Snow King, the popular **43 North** (645 S. Cache, 307/733-0043, www.43northmusic.com) has live music most nights, including Monday jam sessions; cover charge on Friday and Saturday nights. At last count they had 17 beers—including all the regional brews—on draught.

The Granary (307/733-8833) atop East Gros Ventre Butte has mellow jazz and classics on Friday nights.

Over in Wilson, **The Stagecoach Bar** (307/733-4407) is *the* place to be on Sunday nights 6–10 P.M., when locals call it "the church." In the 1970s, when hippies risked getting their heads shaved by rednecks at Jackson's Cowboy Bar, they found the 'Coach a more tolerant place. Today tobacco-chewing cowpokes show their partners slick moves on the tiny dance floor as the Stagecoach Band (jokingly known as the "worst country-western band in the U.S.") runs through the country tunes one more time; the band has performed here every Sunday since 1969! Outside you'll find picnic tables and a volleyball court for pickup games in the summer, or pick up a cue stick and show off your billiard skills indoors. The Mexican-infused bar food comes from Pica's Taqueria, with burritos, tacos, quesadillas, and more. Also popular are the Thursday-night disco parties (a great time to dress up in *Saturday Night Fever* garb) and Wednesday-night reggae refrains.

Other spots with occasional live music (or DJs) are two places in Grand Teton National Park: **Spur Bar** (307/733-2415, ext. 200) at Dornan's in Moose and **Leek's Marina Restaurant** (307/543-2494) along Jackson Lake.

CLASSICAL MUSIC

In existence since 1962, the **Grand Teton Music Festival** (307/733-3050, www.gtmf .org) takes place at Walk Festival Hall in Teton Village, with performances of classical and modern works by a cast of 200 world-renowned symphony musicians. Concerts take place at 8 p.m. from the first of July to mid-August each year, with chamber music on Tuesday and Wednesday, small ensembles on Thursday, and festival orchestra concerts on Friday and Saturday ($50 adults, $10 kids). They also perform a free outdoor **Music in the Hole** patriotic concert on the Fourth of July for an audience that tops 8,000, plus special youth concerts and other events. The three-hour-long Friday morning rehearsals are just $10.

MUSICALS AND MOVIES

In addition to the bar scene, summers bring several lighthearted acting ventures to Jackson. For family musicals such as *Paint Your Wagon, Nunsense,* or *The Ballad of Cat Ballou,* head to **Jackson Hole Playhouse** (145 W. Deloney, 307/733-6994, www.jh playhouse.com). Shows take place Monday–Saturday evenings in a campy 1890s-style setting; $26 adults, $19 kids. A family saloon (no

alcohol; what kind of a saloon is that?) and restaurant are next door.

Located in the Pink Garter Plaza at 50 W. Broadway, the **Pink-Garter Theatre** (307/200-4407, www.pinkgartertheatre.com) puts on three Broadway shows each week throughout the summer, featuring such favorites as *Oklahoma* or *Singin' in the Rain.* Seats are $15–25.

A professional repertory group, the **Off Square Theatre Company** (307/733-3670, www.offsquare.org) stages Broadway comedies in the summer at the Jackson Hole Center for the Arts, with dramatic productions the rest of the year.

Watch flicks downtown at **Teton Theatre** (120 N. Cache Dr.) and **Jackson Hole Twin Cinema** (295 W. Pearl St.), or south of town at **MovieWorks** (860 S. U.S. Hwy. 89). All three of these have the same movie line: 307/733-4939. Find this week's films on the Web at www.jacksonhole.net/movies.htm.

RODEO

On Wednesday and Saturday nights in summer you can watch bucking broncs, bull riders, barrel racers, rodeo clowns, and hard-riding cowboys at the **Jackson Hole Rodeo** (307/733-2805, www.jhrodeo.com, early June–early Sept., starting at 8 p.m., $12 adults, $8 ages 4–12, free for kids under four, or $40 for the whole family) on the Teton County Fair Grounds. Kids get to join in the amusing calf scramble.

CHUCK WAGON COOKOUTS

Jackson Hole is home to several chuck wagon affairs offering all-you-can-eat barbecue cookouts and Western musical performances in the summer. Each has its own advantages, but reservations are highly recommended at all of these.

Run by the Thomas family since 1973, **Bar-T-Five** (790 Cache Creek Rd., 307/733-5386 or 800/772-5386, www.bart5.com) is one of the best chuck wagon feeds. Horse-drawn Conestoga-style wagons depart just east of Snow King, carrying visitors along Cache Creek past costumed mountain men, cowboys,

© DON PITCHER

Bar-T-Five chuck wagon

and Indians. At the in-the-trees cookout site (chicken, roast beef, salad, rolls, corn, beans, dessert, and lemonade), cowboys serenade your meal, tell stories, and crack corny jokes that aren't entirely politically correct. It's great fun for families and busloads of Japanese tourists. Rates are $42 adults, $35 ages 5–12, and free for kids under five. Open mid-May–September, with departures Monday–Saturday at 5:15 and 6:30 P.M. Reservations are recommended.

Along the Teton Village Road near Teton Pines, the **Bar J Chuckwagon** (307/733-3370 or 800/905-2275, www.barjchuckwagon.com) does a land-office business throughout the summer, with seating for over 700 people in a cavernous building, including busloads of gray-haired Gray Liners. In existence for more than 30 years, Bar J is famous for its first-rate musicians who fiddle (one is a two-time national fiddle champion), sing, yodel, and regale the audience with cornball jokes and dollops of cowboy poetry. Before the show everyone queues up for heaping servings of barbecued beef, roast chicken, pork rib, or rib-eye steak

served with baked potatoes, beans, biscuits, applesauce, spice cake, and lemonade (but no alcohol). Amazingly, Bar J manages to feed the entire crowd in a half hour. The picnic-table seating is cramped, but after dinner you're treated to 90 minutes of rollicking entertainment. The cost is $20–30 for adults (depending on your meal), $10 for kids under eight, or free for tots. Bar J is open late May–September, with dinner at 7 P.M.; many folks arrive an hour or so earlier to get front-row seats for the show. It's a good idea to make reservations at least one week ahead. The Bar J does not offer wagon or horseback rides.

In beautiful Buffalo Valley, 45 miles northeast of Jackson, **Castagno Outfitters Covered Wagon Cookouts** (307/543-2407, www.castagno outfitters.com) start with a 30-minute ride in covered wagons. The wagons stop at an isolated aspen grove, where guests enjoy a dinner of steak, BBQ beans, baked potato, corn bread, watermelon, and dessert. Dinners cost $30 adults, $25 kids, and run mid-June–late August; closed Sunday. It also has breakfast rides for $15 adults, $12 kids. Call the day before for reservations.

EVENTS

Jackson Hole is packed with entertaining events almost every day of the year. Some of these are homegrown affairs such as the county fair, whereas others attract people from near and far. Of particular note are the International Pedigree Stage Stop Sled Dog Race (IPSSSDR), the Pole-Pedal-Paddle Race, the Elk Antler Auction, the Grand Teton Music Festival, and the Jackson Hole Fall Arts Festival. (In addition to the events listed, Grand Targhee Ski Resort has a year-round calendar of events on the other side of the Tetons.)

Winter

December is a particularly beautiful time in downtown Jackson. Lights decorate the elk antler arches, and a variety of events take place. Buy arts and crafts during the **Christmas Bazaar** early in the month, or take the kids to visit Saint Nick and his elves on Town Square starting in mid-December; they're there daily 5–7 P.M.

Kick the year off by watching (or participating in) the annual **torchlight ski parades** at all three local ski areas. They take place on Christmas evening and New Year's Eve at both Jackson Hole Mountain Resort and Grand Targhee Ski Resort, and on New Year's Eve at Snow King.

In existence since 1996, the **International Pedigree Stage Stop Sled Dog Race** (IPSSSDR, pronounced IPS-der, 307/734-1163, www.wyomingstagestop.org) is the largest sled dog race in the lower 48 states and a qualifying event for Alaska's Iditarod. Unlike the Iditarod and most other mushing events, this one is run in short 30- to 60-mile legs, with teams operating from a different town each day. As with the Tour de France, it's the total time that counts in this stage race. The race is the creation of Iditarod musher Frank Teasley and nurse Jayne Ottman, who came up with the idea as a way to raise awareness of the need to immunize children; it's unofficially called "The Race to Immunize." IPSSSDR starts in

Jackson and then goes on to Lander, Pinedale, Big Piney, Alpine, Kemmerer, Evanston, and Lyman, before ending in Park City, Utah. The race boasts a $50,000 purse and has attracted some of the top names in dog mushing, including Iditarod winners Jeff King, Rick Swenson, and Susan Butcher. It's held over eight days in late January and early February.

Each February, local Shriners hold horse-drawn **cutter races** (307/733-4052)—essentially a wild chariot race on 0.25 mile of ice—at Melody Ranch, six miles south of Jackson.

In February, the **Cowboy Ski Challenge** (307/739-2770) provides a different kind of race, with skiers pulled behind a horse and rider at speeds of up to 40 miles per hour. The race takes place at the base of Jackson Hole Mountain Resort.

Ski and snowboard races take place all winter long, varying from elegant "Powder Eight" Championships in early March to blazingly fast downhill races. (Volunteer to work one of the gates at a downhill race and you get to ski free the rest of the day.)

One of the most popular (and dumbest) Jackson events is the **World Championship Snowmobile Hillclimb,** in which man (or woman) and machine churn up the slopes at Snow King Resort. The event takes place in late March.

The ski season ends the first weekend of April with the **Pole-Pedal-Paddle Race** (307/733-6433, www.polepedalpaddle.com), combining alpine skiing, cross-country skiing, cycling, and canoeing in a wild, tough competition. It's the largest such event in the West and great fun for spectators and contestants, many of whom dress up in goofy costumes.

Spring

Spring in Jackson Hole is the least favorite time of the year for many locals. The snow is going, leaving behind brown grass and trees; biking and hiking trails aren't yet passable; and the river is too cold to enjoy. For many folks, this is the time to load up the car and head to Utah for a desert hike in Canyonlands. Despite these conditions, April and May can be a good time to visit, especially if you want to avoid the crowds, need to save money on lodging, or are planning to stay for the summer and need a job and a place to live. (Housing gets progressively more difficult to find after April.)

Summer

Summer begins with a series of events during **Elkfest** (307/733-3316, www.elkfest.org) on the third weekend of May, including a **mountain-man rendezvous** and chili cook-off. The main event, however, is the world's only public **elk antler auction,** which attracts hundreds of buyers from all over the globe to Jackson's Town Square. Local Boy Scouts collect five tons of antlers from the nearby National Elk Refuge each spring, with 80 percent of the proceeds helping to fund feeding of the elk. This may sound like an odd event, but the take is more than $60,000! Prices average $11 per pound, and the bidding gets highly competitive; perfectly matched pairs can go for more than $1,500. The antlers are primarily used in taxidermy, belt buckles, and furniture.

Memorial Day weekend brings **Old West Days** (307/733-3316), complete with a mountain-man rendezvous, horse-drawn parade, brew fest, carriage show, and antler crafts fair. The **Jackson Hole Film Festival** (307/733-8144, www.jhff.org) showcases dozens of independent films, shorts, and world premiers for five days in early June. Later that same month, the **Jackson Hole Writers Conference** (307/413-3332, www.jacksonholewritersconference.com) attracts nationally known authors and wannabes to the Center for the Arts.

Fourth of July is another big event in Jackson, with a parade, rodeo, and an impressive fireworks show from Snow King Mountain. Another very popular Independence Day event is the free **Music in the Hole** (307/733-1128, www.gtmf.org) outdoor classical concert by the Grand Teton Music Festival orchestra.

If you have a burning desire for something hot, don't miss the **Jackson Hole Fire Festival** on summer solstice (June 21), when the city partners with Fujiyoshida, Japan. You'll see traditional Japanese drumming, dancing, and street torches.

The **Jackson Hole Rodeo** (307/733-2805, www.jhrodeo.com) brings spills and thrills to town, with Wednesday and Saturday night rodeos all summer. Another ongoing event is the **Grand Teton Music Festival** (307/733-3050, www.gtmf.org), providing summertime classical music at Teton Village. (These latter two activities are detailed in the earlier section.)

The **Art Fair of Jackson Hole** (307/733-8792, www.jhartfair.org) features 170 artisans displaying their works at Miller Park. This highly competitive, juried event takes place in mid-July and again in mid-August.

The last week of July brings an always fun **Teton County Fair** (307/733-5289, www .tetoncountyfair.com) with 4-H exhibits (from lambs to photography), pig wrestling in the mud, a horse show, pony rides and a petting farm, watermelon- and pie-eating contests, live music and comedy acts, a carnival, rodeos, and everyone's favorite: a bang-up **demolition derby** on the final Sunday night.

In mid-August the **Jackson Hole Music Festival** (www.festivalnetwork.com/jhmf) brings such alt-rock favorites as The Black Crowes, Ben Harper, Son Volt, and Wilco to Teton Village for two days of partying.

During the second weekend of September, the invitation-only **Jackson Hole One-Fly Contest** (307/733-3270 or 800/570-3270, www.jhonefly.com) attracts anglers from all over, including several celebrity competitors. Another charity event is **Old Bill's Fun Run** (307/739-1026, www.oldbills.org) the second Saturday of September; it's raised more than $50 million over the last decade or so!

Fall

Jackson Hole is at its most glorious in the fall, as aspens and cottonwoods turn into a fire of yellow and orange against the Teton backdrop. Most tourists have fled back home, leaving locals and hardier visitors to savor the cool autumn nights. The peak time for **fall colors** is generally the first week of October— considerably later than most people expect.

The primary autumn event is the **Jackson Hole Fall Arts Festival** (307/733-3316, www.jacksonholechamber.com/events), which takes place over a 17-day period in September. Featured activities include exhibits at the National Museum of Wildlife Art and local galleries, a juried art fair, art auction, Western fashion and furniture shows, a miniature art show, cowboy poetry and old-time cowboy music, "Taste of the Tetons" with delectable food from local restaurants, and tours of historic ranches. Also fun is a "quickdraw" in which artists paint, draw, and sculpt while you watch; the pieces are then auctioned off.

In early October, **Quilting in the Tetons** (307/733-3087, www.quiltthetetons.org) brings a week of exhibits, classes, workshops, and quilting demonstrations.

Shopping

If you have the money (or a credit card), Jackson is a great place to buy everything from artwork to mountain bikes. Even if you just hitchhiked in and have no cash to spare, it's always fun to wander through the shops and galleries surrounding Town Square.

Fans of classic Old West furniture should not miss **Fighting Bear Antiques** (375 S. Cache, 307/733-2669 or 866/690-2669, www.fightingbear.com), famed for its collection of Thomas Molesworth pieces. Owner Terry Winchell literally wrote the book on this creator of uniquely American furniture.

Lots of T-shirt places in town, but **Lee's Tees** (80 W. Broadway, 307/733-6671, www.leestees.com) sells the high-quality versions.

OUTDOOR GEAR

Outdoor enthusiasts will discover several excellent shops in Jackson. Climbers, backpackers, and cross-country skiers head to America's oldest climbing shop, **Teton Mountaineering** (170 N. Cache Dr., 307/733-3595 or 800/850-3595, www.tetonmtn.com), for quality equipment, maps, and travel guides. They also rent tents, sleeping bags, pads, backpacks, climbing shoes, crampons, and ice axes in the summer, along with snowshoes, cross-country skis, telemark, and alpine touring skis in winter. Check the bulletin board for used items.

Jack Dennis' Outdoor Shop (50 E. Broadway, 307/733-3270 or 800/570-3270, www.jackdennis.com) is a large upscale store with fly-fishing and camping gear in summer and skis and warm clothes during winter. The store also rents almost anything: tents, stoves, lanterns, cookware, sleeping bags, fishing poles, fly rods, waders, float tubes, backpacks, skis, snowboards, snowshoes, and more.

Skinny Skis (65 W. Deloney Ave., 307/733-6094 or 888/733-7205, www.skinnyskis.com) has more in the way of high-quality clothing and supplies, especially cross-country ski gear. Rent sleeping bags, tents, climbing shoes, ice axes, baby carriers, and backpacks here. The same folks run the summer-only **Moosely Seconds** (307/739-1801) in Moose, with climbing and outdoor gear, along with rentals of trekking poles, ice axes, crampons, rock shoes, approach shoes, plastic boots, and snowshoes.

Another place to rent outdoor gear of all types—including volleyball sets, fishing gear, float tubes, tents, sleeping bags, backpacks, camp stoves, and lanterns—is **Leisure Sports** (1075 S. U.S. Hwy. 89, 307/733-3040, www.leisuresportsadventure.com).

Gart Sports (485 W. Broadway, 307/733-4449, www.gartsports.com) is a large store with a variety of outdoor and sports gear. The least expensive place to buy rugged outdoor wear, cowboy boots, and cowboy hats is **Corral West** (840 W. Broadway, 307/733-0247, www.corralwest.com).

BARGAINS

Buy used clothing and other items at **Browse 'N Buy Thrift Shop** (139 N. Cache Dr., 307/733-7524) or the more chaotic **Orville's** (385 N. Cache Dr., 307/733-2684).

BOOKS

Unlike many Wyoming towns where the book selection consists of a few bodice-buster romance novels in the local pharmacy, Jackson is blessed with several fine bookstores. **Valley Bookstore** (125 N. Cache Dr., 307/733-4533, .valleybook.com) is the largest local bookshop, with a big choice of regional titles, plus occasional author signings and readings. **Main Event** (980 W. Broadway, 307/733-7112) in the Powderhorn Mall sells new books and CDs and rents videos. A few doors away in the mall is **Jackson Hole Book Traders** (307/734-6001 or 800/722-2710, www.jacksonholebook traders.com), with a surprising selection of used and rare books. Up in Grand Teton National Park, find natural-history books and maps at the **Craig Thomas Discovery and Visitor Center** (307/739-3399) and **Colter Bay Indian Arts Museum** (307/543-2467).

Accommodations

As one of the premier centers for tourism in Wyoming, Jackson Hole is jam-packed with more than 70 different motels, hotels, and B&Bs, plus many more condominiums and guest ranches. Other lodging can be found just to the north within or near Grand Teton National Park. The Jackson Hole Chamber of Commerce's website (www .jacksonholechamber.com) has brief descriptions and Web links for most local places.

Because of the town's popularity, Jackson accommodations command premium prices. With a few exceptions, you'll pay at least $100 d during the peak visitor seasons of July–August and late December–early January. Rates can drop more than 50 percent in the off-season, so if you can visit March–May or late September–mid-December, you'll save a lot of cash. (The same Super 8 Motel rooms that go for $199 in July cost just $65 in early November!) In the town of Jackson, the highest rates are usually in July and August, while at Teton Village, skiers and snowboarders send room rates to their peak between mid-December and early January. You will need to add a 6 percent sales tax to all the lodging rates below.

Reservations are highly recommended. For midsummer, book rooms at least two months ahead, or longer if you really want to be certain of a place. During the Christmas–New Year's period you should probably reserve six months in advance to ensure a spot. Summer weekends tend to be the most crowded, with many families driving up from Salt Lake City for a cooling break in the mountains.

If you're overwhelmed by all the lodging choices, try one of the reservation services, such as **Jackson Hole Central Reservations** (307/733-4005 or 800/443-6931, www.jackson holewy.com). Looking for other opinions? Head online to Tripadvisor (www.tripadvisor .com) for reviews of many Jackson Hole lodging places.

HOTELS AND MOTELS
Under $100

Jackson's least-expensive option, the **Bunkhouse** (307/733-3668 or 800/234-4507, www.anvilmotel.com) is in the basement of the Anvil Motel (215 North Cache Drive). Right in town, the year-round hostel generally has space, but get there early in the peak of summer to be sure. It costs $25 per person and includes a TV room and a kitchen with a refrigerator and microwave and hotplate (but no dishes). The big sleeping room contains 11 twin beds with linen, towels, and adjacent storage lockers; bring your own lock. No kids under 16. Although men's and women's showers and restrooms are separate, the sleeping space is coed. It can get pretty noisy with all those snoring bodies in one room at night, so earplugs are a smart buy. Check in after 3 P.M. and be out by 11 A.M. Alcohol is not allowed, but there is no curfew. No advance reservations (except for groups of 10 or more), but you can call the day

JACKSON HOLE

of your arrival to reserve a bed. Hostel guests also have access to the Anvil Motel hot tub, upstairs. Backpackers and others who aren't staying here can take showers for $6.

Despite the name, **The Hostel** (307/733-3415, www.thehostel.us) really isn't a hostel, though it does provide budget rates in a scenic location. Private rooms cost $89 s or d, or $99 for up to four people. The very small plain-vanilla rooms lack TV or phones, but there's a central lounge for camaraderie and Wi-Fi for $5 more. The lounge includes a TV, pay phones, pool table, table tennis, a children's play area, fireplace, microwave, games, Wi-Fi, and ski-waxing room. Because of its Teton Village location at the foot of Jackson Hole Mountain Resort, The Hostel is very popular with skiers on a budget, so reserve three months ahead for midwinter rooms. Winter stays require a five-night minimum stay. Space is typically available in the summer, with no minimum stay.

Two older motels—The Cottages at Snow King and Alpine Motel—offer the cheapest rates in town and have the same owners. Both are located in quiet residential areas, but they don't take advance reservations and are often booked up by summertime workers. They're a good last-minute option if you roll into town without reservations and not a lot of cash. No cottages at **The Cottages at Snow King** (470 King St., 307/733-3480, $78–88 d), but the modest rooms include a queen bed, fridge, and microwave. Pets are welcome at no extra charge. **Alpine Motel** (70 S. Jean St., 307/739-3200, $88 d) is just a few blocks from Town Square. The furnishings may not be the newest, but rooms are clean, and a small outdoor pool (heated but seasonal) is on the premises. Both motels rent rooms only on a monthly basis October–April.

One of Jackson's better deals for standard motel rooms is—not surprisingly—**Motel 6** (1370 W. Broadway, 307/733-1620 or 800/466-8356, www.motel6.com, $100 d), but even here the summertime rates are high. You'll find humdrum rooms and an outdoor pool; reserve six months in advance for July

and August. Off-season prices ($52 d) are a much better bargain.

Family owned ⟨ **Kudar's Motel** (260 N. Cache Dr., 307/733-2823, $85 d) is a holdover from a quieter era when Jackson's motels were simple and unpretentious. You'll find 14 basic motel units with king beds and TVs; three contain the original 1950s furnishings. Of considerably more interest are Kudar's 17 rustic but nicely maintained and spotless log cabins. Built in 1938, these go for $100–120 d, and the larger two-room cabins can sleep five. No phones in any of the units, but the cabins contain fridges and microwaves, and Wi-Fi works in most rooms. There's air conditioning in all units except five cabins now on the National Register of Historic Places. Travelers love Kudar's, with many returning year after year, including some who've returned annually since the 1950s. Open early May–early October.

$100-200

Many Jackson accommodations fall in the $100–200 range, with pricing factors being location, type of room, quality of furnishings, and presence of amenities such as pools and hot tubs. Several comfortable midrange options are described as follows. These are not the corporate lodging giants, but they offer good value and down-home friendliness.

Downtown: Justifiably popular with families, **Elk Country Inn** (480 W. Pearl, 307/733-2364 or 800/483-8667, www.elkcountryinn.com) is a fine option. Spacious motel rooms with two queen beds are $134 s or $140 d, or choose a room with three queen beds (one in an upstairs loft) for $160 d or $184 for six guests. Add $10 to these prices for a kitchenette unit. A luxury suite with a king bed and kitchen is $210 d. Out back are two-dozen modern log cabins with full kitchenettes (including dishes) and lodgepole furnishings: $194 d or $204 for four. Guests appreciate the indoor hot tub, shady picnic area with a small playground, Wi-Fi, morning fruit and coffee, plus a free wintertime shuttle to Teton Village. Elk Country is one of the better bargains in Jackson.

At **Anvil Motel** (215 N. Cache Dr.,

307/733-3668 or 800/234-4507, www.anvil motel.com), $128 d gets you a little room with one queen, or pay $148 for up to four people in a larger unit with two queen beds. Two suites ($192 and $310) are also available, and all rooms here have microwaves and small fridges, along with Wi-Fi and access to the outdoor hot tub.

Ranch Inn (45 E. Pearl St., 307/733-6363 or 800/348-5599, www.ranchinn.com) offers a wide variety of accommodations just one block off Town Square. These include standard rooms ($115 d), tower rooms with balconies facing Snow King, fridges, and microwaves ($170 d), and suites with king beds, wood-burning fireplaces, balconies, and jetted tubs ($190–195 d). Amenities include indoor and outdoor hot tubs, Wi-Fi, plus a continental breakfast. Some of the tower rooms are wheelchair-accessible.

Golden Eagle Inn (325 E. Broadway, 307/733-2042 or 888/748-6937, www.golden eagleinn.com) is a quiet out-of-the-way family motel with standard rooms for $135 d, and larger rooms for $148–191 d. All include microwaves, small refrigerators, Wi-Fi, and access to a heated outdoor pool. Adjacent is a two-bedroom house with a full kitchen that sleeps four for $290. Same owner at **Four Winds Motel** (150 N. Millward St., 307/733-2474 or 800/228-6461, www.jacksonholefour winds.com, $120 d), just a few blocks from Town Square and across the street from a city park (with a popular children's playground). Nothing-fancy rooms, but they're exceptionally clean and affordably priced. Free Wi-Fi. Both Golden Eagle and Four Winds are open April–November.

A couple of blocks off Town Square, cozy **Anglers Inn** (265 N. Millward St., 307/733-3682 or 800/867-4667, www.anglers inn.net, $130–150 d) has pleasant rooms with Western-style fixtures, lodgepole beds and chairs, and small baths. All rooms contain fridges, microwaves, and free Wi-Fi access.

Find a diverse mixture of room styles at **Jackson Hole Lodge** (420 W. Broadway, 307/733-2992 or 800/604-9404, www .jacksonholelodge.com), where featured attractions are a large indoor swimming pool, wading pool, two hot tubs, sauna, and game room on attractive grounds. Standard motel rooms cost $129 d. Condo-type units are much nicer, with an upscale decor that includes log furniture; $169 for a studio unit, $269 for a one-bedroom unit (sleeps four to six) with a living room, fireplace, and full kitchen. Two-bedroom units cost $329 for up to eight people. A computer is available in the lobby, which also has free Wi-Fi.

Located in a peaceful neighborhood six blocks from Town Square, family-owned **Buckrail Lodge** (110 E. Karns Ave., 307/733-2079, www.buckraillodge.com) has faux-log-cabin units on immaculate park-like grounds; portions of Clint Eastwood's *Any Which Way You Can* were filmed here. Relax in the large outdoor hot tub, and plunk down for the night in one of the dozen lovingly maintained motel rooms ($125 d with two queen beds, or $100 d with one queen), all decorated with Western-style furnishings. No in-room phones (you're probably carrying a cell phone anyway), and the walls are thin, but baths are spacious and guests can use the computer in the lobby or open a laptop to find free Wi-Fi. Buckrail is closed mid-October–April.

Antler Inn (50 W. Pearl Ave., 307/733-2535 or 800/522-2406, www.townsquareinns.com) is a large property with 110 rooms just one block off Town Square. Most contain two queen beds and cost $140 d, but also available are a dozen large family rooms/suites ($180) with three beds and space for six people. Most of these have wood-burning fireplaces. Rounding out the options are attractive (but small) log-walled rooms for $125 d. All guests have access to Wi-Fi, plus access to the exercise room, sauna, and large indoor hot tub. There's a free winter shuttle to Teton Village.

Rawhide Motel (75 S. Millward St., 307/733-1216 or 800/835-2999, www.raw hidemotel.com, $145 d) is a fine midtown place with large rooms containing handmade lodgepole furniture, plus Wi-Fi and fridges. Open May–October.

The rooms are a bit cramped, but guests appreciate the friendly service and extra touches at **Sundance Inn** (135 W. Broadway, 307/733-3444 or 888/478-6326, www.sundance innjackson.com). The motel is close to Town Square and serves a light homemade breakfast plus evening cookies and lemonade. Guests can also use the outdoor hot tub (with alleyway ambience, alas). Standard rooms cost $139 d, while two-room suites are $199 for up to four people. Wireless Internet is available in the lobby and most rooms.

On the north side of town, **Cache Creek Motel** (390 N. Glenwood, 307/733-7781 or 800/843-4788, www.cachecreekmotel.com) is another well-kept, moderately priced choice. All rooms include full kitchens (with dishes and pans). Standard rooms start at $125 d, with two-bedroom suites that sleep up to six for $150.

A large heart-of-town place is **49'er Inn and Suites/Quality Inn** (330 W. Pearl, 307/733-7550 or 800/451-2980, www.49erinn .com) with 142 rooms spread across several buildings. Standard rooms have two queen beds and a nothing-special decor for $155 d. Newer and considerably nicer are five-person units with kitchenettes for $195–225; some include fireplaces. Two luxury suites—with hot tub and fireplace—are available for $329 d. All guests have access to outdoor and indoor hot tubs, sauna, and exercise room, plus a continental breakfast and free Wi-Fi.

Outside Downtown: On the south end of Jackson at the Y intersection of highways 89 and 22, **Pony Express West Motel** (1075 W. Broadway, 307/733-3835 or 800/526-2658, www.ponyexpresswest.com) is a good family option. Kitchen units with a queen bed are $115 d, while family units with a queen bed and a bunk bed for the kids, plus microwave and fridge cost $135. Free Wi-Fi, but the main attraction is a heated outdoor pool. Open May–September.

Right across the highway from Pony Express, **Teton Gables Motel** (1140 W. Broadway, 307/733-3723, www.tetongables.com, $110 d) is another reasonably priced place with older

rooms, all with microwaves, fridges, and free Wi-Fi. Open May–mid-November.

With 170 guest rooms, **Virginian Lodge** (750 W. Broadway, 307/733-2792 or 800/262-4999, www.virginianlodge.com) is one of the larger local motels. The rooms cluster around a grassy central space with a seasonal heated pool, year-round hot tub, and Wi-Fi in the lobby. A variety of ho-hum rooms are available, including standard units for $109 d, kitchenette suites for $150 d, Jacuzzi suites for $190 d, and two-bedroom suites for $211 d. Virginian RV Park is right behind the motel.

Two mid-priced motels are adjacent to each other and one mile north of Jackson on U.S. 89. Both face the Elk Refuge (and the busy highway). **Elk Refuge Inn** (307/733-3582 or 800/544-3582, www.elkrefugeinn.com) is the smaller and more homey of the two, with a mixture of rooms and friendly management, plus corrals where horses can be boarded. Rates are $160 d for downstairs rooms or $196 for upstairs units with kitchenettes and private balconies. A six-person family unit is $226. All rooms include drive-up access, fridges, microwaves, continental breakfast, and computer access.

Flat Creek Inn (307/733-5276 or 800/438-9338, www.flatcreekinn.com) is a large two-level motel just a few hundred feet north of Elk Refuge Inn. Rooms are functionally furnished, with microwaves and small fridges. Standard rooms are an affordable $131 d or $158–169 for up to four guests, while spacious kitchenettes cost $199 for up to five. A continental breakfast and Wi-Fi are included. Three suites ($169–299) are more spacious, and the largest includes a separate bedroom with king bed, kitchen, flat screen TV, and other comforts. Guests in the suites have access to an indoor hot tub, and all guests get a continental breakfast and Wi-Fi.

Teton Village: In the heart of Teton Village action, **Village Center Inn** (307/733-3990 or 800/443-8613, www.jhrl.com) charges $170 d for studio or loft units and $230 for two-bedroom units that sleep six. All units include full kitchens, but no Wi-Fi (though it's available nearby). Peak-season winter rates rise to $250 d for a one-bedroom unit, up to $330 for two bedrooms. The decor is fairly utilitarian, but other than The Hostel, this is the cheapest Teton Village accommodation.

Over $200

It should come as no surprise that tony Jackson Hole has several elaborate, pricey, and sumptuous places to stay, with rooms starting around $200 and hitting the stratosphere at $4,000 per night!

Downtown: Close to Town Square, the **Wort Hotel** (50 N. Glenwood St., 307/733-2190 or 800/322-2727, www.worthotel.com) has been a Jackson favorite since 1941. A disastrous 1980 fire—started by a bird that built a nest too close to a neon sign—destroyed the roof and upper floor. The hotel was completely restored within a year, and today it's better than ever, with such amenities as a fitness center, valet parking, Wi-Fi, business center, and two small hot tubs. The lobby, with its grand central staircase and stone fireplace with crackling fire, makes a fine place to meet friends. The Silver Dollar Bar and Grill serves meals, or you can sidle up to the famous curving bar—inlaid with 2,032 uncirculated silver dollars from 1921. The Wort's spacious rooms are attractively decorated with a New West motif that includes lodgepole-pine beds and creative fixtures. Rates are $339 d for standard rooms (with two queens or one king bed), or $379 d for larger and more luxurious rooms. Spacious junior suites with king beds and wet bars cost $449, while the luxury suite will set you back $769 d.

Greatly expanded and updated in the last few years **Trapper Inn** (235 N. Cache Dr., 307/733-2648 or 888/771-2648, www .trapperinn.com) sprawls across four buildings with very comfortable guest rooms and a friendly staff. Large units with two queen beds or one king bed are $219 d, while two-room suites cost $269 d, or $289 d for units with kitchenettes; add $12 for each additional adult. Other amenities include an indoor family pool and hot tub, light breakfast, small fridges

and microwaves in rooms, a computer in the lobby, and Wi-Fi.

An outstanding in-town choice is **Parkway Inn** (125 N. Jackson St., 307/733-3143 or 800/247-8390, www.parkwayinn.com). This immaculate, midsize lodge has a delightful Victorian ambience with antique furniture and quilts in many rooms, along with jetted tubs and flat-screen TVs in the some units. Guests will also enjoy a small indoor lap pool, two hot tubs, two saunas, and a gym in the basement, along with Wi-Fi. A light breakfast is served in the lobby. Rates are $239–259 d for standard rooms with two queen beds or a king bed, $299 for larger suites, or $329 d for two-room suites; $25 each for additional guests (maximum of four per room).

An excellent nine-room lodge just a few blocks from Town Square, **Inn on the Creek** (295 N. Millward, 307/739-1565 or 800/669-9534, www.innonthecreek.com) has a peaceful location beside Flat Creek. Standard rooms ($199 d) feature designer furnishings and down comforters. The deluxe rooms ($309 d) also include fireplaces and in-room hot tubs, while a gorgeous suite ($509) sleeps four and has a full kitchen, jetted tub, and private patio. A light breakfast is delivered to your door each morning, and all guests have access to the outdoor hot tub facing the creek. Free Wi-Fi is available, along with a guest computer.

Another downtown option is **Grand Victorian Lodge** (85 Perry Ave., 307/739-2294 or 800/584-0532, www.grandvictorianlodge .com), a "boutique hotel with a bed and breakfast ambience." Choose from standard rooms ($189–199 d), deluxe rooms ($279–299 d), or a large two-room suite ($339 d) that features a four-poster king bed, jetted tub, and gas fireplace. A delicious full breakfast is a morning highlight, and guests can relax in the outdoor hot tub or surf the Web wirelessly. Closed during November and April.

You'll find outdoorsy owners at **Alpine House Country Inn** (285 N. Glenwood, 307/739-1570 or 800/753-1421, www.alpine house.com); both Hans and Nancy Johnstone were skiers for U.S. Olympic teams and are highly knowledgeable about adventure options in the Tetons. The modern timber-frame lodge is just two blocks from Jackson's Town Square and has 22 guest rooms in two connected buildings. Both are bright and modern, accented by Swedish-style stenciling on the walls. All rooms have private balconies and deep soaking tubs, plus access to the outdoor hot tub and a central computer and Wi-Fi. A healthy full breakfast is served. Rates are $175 d in the original rooms (no TV or air conditioning), or $215–260 d in the new building, which also features gas fireplaces in most rooms. The two suites cost $295 for up to four guests. Closed in November and April.

The acclaimed (C Rusty Parrot Lodge and Spa (175 N. Jackson, 307/733-2000 or 888/739-1749, www.rustyparrot.com) has sumptuous accommodation just two blocks from Town Square. The 31 rooms are highlighted with handcrafted furniture, original artwork, oversize tubs, and goose-down comforters; some also contain wood-burning fireplaces or jetted tubs. An unforgettable breakfast—it's never the same—is served each morning in the cozy dining room, and guests can relax in the hot tub on a deck overlooking Jackson, borrow a book from the library, or pamper themselves with a massage, aromatherapy session, or facial from Body Sage Spa (extra charges). Rates are $405 d for standard rooms, or $750 d for the luxurious master suite. No children under age 12. The lodge also serves epicurean dinners at Wild Sage Restaurant each evening. It doesn't get much better than this.

One of Jackson's newest and fanciest lodging places is **Homewood Suites by Hilton** (207 N. Millward St., 307/739-0808 or 800/225-5466, www.homewoodsuites.com, $319–389 d). All units are two-room suites with separate living and sleeping areas, top-of-the-line beds, a fireplace, two TVs and phones, free airport shuttle, an indoor pool, fitness center, and hot tub, plus fully equipped kitchens, Wi-Fi, and a big breakfast buffet. Guests are served light dinner entrées and salads Monday–Thursday.

Southside: Days Inn of Jackson Hole (1280 W. Broadway, 307/733-0033 or 800/329-7466, www.daysinnjacksonhole .com) has comfortable rooms at the south end of town. Standard rooms cost $169 d, while Western-style suites with fireplaces and hot tubs go for $209–219 d. Amenities include a light breakfast, large hot tub, sauna, Wi-Fi, guest computers, ski-racks, plus microwaves and fridges in most rooms.

A modern hotel with an ostentatious lobby and southside location, **Wyoming Inn of Jackson Hole** (930 W. Broadway, 307/734-0035 or 800/844-0035, www .wyoming-inn.com) has large and comfortable rooms for $300 d, including a big breakfast. The finest rooms ($380 d) also include fireplaces and jetted tubs. Guests appreciate Wi-Fi, guest computers, and airport shuttle, all at no extra charge.

A three-story building sandwiched between strip malls on the south end of Jackson, **The Lodge at Jackson Hole (Best Western)** (80 S. Scott La., 307/739-9703 or 800/458-3866, www.lodgeatjh.com) has big guest rooms featuring fridges, microwaves, safes, Wi-Fi, and two queen beds (or a king) for $279 d. Hotel guests are treated to a buffet breakfast, a unique indoor/outdoor heated pool, hot tubs, and a sauna, plus access to the Jackson Hole Athletic Club and a free winter shuttle to Teton Village.

Log Cabin Motels

Several local motels offer log-cabin accommodations for a step back to the Old West while keeping such newer amenities as televisions, private baths, and Wi-Fi.

Set amid tall cottonwood trees along Flat Creek, **Rustic Inn** (475 N. Cache Dr., 307/733-2357 or 800/323-9279, www.rustic innatjh.com) has a mixture of cozy log cabins, log motel units, and newer log-sided units. Old timers remember these as Wagon Wheel Village, a funky place that underwent a major transformation in 2008. Seventy-five of the original structures remain, with 70 brand new ones added. Unfortunately, prices were jacked up dramatically, even for the historic cabins. Check their website for specifics on all the cabin choices, ranging from older cabins containing two queen beds and a fireplace for $339 d, larger ones with flat-screen TVs, fridges, and microwaves for $389 d, up to the "superior" new cabins with private decks, rain showers, flat-screen TVs, and king beds for $459 d. Add $10 per person for additional guests (max four). All guests have access to the sauna, gym, outdoor pool, and hot tub, plus Wi-Fi, concierge service, and a hot breakfast.

Near a busy Jackson intersection, **Cowboy Village Resort** (120 Flat Creek Dr., 307/733-3121 or 800/962-4988, www.cowboy village.com) has 82 modern but jammed-together cabins with kitchenettes and sleeper sofas. The cabins cost $158 for up to four people in a studio unit with two queen bunk beds, or $188 for a cabin with a separate bedroom (one king or two queens). Two hotel rooms are available, one with a king bed for $188 d, and a larger unit with two queens, a bunk bed, and full kitchen; $238 for up to six. Guests have access to a covered outdoor pool, an inside hot tub, office computer, and Wi-Fi. In winter a continental breakfast is available, along with a free shuttle to Teton Village.

Other motels with log cabins units include Elk Country Inn and Kudar's Motel; both described above. Additional places with cabins—including Hatchet Resort, Anne Kent Cabins, Moulton Ranch on Historic Mormon Row, and Budges' Slide Lake Cabins—are described under *Accommodations* in the *Grand Teton* chapter.

TETON VILLAGE LODGING

If you're looking for beautifully appointed accommodations in Teton Village instead of downtown Jackson, you can't go wrong at ◖ **Snake River Lodge and Spa** (307/732-6000 or 800/445-4655, www .snakeriverlodge.com). The lodge features a New West–style lobby with stone fireplaces and whimsically carved bears, plus rooms that follow the theme with rustic lamps, pine furniture, and colorful prints. A distinctive free-form indoor/outdoor heated pool has a cascading waterfall, and other attractions

include indoor and outdoor hot tubs, a sauna, ski lockers, a ski-in concierge service, Wi-Fi, and a five-story spa and health club with exercise equipment, facials, manicures, hydrotherapy, massages, soaking tubs, and steam baths. Peak-season summertime rates are $395–579 d in the guest rooms, $715 d for a one-bedroom suite or condo, up to a $1,155 for a three-bedroom unit. Peak winter rates run $405–619 for guest rooms, $1,095 for a suite or one-bedroom condo, up to $2,650 nightly for three-bedroom units. Add a $25 per night resort fee to all the rates. Snake River Lodge is owned by RockResorts.

Alpenhof Lodge (307/733-3242 or 800/732-3244, www.alpenhoflodge.com) exudes a European ambience, and its owners come from Switzerland and Germany. Summertime rates start at $229 d for the simplest rooms on the top floor with sloping ceilings, or $289–379 for rooms with Bavarian furnishings and space for four guests. A two-room suite is $539. Peak winter ski-season rates are $279–649 d. Guests have access to the heated year-round outdoor pool, hot tub, sauna, Wi-Fi, and guest computer. The resident golden retrievers are a bonus.

Another Teton Village option with the same management, **The Inn at Jackson Hole/Best Western** (307/733-2311 or 800/842-7666, www.innatjh.com) has standard rooms with log furnishings at $249 d, and units with kitchenettes and fireplaces for $279 d. Add $10 per person for additional adults. Family-friendly loft suites with fireplaces and kitchenettes cost $379 for up to six guests. Guests can use the hotel's outdoor heated pool and hot tub, sauna, and ski lockers. There's an upscale restaurant and Wi-Fi.

Four Seasons Resort (307/732-5000 or 800/732-5000, www.fourseasons.com/ jacksonhole) includes a 124-room luxury hotel with ski-in access, an elegant restaurant (Westbank Grill), après-ski bar for slope-side drinks, gorgeous outdoor heated pool, three whirlpools, full health club, spa, and concierge all under one roof. Summertime rates start at $800 d for not-so-standard, standard rooms—which come with a king bed, marble bath and soaking tub, in-room safe, minibar, private terrace or gas fireplace—all the way up to $4,600 for the presidential suite. At 2,200 square feet, it's bigger than many houses. A full breakfast is included during the summer.

Another of Jackson Hole's up-market lodging options, **Teton Mountain Lodge** (307/734-7111 or 800/801-6615, www.teton lodge.com) sits at the base of the mountain in Teton Village. The lodge offers an impressive array of amenities and services: indoor and outdoor heated pools, hot tubs (including an adults-only version on the rooftop), a fitness center/spa, concierge service, valet parking, Wi-Fi, and underground parking. Guests can choose lodge rooms or studios for $329–339 d, or one-, two-, or three-bedroom suites for $679–1,530 d, all the way up to the penthouse suite for $2,030 nightly.

The newest high-end lodge in Teton Village, **Hotel Terra** (307/739-4000 or 800/631-6281, www.hotelterrajacksonhole.com), has a splashy modern design with an eco-boutique emphasis. Rooms are sumptuously appointed, with organic cotton sheets and bathrobes, Wi-Fi, safes, twice-daily maid service, and all sorts of techie treats, from "rain showers" in the bath and in-floor heating to iPod docking stations and flat-screen TVs. Guests have access to the pools, fitness center, and hot tubs at adjacent Teton Mountain Lodge (same owners). Standard rooms are $319 d, studios with kitchens cost $339 d, and suites start at $495 d, up to a magnificent three-bedroom suite for $1,335.

RESORTS

At the base of Jackson's in-town ski hill, and just a few blocks from downtown, **Snow King Resort** (400 E. Snow King Ave., 307/733-5200 or 800/522-5464, www.snowking.com) includes more than 200 hotel rooms and 130 condos, plus such amenities as a year-round heated outdoor pool and two hot tubs, a sauna, an exercise facility, restaurants facing the slopes, a bar, a concierge, a business center (with Internet access), game room, spa, and Wi-Fi. Additional condos, a spa, and an upscale restaurant open

in 2009. A free shuttle provides connections to the airport and Teton Village (winters), and guests receive discounted passes for Snow King Ski Area. The lodge offers reasonable ski-and-stay packages, starting around $600 d for three nights of lodging, plus breakfasts and two days of skiing (add $360 to this for the holiday season). When the snow is gone, Snow King is a popular destination for meetings, offering 40,000 square feet of conference space. A winter ice rink is close by, and in summer a slide and miniature golf course attract the kids. The main resort building has a 1970s feel, but guest rooms are comfortable and updated. Hotel rooms at Snow King cost $260 d in the summer, and condos start at $220 d, up to an ultraluxurious three-bedroom Love Ridge condo that will set you back $720 per night.

Some of the most dramatic vistas of the Tetons are from the luxurious **Spring Creek Ranch** (307/733-8833 or 800/443-6139, www .springcreekranch.com). On a 1,000-acre estate, the resort sits high atop Gros Ventre Butte four miles west of Jackson and includes a wide range of lodging options. Hotel rooms and studios are $340 d in the summer, and two-bedroom suites cost $360 for four people. One-bedroom condos run $410 d; two- and three-bedroom condos range from $575 to $1,000 nightly, with the largest sleeping eight comfortably. Also available are executive four-bedroom homes (one covers 6,300 square feet!) that cost a mere $2,250 per night. All rooms at Spring Creek Ranch contain fireplaces and lodgepole furnishings, and the condos and studios include full kitchens. Other amenities include a private pond, tennis courts, an outdoor pool, hot tub, fitness center, and day spa with massage and other offerings (for a fee).

Four miles south of Teton Village, **Teton Pines Resort and Country Club** (307/733-1005 or 800/238-2223, www.teton pines.com) features the amenities you'd expect in a year-round resort, including an 18-hole golf course, tennis center, and classy restaurant. The accommodations are varied, but all include a continental breakfast, access to the outdoor pool and hot tub, athletic-club privileges, concierge

© DON PITCHER

Spring Creek Ranch

service, and an airport shuttle. Most of the resort's condos are now privately owned, but two large (2,100-square-foot) three-bedroom town houses are offered on a nightly basis. Each includes a kitchen, dining room, two decks, three baths, a fireplace, hot tub, washer, dryer, and attached garage. These sleep up to eight for $1,050 per night. Golf packages are also available.

Atop Gros Ventre Butte near Spring Creek Ranch is stunning **Amangani** (307/734-7333 or 877/734-7333, www.amangani.com) the only representative of Amanresorts in America. (Most of the company's other lavish resorts are in Southeast Asia.) Aman groupies and business travelers know to expect the utmost in luxury, and they will certainly not be disappointed here, starting with dressed-in-black employees and spare-no-expenses construction. Guests who come here expect pampering, and the somewhat snooty staff obliges. The three-story sandstone-faced hotel contains 40 suites, each with a patined-metal fireplace, mountain-facing balcony, king-size bed, deep soaking tub (with a window view), minibar, and terrazzo dining table. Amangani's central lobby is particularly impressive, blending sandstone columns, redwood accents, custom furnishings, and soaring two-story windows. Outside, those soaking in a whirlpool and heated 35-meter pool enjoy a remarkable view of the Tetons. Among other amenities are a complete health center, a gourmet restaurant, and a lounge. Amangani's accommodations include suites ($875 d), five deluxe suites ($1,100 d), five large luxury suites with two baths and spacious balconies ($1,400–1,700 d), and a four-bedroom home ($4,800) for the utmost in sumptuousness. A three-night minimum is required in the summer. The health center and restaurant are open to the general public.

BED-AND-BREAKFASTS

Jackson hosts many fine B&Bs, where those who can afford it can relax in comfort at the homes of locals. Be sure to reserve space far ahead during the peak summer season, although you might get lucky at the last minute if someone cancels. The **Jackson Hole Bed and Breakfast Association's** website (www.jacksonholebnb.com) has links to a number of local B&Bs.

Near the Aspens along the road to Teton

Village, **The Sassy Moose Inn** (307/733-1277 or 800/356-1277, www.sassymoose.com) is a modest log house with five guest rooms, each with private bath, TV, and Wi-Fi. A full breakfast is served each morning. Guests can soak in the outdoor hot tub, and an on-site spa provides massage and other treats. Rates are $169–199 d; the larger have two beds and are fine for families. Pets are welcome (a rarity for B&Bs).

A personal favorite is **Teton Treehouse B&B** (307/733-3233, www.atetontreehouse .com) a gorgeous four-story hillside home in Wilson. This spacious open-beam B&B sits up 95 steps—needless to say, it's not accessible for people with disabilities—and contains six guest rooms with private baths. It really does offer the feeling of living in a tree house, and it's a great place for bird-watchers. Decks provide impressive views across the valley below, and guests enjoy a healthy full breakfast each morning along with Wi-Fi access. Rooms cost $215–250 d. No young children, but ages 10 and older are welcome. There's a three-night minimum stay in July and August, and the B&B is open May–September.

On the way to Teton Village, **Teton View B&B** (2136 Coyote Loop, 307/733-7954 or 866/504-7954, www.tetonview.com) features a guest room ($189 d) and suite ($249 d), both with private baths. Guests enjoy a big breakfast, Wi-Fi, and a dramatic view of the Tetons from both the indoor whirlpool tub and outdoor hot tub. The owners also offer a perfect-for-families cabin with a kitchen, wood-burning stove, and private bath; $289 d. For additional guests, add $25 per adult or $15 per child. Open June–October.

The rambling **Wildflower Inn** (307/733-4710, www.jacksonholewildflower.com) sits on three acres of country land along Teton Village Road, with five bright guest rooms. Four rooms have private decks, and all contain private baths and handcrafted lodgepole beds. One of the rooms is actually a suite with a separate sitting room, hot tub, and gas fireplace. Wildflower's hot tub occupies a plant-filled solarium. Ken and Sherrie Jern built and manage the B&B, and bring a wealth of local knowledge; both were

ski instructors at Vail, and he's a long-time Exum climbing guide. Rates are $320–360 d ($420 d for the suite) and include a memorable family style breakfast. Children are welcome and Wi-Fi is available.

One of the most impressive local lodging options is ◀ **Bentwood B&B** (307/739-1411, www.bentwoodinn.com), just north of the junction on the road to Teton Village. This massive 6,000-square-foot log home sits amid tall cottonwood trees and is a favorite place for weddings and receptions. The interior is filled with Western styling and English antiques. The grand living room is centered on a three-story stone fireplace, and each of the five elegant guest rooms has a fireplace, flat-screen TV, deck or balcony, jetted tub, and Wi-Fi. The loft room is perfect for families. Wine and hors d'oeuvres are served each evening, and morning brings a creative breakfast. Innkeepers Jennifer and Peter Tignor are gracious hosts. A professional chef, Peter's expertise shows in the special four-course dinners (around $40 per person) offered on Tuesday and Saturday nights. Lodging rates are $350 d, or $365 for up to four in the family room. Both children and pets are welcome in this very special place. A three-night minimum stay is generally required in the summer, but single nights are sometimes available.

GUEST RANCHES

Several of Wyoming's best-known and most luxurious dude ranches are in Jackson Hole, providing wonderful places for families who are looking to rough it in style. In addition to the local places listed, many more guest ranches are just over Togwotee Pass in the Dubois area and to the south in the Pinedale area. See the *Grand Teton National Park* chapter for details on several of the most popular dude ranches: **Triangle X Ranch** (www.trianglex.com), **Moose Head Ranch** (www.ranchweb.com/moose-head-ranch), **Lost Creek Ranch** (www.lostcreek.com), **Turpin Meadow Ranch** (www.turpinmeadowranch .com), **Heart Six Ranch** (www.heartsix.com), **Goosewing Ranch** (www.goosewingranch

.com), **Gros Ventre River Ranch** (www .grosventreriverranch.com), and **Red Rock Ranch** (www.theredrockranch.com).

At the base of Sheep Mountain, **Flat Creek Ranch** (307/733-0603 or 866/522-3344, www.flatcreekranch.com) is packed with history. The land was originally homesteaded by cowboy, hunting guide, and rustler Cal Carrington, but he sold it to his close friend, "Countess" Cissy Patterson, in 1923. Previously married to a Polish count, Cissy came from a wealthy Chicago newspaper family, but her love of the West and horses matched Cal's. For two decades Cissy and Cal were grist for the gossip mill, mostly during her trips to Wyoming, but also when she took him along on a grand tour of Europe. Cissy died in 1948, and her relatives now own the ranch. After a long hiatus and extensive improvements, this historic ranch in a gorgeous setting is once again open for guests, with five renovated cabins and three gourmet meals daily. The emphasis is on fly-fishing in legendary Flat Creek; the ranch owns 1.5 miles along the stream. Other activities include horseback rides and hikes into the Gros Ventre Wilderness, canoeing, and a wood-fired sauna for chilly evenings. There's a three-night minimum stay in the summer; $625 for two people per night, all-inclusive. The ranch is 15 miles up a bumpy dirt road, but the ranch provides transportation (Mon. and Fri. only) if you don't have a four-wheel-drive with high clearance. Open late May–late September.

Another historic dude ranch is **R Lazy S Ranch** (near Teton Village along the Moose-Wilson Rd., 307/733-2655, www.rlazys.com), with space for 45 guests, who enjoy horseback rides, fishing, and other Western adventures. A one-week minimum stay is required. All-inclusive rates range widely depending upon the cabin: $2,815–3,800 for two people per week. Lazy S is open mid-June–September. Tykes under age seven are not allowed.

On the banks of the Hoback River, 16 miles south of Jackson, **Spotted Horse Ranch** (307/733-2097 or 800/528-2084, www.spotted horseranch.com) exudes a comfortable rusticity.

The main lodge and cabins contain lodgepole furniture, and a maximum of 35 guests stay in log cabins with modern conveniences. Activities include horseback riding (some Appaloosas), fly-fishing, cookouts, and river trips, and you can unwind in the hot tub or sauna. A one-week minimum stay is required; $4,500 d per week, all-inclusive. Open mid-May–October. The ranch also offers wintertime sleigh rides.

MOUNTAIN RESORTS

East of Moran Junction at Togwotee Pass (9,658 feet), U.S. Hwy. 26/287 tops the Continental Divide and then slides eastward toward Dubois and the Wind River Valley. The Togwotee Pass area is famous for luxuriously deep snow all winter and is a destination for snowmobilers, cross-country skiers, and dogsledding enthusiasts. Just north of the pass is Teton Wilderness, a place to discover what solitude means. As you face west from the pass, the Teton Range offers a jagged horizon line. This entire area provides a delicious escape from hectic Jackson and is home to two noteworthy, attractive high-elevation resorts: Togwotee Mountain Lodge and Brooks Lake Lodge.

Forty-eight miles northeast of Jackson and just a few miles west of Togwotee Pass is **Togwotee Mountain Lodge** (307/543-2847 or 800/543-2847, www.togwoteelodge.com), a pleasantly rustic place to spend a night or a week. The resort offers horseback rides, and the staff can set up mountain-bike trips, whitewater rafting, fly-fishing, backcountry pack trips, and other summertime adventures, along with wintertime snowmobiling (the primary winter activity), dogsledding, and cross-country skiing when the snow flies. Togwotee has a variety of accommodations, and guests will enjoy the sauna and two large hot tubs. Summer rates are $179 d for rooms in the lodge, $189 d for family rooms with bunk beds for the kids, and $225–235 d for one-bedroom cabins. The mini-suites and cabins sleep up to six people ($10 per person for more than two). In winter, the resort specializes in package deals that include lodging, breakfast and dinner, snowmobile guide, and free airport shuttle. The resort also houses a steak house (open three meals a day; dinners $16–27), bar, gas station, gift shop, and convenience store. Togwotee is closed early April–mid-May, and mid-October–November.

Brooks Lake Lodge (307/455-2121, www.brookslake.com) may have the finest location of any Wyoming resort, with a placid lake in front and the cliffs of Pinnacle Buttes nearby. Built in 1922, it has long served travelers en route to Yellowstone, and its enormous great hall contains big-game trophies from all over the world. Completely restored, the lodge is now on the National Register of Historic Places. Seven guest rooms are available in the main lodge, and eight attractive cabins hide in the trees; all are tastefully furnished with handmade lodgepole furniture. The cabins also have woodstoves.

The turnoff for Brooks Lake Lodge is 65 miles northeast of Jackson (34 miles east of Moran Junction) and another five miles off the highway via Brooks Lake Road. The lodge is open mid-June–mid-September and late December–mid-March. There's a three-night minimum stay, and rates are $600–750 per day for two guests in the lodge or cabins. The largest and most luxurious cabin has a full living room, kitchen, jetted tub, king bed, and more for $1,600 nightly. All rates include gourmet meals, horseback riding, guided hiking, canoeing, fly-fishing, and Wi-Fi in the summer. A stocked casting pond is available for working on your technique. The spa features a small workout room, sauna, and outdoor hot tub; massage and facials are extra. Winter stays include three meals, cross-country skis, ice-fishing, and snowshoes, plus spa access for $500–600 per day for two people (two-night minimum). Snowmobile rentals and dogsled tours are also available. Brooks Lake Lodge is open to the public for winter lunches (burgers, sandwiches, salads, and daily specials), making this a popular stop for snowmobilers and X-C skiers.

RENTALS
Condominiums

Condominiums provide a popular option for families and groups visiting Jackson Hole. These privately owned places are maintained by several local property-management companies and vary from small studio apartments to spacious five-bedroom houses. All are completely furnished (including dishes) and have fireplaces, cable TV, phones, and mid-stay maid service if you remain more than five nights. The nicest also include access to pools and hot tubs and have balconies overlooking the spectacular Tetons. Many of the condominiums are in Teton Village (adjacent to the ski area) or a couple miles south in Teton Pines or the Aspens; others are scattered around Jackson Hole, so make sure you get a place close to your interests.

Condo prices vary widely depending upon location and amenities, but during the winter holiday season (Christmas–early Jan.), expect to pay $235–540 per night for studio or one-bedroom condos (1–2 people). Two-bedroom units (up to four people) cost $370–710 per night, and full four-bedroom/four-bath condos (these sleep eight) start around $1,000 per night. The most sumptuous places will set you back $3,000 nightly in the peak winter season, but if you're feeling flush with cash rent one of the finer homes for a mere $30,000 a month! Summer and off-peak winter rates are often 35–50 percent lower, with spring and fall rates 50–70 percent less than peak-season prices. In fall or spring, condos offer a real bargain for traveling families looking to stay several nights in the area. Minimum stays of 3–7 nights are required throughout the year, with the longest minimum stays required in the peak winter season.

If you have the luxury of time, do a little comparison shopping before renting a condo. Things to ask include whether you have access to a pool and hot tub, how close you are to the ski slopes, how frequent the maid service is, and whether the units include such amenities as Wi-Fi, DVD players, flat-screen TVs, and washing machines. Also be sure to find out what beds are in the rooms because couples might not enjoy sleeping in twin bunk beds. Ask about the age and condition of the condos since some are dated. Some of the newest units are at Love Ridge (next to Snow King Resort) and White Buffalo Club (downtown). Fortunately, the rental companies provide helpful online photos, floor plans, and other details for the various styles of condos.

Contact the following companies for details:

Grand View Lodge & Spa (at Snow King Resort, 307/733-3186 or 800/522-5464, www.grandviewlodgeandspa.com)

OK Rentals (307/733-8604 or 800/735-8310, www.jackson-hole-vacations.com)

Jackson Hole Lodge (307/733-2992 or 800/604-9404, www.jacksonholelodge.com)

Jackson Hole Resort Lodging (307/733-3990 or 800/443-8613, www.jhrl.com)

Love Ridge Resort Lodges (at Snow King Resort, 307/733-5200 or 800/533-7669, www.loveridgelodge.com)

Mountain Property Management (307/733-1684 or 800/992-9948, www.mpmjh.com)

Property Management of Jackson Hole (307/733-4969 or 800/687-1154, www.jacksonhole.net)

Rendezvous Mountain Rentals (307/739-9050 or 888/739-2565, www.rmrentals.com)

Snow King Resort Condominiums (307/733-5200 or 800/522-5464, www.snowking.com)

Spring Creek Ranch (307/733-8833 or 800/443-6139, www.springcreekranch.com)

Teton Pines Resort and Country Club (307/733-1005 or 800/238-2223, www.tetonpines.com)

The largest of these businesses—and a good place to begin your search—is Jackson Hole Resort Lodging. Owned by Jackson Hole Mountain Resort, it manages about 200 places. Other large management companies include Rendezvous Mountain Rentals and Snow King Resort Condominiums. The last of these also owns (and can book condos at) Grand View Lodge & Spa and Love Ridge Resort Lodging.

Two resorts offer fractional-ownership condos in Jackson Hole: **The Residence Club at Teton Pines** (307/733-1005 or 800/238-2223, www.tetonpinesresidenceclub.com) and **The Teton Club** (307/734-7679 or 877/838-6677, www.tetonclub.com). The Teton Club is right at the base of Jackson Hole Resort, making it perfect for skiers, while Teton Pines offers an upscale country club with a golf course and other amenities. Members typically share ownership and stay for 4–12 weeks per year. Also check out the recently opened **White Buffalo Club** (160 W. Gill Ave., 888/256-8182, www.whitebuffaloclub.com), a member-only operation in the heart of Jackson.

Home Rentals and Swaps

Jackson Hole home rentals—both short and long-term—are available from **OK Rentals** (307/733-8604 or 800/735-8310, www.jackson-hole-vacations.com), **Mountain Property Management** (307/733-1684 or 800/992-9948, www.mpmjh.com), **Prime Properties of Jackson Hole** (307/733-7440 or 800/800-6455, www.jackson-hole-wyoming-real-estate.com), **Rendezvous Mountain Rentals** (307/739-9050 or 888/739-2565, www.rmrentals.com), **Mountain Haus** (307/690-1034, www.jhmountainhaus.com), and **Rocking-V Lodge** (307/733-7319, www.rocking-v.com).

Rancho Alegre Lodge (3600 S. Park Loop Rd., 307/733-7988, www.ranchoalegre.com) offers Jackson's most expensive lodging. On a 50-acre spread facing the Tetons, this 10,000-square-foot structure houses seven bedrooms (each with its own TV/VCR, phone, and fridge) and offers an upscale hunting lodge decor along with such amenities as concierge service, a private chef available for hire, seven fireplaces, extensive decks, a hot tub, and a pool table. Full-house rentals are $2,500 per night, including breakfast, with a five-night minimum stay in the summer (and five times $2,500 is $12,500…). Up to 14 people can stay for this price, or save money and rent it all month for the bargain rate of just $60,000! At these prices, the lodge is primarily used for weddings, corporate retreats, large (and wealthy) families, and ski groups.

At the base of the mountains in Wilson, **Trail Creek Ranch** (307/733-2610, www.jackson holetrailcreekranch.com) operated as a dude ranch for 50 years. Lodging on this 270-acre spread ranges from a double room with a king bed ($910 per week; no kitchen) to a two-bedroom cabin ($1,700 per week) with full kitchen that's perfect for families. All units have private baths and Wi-Fi, but no distracting TVs. Families love the heated outdoor pool. Trail Creek is open June–mid-October, with a four-day minimum stay.

In addition to the lodging places described, visitors to Jackson Hole may want to investigate a house exchange. Several online companies list homeowners in Jackson who are interested in a trade if you have an upscale home, especially one on the beach in midwinter! If you live in Hawaii or Costa Rica and want to go skiing, your home might be a hot property. If you live in North Dakota or South Ossetia, good luck. Companies worth investigating include **Home Exchange** (310/798-3864 or 800/877-8723, www.homeexchange.com), **Home Link** 954/566-2687 or 800/638-3841, www.swapnow .com), and **Intervac** (415/839-9670 or 800/756-4663, www.intervac.com).

Another option is through one of the online vacation rental brokers, such as **Vacation Rentals by Owner** (www.vrbo.com), **CyberRentals** (www.cyberrentals.com), or **Vacation Homes** (www.vacationhomes.com).

Camping

Fully 97 percent of Jackson Hole is publicly owned, primarily within Grand Teton National Park and Bridger-Teton National Forest. So many options exist, that campers can pitch their tent in a new campground every night for three weeks. Private RV parks are considerably more limited, but a half-dozen are scattered around the valley.

PUBLIC CAMPGROUNDS

Most public campgrounds on Forest Service and Park Service lands around Jackson Hole are on a first-come, first-camp basis with no reservations. In addition to the sites described below, many people camp for free on dispersed sites on Forest Service lands; but contact the agency for locations and restrictions.

Bridger-Teton Campgrounds

Bridger-Teton National Forest (307/739-5400, www.fs.fed.us/r4/btnf) has a number of campgrounds ($12–15; open mid-May–Sept.) located around Jackson Hole. Closest is **Curtis Canyon Campground,** seven miles northeast of Jackson up a gravel road with a fine view of the Tetons.

Three popular Bridger-Teton campgrounds are southwest of Jackson in the Snake River Canyon, with access via U.S. Hwy. 26/89. They include **East Table Creek Campground** and **Station Creek Campground,** both 24 miles south of Jackson and 11 miles southwest of Hoback Junction, along with **Wolf Creek Campground,** 26 miles southwest of Jackson and six miles from Hoback Junction.

Three more campgrounds are northeast of Jackson in the Gros Ventre Valley. **Atherton Creek Campground,** sits along Slide Lake 18 miles northeast of Jackson and seven miles northeast of Kelly up Gros Ventre Road. **Red Hills Campground,** and **Crystal Creek Campground** are near each other along the Gros Ventre River approximately 23 miles northeast of Jackson and 13 miles up the partly gravel Gros Ventre Road.

In the Buffalo Valley area 45 miles northeast of Jackson, pitch your tent at **Hatchet Campground,** eight miles east of Moran Junction, **Turpin Meadow Campground,** 10 miles east of Moran Junction, or **Box Creek Campground,** along Buffalo Valley Road.

Forty-nine miles north of Jackson, **Angles Campground** is a small site just uphill from Togwotee Mountain Resort on U.S. Hwy. 287. Another small camping place, **Sheffield Creek**

Campground, 55 miles north of Jackson, is off U.S. Hwy. 89/191/287 near Flagg Ranch Resort (poor road access until late summer). **Pacific Creek Campground**is 46 miles north of Jackson and nine miles up Pacific Creek Rd., with access through Grand Teton National Park.

Two campgrounds are approximately 20 miles southeast of Jackson along the Hoback River: **Kozy Campground,** seven miles southeast of Hoback Junction, and **Hoback Campground,** eight miles east of Hoback Junction.

Close to Granite Hot Springs—a delightful place for a soak—**Granite Campground** is 35 miles southeast of Jackson and nine miles up the gravel Granite Creek Road.

Caribou-Targhee Campgrounds

Trail Creek Campground and **Mike Harris Campground** are in the **Caribou-Targhee National Forest** (208/354-2312, www.fs.fed.us/r4/caribou-targhee, $10) on the west side of Teton Pass, approximately 20 miles west of Jackson. Both are open mid-May–mid-September, with reservations ($10 fee) available at 518/885-3639 or 877/444-6777, www.recreation.gov.

RV PARKS

As land values have soared, the number of RV parks in Jackson has dropped. Today, only one RV resort remains, with two more a dozen miles to the south and three more north of town in or near Grand Teton National Park.

None of the private RV parks around Jackson is really noteworthy; "parking lots" would be a better term. They can also be surprisingly expensive: Some places charge more for a tent space than it would cost to stay in a motel room in many Wyoming towns! Even more expensive is a ticket for parking RVs overnight on Jackson city streets. It's illegal to do so, and local police strictly enforce the ordinance.

On the south end of town behind the Virginian Lodge, **Virginian RV Park** (750 W. Broadway, 307/733-7189 or 800/321-6982 in summer or 800/262-4999 in winter, www.virginianlodge.com) is the biggest RV parking lot in the area. Full hookups at more than 100 sites (many pull-through spaces) cost $65; no tents. Guests at the RV park can use the Virginian Lodge's outdoor pool and hot tub. The park is open May–mid-October.

Two private campgrounds are in the Hoback Junction area, 12 miles south of Jackson. **Lazy J Corral** (307/733-1554) is right on the highway at Hoback Junction, but the rates are low: RV sites with full hookups are just $25. It does not have tent spaces but is open year-round.

Snake River Park KOA (307/733-7078 or 800/562-1878, www.srpkoa.com), 12 miles south of Jackson at Hoback Junction, has RV spaces for $60 d, tent sites for $39 d, tepees for $38, and simple "kamping kabins" for $71–81 d. Open early April–mid-October. The KOA has a riverside location and a game room. Snake River Park Whitewater rafting company is also based here.

Food

Jackson stands out from the rest of Wyoming on the culinary scene: Chicken-fried steak may be available, but it certainly isn't the house specialty! You won't need to look far to find good food; in fact, the town seems to overflow with memorable (and even more memorably priced) eateries. If you stood in Town Square and walked in any direction for a block you would find at least one restaurant that would be a standout in any other Wyoming town. More than 70 local restaurants do business here—in a town that contains just 9,000 people.

To get an idea of what to expect at local restaurants, pick up a copy of the free *Jackson Hole Dining Guide* (www.focusproductions.com) at the visitor center or local restaurants. The guide includes sample menus and brief descriptions of many local establishments. All local restaurants are entirely smoke-free.

BREAKFAST

The best breakfast place in Jackson isn't in Jackson, but in Wilson, where (**Nora's Fish Creek Inn** (307/733-8288, Mon.–Fri. 6:30 A.M.–2 P.M. and 5:30–9 P.M., Sat.–Sun. 6:30 A.M.–1:30 P.M. and 5:30–9 P.M., $19–28) attracts a full house each morning. The food (including *huevos rancheros,* biscuits and gravy, and omelettes) is great, the setting is authentically rustic, and the waitresses are friendly and fast. Nora's also serves tried-and-true lunches and dinners at fair prices, from $8 patty melts to nut-crusted trout for $20. Dinner reservations are required.

Very popular for breakfast and lunch is **Jedediah's House of Sourdough** (135 E. Broadway, 307/733-5671, daily 7 A.M.–2 P.M., $5–11), where, as the name implies, sourdough pancakes are the morning specialty. Lots of other choices, from eggs benedict to steak and eggs. Housed in a 1910 log cabin, the restaurant gets noisy and crowded in the morning, making it perfect for families with young kids. The lunch menu stars burgers, sandwiches, and salads. A half-dozen tables are on the deck, shaded by tall cottonwoods, and there's a second Jedediah's inside the airport.

Another longtime morning standout is **The Bunnery** (130 N. Cache Dr., 307/733-5474 or 800/349-0492, www.bunnery.com, daily 7 A.M.–3 P.M. and 5–9 P.M., $6–9), with good omelets and fresh-squeezed juices, plus delicious sandwiches on freshly baked breads, salads, burgers, and homemade soups. The Bunnery bakes a big variety of treats and sweets, but it's best known for its hearty-flavored OSM (oat, sunflower, and millet) bread—on the pricey side at almost $6 a loaf.

Teton Steakhouse (40 W. Pearl St., 307/733-2639, www.tetonsteakhouse.com, daily 6:30 A.M.–11 P.M.) serves a two-notches-on-your-belt breakfast buffet, with pancakes, bacon, sausage, potatoes, fruits, and more for $6 (not including coffee and juice).

Bubba's Bar-B-Que Restaurant (515 W. Broadway, 307/733-2288, daily 6:30 A.M.–10 P.M. in summer, daily 6:30 A.M.–8:30 P.M. in winter) is another cheap and tasty option, with a very filling worker's special for under $7. Ask for it, since you won't find it on the menu.

In Teton Village, head downstairs at the Mangy Moose to **RMO Café** (307/734-9438, www.mangymoose.net, daily 7 A.M.–5 P.M.), offering killer breakfasts along with inexpensive burgers, pizza-by-the-slice, and sandwiches for lunch. Breakfasts are $5–7; lunches $6–11.

E. Leven & Food Co. (175 N. Center St., 307/733-5603, www.elevenfood.com, daily 6:30 A.M.–3 P.M., $6–11) has a bright location a block off the Square. Take an indoor table next to the tall windows lining the street, or sit outside on the side patio. Breakfast omelettes, quiche, bagels, waffles, and monster cinnamon rolls are followed by lunchtime hot and cold sandwiches and salads. Good espresso too.

COFFEE, LIGHT MEALS, AND SWEETS

Housed in a tiny log cabin a block off the Square, **Shades Café** (82 S. King St., 307/733-2015, daily 7:30 A.M.–4 P.M.) has a shady summer-only side patio. Breakfasts feature eggs benedict, muesli, and fresh-baked croissants, plus lattes, mochas, and other coffee drinks. Lunch standouts are salads, quiches, burritos, and paninis. Shades is a relaxing place to hang out with the latte habitués, although it does close early in the fall, winter, and spring.

Surprisingly, Jackson Hole's best coffee is a dozen miles northeast of town in miniscule Kelly, where Al and Heather Hunter have opened **Kelly on the Gros Ventre** (307/732-9837, Mon.–Sat. 7 A.M.–3 P.M. and Sun. 9 A.M.–2 P.M.), using Alaska's justly famous Kaladi Bros. Coffee beans. No inside seating, so take your espresso and bagel outdoors to take in the amazing Teton vistas.

(**Cioccolato Pastry Shop** (130 W. Broadway, 307/734-6400, www.cioccolatopastryshop.com, daily 11 A.M.–8 P.M.) is the creation of Mexican-born Oscar Ortega, a master pastry chef whose accolades include several international awards. Crème brûlée, truffles, and other luscious confections await true chocoholics. These are heavenly works of art, almost too perfect to eat.

LUNCH

One of the most popular noontime spots in Jackson—it's been here more than 30 years—is **Sweetwater Restaurant** (85 King St., 307/733-3553, daily 11:30 A.M.–3 P.M. and 5:30–10 P.M. in summer, daily 11:30 A.M.–3 P.M. and 5:30–9 P.M. in winter). The cozy log cabin has several tables on the front deck and a lunch menu ($10–13) of dependably good salads, homemade soups, and earthy sandwiches. For dinner, try pesto pork chops, spinach and feta soufflé, or mustard-marinated pork tenderloin. Entrées are $22–30.

Better known as DOG, **(Down on Glen** (307/733-4422 daily 6:30 A.M.–2 P.M., Fri.–Sun. 5–9 P.M.) is a miniscule eatery next to Mountain High Pizza at Glenwood and Broadway with a schizophrenic personality. Locals—and in-the-know tourists—crowd in for tasty and cheap breakfast burritos (just $5), organic buffalo burgers, and Philly cheesesteaks early in the day. Owner Sange Sherpa's roots emerge in the evening, when DOG becomes Everest Momo Shack, with Nepalese specialties ($9–12), including curry dishes, tikka masala, and momo dumplings, all served with naan bread on the side. Delicious, but because everything is freshly made you'll need to wait. Primarily a to-go spot, DOG has a couple of picnic tables on the adjacent patio.

Find delicious sub sandwiches on tangy homemade bread at **New York City Sub Shop** (20 N. Jackson St., 307/733-4414, www.newyorkcitysubshop.com, Mon.–Fri. 10 A.M.–7 P.M., Sat. 10 A.M.–6 P.M., Sun. 10 A.M.–5 P.M. in summer, reduced winter hours). It's a little pricey ($7 for a half hoagie or $12 for a whole), but the service is fast, and the hot sandwiches are vastly better than at Subway. You'll recognize owner Bruce Tlougan by his famous handlebar mustache.

Pearl Street Bagels (145 Pearl St., 307/739-1218, daily 6:30 A.M.–6 P.M.) serves home-baked bagels—they're on the small side, however—along with good espresso and juices. There's a second Pearl Street over in Wilson (307/739-1261); it's *the* groovy place to be seen in Wilson (OK, so are Nora's and the 'Coach).

For lunches in the Teton Village area, stop by **Westside Store and Deli** (307/733-6202, daily 7 A.M.–7 P.M.), in the Aspens. The deli will be glad to pack you a big picnic lunch, and it also sells such entrées (around $5 per person) as lemon dijon chicken, lasagna, and ribs.

The National Museum of Wildlife Art, two miles north of Jackson on U.S. Hwy. 26/89, houses a bright little restaurant with windows facing the National Elk Refuge. Called **Rising Sage Café** (307/733-8649, www.risingsagecafe.com, daily 11 A.M.–3 P.M., $5–10), it has a lunch menu of sandwiches (try the chicken croissant), buffalo burgers, homemade soups, chili, salads, and espresso.

AMERICAN

Jackson's most popular family eatery is **(Bubba's Bar-B-Que Restaurant** (515 W. Broadway, 307/733-2288, daily 6:30 A.M.–10 P.M. in summer, daily 6:30 A.M.–8:30 P.M. in winter). Each evening the parking lot out front is jammed with folks waiting patiently for a chance to gnaw on barbecued spare ribs, savor the spicy chicken wings, or gobble up the turkey plate; $11–20 entrées. The big salad bar is just $7, but get here before 6:30 P.M. for shorter lines. Lunch is a real bargain, with specials for less than $8. Drinks come in recycled Mason jars, but Bubba's doesn't serve alcohol, so BYOB (no corkage fee). Cheap and tasty breakfasts, too.

Get great all-American burgers at the 1950s-style **Billy's Burgers** (55 N. Cache Dr., 307/733-3279, www.cadillac-grille.com, daily 11:30 A.M.–10:30 P.M.), adjacent to the more upscale Cadillac Grille. The Billy burger ($6) is a half-pound monster. Not on the menu, but recommended if you aren't absolutely famished, is the smaller Betty burger. Ask for it.

Next door to Billy's and in the basement of

the bar of the same name, the **Million Dollar Cowboy Steakhouse** (307/733-4790, www .cowboysteakhouse.net, daily 5:30–10 P.M.) specializes in "casual Western elegance" and great steaks, from sirloin to filet mignon. In addition, the menu includes salads, buffalo meatloaf, seafood, pasta, ribs, and a few lonely vegetarian specials. The bar offers a dozen different single-malt scotches, plus seasonal drink specials. Not for kids, and not cheap: steaks are $25–49. Reservations advised.

Also recommended is **Gun Barrel Steakhouse** (862 W. Broadway, 307/733-3287, www.gunbarrel.com, daily 5:30–10 P.M., closed in Nov.), where the meaty mesquite-grilled steaks, elk, and buffalo are served in a delightful hunting-lodge atmosphere with trophy game mounts; they came from a wildlife museum that previously occupied the site. You'll find lots of historic guns and other Old West paraphernalia around the Gun Barrel too, making this an interesting place to explore even if you aren't hungry. Gun Barrel is a bit on the pricey side, with entrées for $17–37. The bar has a wide choice of beers on tap.

Another fine place is **Camp Creek Inn** (16 miles south of Jackson in Hoback Canyon, 307/732-2222, www.campcreekinn.com, Wed.–Sun. 5–9:30 P.M. in summer, reduced winter hours). The cozy fireplace and rustic Old West setting make this a good place to escape the Jackson Hole crowds. Very good steaks, St. Louis–style barbecue ribs, and "no mercy" one-pound burgers are big enough to fill the hungriest appetite. Friday and Saturday nights bring prime rib. Prices run $9–24. Sunday brunches (10 A.M.–2 P.M.) are all-you-can-eat affairs for $12. Outside dining is available in the summer, along with sleigh-ride dinners ($45) in winter.

A very popular place with both locals and ski bums is the **Mangy Moose Restaurant & Saloon** (Teton Village, 307/733-4913, www .mangymoose.net, daily 5–10 P.M. restaurant, daily noon–1:30 A.M. saloon), where you'll find a big salad bar and steak, prime rib, pasta, chicken, and fresh fish ($15–28). It's a fun and lively place, with a menu that changes weekly.

The menu and setting at **Teton Steakhouse** (40 W. Pearl St., 307/733-2639, www.teton steakhouse.com, daily 6:30 A.M.–11 P.M.–) reflect this restaurant's previous incarnation as a Sizzler, but that doesn't faze anyone. The central location (one block off Town Square), stuff-yourself meals, and noisy, kid-friendly setting bring a crowd every day, even if the food isn't notable. Line up to put in your order for steaks, ribs, or chicken, or just sidle up to the big salad, soup, and dessert bar to fill your plate. Steaks are $17–30, and there also is a breakfast buffet. Free Wi-Fi too. This place is very popular with hogs who park their Hogs (Harleys) and waddle in, along with swarms of motorcoach tourists.

Housed in an old Denny's building next to Albertson's, **Rendezvous Bistro** (380 South U.S. Hwy. 89, 307/739-1100, www .rendezvousbistro.net, daily 5:30–11 P.M. in summer, closed Sun. in winter, $17–33) has a strong local following for all-better-than-mom's meatloaf, veal marsala, crispy risotto cake, duck confit, and a rather pricey oyster bar. Definitely recommended.

At the base of Snow King Mountain, **43 North** (645 S. Cache, 307/733-0043, www.43 northmusic.com, daily 11:30 A.M.–10 P.M., $10–30) established itself with locals who appreciate the away-from-the-Square setting, good food, lively pub atmosphere, music most nights (the main attraction), and a rooftop deck and front patio for summertime dining. The restaurant is open for lunch and dinner, with burgers, fish tacos, open-faced sandwiches, salads, seafood, and chicken dishes. Good drinks, too, especially the Irish coffees and martinis.

PASTA AND PIZZA

Hidden away on the north end of town next to Anvil Motel, **Nani's Genuine Pasta House** (242 N. Glenwood, 307/733-3888, www.nanis .com, daily 5–10 P.M., $19–45) is a long-time favorite. Flowers cover the exterior in summer, and inside it's quiet and romantic. In addition to the standards, Nani's features a menu of specialties from a different region of Italy each month. The wine bar (Enoteca Sicula) has an extensive choice of Italian and California vintages. Reservations recommended.

Owned by acclaimed chef Roger Freedman—formerly of Snake River Grill—**[** **Il Villagio Osteria** (307/739-4100, www.jhosteria.com, daily noon–2 P.M. and 5:30–10 P.M.) specializes in Italian cuisine, including housemade gnocchi, veal Milanese, and wonderful pizzas and paninis from the wood-fired oven. The 12-seat wine bar is a delightful place for something less formal; plenty of Italian wines available by the glass or bottle. Entrées are $18–39, with pizzas around $18. The restaurant is downstairs in the luxurious Hotel Terra in Teton Village.

Several other pizza places stand out in Jackson. You'll find **Calico Italian Restaurant & Bar** (307/733-2460, www.calicorestaurant.com, daily 5–10 P.M. restaurant, 5 P.M.–midnight bar) in the garish red-and-white building 0.75 mile north on Teton Village Road. The menu has gone a bit upscale, but prices are still manageable: $16–28 entrées, including such faves as linguini with spinach and chicken or Italian sausage lasagna. A 12-inch personal pizza is 12 bucks. The bar at Calico is a locals' watering hole, and kids love the 2.5-acre lawn/playground and old-fashioned porch, and flower-bedecked patio affording Teton vistas. START buses stop right out front, making this an easy destination even if you're without a car.

Mountain High Pizza Pie (120 W. Broadway, 307/733-3646, daily 11 A.M.–11 P.M.) is a convenient downtown place offering all the usual toppings (and some not so, including the Thai pie), plus calzones, subs, salads, and free delivery in Jackson and Teton Village. Large pizzas start around $16.

FINE DINING

If you want fine continental dining and aren't deterred by entrées costing $25 or more, Jackson has much to offer you.

Just off Town Square, **Snake River Grill** (upstairs at 84 E. Broadway, 307/733-0557, www.snakerivergrill.com, daily 5:30–10 P.M.) is one of Jackson's finest gourmet restaurants—with prices to match ($25–54 entrées). Meals are exquisite, and the seasonal menu typically contains a variety of seafood, free-range beef, and organic vegetables that are artfully presented. The wine list is equally impressive, and a few outside tables face the square. Try the bourbon crème brûlée for dessert. Reservations are a must; reserve two weeks in advance for primetime seatings in the summer. Snake River Grill is a good place to scan for Jackson's best-known residents, Harrison Ford and Calista Flockhart. Closed November and April.

For views so spectacular they make it difficult to concentrate on your meal, don't miss **The Granary Restaurant** (307/733-8833 or 800/443-6139, www.springcreekranch.com, daily 7–11 A.M., noon–2 P.M., and 5–9 P.M., closed Sun.–Tues. mid-Oct.–mid-Dec.), atop East Gros Ventre Butte west of Jackson with tall windows opening to the Tetons. This is also a great place for evening cocktails and romantic dining. Entrées run $26–55 and include Idaho trout, buffalo ribeye, and a popular Cajun spiced elk tenderloin. The separate lounge menu offers lighter fare, including happy hour specials 4–7 P.M. nightly; Sunday specials include a tasty $7 burger (normally twice that price).

Jackson's popular nouvelle cuisine restaurant—**[** **Cadillac Grille** (55 N. Cache on the square, 307/733-3279, www.cadillac-grille.com, daily 11:30 A.M.–3 P.M. and 5:30–10 P.M., $18–35)—serves artfully prepared meals, with a changing menu of seafood, grilled meats, and wild game. The art deco decor of the Cadillac helps make it one of the most crowded tourist hangouts in town, but it also attracts a devoted following of locals, especially during the nightly happy hour when two-for-one drinks are the draw. The restaurant includes a bar called Munchies with lighter fare ($7–9 salads, ribs, and chicken wings), Billy's Burgers (described above), and a covered rear patio for summertime dining.

Owned by a trio of local chefs, **[** **Trio, An American Bistro** (45 S. Glenwood, 307/734-8038, www.bistrotrio.com, daily 5:30–10 P.M.) is the hot new downtown eatery. House specialties include Tuscan grilled

New York steak, forever roasted pork, wood-fired roasted half chickens, butternut squash risotto, and buffalo burgers. Reservations advised. Most entrées are $18–30, but $10 will get you a simple mozzarella, marinara, and basil pizza. Trio may also be open for lunch during the summer season.

Housed within Rusty Parrot Lodge, the acclaimed **(Wild Sage Restaurant** (175 N. Jackson, 307/733-2000 or 888/739-1749, www.rustyparrot.com, 5:30–9:30 P.M.) serves gourmet dinners in an intimate setting (just 26 seats). One of two AAA four-diamond restaurants in Jackson Hole, Wild Sage offers a delectable array of regional cuisine and fresh seafood. The menu changes, but typically includes pan-seared beef tenderloin, herb marinated bison rib-eye and ginger and citron crème brûlée, plus a fine choice of wines. Entrées are $40–52, and reservations are required; call a month ahead in midsummer. Breakfast is only for lodge guests all summer, but open to the public October–May 7–10 A.M., $20 for an all-you-can-eat spread that changes daily.

Located atop Bridger gondola at Jackson Hole Resort, **(Couloir Restaurant** (307/739-2675, www.couloirrestaurant.com, daily 11 A.M.–3 P.M. and Thurs.–Sat. with seatings at 5:15 and 8 P.M. Memorial Day–Sept., no lunches in winter) gained accolades from both *Condé Nast* and *Food and Wine*. This special-occasion spot features views of Corbet's Couloir and the valley of Jackson Hole 2,800 feet below, with four-course dinners for $85 adults or $40 kids. Signature dishes include house-smoked tenderloin of buffalo and sun-dried tomato crusted Alaskan halibut, but the desserts and cocktails are equally notable. For lunch ($15–21) the restaurant serves distinctive sandwiches, salads, and seafood. The setting is contemporary, with an outdoor deck to take in the views. Reservations highly recommended. For dinner guests the gondola price is included in your set-price meal. Lunchtime visitors pay $18 adults; free for kids under 13. Downstairs from Couloir is **Headwall Deli,** serving a simpler menu of pizzas and sandwiches.

MEXICAN

For the fastest Mexican food in town (with the possible exception of Taco Bell), drop by **Pica's Mexican Taqueria** (1160 Alpine La., 307/734-4457, Mon.–Sat. 11 A.M.–10 P.M., Sat.–Sun. 8 A.M.–11 P.M., $8–15). You'll find tasty tacos, bodacious burritos, enchanting enchiladas, and tempting *tortas* in a hip setting packed with locals. There's also a morning menu of breakfast burritos, huevos rancheros, and more on weekends. The shop is in Buffalo Junction strip mall near Albertson's, with a second inside the Stagecoach Bar in Wilson.

In business since 1969, **The Merry Piglets** (160 N. Cache Dr., 307/733-2966, www.merrypiglets.com, daily 11:30 A.M.–10 P.M.) is a very busy place with a heart-of-town location. The menu features Tex-Mex meals, fajitas, wraps, quesadillas, and cheese crisps—the house specialty. Excellent margaritas, pitchers of beer, and a sky-lit front section add to the appeal. Most plates run $10–20, but you can get a simple burrito for $6.

ASIAN
Chinese

In Grand Teton Plaza on the south end of town, **Chinatown Restaurant** (850 W. Broadway, 307/733-8856, daily 11 A.M.–10 P.M.) serves good Chinese dishes—particularly the *mu shu* vegetables, lemon chicken, and pot stickers—and offers $6.50 weekday lunch specials.

Ocean City China Bistro (340 W. Broadway, 307/734-9768, daily 11:30 A.M.–9:30 P.M.) provides a pleasant downtown setting and more than 120 choices—from honey walnut prawns with pork to Szechwan Three Delight—for $8–13. Weekday lunch combo plates are a bargain at $6.

Hong Kong Buffet (826 W. Broadway, 307/734-8988, Mon.–Sat. 10:30 A.M.–10 P.M., Sun. 11:30 A.M.–10 P.M.) has a big 50-item buffet: $7.50 at lunch or $12 for dinner and all day Sunday.

Japanese

Get delicious freshly rolled sushi—including vegetarian rolls and a unique hot spicy tuna roll—at **Masa Sushi** (307/733-2311, daily 6–10 P.M., $18–25 entrées), located inside The Inn at Jackson Hole in Teton Village. The setting is intimate and inviting.

Long a favorite with locals and visitors, **Nikai** (225 N. Cache, 307/734-6490, www.nikaisushi.com, daily 6–9:30 P.M.) serves creatively prepared sushi as the main attraction, but also has a menu of Asian fusion items from the open kitchen, including miso-glazed black cod, coconut fried chicken, and *wakame* seaweed salad. The atmosphere is contemporary and stylish. Most items are priced $10–20. Reservations advised.

Housed within the Jackson Hole Wine Company, **Koshu Wine Bar** (200 W. Broadway, 307/733-5283, www.koshuwinebar.com, daily 6–10 P.M.) serves pan-Asian cuisine nightly in a classy setting. The menu changes often; most items are $14–22. You can choose from more than a dozen wines by the glass, or buy a bottle from the shop's extensive selection ($10 corkage fee).

Thai

In an alley across the street from Teton Theater, **Teton Thai Restaurant** (135 N. Cache Dr., 307/733-0022, www.tetonthai.com, $14–16) is a favorite spot for the 20-something crowd. All seating is outdoors, though some is under a deck, and a DJ spins tunes most nights to amp up the festive atmosphere. Pick a rice, noodle, or curry dish and add your choice of chicken, beef, shrimp, or tofu. Service can be haphazard and it may take time to get served, but you'll be glad you waited. Open for lunch 11:30 A.M.–2:30 P.M. and dinner 5:30–9:30 P.M., but folks often hang around till 11 P.M. listening to the tunes on a summer evening. Everything moves inside the tiny eatery when winter comes, with customers filling a handful of stools along the counter. No credit cards or alcohol, but it's fine to BYOB.

Thai Me Up (75 E. Pearl St., 307/733-0005, Mon.–Fri. 11:30 A.M.–2:30 P.M., Mon.–Sat. 5:30–10 P.M., closed Apr. and Nov.) has a gimmicky name and a U.S.-born chef, but the food is spicy, creative, and delicious. It has a few sidewalk tables, plus a tiny bar with great drinks, including the Bigglesworth Typhoon, a blow-me-down 45-ounce blend of seven different alcohols that's set afire. The location is a bit quieter than places on the Square. Entrées are $13–16, and lunches are more reasonable, starting around $8. Try the drunken noodles (pad kee mow) for a spicy favorite.

Run by a young Thai couple, **Bon Appe Thai** (245 W. Pearl St., 307/734-0245, daily 11 A.M.–5 P.M.) is another option, with fast Thai lunches and reasonably priced dinners ($12–14).

BREWERIES

Before Prohibition in 1920, nearly every town in Wyoming had its own brewery, making such local favorites as Hillcrest, Schoenhofen, and Sweetwater. After repeal of "the noble experiment," breweries again popped up, but competition from industrial giants such as Anheuser-Busch and Coors forced the last Wyoming operation—Sheridan Brewing—out of business in 1954. It was another 34 years before commercial beermaking returned. In 1988, Charlie Otto started a tiny backyard operation in Wilson. His **Grand Teton Brewing Company** (208/787-4000 or 888/899-1656, www.grandtetonbrewing.com) brews just over Teton Pass in Victor, Idaho, where you can sample Teton Ale, Old Faithful Ale, Moose Juice Stout, Teton Golden Ale, Teton Huckleberry Wheat, and Sweetgrass IPA. You'll find them on tap at many Jackson-area bars and restaurants and for sale in six-pack bottles throughout the region.

An old warehouse two blocks from Town Square has been beautifully transformed into **C Snake River Brewing Co. and Restaurant** (265 S. Millward St., 307/739-2337, www.snakeriverbrewing.com, daily 11:30 A.M.–1 A.M.). The bright and cavernous setting fills with a convivial crowd of young outdoors enthusiasts most evenings, and the bar generally has seven or eight of its award-winning beers on tap. Particularly notable—they've all won gold medals at various brew festivals—are Zonker Stout, Rock Chuck Rye, and Snake River Pale Ale. The

© DON PITCHER

Snake River Brewing Co. and Restaurant

lunch and dinner café menu includes delicious thin-crust pizzas baked in the apple-wood–fired oven, flavorful appetizers, daily pasta specials, panini sandwiches, and salads. It's great food in a lively atmosphere, and one of *the* places to be seen in Jackson. Most entrées run $9–14, but the brewery also serves a number of $7 lunch specials. Pick up the brochure for a self-guided brewery tour.

WINE SHOPS

The most complete local wine and beer shops are **Westside Wine and Spirits** (307/733-5038, www.westsidewineand spirits.com) in the Aspens along Teton Village Road, **The Liquor Store** (next to Albertson's on W. Broadway, 307/733-4466, www .wineliquorbeer.com), and **Dornan's Wine Shoppe** (307/733-2415, ext. 202, www.dornans .com) in Moose. The Liquor Store features an impressive upstairs wine department, plus a wine bar with free wine tastings Fridays 4–7 P.M. **Jackson Hole Wine Company** (200 W. Broadway, 307/739-9463, www

.jacksonholewinecompany.com) also has a fine selection, with Koshu Wine Bar in the back.

GROCERIES AND NATURAL FOODS

Get groceries from the large **Albertson's** (307/733-5950, www.albertsons.com) on the south end of town at the corner of Buffalo Way and Broadway. Inside you'll find a bakery, pharmacy, deli, one-hour photo lab, bank branch, and coffee bar. This is the most lucrative Albertson's in the entire chain of 2,300 stores; sales are said to be three times higher than the second-most-successful store! A few blocks farther south (right in front of the high school) is an even larger **Smith's** (1425 S. U.S. Hwy. 89, 307/733-8908, www.smiths foodanddrug.com), with the same features as Albertson's and a deli serving fresh sushi.

In Powderhorn Mall, **Jackson Whole Grocer** (974 W. Broadway, 307/733-0450, www.jacksonwholegrocer.com, open daily 7 A.M.–11 P.M.) is a hybrid of sorts between an organic grocer and a traditional supermarket. The emphasis is upon fresh and local items, but there's also a great bakery, full deli, and espresso.

The popular **Jackson Hole Farmers Market** (307/690-1759, www.jacksonhole farmersmarket.org) comes to Town Square Saturdays 8–11 A.M. July–September. Shop for fresh veggies, fruits, food, and flowers. Live music and cooking demonstrations add to the attraction.

For a side of Jackson most tourists don't see, drop by **Tienda Guadalupana** (975 Alpine Ave.), where you'll find Mexican pastries, meats, and specialty groceries. Like the hundreds of low-paid Mexican and Central American workers who make Jackson run, the shop is hidden away in a tiny backstreet location.

In business since 1947, **Jackson Hole Buffalo Meat Company** (1325 S. Hwy. 89, 307/733-4159 or 800/543-6328, www.jh buffalomeat.com) sells smoked buffalo salami, jerky, sausage, steaks, and burgers, along with buffalo meat gift packs and New Zealand elk steaks. It's in the Smith's mall.

Getting There and Around

Access to Jackson Hole has become easier in recent years, with several airlines and daily buses now serving the valley. Most summer visitors arrive by car, although a few more adventurous souls pedal in on bikes. If you're looking for or offering a ride, KMTN (96.9 FM, 307/733-4500, www.kmtnthemountain.com) has daily ride-finder announcements during its Trash and Treasure radio program. Tune in weekdays 9:30–9:50 A.M.

Several local travel agencies offer reservation services for those who prefer to leave the planning to someone else. They can set up airline tickets, rental cars, lodging, horseback riding, fishing trips, whitewater rafting, ski vacations, and all sorts of other packages. The biggest is the long-established **Jackson Hole Central Reservations** (307/733-4005 or 800/443-6931, www.jacksonholewy.com), which produces a

slick glossy publication of featured properties. **Jackson Hole Reservations** (307/733-6331 or 800/329-9205, www.jacksonhole.net) has an equally complete listing of local places.

BY AIR

Jackson Hole Airport (307/733-7682, www .jacksonholeairport.com) is eight miles north of Jackson inside Grand Teton National Park. The airport is small and cozy but offers daily jet service to several U.S. cities. It's the only commercial airport within any national park, and the Grand Teton Association maintains a gift shop here. Stop by the **Ground Transportation Information Desk** (open daily 9 A.M.–5 P.M. year-round) for helpful maps and advice. Nearby are courtesy phones for local businesses and racks of brochures. You'll also find free Wi-Fi and a restaurant.

LONE HIGHWAYMAN OF YELLOWSTONE

Because of its remote location, Teton Valley became a rendezvous place for rustlers and outlaws in the 1880s. Horses stolen from the soldiers at Fort Hall, along with cattle "liberated" from Wyoming and Montana ranches, made their way through Pierre's Hole to the railroads. Hiram C. Lapham was the first to try his hand at ranching in the valley, but his cattle quickly disappeared. With the help of a posse from Rexburg, Lapham tracked down the culprits, one of whom was killed in the ensuing gunfight. The others surrendered but escaped from jail when the wife of bandit Ed Harrington smuggled a gun to her husband in clothing worn by his baby. Harrington and partner Lum Nickerson were eventually tracked down and sent to jail.

Although Harrington was sentenced to 25 years, the governor pardoned him after just three. Harrington went on to become Teton Valley's first postman, but his criminal activity continued. Using the alias Ed Trafton, Harrington went on to rob stores throughout Teton Valley and eventually spent another

two years behind bars. After getting out, he turned his attention to the tourism business in Yellowstone, but not in the standard way. Although it was never proven, he was suspected of being behind a string of stagecoach robberies in 1908 in which cash and jewelry were taken from tourists at gunpoint. Harrington's most brazen feat came on July 29, 1914, when he single-handedly robbed 15 stages, earning the nickname "the lone highwayman of Yellowstone." The tourists were particularly impressed with his gentlemanly manner as he asked them to "please" hand over all their cash and jewelry. Harrington made off with $915.35 in cash and $130 in jewelry, but he made the mistake of posing for photos in the process. He was caught the following year and spent five years in Leavenworth Prison.

When Harrington died, a letter in his pocket claimed that he had been Owen Wister's model for the Virginian in the famous novel of the same name. Others suspected that he was more likely to have been Wister's model for the villain, Trampas.

Delta/Skywest (800/221-1212, www.delta
.com) has year-round flights from Salt Lake
City, and seasonal flights from Atlanta and
Cincinnati. Some of the Salt Lake flights are
in smaller turboprops, others in jets; all Atlanta
and Cincinnati flights are jets. **American**
(800/433-7300, www.aa.com) has non-
stop summer and winter service from Dallas
and Chicago. **Northwest** (800/225-2525,
www.nwa.com) flies from Minneapolis/St.
Paul year-round. **United/United Express**
(800/241-6522, www.ual.com) offers year-
round service from Denver and seasonal
flights from Los Angeles. **Frontier Airlines**
(800/432-1359, www.frontierairlines.com) has
daily summer-only flights from Denver. In addition, the tarmac is often crowded with Lear
and Gulfstream jets and other noisy transportation symbols of the elite.

Jackson Hole Aviation (307/733-4767 or
800/437-5387, www.jhaviation.com) provides
charter air service.

If you're flying in from the Pacific
Northwest, you will need to go through either
Salt Lake City or Idaho Falls. The latter airport is served by Horizon Air (Alaska Airlines).
Many Seattle or Portland-based travelers opt to
fly to either Salt Lake (275 miles from Jackson)
or Idaho Falls (90 miles away) and pick up a
rental car for the drive to Jackson.

Airport Shuttles and Taxis
Alltrans/Gray Line of Jackson Hole
(307/733-3135 or 800/443-6133, www.jackson
holealltrans.com) provides airport shuttle service to and from motels in Jackson ($16 one-way
or $31 round-trip per person) and Teton Village
($26 one-way or $47 round-trip per person).
The shuttles meet nearly all commercial airline
flights in winter and most summertime flights,
but you should make reservations to be sure of
an airport pickup. Make outgoing reservations
for a motel pickup 24 hours in advance.

Local taxis provide direct service from the
airport to your hotel. The one-way rates for
one or two people are $32 to Jackson, or $55
to Teton Village. At last count there were
almost 20 local taxi companies, including

Buckboard Transportation (307/733-1112
or 877/791-0211, www.buckboardtrans
.com), **Bullseye Taxi** (307/730-5000),
Cowboy Cab (307/413-1000), **Old West Taxi**
(307/690-8898), **Teton Taxi** (307/733-1506,
www.tetontaxi.com), and **Westbank Cab**
(307/690-0112).

LONG-DISTANCE BUSES
Greyhound buses don't come even close to
Jackson; the nearest stopping place is the re-
gional hub at Salt Lake City. **Alltrans/Jackson
Hole Express** (307/733-3135 or 800/443-6133,
www.jacksonholealltrans.com) connects
Jackson with Salt Lake City ($80 one-way),
Idaho Falls ($40 one-way), and Pocatello ($48
one-way) daily. Buses operate year-round.

Salt Lake Express (207/736-8824 or
800/356-9796, www.saltlakeexpress.com)
runs shuttle vans connecting Jackson with
Idaho Falls four times daily for $46 one-way.
The company also has daily service continuing
south to Salt Lake, north to West Yellowstone
and Butte, and west to Twin Falls and Boise.

START BUSES
Local buses are operated by Southern Teton
Area Rapid Transit (START, 307/733-4521,
www.startbus.com) and serve Jackson and
Teton Village all year. START fares are **free**
within town and $3 one-way to Teton Village
($1.50 for seniors and children). Discount cou-
pons are available for multiple rides. Hours
of operation are generally 6 A.M.–10:30 P.M.
During summer and winter, buses run seven
days a week, with in-town service every half-
hour. Service to Teton Village is hourly (more
or less) in summer and two or three times an
hour in winter. Reduced bus service is available in fall and spring. Get schedules and route
maps in the visitor center. Buses stop near most
Jackson hotels and motels and are equipped to
carry skis (in winter) and bikes (in summer)
on outside racks. Unfortunately, START buses
do not run to the airport, Kelly, or Moose, but
commuter buses ($7 one-way) provide morn-
ing and evening service to Teton Valley, Idaho
(Driggs and Victor), as well as Star Valley.

CAR AND RV RENTALS

Most of the national chains offer rental cars in town or at the airport. These include **Alamo** (307/733-0671 or 888/426-3299, www.alamo.com), **Avis** (307/733-3422 or 800/831-2847, www.avis.com), **Budget** (270 W. Pearl St., 307/733-2206 or 800/237-7251, www.budget.com), **Dollar** (345 W. Broadway, 307/733-9224 or 877/222-7736, www.dollar.com), **Hertz** (307/733-2272 or 800/654-3131, www.hertz.com), **National** (220 N. Millward St., 307/733-7961 or 888/868-6204, www.nationalcar.com), and **Thrifty** (307/734-9306 or 800/847-4389, www.jackson.thrifty.com). Alamo, Avis, Hertz, and Budget all have counters at the airport, while the others provide a free shuttle to their offices in town. **Leisure Sports** (1075 S. Hwy. 89, 307/733-3040, www.leisuresportsadventure.com) also has a few rental cars.

The best deals are often from Dollar or Thrifty, but check one of the online reservation sources (www.travelocity.com or www.expedia.com) to see who currently has the best rates. You may be better off getting a car in town, where you don't have to pay the additional taxes imposed at the airport. Taxes and fees (especially for airport rentals) can add another 21 percent to your charges, so read the fine print! Reserve cars at least one month ahead during summer and two months ahead for midsummer or the Christmas-New Year's holiday period. Be sure to mention any discounts; an AAA membership generally cuts 10 percent from the bill.

Despite the Rent-A-Car in their name, **Eagle Rent-A-Car** (1875 N. Hwy. 89, 307/739-9999 or 800/582-2128) doesn't rent cars. Instead they provide RV rentals through Cruise America (www.cruiseamerica.com), ranging from 22-foot compact versions to spacious 30-foot behemoths.

PARK TOURS

Summertime bus tours of Grand Teton and Yellowstone national parks are available several times a week from **Alltrans/Gray Line of Jackson Hole** (307/733-3135 or 800/443-6133, www.jacksonholealltrans.com). Yellowstone tours last 11 hours and cost

$106 plus $12 for the park entrance. Eight-hour Grand Teton tours are $90 plus the $12 park entrance. Those without vehicles can use these tours for access to the parks; reserve to schedule a pickup in Jackson, Grand Teton, or Yellowstone. In Yellowstone, travelers can connect with other buses to West Yellowstone or Gardiner, Montana. During winter, Alltrans/Gray Line has daily bus runs to Flagg Ranch Resort for $58 one-way ($106 round-trip), arriving in time to meet the snowcoach departures for Yellowstone. Reservations required. Jackson taxi companies also offer shuttle services within the park and guided tours.

Operated by Teton Science School, **Wildlife Expeditions** (307/733-2623 or 888/945-3567, www.wildlifeexpeditions.org) leads an array of wildlife-viewing safaris throughout the region, from four-hour sunset trips for $125 to four-day tours through Yellowstone and Grand Teton for $1,895. Their trips change seasonally—depending upon which animals are visible—and are offered in customized vehicles with multiple roof hatches for better wildlife viewing.

Get a geologist's perspective on the area from **Earth Tours** (307/733-4261, www.earth-tours.com), with outstanding tours and hikes led by Dr. Keith Watts. He also guides full-day trips into Yellowstone and longer trips to southern Utah parks.

Other companies with guided van tours of the area include **Brushbuck Guide Services** (888/282-5868, www.brushbuckphototours.com), **Callowishus Park Touring Company** (307/413-5483, www.callowishus.com), **EcoTour Adventures** (307/690-9533, www.jhecotouradventures.com), **Jackson's Hole Adventure** (307/654-7849 or 800/392-3165, www.jacksonholeadventure.com), **Upstream Anglers and Outdoor Adventures** (307/739-9443 or 800/642-8979, www.upstreamanglers.com), **Grand Teton Adventure Company** (307/734-4454 or 800/700-1558, www.grandtetonadventures.com), **The Hole Hiking Experience** (307/690-4453 or 866/733-4453, www.holehike.com), and **Wyoming Photo Experience** (307/413-3777, www.wyomingphotoexperience.com).

JACKSON HOLE

Information and Services

INFORMATION

On the north side of town is the **Jackson Hole & Greater Yellowstone Visitor Center** (532 N. Cache Dr., 307/733-3316, www.jackson holechamber.com, open daily; see details above in *Sights*). Brochures are also available at the airport, the stagecoach stop on Town Square, next to the downtown public restrooms at Cache and Gill, and the Mangy Moose in Teton Village. Immediately south of the visitor center is an impressive building housing the **Wyoming Game and Fish** (307/733-2321) offices.

The **Bridger-Teton National Forest** supervisor's office (340 N. Cache Dr., 307/739-5500, www.fs.fed.us/r4/btnf) is open Monday–Friday 8 A.M.–4:30 P.M. Get information and Forest Service maps at the visitor center.

News

Find **National Public Radio's KUWJ** on your dial at 90.3 FM (www.wyomingpublic radio.net). The locals' commercial station is **KMTN** (www.kmtnthemountain.com) at 96.9 FM.

At 89.1 FM, radio station **KHOL** (www.jhcr.org) is a non-profit community station with a wide variety of music—free from ads—hosted by local DJs. Other Jackson Hole radio stations are KZJH 95.3 FM and KSGT 1340 AM. See www.jacksonholeradio.com for details on the commercial stations.

Jackson's outstanding local newspaper—the *Jackson Hole News and Guide* (307/733-2047, www.jhnewsandguide.com)—is produced in tabloid format. Free Monday–Saturday editions can be found all over the valley, and a fat weekly edition ($0.50) comes out on Wednesdays with more detailed local and regional coverage, including the weekly entertainment paper, *Stepping Out. Planet Jackson Hole* (307/732-0299, www.planetjh.com) is a free weekly that focuses on local music and entertainment.

Library

Spacious **Teton County Library** (125 Virginian La., 307/733-2164, www.tclib.org) is the kind of library every town should have. Inside this modern building is a large collection of books about Wyoming and the West, plus a great kids' section (complete with a fenced-in children's garden with a tepee). Computers provide free Internet access and are available by reservation or on a walk-up-and-wait basis. In the summer the queue can get long if you don't have a reservation. The library takes reservations up to one week in advance. Library hours are Monday–Thursday 10 A.M.–9 P.M., Friday 10 A.M.–5:30 P.M., Saturday 10 A.M.–5 P.M., and Sunday 1–5 P.M. If you plan to be in the Jackson area for a week or more, it may be worth your while to get a visitor's library card. For a one-time fee of $5 you can check out up to four books at a time.

Kid-Friendly Jackson

During summer, older kids will enjoy hiking, mountain biking, Snake River float and whitewater trips, and the putting course at Alpine Miniature Golf. In winter, snowboarding and skiing are favorites of older kids, but sleigh rides, dogsledding, ice-skating, and snowshoeing are also fun.

For those traveling with tots, **Baby's Away** (307/739-4711 or 888/616-8495) and **Babies on the Go** (307/690-8895, www.babies onthego-jh.com) rent all sorts of baby supplies, including car seats, cribs, gates, joggers, backpacks, swings, and high chairs.

You'll find more stroller and backpack rentals—along with trendy kids' clothing—at **Teton Kids** (130 E. Broadway, 307/739-2176). **Second Helpings** (141 E. Pearl Ave., 307/733-9466) has an excellent selection of quality used baby and children's clothes.

For child care, contact **Babysitting by the Tetons** (307/733-0754 or 866/733-0754, www.babysittingbythetetons.com), **Jackson Hole Babysitting** (307/732-7720, www.jacksonholebabysitting.com), or **Snake River Babysitting and Nannies** (307/699-1195, www.snakeriversitters.com).

Jackson Hole Mountain Resort (307/733-2292 or 888/333-7766, www.jackson hole.com, Mon.–Sat. mid-June–early Sept. and daily late Nov.–early Apr.) operates a Kids Ranch day camp with activities and child care for ages 6 months–11 years old. Programs are geared to different ages, and cost $95 per day.

Weddings

Jackson Hole makes a wonderful spot for a mountain wedding, with a grand setting, an abundance of fine lodging places and upscale caterers, plus easy access from anywhere in the nation. You can choose the simple back-to-nature version with a couple of family members along Jenny Lake or the full-blown variety at such places as Rancho Alegre Lodge ($12,500 per night, with a five-night minimum). A local company produces a slick 100-page free magazine called *A Grand Wedding* (www.jackson holewedding.com), filled with advice and ads for Jackson Hole caterers, locations, musicians, DJs, photographers, wedding consultants, spas, tent and carriage rentals, wedding cakes, limos,

and yes, even portable toilets. Also check out **Destination Jackson Hole** (307/734-5007, www.destinationjacksonhole.com) for wedding planning.

Looking for a stunning natural setting to tie the knot? Book your wedding at **Chapel of the Transfiguration** (307/733-2603) or **Chapel of the Sacred Heart** (307/733-2516) within Grand Teton National Park, but be ready to drop $2,000 or so to reserve a date.

SERVICES

Jackson's main **post office** (1070 Maple Way, 307/733-3650) near Powderhorn Lane is open Monday–Friday 8:30 A.M.–5 P.M., Saturday 10 A.M.–1 P.M. Other post offices are downtown (220 W. Pearl Ave., 307/739-1740), in Teton Village (307/733-3575), in Wilson (307/733-3335), and in Kelly (307/733-8884).

For shipping, packaging, and copying needs, head to the **UPS Stores** at 970 W. Broadway, 307/733-9250, and 3465 N. Pines Way, 307/733-7110.

Wash clothes at **Ryan Cleaners** (545 N.

JACKSON HOLE

© DON PITCHER

The Chapel of the Transfiguration is a wonderful spot for a wedding.

Cache Dr., 307/733-2938), or **Missing Sock** (1325 S. Hwy. 89, 307/739-9274). Showers ($6 with a towel) are available in the Bunkhouse section of **Anvil Motel** (215 N. Cache Dr., 307/733-3668 or 800/234-4507, www.anvil motel.com).

Going Green

Jackson has been at the forefront of the movement to practice the three R's: reduce, reuse, and recycle. Many businesses have attempted to go green (or at least to gain good publicity by saying all the right things). Even the ski resorts have gotten in on the action. Jackson Hole Mountain Resort—one of the largest users of energy in the valley—is committed to getting 50 percent of its energy from renewables such as wind, biomass, small hydro, and geothermal. **Reduce, Reuse, Recycle Jackson Hole** (www.howdoyourrr.com) recognizes local businesses that promote conservation.

Just because you're on vacation doesn't mean you should just chuck everything in the trash. If you don't need that extra plastic bag or napkin, don't take it. Bring your coffee mug instead of getting a throwaway cup. Walk or bike

SAVING JACKSON HOLE

The Jackson Hole economy has been stuck in permanent high gear for the last few decades as Jackson has grown from a sleepy burg to a national focal point for outdoor fun. From 1990 to 2000, the population nearly doubled, and today the area is home is approaching 10,000 people. Expensive homes now spread across old ranch lands, retailers such as Kmart have moved in, and development reaches for miles south from Jackson itself. Surrounding towns such as Alpine and Driggs have become bedroom communities for those willing to endure the long commute to Jackson, and their growth spreads the problems outward from Jackson.

Although 97 percent of the land in Teton County is in the public domain, the 70,000 acres of private land that remain are rapidly being developed, and Jackson Hole is in grave danger of losing the wild beauty that has attracted visitors for more than a century. This dilemma is immediately obvious to anyone arriving in Jackson. Instead of the wide-open spaces that remain protected by public land ownership, the edges of Jackson are falling under a proliferation of trophy homes, real-estate offices, chain motels, fast-food outlets, megamarts, gas stations, and elaborate banks, all competing beneath a thicket of signs. Summertime traffic jams are becoming all too common in this once-quiet place, where more than 35,000 visitors can be found on a summer afternoon.

Way back in 1994, Jackson voters got fed up with the pace of development and voted to scrap the town's 2 percent lodging tax, which had provided more than $1 million per year in funding to promote Jackson Hole around the world. Despite this lack of promotional effort, growth shows no signs of slowing down. Housing costs continue to spiral upward, pushed by a wealthy clientele willing to drop $2 million or more for a Jackson Hole home. A moratorium on large commercial developments went into effect in 2008, but smaller developments with housing for employees will be allowed.

The **Jackson Hole Conservation Alliance** (307/733-9417, www.jhalliance.com) is an 1,800-member environmental group that works to preserve the remaining natural areas of Jackson Hole. Membership starts at $30 per year and includes triannual newsletters and a chance to help control the many developments that threaten this still-beautiful valley.

Another influential local group is the **Jackson Hole Land Trust** (307/733-4707, www .jhlandtrust.org). Established in 1980, this nonprofit organization obtains conservation easements to maintain ranches and other land threatened by development. The group has protected more than 20,000 acres in the valley in this way, including the 1,740-acre Walton Ranch, visible along the highway between Jackson and Wilson.

instead of driving around town. Even the small steps add up.

Jackson has a good recycling program and accepts newspaper, aluminum cans, glass, tin cans, plastic milk jugs, magazines, catalogs, cardboard, and office paper. The **recycling center** (307/733-7678, www.tetonwyo.org/recycling) is the big brown building two miles south of the high school on U.S. Hwy. 89, but bins are also located on the rodeo grounds on the corner of Snow King Ave. and Flat Creek Drive.

Banking

Get fast cash from **ATMs** at many locations around town, including banks, grocers, downtown shops, the airport, plus in Teton Village and the Aspens.

International travelers will appreciate the currency exchange where you can swap those Euros, Japanese yens, or colorful Canadian dollars at all four **Wells Fargo** (307/733-3737, www.wellsfargo.com) locations: 112 Center Street, 50 Buffalo Way, Teton Village, and in the Aspens on Teton Village Road. (Formerly called Jackson State Bank, the largest local bank was swallowed up by Wells Fargo in 2008. The town still does have one independent bank, the Bank of Jackson Hole.)

Photography

D. D. Camera Corral (60 S. Cache, 307/733-3831) is the local photo shop, with a good selection of professional and point-and-shoot equipment.

Serious professional or semipro photographers should not miss **Photography at the Summit** (303/295-7770 or 800/745-3211, www.photographyatthesummit.com), an extraordinary five-day series of workshops led by internationally famous photographers and photo editors. The staff always includes a contingent of *National Geographic* photographers. Evening talks—held at the National Museum of Wildlife Art—are open to the public. Also notable are photography workshops through **Jackson Hole Center for the Arts** (240 S. Glenwood, 307/734-8956, www.jhcenterforthearts.org).

Internet

To keep in touch with folks via email, use the free terminals in the **public library.** Another option is **Mountunes** (265 W. Broadway, 307/733-4514, www.mountunes.com). In addition to a diverse collection of new and used CDs for sale, it has an Internet café where computer time costs $5 per half hour. Wi-Fi is free if you buy an espresso drink. Open daily 11 A.M.–7 P.M. in summer; reduced hours the rest of the year.

Check out the current conditions around Jackson at the following **Web camera** sites: www.wyoroad.info and www.alltravelcams .com; the latter includes cameras in Town Square, the airport, Spring Creek Ranch, and Teton Valley, plus other regional webcams.

Across from the post office on the south end of town, **Hard Drive Café** (1110 Maple Way, 307/733-5282, www.harddrivecafe.biz, daily 6 A.M.–3 P.M.) has free Wi-Fi plus rental computers ($6 per half hour).

A great place to begin your Web tour is the chamber of commerce site: www.jackson holechamber.com. Also very useful are www .jacksonholetraveler.com and www.jackson holenet.com. All three of these contain links to dozens of local businesses of all types. You may also want to check out the Teton County website, www.tetonwyo.org. Federal government websites for the local area include Grand Teton National Park at www.nps.gov/grte, Yellowstone National Park at www.nps.gov/yell, Bridger-Teton National Forest at www.fs.fed.us/ r4/btnf, and Caribou-Targhee National Forest at www.fs.fed.us/r4/caribou-targhee.

Medical

Because of the abundance of ski and snowboard accidents, orthopedic specialists are in high demand in Jackson and are some of the best around. The specialists at **Teton Orthopaedics** (555 E. Broadway, 307/733-3900 or 800/659-1335, www.teton ortho.com) are official physicians for the U.S. and French national ski teams!

St. John's Medical Center (625 E. Broadway, 307/733-3636, www.tetonhospital.org) has emergency medical services. They also operate a winter-only ski-in clinic at Teton Village, 307/739-7346. Medical service on a walk-in basis is available at **Emerg-A-Care** (982 W. Broadway, 307/733-8002) in Powderhorn Mall or **Urgent Care of Jackson Hole** (1415 S. Hwy. 89, 307/739-8999, www.urgentcare ofjh.com) next to the Smith's store.

Pets

Several local kennels in Jackson will keep an eye on Fido for you. **Happy Tails Pet Resort/ Spring Creek Animal Hospital** (1035 W. Broadway, 307/733-1606, www.springcreek animalhospital.com) provides veterinary care and kennels for Fido. **Critter Camp/Jackson Hole Veterinary Clinic** (2950 Big Trail Dr., 307/733-4279) has a small pet boarding facility, and **Rally's Pet Garage** (520 S. Hwy. 89, 307/733-7704, www.rallyspetgarage.com) is a unique service with "doggie daycare," boarding, dog baths, and grooming.

Bridger-Teton National Forest

One of the largest national forests in the Lower 48, Bridger-Teton ("the B-T") National Forest stretches southward for 135 miles from the Yellowstone border and covers 3.4 million acres. In Jackson Hole, the two areas of most interest for recreation are the Teton Wilderness and the Gros Ventre Wilderness, but nonwilderness areas offer additional opportunities for recreation.

The Bridger-Teton National Forest **supervisor's office** (307/739-5500, www .fs.fed.us/r4/btnf) is at 340 North Cache Drive in Jackson. The visitor center, a couple of blocks north on Cache, usually has a Forest Service worker on duty who can provide recreation information. The center also sells Bridger-Teton maps and has a good choice of outdoor books. Local ranger stations are the **Jackson Ranger District** (directly behind the supervisor's office, 307/739-5400) and the **Blackrock Ranger Station** (nine miles east of Moran Junction, 307/543-2386).

TETON WILDERNESS

The Teton Wilderness covers 585,468 acres of mountain country, bordered to the north by Yellowstone National Park, to the west by Grand Teton National Park, and to the east by the Washakie Wilderness. Established as a primitive area in 1934, it was declared one of the nation's first wilderness areas upon passage of the 1964 Wilderness Act. The Teton Wilderness offers a diverse mixture of rolling lands carpeted with lodgepole pine, spacious grassy meadows, roaring rivers, and dramatic mountains. Elevations range from 7,500 feet to the 12,165-foot summit of Younts Peak. The Continental Divide slices across the wilderness, with headwaters of the Yellowstone River draining the eastern half and headwaters of the Buffalo and Snake rivers flowing down the western side. Teton Wilderness has a considerable amount of bear activity, so make sure you know how to avoid bear encounters and bring pepper spray.

One of the most unusual places within Teton Wilderness is **Two Ocean Creek,** where a creek abruptly splits at a rock and the two branches never rejoin. One branch becomes Atlantic Creek, and its waters eventually reach the Atlantic Ocean, while the other becomes Pacific Creek and its waters flow to the Snake River, the Columbia River, and thence into the Pacific Ocean! Mountain man Osborne Russell described this phenomenon in 1835:

On the South side about midway of the prairie stands a high snowy peak from whence issues a Stream of water which after entering the plain it divides equally one half running West and other East thus bidding adieu to each other one bound for the Pacific and the other for the Atlantic ocean. Here a trout of 12 inches in length may cross the mountains in safety. Poets have sung of the "meeting of the waters" and fish climbing cataracts but the "parting of the waters and fish crossing mountains" I believe remains unsung yet by all except the solitary Trapper who sits under the shade of a spreading pine whistling blank-verse and beating time to the tune with a whip on his trap sack whilst musing on the parting advice of these waters.

Natural events have had a major effect on the Teton Wilderness. On July 21, 1987, a world-record high-elevation tornado created a 10,000-acre blowdown of trees around the Enos Lake area, and it took years to rebuild the trails. A series of fires followed—including the Huck and Mink Creek fires that burned 200,000 acres. Don't let these incidents dissuade you from visiting; this is still a marvelous and little-used area, and more than 60 percent of the land was not burned. Herds of elk graze in alpine areas, and many consider the Thorofare country abutting Yellowstone National Park the most remote place in the Lower 48. This is prime grizzly habitat and you may well encounter them, so be very cautious at all times. Poles for hanging food have been placed at most campsites, as have bear-resistant boxes or barrels. Use them, and always keep a clean camp. You can rent bear-resistant backpacker food tubes or horse panniers from the Blackrock Ranger District (307/543-2386), but it's a good idea to make reservations for these items before your trip.

Access

Three primary trailheads provide access to the Teton Wilderness: Pacific Creek on the southwestern end, Turpin Meadow on the Buffalo Fork River, and Brooks Lake just east of the Continental Divide. Campgrounds are at each of these trailheads. Teton Wilderness is a favorite of Wyomingites, particularly those with horses, and in the fall elk hunters from across

the nation come here. Distances are so great and some of the stream crossings so intimidating that few backpackers head into this wilderness area. No permits are needed, but it's a good idea to stop in at the **Blackrock Ranger District** (307/543-2386) nine miles east of Moran Junction on U.S. Hwy. 26/287, for topographic maps and information on current trail conditions, bear problems, regulations, and a list of permitted outfitters offering horse or llama trips.

For a shorter trip, you could take a guided horseback ride at the Turpin Meadow Trailhead with **Yellowstone Outfitters** (307/543-2418 or 800/447-4711, www.yellowstoneoutfitters .com) or **Buffalo Valley Ranch** (307/543-2062 or 888/543-2477, www.buffalovalleyranch .com). **Teton Horseback Adventures** (307/730-8829 or 307/367-3291, www.horse backadv.com) heads out from the Pacific Creek Trailhead. All three of these outfitters offer pack trips into the Teton Wilderness.

Unfortunately, USGS maps don't show the many Teton Wilderness trails built and maintained (or not maintained) by private outfitters and hunters. These can make hiking confusing since not every junction is signed. Forest Service maps for the wilderness have been updated with most trail locations. A few of the many possible hikes are described as follows.

Whetstone Creek

Whetstone Creek Trail begins at the Pacific Creek Trailhead, on the southwest side of Teton Wilderness. An enjoyable 20-mile round-trip hike leaves the trailhead and follows Pacific Creek for 1.5 miles before splitting left to follow Whetstone Creek. Bear left when the trail splits again another three miles upstream and continue through a series of small meadows to the junction with Pilgrim Creek Trail. Turn right here and follow this trail two more miles to Coulter Creek Trail, climbing up Coulter Creek to scenic Coulter Basin and then dropping along the East Fork of Whetstone Creek. This rejoins the Whetstone

Creek Trail and returns you to the trailhead, passing many attractive small meadows along the way. The upper half of this loop hike was burned in 1988; some areas were heavily scorched, while others are patchy. Flowers are abundant in the burned areas, and this is important elk habitat.

South Fork to Soda Fork

A fine loop hike leaves Turpin Meadow and follows South Buffalo Fork River to South Fork Falls. Just above this point, a trail splits off and climbs to Nowlin Meadow (excellent views of Smokehouse Mountain) and then down to Soda Fork River, where it joins the Soda Fork Trail. Follow this trail back downstream to huge Soda Fork Meadow (a good place to see moose and occasionally grizzlies) and then back to Turpin Meadow, a distance of approximately 23 miles round-trip. For a fascinating side trip from this route, head up the Soda Fork into the alpine at Crater Lake, a six-mile hike above the Nowlin Meadow-Soda Fork Trail junction. The outlet stream at Crater Lake disappears into a gaping hole, emerging as a large creek two miles below at Big Springs. It's an incredible sight.

Cub Creek Area

The Brooks Lake area just east of Togwotee Pass is a popular summertime camping and fishing place with magnificent views. Brooks Lake Trail follows the western shore of Brooks Lake and continues past Upper Brooks Lakes to Bear Cub Pass. From here, the trail drops to Cub Creek, where you'll find several good campsites. You can make a long and scenic loop by following the trail up Cub Creek into the alpine country and then back down along the South Buffalo Fork River to Lower Pendergraft Meadow. From here, take the Cub Creek Trail back up along Cub Creek to Bear Cub Pass and back out to Brooks Lake. Get a topographic map before heading into this remote country. Total distance is approximately 33 miles round-trip.

GROS VENTRE WILDERNESS

The 287,000-acre Gros Ventre Wilderness was established in 1984 and covers the mountain country just east of Jackson Hole. This range trends mainly in a northwest-southeast direction and is probably best known for Sleeping Indian Mountain (maps now call it Sheep Mountain, but locals never use that appellation), the distinctive rocky summit visible from Jackson Hole. Although there are densely forested areas at lower elevations, the central section of the wilderness lies above timberline, and many peaks top 10,000 feet. The tallest is Doubletop Peak at 11,682 feet. The Tetons are visible from almost any high point in the Gros Ventre, and meadows line the lower-elevation streams. Elk, mule deer, bighorn sheep, moose, and black bears are found here, and a few grizzlies have been reported. The Forest Service office in Jackson has more information on the wilderness, including brief trail descriptions and maps.

Access and Trails

Several roads provide good access to the Gros Ventre Wilderness: Gros Ventre River Road on the northern border; Curtis Canyon Road on the western margin; and Granite Creek Road to the south. Flat Creek is rough and accessible only in a 4WD vehicle. Hikes beginning or ending in the Granite Creek area have the added advantage of nearby Granite Hot Springs, a great place to soak tired muscles.

For a beautiful hike, follow **Highline Trail** from the Granite Creek area across to Cache Creek, a distance of 16 miles. This route passes just below a row of high and rugged mountains, but because it isn't a loop route, you'll need to hitchhike or set up a shuttle back. Plan on three days for this hike. The area is crisscrossed with game and cattle trails, making it easy to get lost, especially on the headwaters of Little Granite Creek. Talk with Forest Service folks before heading out, and make sure that you know how to read a map and compass.

A third hike begins at the **Goosewing**

© DON PITCHER

Granite Hot Springs

Ranger Station, 12 miles east of Slide Lake on Gros Ventre River Road. Take the trail from here to Two Echo Park (a fine camping spot) and then continue up to Six Lakes. You can return via the same trail or take the Crystal Creek Trail back to Red Rock Ranch and hitch back to Goosewing. The trail distance is approximately 23 miles round-trip.

GRANITE HOT SPRINGS
At the head of a gorgeous mountain valley, Granite Hot Springs (307/734-7400) is a wonderful escape both summer and winter. Get here by driving south from Jackson 12 miles to Hoback Junction and then another 12 miles east on U.S. Hwy. 189 to the turnoff at Granite Creek Road. This well-maintained gravel road follows Granite Creek for 10 miles, affording impressive views of the Gros Ventre Range and the 50-foot drop of **Granite Falls.** The road ends at a parking lot just a short walk from the

hot springs. The deep pool was built in 1933 by the CCC and recently improved with a deck and changing rooms. The pool stays around 93°F in the summer but rises to 112°F in winter when the water flow slows. The springs are open daily 10 A.M.–8 P.M. June–October, and 11 A.M.–5 P.M. December–March; closed in the fall and spring. No showers or running water are available at the pool, but vault toilets are nearby. The cost is $6 adults, $4 ages 3–12, and free for infants. Suits and towels can be rented, and a few snacks are sold here. Granite Canyon Road is not plowed in winter but is groomed for use by both snowmobilers and cross-country skiers. A nearby campground ($15) is open mid-May–September. The campground almost never fills up and is managed by folks from the hot springs; no reservations. Dispersed camping is allowed on the road to Granite Hot Springs, except along the final 1.3 miles before the springs.

Caribou-Targhee National Forest

Covering nearly three million acres, Caribou-Targhee National Forest extends from Montana to Utah. Most of the forest lies within Idaho, but it also includes the western edge of Wyoming along the Tetons. Much of the forest is heavily logged, but two wilderness areas protect most of the Wyoming section. Contact the Forest Service office in Driggs, Idaho (208/354-2312, www.fs.fed.us/r4/caribou-targhee) for more recreation information.

Hiking

Many short hiking options are available on the west side of the Tetons, and the Forest Service office in Driggs has a handout that describes more than 20 of these hikes. A few of the best include the following. From Darby Canyon Trailhead, you can choose either the **Aspen Trail** (3.6 miles one-way; especially pretty in the fall) or the **South Darby Trail** (2.7 miles one-way; with nice waterfalls and flowered meadows).

From the South Teton Trailhead, you can opt to climb **Table Mountain** (6.4 miles one-way), visit gorgeous **Alaska Basin** (7.7 miles one-way), or ascend the **Devil's Stairs** to Teton Shelf (6.8 miles one-way). All three of these hikes take you high into the alpine, but many families just hike until the kids get tired, eat lunch, and then head back to the car.

Several trails take off from the Teton Pass area along Wyoming Hwy. 22/Idaho Hwy. 33, including **Moose Creek Trail,** which leads to Moose Meadows (5.4 miles one-way), and the **Teton Crest Trail** if you're feeling very ambitious (nine miles one-way). It joins another popular hiking route, the **Coal Creek Trail,** for an alternative return route to the highway.

JEDEDIAH SMITH WILDERNESS

The 123,451-acre Jedediah Smith Wilderness lies on the west side of the Teton Range, facing Idaho but lying entirely within Wyoming. Access is primarily from the Idaho side, although trails breach the mountain passes at various points, making it possible to enter from Grand Teton National Park. This area was not declared a wilderness until 1984. A second wilderness area, the 10,820-acre **Winegar Hole Wilderness** (pronounced WINE-a-gur), lies along the southern border of Yellowstone National Park. Grizzlies love this country, but hikers will find it uninteresting and without trails. In contrast, the Jedediah Smith Wilderness contains nearly 200 miles of paths and some incredible high-mountain scenery.

Several mostly gravel roads lead up from the Driggs and Victor areas into the Tetons. Get a map ($7) showing wilderness trails and access points from the Caribou-Targhee National Forest ranger station in Driggs, Idaho (208/354-2312) or from the Forest Service offices in Jackson. Be sure to camp at least 200 feet from lakes and 100 feet from streams. Group size limits are also in place; check with the Forest Service for specifics on these and other backcountry regulations. In addition, anyone planning to cross into Grand Teton National Park from the west side will need to get a park camping permit in advance. Wilderness permits are not required for the Jedediah Smith Wilderness. Both grizzly and black bears are present throughout the Tetons, so all food must be either hung out of reach or stored in bear-resistant containers.

Hidden Corral Basin

At the northern end of the wilderness, Hidden Corral Basin provides a fine loop hike. Locals (primarily those on horseback) crowd this area on late-summer weekends. Get to the trailhead by driving north from Tetonia on Idaho Hwy. 32 to Lamont, then turn north on a gravel road. Follow it one mile and then turn right (east) onto Coyote Meadows Road. The trailhead is approximately 10 miles up, where the road dead-ends. An eight-mile trail parallels South Bitch Creek (the name Bitch Creek comes from the French word for a female deer, *biche*) to Hidden Corral, where you may see moose. Be sure to bring a fishing pole to try for the cutthroats.

Above Hidden Corral you can make a pleasant loop back by turning north onto the trail to Nord Pass and then dropping along the Carrot Ridge and Conant Basin trails to Bitch Creek Trail and then on to Coyote Meadows, a distance of 21 miles round-trip. Note that this is grizzly and black bear country, and bear-resistant containers are required. By the way, Hidden Corral received its name in the outlaw days, when rustlers would steal horses in Idaho, change the brands, and hold the horses in this natural corral until the branding wounds healed. The horses were then sold to Wyoming ranchers. Owen Wister's *The Virginian* describes a pursuit of horse thieves through Bitch Creek country.

(Alaska Basin

The most popular hiking trail in the Jedediah Smith begins near the **Teton Canyon Campground** (518/885-3639 or 877/444-6777 for reservations, www.reservations.gov, open late-May–mid-Sept., $10–18) and leads through flower-bedecked meadows to mountain-rimmed Alaska Basin. It's great country, but don't expect a true wilderness experience because many others will also be hiking and camping here. Get to the campground by following the Grand Targhee Ski Resort signs east from Driggs, Idaho. A gravel road splits off to the right approximately three miles beyond the little settlement of Alta. Follow it to the campground. (If you miss the turn, you'll end up at the ski area.) For an enjoyable loop, follow Alaska Basin Trail up the canyon to Basin Lakes and then head southwest along the Teton Crest Trail to the Teton Shelf Trail. Follow this trail back to its junction with the Alaska Basin Trail, dropping down the Devils Stairs—a series of very steep switchbacks. You can then take the Alaska Basin Trail back to Teton Campground, a round-trip distance of approximately 19 miles. You could also use these trails to reach the high peaks of the Tetons or to cross the mountains into Death Canyon within Grand Teton National Park (camping permit required). Campfires and horse camping are not allowed in Alaska Basin.

Moose Meadows

For a somewhat less crowded hiking experience, check out the Moose Meadows area on the southern end of the Jedediah Smith Wilderness. Get to the trailhead by going three miles southeast of Victor on Idaho Hwy. 33. Turn north (left) on Moose Creek Road and follow it to the trailhead. The trail parallels Moose Creek to Moose Meadows, a good place to camp. You'll need to ford the creek twice, so this trail is best hiked in late summer. At the meadows, the trail deadends into Teton Crest Trail, providing access to Grand Teton National Park through some gorgeous alpine country. A nice loop can be made by heading south along this trail to flower-covered Coal Creek Meadows. A trail leads from here past 10,068-foot Taylor Mountain (an easy side trip with magnificent views), down to Taylor Basin, through lodgepole forests, and then back to your starting point. This loop hike will take you 15 miles round-trip.

JACKSON HOLE

Teton Valley, Idaho

The west side of the Tetons differs dramatically from nearby Jackson Hole. As the road descends from Teton Pass into Teton Valley, Idaho (a.k.a. Pierre's Hole), the lush farming country spreads out before you, 30 miles long and 15 miles across. This, the "quiet side" of the Tetons, offers a slower pace than bustling Jackson, but the Teton Range vistas are equally dramatic.

In recent years the growth in Jackson Hole has spilled across the mountains. The potato farms, horse pastures, and country towns are now undergoing the same transformation that first hit Jackson in the 1970s. As land prices soar and affordable housing becomes more difficult to find in Jackson, more people have opted to move over the pass and commute from Idaho.

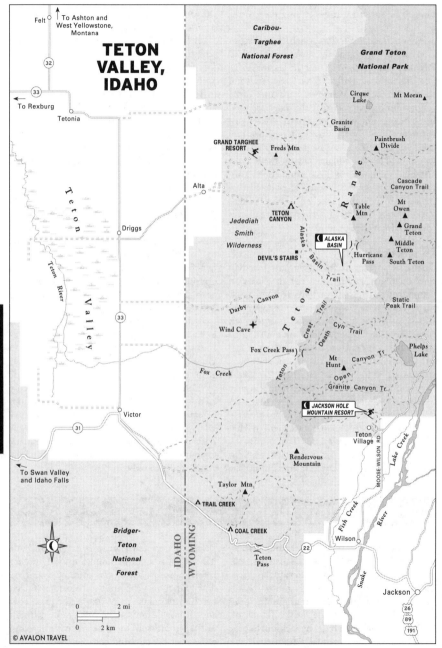

Felt

To Ashton and
West Yellowstone,
Montana

TETON
VALLEY,
IDAHO

32

33

To Rexburg

Tetonia

Caribou-
Targhee
National Forest

Grand Teton
National Park

Cirque
Lake

Mt Moran

Granite
Basin

GRAND TARGHEE
RESORT

Freds Mtn

Paintbrush
Divide

Alta

Cascade
Canyon Trail

Teton

Jedediah
Smith
Wilderness

TETON
CANYON

Table
Mtn

Mt
Owen

Grand
Teton

Range

DEVIL'S STAIRS

ALASKA
BASIN

Middle
Teton

Alaska Basin Trail

Hurricane
Pass

South Teton

Driggs

Teton River

V a l l e y

33

Darby Canyon

Wind Cave

Static
Peak Trail

Teton Crest Trail

Death Cyn Trail

Phelps
Lake

Fox Creek Pass

Fox Creek

Mt
Hunt

Canyon Tr

Open
Granite Canyon Tr.

JACKSON HOLE
MOUNTAIN RESORT

Victor

31

To Swan Valley
and Idaho Falls

Teton
Village

MOOSE-WILSON RD

Lake Creek

Rendezvous
Mountain

Taylor Mtn

TRAIL CREEK

COAL CREEK

Teton
Pass

22

Wilson

Fish Creek

Snake River

IDAHO

WYOMING

Bridger-
Teton
National
Forest

Jackson

26

89

191

0   2 mi

0   2 km

© AVALON TRAVEL

Glossy ads now fill *Teton Valley Magazine,* offering ranchland with a view, luxurious log homes, cozy second homes, private aircraft hangars, espresso coffee, mountain-bike rentals, and handmade lodgepole furniture. Despite these changes, Teton Valley remains a laid-back place, and spud farming is still a part of the local economy. The primary town here—it's the county seat—is Driggs, with Victor nine miles south and tiny Tetonia eight miles north.

History

The area now known as Teton Valley was used for centuries by various Indian tribes, including the Bannock, Blackfeet, Crow, Gros Ventre, Shoshone, and Nez Perce. John Colter—a member of the Lewis and Clark expedition—was the first white man to reach this area, wandering through in the winter of 1807–1808. In 1931, an Idaho farmer claimed to have plowed up a stone carved into the shape of a human face, with "John Colter 1808" etched into the sides. The rock later turned out to be a hoax created by a man anxious to obtain a horse concession with Grand Teton National Park. He got the concession after donating the rock to the park museum.

Vieux Pierre, an Iroquois fur trapper for the Hudson's Bay Company, made this area his base in the 1820s, but was later killed by Blackfeet Indians in Montana. Many people still call the valley Pierre's Hole. Two fur trapper rendezvous took place in Pierre's Hole, but the 1832 event proved pivotal. About 1,000 Indians, trappers, and traders gathered for an annual orgy of trading, imbibing, and general partying. When a column of men on horseback appeared, two white trappers headed out for a meeting. The column turned out to be a group of Gros Ventre Indians, and the meeting quickly turned sour. One trapper shot the Gros Ventre chief point-blank, killing him. A battle quickly ensued that left 38 people dead on both sides and forced rendezvous participants to scatter. Later rendezvous were held in valleys where the animosities were not as high. For the next 50 years, virtually the only whites in Pierre's Hole were horse thieves and outlaws. Hiram C. Lapham was the first to

try his hand at ranching in the valley, but his cattle were rustled by three outlaws, including Ed Harrington, alias Ed Trafton.

In 1888, a lawyer from Salt Lake City, B. W. Driggs, came to the valley and liked what he found. With his encouragement, a flood of Mormon settlers arrived in the next few years, establishing farms along the entire length of Teton Valley. By the 1940s the valley was home to a cheese factory, sawmills, a railroad line, and numerous sprawling ranches. Teton Valley's population plummeted in the 1960s, but in 1969 development began at Grand Targhee Ski Resort, and the economy started to turn around. Recent years have seen the area come into its own as tourism-related businesses began to eclipse farming and ranching. Over the last decade or so the valley has boomed, making Teton County, Idaho one of the fastest-growing counties (on a percentage basis) in the nation.

Teton Valley Recreation

Outdoor enthusiasts will discover all sorts of activities at all times of the year in the Driggs area. The Teton River runs the entire length of Teton Valley and is renowned among fly-fishing enthusiasts, canoeists, and bird-watchers. A plethora of hikes can be found both to the east in the Tetons and to the west in the Big Hole Mountains. (See the *Caribou-Targhee National Forest* section for details on *Alaska Basin;* it's one of the most popular day—or multi-night—hikes in the area.) The Forest Service office in Driggs has details on other hiking options if you're looking for a less crowded experience.

Friends of the Teton River (36 E. Little Ave., 208/354-3871, www.tetonwater.org) is a nonprofit group that works to preserve the Teton Basin. Its office also exhibits works by local artists.

The **National Outdoor Leadership School** (NOLS, 166 E. 200 S., 208/354-8443, www .nols.edu) has an office off the main road south of Driggs; headquarters is in Lander, Wyoming. The Driggs office runs summertime backpacking and whitewater training, plus backcountry skiing classes in the winter. Courses last two weeks to three months.

JACKSON HOLE

© DON PITCHER

Teton Range, as seen from Teton Valley

Kids and their parents will appreciate the **Driggs Town Park,** with an attractive playground and sprinklers that make for impromptu summer fun. It's on Ashley Street. A paved **bike path** parallels Hwy. 33 between Victor and Driggs, providing a pleasant running, cycling, or inline skating opportunity. A wide bike lane heads east from Driggs all the way to the Targhee Resort. The non-profit **Teton Valley Trails & Pathways** (208/201-1622, www.tvtap .org) has online maps showing local routes.

Peaked Sports (70 E. Little Ave., 208/354-2354 or 800/705-2354, www.peaked sports.com) rents mountain bikes, bike trailers, and kayaks in the summer, along with skis, snowboards, and snowshoes in the winter. Stop by for a helpful biking map of the area.

High Peaks Health and Fitness Center (50 Ski Hill Rd., 208/354-3128, www.high peakspt.com) has $10 day passes. **The Links at Teton Peaks** (127 N. 400 W., 208/456-2374) is a Scottish-style nine-hole golf course. It's one of five golf courses in Teton Valley, with two more expected to open by 2010.

Horseback rides and pack trips are available from **Dry Ridge Outfitters** (208/354-2284, www.dryridge.com) or nearby Grand Targhee Ski Resort. For horseback rides and winter sleigh rides, head to **Linn Canyon Ranch** (130 E. 600 South, 208/787-5466, www.linn canyonranch.com).

Bagley's Teton Mountain Ranch (265 W. 800 S., 208/787-9005 or 866/787-9005, www .elkadventures.com) raises more than 100 elk as breeding stock and for their antlers. It offers summertime wagon rides and wintertime sleigh rides among the elk for $9, plus horseback rides (starting at $35 for a one-hour ride).

Teton Aviation Center (208/354-3100 or 800/472-6382, www.tetonaviation.com) is best known for its scenic glider flights ($250 for a one-hour flight) past the Tetons, but it also offers airplane rides and has an impressive collection of vintage military aircraft.

Teton Balloon Flights (208/787-5500 or 866/533-6404, www.tetonballooning.com) offers one-hour hot-air balloon flights over Teton Valley for $250 per person in the summer.

Teton Valley Events

The main summer event, the **Teton Valley Summer Festival** (208/354-2500), comes on

Fourth of July weekend. Highlights include hot-air balloon launches (more than 40 balloons) and tethered rides for the kids at the airport, a parade and crafts fair in Victor, a rodeo in Tetonia, arts exhibits, a pig roast, live music, and evening fireworks in Driggs.

Grand Targhee Ski Resort pulls out the stops for the always-popular **Targhee Bluegrass Festival** (307/353-2300 or 800/827-4433, www.grandtarghee.com) in mid-August, with nationally known acts. The music attracts a throng, so make camping or lodging reservations well ahead of time.

In mid-August, the **Teton County Fair** (208/354-2961) brings down-home fun with livestock judging, arts and crafts, quilts, and pies, jams, and other fare on display. One of the unique local events is **Spudfest** (www.spudfest.org), with independent features, documentary and short films, some of which are shown at the Spud Drive-In in mid-August.

On Thursday evenings in July and August, **Music on Main** (208/201-5356, www.tetonvalleyfoundation.org) brings free concerts (two bands nightly) to downtown Driggs. This is a surprisingly big deal, attracting some nationally known acts.

VICTOR

Twenty-four miles west of Jackson, the town of Victor, Idaho, was—until recently—little more than the proverbial wide spot in the road. But things have changed dramatically as the population doubled in just five years and an ugly sprawl of homes and businesses covered former ranchland. Despite this, the town does have a couple of places worth noting.

Pierre's Playhouse (on Main St. in Victor, 208/787-2249, www.pierresplayhouse.com) puts on old-fashioned melodramas Thursday–Saturday mid-June–early September. An optional Dutch-oven chicken dinner is served before the show. You know you're in for a serious production when the villain is named Gustavo Scumsuckler.

Accommodations

Trails End Motel (208/787-2973, $90) rents

simple four-person log cabin units with microwaves and fridges and is open May–mid-October.

Two miles south of town on Pole Canyon Rd., **Kasper's Kountryside Inn** (208/787-2726, www.tetonvalleychamber.com/kountrysideinn.htm, $99 for up to four) is a barn-like building with two modern apartments with full kitchens.

Teton Springs is more evidence of the spillover effect from Jackson. This private club for the moneyed class includes 500 homes and condos, a golf course, spa, tennis courts, swimming pool, and an "old town village" with shopping, dining, lodging, and more. A heliport waits for those who can afford the helicopter flight over to Jackson for the evening. Various lodging options are offered at **Teton Springs Lodge & Spa** (208/787-7888 or 877/787-8757, www.tetonspringslodge.com), including luxurious hotel rooms ($289 d) and suites ($379 d). Condos and sprawling four-bedroom "cabins" are also available on a nightly or weekly basis.

On the north end of town, **Cowboy Roadhouse Lodge** (381 N. Agate St., 208/787-2755, www.cowboyroadhouselodge.com, $110 d) is a modern two-story motel with log beds, Wi-Fi, and two queen or one king bed.

Set on four acres and surrounded by cottonwood trees, **Fox Creek Inn Bed and Breakfast** (27 E. 550 South, 208/787-3333, www.thefoxcreekinn.com) has three guest rooms with queen beds and private baths for $99 d, plus a more spacious room with king bed, private bath, and indoor Jacuzzi for $175 d. All include a full breakfast, access to the outdoor hot tub, and Wi-Fi. Fox Creek is halfway between Victor and Driggs.

Camping

The Forest Service's pleasant **Trail Creek Campground** (518/885-3639 or 877/444-6777, www.recreation.gov, open late-May–mid-Sept., $10) is six miles southeast of Victor and just across the Wyoming state line. **Teton Valley Campground** (208/787-2647 or 877/787-3036, www.tetonvalleycampground.com), one mile west of Victor on Idaho Hwy. 31, has RV hookups ($34–38), tent sites ($20), basic cabins ($44), and a small outdoor pool and playground, plus Wi-Fi.

Food

Victor Emporium (208/787-2221, daily 8 A.M.–6 P.M.) houses an old-fashioned soda fountain with huckleberry shakes in season, plus sundaes, banana splits, and cones year-round. It's been in business since 1949, and also sells fishing supplies and Idaho souvenirs.

Housed in an old one-car garage, **Grumpy's Goat Shack** (37 S. Main St., 208/787-2092, www.goatshack.com, daily 11 A.M.–11 P.M. Apr.–Oct.) is a fun hot dog stand/wine bar where Mike and Liz serve the best brats you'll ever taste, along with hot Italian beef sandwiches, chili-cheese dogs, and Chicago-style hot dogs. They're the real deal; even true Chicagoans love 'em. The owners' goat produces milk for homemade goat cheese, served with roasted garlic and bread. The ceiling is crowded with bras and panties left by previous female customers (free drinks are the incitement). Sit outside around the patio tables. No credit cards, but everything's under $8.

Thai food has finally spilled over the mountains into Idaho. At **Teton Thai Restaurant** (208/787-8424, www.tetonthai.com, daily 11:30 A.M.–2:30 P.M., 5:30–9:30 P.M.) a Jackson Hole favorite has expanded, offering the same menu of South Asian favorites—including noodle, rice, and curry dishes—in a busy setting on the south end of Victor. Most entrées are $14–16, but lighter options such as satae chicken or tom kha gai are a few bucks less.

Next to the golf course at Teton Springs just south of town, **Headwaters Grille** (208/787-3600 or 866/445-3328, www.teton springs.com, daily 11 A.M.–9 P.M.) serves upscale lunches and dinners daily, including seared duck breast and almond-encrusted halibut; $18–24 entrées.

Also in Victor is **Knotty Pine Supper Club** (208/787-2866, daily 4–10 P.M., bar is open until 1 A.M.), with hearty ribs, steaks, and rack of lamb. Most entrées are $13–27, but you can always choose the $10 dinner of hot turkey,

meat loaf, mashed potatoes, and gravy. Knotty Pine is an old-fashioned place with low ceilings, log walls, and a dark interior brightened by blue Christmas lights. Dining is also available on the outside deck. Live bands crank out the dance tunes Wednesday–Saturday nights all summer. Now entirely smoke-free.

Amazingly, there are two microbreweries in Victor. In existence since 1988, **Grand Teton Brewing Company** (208/787-9000 or 888/899-1656, www.grandtetonbrewing.com, Mon.–Fri. 8 A.M.–7 P.M. in summer, Mon.–Fri. 8 A.M.–6 P.M. in winter) is on the east end of town. Drop by weekdays for a free tour or to sample Teton Ale, Old Faithful Ale, Bitch Creek ESB, Workhorse Wheat, or Sweetgrass IPA. The gift shop sells T-shirts, glasses, and beer to go.

Much smaller is **Wildlife Brewing and Pizza** (208/787-2623, daily 4–10:30 P.M.), a busy spot with crunchy pizzas by the slice or pie, plus fresh beers from the on-the-premises brewery.

DRIGGS

Driggs (pop. 1,500) is an odd conglomeration, mixing an old-time farming settlement and new-fangled recreation mecca. It's also fast becoming a bedroom community for commuters to Jackson Hole. A major development on the south end of town brought many more homes and businesses, and the airport keeps expanding with giant hangars for all those private jets. There isn't much to downtown Driggs, so it's pretty easy to find your way around. But don't expect things to stay small for long because the area has been discovered. In 2002, *Men's Journal* put Driggs at the top of its list for best small towns in America, and today it seems every other downtown building is a mortgage company, realtor, or title company. You know the valley has arrived when Sotheby's opens a big real-estate office.

Sights

Driggs is perhaps best known as home to the delightfully amusing **Spud Drive-In** (208/354-2727 or 800/799-7783, www.spud drivein.com, here since 1953. You can't miss the big truck out front with a flatbed-size

© DON PITCHER

the Spud Drive-In, Driggs

"potato" on the back. The drive-in even attracts folks from Jackson, who cross the pass for an evening of fun beneath the stars. The drive-in is locally famous for Gladys burgers and Spud buds—served by carhops.

The spacious **Teton Valley Museum** (137 N. Hwy. 33, 208/354-6000, Tues.–Wed. 1–6 P.M. and Thurs.–Sat. 10 A.M.–6 P.M. late May–Oct. only, $5 adults, $2 kids, $15 families) houses historical displays from the valley's past on two floors. It's on the north side of town just beyond the Super 8 Motel.

At the airport just north of town, **Warbirds Museum** houses an interesting collection of restored historic planes in a hangar at the Teton Aviation Center (208/354-3100 or 800/472-6382, www.tetonaviation.com, free). Access is through the adjacent Warbirds Café. The collection includes several unusual fighter aircraft—including a T-28 Trojan and a Mig 15—but only four are displayed at any given time.

A new downtown visitor center and museum is expected to open in 2010. The centerpiece will be the influential Yellowstone paintings by Thomas Moran and the photos by William Henry Jackson.

Shopping

Yöstmark Mountain Equipment (285 E. Little Ave., 208/354-2828, www.yostmark .com) sells a wide range of outdoor equipment. They also rent cross-country skis, skate skis, snowboards, and telemark and alpine touring skis in winter.

Browse the eclectic selection of regional books at the friendly **Dark Horse Books** (76 N. Main St., 208/354-8882 or 888/434-8882). The **Community Art Center** (8 Rodeo Dr., 208/354-4278, www.tetonartscouncil.com) exhibits works by regional artists.

Accommodations

A delightful European-style guesthouse built in 1900, **The Pines Motel Guest Haus** (105 S. Main St., 208/354-2774 or 800/354-2778, www.travelassist.com/reg/id101s.html) is run by the Nielson family. The home has seven rooms with private baths, each different but all

JACKSON HOLE

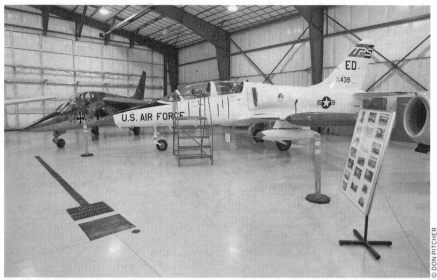

© DON PITCHER

Warbirds Museum

nicely appointed with tasteful touches such as handmade quilts. A hot tub is available outside. Rates are very reasonable, starting at $60 d, or $100 for a two-room suite that sleeps eight. Kids are welcome.

On the north side of Driggs, **Super 8 Motel,** (133 Hwy. 33, 208/354-8888 or 800/800-8000, www.super8.com), has standard rooms for $98 d and suites that sleep four for $166 d. Amenities include large rooms, an indoor pool, sauna, hot tub, Wi-Fi, and continental breakfast.

On the north side of Driggs, **Best Western Teton West** (476 N. Main St., 208/354-2363 or 800/528-1234, www.bestwestern.com, $99–119 d) features a light breakfast, indoor pool, hot tub, and Wi-Fi. Closed mid-October–mid-November.

Located a mile east of town, **Teton Valley Cabins** (34 E. Ski Hill Rd., 208/354-8153 or 866/687-1522, www.tetonvalleycabins.com, $99–119 d) has comfortable and modern duplex cabins that sleep six. Most include kitchenettes, and families appreciate those with bunk beds.

Short-term bookings for town houses, homes, cabins, and condos in the area are provided by **Grand Valley Lodging** (208/354-8890 or 800/746-5518, www.grandvalleylodging.com) and **Teton Valley Property Management** (208/354-8881 or 888/354-8881, www.teton valleyidaho.com). Rates range $150–400 per night (higher around Christmas and the Fourth of July). These accommodations are popular with families and ski groups heading to Grand Targhee Ski Resort.

Camping

The nearest public campsites are at **Teton Canyon Campground** (open late May–mid-Sept., $10–18), 11 miles east of Driggs in the Tetons. This is a delightful camping spot, and the trailhead into beautiful (and very popular) Alaska Basin is nearby. Make reservations ($10 fee) at 518/885-3639 or 877/444-6777, www.recreation.gov.

Food

One benefit of Teton Valley's rapid growth is a dramatic improvement in the local restaurant scene. Driggs now has several good dining places, and another standout—Lost Horizon Dinner Club—is just up the hill in Alta, Wyoming.

You won't find burgers or steaks at **Miso Hungry Café** (165 N. Main St., 208/354-8015, breakfast Mon.–Fri. 7:30–10:30 A.M., lunch Mon.–Sat. 11 A.M.–3 P.M., dinner Thurs.–Sat. 4:30–9 P.M., $12–25), a playful spot with covered tables on the front porch and a flavorful globe-trotting fare. The menu changes seasonally, but might include Thai noodle bowl, Greek Athenian plate, chicken curry sandwich, and a variety of soups, salads, homemade breads, espresso, and desserts. Even the potato chips are made on the premises from local (of course) Idaho potatoes. Check the chalkboard for lunch and dinner specials, typically around $15.

An aviation-themed restaurant at—appropriately enough—Driggs Airport just north of town, **Warbirds Café** (208/354-2550, www.tetonaviation.com, Sat.–Sun. 7 A.M.–9 P.M., Mon.–Fri. 11 A.M.–2 P.M. and 5–9 P.M., $15–30) has windows facing the taxiway and several tables on the patio providing an even closer view. The café is open daily for lunch and dinner, plus summer weekends for breakfast (no winter breakfasts). The menu includes such treats as grilled elk tenderloin in a blackberry port-wine sauce or braised Alaskan halibut with hearts of palm. For breakfast, try crab cakes benedict, or for lunch the buffalo burgers. Several restored planes are in the adjacent hangar. Warbirds Café is popular with pilots who can fly in for lunch with a view and upscale meal. Or, as one local pointed out, it represents "all the things we ran away from when we moved here from Jackson." Dinner reservations recommended.

Find Martha Pendl's amazing Austrian pastries and other treats at **[** **Pendal's Bakery & Café** (40 Depot St., 208/354-5623, www .pendlspastries.com, Mon.–Sat. 7 A.M.–3 P.M., Sun. 8 A.M.–3 P.M.). Ignore the official address; it's actually at the back of the public parking lot on Bates Rd. (and almost directly behind the bookstore). Get a continental breakfast coffee (best espresso in Teton Valley) and one of the incredibly delectable treats: Nussknacker, Linzertorte, or Florentiner pastries. Lunchtime soups, sandwiches, and quiches follow. Pendl's is occasionally open for dinner, depending upon the owner's mood.

Get malts, shakes, and hot fudge sundaes at the old soda fountain inside **Corner Drug** (10 S. Main St., 208/354-2334, Mon.–Sat. 9 A.M.–6:30 P.M.). Lime freezes are their claim to fame.

Latino's Delights (190 N. Main St., 208/354-2718, daily 9 A.M.–9 P.M.) is the real thing, with tamales, enchiladas, *guaraches, gorditos, flautas,* and Mexican pastries, along with a TV blaring soccer games. It's a good place to bone up on your Spanish. Nothing over $10, and the adjacent tienda sells items from south of the border.

For a more formal setting, **Guadalajara Mexican Restaurant** (355 N. Main St., 208/354-9000, Mon.–Fri. 11 A.M.–10 P.M.) serves a wide choice of specials—including steak ranchero, chicken fajitas, and various combo plates, plus margaritas. There's a comfy deck for outside dining.

For late-night foraging—and all-round wonderful meals—head to **[** **Forage Bistro & Lounge** (385 Little Ave., 208/354-2858, daily 3 P.M.–midnight, $8–16 entrées) a few blocks east of downtown. This trendy and very hip spot has a brick-paved deck out front and a curvy bar inside with a handful of tables. The moderately priced menu changes seasonally and has limited choices. When I last stopped by, specials included pan-seared coconut scallops, several kinds of salads, panko-crusted hoki fish with vegetable curry, and a savory cheese plate with fresh pesto, olives, fruit, and artisan bread.

Shop for groceries at **Broulim's** (52 S. Main St., 208/354-2350, www.broulims.com, daily 7 A.M.–11 P.M.). There's a sushi bar and café with upstairs seating. Head across the parking lot to **Barrels and Bins** (208/354-2307), selling health foods and other earthy fare.

The **Teton Valley Farmers Market** (208/787-3025) comes to downtown Driggs Wednesdays 4–7 P.M. and Fridays 9 A.M.–2 P.M.

late June–September, with produce, crafts, flowers, and baked goods.

Information and Services

The **Teton Valley Chamber of Commerce** (91 E. Little Ave., 208/354-2500, www.tetonvalley chamber.com) is in downtown Driggs. Its hours are officially Monday–Friday 10 A.M.–4 P.M., but call first to make sure someone is around since the office is staffed by volunteers.

Get Caribou-Targhee National Forest information from the **Teton Basin Ranger District Office** (just south of town at 525 S. Main St., 208/354-2312, www.fs.fed.us/r4/caribou-targhee). Wash clothes at the appropriately named **Coin Laundry** next to Latino's Delight (190 N. Main St.).

Teton Valley Hospital (120 E. Howard Ave., 208/354-2383, www.tetonvalley hospital.com) is available for emergencies.

Rent cars from **Basin Auto** (180 N. Main St., 208/354-2297).

TETONIA

Eight miles north of Driggs, sleepy Tetonia is dominated by a big LDS church, with dirt side streets. Potato farms and grand old barns spread across the surrounding landscape; it's a good place to see kids riding horseback. The crest of the tourist wave is just starting to lap at the shores of Tetonia, and at last check no local place sold espresso, focaccia, or cell phones.

However, a couple of miles south of Tetonia, **Drawknife Billiards** (516 N. Hwy. 33, 800/320-0527, www.drawknife.com) creates one-of-a-kind pool tables using hand-carved lodgepole bases and top-quality tabletops.

Three miles south of Tetonia, **Blue Fly Gallery** (208/456-0900, www.kenmorrison fineart.com) exhibits the colorful paintings and sculptures of Ken Morrison.

Steve Horn Mountain Gallery (112 S. Main St., 307/734-5664 or 888/345-7469, www .stevehorn.com) exhibits rugged Old West-style furniture and relief carvings.

North End Bar & Grill (208/456-2202, daily 7 A.M.–10 P.M. in summer, till 9 P.M. in winter) attracts local farmers (and travelers) with filling biscuits and gravy breakfasts (along with some lighter fare), lunchtime fish tacos, burgers, sandwiches, salads, and chicken fried steak, and dinners that include shrimp scampi, BBQ ribs, and filet mignon. Dinners start around $12 for grilled chicken, up to $22 for Alaskan king crab.

Alta, Wyoming

The little place called Alta sits right along the Wyoming border and just six miles northeast of Driggs, Idaho. There are no stores in Alta, but the settlement does have a stellar restaurant and several places to stay. East from Alta, the road climbs through heavily timbered country, with periodic views of the Big Hole Mountains to the west and up-close looks at the Teton Range.

GRAND TARGHEE SKI RESORT

On the west side of the Tetons 42 miles from Jackson, Grand Targhee Ski Resort (307/353-2300 or 800/827-4433, www.grand targhee.com) offers the friendliness of a small resort with the amenities and snow you'd expect at a major one. To get here you'll need to drive into Idaho and turn east at Driggs. The resort sits at the end of a beautiful road (recently rebuilt) 12 miles east of Driggs and just six miles inside Wyoming. Its motto says it all: "Snow from heaven, not from hoses." With an annual snowfall topping 500 inches (42 feet!)—most of which is champagne powder—Targhee became the spot where powderhounds got all they could ever want. Ski magazines consistently rank it as having North America's best (or second-best) snow. In fact, the resort guarantees its snow: If you find conditions not to your liking, you can turn in your ticket within an hour of purchase and get a "snow check" good for another day of skiing.

By the way, the official name is Grand Targhee Ski and Summer Resort, but most folks call it Grand Targhee, or simply Targhee.

The biggest drawback to Grand Targhee Ski Resort is the same thing that makes it so great—the weather. Lots of snow means lots of clouds and storms, and because it snows so much there are many days when the name cynics apply—"Grand Foghee"—seems more appropriate. Many folks who have returned to Targhee year after year have still not seen the magnificent Grand Teton backdrop behind the ski area! Be sure to bring your goggles. The quad lift up Peaked Mountain provides intermediate skiing on slopes that are more protected and suffer less wind and fog.

Skiing and Snowboarding

The resort has two quads, one double chairlift, and a surface lift on Fred's Mountain, plus a quad on adjacent Peaked Mountain. The top elevation is 10,230 feet, with the longest run dropping 2,822 feet over almost three miles. About 750 acres are groomed, but you'll always find track-free skiing on the remaining 2,250 acres of ungroomed powder, so bring your snorkel. In addition, snowcat skiing ($399 per day including lunch and guide) is offered on a 1,000-acre section of Peaked Mountain reserved for powderhounds.

Lift tickets at Grand Targhee cost $69 per day ($59 half day) for adults and $39 per day for children ages 6–14 and seniors (free under age six). Substantial discounts are offered for multi-day lift tickets or lodging-and-ski packages.

Fully 70 percent of Targhee's groomed runs are intermediate to advanced-intermediate, but advanced skiers will find an extraordinary number of deep-powder faces to explore. The ski school offers lessons for all abilities, and children's programs make it possible for parents to leave their kids behind. Cross-country skiers enjoy the Nordic center, and ski and snowboard rentals are available at the base of the mountain. The ski area usually opens in mid-November and closes in mid-April, although some years you may be able to ski even into July. Lifts operate daily 9:30 A.M.–4 P.M.

Winter Activities

Excellent guided **snowshoe wildlife tours** (free if you have snowshoes, $25 to rent them) will appeal to amateur naturalists, and on the **sleigh-ride dinner** ($35 adults, $15 kids), you'll ride in a horse-drawn sleigh to a yurt where a Western-style meal is served. Targhee's **tubing park** ($8 per hour; opens at 5 P.M.) is a fun place for kids to slide down a snowy hill, and the resort also has an outdoor **skating pond** and skate rentals. A **Kid's Club** at Targhee provides supervised child care for children under six, and teens can join special programs that include skiing and other fun on the mountain.

Summer Activities

Not far from Grand Targhee are several popular summertime hiking trails within the Jedediah Smith Wilderness.

The resort is a popular place to relax in the summer and offers many activities. A quad chairlift ($13 adults, $6 kids) takes you up the 10,200-foot summit of Fred's Mountain for strikingly close views of the Tetons. The lift operates daily late June–mid-September. A Forest Service naturalist leads guided walks twice daily.

Horseback rides and lessons are a favorite Targhee summertime activity; one-hour rides are $33. The area is also a fun mountain-biking destination, with bike rentals; you can also take them up the chair lift. The big climbing wall ($7 for an introductory climb) is open to all abilities and is a good place to learn some basic—or advanced—moves. Other summer activities and facilities at Targhee include basketball courts, an outdoor swimming pool and hot tubs, a fitness center, horseshoes, tennis, disc golf, archery, and volleyball. The nine-hole **Targhee Village Golf Course** (208/354-8577 or 307/353-8577) is just down the road. After all this excitement, you'll probably want to relax with a massage, aromatherapy, facial, or steam bath from the on-site spa.

Events

End the year—and start a new one—with

JACKSON HOLE

Torch Light Parades at Grand Targhee on the evenings of December 25 and 31. Also on New Year's Eve is a fireworks display over the mountain. Each March, the resort celebrates telemark skiing with the **Tele Fest.** Ski races of all sorts take place, and Targhee rocks to great music, an outdoor barbecue, and fun events. The **Spring Snow Games** is a three-day mid-March event with races and other play for all ages. It's followed over the closing weekend in mid-April by the **Cardboard Box Derby,** with participants swooshing down the ski hill on cardboard creations of all types.

The resort pulls out the stops for two very popular musical events: **Targhee Fest** in mid-July with a mix of nationally known Americana and folk artists, plus **Targhee Bluegrass Festival** in mid-August. Bring your dancin' shoes! The music attracts hundreds of people, so call the resort well ahead of time for camping or lodging reservations.

ACCOMMODATIONS

Wilson Creekside Inn B&B (130 Alta North Rd., 307/353-2409) is a century-old home on a 200-acre sheep farm. Four guest rooms are available and all contain family heirlooms. One costs $85 d and includes a king-size bed and private bath; the others share a bath and run $75 d or $85 for four. Guests are served an ample country breakfast and kids are welcome. The owner's son raises about 150 ewes on the ranch.

Grand Targhee

Contact Targhee (307/353-2300 or 800/827-4433, www.grandtarghee.com) for details on lodging options at or near the resort. The three lodges at the base of the mountain—Targhee Lodge, Teewinot Lodge, and Sioux Lodge—offer ski-in, ski-out access, a large heated outdoor pool, a hot tub, and a workout room. Rates quoted are for the winter holiday season; they're approximately 40 percent lower in summertime. Most lodging places are closed October–mid-November, and mid-April–mid-June.

Get standard motel accommodations at **Targhee Lodge** with holiday winter rates of $129 for up to four. Deluxe hotel rooms with lodgepole furnishings and access to an indoor hot tub are $200 d at **Teewinot Lodge.** The lobby here is a fine place to relax in front of the fire on winter evenings. **Sioux Lodge** continues the Western theme with lodgepole furnishings, but it also has kitchenettes, adobe-style fireplaces, and small balconies. Studio units are $220 for up to four people, loft units $262 for four people, and two-bedroom units run $367.

Off-site lodging (approximately 10 miles downhill from Grand Targhee) includes one-, two-, and three-bedroom condominiums and townhouses. Nightly holiday-season rates start at $210 d for one-bedroom condos up to $390 for three-bedroom townhouses. The minimum stay at all Targhee-managed lodging places is two nights most of the year, or five nights during peak winter periods.

You can cut these lodging rates by avoiding the Christmas-New Year's and Spring Break rush periods. More substantial discounts are available if you ski or snowboard during the value season before mid-December or after late March.

Ski packages are a fine bargain, starting around $1,500 for a five-night family rate at Targhee Lodge in the peak season. Packages include lodging and lift tickets for two adults and two kids under age 13. Summer lodging is surprisingly reasonable, with such options as rafting trips, scenic chairlift, and spa amenities.

FOOD

Lost Horizon Dinner Club (307/353-8226) is one of the standout places in the Teton Valley area. This fun and funky restaurant/home has space for just a dozen guests, who sit down to a memorable nine-course Japanese and Chinese meal ($45 per person plus wine) prepared by co-owner and chef Shigako Irwin. Lost Horizon isn't for vegetarians or for those in a hurry; expect to be here for three or four leisurely hours. Dinners are served Friday and Saturday nights at 7, with reservations required. Formal dress isn't necessary, but don't come in shorts, sandals, or T-shirts. No credit cards, but checks (even out of state) are accepted.

At the base of Grand Targhee is a compact cluster of shops. You won't have to walk far to find a cafeteria, pizza place, sandwich shop, burger joint, and general store. The nicest place is **Targhee Steakhouse,** serving hearty breakfasts and lunches, along with cozy dinners. Grand Targhee's social center is the **Trap Bar,** featuring live music Thursday–Saturday all winter, along with pub grub on the menu all the time. Guests at Targhee can also take a **horse-drawn sleigh** on a 15-minute ride to a Mongolian-style yurt for a home-cooked steak or chicken dinner. The price is $35 ($15 for kids ages 7–12), and reservations are required. Other shops here sell groceries, ski and snowboard gear, clothing, and gifts.

GETTING THERE AND AROUND

Grand Targhee is 42 miles northwest of Jackson on the western side of the Tetons in Alta, Wyoming. Get there by driving over Teton Pass (occasionally closed by winter storms), north through Victor and Driggs, Idaho, and then east back into Wyoming.

The **Targhee Express/Alltrans** bus makes daily wintertime trips (90 minutes each way) to Grand Targhee from Jackson Hole. Buses pick up skiers from Jackson and Teton Village hotels shortly after 7 A.M., returning from Targhee at 4:30 P.M. for a round-trip fare of $84, including a full-day lift ticket. Round-trip bus fare without a lift ticket costs $44. Reservations are required; make them before 9 P.M. on the night before by calling 307/733-3135 or 800/443-6133, or book online at www.jacksonholealltrans .com. Van service is also available year-round to airports in Jackson or Idaho Falls, Idaho.

GATEWAYS TO YELLOWSTONE

Yellowstone National Park is most commonly entered via one of several Wyoming or Montana towns. From the south, people generally arrive from the energetic town of Jackson (see the *Jackson Hole* chapter). Described in this chapter are four Montana towns that act as park gateways: West Yellowstone, which predictably enough is immediately west of Yellowstone; Gardiner, at the northwest gate just a few miles from Mammoth Hot Springs; and the twin towns of Cooke City and Silver Gate just beyond the Northeast Entrance to Yellowstone. Also described are two Wyoming towns: Cody, which provides access through Wapiti Valley to Yellowstone's East Entrance, and the Wind River Valley town of Dubois on the east side of Togwotee Pass.

For points to the east and south—including the towns of Lander, Pinedale, Alpine, and Afton—see Don Pitcher's *Moon Wyoming*. Nearby towns in Montana, including Red Lodge, Bozeman, Billings, and Livingston, are fully covered in *Moon Montana,* by W. C. McRae and Judy Jewell. See Don Root's *Moon Idaho* for coverage of Island Park, Swan Valley, and the scoop on the tater state. Avalon Travel Publishing (www.moon.com) publishes all three of these books.

PLANNING YOUR TIME

Three Montana towns are just outside Yellowstone National Park entrance roads. Immediately west of the park is the appropriately named **West Yellowstone,** a popular and family friendly town with moderately priced motels, RV parks, restaurants, and trinket

© DON PITCHER

HIGHLIGHTS

◖ Yellowstone Historic Center: There's a fine historical collection inside this stone-and-log building that once served as a railroad depot (page 245).

◖ Beartooth Highway: Some call this the most scenic highway in America. It's high (10,947 feet), dramatic, and closed September–May (page 274).

◖ Buffalo Bill Historical Center: The center started with items from Buffalo Bill's life but now covers 300,000 square feet in five distinct museums focusing on Western art, the Plains Indians, natural history, firearms, and, of course, Buffalo Bill. It's one of the finest museums in North America (page 281).

◖ Trail Town: The perfect counterpoint to the Historical Center, with old wagons, rustic cabins – including one used by Butch Cassidy and the Sundance Kid – plus a treasure trove of other items. Check out the dugout canoe that just might have been used by Lewis and Clark (page 286).

◖ Cody Nite Rodeo: Still going strong after seven decades, the popular rodeos take place nightly all summer. Get there early for a seat in "buzzards roost" (page 294).

◖ National Bighorn Sheep Center: After exploring the museum, displays, and theater, head out to Whiskey Basin to see the live version (but they're in the high country by June) (page 306).

◖ Togwotee Pass: One of the prettiest mountain passes in Wyoming, Togwotee provides a grand entryway into Grand Teton and Yellowstone national parks (page 316).

LOOK FOR ◖ TO FIND RECOMMENDED SIGHTS, ACTIVITIES, DINING, AND LODGING.

shops. West (as it's called) has a fine museum, the Yellowstone Historic Center, but it is better known for the IMAX Theatre that shows big-screen movies about Yellowstone, and the zoolike Grizzly and Wolf Discovery Center.

The smaller town of **Gardiner, Montana** lies just outside Yellowstone's northwest corner and five miles from Mammoth Hot Springs. A dramatic stone structure, Roosevelt Arch, provides a grand entry point into the park, and Gardiner offers a full range of services, from lodging and

dining to horseback rides and rafting down the Yellowstone River. If you exit the park from the wooded northeast corner, you'll pass through a pair of rustic settlements: **Silver Gate,** where virtually all the buildings are built from logs, and the larger burg of **Cooke City.** Food, lodging, gas, and other basics are here, but the main draw is their homespun and genuine feel.

Yellowstone's east entrance road drops through the wilds of Shoshone National Forest and past the dude ranches and summer

GREATER YELLOWSTONE AREA

Absaroka Range

Shoshone National Forest

WIND RIVER INDIAN RESERVATION

To Lander and Riverton

Bull Lake

Bear Pk 10,755ft

Roberts Mtn 12,767ft

Shoshone National Forest

Valley

South Fork

DUBOIS

NATIONAL BIGHORN SHEEP CENTER

Wind River

Burris

Crowheart

Wolverine Pk 12,360ft

Continental

Divide

26 287

Younts Peak 12,156ft

Wind River

Mountains

Gannett Peak 13,804ft

Continental

WHITE PINE

Boulder Lake

Boulder

191

TOGWOTEE PASS

New Fork Lakes

Willow Lake

Fremont Lake

Pinedale

Cora

352

189

Bridger-Teton National Forest

Mt Hancock 10,214ft

Moran Junction

Mt Leidy 10,326ft

Doubletop Pk 11,682ft

Daniel

354

26 89

Jackson Lake

Gros Ventre Range

Bondurant

Merna

Halfway

John D. Rockefeller Jr. Memorial Parkway

Grand Teton National Park

89 191

Kelly

National Elk Refuge

JACKSON

SNOW KING

Hoback Junction

189

191

Hogback Pk 10,862ft

Bridger-Teton National Forest

Range

Jenny Lake

Teton Village

JACKSON HOLE

89 26

Wyoming

GRAND TARGHEE

Grand Teton 13,772ft

Moose Junction

22

Turnerville

Grover

Alta

Etna

Thayne

Bedford

89

IDAHO / **WYOMING**

Freedom

Auburn

32

Tetonia

Driggs

Victor

31

Swan Valley

Alpine

Palisades Reservoir

34

Wayan

Caribou-Targhee National Forest

Ashton

33

St. Anthony

Rexburg

To Idaho Falls

Snake River

26

Grays Lake

Henry

10 mi

10 km

0

0

© AVALON TRAVEL

homes within scenic **Wapiti Valley** before emerging into the prosperous and busy town of **Cody, Wyoming.** It's named for Buffalo Bill Cody, and his old lodging place (Irma Hotel) is a downtown fixture. The main draw, however, is massive Buffalo Bill Historical Center, which houses five museums focusing on Plains Indians, the life of Buffalo Bill, Western art, natural history, and firearms. Up the road is the low-key Trail Town with historic cabins and wagons. The Cody Nite Rodeo takes place nightly all summer, and whitewater rafting on the Shoshone River lets visitors do their own bucking.

The Upper Wind River Valley town of **Dubois, Wyoming,** is a fine stopping place for travelers heading into Grand Teton and Yellowstone national parks from the east. The town hosts a small museum and the National Bighorn Sheep Center, with exhibits on these majestic animals that live in the surrounding mountains. Dubois is unpretentious, with old-time dude ranches nearby and a good choice of family restaurants. East from Dubois, U.S. 26/287 climbs over beautiful **Togwotee Pass** into the parks. Visitors could easily spend at least two days in Cody or one in Dubois before heading into Yellowstone.

West Yellowstone, Montana

West Yellowstone (elev. 6,650) is the definitive Western tourist town. With a year-round population of only 1,000 (three times that in the summer) but more than 50 places to stay, it's pretty easy to see what makes the West Yellowstone cash registers ring. The West Entrance gate—most popular of all Yellowstone entrances—lies just a couple of hundred feet away. "West," as the town is known locally, isn't particularly attractive, and in the 1990s a major development brought several corporate hotels and other ugly additions to an already crowded mix of restaurants, motels, T-shirt stores, and gift shops.

West Yellowstone may be decidedly middle-brow, but the surrounding land is anything but, with Gallatin (GAL-a-tin) National Forest lying north and west, Caribou-Targhee National Forest just a few miles to the south, and Yellowstone National Park just a few feet to the east. It's just a couple of miles east from West Yellowstone to the Wyoming border, and the Idaho border lies only nine miles west.

HISTORY
In 1907, the Union Pacific Railroad completed laying tracks for its Oregon Short Line to the western border of Yellowstone. The following summer, Yellowstone Special trains began

rolling in from Salt Lake City, dropping tourists for their stagecoach tours of the park. A small town—West Yellowstone—quickly developed on the margins of the park, providing lodging, meals, and tourist trinkets. After World War II, interest in rail travel declined and more people came to Yellowstone by automobile. Although the last passengers stepped off the train in 1960, the Union Pacific's historic stone depot and neighboring buildings still stand; they now house a museum, library, police station, jail, medical clinic, and other offices.

The West Yellowstone area was rocked by a devastating magnitude-7.5 earthquake on August 17, 1959. One of the most powerful temblors ever recorded in the Lower 48 states, the quake cracked Hebgen Dam and caused a massive landslide (estimated at more than 80 million tons of debris!) that generated a 20-foot-high tsunami and created Earthquake Lake. Twenty-eight people died, and the geysers and hot springs of Yellowstone were dramatically affected for years.

Evidence of the powerful 1959 earthquake is still visible north of West Yellowstone along Hebgen Lake. The Forest Service has an **Earthquake Visitor Center;** get there by heading eight miles north on U.S. Hwy. 191

and turning left on U.S. Hwy. 287. Continue another 17 miles west to the center; open daily 8:30 A.M.–6 P.M. Memorial Day–late September only.

SIGHTS
☑ Yellowstone Historic Center

The Yellowstone Historic Center (104 Yellowstone Ave., 406/646-1100, www.yellowstonehistoriccenter.org, daily 9 A.M.–9 P.M. mid-May–early Sept., daily 9 A.M.–6 P.M. the rest of Sept.–mid-Oct., and closed the rest of the year, $5 adults, $4 seniors, and $3 students and kids; free for kids under three) is a stone-

and-log structure from the railroad days that served for decades as the town's train depot. Inside are exhibits on the history of park transportation, the 1959 Hebgen Lake earthquake, the fires of 1988, and "Old Snaggletooth" the grizzly. Videos and movies about Yellowstone are shown in the theater, and the museum offers historic walking tours when enough people are interested.

Right next door is another wonderful stone structure (built in 1925) that served until the late 1950s as an elegant Union Pacific Dining Lodge. The building has a spacious dining hall containing an enormous fireplace, a 45-foot-tall vaulted ceiling, and handmade light fixtures. Also worth a look-see is an **Oregon Short Line Railroad car** housed at the Holiday Inn Sunspree Resort (315 Yellowstone Ave., 406/646-7365, www .doyellowstone.com). Built in 1903, the beautifully restored railroad car forms a centerpiece for the restaurant and lounge here.

Grizzly and Wolf Discovery Center

In the early 1990s, a massive $50 million project covering 67 acres transformed (some might prefer the term decimated) the town of West Yellowstone. Included are a grizzly and wolf theme park, an IMAX theater, three major hotels, cabins, a restaurant, fast-food joints, an RV park, and a post office. The centerpiece is the Grizzly and Wolf Discovery Center (201 S. Canyon St., 406/646-7001 or 800/257-2570, www.grizzlydiscoveryctr.com, open daily 8 A.M.–dusk all year), home to eight Alaskan and Canadian grizzlies and 11 captive-born gray wolves. Not all of the bears are visible at any given time, but visitors are bound to see at least one in the pseudo-natural habitat. This center attracts throngs of visitors and photographers who might otherwise never see a grizzly or wolf, and there's always a staff member out to answer any questions. Park Service rangers provide daily presentations in the summer. The center remains controversial, however. Scientists note that the bears here are genetically distinct from those in Yellowstone, and anyone who has spent time around grizzlies in the wild will be dismayed to see them in captivity, even in a facility less oppressive than traditional zoos. The folks at Grizzly and Wolf Discovery Center counter that all these bears were either raised in captivity or were "problem" bears that would almost certainly have been killed had they not been moved here. In addition to the bears and wolves, the center has wildlife exhibits, bear safety tips, a video on bears, plus the obligatory gift shop. Entrance—good for two consecutive days—is $10 adults, $9 seniors, $5 ages 5–12, free for kids under five.

Yellowstone IMAX Theatre

Directly in front of the Grizzly and Wolf Discovery Center is the Yellowstone IMAX Theatre (406/646-4100 or 888/854-5862, www .yellowstoneimax.com, daily 8:30 A.M.–9 P.M. late May–early Oct., reduced hours the rest of the year, $10 adults, $5 ages 5–12, free for younger children), where you can watch the big-budget production of *Yellowstone* on the 60- by 80-foot screen; other movies typically are on wolves, bears, Lewis and Clark, or some other nature or Old West topic. The featured attraction is a 35-minute movie that presents Yellowstone history and geology, complete with stirring music and a cast of dozens. If you haven't seen IMAX flicks before, hold onto your seat—lots of jaw-dropping scenes here. The movie packs in the crowds on summer days, but the film seems to be a Disneylandish version of reality, ignoring many of the things you're likely to see in the park—such as burned forests and crowds of visitors—and putting history into a pretty little box. Reality wasn't—and isn't—quite like this. Even more disconcerting is that this glorification of the park stands right next to the park. To me it symbolizes the make-a-buck attitude that holds Yellowstone up as an attraction while developing a massive complex on its very margin. But hey, the movies are still fun to watch.

SUMMER RECREATION
Horses and Bikes

Horseback trail rides are available from **Parade Rest Guest Ranch** (seven miles north of town, 406/646-7217 or 800/753-5934, www.parade restranch.com), **Diamond P Ranch** (seven miles to the west, 406/646-7246, www.yellow stonehorse.com), **Yellowstone Mountain Guides** (406/646-7230, www.yellowstone-guides.com), and **Yellowstone Horseback Trail Rides and Van Tours** (406/646-9022, www.allyellowstone.com). Diamond P and Parade Rest both also offer evening wagon rides with Old West chuckwagon suppers.

The 30-km Rendezvous Trail System becomes mountain-bike central when summer rolls around. It starts from the southern edge of town; get a map at the visitor center. Rent mountain bikes from **Free Heel and Wheel**

(40 Yellowstone Ave., 406/646-7744, www.freeheelandwheel.com). Free Heel also rents strollers and child carrier backpacks.

Fishing

You'll find six fly-fishing shops in town, a reflection of the sport's importance in the Yellowstone area. In business for more than 50 years, **Bud Lilly's Trout Shop** (39 Madison Ave., 406/646-7801 or 800/854-9559, www.budlillys.com) is the best-known local place, with fishing tackle, clothing, guides, and even a gallery. Also well worth a look are **Arrick's Fly Shop** (37 Canyon St., 406/646-7290, www.arricks.com), **Eagle's Tackle Shop** (3 Canyon St., 406/646-7521, www.eagles-store.com), **Jacklin's Fly Shop** (105 Yellowstone Ave., 406/646-7336, www.jacklinsflyshop.com), and **West Yellowstone Fly Shop** (140 Madison Ave., 406/646-1181, www.wyflyshop.com), **Madison River Outfitters** (117 Canyon St., 406/646-9644, www.flyfishingyellowstone.com). All of these offer guided fishing ($400–450 for two people per day) and equipment.

River Rafting

Two rafting companies run all-day and half-day whitewater trips down the Gallatin River approximately 50 miles north of West Yellowstone (near Big Sky). The rafting season is generally late May–September, and you'll pay around $85 for all day or $50 for a half-day trip. The companies are **Geyser Whitewater Expeditions** (406/995-4989 or 800/914-9031, www.raftmontana.com), and **Montana Whitewater** (406/763-4465 or 800/799-4465, www.montanawhitewater.com). Both companies also offer sit-on-top kayaks for those who'd rather paddle it themselves. Montana Whitewater also leads trips down the challenging Madison River northwest of West Yellowstone, and Geyser Whitewater has gentle scenic floats for those who'd rather relax.

WINTER RECREATION
Cross-Country Skiing

West Yellowstone is infamous for its bitterly cold winters, when the thermometer can drop to -50°F. Fortunately, it doesn't always stay there, and by March the days have often warmed to a balmy 20°F. In November, West Yellowstone becomes a national center for cross-country skiers, with the U.S. Nordic and biathlon ski teams training here. Pick up a map of local ski trails at the visitor center.

Two trail systems provide a wide variety of Nordic skiing conditions, with trails groomed for both classical and skate skiing. The 50-km **Rendezvous Ski Trail** system (www.rendezvousskitrails.com) takes off from the southern edge of town and is groomed early November–April. The nine-kilometer **Riverside Trail** begins on the east side of town and leads to the Madison River within Yellowstone National Park. This trail provides a good opportunity to see bison, elk, and possibly moose. You can also ski the snowpacked streets in winter. Find many more places for flat tracking or telemarking in adjacent Yellowstone National Park and the Gallatin and Caribou-Targhee national forests. Before heading out into remote areas, get recorded avalanche-safety information from the **Avalanche Advisory Hotline** (406/587-6981). It's updated daily in the winter.

Rent skinny skis from **Bud Lilly's Trout Shop** (39 Madison Ave., 406/646-7801 or 800/854-9559, www.budlillys.com), or **Free Heel and Wheel** (40 Yellowstone Ave., 406/646-7744, www.freeheelandwheel.com). FreeHeel also rents snowshoes.

The closest downhill ski and snowboard area is the world-class **Big Sky Resort** (800/548-4486, www.bigskyresort.com), 57 miles north of West Yellowstone. The resort features 15 lifts and more than 3,500 acres of terrain. You will find excellent cross-country trails at **Lone Mountain Ranch** (406/995-4644 or 800/514-4644, www.lmranch.com) near Big Sky.

The Forest Service leads Hebgen Lake **snowshoe walks** during the winter months.

Dogsledding

For a delightfully different way to explore the Gallatin National Forest backcountry, take a sled dog tour from **Spirit of the North Sled Dog Adventure** (406/682-7994, www.husky power.com). Half-day tours are $150 adults or $90 kids.

Snowcoach Trips

Yellowstone Alpen Guides (406/646-9591 or 800/858-3502, www.yellowstoneguides.com) leads snowcoach tours from West Yellowstone. All-day trips are $110 adults, $100 seniors, $90 kids to either Grand Canyon of the Yellowstone or Old Faithful. Guests on the latter run have an option of getting dropped at Biscuit Basin, where they can ski to Old Faithful and meet up with others. Ski or snowshoe rentals are available. The company's eight classic Bombardier snowcoaches (one built in 1953) have been modernized but are still a charming anachronism.

Other companies offering wintertime van tours into Yellowstone include **All Yellowstone Sports/Yellowstone Van Tours** (406/646-9022 or 800/548-9551, www.allyellowstone.com), **See Yellowstone** (800/221-1151, www.seeyellowstone.com), **Back Country Adventure** (406/646-9317 or 800/924-7669, www.backcountry-adventures .com), and **Snowcoach Yellowstone/ Buffalo Bus Touring Co.** (429 Yellowstone, 406/646-9564 or 800/426-7669, www.yellow stonevacations.com).

For a truly unique experience, book a winter trip with another West Yellowstone–based company, **Yellowstone Expeditions** (406/646-9333 or 800/728-9333, www.yellow stoneexpeditions.com). The company has day tours of the park, but specializes in homey yurts at the Canyon area during the winter. Choose from a variety of multi-night adventures for skiers, starting at $1,900 for two people for three nights and four days.

Snowmobiles

Enthusiasts refer to West as "snowmobile capital of the world," and each winter day hundreds of 'bilers show up to roar across nearby Forest Service lands or to join park tours. All trips inside Yellowstone must be

with guided groups, and a number of local companies provide these tours. Drop by the West Yellowstone Chamber of Commerce (406/646-7701, www.westyellowstone chamber.com) office for current snow and trail conditions, a detailed map of local trails, and brochures from companies that offer guided snowmobile trips into the park.

Snowmobile rentals for use on Forest Service lands outside the park are available from more than a dozen local companies. Hundreds more folks bring in their own "crotch rockets" to ride on national forest lands, and local motels offer snowmobile/lodging packages.

ENTERTAINMENT

During summer, you can attend lighthearted comedies and musicals such as *Hello Dolly* or *Oklahoma* for the whole family at **Playmill Theatre** (124 Madison Ave., 406/646-7757, www.playmill.com). It's been in operation for more than four decades.

Watch flicks at **Bears Den Cinema** (15 Electric St., 406/646-7777). **Yellowstone IMAX Theatre** (406/646-4100 or 888/854-5862, www.yellowstoneimax.com) shows movies especially formatted for the three-story screen.

The bar at **Stage Coach Inn** (209 Madison Ave., 406/646-7381) has a pool table and the occasional live band, or try **Iron Horse Saloon** inside the West Yellowstone Conference Hotel (315 Yellowstone Ave., 406/646-7365).

On the shores of Hebgen Lake 15 miles north of West Yellowstone, **Happy Hour Bar and Restaurant** (15475 Hebgen Lake Rd., 406/646-5100, www.happyhourbar.com) is a destination for country meals (steaks, burgers, and shrimp). The ceiling is coated with ball caps, and two walls are dedicated to bare boobs and butts (don't ask). Open May–September and late December–mid-March.

EVENTS

On the second weekend of March, the **Rendezvous Marathon Ski Race** (406/646-7245, www.rendezvousrace.com), a nationally known Nordic ski race, attracts hundreds of participants. Motorheads arrive the following weekend for the **World Snowmobile Expo** (406/646-7001, www.snowmobileexpo .com), with races, demos, and other activities.

A fun parade, live music, BBQ, and fireworks highlight the town's **Fourth of July** festivities. The **Yellowstone Rod Run** on the first full weekend of August brings vintage cars of all types to the oldest such event in the Pacific Northwest; it's been a summer staple since 1970.

The **Wild West Yellowstone Rodeo** (406/560-6913, www.yellowstonerodeo.com) features bareback riding, team roping, saddle bronc riding, bull riding, barrel racing, a calf scramble, and more in the rodeo arena six miles west of town. Rodeos take place three times weekly June–August.

The ever-popular **Knothead Jamboree** attracts more than 1,000 square dancing enthusiasts for calling, clapping, and fun on Labor Day weekend; it's been happening annually since 1955.

Thanksgiving weekend in November means **Yellowstone Ski Festival** (www.yellow stoneskifestival.com), attracting hundreds of spandex-clad cross-country ski enthusiasts. The event also attracts major Nordic ski manufacturers, giving the public a chance to demo their latest toys.

SHOPPING

Many West Yellowstone shops sell the obligatory Yellowstone souvenirs, corny T-shirts, and other items with mass appeal. You'll probably get bored after one or two of these gift shops, but many more await your exploration. Fortunately, the town does have several more distinctive places.

Family-run **Eagle's Store** (406/646-9300, www.eagles-store.com) on the corner of Canyon and Yellowstone, is definitely worth a stop. Built in the 1920s, this historic log building contains all of the standard tourist knick-knacks, along with quality Western clothing, jewelry, fishing tackle, and a delightful old-fashioned soda fountain open in summer.

Seldom Seen Knives (115 Yellowstone Ave.,

406/646-4116, www.seldomseenknives.com) is worth a look, not only for Steve Hulett's distinctive knives, but also for his multicolor wooden letter openers and other locally crafted items, including offbeat fencepost vases.

Books

A book-lover's shop, **Bookworm Books** (14 Canyon St., 406/646-9736) is packed with both new and used titles, including many first editions. Don't miss the extraordinary collection of Yellowstone memorabilia, notably the postcards, collectable spoons, plates, and stereo views. Owner Scott Clewell also carries English stained glass from the 1890s. The shop is open late: daily till 11 P.M. in the summer and 10 P.M. at other times of the year when the Yellowstone National Park entrance is open.

In business for more than 25 years, **The Book Peddler** (106 Canyon St., 406/646-9358, daily 7:30 A.M.–9 P.M. in summer, daily 9 A.M.–5 P.M. the rest of the year) is a large and attractive bookstore with an abundance of regional titles. A pleasant café sells espresso, bagels, and pastries in the back.

The sparkling new **West Yellowstone Library** (23 N. Dunraven St., 406/646-9017) has Internet access.

ACCOMMODATIONS

The proximity to Yellowstone makes the town of West Yellowstone an extremely popular stopping place for vacationers in both summer and winter. More than 1,700 rooms are available, starting around $60–70 in midsummer. The streets are lined with more than three-dozen motels, so I won't try to describe all of them, although you'll find general information and links from the **West Yellowstone Chamber of Commerce** (406/646-7701, www.westyellow stonechamber.com). Add a 10 percent lodging tax to all rates quoted below.

Although rooms are generally available most summer nights, reservations are advisable; motels can even be full on late September weekends. To ensure your best choice of accommodations, reserve a room in May for the peak summer season. **West Yellowstone**

Central Reservations (406/646-7077 or 888/646-7077, www.yellowstonereservation .com) books rooms at many local places and can also set up a range of activities, from snowcoach tours to whitewater rafting.

Hostel

Budget travelers will be happy to discover the West Yellowstone International Hostel (not affiliated with AYH) in the historic **Madison Hotel** (139 Yellowstone Ave., 406/646-7745 or 800/838-7745, www.madisonhotelmotel.com). On the National Register of Historic Places, the hotel has friendly owners and a delightfully rustic lobby crowded with deer and moose heads. Presidents Harding and Hoover stayed here (though it wasn't a hostel at the time, of course). Travelers stay in clean and comfortable bedrooms (three beds in each, with bedding provided) that have been furnished with handmade lodgepole furniture. The classic hotel rooms are a delightful mix of old and new, providing the ambience of a place that has been here since 1912. The creaky floors and burled log railings add to the charm. No televisions or phones are provided in the rooms, but there is a small fridge and microwave for hostelers in the back, plus a TV in the lobby and a barbecue grill out back. A computer is available to check your email ($5 per day), and free Wi-Fi is available in some rooms. Lodging costs $30 per person in three-bed dorm rooms. Make hostel reservations a few days ahead in midsummer or get here before evening to be sure of a space in the dorms.

In addition to hostel rooms, the hotel has a range of other economical options. Rooms with a bath down the hall and no TV or phone are $48 s or $55 d. Larger units with private baths and space for four cost $79. Behind the hotel is a separate building with standard motel accommodations (private baths, TVs, and phones) for $89–99 d or $115 for a room with three double beds. The Madison Hotel is open late May–early October only.

$50-100

A fine economy choice, **Lazy G Motel** (123 Hayden, 406/646-7586, www.lazygmotel.com, $61–74 d) offers clean and quiet rooms with fridges, Wi-Fi, and phones (but no air-conditioning); kitchenettes are $10 extra. Friendly owners too. It's a five-block walk from town center. Closed mid-October–mid-November and the month of April.

Also recommended is another affordable place, **Al's Westward Ho Motel** (16 Boundary St., 406/646-7331 or 888/646-7331, www .alswestwardhomotel.net), which charges $79 d for rooms with one queen, $99 for those with two queen beds, and $129 for three-room family suites. Many units include kitchenettes. Open May–October; no in-room phones or air-conditioning.

Alpine Motel (120 Madison Ave., 406/646-7544, www.alpinemotelwestyellow stone.com) is similar: $74–94 d. The Alpine also has a family suite that sleeps six with a full kitchen for $145. No phones, but it does have air conditioning, Wi-Fi, and gracious owners. Open mid-May–mid-October.

Pony Express Motel (4 Firehole Ave., 406/646-7644 or 800/323-9708, www.yellow stonevacations.com) has a quiet location but no phones; $59 for one queen bed or $69 for two queens. A kitchenette is $99 for up to four people, and a deluxe two-bedroom suite with space for eight costs $179. Rooms are clean with air conditioning, but very simple, with old furnishings. Free Wi-Fi. Open mid-May–mid-October.

A little nicer but still reasonably priced is another property with the same owners, **City Center Motel** (214 Madison Ave., 408/646-7337 or 800/742-0665, www.yellow stonevacations.com), where the big rooms (no phones) are $79 for one queen bed or $89 for two. Family suites sleep up to eight for $129. A community kitchen, indoor hot tub, and Wi-Fi are available for guests. Open mid-May–mid-October.

◀ **Wagon Wheel Cabins and Campground** (408 Gibbon, 406/646-7872, www.wagon wheelrv.com) has a unique collection of 10 attractive cabins, most containing full kitchens. The cabins are on large lots surrounded by trees, and each has a barbecue grill and picnic table. Basic bring-your-sleeping-bag cabins cost $60 d, and a one-bedroom unit starts at $96 d. The largest unit (cabin 7) is really a small log house with three bedrooms, a full kitchen, and a den with fireplace; it sleeps six for $219. There's a four-night summertime minimum on the larger cabins or three nights for the smaller ones. Cabins at Wagon Wheel fill early, so book several months ahead, especially for cabins 1 and 7. The cabins are often closed in the winter.

Family-run **One Horse Motel** (216 N. Dunraven St., 406/646-7677 or 800/488-2750 www.onehorsemotel.com, $89–99 d) is another good bargain, where all rooms contain microwaves, fridges, and Wi-Fi, but no phones. There's a winter-only indoor hot tub to soak away the chill. Closed mid-March through April and November–mid-December. Same owners for another property with comfortable and clean rooms: **Evergreen Motel** (229 Firehole Ave., 406/646-7655 or 800/488-2750, www.evergreenmotel.info, $79–99 d). It has fridges, microwaves, Wi-Fi, and a couple of kitchenettes, but no air conditioning or phones. Open May–September.

Over $100

You'll find very good accommodations at **Brandin' Iron Inn** (201 Canyon St., 406/646-9411 or 800/217-4613, www.brandiniron.com). Spacious, clean rooms include fridges, a big hot breakfast, Wi-Fi, and access to two indoor hot tubs. Standard rooms are $119–129, with suites for $136–146.

Three Bear Lodge (217 Yellowstone Ave., 406/646-7353 or 800/646-7353, www.threebearlodge.com) is probably best known for its popular restaurant of the same name. The 73-room motel features contemporary rooms, plus two indoor hot tubs, Wi-Fi, an exercise room, and outdoor pool. A wide variety of rooms are available, starting at $109 for standard rooms that sleep four, up to $139 d for units that include a king bed and jetted tub. Two-room family units with fridges and microwaves are $158; the largest sleeps six. Open

year-round. (Note: after a 2008 fire, half the rooms were completely rebuilt as deluxe units with the latest amenities. Rates for these will be higher than the rooms listed above; contact the hotel for details.)

Days Inn (118 Electric St., 406/646-7656 or 800/548-9551, www.allyellowstone.com) is a large motel with standard older rooms ($140–169 d), plus deluxe suites containing two queen beds, a sleeper sofa, microwave, and fridge ($180 d). The nicest rooms have king beds and in-room hot tubs for $215 d. Days Inn also has Wi-Fi, plus two hot tubs and an indoor pool that features the star attraction: a 90-foot corkscrew water slide. (It's the only water slide in town.) Hotel guests receive a coupon for two free breakfasts at Trappers Family Restaurant, downstairs.

Other moderately priced lodging choices in West Yellowstone with good reputations include **Yellowstone Country Inn** (234 Firehole Ave., 406/646-7622, www.yellowstonecountryinn.net, $109–149 d), with a seasonal outdoor pool, hot tub, and sauna. Also check out **Roundup Motel/Dude Motor Inn** (3 Madison Ave., 406/646-7301 or 877/949-7669, www.yellowstonedudemotel.com, $109–129 d), with a hot tub and sauna.

Yellowstone Lodge (251 Electric St., 406/646-0020 or 877/239-9298, www.yellowstonelodge.com) is one of the newer places in town, with oversized rooms, an indoor pool, Jacuzzi, Wi-Fi, guest computer, and light breakfast. Standard rooms with two queens cost $179 d; add $10 for units with a king or two queens plus a fridge and microwave. Suites are $209 d, and a big family unit sleeps six for $229.

Stage Coach Inn (209 Madison Ave., 406/646-7381 or 800/842-2882, www.yellowstoneinn.com), extending almost an entire downtown block, features an impressive Western-style lobby with fireplace, plus a restaurant and heated underground parking (a big plus in winter). Nothing-special older rooms go for $125 d, and updated, larger units are $143–152 d. Guests have access to a sauna and two hot tubs.

At **Hibernation Station** (212 Gray Wolf Ave., 406/646-4200 or 800/580-3557, www .hibernationstation.com) the 50 modern cabins—each a bit different inside—feature handmade log furniture and down comforters. Half also contain kitchenettes. Prices start at $119 d for a cabin with a queen bed, or $149 for one that sleeps four and contains a queen-size bunk bed, fireplace, and kitchenette. Spacious suites with fireplace, king bed, jetted tub, and kitchenette run $239–259 d. Families (not on a budget) will appreciate the large condo unit with room for six, a full kitchen and dining area, fireplace, and jetted tubs for $289–299. Free Wi-Fi. A big outdoor hot tub is available for all guests, and pets are allowed ($10 extra).

The motel chains have moved into West Yellowstone in a big way. One of the nicest is **Comfort Inn** (638 Madison Ave., 406/646-4212 or 888/264-2466, www .westyellowstonecomfortinn.com). The featured attraction here is the biggest indoor pool in town, but the motel also has large rooms, a hot tub, exercise room, hot breakfasts, a guest computer, and Wi-Fi. Rates are $190 d in standard rooms, or $229 for six-person suites.

The large **Gray Wolf Inn and Suites** (250 S. Canyon, 406/646-0000 or 800/852-8602, www.graywolf-inn.com) features a hot tub, sauna, and a small indoor pool, plus a breakfast buffet. An added attraction, especially in the winter, is the heated underground parking garage. Rates are $179 d in standard rooms, $269–309 for one- and two-bedroom suites that come with full kitchens.

The most elaborate local place is the ludicrously named **West Yellowstone Conference Hotel Holiday Inn Sunspree Resort** (315 Yellowstone Ave., 406/646-7365 or 888/633-1724, www.doyellowstone.com), with spacious rooms with fridges and microwaves, Wi-Fi, an indoor pool, exercise room, and hot tub. Standard rooms cost $199 d, two-room family suites are $249–269 and sleep six, and luxurious executive suites (king bed, jetted tub, and wet bar) run $269.

Yellowstone Clubhouse Inn (105 S. Electric St., 406/646-4892 or 800/565-6803, www.yellowstoneclubhouseinn.com, $179 d in standard rooms, $229 d for king rooms with jetted tub, $249 for family suites) is an attractive hotel with modern rooms, fridges, microwaves, an indoor pool and whirlpool bath, small fitness center, guest computer, Wi-Fi, and light breakfast (with waffles). Closed late October–April.

Another relatively new place with a fine reputation is **Kelly Inn West Yellowstone** (104 S. Canyon St., 406/646-4544 or 800/259-4672, www.yellowstonekellyinn.com, $189–209 in standard rooms, $259 for suites with king beds and jetted tubs), which features huge rooms, fridges, microwaves, an indoor pool, sauna, Wi-Fi, a guest computer, and hot breakfast.

Bed-and-Breakfast and Guesthouses

Four miles west of town, **West Yellowstone Bed and Breakfast** (20 Crane Lane, 406/646-7754, www.westyellowstonebandb.com, $135–139 d) features three rooms, all with private baths and entrances, along with a home-cooked breakfast. Kids are welcome.

Six miles west of West Yellowstone and right along the Madison River, **Bar N Ranch** (Hwy. 20, 406/646-0300, www.bar-n-ranch .com) is a luxurious way to rough-it. The main lodge features a three-side fireplace in the great room, with windows framing the mountains. Guests stay in elegant cabins ($273–345 d) with private hot tubs, or in rooms ($199–238 d) in the main lodge. Other amenities include jetted tubs and wood-burning fireplaces in all units, a heated outdoor pool, hot tub, Wi-Fi, and filling breakfasts. Friendly owners too. A three-night minimum is required in the summer.

A number of local companies rent homes, cabins, condos, and town houses of all types, ranging from simple $120 condos to an 18-person log home with eight bedrooms and five baths for $475 per night. The companies include **Yellowstone Townhouses** (406/646-9331 or 866/252-6636, www.yellow stonetownhouses.com), **Moose Haven Vacation Cabin** (714/397-6486, www.moose-haven

.com), **Angler's Rest** (406/646-7778, www.burkinc.net/anglersrest), **LL Western Adventures** (406/646-9730, www.ll westernadventures.com), **Faithful St. Inn** (406/646-1010 or 866/646-4329, www.faithful streetinn.com), **Moose Creek Cabins & Inn** (406/646-7952, www.moosecreek cabin.com), **Eino's Tavern** (406/646-9344), and **Yellowstone Village Condominiums** (406/646-7335 or 800/276-7335, www.west yellowstonerentals.com). A three-night minimum stay is required for most of these places.

CAMPING
Public Campgrounds
The nearest Park Service camping place is inside Yellowstone at **Madison Campground,** 14 miles east of West Yellowstone. The cost is $19, and it's open May–October. Make reservations (advised) at 307/344-7311 or 866/439-7375, www.travelyellowstone.com.

Gallatin National Forest (406/823-6961, www.fs.fed.us/r1/gallatin) has several campgrounds in the West Yellowstone area. The closest camping spot is **Baker's Hole Campground** (open mid-May–mid-Sept., $14), just three miles north of West Yellowstone. It's open for RVs and other hard-sided vehicles only because of bear problems. Tent campers will need to go north of town to **Hebgen Lake,** where five different tenting areas are strung westward along the lake; closest is the **Lonesomehurst Campground** (open mid-May–mid-Sept., $14), 12 miles from West Yellowstone. No reservations are taken at these Forest Service sites.

The Forest Service maintains four public-use cabins ($30 a night for four people) in the country around West Yellowstone. Three of these are open year-round. The closest is **Basin Station Cabin,** eight miles west of town. Make reservations ($10 fee) at 518/885-3639 or 877/444-6777, www.recreation.gov.

RV Parks
West Yellowstone has a half dozen private campgrounds right in town, and several more are west or north of town. Most of the in-town places are just RV parking lots. Far nicer are

two places with shady trees and quiet sites: **Rustic Wagon Campground** (634 U.S. Hwy. 20, 406/646-7387, www.rusticwagonrv.com, $29 for tents or $36–40 for RVs); and **Wagon Wheel Cabins and Campground** (408 Gibbon Ave., 406/646-7872, www.wagonwheelrv .com, $29 tents, $36–40 RVs). Non-campers can shower at either of these for a few dollars. Rustic Wagon is open mid-April–mid-November, and Wagon Wheel is open late May–September. Both are owned by the same family and recommended.

The other in-town RV parks are **Pony Express RV Park** (4 Firehole Ave., 406/646-7644 or 800/323-9708, www.yellow stonevacations.com, $40 RVs, no tents, open year-round), **Hideaway RV Campground** (310 Electric St., 406/646-9049, www.hideaway rv.com, $19 tents, $28–32 RVs, open May–mid-Oct.), **Yellowstone Cabins and RV Park** (504 U.S. Hwy. 20 W., 406/646-9350 or 866/646-9350, www.yellowstonecabins andrv.com, $30 RVs, no tents, open May–Oct.), and **Yellowstone Grizzly RV Park** (210 S. Electric, 406/646-4466, www.grizzlyrv.com, $30 tents, $45–55 RVs, open May–Oct.).

Yellowstone Park KOA (406/646-7606 or 800/562-7591, www.yellowstonekoa.com, $38–43 tents, $48–65 RVs, open May–Sept.) is six miles west of town on U.S. Hwy. 20, with an outdoor pool, game room, and Wi-Fi. Seven miles west of West Yellowstone is **Lionshead RV Park** (406/646-7662, www.lionsheadrv .com, $40–43 for RVs, $25 d for tents, open May–Sept.), adjacent to the Super 8 Motel. **Yellowstone Holiday RV Campground & Marina** (406/646-4242 or 800/643-4227, www.yellowstoneholiday.com, $37–47 RVs) is an RV campground along Hebgen Lake, 13 miles north of West Yellowstone. Cabins are also available; $67 for simple units or $115 for nicer cabins.

FOOD
West Yellowstone has a decidedly middle-brow dining reputation, but the situation has improved in recent years, and you'll be pleased with the choices. Don't expect anything on

the order of Jackson's high-end restaurants, but some local places are really very good. Of course, you can always head to the Dairy Queen if a milkshake and burger fill your hunger pangs.

Breakfast and Lunch

For omelettes, buckwheat pancakes, biscuits and sausage gravy, or other breakfast faves, run—don't walk—over to ◖ **Running Bear Pancake House** (538 Madison Ave., 406/646-7703, daily 7 A.M.–2 P.M.) but be ready for a long wait in midsummer. Five blocks from town center on the west side, this is a great family place with plenty of kid-friendly choices (not to mention the kid-generated noise), and substantive portions. Prices start around $3 for a pancake, up to $10 for the full-cholesterol steak and eggs.

A bit off the beaten path but worth the detour, **Ernie's Deli and Bakery** (406 U.S. Hwy. 20 W., 406/646-9467, www.erniesbakery .com, daily 7 A.M.–3 P.M.) is open for reasonable breakfasts ($6 for two eggs, hash browns, bacon, and a buttermilk biscuit), doughnuts, and unbeatable lunchtime sandwiches (around $7) on freshly baked bread. Heading into the park? Ernie's will put together a box lunch ($9) if you want to leave the sandwiches to the experts. Recommended.

On the corner of Electric and U.S. Hwy. 20, **Kiwi Takeaway** (406/646-7040, Wed.–Mon. 11:30 A.M.–11:30 P.M.) has to be the only New Zealand restaurant for hundreds of miles in any direction. Meat pies (try the chicken curry) are fresh daily, but they often sell out early. The small menu also includes deep-fried tilapia, a blue-cheese burger, and veggie-friendly toasted cheese with pineapple sandwiches.

Coffee and Sweets

Stop by **Tubby's Bakery** (29 Canyon St., 406/646-9737, daily 7 A.M.–9 P.M. in summer, Tues.–Sat. 7 A.M.–2 P.M. in winter) for a morning cup of coffee and fresh-from-the-oven pastry. If you're lucky, Turtle will be the barista pulling your espresso shots and foo-foo drinks; he really knows coffee. Also here are

Baja burritos and bagel sandwiches for breakfast, along with unusual lunch sandwiches such as the Caribbean chickadee with chicken, mango peach salsa, black beans, and cheese wrapped in a tortilla and toasted. Get a fisherman's lunch to go ($12) if you're really hungry and heading out for a day in Yellowstone. By the way, Tubby is the big teddy bear sitting atop the fridge.

Another good latte destination is **The Book Peddler** (106 Canyon St., 406/646-9358, daily 7:30 A.M.–9 P.M. in summer, daily 9 A.M.–5 P.M. the rest of the year) with several tables in the back for bagels, sweets, and coffee.

For sweet treats, head to **Mooseberry's Ice Cream Parlor** (29 Canyon St., 406/646-9776, daily 11 A.M.–11 P.M. late May –Oct., closed Sun.–Mon. in winter). They blend their own flavors, and are best known for shakes, banana splits, and waffle cones.

American

With a downtown location, friendly service, and an eclectic menu, ◖ **Sydney's Mountain Bistro** (38 Canyon St., 406/646-7660, Mon.–Fri. 11 A.M.–3 P.M. and Tues.–Sat. 5–10 P.M.) is a local standout. The butternut squash ravioli is made on the premises, and daily seafood specials are always worth a look. Order a crab cake sandwich for lunch or try Panang chicken or a ribeye steak at dinner, when entrée prices are $14–26. Patio seating is available for dinner.

Beartooth BBQ (111 Canyon St., 406/646-0227, daily 11 A.M.–10 P.M. May–Oct., closed in winter) is a justly popular eatery with a top-carnivore menu of pulled beef brisket sandwiches, finger-lickin' spare ribs, and smoked sausage. Consistently good, it's a favorite of both locals and travelers. Sandwiches are $9–10, with ribs for $15–18.

Three similar family dining places—all with salad bars and three hearty meals a day—are within a block of each other on Yellowstone Avenue: Three Bear, Timberline, and Outpost. **Three Bear Restaurant** (205 Yellowstone Ave., 406/646-7811, www.threebearlodge.com, daily 6:30–11 A.M. and 5–10 P.M., ($18–30)) is a friendly place with an up-market dinner menu of shrimp, fresh seafood, trout, chicken, and steaks. It has a good salad-and-soup bar, a children's menu, and apple brown Betty à la mode for dessert. Open for breakfast and dinner.

Timberline Café (135 Yellowstone Ave. next to the Madison Hotel, 406/646-9349, daily 6:30 A.M.–10 P.M. mid-May–mid-Oct. closed in winter) is an oft-crowded family place for home-cooked breakfast, lunch, and dinner, with a small salad and potato bar ($9), tasty entrées ($16–30) that include homemade lasagna and buffalo meatloaf, a kid's menu, and daily specials. The food is always good.

Outpost Restaurant (115 Yellowstone Ave., 406/646-7303, daily 6:30 A.M.–10 P.M. May–Sept., closed in winter) is another good option serving three meals a day, with a decent salad bar ($9 for all you can eat) and all the dinner favorites: steaks, pork chops, trout, chicken Parmesan, buffalo burgers, and country-fried steak. Daily specials—look for the buffalo steaks—are a good bet. Entrées are $15–24, with "Old Faithfuls" such as baked chicken or homemade beef stew under $12.

The most unusual local eatery is the eccentric **Eino's Tavern** (406/646-9344, open lunch and dinner year-round), nine miles north of town on U.S. Hwy. 191. It's a cook-your-own steak, burger, and chicken place with a big indoor grill and a motley, hard-drinking crowd. Prices are reasonable *(but you are cooking your own food after all)* and the bar is famous for its Bloody Marys. The patio faces Hebgen Lake, and the bar has a big-screen TV and pool tables.

If gourmet meals are your goal, your best bet is ◖ **Bar N Ranch** (406/646-0300, www .bar-n-ranch.com, daily 7–10 A.M. and 5–9 P.M. year-round), serving big breakfasts ($5–8) and fine dinners ($20–38). Check for today's dinner specials, or try the New York steak or lingonberry-orange chicken breast, but save space for their delectable desserts.

Right in the heart of the action, **Dairy Queen** (40 N. Canyon St., 406/646-4106) is the quintessential American joint (though it's probably staffed by seasonal workers from Russia or Poland). Join the line on a warm summer evening for burgers, onion rings, parfaits, and blizzards. DQ is open till 11:30 P.M. daily in the summer, with a couple of picnic tables out front.

Pizza and International

Unlike other local pizza joints, **Wild West Pizza** (20 Madison Ave., 406/646-4400, www.wildwestpizza.com, Sun.–Thurs. 11 A.M.–10 P.M., Fri.–Sat. 11 A.M.–11 P.M.) makes from-scratch pizzas with fresh dough and some odd toppings. I'm not sure how they came up with the pizza names, but somehow the "Sacajawea" has fresh spinach, feta, kalamata olives, and artichoke hearts! Sixteen-inch pizzas run $14–21, and the menu also includes lasagna, calzones, and hot sandwiches on garlic bread. Free local delivery after 5 P.M.

Chinatown (110 Madison Ave., 406/646-7088, daily 11 A.M.–10 P.M.) serves okay Chinese meals and has $6 lunch specials—best deal in town. Dinners run $9–12.

GROCERS

Market Place (22 Madison Ave., 406/646-9600), and **Food Roundup Supermarket** (107 Dunraven, 406/646-7501, daily 7 A.M.–10 P.M.) are the local grocery stores. Market Place also contains a deli and bakery.

INFORMATION AND SERVICES

The **West Yellowstone Chamber of Commerce Visitor Center** (30 Yellowstone Ave., 406/646-7701, www.destinationyellowstone.com, daily 8 A.M.–8 P.M. Memorial Day–Labor Day, daily 8 A.M.–5 P.M. in May and Labor Day–Oct., and Mon.–Fri. 8 A.M.–5 P.M. the rest of the year) is a one-stop destination for regional information. The office is also staffed by Park Service employees (406/646-4403) whenever Yellowstone is open. Daily **ranger talks** (9:30 A.M.) are a feature late May–mid-September, and in winter rangers lead twice-weekly snowshoe walks. Forest Service employees are here Thursday–Saturday in the summer, with details on nearby Gallatin National Forest.

In addition to the chamber's website, you'll find useful information at www.westyellowstonetraveler.com and Yellowstone Park's www.westyellowstonenet.com. The chamber office has a computer to surf the Web, along with free Wi-Fi if you brought a laptop. The **library** (a block west at 200 Yellowstone Ave.) also has free computers. Other options for Wi-Fi and computer rentals include **Madison Hotel** (139 Yellowstone Ave., 406/646-7745 or 800/838-7745, www.madisonhotelmotel.com) and **Send-It-Home** (30 Madison Ave., 406/646-7300, www.send-it-home.com). Drop by the latter to check out the largest keychain collection in the area—800 at last count!

The **Hebgen Lake Ranger District Office** (406/646-7369, www.fs.fed.us/r1/gallatin, Mon.–Fri. 8 A.M.–4:30 P.M.) is just north of town on U.S. Hwy. 191/287. Pick up maps of Gallatin National Forest, along with an interesting brochure on the Madison River Canyon Earthquake Area.

West Yellowstone's **post office** (406/646-7704) is at 209 Grizzly Avenue.

Wash clothes at **Swan Cleaners and Laundromat** (520 Madison Ave., 406/646-7892). Grizzly RV Park and Madison Hotel have public showers.

West Yellowstone Family Medical Clinic (236 Yellowstone Ave., 406/646-0200) takes walk-in patients. It generally has a nurse practitioner or a doctor on duty, and it is open weekdays.

GETTING THERE AND AROUND
By Air
The West Yellowstone airport is two miles north of town off Hwy. 141. **Delta/Skywest** (406/646-7351 or 800/453-9417, www.delta.com) has three flights a day to West Yellowstone from Salt Lake City June–September. The rest of the year, the closest air service is in Bozeman, Idaho Falls, or Jackson Hole.

By Bus and Car
Karst Stage (406/556-3500 or 800/287-4759, www.karststage.com) provides winter shuttles three times daily between the Bozeman airport

and West Yellowstone ($57 one-way, $87 round-trip). Shuttles operate mid-December through April. No scheduled summertime shuttles, but Karst provides custom service from Bozeman to West Yellowstone: $186 one-way for one person, dropping to $118 one-way per person for three travelers. For all Karst trips be sure to make reservations at least three days ahead.

Salt Lake Express (207/736-8824 or 800/356-9796, www.saltlakeexpress.com) runs shuttle vans connecting West Yellowstone with Rexburg, Pocatello, and Boise, Idaho, with connections to Jackson, Salt Lake City, and Butte. The cost is $60 one-way to Salt Lake City.

West Yellowstone has some of the highest gas prices in the region; fill up before you get here! Rental cars are available at the airport from **Avis** (406/646-7635 or 800/831-2847, www.avis.com) and **Budget** (406/646-7882 or 800/527-0700, www.budget.com), or in town from **Big Sky Car Rentals** (415 Yellowstone Ave., 406/646-9564 or 800/426-7669, www.yellowstonevacations.com).

Park Tours
Buffalo Bus Touring Co. (429 Yellowstone, 406/646-9564 or 800/426-7669, www.yellowstonevacations.com) has summertime tours into Yellowstone, with daily lower park loop tours, plus upper loop tours on Mondays, Wednesdays, and Fridays. Rates are $58 adults or $45 kids for the lower loop, or $111 adults, $90 kids for tours that include both loops.

See Yellowstone (406/646-9310 or 800/221-1151, www.seeyellowstone.com) takes smaller groups (maximum 12) on van tours of the park for a bit more: $65 for the lower loop, $70 for an evening wildlife tour of the upper loop (including Lamar Valley), and $88 for a tour to Grand Teton and Jackson Hole.

Also offering small-group van tours and private trips from West Yellowstone are **Yellowstone Tour Guides** (406/646-1092 or 888/493-2260, www.yellowstonetourguides.com), **All Yellowstone Sports/ Yellowstone Van Tours** (406/646-9022 or 800/548-9551, www.allyellowstone.com), and **Caldera Adventures** (406/640-0116, www.yellowstonesummertours.com). Park entrance fees are additional for all tours.

Yellowstone Alpen Guides (555 Yellowstone Ave., 406/646-9591 or 800/858-3502, www .yellowstoneguides.com) leads a range of van tours into Yellowstone, but specializes in personalized tours; $425 for eight hours. The company provides the naturalist-guide, and you travel around the park in your own car or the company van. Linda Wallace of **Yellowstone Country Adventures** (406/581-7476, www .yellowstonecountry-adventures.com) provides a similar personalized tour of the park; she has more than 30 years experience in the park.

Gardiner, Montana

The little tourist town of Gardiner, Montana (pop. 800), lies barely outside the northwest entrance to Yellowstone, just three miles from the Wyoming line. The Yellowstone River slices right through town. Park headquarters at Mammoth Hot Springs is just five miles away, and the large warehouses of park concessioner Xanterra Parks and Resorts dominate the vicinity. Gardiner is the only year-round entrance to Yellowstone, and the Absaroka-Beartooth Wilderness lies just north of here. The town sits at an elevation of 5,300 feet—about 900 feet lower than Mammoth—and has warm, dry summers and relatively mild winters.

SIGHTS
Roosevelt Arch

Gardiner was founded in 1880, and three years later the Northern Pacific Railroad extended a line to the edge of Yellowstone, making the town the first major entryway into the park. A reporter of that era described Gardiner as having "200 hardy souls, with 6 restaurants, 1 billiard hall, 2 dance halls, 4 houses of ill-fame, 1 milk man and 21 saloons." Today, the most distinctive structure in town is the monumental stone park entryway—similar to France's Arc de Triomphe—which was the primary entry point into Yellowstone for many years. Built in 1903, Roosevelt Arch was dedicated by President Theodore Roosevelt, a man regarded by many as Yellowstone's patron saint. A tablet above the keystone is inscribed, "For the Benefit and Enjoyment of the People." (The arch was actually built to offset the park visitors' initial disappointment at finding the rather ordinary country in this part of Yellowstone!) Just downhill from the arch is a small park with picnic tables.

Yellowstone Heritage and Research Center

On the edge of town is the Park Service's massive 32,000-square-foot Yellowstone Heritage and Research Center (307/344-2664, www .nps.gov/yell/historyculture/collections.htm), home to archives, museum collections, and the park library. The 5.3 million (!) artifacts

© DON PITCHER

Roosevelt Arch, Gardiner

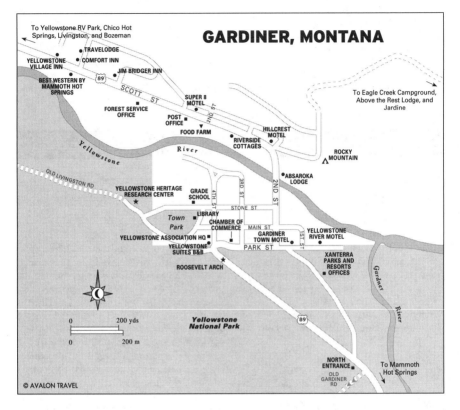

include Thomas Moran watercolors, rare books, early park souvenirs and postcards, more than 90,000 historic photos, and even wolf skulls. It's hard to miss the building, just below the Roosevelt Arch; it's easily the largest structure in town. The library is open Tuesday–Friday 9 A.M.–4 P.M., but the collection is for research purposes by appointment only. Free one-hour tours are, however, offered Wednesday at 10 A.M. in the summer.

RECREATION

Kids will appreciate the **playground** behind the K-12 school in Gardiner; it's just downhill from the arch. Get fishing gear at **Park's Fly Shop** (406/848-7314, www.parksflyshop.com). During the winter, the store also rents cross-country skis.

For horseback rides and backcountry pack trips, contact **Rendezvous Outfitters** (406/848-7697 or 800/565-7110), **Slip & Slide Ranch** (406/848-7076, www.goride montana.com), **Hell's A-Roarin Outfitters** (406/848-7578, www.hellsaroarinoutfitters .com), and **Yellowstone Wilderness Outfitters** (406/223-3300, www.yellowstone.ws).

River Rafting

During summer, four rafting companies offer whitewater trips from Gardiner down the Yellowstone River. **Yellowstone Raft Company** (406/848-7777 or 800/858-7781, www.yellow stoneraft.com) has been running trips since 1978. Other good companies are **Flying Pig Adventure Company** (406/848-7510 or 866/807-0744, www.flyingpigrafting.com),

Montana Whitewater (406/763-4465 or 800/799-4465, www.montanawhitewater.com), and **Wild West Rafting** (406/848-2252 or 800/862-0557, www.wildwestrafting.com).

The rapids in this stretch of the Yellowstone River are relatively gentle, in the Class II–III range, and the featured attractions are half-day eight-mile trips or all-day 17-mile trips. Expect to pay around $38 adults, $27 kids for three-hour trips, or $75 adults, $55 kids for a full-day voyage. Sit-on-top kayaks are a fun option, along with trips that combine rafting with horseback rides. Wild West offers scenic float trips in Paradise Valley north of Gardiner, and Flying Pig has overnight trips that include a night of riverside camping.

Mountain Biking

No local bike rentals, but if you brought your mountain bike, be sure to check out the **Old Gardiner Road.** This narrow dirt road gains 900 feet in elevation on the five-mile ride to Mammoth and makes for a speedy ride back down—not recommended for children. (Cars are only allowed in the downhill direction.) Also worth a ride is the old road to Livingston, a gravel road that follows the west side of the Yellowstone River out of Gardiner. It starts near the arch and passes an interesting cemetery with century-old graves a few miles up.

ENTERTAINMENT AND EVENTS

The big annual event in town is the **Gardiner Rodeo,** which comes around the third weekend of June; it's part of the National Rodeo Association circuit.

End summer with a Labor Day blast at the **Yellowstone Music Festival** (www.yellowstonemusicfest.com), offering plenty of live folk, bluegrass, rock, and roots music in Arch Park. In late September, return for the **Gardiner Brew Fest,** an event that combines food, beers from regional breweries, and live bands.

SHOPPING

Tumbleweed Bookstore and Café (501 Scott St., 406/848-2225) sells new and used titles

and serves paninis, wraps, sandwiches, espresso, salads, and smoothies. It also has rental computers for Web surfing, but lacks Wi-Fi. You'll also find Western books and gifts—along with espresso—downtown on Park Street at **High Country Trading** (406/848-7707).

Yellowstone Gallery and Frameworks (406/848-7306, www.yellowstonegallery.com) is an excellent place for quality pottery, jewelry, paintings, and photography.

Flying Pig Camp Store (406/848-7510 or 866/807-0744, www.flyingpigrafting.com) sells quality outdoor gear, offers river-rafting trips, and has rental computers and Wi-Fi to check your email.

ACCOMMODATIONS

Gardiner has many places to stay, but be sure to make reservations in the summer; rooms may be hard to find even in mid-September. Rates plummet after (and before) the gold rush of seasonal tourists; $90 summertime rooms suddenly go for $45! For a complete listing of local lodging options, visit the Gardiner Chamber of Commerce website, www.gardinerchamber.com.

Under $100

Yellowstone River Motel (14 Park St., 406/848-7303 or 888/797-4837, www.yellowstonerivermotel.com, open May–Oct.) has a garden patio overlooking the river. Economy rooms in the older building are $76 d, or $106 for up to six people in a three-bedroom family unit with full kitchen. Rooms (with fridges and microwaves) in the newer building are $95 d. Wi-Fi is available.

Jim Bridger Motor Court (901 Scott St. W, 406/848-7371 or 888/858-7508) is a classic Western place with cute log cabins built in 1937. Smaller cabins are $89–99 d, or $109 for two-room units that sleep six. No phones or air-conditioning in the cabins, but they do have fans and the larger ones include small fridges. Open late May–mid-October.

Originally built in the 1950s but updated with newer furnishings, **Hillcrest Cottages** (200 Scott St., 406/848-7353 or 800/970-7353, www.hillcrestcottages.com) has 17 cozy little units, all with functional kitchenettes and picnic tables. Most have tiny showers, but a few contain tubs. Rates are $76–88 d in the smaller units, $96 d or $120 for six in a two-room cottage, and $150 for a duplex unit that sleeps eight in two adjoining rooms. No phones, but the cottages have Wi-Fi and air conditioning. Open May– mid-October.

For economical lodging, **Westernaire Motel** (406/848-7397 or 888/273-0358, www.yellowstonemotel.com, $85–95 d) has attractive grounds and clean rooms but dated furnishings. You're likely to see elk hanging out here most of the summer; guess they like the owner's plants better than the surrounding places.

Riverside Cottages (406/848-7719 or 877/774-2836, www.riversidecottages.com) has a mix of motel units ($89–99 d), cottages ($149 d) with full kitchens, and a family suite ($185 for up to six) with jetted tub and full kitchen. Rooms are in good condition, and guests will appreciate the deck out back with a hot tub overlooking the Yellowstone River and free Wi-Fi. Open year-round.

On the north end of town next to the rodeo grounds, **Yellowstone Village Inn** (406/848-7417 or 800/228-8158, www.yellowstonevinn.com) features themed rooms for $122–165 d and kitchenette suites for $172–239; the larger suites sleep six. Amenities include a quiet location, indoor pool, Wi-Fi, fridges, and a continental breakfast.

Over $100

A modern motel close to the bridge, ◖ **Absaroka Lodge** (310 Scott St. W., 406/848-7414 or 800/755-7414, www.yellowstonemotel.com) has immaculate rooms for $110 d, and suites with kitchenettes that cost $130 d, or $140 for four people. All rooms have balconies or decks with a great view of the Yellowstone River. The hotel is especially popular with families. Free Wi-Fi too.

On the north side of the river, **Best Western by Mammoth Hot Springs** (406/848-7311 or 800/828-9080, www.bestwestern.com/mammothhotsprings) has a fine indoor pool,

two saunas, a hot tub, and Wi-Fi. Rooms are $145–170 d, and big family suites with kitchens cost $250. Rooms on the first level have balconies facing the river and pets are welcome.

Out in the country four miles northwest of Gardiner, **Yellowstone Basin Inn** (406/848-7080 or 800/624-3364, www.yellowstonebasininn.com) is a charming, recently built lodge with a variety of accommodations. Standard rooms start at $160 d, and other options include one-bedroom and two-bedroom suites ($245–295), up to a three-bedroom cottage suite ($360) with space for six. All units have private decks where you can sit on a rocking chair with a view of Electric Peak inside Yellowstone. An outdoor hot tub is available, along with Wi-Fi, and a light breakfast is served in the lobby. The inn is open mid-May–mid-October, with limited availability in the off season. Well behaved kids accepted.

Bed-and-Breakfasts

Yellowstone Suites B&B (506 4th St., 406/848-7937 or 800/948-7937, www.yellowstonesuites.com, $112–158 d) is a stone house built in 1904. Features include Victorian antique furnishings, hardwood floors, a veranda, full breakfasts, and Wi-Fi. The four guest rooms have shared or two private baths; one contains a kitchenette. Kids are welcome, and it's open year-round.

North Yellowstone Cabins (406/848-7651, www.northyellowstone.com) is a delightful country place, with two modern log cabins two miles up Jardine Road. The cabins are $90 for up to four. No phones and only a TV are provided, but the cabins have private baths, small fridges, microwaves, and barbecue grills. Outside, weeping willow trees provide shade, and gorgeous sagebrush country heads out in all directions. Open May–September. A two-bedroom vacation home is also available here; four-night minimum stay.

A large house on three acres of land along the Yellowstone River, ◖ **Headwaters of the Yellowstone B&B** (406/848-7073 or 888/848-7220, www.headwatersbandb.com) is a mile north of the Gardiner airport. Inside are four guest rooms ($140 d) and nearby find two modern cabins with full kitchens ($160 for four and $195 for up to six); the riverview cabin fills quickly so call ahead. All of these units have private baths and Wi-Fi, and the rate includes a big homemade breakfast for guests in the rooms and suites (but not the cabins). Kids are welcome. Headwaters has a quiet location next to the park, with a fine view of Electric Peak from the deck and vintage Yellowstone souvenirs inside. Owners Tim and Charissa Reid are especially knowledgeable about the area; she's the author of an authoritative Yellowstone book and he works for the Park Service.

Guesthouses and Vacation Rentals

◖ **Above the Rest Lodge** (406/848-7747 or 800/406-7748, www.abovetherestlodge .com) has five modern and well-appointed cabins less than two miles north of Gardiner up Jardine Road. Smallest is a one-bedroom unit with a spiral staircase and full kitchen; $125 d. Largest is a spacious three-bedroom home that sleeps eight people for $260 per night ($350 nightly for 14 guests). All of these have full kitchens and decks facing Yellowstone. Open year-round. This is a great, secluded place to get away from it all, and is big enough for weddings and other special occasions.

Five miles north of town on Jardine Road is another gorgeous place in a quiet setting: **Bear Creek Hideaway** (406/848-9809, www .bearcreekhideaway.com). This beautiful large guesthouse (seven bedrooms, three baths, kitchen, formal dining room, and living room) has room for 17, and costs $500 per night with a five-night minimum.

Five miles up Jardine Rd. from Gardiner, **Bear Lair Lodge** (406/223-7939, www.yellow stonevacationrental.net) is equally remote. The main 2,000-square-foot lodge sleeps groups of five comfortably for $350 per night, while a smaller cabin sleeps four for $150. Both include full kitchens, woodstove, Wi-Fi, and comfortable beds. A special treat is the owners' alpaca ranch, pegging the cuteness meter for most kids.

Yellowstone Riverbend Cabin (406/586-0600, www.yellowstoneriverbend cabin.com, $185 d) is a recently constructed cabin along the river with two bedrooms, a gas fireplace, flat-screen TV, porch, and kitchen. Open May–mid-October with a three-night minimum.

Chico Hot Springs

Besides lodging in Gardiner, several places are available in Paradise Valley, 20 miles to the north. Farther away, but worth a visit if you're heading north, is Chico Hot Springs (406/333-4933 or 800/468-9232, www.chico hotsprings.com), 30 miles north of Gardiner in Pray, Montana. This classic old hotel sits adjacent to a hot springs–fed pool (open 7 A.M.–10:30 P.M., $6.50 adults, $4.50 kids, $2 seniors), and the restaurant is an attraction in its own right. Dinner reservations are required. Rooms in the main hotel start at $49 d for those with a bath down the hall, while nicer ones in the lower lodge are $125–225 d. A variety of cabins and houses are also available, all the way up to a five-bedroom log home (popular with wedding parties and family reunions) that sleeps 17 for $355 per night. The Dining Room at Chico (7–10:30 A.M. and 5:30–10 P.M.) serves $9 breakfast buffets along with fine dining in the evenings ($25–30 entrées). There's a day spa on the premises, along with summertime horseback rides and fly-fishing, plus wintertime dog sledding. The saloon swings to live bands on weekends year-round.

CAMPING

Yellowstone National Park's **Mammoth Campground** is five miles up the hill at Mammoth Hot Springs and costs $14. The campground is open year-round but sits close to a busy road. No reservations are taken.

Closer—and more peaceful—is the small **Eagle Creek Campground** (open year-round, $7), less than two miles northeast of Gardiner up the gravel road on the way to Jardine. This Gallatin National Forest campground (406/848-7375, www.fs.fed.us/r1/gallatin) is approximately 500 feet higher than Gardiner, and you will need to bring water from town or treat water from the creek here. Two other Forest Service campgrounds (free; open mid-June–Oct.) are a few miles up Jardine Road.

Park RVs at **Rocky Mountain Campground** (406/848-7251 or 877/534-6931, www.rocky mountaincampground.com, open mid-Apr.–mid-Oct., $28 tents, $42–46 RVs), with free Wi-Fi. Showers for noncampers are available, and a coin launderette is on the site. Simple cabins cost $40–50 d.

Campsites are also available in crowded, along-the-river sites at **Yellowstone RV Park** (406/848-7496, www.ventureswestinc.com, open May–Oct.) on the northwest end of town. Laundry and Wi-Fi available.

FOOD

K-Bar & Café (202 Main St., 406/848-9995, daily 11 A.M.–10 P.M.) doesn't look like much either outside or inside, but the from-scratch pizzas are very good in this locals' hangout; kids and families are welcome. Pizzas start at $7 for the mini version, up to $17 for a 16-inch combo. Also popular with families is **Outlaw's Pizza** (in the Outpost Mall on the northwest end of town, 406/848-7733, 11 A.M.–10:30 P.M.) for pizzas ($14 for a medium), pasta, and calzones, plus a small salad and soup bar ($6) for something less filling.

The downtown **Sawtooth Deli** (220 W. Park St., 406/848-7600, Tues.–Sat. 8 A.M.–4 P.M. in summer, reduced winter hours, $6–8) serves tasty breakfasts, along with subs, grilled sandwiches, soups, and salads for lunch (no dinners). Daily specials are generally your best bet. The covered deck is a favorite hangout. Closed Sunday and Monday and mid-October–May.

At the aging yellow **Corral Drive Inn** (711 Scott St. W., 406/848-7627, daily 11 A.M.–11 P.M. in summer, $7–14), Helen and her sons serve the biggest, juiciest, and messiest (grab a handful of napkins) hamburgers anywhere around. Chicken, fish and chips, grilled cheese sandwiches, and shrimp baskets fill out the menu.

Find a good choice of Italian dishes at

Pedalino's Restaurant (204 West Park St., 406/848-9950, www.pedalinositalian.com, Wed.–Mon. 5–9 P.M., closed Tues., $15–28), including the signature dish: "crazy pasta" with chicken, sausage, soppresata, cream, cheeses, and red chili peppers. Meals come with a big house salad, and fresh-baked bread. Closed October–April.

The presentation is simple—picnic tables, paper plates, and a screened-in porch out front of Two Bit Saloon—but meat lovers should not miss ◀ **Raven Grill** (107 Hwy. 89 S, 406/848-7743, daily 5–10 P.M. late May–early Oct., $13–19). Owner/chef Philip Currie grills choice steaks, including buffalo sirloin, and also has Jamaican jerk chicken, jumbo shrimp (is that an oxymoron?), and other affordable meals. Entrées come with Cajun corn on the cob, baked beans, garlic bread, and fresh strawberries. This one's a real find!

Shop for groceries, fresh baked goods, and deli items at **Food Farm** (406/848-7524, Sun. 8 A.M.–8 P.M., Mon.–Sat. 7 A.M.–9 P.M.) across the river on the northwest end of town.

INFORMATION AND SERVICES

The **Gardiner Chamber of Commerce** (222 W. Park St., 406/848-7971, www.gardiner chamber.com, Mon.–Fri. 9 A.M.–7 P.M. and Sat.–Sun. 10 A.M.–3 P.M. late May–early Sept., and Mon.–Thurs. 10 A.M.–5 P.M. the rest of the year) has local information. If the office is closed, check the information kiosk next to Outlaw Pizza on the north end of town for maps, brochures, and events. Located adjacent to Arch Park, the tiny **Gardiner Library** (406/848-7835, Tues. 10 A.M.–5 P.M. plus Tues. and Thurs. 6–8 P.M.) has one computer with free Internet access (but no Wi-Fi).

For computer rentals and Wi-Fi head to **Yellowstone Perk** (208 Park St., 406/848-2240), **Tumbleweed Bookstore and Café** (501 Scott St., 406/848-2225), **High Country Trading** (406/848-7707), or **The Silvertip** (505 Scott St., 406/600-4730, www.the-silvertip.com).

The **Gardiner District Office** of Gallatin National Forest (406/848-7375, www.fs.fed

.us/r1/gallatin) has maps and information on the 930,584-acre **Absaroka-Beartooth Wilderness.** The area around Gardiner is lower in elevation and covered with forests, while farther east are the alpine peaks of the Beartooth Mountains.

The **post office** is on the north end of town (along U.S. Hwy. 89, 406/848-7579). Get fast cash at the ATM inside the Cenex station just north of the river, the Sinclair station in town, or from the First Interstate Bank on the northwest end of town. Wash clothes or take a shower at the **North Entrance Wash Tub** (209 Main St. W., 406/848-9870). Both Yellowstone Village Inn and Rocky Mountain Campground also have washers and driers available to the public. The closest medical facility is in Mammoth Hot Springs.

If you get to Gardiner without a vehicle, but call **Enterprise Rent-A-Car** in Livingston (406/222-0506). They'll pick you up in Gardiner and provide a rental car.

GETTING THERE AND AROUND

Karst Stage (406/388-2293 or 800/287-4759, www.karststage.com) has daily wintertime shuttles between the Bozeman airport and Gardiner: $159 one-way or $311 round-trip per person (prices drop substantially for more than one passenger). No summertime shuttles, but Karst provides custom service from Bozeman to Gardiner or Mammoth Hot Springs: $186 one-way for one person, dropping to $118 per person for three travelers. For all Karst trips be sure to make reservations at least three days ahead.

Late May–mid-September, Xanterra Parks and Resorts (307/344-7311 or 866/439-7375, www.travelyellowstone.com) operates full-day bus tours of Yellowstone out of Gardiner. Rates are $70 adults, $35 ages 8–15, and free for younger kids; park entrance fees are extra. These tours are a bit grueling because you leave at 7:45 A.M. and don't get back until 6:15 P.M.

Cooke City and Silver Gate, Montana

Shortly after you exit Yellowstone's northeast corner along U.S. Hwy. 212, the road widens slightly as it passes through two settlements: Silver Gate and the larger Cooke City, Montana. The towns are just three miles apart and almost within spitting distance of the Wyoming line. The area code—406—is larger than the combined population of both settlements! Although they depend on tourism, these quiet, homespun places lack the hustle and bustle of West Yellowstone and have a more authentic feel. No leash laws exist here, so you're likely to see dogs sleeping on the sidewalks or wandering lazily down the middle of the road. Most establishments are built of log, befitting the mining heritage of this area. Silver Gate even has a building code that requires all structures to be of log or rustic architecture—it's the only municipality in the country with such a code. Pilot Peak and Index Peak are the prominent rocky spires visible along the highway east

of Cooke City. Dramatic Amphitheater Peak juts out just south of Silver Gate.

During winter, the road is plowed all the way from Gardiner, through the northern part of Yellowstone, and into Cooke City, making this a popular staging area for snowmobilers and skiers heading into the Beartooth Mountains. East of Cooke City, the Beartooth Highway across 10,947-foot Beartooth Pass is closed by the first of November (often earlier) and doesn't open again until late May.

HISTORY

The town of Cooke City was first called Shoo-Fly, but the name was changed in honor of Jay Cooke Jr., a promoter of the Northern Pacific Railroad. The promised railroad never materialized, but the name stuck. Cooke City had its start in 1882 when the boundaries of the Crow Reservation were shifted to the east, opening this area to mining. A small gold rush ensued, the spire of Beartooth Mountain near Cooke City

and by the following summer, Cooke City had grown to hold several hundred miners, along with two smelters, two sawmills, and a cluster of businesses. At its peak, the town was also home to 13 saloons. As with many 19th-century mining towns, the population of Cooke City had wild swings, with up to 1,000 people at one time, but just 20 souls a few years later. The isolation, modest gold and silver strikes, and high transportation costs (no railroad was ever built into the settlement) kept mining from ever really booming. Today fewer than 100 people live in Cooke City year-round, but the population triples with the arrival of summer residents.

The town of Silver Gate has a briefer history. The land here was first homesteaded in the 1890s, but the town didn't appear until 1932 when John Taylor and J. J. White founded it as a haven for summer residents looking for a home close to Yellowstone. Only a handful of folks live here in the winter, but that swells to 100 or so when the long days of summer return.

The country around Silver Gate and Cooke City was torched in the Storm Creek Fire of 1988, leaving charred hills just a couple of hundred feet to the north and prompting alterations in the road signs to read "Cooked City." Today, tourism is the ticket to ride for both Cooke City and Silver Gate. In summer the towns are crowded with folks en route to (or from) Yellowstone. Both Soda Butte Lodge and Miners Saloon in Cooke City have one-armed bandits with slot-machine poker and keno gambling, along with live poker. In the fall, hunters head into the surrounding mountains, and when the snow flies, the snowmobiles come out of hibernation.

Reminders of the mining era abound in the surrounding country, but not all of it is benign. Reclamation ponds catch toxic runoff from some of these old mines.

SIGHTS

It's hard to miss the red **Cooke City Store** (406/838-2234, www.cookecitystore.com, daily 8 A.M.–9 P.M. in July and Aug., till 6 P.M. May, June, and Sept.), one of the oldest buildings in the area. Built in 1886, this classic country market sells groceries, quality T-shirts, and gifts. It also carries Yellowstone and Wyoming fishing licenses. Open May–September only. Up the street is another seasonal place that's well worth a look. **Blain Gallery** (406/838-2474, www.artmontana.com/Blain) features original watercolors by Mary Blain, along with pottery, jewelry, and photographs.

RECREATION

Yellowstone is less than four miles away, and it's the obvious site for recreation in the Cooke City-Silver Gate area during the summer. The **Absaroka-Beartooth Wilderness** is accessible from Cooke City and various points to the east along the gorgeous Beartooth Highway. One of the more unusual sights is **Grasshopper Glacier,** eight miles north of Cooke City and 4,000 feet higher. The glacier contained the remains of a swarm of locusts that was apparently caught in a snowstorm while flying over the mountains. Unfortunately, most have now melted out and decayed.

Summertime horseback rides, pack trips into the Absaroka-Beartooth Wilderness, and guided fly-fishing expeditions are provided by several local outfitters: **Beartooth Plateau Outfitters** (406/445-2328 or 800/253-8545, www.beartoothoutfitters.com), **Castle Creek Outfitters** (406/838-2301), **K Bar Z Guest Ranch** (307/587-4410, www.agonline.com/kbarz), **Skyline Guest Ranch & Guide Service** (406/838-2380 or 877/238-8885, www.flyfishyellowstone.com), and **Stillwater Outfitters** (406/855-0016, www.stillwateroutfitters.com).

Hiking, Skiing, and Snowshoeing

Visit **Silvertip Mountain Center** (406/838-2125 or 800/863-0807, www.silvertipmountaincenter.com) in Silver Gate for outdoor gear, climbing equipment, bear spray, maps, and other supplies. They rent skis and snowshoes in winter, along with all sorts of other gear (from tents to rock climbing shoes) in summer. The owners also run Log Cabin Café (adjacent), and can provide details on nearby hiking and snowshoe trails, plus vehicle drop-offs. Open late May–mid-September.

Snowmobiling

Cooke City has become a hub for winter sports. Pick up a map of groomed cross-country ski trails and snowmobile routes from local businesses. The area consistently ranks among the top snowmobiling destinations in America. Snowmobile rentals (and summertime ATV rentals) are available from **Cooke City Exxon** (406/838-2244, www.cookecityexxon.com) and **Cooke City Motorsports** (406/838-2231). The local snowmobile club grooms approximately 60 miles of trails in the surrounding mountains. Be sure to also check the **Avalanche Advisory Hotline** (406/587-6981, www.mtavalanche.com) for the latest on backcountry conditions before heading out.

ENTERTAINMENT AND EVENTS

The twin towns have a fun **Fireman's Picnic and Fourth of July fireworks,** and Silver Gate is home to **Shakespeare in the Park** in late August. Mid-August brings the **Fish Fry and Big Fish Contest** to Cooke City.

ACCOMMODATIONS

Cooke City and Silver Gate have quite a few old-fashioned motels and cabins that provide a delightful Old West feeling. As with other towns surrounding Yellowstone, reservations are always a good idea in midsummer or midwinter.

Cooke City

You'll find spacious, clean, and comfortable rooms and cabins at **High Country Motel** (406/838-2272, www.cookecityhighcountry.com, $60–90 d). Some units contain kitchenettes. Open all year. **Hoosier's Motel** (406/838-2241, $85 d) has clean older rooms and is open mid-May–mid-October.

Alpine Motel (406/838-2262 or 888/838-1190, www.cookecityalpine.com) is also open all year and has rooms for $65–88 d, plus apartment-style units with two bedrooms and full kitchens for $95 d, plus $4 per person for additional guests (max of six). Free Wi-Fi.

Three miles east of Cooke City, **Big Moose**

Resort (406/838-2393, www.bigmooseresort
.com, $95–110 for up to five) has a mix of eight
old and new year-round cabins; two include
kitchenettes 110 for up to five. Guests have access to an outdoor hot tub and free Wi-Fi, but
no in-room phones. Open mid-May through
October and January–March.

Right across the road, **Stillwater Outfitters
Lodge** (406/838-2267 or 888/341-2267, www
.stillwateroutfitters.com) is primarily a fishing,
hiking, and hunting lodge but offers nightly accommodations throughout the year. Guests stay
in six older but well-kept log cabins ($70–80 d),
each with two double beds and private baths.
Open June–mid-October and January–March.
Stillwater Outfitters leads all sorts of horse-based trips, including day rides and horse-packing into Yellowstone National Park.

Also on the east end of town, **Super 8 Motel**
(406/838-2070 or 877/338-2070, www.cooke
citysuper8.com, $75–85 d) is a modern and
clean place where amenities include a light
breakfast and Wi-Fi.

Friendly **Elk Horn Lodge** (406/838-2332,
www.elkhornlodgemt.com) has attractive and
spotless motel rooms ($89 d) with microwaves
and fridges, plus two cabins ($109 d or $119
for four guests) with kitchenettes. Open year-round, with free Wi-Fi.

Antler's Lodge & Cabins (406/838-2432
or 866/738-2432, www.cookecityantlerslodge
.com, $75–135 d) has 15 cabins in various sizes
and configurations, most with kitchens and
some containing lofts. The largest sleeps six
for $135. Wi-Fi is available; open year-round.

Skyline Guest Ranch (406/838-2380 or
877/238-8885, www.flyfishyellowstone.com)
has five spacious guest rooms in a three-story
lodge, each with private bath and access to a
hot tub on the deck. Rates—with a full breakfast—are $83 for one queen bed or $105 for
rooms with two queens. Open June–October
and January–March.

A few miles north of Cooke City and 1.5
miles up a jeep/hiking trail, the Forest Service's
Round Lake Cabin sleeps four and costs just
$30. It's open mid-July–mid-September and
mid-December–March. Make reservations

($10 fee) at 518/885-3639 or 877/444-6777,
www.recreation.gov.

A number of vacation rentals are available
in the Cooke City area. Located three miles
east of town, **Montana Rocky Top Cabin**
(863/465-2966, www.montanarockytopcabin
.com) is an elegant log home with a bedroom
and loft; it sleeps up to five for $225 nightly
with a four-night minimum stay. Other options include **Two Rib Cabin** (406/721-6986,
www.vrbo.com/35554, $220 per night with a
three-night minimum) and **All Seasons Cabin**
(406/838-2433, www.allseasonscabin.com).

Silver Gate

For a quiet step into the past, book one of the 24
cabins maintained by ◖ **Silver Gate Lodging**
(406/838-2371, www.pineedgecabins.com), just
a few minutes from the entrance to Yellowstone
National Park. Most of these were built in the
1930s, but they've been updated with small private baths and Wi-Fi, but no TVs or phones.
Most include kitchenettes with dishes and
pans, and pets are welcome. The cabins vary
widely, from rustic two-person units ($72), to
an attractive six-person cabin ($170). The five
motel units are $72 d. Outside, you'll find barbecue grills, volleyball and horseshoes, and a
playground for kids. Some cabins remain open
year-round. This is a quiet place where snowmobiles and four-wheelers are not allowed.
Also on the premises is **Silver Gate General
Store & Cabins,** with supplies, a good selection of books, and Montana-made products.
The store rents high-quality **spotting scopes**
($25/day) and binoculars for folks heading into
Yellowstone to watch wolves. The adjacent
Range Rider Lodge—a classic log building
from 1937—serves spirits on weekends.

Right on the river and close to the
Yellowstone border in Silver Gate, **Grizzly
Lodge** (406/838-2219, www.yellowstone
lodges.com, $73–87) centers around a 1937 log
building with a comfortable lounge and wood
stove. Guests stay in a variety of rather basic
motel-style rooms (including kitchenettes, two-bedroom units) with access to a sauna, hot tub,
and free Wi-Fi. Open late May–September.

© DON PITCHER

Silver Gate

Log Cabin Café (406/838-2367 or 800/863-0807, $115 d or $155 for four) rents two restored cabins from the 1930s; open mid-May–mid-September. A free breakfast at the café is included.

CAMPING

Heading east from Cooke City, you'll find four Forest Service campgrounds (open July–Sept., $8) within 10 miles of town. Closest is **Soda Butte Campground,** just 0.5 mile from town; another mile to the east is **Colter Campground** (406/848-7375, www.fs.fed.us/r1/gallatin). Showers are available from Soda Butte Lodge in Cooke City.

No RV parks are in the area, but **Big Moose Resort** (406/838-2393, www.bigmooseresort.com, $35) has summertime RV sites with water, showers, and electric hookups.

FOOD

Inside Cooke City's Soda Butte Lodge, **Prospector Restaurant**(406/838-2251 or 800/527-6462, www.cookecity.com, daily 7 A.M.–10 P.M. in mid-summer) is well known for steak and prime rib cooked to perfection,

but it's also open for breakfast and lunch. Entrées are $14–30. Smoke from the bar may drift into the restaurant. Also here is the **Ore House Saloon,** with sports on the TV and video poker and keno machines to take your money. Everything at Soda Butte Lodge is open year-round, and they pull out the poker tables in winter.

Cooke City Bike Shack (406/838-2412) cranks out espresso coffees and also serves sandwiches and burritos. Not much in the way of bikes anymore—despite the name—but the shop has a few cycling supplies.

Cooke City's **Bistro Café** (406/838-2160, daily 7:30 A.M.–10 P.M. in mid-summer, daily 8 A.M.–8 P.M. in winter) serves American standards for breakfast and lunch, but dinner is when this bistro shines, with quality steaks, pork chops, and rack of lamb; $15–30. Closed mid-October–December.

In business since for over 30 years, (**Beartooth Café** in Cooke City (406/838-2475, www.beartoothcafe.com, daily 11 A.M.–9 P.M. mid-May–Sept.) is a perpetually busy place all summer. The lunch menu includes soups, salads, burgers, and sandwiches;

try the French dip sandwich or the half-pound funk burger. Dinners ($16–30 entrées) include BBQ ribs, thick steaks, Angus prime rib, teriyaki chicken, and a popular rainbow trout, served with all the fixin's. Everything is freshly made on the premises. Beer connoisseurs can choose from 130 brews from all over the planet. Eat out on the front patio for the full-on Beartooth experience.

Next door is **Buns 'N Beds Deli** (406/838-2030, $8–9), a lunch-only place with year-round deli sandwiches, soups, and salads.

In peaceful Silver Gate, **Log Cabin Café** (406/838-2367, daily 7:30 A.M.–10 P.M. Memorial Day–Labor Day, $15–24) is a consistent favorite, with locally famous rainbow trout, steak with crab, and organic salads for dinner, along with big breakfasts and lunches featuring barbecued beef and homemade soups. It's been here since 1937. Owners Laurie Hinck and Jay Schifferdecker are long-time residents with a deep knowledge of the area.

Cooke City's **Miner's Saloon** (406/838-2214, Sun.–Thurs. noon–10 P.M., Fri.–Sat. noon–11 P.M., with reduced winter hours; closed fall in spring) is a classic Old West bar where the stools are filled with locals and tourists. Pull the handles on the keno and poker machines, or try a game of pool or foosball. The menu includes surprisingly good pizzas, burgers, fish tacos, and Caesar salads for $8–19.

For groceries and supplies, head to historic **Cooke City Store** (406/838-2234, www.cookecitystore.com).

INFORMATION AND SERVICES

The **Cooke City, Colter Pass, and Silver Gate Chamber of Commerce** (406/838-2495, www.cookecitychamber.org) has a small visitor center in Cooke City that's staffed daily 10 A.M.–6 P.M. late May–mid-September. In winter, the office is open some weekday afternoons, but call ahead to be sure. Put away your **cell phone** in Cooke City and Silver Gate; there's no service here. If you're heading here from other areas, fill your tank because gas prices here are some of the highest in the region. The Exxon station's website—www.cookecityexxon.com—has live Web cams if you want to see what's happening in Cooke City right now.

Despite its remoteness, you'll discover several ATMs in Cooke City. Laundry facilities are inside Soda Butte Lodge and **Cooke City Sinclair** (406/838-2000, www.cookecitysinclair.com) has Internet access.

Shoshone National Forest

Shoshone National Forest encompasses more than 2.4 million acres and extends along a 180-mile strip from the Montana border to the Wind River Mountains. Sagebrush dominates at the lowest elevations, but as you climb, lodgepole, Douglas fir, Engelmann spruce, and subalpine fir cover the slopes. Above 10,000 feet, the land opens into alpine vegetation and barren rocky peaks. The **Shoshone National Forest Supervisor's Office** (307/578-1200, www.fs.fed.us/r2/shoshone) is in Cody. Get information and forest maps there or from ranger stations in Cody, Dubois, and Lander.

History

Shoshone is America's oldest national forest. On March 30, 1891, President Benjamin Harrison signed a proclamation creating Yellowstone Park Timberland Reserve adjacent to Yellowstone National Park. At first this title meant very little, but in 1902 President Theodore Roosevelt appointed rancher and artist A. A. Anderson to control grazing and logging and catch poachers. His strong management almost got him lynched. Three years later under Gifford Pinchot, the forest reserves were transferred to the Department of Agriculture and renamed national forests. The land was renamed Shoshone National Forest in 1908.

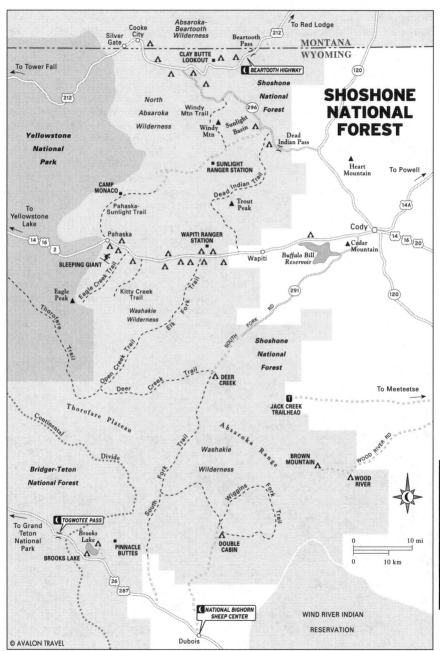

SHOSHONE
NATIONAL
FOREST

Yellowstone
National
Park

North
Absaroka
Wilderness

Silver
Gate

Cooke
City

Absaroka-
Beartooth
Wilderness

Beartooth
Pass

To Red Lodge

To Tower Fall

MONTANA
WYOMING

CLAY BUTTE
LOOKOUT

BEARTOOTH HIGHWAY

Shoshone
National
Forest

Windy
Mtn Trail

Windy
Mtn

Sunlight
Basin

Dead
Indian Pass

Heart
Mountain

To Powell

SUNLIGHT
RANGER STATION

CAMP
MONACO

Dead Indian Trail

Trout
Peak

Pahaska-
Sunlight Trail

To
Yellowstone
Lake

Pahaska

WAPITI RANGER
STATION

Cody

Cedar
Mountain

SLEEPING GIANT

Wapiti

Buffalo Bill
Reservoir

Eagle
Peak

Eagle Creek Trail

Kitty Creek
Trail

Washakie
Wilderness

Elk Fork Trail

Thorofare Trail

Open Creek Trail

Deer Creek Trail

Shoshone
National
Forest

DEER
CREEK

To Meeteetse

JACK CREEK
TRAILHEAD

Thorofare Plateau

Continental

Divide

Bridger-Teton
National Forest

South Fork Trail

Washakie
Wilderness

Absaroka Range

BROWN
MOUNTAIN

WOOD RIVER RD

WOOD
RIVER

To Grand
Teton
National
Park

TOGWOTEE PASS

Brooks
Lake

PINNACLE
BUTTES

Wiggins Fork Trail

DOUBLE
CABIN

BROOKS LAKE

GATEWAYS TO YELLOWSTONE

0   10 mi

0   10 km

NATIONAL BIGHORN
SHEEP CENTER

WIND RIVER INDIAN

RESERVATION

Dubois

© AVALON TRAVEL

Recreation

More than half of Shoshone National Forest lies inside wilderness boundaries; the Absaroka-Beartooth, North Absaroka, and Washakie wilderness areas cover much of the country east of Yellowstone National Park, while the Wind River Mountains contain the Fitzpatrick and Popo Agie wildernesses. Part of the credit for the surprising expanse of wilderness areas in the national forest goes to Buffalo Bill. By bringing people into the area to hunt, fish, and explore, he helped create what one author called a "dude's forest." In addition, the Buffalo Bill Dam (which he vociferously supported) prevented logs from being sent down the North Fork of the Shoshone River and thus made logging less important.

More than 1,500 miles of trails offer hiking and horseback access to much of this country. Shoshone has more than 50 campgrounds for $10–15 per night. Once the water has been shut off for winter (generally Oct.–Apr.), you can camp for free but will have to haul out your own trash. Space is generally available even at the busiest times of year. In addition, free dispersed camping is possible at undeveloped sites throughout the forest, with the exception of heavily traveled U.S. Hwy. 14/16/20, where you must be 0.5 mile off the road.

Although uncommon, black bears roam throughout the forest, and grizzlies are found within the northern sections, including the North Absaroka and Washakie wilderness areas. Be sure to take the necessary bear precautions anywhere in the backcountry. Bears also sometimes wander into campgrounds along U.S. Hwy. 14/16/20 near Yellowstone National Park. You are much more likely to encounter mosquitoes, deer flies, and horse flies in midsummer, so be sure to bring insect repellent.

NORTH ABSAROKA WILDERNESS

The 350,488-acre North Absaroka Wilderness is one of the lesser-known wild places in Wyoming. It abuts Yellowstone National Park to the west and is bordered by the Sunlight Basin Highway and Beartooth Highway to the north and U.S. Hwy. 14/16/20 to the south. North Absaroka Wilderness is primarily used

© DON PITCHER

Volcanic rocks border U.S. Hwy. 14/16/20 in Shoshone National Forest.

by hunters who arrive on horseback. The few hikers here tend to be quite experienced with backcountry travel and willing to tolerate the lack of trail signs and the steep and frequently washed-out paths. Much of the wilderness is relatively inaccessible, and snow may be present on passes until mid-July. Ask at the ranger stations for current trail conditions, and be sure to get topographic maps before heading out. Large populations of grizzly and black bears, bighorn sheep, moose, and elk are found in the Absaroka Mountains, and golden eagles are a common sight. The tough landscape is of volcanic origin, and the topsoil erodes easily, turning mountain creeks into churning rivers of mud after heavy summer rainstorms.

Hiking

The 1988 Clover-Mist Fire that began in Yellowstone burned through a large section of the North Absaroka Wilderness, but the land is recovering. Many hikers begin from trailheads near the Crandall Ranger Station along the Chief Joseph Scenic Highway. The **North Crandall Trail** is the most popular, a 16-mile hike up the North Fork of Crandall Creek. It is primarily used by horsepackers and offers great views of Hurricane Mesa along the way. Another popular wilderness path is **Pahaska-Sunlight Trail,** an 18-mile trek that begins at Pahaska Campground on U.S. Hwy. 14/16/20 and heads north through historic Camp Monaco to Sunlight Basin.

WASHAKIE WILDERNESS

Covering 704,529 acres, Washakie Wilderness is one of the largest chunks of wild land in Wyoming. Named for Shoshone Chief Washakie, it lies between U.S. Hwy. 14/16/20 (the road connecting Yellowstone and Cody) and U.S. Hwy. 26/287 (Dubois area). To the west are Yellowstone National Park and Teton Wilderness. The Washakie is a land of deep narrow valleys, mountains of highly erodible volcanic material, and steplike buttes. The mountains—a few top 13,000 feet—are part of the Absaroka Range. About half of the land is forested. One of the unique features of

Washakie Wilderness is a petrified forest, a reminder of the region's volcanic past.

Hiking

Numerous trails run through the Washakie Wilderness, but most require that you either return the same way or end at a location far from your starting point. Several trails stretch into Yellowstone National Park and are popular with extended horsepacking trips. The most popular Washakie Wilderness hikes are from U.S. Hwy. 14/16/20 in Wapiti Valley. Most folks use them for short day hikes or horseback rides rather than attempting longer backcountry treks.

Kitty Creek Trail leaves from the Kitty Creek summer home area, nine miles east of Yellowstone. Low-clearance vehicles will need to park along the highway. The trail follows the creek past two large scenic meadows to Flora Lake, 6.5 miles and 2,500 feet higher. This is the shortest hike in the area and one of the most popular.

The 21-mile-long **Elk Fork Trail** starts at Elk Fork Campground and crosses Elk Creek several times en route to remote Rampart Pass at nearly 11,000 feet. It is steep and rocky in the higher elevations. West of the Continental Divide you enter the Teton Wilderness. For the really ambitious, the Open Creek Trail and Thorofare Trail continue into Yellowstone National Park.

Deer Creek Trail departs from the free Deer Creek Campground, 42 miles southwest of Cody on Hwy. 291 (South Fork Rd.). The trail switchbacks very steeply uphill at first and after two miles reaches an attractive waterfall. Continue another eight miles from here to the Continental Divide and the Thorofare section of the Teton Wilderness. This is probably the quickest route into this remote country and is popular with both horsepackers and hikers.

South Fork Trail takes off from the South Fork Guard Station across the creek from Deer Creek Campground. (Take a signed spur road to get there.) It climbs up along South Fork Creek to Shoshone Pass on the Continental Divide (9,858 feet). From here you can continue on several trails to the south, rambling over three more passes to eventually reach Double

Cabin Campground, 27 miles north of Dubois. Another long hike into Washakie Wilderness leaves from this campground and follows the **Wiggins Fork Trail** up into a connecting series of paths: Absaroka, Nine Mile, East Fork, and Bug Creek trails. It ends back at Double Cabin Campground. Total length is 60 miles. Along the way you're likely to see hundreds of elk in the high country as well as bighorn sheep.

SUNLIGHT BASIN

The **Chief Joseph Scenic Highway** (Hwy. 296) is a 46-mile route through a magnificent Wyoming landscape. Popularly known as Sunlight Basin Road, it is paved and most of it remains open year-round, providing access for backcountry skiers and snowmobilers to the beautiful Beartooth Pass area. (An eight-mile section between Cooke City, Montana, and Pilot Creek, Wyoming, is not plowed in the winter. It typically opens by early May.) Chief Joseph Highway begins 17 miles north of Cody off Hwy. 120, with Heart Mountain prominent to the southeast, and climbs sharply from the dry east side, passing a brilliant red butte en route to **Dead Indian Pass,** named for an incident during an 1878 fight between Bannocks and the U.S. Army. After the battle, Crow scouts found a wounded old Bannock warrior here. They killed and scalped him, burying the body under a pile of rocks. Other tales claim that the name came from the body of an Indian propped up as a ruse to trick the army during Chief Joseph's attempted escape to Canada in 1877. Chief Joseph *did* lead the Nez Perce through this country, avoiding the cavalry by heading up Clarks Fork Canyon, a route the army had considered impassable. An overlook on top of Dead Indian Pass provides a panoramic vista of the rugged mountains and valleys below. The river forms a boundary between the volcanic Absarokas to the south and the granitic Beartooth Mountains to the north.

Indians weren't the only ones killed in this era. In 1870, two miners, Marvin Crandall and T. Dougherty, headed into the Upper Clarks Fork after reports of gold in the area. When they failed to meet up with other miners, a search party was sent out. The searchers were themselves attacked by Indians, but they later found the bodies of Crandall and Dougherty—scalped and decapitated, with their heads atop mining picks. In a macabre bit of humor, tin cups sat in front of each skull and the right hand of each man held a spoon. The men had apparently been killed while eating and the bodies were left as a warning against further white exploration of the area.

West of the overlook, the road switchbacks down hairpin turns into remote and beautiful Sunlight Basin. The name came about in the 1840s. Fur trappers worked this area for beaver and discovered a place flooded with light, but it was so remote that "the only thing that can get into this valley most of the year is sunlight." Today it is considerably more accessible but still just as beautiful. A gravel side road leads seven miles up the valley to **Sunlight Ranger Station,** built in 1936 by the CCC. It's open summers only. This is some of the finest elk winter range anywhere and the home of several scenic old guest ranches.

Back on the main road, a bridge—highest in Wyoming at 300 feet above Sunlight Creek—spans deep, cliff-walled **Sunlight Gorge.** Sorry, no bungee jumping allowed. The highway then continues northwest past Cathedral Cliffs and through a scenic ranching and timbering valley, offering views into the deep gorge that belongs to the Clarks Fork of the Yellowstone River. In some sections, sheer cliffs tower 1,200 feet above the water. Part of the area burned by the 1988 Clover-Mist Fire is visible near **Crandall Ranger Station.** This area also contains the only large herd of mountain goats in Wyoming. Eventually you reach the junction with U.S. Hwy. 212, the Beartooth Highway.

Camping and Hiking

The Forest Service's Lake Creek, Hunter Peak, and Dead Indian campgrounds (open mid-May–Sept., $10–15) are found along Chief Joseph Scenic Highway. **Dead Indian Trail** (just uphill from Dead Indian Campground) goes two miles to a fine overlook into Clarks Fork Canyon. Also of interest is **Windy Mountain**

Trail which climbs 10,262-foot Windy Mountain. It starts from a trailhead four miles east of the Crandall Ranger Station (interesting old log buildings here), is approximately seven miles one-way, and gains 3,700 feet in elevation. Windy Mountain can also be climbed from the other side near the Sunlight Ranger Station. Trailheads into the North Absaroka Wilderness are at the Crandall Ranger Station and beyond the Little Sunlight Campground (open year-round, free) on Forest Road 101.

River-Running
Clarks Fork of the Yellowstone River (named for William Clark, of the Lewis and Clark expedition) is Wyoming's only designated Wild and Scenic River. Experienced kayakers will find a couple of great stretches of Class IV–V white water in the upper Clarks Fork; however, use considerable caution because there are several big drops. Be sure to pull out before dangerous Box Canyon, which is considered unrunnable. Find more Class IV waters farther down the river. Check with the Forest Service for specifics. Below the rapids are quieter stretches.

Accommodations
In the heart of beautiful Sunlight Basin, **7 D Ranch** (307/587-9885 or 888/, www.7dranch.com) is a family-oriented guest ranch offering horseback rides, cookouts, fly-fishing, hiking, pack trips, and something parents will really appreciate: child care for tots during riding periods, along with a special program for older kids. The setting is spectacular—it's where some of the Marlboro ads were shot—and the cabins are comfortable and cozy. Weekly all-inclusive rates are $3,640 for two people. The ranch has space for a maximum of 32 guests. Open early June–late September; adults only in September.

K Bar Z Guest Ranch (307/587-4410, www.agonline.com/kbarz) is off the Chief Joseph Scenic Highway in the Crandall Creek area. Nightly log-cabin accommodations are available for $95 d (lodging only), or two people can stay for six nights for $2,800, including meals, lodging, horseback rides, and Yellowstone sightseeing; extra charge for

backcountry pack trips and guided fishing trips. The ranch is open May–mid-December and has room for a maximum of 30 guests.

Hunter Peak Ranch (4027 Crandall Rd., 307/587-3711, www.hunterpeakranch.com) is on the banks of the upper Clarks Fork River and offers lodging in rustic log cabins or motel-style rooms. Unlike most dude ranches, this one operates on an à la carte basis. Lodging starts at $135 d per night or $810 d per week, with extra charges for meals, horseback rides, and pack trips. The main lodge was built from hand-hewn logs in 1917. Open May–November.

Also in Sunlight Basin, **Elk Creek Ranch** (307/587-3902 in summers or 307/587-8828 in winter, www.elkcreekranch.com) provides a unique coed opportunity for teenagers to gain a wide range of ranching and wilderness skills. Ranch stays include lots of time on horseback; they also build cabins, cut hay, and learn other ranch work. The backpacking adventures give kids plenty of time in the backcountry, where they learn a range of outdoor and mountain-climbing skills—including a chance to summit Grand Teton. Two month-long sessions are offered each summer with a maximum of 30 kids at a time. The cost is $3,750 per person for all-inclusive four-week sessions.

Services
The miniscule settlement called **Painter** is 21 miles southeast of Cooke City on Chief Joseph Highway and right along the Clarks Fork River. Here you'll find a convenience store, liquor, and gas, along with year-round campsites ($25 for RVs, $11 for tents) at **Painter Outpost** (307/527-5510, www.painteroutpost.com). Its restaurant, named—appropriately enough—**Clark's Fork and Spoon,** serves three home-style meals a day; open daily 8 A.M.–7 P.M. Dine on the deck with a view overlooking the river. Showers are $6 if you aren't camping here.

SOUTH FORK AREA
South Fork Road heads southwest from Cody and follows the South Fork of the Shoshone River for 42 miles to the edge of the Washakie Wilderness. It's a beautiful drive through

definitive Western country with tree-covered mountains and the rich valley below. During winter, the South Fork area has one of the largest collections of frozen waterfalls in the Lower 48, with more than 200 world-class multipitch climbs. Ice climbers are here all winter, and the **Water Fall Ice Festival** (www.southforkice .com) takes place each February.

Accommodations
Bison Willy's Bunkhouse (307/587-0629, www.bisonwillys.com) is open November–April and is primarily used by ice climbers. The hostel has a co-ed bunk room at $25 per person, plus kitchenettes and showers. You'll need to bring your own sleeping bag. It's part of the American Alpine Club's national hut system (www.americanalpineclub.org). Call ahead for reservations at this very popular spot.

Rustler's Roost Guest House (307/587-8171 or 800/667-6352, www.rustlersroost.home stead.com/guesthouse.html) is a small furnished house with a deck overlooking the South Fork, plus a full kitchen and a bath with jetted tub. It sleeps four for $130, with a two-night minimum stay.

BEARTOOTH MOUNTAINS
Spectacular Beartooth Highway (U.S. Hwy. 212) connects Cooke City and Yellowstone National Park with the historic mining town of **Red Lodge, Montana** (www.redlodge.com). Along the way, it passes through the Beartooth Mountains on a road built by the CCC in the 1930s. Some have called this the most scenic route in America. If you like alpine country, towering rocky spires, and a landscaped dotted with small lakes and scraggly trees, you're going to love this drive. A small corner (23,750 acres out of a total of 945,334 acres) of the **Absaroka-Beartooth Wilderness** lies in Wyoming just north of the highway—the rest is right across the Montana border.

◖ Beartooth Highway
Designated both as a National Scenic Byway and All-American Road, the Beartooth Highway sails across a high plateau and then over the twin summits of **Beartooth Pass.** The east summit is 10,936 feet, and a short distance farther is the west summit at 10,947 feet. A scenic overlook at west summit provides views of the Absarokas to the south and west, the Beartooths to the north, and Bighorn Basin to the east. Majestic rock faces rise in all directions, the most obvious being Beartooth Mountain (its sharp point resembles the tooth of a bear), Pilot Peak, and Index Peak. This is the highest highway pass in Wyoming and one of the highest in North America. A major reconstruction of the highway won't be completed until 2015. Call 888/285-4636 for details on construction delays, or visit www.wfl .fhwa.dot.gov/projects/beartooth.

As the road enters Montana, it passes Beartooth Mountain and begins a rapid elevator ride down folded ribbon curves into the resort town of Red Lodge. On top, keep your eyes open for moose, mule deer, mountain goats, bighorn sheep, marmots, and pikas. Be ready for strange weather at this elevation, including snow at any time of year. The highway is closed with the first heavy snowfall (generally in September) and doesn't open until May. The flowers don't really get going until mid-July.

Red Lodge International Ski and Snowboard Camp (www.rlissc.com) near the Wyoming-Montana border, provides Olympic ski training for teens in June and July. South of the summit is the Top of the World Store, and another mile or so farther south is the turnoff to an old fire lookout tower at **Clay Butte,** where you'll discover horizon-to-horizon views of the surrounding countryside. A narrow gravel road climbs three miles to the tower, perched at an elevation of 9,811 feet. The small visitor center here is staffed July–mid-September.

Hiking
The open country at this elevation is dotted with whitebark pines and Engelmann spruce, and it delivers marvelous cross-country hiking opportunities. Anglers should bring a fishing pole to take a few casts for the brook, cutthroat, and rainbow trout in the alpine lakes. Two major trail systems are found in the High Lakes area. The **Beartooth High Lakes Trail**—actually

a series of trails—connects Island Lake, Beartooth Lake, Beauty Lake, and many smaller alpine ponds and puddles. A good place to start is from the boat ramp at Island Lake; see topographic maps for specific routes. This is a very popular late-summer area for day hiking or for access to the Absaroka-Beartooth Wilderness. Be sure to bring a compass, topo map, and warm clothes before heading out on a day hike; the weather can close in very quickly at this elevation, and afternoon thunderstorms are frequent. Always be aware of lightning activity when hiking in this exposed country.

Beartooth Loop National Recreation Trail is just two miles east of Beartooth Pass. This 15-mile loop traverses alpine tundra and passes several lakes and a century-old log stockade of unknown origins.

Camping and Supplies

There are four developed campgrounds (open July–Labor Day, $10–15) along this stretch of U.S. Hwy. 212, and more once you drop into Montana. **Beartooth Lake** and **Island Lake** campgrounds border alpine lakes. In addition, dispersed camping is allowed for free once you get off the main roads. Grizzlies inhabit this country, so be sure to store your food safely.

Top of the World Store (307/587-5368, www.topoftheworldresort.com) sits along the highway between the two Forest Service campgrounds. It's a popular stopping point for cyclists and other travelers crossing the pass. The general store has a limited selection of food, gifts, camping supplies, plus gas pumps. The store also rents mountain bikes, fishing gear, canoes, paddle boats, and four-wheelers. Three motel rooms ($55 d, add $15 for additional guests) and a handful of RV spaces ($24 with water and sewer) are also available. The store and motel are open daily mid-May–mid-October.

Wapiti Valley

Wapiti Valley provides one of the most popular and scenic routes into or out of Yellowstone National Park, connecting Cody with the park's East Entrance. President Theodore Roosevelt came here often and called it "the most scenic 50 miles in the U.S." The valley is bisected by the North Fork of the Shoshone River, which U.S. Hwy. 14/16/20 parallels for the entire 50 miles from Yellowstone to Cody. Heading east out of Yellowstone, the highway drops through high forests and past an array of volcanic pinnacles and cliffs as the country becomes drier and more open. Cottonwoods line the gradually widening river, and Douglas firs intermix with sage, grass, and rock at lower elevations. Trailheads provide access to two backcountry areas that border the highway: North Absaroka Wilderness and Washakie Wilderness. The road is in excellent condition the entire distance from Cody to Yellowstone.

Wapiti Valley is dotted with lodges, dude ranches, and resorts, many of which offer family-style meals, barbecue cookouts, horseback rides, pack trips, fishing, hiking, river rafting, and other outdoor recreation. If you aren't staying on an all-inclusive plan, most of these perks will cost extra, and some—such as meals or horseback rides—are often available to both guests and the general public. The lodges generally do not have TVs or phones in the rooms, but most will provide transportation from Cody on request. Get additional lodge information from the **Wapiti Valley Association** (307/587-9595, www.yellowstone-lodging.com).

On the western end of the valley are Shoshone National Forest campgrounds and hiking trails. The fishing is great in the river and at Buffalo Bill Reservoir on the eastern end of Wapiti Valley.

SIGHTS

Heading east from the Yellowstone National Park's east entrance, U.S. 14/16/20 drops in elevation, passing Pahaska Teepee and Sleeping

The east end of Wapiti Valley is open and lush.

Giant Ski Area, before descending towards Wapiti Valley. Along the way, the road passes a whole series of delightfully weird volcanic rock formations. Signs point out several of the most obvious. Stop at the **Firefighters' Memorial,** which honors 15 firefighters who were killed nearby in the Blackwater Fire of 1937. The picnic area here has a special pond for anglers with disabilities.

Eight miles farther east is the historic **Wapiti Ranger Station.** Built in 1903, it was the nation's first Forest Service ranger station. Just a few hundred feet away and right along the highway is **Wapiti Wayside Visitor Center** (307/587-3925, Fri.–Sun. 10 A.M.–4 P.M. late May–early Sept.). Pull in for details on local camping and recreation opportunities, and to watch the informative video on safety in bear country. A few miles to the west (not marked) is **Mummy Cave,** where a 1,300-year-old mummified body was discovered in 1957. The site contains 38 different levels of Indian occupation covering 9,000 years.

Next up is a parking area at **Holy City,** an impressive group of dark red volcanic rocks with the North Fork of the Shoshone River cutting away at their base. Try to pick out Anvil Rock, Goose Rock, and Slipper Rock

here. The highway leaves Shoshone National Forest and then passes the scattered settlement called **Wapiti**—an Indian word meaning "elk"—20 miles east of Cody. As you might guess, a large elk herd winters in this valley. An unusual volcanic rock ridge near here is locally called the Great Wall of China; scan the slopes for bighorn sheep. The eastern half of the road between Cody and Yellowstone passes through this broad and fertile valley; it's quite a change from the rock-lined route to the west. On the east end, the road borders Buffalo Bill Reservoir (see *Buffalo Bill State Park* in the *Cody* section) before plunging through three tunnels on the descent into Cody.

Pahaska Tepee

Less than three miles from Yellowstone's East Entrance (48 miles west of Cody), Pahaska Tepee (307/527-7701 or 800/628-7791, www.pahaska.com) was built in 1904 to house Buffalo Bill's guests and others on their way to the park. Pahaska (pa-HAZ-ka) was Buffalo Bill's nickname, a Crow Indian word meaning "Long Hair."

The original Pahaska Tepee is a two-story log building that contains a few of Buffalo

Bill's original items, including an old buffalo skull over the stone fireplace and several flags that were given to him. Although it is no longer used and in need of major repairs, the remarkable main lodge is open for fascinating tours ($2) on most summer days. The bar inside Pahaska Tepee is small but contains a stunning Thomas Molesworth chandelier crafted in 1938; it's said to be worth $2 million. Look around for other furnishings from Molesworth along with a beautiful stained-glass window.

On one of Buffalo Bill's many hunting treks with European royalty, he led the Prince of Monaco into the North Fork country. **Camp Monaco,** 15 miles up the Pahaska-Sunlight Trail from Pahaska Tepee, was named in his honor. Unfortunately, the old spruce tree inscribed with the words "Camp Monaco" was killed when the Clover-Mist Fire burned through here in 1988.

Pahaska Tepee Resort has a mix of old and newer cabins, along with A-frame motel rooms and duplexes. Summer rates start at $110 d in a little housekeeping cabin up to $175 for a two-bedroom condo (two-night minimum for this one). Also here are a full-service restaurant, gift shop, gas pumps, and limited supplies. Pahaska is open May–October. In winter the road is not plowed beyond Pahaska.

RECREATION

Just four miles from Yellowstone's East Gate, **Sleeping Giant Ski Area** (307/587-3125, www.skisg.com), reopened in 2009 after being closed for several years. Operated by a nonprofit foundation, Sleeping Giant has new lifts (one double chair, a triple chair, and a kiddie conveyor), along with snowmaking capabilities and a 1,000-foot vertical drop.

Not far away are 25 km of groomed trails maintained by the **Park County Nordic Ski Association** (www.nordicskiclub.com) for both classical and skate skiing. No charge (but donations are welcome), and the grooming is generally completed in time for the weekend rush of skiers. Trails cover a widely varied terrain along the river and right to the edge of Yellowstone National Park. Access is from Pahaska Tepee or Sleeping Giant.

ACCOMMODATIONS
Upper North Fork Ranches

More than 20 lodges, motels, and guest ranches line the road between Yellowstone and Cody. Lodging places west of the midpoint between Cody and Yellowstone are in the more secluded and wooded canyon country of the upper North Fork of the Shoshone River. These places are listed as follows, arranged by their distance from downtown Cody on U.S. Hwy. 14/16/20, starting with those nearest the East Entrance to Yellowstone. Places east of the midpoint between Cody and Yellowstone are situated in the broad and beautiful Wapiti Valley and are typically visible from the highway. Pahaska Tepee (above) is the closest lodge to Yellowstone.

A classic mountain lodge, **Shoshone Lodge** (46 miles west of Cody, four miles east of Yellowstone, 307/587-4044, www.shoshone lodge.com) has rustic log cabins and home-cooked meals ($15–20) served in the main lodge. Cabins have been updated with Western furnishings, and range in size from 1–3 rooms; some contain kitchens. Nightly lodging rates start at $130 d or $160 for four guests, although the nicest cabins are considerably more expensive: up to $300 for a three-bedroom cabin that sleeps seven. Horseback rides are available, and Shoshone Lodge is open May–mid-October.

Established in 1898 and completely rebuilt after a 2004 fire, **Crossed Sabres Ranch** (307/587-3750, www.crossedsabresranch.com), 42 miles west of Cody or eight miles east of Yellowstone, has a beautiful main lodge, plus space for 50 guests in modern two-bedroom cabins with log furniture and Western decor. After a day of horseback riding, hiking, fly-fishing, or exploring Yellowstone, guests can relax with an evening cookout. A children's program is available, along with wilderness pack trips. Nightly stays cost $145 d with breakfast, and all-inclusive weekly packages run $2,900 for two adults; open late May–mid-September.

Stay in deluxe log cabins at **Goff Creek Lodge** (307/587-3753 or 800/859-3985, www .goffcreek.com) 40 miles west of Cody or 10 miles east of Yellowstone. Cabins are offered on either a nightly basis ($119 d) with activities and meals extra. Goff Creek is open mid-May–mid-September. A variety of outdoor adventures fill the bill here, including horseback rides, fly-fishing, river rafting, trips to Yellowstone, and chuck wagon cookouts. All of these options, including meals at the restaurant, are also open to the general public.

Forty miles west of Cody or 10 miles east of Yellowstone, **Elephant Head Lodge** (307/587-3980, www.elephantheadlodge .com) is a no-frills dude ranch with a gracious main lodge built in 1910. Guests stay in 15 modernized cabins, all with private baths and most with decks. Because of its proximity to the park, Elephant Head makes a good base for exploring Yellowstone. Peak-season lodging-only rates start at $155 d per day, and the largest cabin—it's actually more like a luxury apartment—sleeps eight people comfortably and has a full kitchen for $350. Elephant Head's restaurant is open for breakfast and dinner and is locally famous for steaks, pork chops, and other carnivorous fare. It's a frequent destination for Cody folks looking for an evening out. Horseback rides are also available for both guests and the general public. The ranch is open mid-May–October.

Find old-time hospitality and adventure at **Absaroka Mountain Lodge** (307/587-3963 in summer, 406/932-6895 in winter, www .absarokamtlodge.com), 38 miles west of Cody or 12 miles east of Yellowstone. Guests stay in comfortable log cabins with private baths and dine in the historic main lodge, built in 1910. Nightly rates start at $110 for a cabin with one queen bed, up to $199 for a two-bedroom cabin that sleeps eight. The package plan includes lodging, three meals a day, and four hours per day of horseback rides for $198 per adult ($156 kids) per day. Open mid-May–September. Folks who aren't staying here can join the trail rides of all types, including four-hour lunch cookout rides for $85. The restaurant is open for breakfast or dinner daily 7–9:30 A.M. and 6–8:30 P.M., serving everything from $6 burgers to $23 steaks. Wednesday night outdoor barbecues ($16) and Saturday evening Dutch oven beef stew ($13) are favorites.

Thirty-five miles west of Cody (15 miles east of Yellowstone), **Blackwater Creek Ranch** (307/587-5201, www.blackwatercreekranch .com), is a fine place to relax amid the natural beauty of the area. Featured attractions include horseback rides, trout fishing, hiking, games, barbecues, and plenty of kid activities. The gracious log cabins contain fireplaces, and meals are served in the modern Old West-style lodge. Also here are an outdoor pool, a large hot tub, and a game room with pool and ping-pong tables. All-inclusive one-week stays cost $2,400 for two people, and the ranch is open May–September.

Halfway between Cody and Yellowstone—25 miles in either direction—**Bill Cody Ranch** (307/587-2097 or 800/615-2934, www.bill codyranch.com) has attractive log cabins, a comfortable lodge, horseback rides, creekside cookouts, and trout fishing. All-inclusive stays (lodging, meals, and horseback riding) are $490 for two people per night; lodging-only rates range widely depending upon the cabin and the number of guests, starting at $100 d. Looking for additional room and privacy? The ranch also rents out two comfortable fully furnished homes with space for up to 13 guests at $430 per day, with a three-night minimum stay. Horseback rides, meals (breakfast and dinner daily, $11–23), and chuck wagon BBQ cookouts on Wednesday and Saturday nights are also available for those not staying at Bill Cody Ranch. The guest ranch is open mid-May–September.

Similarly positioned halfway between Cody and Yellowstone, **Rimrock Dude Ranch** (307/587-3970, www.rimrockranch.com) is a classic western ranch with creekside log cabins, horseback riding, a large swimming pool and hot tub, river rafting, hearty family-style meals, and grand mountain country. Weekly all-inclusive stays are $3,300 for two people. Open May–mid-September.

Lower Wapiti Valley

The places listed below are east of the midpoint between Yellowstone and Cody, in the broad and open part of Wapiti Valley.

Green Creek Inn and RV Park (307/587-5004 or 877/587-5004, www.greencreekinn.com), 22 miles west of Cody or 28 miles east of Yellowstone, has roadside motel rooms with rustic log furniture for $89 d. Also available is a six-person log cabin with bunk beds for $147. The setting is pretty, and children will appreciate the playground and horseshoe pit. RV sites (no tents) are $40, but they lack showers or a restroom. Open May–mid-November, and possibly through the winter.

At **Yellowstone Valley Inn** (307/587-3961 or 877/587-3961, www.yellowstonevalleyinn.com), 18 miles west of Cody or 32 miles east of Yellowstone, small cabins are $114–124 d, tent spaces are $22, and RV sites with full hookups run $40. The attractive inn—often filled with RVs—sits right on the North Fork Shoshone River and has an outdoor heated pool (only heated pool in Wapiti Valley), indoor hot tub, restaurant, launderette, and lounge. Open May–October. The breakfast buffet is just $4 in the restaurant for cabin guests or $6 for RV guests. The restaurant is open daily 7 A.M.–9 P.M. Memorial Day–Labor Day, and specializes in steak, pasta, and seafood (including crab), with $13–24 entrées.

Red Pole Ranch (307/587-5929 or 800/587-5929, www.redpoleranch.com), 11 miles west of Cody or 39 miles east of Yellowstone, has eight updated log cabins starting for $89–99 d, up to $129 for units that sleep five and include a full kitchen.

CAMPING

Nine different Shoshone National Forest campgrounds provide rustic accommodations along the North Fork of the Shoshone River. Most of these are open mid-May–September (some remain open through Oct.) and cost $10–15 per site; no reservations are taken. All sites have picnic tables, fire rings, potable water, and outhouses. The Wapiti Campground ($15–40) has both tent sites and RV sites with electricity. In areas where bears are a problem, the campgrounds also contain bearproof food-storage boxes. All of these Forest Service campgrounds are on the west half of the 50-mile stretch of highway between Cody and Yellowstone. Of these, **Big Game Campground** is closest to Cody at 25 miles to the west, and **Three Mile Campground** is closest to the park, just three miles from Yellowstone's East Gate. Three of these can be reserved ($10 fee) at 518/885-3639 or 877/444-6777, www.recreation.gov.

Get details on public campgrounds from the Forest Service's Wapiti Wayside Visitor Center (see *Sights* earlier in this section). Dispersed camping outside designated campsites is not allowed anywhere between Cody and Yellowstone along U.S. Hwy. 14/16/20.

Two campgrounds are within Buffalo Bill State Park. There are also two Wapiti Valley lodges that have RV campgrounds: Green River Inn and Yellowstone Valley Inn.

Cody

The city of Cody (pop. 9,000, elev. 5,095 ft) marks the transition point between the forested mountains of northwest Wyoming and the sage-covered plains of Bighorn Basin. It's a favorite stopping place for Yellowstone tourists. The park is just 50 miles due west of town, and other magnificent country spreads in all directions—the Beartooth Mountains and Sunlight Basin to the north, the Absaroka Range and Wapiti Valley to the west and south. Established as an agricultural and tourism center, Cody retains both roles today, although tourism gains in importance with each passing year.

Cody has several attractions, including the justly famous Buffalo Bill Historical Center, along with Trail Town and other local sights. The Shoshone River flows right through town, providing the opportunity for scenic float trips. Lots of events crowd the summer calendar, from nightly rodeos and shoot-outs to parades and powwows; biggest of all is the annual Cody

Stampede in July. The town also takes pride in a long list of artists that includes Charles Cary Rumsey and Harry Jackson. Famed abstract expressionist Jackson Pollock was born here but achieved his reputation in New York and never returned to his birthplace.

HISTORY

Just west of Cody—past the Wal-Mart, RV parks, fireworks stands, and gas stations—are the Absaroka Mountains, named for the Native Americans who first lived here. They called themselves the Absaroka, or "Children of the Large Beaked Bird." Whites interpreted this as crow, and the natives have been called Crow Indians ever since. Explorer John Colter

passed through this region in 1808 while recruiting Indians to supply beaver furs. When Colter returned to the semblance of civilization called Fort Manual Lisa, everyone laughed at his tales of a spectacular geothermal area along the "Stinkingwater River." Soon everyone was calling it "Colter's Hell." But the geysers were real, and they still steam along the Shoshone (formerly the Stinkingwater) just west of present-day Cody. Other mountain men came later, followed by miners who found copper and sulfur in Sunlight Basin. The first real settler in the area was a Prussian, Otto Franc, who developed a large cattle spread at the famous Pitchfork Ranch. (Franc is said to have helped finance the Wyoming Stock Growers during the infamous Johnson County War. He was later murdered, and some blamed men affiliated with the homesteaders.)

Because of desertlike conditions, Bighorn Basin was one of the last parts of Wyoming to be settled, and most of the towns did not spring up until the 1890s, when passage of the Carey Act brought a flood of irrigation speculators, investors, and farmers. In 1895, William F. "Buffalo Bill" Cody and two partners began plans for the Shoshone Land and Irrigation Company, with headquarters along the Shoshone River just west of the present city of Cody. Cody had spent much time in the Bighorn Basin, guiding parties of wealthy sportsmen, and was convinced that a

combination of tourism and irrigated farming could transform this desert land. The name Cody was a natural choice for this new settlement, officially founded in 1896. At the urging of Buffalo Bill, the Chicago, Burlington, and Quincy Railroad arrived in 1901, bringing in thousands of tourists who continued west up Shoshone Canyon to Yellowstone by stagecoach. Between 1904 and 1909, construction of massive Buffalo Bill Dam employed hundreds of workers, and the reservoir later provided water to irrigate farmland in Bighorn Basin. Oil was first discovered near Cody in 1904, and Park County remains an important oil producer. Other local businesses include a wallboard manufacturing plant, and a pharmaceutical manufacturer. One of the biggest employers (after the hospital, the school district, and Wal-Mart) makes—I kid you not—ear tags for livestock. Tourism remains a cornerstone of Cody's economy, fueled both by its status as an entry point into the park, and also because of the world-famous Buffalo Bill Historical Center. Interestingly, the town is also attracting quite a few retirees who appreciate the mild weather and abundant recreational opportunities.

◖ BUFFALO BILL HISTORICAL CENTER

Each year, more than 220,000 people visit Cody's main attraction, the Buffalo Bill Historical Center (BBHC). The center actually houses five separate museums covering Buffalo Bill, the Plains Indians, Western art, firearms, and natural history, plus a research library, the boyhood home of Buffalo Bill, and two sculpture gardens. This is the largest and most impressive museum in Wyoming and the finest Western museum in the world. Nowhere else in America is such a major museum situated in a town with so few people. The late author James Michener once labeled the BBHC "the Smithsonian of the West," and his term is even truer today with the addition of a natural-history wing a few years back. The museum's collection focuses—not surprisingly—on the Western frontier and includes thousands of artifacts and works of art, culture, and natural history spread throughout more than 300,000 square feet of space.

The original Buffalo Bill Museum opened in 1927 in what is now the chamber of commerce log cabin. Opening in 1959, the Whitney Gallery of Western Art formed a nucleus for the current museum location; later additions included the Buffalo Bill Museum, the Plains Indian Museum, the Cody Firearms Museum, and the Draper Museum of Natural History.

Practicalities

Buffalo Bill Historical Center (307/587-4771 or 800/227-8483, www.bbhc.org) is open year-round. In the busy summer season, May–mid-September, it's open daily 8 A.M.–8 P.M. At other times, hours are reduced: daily 8 A.M.–5 P.M. mid-September–October; Tuesday–Sunday 10 A.M.–3 P.M. November–March; and daily 10 A.M.–5 P.M. in April. Closed Thanksgiving, Christmas, and New Year's Day.

Admission costs $15 adults, $13 seniors, $10 students age 13–17, $6 ages 5–12, and free for children under five. The $40 family rate is a great value. Admission is good for two

Buffalo Bill Historical Center

days, and it may well take you that long to explore this massive collection! Tours are generally offered only for school groups and VIPs, but the historical center often has summertime demonstrations, and the helpful docents can provide additional information. If you have kids in tow, be sure to pick up the Art Gallery Family Guide, with activities specifically directed at children.

On the Museum Grounds

Flanking the museum on the right side is *The Scout,* a dramatic, larger-than-life statue of larger-than-life Buffalo Bill. This tall bronze piece was created by New York sculptor Gertrude Vanderbilt Whitney and was unveiled in 1924. Her family later donated 40 acres of surrounding land to the Buffalo Bill Museum. Directly in front of the historical center are three colorfully painted tepees, a treat for kids.

Buffalo Bill Museum

The Buffalo Bill Museum is a real joy. In it, the life of Buffalo Bill Cody is briefly sketched with all sorts of memorabilia from his Wild West Show, including the famous Deadwood Stage, silver-laden saddles, enormous posters, furniture, guns, wagons, and buffalo hide coats. Be sure to look for "Lucretia Borgia," the Springfield rifle that helped William Cody gain his nickname. Also here are some of the gifts given to Buffalo Bill by European heads of state—including a fur carriage robe from Czar Alexander II—and by Wild Bill Hickok and Sitting Bull. Original film footage from the Wild West Show runs continuously, offering a fascinating and sometimes unintentionally comical glimpse into the past. Amazingly choreographed marching soldiers, fake Indian battles, sign-language conversations, and bucking broncos make it easy to see how the Wild West Show helped inspire Western movies.

YOUNG BUFFALO BILL CODY

For many people today, the name "Buffalo Bill" brings to mind a man who helped slaughter the vast herds of wild bison that once filled the West. But William F. Cody cannot be so easily pigeon-holed, for here was one of the most remarkable men of his or any other era – a man who almost single-handedly established the aura of the "Wild West." More than 800 books – many of them the dime-store novels that thrilled generations of youngsters – have been written about Cody. In many of these, the truth was stretched far beyond any semblance of reality, but the real life of William Cody contains so many adventures and plot twists that it seems hard to believe one person could have done so much.

Born to an Iowa farm family in 1846, William Cody started life as had many others of his era. His parents moved to Kansas when he was six, but his abolitionist father, Isaac Cody, soon became embroiled in arguments with the many slaveholders. While defending his views at a public meeting, Isaac Cody was stabbed in the

back and fled for his life. When a mob learned of his father's whereabouts, the eight-year-old Will Cody rode on his first venture through enemy lines, galloping 35 miles to warn of the impending attack. Three years later, when Isaac Cody died of complications from the stabbing, 11-year-old Will Cody became the family's breadwinner. There were four other children to feed. Will quickly joined the company of Alexander Majors, running dispatches between army supply wagons and giving his $40 monthly wages to his mother. In Cody's autobiography he claimed to have killed his first Indian on this trip, an action that gave him the then-enviable title "youngest Indian slayer of the plains."

On his first long wagon trek west, the army supply wagons were attacked by Mormon zealots who took all the weapons and horses, forcing Cody to walk much of the thousand miles back to his Kansas home. It was apparently on this walk that Cody met Wild Bill Hickok. At Wyoming's Fort Laramie, young Will sat in

Whitney Gallery of Western Art

The Whitney Gallery contains a stunning collection of masterworks by such Western artists and sculptors as Charles Russell, Frederic Remington, Carl Bodmer, George Catlin, Maynard Dixon, Harry Jackson, Thomas Moran, Albert Bierstadt, Alfred Jacob Miller, Edgar Paxson, N. C. Wyeth, and others. The studios of Frederic Remington and Alexander Phimister Proctor have been re-created, and Gertrude Vanderbilt Whitney's *The Scout* is visible from a large window on the north end. The collections of both "cowboy artist" Charles Russell and Frederic Remington—best known for his paintings of battles during the Indian wars—are the most complete here; the museum has more than 100 of each man's paintings. Next to the Whitney Gallery is the **Joseph Henry Sharp Garden,** where you'll find his "Absarokee Hut" filled with the painter's paraphernalia. (The Whitney Gallery was set for a major remodeling in 2009.)

The **Kriendler Gallery of Contemporary Western Art** is upstairs from the entrance to the Whitney Gallery and contains a diverse collection of pieces, including several with a delightfully whimsical twist. Well worth the detour.

Plains Indian Museum

The largest exhibition space in the historical center encloses the Plains Indian Museum, with items from the Sioux, Cheyenne, Blackfeet, Crow, Arapaho, Shoshone, and Gros Ventre tribes. At first it may seem incongruous that a museum featuring the man once called the "youngest Indian slayer of the plains" should include so much about the culture of Indians, but Cody's later maturity forced him to the realization that Indians had been severely mistreated and that their culture was of great value. His Wild West Shows recreated some semblance of that lost society, if only for show. Some of the more important awe as famed scouts Jim Bridger and Kit Carson reminisced about their adventures. The experience was a turning point in Cody's life; he resolved to one day become a scout. Cody's next job offered excellent training: he became a rider for the Pony Express. At just 15 years of age he already was one of the finest riders in the West and a crack shot with a rifle. On one of his Pony Express rides, Cody covered a total of 320 miles in just 21 hours and 40 minutes – the longest Pony Express ride ever. The Civil War had begun, and at age 18 Cody joined the Seventh Kansas Regiment, serving as a scout and spy for the Union Army.

In 1867, Cody found work hunting buffalo to supply fresh meat for the railroad construction crews, a job that soon made him famous as "Buffalo Bill" and paid a hefty $500 per month. With 75 million bison spread from northern Canada to Mexico, and herds so vast that they took many days to pass, it seemed impossible that they could ever be killed off.

Cody was one of the best hunters in the West; in just eight months, he slaughtered 4,280 buffalo, often saving transportation by driving the herd toward the camp and dropping them within sight of the workers. Cody's name lives on in the jingle: "Buffalo Bill, Buffalo Bill; never missed and never will; always aims and shoots to kill; and the company pays his buffalo bill . . ."

After this stint, Cody finally got the job he wanted – chief scout for the U.S. Army in the West – a job packed with excitement and danger. Conflicts with Indians had reached a fever pitch as more and more whites moved into the last Indian strongholds. Cody worked as scout for Gen. Philip Sheridan, providing information on the Indians' movements, leading troops in pursuit of the warriors, and joining in the battles, including one in which he supposedly killed Chief Tall Bull. His men considered Buffalo Bill good luck because he managed to keep them out of ambushes.

items here were given to Buffalo Bill by various Indian performers through the years, and the collection of artifacts is now one of the finest in America.

On exhibit are an extraordinary painted buffalo robe from 1890 that depicts the Battle of Little Big Horn, elaborately decorated baby carriers, a ghost-dance dress, beaded arrow quivers, dance shields, leather garments, war bonnets, ceremonial pipes, hand drums, and even a Pawnee grizzly claw necklace. One of the more unusual items is Lone Dog's Winter Count, with figures representing a 71-year sequence of events affecting the Sioux; it was created in 1877. The Hitatsa earth lodge is another highlight.

Walking through this remarkable collection always leaves me with mixed emotions. I'm impressed at the beauty of the items and their historical and cultural significance, but I'm saddened by the way all museums—of necessity—remove things from their environments

and create a visually enticing setting, but one that is devoid of the living, breathing people who created these objects. If only we could step back into the past to see how life really was, dirt and all.

Draper Museum of Natural History

This newest addition to the BBHC opened in 2002 to rave reviews. The $17 million museum covers 55,000 square feet, with state-of-the-art exhibits on the Greater Yellowstone Ecosystem and the integral role of humans. Guests begin at a pair of cabins, one of which serves as a naturalist's field station. The other serves as a classroom (of sorts), with a seismograph and computer stations to learn about glaciers, volcanoes, and other natural forces. The main section of the Draper descends along a spiraling path through a giant rotunda, with exhibits describing alpine areas, forests, meadows, and lowland plains ecosystems in the Yellowstone landscape. It's like taking a virtual safari through the area. Multidisciplinary exhibits invite interaction, with lots of kid-friendly audio and video stations, a walk-in beaver lodge, a wolf den, a prairie dog colony, and much more. The winding path ends at a colorful tile map of the Yellowstone ecosystem and an exhibition of children's art.

Cody Firearms Museum

The Cody Firearms Museum houses one of the most comprehensive collections of American firearms in the world, including everything from 16th-century matchlocks to self-loading semiautomatic pistols. This is one museum where the men outnumber the women. The entire firearms collection is remarkably informative and well worth taking time to view—even for those of us who consider the proliferation of guns a national menace.

The museum contains more than 5,000 weapons, but these aren't just rows of guns in glass cases. Some of the more unusual items include a 10-shot repeating flintlock rifle made for the New York Militia around 1825 and a 17th-century windlass crossbow. There are all sorts of displays to explore, including a colonial gun shop, a Western stage station, an early-1900s firearms factory, and a truly extraordinary collection of embellished arms. The Boone and Crockett Club's collection of trophy animal heads is here, including an elephant-sized moose housed in a re-created hunting lodge. Take the elevator to the basement for even more gun displays. All told, this museum houses more implements of destruction and mayhem than you're likely to see at an NRA convention.

Additional Exhibits

Downstairs from the Buffalo Bill Museum is a spacious gallery used for special exhibitions (always worth a look), along with the **Harold McCracken Research Library,** open Monday–Friday 8 A.M.–noon and 1–5 P.M. May–October, or by appointment. The library houses 250,000 historical photos and 15,000 books, including more than 300 volumes about

Buffalo Bill—mostly dime novels and comic books. Buffalo Bill's **boyhood home**—a tiny yellow building built in 1841 by Isaac Cody—is in the garden area. The house stood in LeClarie, Iowa, for almost a century. In 1933 it was sawed in half, loaded on two railcars, and hauled to Cody to be reassembled and refurbished. The **Photography Gallery** near the entrance to the Draper features changing exhibits.

Other facilities at the Buffalo Bill Historical Center include an excellent **gift shop and bookstore,** plus Mustang Grill and an espresso stand. Get your lunch and head to the sculpture garden for a picnic beneath the aspen trees.

Activities and Events

During summer you'll find a wide range of demonstrations every day, including wool-spinning demonstrations, historical talks, cowboy singing, storytelling, and various lectures. Get a brochure at the front desk for today's activities. The **Larom Summer Institute in Western American Studies** is an in-depth two-week history course with two sessions offered each June. The BBHC also hosts many events (see *Entertainment and Events* for details).

◖ TRAIL TOWN

Point your horses toward the mountains and head 'em two miles west of Cody to a unique collection of historic buildings at Trail Town (307/587-5302, www.museumoftheoldwest .org, open daily 8 A.M.–8 P.M. mid-May–Sept. only, $8 adults, $7 seniors, $4 for kids ages 6–12, tots free). Trail Town is the creation of Bob Edgar, the man who discovered Mummy Cave—one of the most important archaeological finds in the West—in 1957. Edgar bought the old Arland and Corbett trading post, and then began dragging in other historic Wyoming cabins. Some were transported whole, others were disassembled and then put back together at Trail Town. The site now holds 26 buildings dating from 1879 to 1901, plus 100 wagons.

For those who love history, Trail Town is an incredible treasure trove without the fancy gift shops and commercial junk that tag

Trail Town

© DON PITCHER

along with most such endeavors. This is the real thing, low-key and genuine. Probably the most famous building here is an 1883 cabin from the Hole-in-the-Wall country that Butch Cassidy and the Sundance Kid used as a rendezvous spot. Also at Trail Town is the oldest saloon (another hangout of the gang) from this part of Wyoming, complete with bullet holes in the door, and a cabin where Jim White—one of the most famous buffalo hunters—was murdered in 1879. The log home of Crow Indian scout Curley stands along the main street, too. (Curley was the only one of General Custer's command who escaped alive from the Battle of the Little Big Horn.) Be sure to step inside **Museum of the Old West,** a more recent log cabin filled with artifacts that include a black hearse, rifles found at Indian battlefield sites, arrowheads, beaded necklaces, cradleboards, and items from the fur traders—including a gravestone from 1811, when only a few Anglo trappers were in the region. There's a quiver, bow and arrow found in a mountain cave, and a prehistoric fishing net.

Look above the display cases for what may be the most significant discovery, a dugout canoe that had been buried along the Yellowstone River in Montana. It might have belonged to a trapper but is remarkably similar to the ones used by Lewis and Clark. They buried canoes while heading west, planning to dig them up on their return trip. The wood dates to that era; could this be one they left behind?

The bodies of buffalo hunter Jim White and several other historic figures have been reinterred in a small graveyard at Trail Town. One of the most interesting of these is Belle Drewry, a prostitute known as "The Woman in Blue." After bouncing around several 19th-century mining towns, she ended up in the lawless and now-abandoned town of Arland, northwest of Meeteetse. One night in 1897 she shot a cowboy to death during a dance. The following night his outlaw friends took retribution by murdering her. Belle was buried in the blue dress that she always wore. Also buried in the cemetery is **John "Liver Eating" Johnston,** the mountain man portrayed by Robert Redford in the

GATEWAYS TO YELLOWSTONE

movie *Jeremiah Johnston.* Those who have seen the film will be surprised to learn that Johnston died in 1900 at the Old Soldiers' Home in Los Angeles! Friends sent him there by train from Montana when his health deteriorated, but he spent only a month in California before his death at the age of 76. After the movie came out, schoolchildren in Los Angeles helped promote moving Johnston's body closer to his mountain home. Nearly 2,000 people showed up for the reburial in 1974, including Robert Redford. A memorial to explorers John Colter and Jim Bridger also stands near the graveyard. The historic buildings, artifacts, and graves at Trail Town provide a fine counterpoint to the glitzier Buffalo Bill Historical Center. Directly in front of Old Trail Town is **Colter's Hell Trail,** a pleasant half-mile loop through the prairie within Stampede Park.

IRMA HOTEL

Named for Buffalo Bill Cody's daughter, the Irma Hotel was built in 1902 to house tourists arriving by train and was one of three way stations to Yellowstone that Cody built. The luxurious saloon has a French-made cherrywood back bar given to Buffalo Bill by Queen Victoria. The queen spent $100,000 to have it built—no doubt helping to fuel rumors of a romance between her and Buffalo Bill. Many famous people have gathered at the bar through the years.

The **Cody Gunfighters** (307/587-4221, www.irmahotel.com) perform in front of the Irma Monday–Saturday June–September. Cody was established long after the era of gunfights in the streets, so this isn't particularly authentic, but it does attract a crowd each evening. The gunfight officially starts at 6 P.M., but the first 15 minutes or so are typically wasted on ads for local businesses. You know you're in America when the advertising even delays a gunfight!

HARRY JACKSON STUDIOS

Cody's most famous living artist, Harry Jackson (602 Blackburn St., 307/587-5508, www.harryjackson.com, Mon.–Fri. 8 A.M.–5 P.M., free) has a large and interesting gallery. It

Buffalo Bill's Irma Hotel

© DON PITCHER

Cody is one of Wyoming's most prosperous towns.

doesn't look like much outside, but inside you'll discover an amazing diversity of works, covering the palette from abstract expressionist paintings, dark World War II pieces, collages, and cubist studies to his more recent paintings and sculptures (many of which contain distinctively painted surfaces). His other sculptures include the monumental *Sacajawea* at the Buffalo Bill Historical Center and *Horseman* in Beverly Hills. Jackson's pieces have been exhibited throughout the United States and in Italy, where his works are cast. Now something of a living legend, Jackson divides his time between Cody and Italy. Some bronzes (but not his paintings) displayed here are for sale, but they're only for serious art patrons willing to spend thousands of dollars—a 10-foot painted Sacagawea goes for $400,000.

ART GALLERIES

The **Buffalo Bill Historical Center** houses a large gift shop with art prints, Indian jewelry, and reproductions of bronze sculptures. Next to the chamber of commerce office, the

Cody Country Art League (836 Sheridan Ave. 307/587-3597, www.codyart.vcn.com) has paintings, sculptures, photos, and crafts for sale. It also offers workshops and juried art shows.

Simpson Gallagher Gallery (1161 Sheridan Ave., 307/587-4022, www.simpsongallagher gallery.com) is one of the best in Cody, with works that go well beyond the standard Western clichés. View M.C. Poulsen's romantic visions of the West at **Poulsen Studio Gallery** (2319 Larkspur Ct.,307/587-6862, www.mcpoulsen .com). His paintings have been exhibited in galleries across America, and even in the Capitol Rotunda.

Two distinctive photographic galleries are across from each other downtown: **Open Range Images** (1201 Sheridan Ave., 307/587-8870, www.openrangeimages.com), and **Traces of Light Gallery** (1280 Sheridan Ave., 307/527-6912, www.tracesoflight.com).

Of less interest but worth a peek are three shops with more predictable artworks: **Mountain Trails Gallery** (1191 Sheridan Ave., 307/527-9097, www.mtgcody.com),

GATEWAYS TO YELLOWSTONE

Jerico Fine Arts Gallery (1210 Sheridan Ave., 307/587-4006, www.jericogallery.com), and **Big Horn Gallery** (1167 Sheridan Ave., 307/527-7587, www.bighorngalleries.com).

OLD WEST MINIATURE VILLAGE

Cody's most unusual attraction—it's actually worth a visit—is Old West Miniature Village and Museum, a.k.a. Tecumseh's Trading Post (142 W. Yellowstone Ave., 307/587-5362, www.tecumsehs.com, open daily 8 A.M.–8 P.M. mid-May–mid-Sept., with reduced hours the rest of the year, donation requested). Owner Jerry Fick spent decades creating an enormous diorama that offers a truncated version of Wyoming and Montana history. Although the term "kitsch" quickly enters your head when you step inside, you've got to appreciate the effort that went

into creating thousands of hand-carved figures and an array of fanciful miniature villages. Of considerably more interest is his collection of artifacts that includes a knife from the Battle of Little Bighorn, old-time cowboy garb, and many Plains Indian artifacts.

BUFFALO BILL STATE PARK

In 1899, Buffalo Bill Cody acquired the rights to build canals and irrigate 60,000 acres of land near the new town of Cody. With passage of the Reclamation Act of 1902, the project was taken over by the Reclamation Service and an enormous concrete-arch dam was added to provide water. The 328-foot-high dam was begun in 1904 and required five years to finish. It cost nearly $1 million and when finally completed was the tallest dam in the world. Seven men died along the way, including a chief engineer,

BUFFALO BILL CODY: HUNTER AND SCOUT

During the Indian campaigns, Ned Buntline began writing of Cody's exploits for various New York papers, giving Buffalo Bill his first taste of national acclaim. Soon Buntline had cranked out several romantic novels loosely based on Cody's adventures. America had a new national hero. European and Eastern gentry began asking Cody to guide them on buffalo hunts. On the trips, Cody referred to them as "dudes" and to his camps as "dude ranches" – perhaps the first time anyone had used the terms for such hunters. One of the West's most unusual businesses had begun. Cody's knowledge of the land and hunting impressed the men, but they were stunned to also discover in him a natural showman. In 1872, the Grand Duke Alexis of Russia came to the United States and was guided by Cody on a hunt that made national headlines and brought even more fame to the 26-year-old. On a trip to New York in 1872, Cody met Buntline again and watched a wildly distorted theater production called *Buffalo Bill*. Amazingly, Cody adjusted quickly to the new surroundings. Dressed in the finest silk clothes but with his long scout's hair under a Western

hat, Cody suddenly entered the world of high society.

In a short while, Cody was on the stage himself, performing with Ned Buntline and fellow scout Texas Jack in a play called *Scouts of the Plains*. Although meant to be serious, the acting of all three proved so atrocious that the play had audiences rolling in the aisles with laughter. A New York reviewer called the play "so wonderfully bad it was almost good. The whole performance was so far aside of human experience, so wonderful in its daring feebleness, that no ordinary intellect is capable of comprehending it." Audiences packed the theaters for weeks on end. But Cody was suddenly called back west, for the Sioux were again on the warpath.

Shortly after Cody had returned to guide Gen. Eugene Carr's forces, they learned of the massacre of Custer's men at the Battle of the Little Big Horn. In revenge, Carr's men set out to pursue Indians along the border between Nebraska and Wyoming. Under Cody's guidance, they surprised a group of warriors at War Bonnet Creek. Cody shot the chief, Yellow Hand, and immediately scalped him, raising and the first two contractors were forced into bankruptcy as a result of bad weather, floods, engineering difficulties, and labor strife. A lack of sand and crushed gravel forced them to manufacture it from granite, and 200-pound boulders were hand-placed into the concrete to save having to crush more gravel.

Originally named Shoshone Dam, the impoundment was renamed in honor of Buffalo Bill in 1946. A hydroelectric plant and a 25-foot addition to the top were completed in 1993, bringing the total dam height to 353 feet and increasing water storage by 50 percent. The dam irrigates more than 93,000 downstream acres through the Shoshone Reclamation Project, making it one of the only Wyoming irrigation schemes that actually benefits the state's farmers to a large extent.

Buffalo Bill State Park (six miles west of Cody on U.S. Hwy. 14/16/20, 307/587-9227, http://wyoparks.state.wy.us) encompasses the reservoir and includes two campgrounds ($12 for nonresidents or $6 for Wyoming residents, open May–Sept.) on the north shore. Make campsite reservations ($9 fee) at 877/996-7275 (www.usedirect.com/cdweb). Day use of the park is $4 for nonresident vehicles or $2 for those with Wyoming plates.

Atop the dam, the impressive **Buffalo Bill Dam Visitor Center** (307/527-6076, www.bbdvc.org, free) has historical displays and jaw-dropping views into the canyon, which plummets 350 feet below you. Watch the video on the dam, or borrow the headphones for a 30-minute audio tour ($3) of the area. The center is open Monday–Friday 8 A.M.–8 P.M., Saturday 8 A.M.–6 P.M., and Sunday 10 A.M.–6 P.M. June–August, plus

the scalp above his head with the cry "first scalp for Custer!" The Sioux immediately fled. If Cody had been famous before, this event propelled him to even more acclaim. It became the grist for countless dime-store novels and was embellished in so many ways over the years that the true story will never be known.

THE WILD WEST SHOW

Buffalo Bill's days in the real Wild West were over, and he returned to staging shows, eventually starting his famed Wild West extravaganza. This was unlike anything ever done before – an outdoor circus that seemed to transport all who watched to the frontier. One newspaper remarked that Cody had "out-Barnumed Barnum." There were buffalo stampedes, cowboy bronco riding, Indian camps, a Deadwood stage and outlaws, crack shooting by Annie Oakley, and, of course, Buffalo Bill. At its peak in the late 1890s, Buffalo Bill was arguably the world's best-known man. Queen Victoria was a special fan, although rumors of an affair are probably false. The show traveled across America and Europe, attracting crowds of up to 40,000 people and making

Cody more than a million dollars in profit each year. Unfortunately, as movies replaced outdoor extravaganzas the show fell out of favor and eventually went bankrupt. By the time of his death in 1917, Cody was plagued by mounting debts and was working for another western show.

Amazingly, Sitting Bull and Buffalo Bill became good friends. Cody, who had earlier bragged of his many Indian killings, eventually said: "In nine cases out of ten when there is trouble between white men and Indians, it will be found that the white man is responsible." Cody went on to criticize the buffalo hunters for their reckless slaughter, and he became an ardent supporter of game preserves and limitations on hunting seasons.

Cody's life spanned one of the most remarkable eras in American history, and his impact on American culture is still felt today, not just in the image of the West that he created, which lives on in hundreds of Western movies and rodeos, but also in the Boy Scouts (an organization inspired by his exploits), in the city of Cody (which he helped found), and in the dude ranches that dot the West.

Monday–Saturday 8 A.M.–6 P.M. and Sunday 10 A.M.–6 P.M. in May and September; closed the rest of the year. Even if it's shut, stop for the view over the dam.

Buffalo Bill Reservoir is a popular place for local boaters and fishermen. Fishing is good for rainbow, cutthroat, brown, and Mackinaw trout. The lake also offers some of the finest **sailboarding** conditions anywhere, with nearly constant 30 mph winds; *Outside* magazine once rated it among the country's 10 best spots. The water's cold: You'll need a wetsuit.

OTHER SIGHTS

Southeast of Cody near Beck Lake is the **Wyoming Vietnam Veterans Memorial,** a black granite memorial modeled after the one in Washington. It contains the names of 137 Wyoming men who were killed or declared missing in action.

The **Wild Sheep Foundation** (720 Allen Ave., 307/527-6261, www.fnaws.org, Mon.–Fri. 7 A.M.–5 P.M., free) has its national headquarters just south of Buffalo Bill Historical Center. A favorite of wealthy trophy hunters, this nonprofit group funds wild sheep research and conservation. Visitors can view an interesting 15-minute video on bighorn sheep, or check out the wild sheep exhibits and habitat maps.

If you're really desperate for something to do, visit the **Cody Murals** (307/587-3290) on the domed ceiling of the Latter-day Saints (Mormon) church at 1719 Wyoming Avenue. Tours are available daily during summer. No, it isn't the Sistine Chapel. The mural—painted in 1951 by Edward Grigware—offers a rosy-tinted version of Mormon Church history and the Bighorn Basin pioneers.

Wild Horses

The McCullough Peaks area, approximately 20 miles east of Cody on U.S. Hwy. 14-16-20, is home to some 450 wild horses with a variety of coat colors. The easiest way to see these wild horses is via a tour from **Red Canyon Wild Mustang Tours** (307/587-6988 or 800/293-0148, www.wildmustangtours.com, $24 adults or $21 kids). Photographer Ken

Martin leads these highly informative two-hour trips.

RECREATION

Paul Stock Aquatic and Recreation Center (1402 Heart Mountain St., 307/587-0400, www.cityofcody-wy.gov) is an impressive center on the south side of town, housing a large indoor pool with a 150-foot spiral slide, hot tub, wading pool, basketball and racquetball courts, a suspended indoor track, exercise machines, and child care. Nonresident rec center passes are $10 adults, $5 youths. Next door is the **Victor J. Riley Arena and Community Events Center** (307/587-1681, www.codyicearena.com), which serves as a summertime convention center and winter ice rink.

Absaroka Bikes (2201 17th St., 307/527-5566) has mountain-bike rentals and bike trail maps. Skateboarders will appreciate the impressive **Cody Skate Park** in Mentock Park on Blackburn Street in east Cody.

The 18-hole **Olive Glenn Golf and Country Club** (802 Meadow La., 307/587-5308, www.oliveglenngolf.com) is a PGA championship course with a complete golf shop and upscale restaurant. Families enjoy playing **miniature golf** (307/587-3685) at the downtown city park; open seasonally.

River Rafting

One of the most popular summertime activities in Cody is floating the Class I and II Shoshone River. Beware, however, that even with these mild conditions, you should plan on getting soaked in the rapids. Expect to pay around $30 for a seven-mile run that lasts 90 minutes, or $40 for a 13-mile (three-hour) float. Both Wyoming River and Red Canyon offer inflatable kayak trips ($40) for those who want to run the rapids on their own power. In addition, Red Canyon leads scenic float trips down the Clarks Fork ($64). The rafting companies offer half-day whitewater trips down the North Fork above the reservoir for $70 including lunch. These trips run only late May–July, when the water level is high.

Founded in 1978, Wyoming River Trips is

the most experienced company in Cody. Red Canyon River Trips is newer, but the guides are very experienced and use smaller rafts for a more personalized trip. For details, contact **Wyoming River Trips** (233 Yellowstone Hwy., 307/587-6661 or 800/586-6661, www .wyomingrivertrips.com), **River Runners** (1491 Sheridan Ave., 307/527-7238 or 800/535-7238, www.riverrunnersofwyoming.com), or **Red Canyon River Trips** (1374 Sheridan Ave., 307/587-6988 or 800/293-0148, www.imt .net/~rodeo/raft.html).

If you want to try rafting or kayaking on your own, you'll find several miles of technical Class IV water with some Class V drops below the dam and above DeMaris Springs. Above the dam are stretches of Class I and II water with good access from the main highway. Ask locally for flow conditions before heading out because snowmelt and dam releases can dramatically affect water levels.

Most rafters put in three miles west of Cody off Demaris Street. Just upstream from the put-in point is DeMaris Springs, a part of "Colter's Hell" that is on private property and not open to the public. The area was once far more active, with hot springs bubbling out of the river and sulfurous smoke rising all around. People actually died from the poisonous gas. Today the geothermal activity has lessened, but the air still smells of sulfur and small hot springs color the cliff faces. Miners worked over nearby hillsides in search of sulfur; the diggings are still apparent. It's also pretty obvious why they first called this the Stinkingwater River.

Open seasonally, **Gradient Mountain Sports** (1723 Sheridan Ave., 307/587-4659, www.gradientmountainsports.com) has kayak rentals and sales, gear, lessons, and guided trips to Buffalo Bill Reservoir and the Shoshone River.

Heart Mountain

Located 13 miles northwest of Cody on U.S. Hwy. 14, this distinctively shaped 8,123-foot peak is a good spot for an adventurous day-hike. Besides the (slightly) heart-shaped summit, the mountain is also an oddity, with older limestone formations atop younger strata, a mystery that has led to all sorts of geological theories. Access is via County Rd. 19 at the site of the old Heart Mountain World War II Internment Camp (also an oddity, but that's another story). For access details, contact the Nature Conservancy's **Heart Mountain Ranch** (307/587-1655, www.nature.org). This 15,000-acre preserve encompasses a variety of rare plants and is occasionally traversed by grizzlies. Sign in at the ranch for the 3.5-mile hike to the summit. Be sure to bring warm clothes since the top may be dramatically chillier than below. The Conservancy also has an office in Cody at 1128 12th St.; stop there for additional details on Heart Mountain. **Jackson Hole Mountain Guides** (877/587-0629, www .jhmg.com) leads day hikes to Heart Mountain in the summer.

Fishing

North Fork Anglers (1107 Sheridan Ave., 307/527-7274, www.northforkanglers.com) has anything you might need for fly-fishing, including a full-service retail shop, professional fishing guides, and fly-tying clinics. Also of note are **The Humble Fly** (1183 Sheridan Ave., 307/587-2757, www.thehumblefly.com) and **Wyoming Troutmasters** (307/250-0043, www.troutmasters.us). A full day of guided float fishing on nearby rivers costs $400 for two people.

Horse and Wagon Rides

Excellent horseback rides are available from **Cedar Mountain Trail Rides** (307/527-4966) a mile and a half west of the rodeo grounds. Hour-long trail rides are $30. Many of the lodges in Wapiti Valley and the Upper North Fork also offer horseback rides and backcountry pack trips. Get a complete listing of Cody-area outfitters and guides from the **Cody Country Outfitters & Guides Association** (307/587-6178, www.ccoga.org), or from the chamber of commerce.

Jerry Kinkade of **K3 Guest Ranch** (33 Nielsen Trail, 307/587-2080 or 888/587-2080, www.k3guestranch.com) offers half-day ranch adventures for wanna-be cowboys, including time with two trick horses, a visit to the wild mustangs, a hay wagon ride, lunch, and other activities. He really has fun with this, and so do the guests—especially children. The cost is $65 for adults, or $30 for kids under 10. Call ahead for reservations since these are primarily for guests at this B&B.

Climbing

Core Mountain Sports (1019 15th St., 307/527-7354, www.coremountainsports.com) sells ice tools, rock equipment, and climbing gear and has a fun climbing wall. This is the place to get details on winter ice climbing (www.codyice.com) in the South Fork area.

Jackson Hole Mountain Guides (at Core Mountain Sports, 1019 15th St., 877/587-0629, www.jhmg.com) has a summertime operation out of Cody, leading climbing classes in nearby Shoshone River Canyon, plus Heart Mountain day hikes.

Caving

Cedar Mountain, the 7,889-foot-tall summit overlooking Cody from the west, is where Buffalo Bill had wanted to be buried. A winding 4WD trail climbs to the top, but there's no public access at present. Also here is **Spirit Mountain Cave,** one of the first national monuments ever designated (1909). A lack of interest caused the designation to be withdrawn, and Spirit Mountain's lower depths were blocked by a cave-in in the 1980s, but spelunkers can explore three levels of the cave. Get permission to enter and a key from the BLM office in Cody, 307/578-5900.

ENTERTAINMENT AND EVENTS

Summer is a busy time in Cody, with special events nearly every weekend. The **Cody Gunslingers** perform downtown at the Irma Hotel Monday–Saturday at 6 P.M. in the summer. The mock gunfights are Western-style entertainment. They're worth a look if you haven't seen one before, but still corny and quite out of character for settled-down Cody.

Cowboy Songs and Range Ballads (307/587-4771, www.bbhc.org/events) is a unique Western musical festival held the second weekend of April at the Buffalo Bill Historical Center. You'll hear true cowboy music (not country-and-western), along with poetry and stories from cowboys, ranchers, musicians, and folklorists.

Held in the Robbie Powwow Garden in front of the Buffalo Bill Historical Center in mid-June, the **Plains Indian Museum Powwow** (307/587-4771, www.bbhc.org/events) attracts several hundred participants from all over the Rockies and Canada vying for $25,000 in prize money. It includes daylong singing and dancing in tribal regalia and various dance competitions. Visitors can buy Indian arts and crafts and taste Indian tacos and fry bread.

The **Old West Show and Auction** (307/587-9014, www.codyoldwest.com) in late June offers a chance for collectors to buy quality old cowboy gear and paintings. It's considered the finest such event in the nation and attracts a wealthy crowd. More Western fun at the annual **Day of the American Cowboy,** celebrated at the BBHC with cowboy music, poetry, and talk in late July. The **Yellowstone Jazz Festival** (www.yellowstonejazz.com) in mid-July brings both regional and national jazz groups.

In late September, the **Celebration of Arts in Cody** encompasses a number of big events, including the largest art event of the year, the **Buffalo Bill Art Show and Sale** (307/587-5002 or 888/598-8119, www.buffalo billartshow.com), with exhibitions, a symposium, receptions, and an auction. Also featured is **Cody High Style,** with Western furniture, metalwork, and a Western-wear fashion show.

【 Cody Nite Rodeo

Cody calls itself "Rodeo Capital of the World," packing the calendar with nightly summertime rodeos, plus the famous Cody Stampede. After over 70 years of operation, the Cody Nite Rodeo (307/587-5155 or 800/207-0744, www .codyniterodeo.com) is still one of the best in a state filled with rodeos. Shows begin at 8 P.M. nightly June–August and always attract a crowd. A crowd favorite is the calf scramble, starring kids from the stands. Tickets cost $17 adults and $8 children; free for kids under seven. For top-of-the-action seats, be sure to get there early and follow the signs to the "buzzards roost" section. The rodeo grounds are one mile west of town on U.S. Hwy. 14/16/20, and a rodeo bus provides transport from local hotels and RV parks for $4 roundtrip; free for kids under 12.

Cody Stampede

Independence Day sets the stage for Cody's main event, the Cody Stampede (307/587-5155 or 800/207-0744, www.codystampederodeo .org), held July 1–4. Established in 1919—more than 90 years ago—it attracts thousands of visitors from all over the nation. Parade fans are treated to one each morning (including a kiddie parade), with dozens of marching bands, mountain men, vintage autos, floats, cowboys, and enough free candy to keep dentists busy for decades. Special PRCA rodeo performances, craft shows, running events, and fireworks complete the schedule.

Music and Entertainment

Pick up a copy of *Cody Pulse*, a free weekly paper listing local events, arts, and entertainment. The downtown City Park band shell is the place to be for Friday evening **Concerts in the Park** during July and August. These free musical performances—in a variety of genres—start at 6 P.M.

On the West Strip, **Cassie's** (214 Yellowstone Ave., 307/527-5500, www.cassies .com) has country-and-western tunes on Friday and Saturday nights year-round, plus Karaoke in the smaller lounge. Hang around the smoky bar long enough and you can join in that old

THE CRUSADING CAROLINE LOCKHART

The West overflows with famous men, but women sometimes get unjustly shunted aside in the accolades. One of the most interesting was Caroline Lockhart (1871-1962), a woman who began her career as an actress but turned quickly to journalism as a writer for a Boston newspaper. Using the pen name "Suzette," she became one of the country's first female newspaper reporters. The job led her into all sorts of adventures, from entering a circus cage with a lion that had killed his trainer the previous day to testing the Boston Fire Department's new fire nets by jumping out of a fourth-story hotel window. When she heard of a "Home for Intemperate Women" where the women were being severely mistreated, Caroline decided to investigate by posing as a derelict. She got her story all right, but it took considerable convincing from her editor to get her out. "Release!" shouted the matron running the house. "We can't! She's not cured yet." One of Lockhart's most lasting impacts was the creation of Mother's Day. Although Anna Jarvis came up with the concept, Caroline Lockhart made it a reality by tirelessly promoting the idea in the newspapers.

In 1904, Lockhart took a bold step. After an interview with Buffalo Bill Cody in the town named for him, she decided to move to Wyoming. She bought the local newspaper, the *Cody Enterprise*, and quickly made a name for herself as a crusader against Prohibition and "game hogs" (hunters who killed everything in sight). She also founded the Cody Stampede, the big annual event in Bighorn Basin. Lockhart wrote seven novels, including *The Lady Doc*, a book that managed to ruffle local feathers with its too-close-to-the-truth descriptions of real-life Cody people. Despite this controversy, her witty, humorous, and insightful writing gained a national reputation.

In 1925, she sold the *Cody Enterprise* and acquired a ranch that eventually included 7,000 acres of land along the Bighorn River north of Lovell, dividing her time between her Cody home (now the Lockhart Bed and Breakfast) and her ranch. She died at the age of 92. Today her old ranch lies within Bighorn Canyon National Recreation Area.

GATEWAYS TO YELLOWSTONE

Cassie's favorite, barroom brawling. Cassie's has been here since 1922.

Silver Dollar Bar (1313 Sheridan Ave., 307/527-7666, www.codysilverdollarbar.com, daily 11 A.M.–11 P.M.) serves great burgers and accompanies them with rock or C&W bands nightly in the summer. Happy hours are weekdays 5–7 P.M.

Find flicks at **Big Horn Cinemas** (2525 Big Horn Ave., 307/587-8001 or 888/878-3549).

Don't miss **Dan Miller's Cowboy Music Revue** (307/272-7855, www.cowboymusic revue.com, $12 per person) at the Cody Theater, 1171 Sheridan Ave. May–September. Dan and his talented band perform nightly at 8 P.M., with cowboy music and poetry, and lots of humor. (Miller hosted championship rodeo events on TNN for 18 years.)

SHOPPING

As you might expect from a tourist town, Cody has more than its share of shops dealing in clunky jewelry, crass T-shirts, and fake Indian trinkets. Fortunately, it's also home to several places with a bit more class. Get fancy Western duds at **Custom Cowboy Shop** (1286 Sheridan Ave., 307/527-7300, www .customcowboyshop.com), or saunter over to **Corral West Ranchwear** (1625 Stampede Ave., 307/587-4493, www.corralwest.com) for inexpensive hats and clothes. In addition to custom-made Native art replicas, **Indian Territory** (1212 Sheridan Ave., 307/527-5522, www.doublehheaddresses.com) sells fun kid-friendly items for around $5.

Traditions West Antique Mall (1137 12th St., 307/587-7434) next to Irma Hotel, and **Cowboy Story** (1215 Sheridan Ave., 307/587-7592) are good places to look for Western antiques.

New books are available from **Cody Newsstand** (1121 13th St., 307/587-2843) and **The Thistle** (1243 Rumsey, 307/587-6635). Cody Newsstand also has one of the best magazine selections in Bighorn Basin.

Outdoor Gear

For quality backcountry equipment, especially

if you travel by horse, be sure to drop by **Wyoming Outdoor Industries** (1231 13th St., 307/527-6449 or 800/725-6853, www .wyomingoutdoor.com). You won't find Gore-Tex jogging bras here, just tough equipment for backcountry use (especially horsepacking), including folding woodstoves, pack saddles, bear-resistant panniers, and wall tents.

Sunlight Sports (1131 Sheridan Ave., 307/587-9517, www.sunlightsports.com) is the largest outdoors shop in town, with tents, climbing equipment, clothes, topographic maps, and more. It also rents cross-country and downhill skis, snowboards, and snowshoes during the winter.

Sierra Trading Post (1402 8th St., 307/578-5802 or 800/713-4534, www.sierra tradingpost.com) has an outlet store in the large log building across from the Buffalo Bill Historical Center.

ACCOMMODATIONS

The tourist town of Cody is packed with places to stay, but be ready to pay more than anyplace in Wyoming except Jackson Hole. Budget accommodations are hard to find during the summer, although rates plummet with the first cold nights of fall. Most of the year, finding lodging in Cody is not a problem as long as you check in before 4 P.M., but during July and August you should reserve a week ahead—and longer for the Cody Stampede in early July. The **Park County Travel Council**'s website (www.yellowstonecountry.org) has details and links to most local lodging places.

In addition to the places below, you will find many dude ranches and lodges in the mountain country around Cody.

Under $50

Cody's homey hostel, 🄲 **Bison Willy's Base Camp** (1625 Alger Ave., 307/250-0763, www .bisonwillys.com) has a backstreet location just a few blocks from the center of town. It's quiet, with a delightful yard and deck, plus an attractive interior, a full kitchen, and commons area. No TV or phone, but Wi-Fi is available. The little 400-square-foot cottage serves as a coed six-person dorm ($25/person) with bunk beds, a kitchen, and bath. Bedding and towels ($3) are available if you don't bring your own sleeping bag. The hostel is open all year, and reservations are recommended in both summer and winter. Owner and Jackson Hole Mountain Guides climbing guide Kenny Gasch also runs a wintertime ice climbers' hostel in the South Fork area.

$50-100

Skyline Motor Inn (1919 17th St., 307/587-4201 or 800/843-8809, www.sky linemotorinn.com, $76–87 d) has large rooms, Wi-Fi, updated furnishings, and a fenced play area for children.

Uptown Motel (1562 Sheridan Ave., 307/587-4245) is a 10-unit motel with well-maintained rooms; $73 for one queen bed or $85 for two. Half the units contain microwaves and fridges, and Wi-Fi is available.

One of the older local places, **Big Bear Motel** (139 W. Yellowstone Ave., 307/587-3117 or 800/325-7163, www.bigbearmotel.com) has updated, clean rooms and friendly owners. No phones in the rooms (use your cell phone), but Wi-Fi and continental breakfasts are available, and half the rooms include fridges and microwaves. Families love the large outdoor pool and pony rides for kids (small charge). Standard rooms are $99–104 d, and modern family suites can sleep six or more for $159.

Carter Mountain Motel (1701 Central Ave., 307/587-4295, www.cartermountain motel.net), atop the hill near Albertson's, features very nicely maintained rooms. Standard units (all with fridges, microwaves, and Wi-Fi) are $85–95 d. Suites with full kitchens are $119–235; the largest can sleep nine.

At **Buffalo Bill's Antlers Inn** (1213 17th St., 307/587-2084 or 800/388-2084, www .antlersinncody.com) rooms are decorated with hand-crafted furniture in the style of Thomas Molesworth, Cody's famed 20th-century craftsman. Look for the big waterfall out front; you can't miss it. Rooms are large and clean: $95 s or $100 d for standard rooms, or $135 d for the honeymoon suite with a king bed and

jetted tub. Free Wi-Fi. The hotel is closed mid-October–April.

A decent older motel in a quiet part of town, **Budget Host** (1807 Sheridan Ave., 307/587-4258 or 800/283-4678, www.budget host.com, $91–102 d), is open May–late October. Standard rooms are $91–102 d, and a family room sleeps six for $136. Wi-Fi is available.

$100-200

Cody Motor Lodge (1455 Sheridan Ave., 307/527-6291 or 800/340-2639, www.cody motorlodge.net) has large rooms for $110 d, and two apartment-style units (one has a kitchen) for $120 d or $150 for six people. Amenities include fridges, microwaves, Wi-Fi, and continental breakfast. Pets welcome.

C Best Value Inn (720 W. Yellowstone Ave., 307/587-4208 or 888/315-2378, www .bestvalueinn.com) is indeed one of the best values in town, with attractive rooms, a small heated outdoor pool (seasonal), and a continental breakfast. Standard rooms (some with king beds, microwaves, and fridges) are $118–124 d. A two-bedroom family suite sleeps six for $154. Open March–mid-November. Wi-Fi is available in some (but not all) rooms.

On the National Register of Historic Places, Buffalo Bill Cody's **Irma Hotel** (1192 Sheridan Ave., 307/587-4221 or 800/745-4762, www .irmahotel.com) has a fine downtown location and all the ambience you could want. It's the real thing—a classic Old West hotel. Given the historic importance of the Irma, standard guest rooms $110–128 d. here are a major disappointment. Considerably nicer are the unique and spacious rooms in the historic section of the hotel, all named after famous guests; $153 d or $168 for four guests. Book the Buffalo Bill suite a year in advance for the peak of summer. It has corner windows and an historic Victorian décor. Be sure to ask about the ghost (of Buffalo Bill?) that supposedly haunts the Irma.

One of the newest local hotels, **Cody Legacy Inn and Suites** (1801 Mountain View Dr., 307/587-6067, www.codylegacyinn.com)

features 50 plush rooms, most with two queen beds for $149 d. A king suite with jetted tub is $165 d, and luxurious two-bedroom suites cost $179–239. Amenities include an outdoor heated pool (seasonal), indoor hot tub, sauna, Wi-Fi (in some rooms), and light breakfast.

Green Gables Inn (1636 Central Ave., 307/587-6886, www.codysgreengables.com) is a modern and tidy 15-unit motel on the south side of Cody with fridges, microwaves, and pillowtop beds in all units. Standard rooms cost $125 d in the high season, with suites running $142 for up to six guests. A continental breakfast is served each morning. Open mid-May–mid-October. It's owned by Kit Cody, a great grandson of Buffalo Bill; his daughter owns Cody Legacy Inn and Suites.

Sunrise Motor Inn (1407 8th St., 307/587-5566 or 877/587-5566, www.sunrise inncody.com) is another comfortable place, with a heated outdoor pool (seasonal), continental breakfast, and Wi-Fi. Summer rates start at $109 d. Open mid-May–mid-October.

Buffalo Bill Village Resort consists of three separate operations that total nearly 350 rooms: Holiday Inn, Comfort Inn, and Buffalo Bill Village Resort. All three are in the heart of Cody at 1701 Sheridan Avenue and share the same toll-free number and website: 800/527-5544, www.blairhotels.com. Guests at all three facilities can use the outdoor heated pool at the Holiday Inn and are welcome to join the free reception each evening. The attractively remodeled 189-room **Holiday Inn at Buffalo Bill Village Resort** (307/587-5555) charges $199 d for rooms with two double or one king bed. Amenities include Wi-Fi, a guest computer, and fitness center. **Comfort Inn at Buffalo Bill Village Resort** (307/587-5556) charges $179 d, including a filling breakfast and free Wi-Fi (but thin walls). The most distinctive of this Cody lodging triumvirate is **◖ Buffalo Bill Village Cabins** (307/587-5544), which consists of 83 cozy log cabins. These cabins were built in the 1920s to house workers and their families for nearby Buffalo Bill Dam. They were later moved here and have since been updated to include phones,

TVs, private baths, and air-conditioning. Small cabins–decorated in a playful cowboy theme–have a queen or king bed for $149 d. Family cabins ($189) contain two bedrooms with three or four double beds. The cabins are open May–September, and Wi-Fi is available in some (but not all) units.

One of Cody's nicer motels, **Beartooth Inn** (2513 Greybull Hwy., 307/527-5505 or 800/807-8522, www.beartoothinn.com) is a mile east of town near the airport. Spacious standard rooms (biggest in town) are $121 d, six-person family rooms go for $139–149, and minisuites with hot tubs cost $149 d. Hotel amenities include a sauna and indoor hot tub, exercise equipment, Wi-Fi, guest computer, airport shuttle, and a big breakfast (fresh waffles), plus microwaves and fridges in all rooms. Ground-floor rooms have both outside and interior entrances.

You'll find excellent accommodations at **Best Western Sunset Motor Inn** (1601 8th St., 307/587-4265 or 800/624-2727, www .bestwestern.com/sunsetmotorinn), where standard rooms start at $165 d, up to $215 for family suites that sleep six. Amenities include indoor and outdoor pools, a hot tub, continental breakfast, Wi-Fi, guest computers, a playground, and fitness facility. The adjacent restaurant (Sunset House) serves family style meals.

New in 2006, **Cody Cowboy Village** (203 W. Yellowstone Ave., 307/587-7555, www .codycowboyvillage.com) has 40 log cabin-style rooms ($139–149 d) and 10 luxury cabin suites ($199 for up to six) on the west end of town near the rodeo grounds. All rooms are furnished with high-end beds and linen, and guests appreciate the big outdoor hot tub (with a waterfall), flat screen TVs, light breakfast, concierge service, and limited Wi-Fi. Ultra-friendly management too.

Over $200

With its concierge service, luxurious linens, turndown service, robes, microwaves, fridges, flat-screen TVs, indoor pool, hot tub, sauna, Wi-Fi, shuttle service, iPod docking stations, and organic breakfast buffet, **The Cody** (232 W. Yellowstone, 307/587-5915, www.thecody .com) would seem more at home in Jackson Hole than Cody. Choose from suites—some with private patios—for $209–219 d, up to king suites with electric (!) fireplaces and jetted tubs for $259 d. There's a player grand piano in the lobby and a patio with a small waterfall and fireplace for chilly evenings. The pool, hot tub, and sauna are open 24 hours.

When it first opened in 1903, the Chamberlin Hotel was one of Cody's finest lodging places, and its guests included Ernest Hemingway, who stayed here in 1932 after completing *Death in the Afternoon.* In later years the hotel was renamed the Pawnee Hotel, but the luster had long passed by the time new owners bought the neglected property in 2005. A year later the hotel reemerged with its original moniker, but entirely transformed into a luxurious boutique hotel. Today, ◖ **Chamberlin Inn** (1032 12th St., 307/5876-0202 or 888/587-2020, www .chamberlininn.com) provides elegant

downtown lodging just a block off the main route through town. Each of the 23 rooms has its own personality. Standard queen rooms with shower start at $155–175 d, with king rooms for $175 d, and suites costing $285–345 d. A grassy, flower-filled courtyard is a relaxing focal point for the hotel, and three smaller buildings are set up as more spacious units, ranging from a cozy garden cottage ($255 d) to a building that once housed Cody's courthouse. The latter has French beveled glass doors, fireplaces, a full kitchen and bar, three baths, a living room, and office. It sleeps six in comfort for $675 nightly with a two-night minimum. Other amenities available to all guests include a library, central kitchen, Wi-Fi, fresh flowers in all rooms, and flat screen TVs. Check out Hemingway's signature in the guest register and a cigar box he left behind.

Vacation Rentals

Cody has an abundance of vacation rentals available on a nightly or weekly basis. For an overview of the options, contact **Cody Lodging**

© DON PITCHER

the courtyard at Chamberlin Inn

Company (1102 Beck Ave., 307/587-6000 or 800/587-6560, www.codylodgingcompany .com), which offers more than 70 furnished homes, cottages, condos, and mountain lodges. Prices range from $125 two-person guest cottages up to $500 for a luxurious three-bedroom home near Buffalo Bill State Park. Two other companies also have with vacation rentals in Cody: **Moose Alley Lodging** (1407 Wyoming Ave., 307/587-6159 or 877/511-4438, www.moosealleylodging.com) and **Duck Inn** (1231 12th St., 307/527-7707, www.duckinncody.com).

Bed-and-Breakfasts

Several historic buildings are now part of the Cody B&B scene, offering a taste of the genteel past. The website for **Cody Country Bed and Breakfast Association** (www.cody bedandbreakfast.com) has links to most local B&Bs.

Cole House B&B (1519 Beck Ave., 307/578-8193, www.colehousecody.com, $140–190 d) has three guest rooms with private baths, Wi-Fi, and a brick patio and wood deck. One elegant room comes with a private spa. Built more than a century ago, the home has been tastefully restored with Victorian antiques and Old West art. A full breakfast is included.

Built in 1924 by Cody Mayor P. E. Markham, **Lambright Place B&B** (1501 Beck Ave., 307/527-5310 or 800/241-5310, www .lambrightplace.com) exudes an old-fashioned charm. Three rooms in the large main house are available for $105–135 d, and a Western-themed cottage/bunkhouse sleeps five for $170. All rooms have private baths and Wi-Fi, and the breakfasts are memorable. Kids are welcome, and the bunkhouse works well for families and small groups.

For lodging in a classic Cody home, stay at (**The Mayor's Inn** (1413 Rumsey Ave., 307/587-0887 or 888/217-3001, www.mayors inn.com), built in 1909 by Frank Houx, the town's first mayor. In 1997 it was moved to the present site and restored to its original opulence. The four guest rooms ($120–210 d)

include private baths with jetted tubs, down comforters, terrycloth robes, and heated floors. The nicest room has a king bed and jetted tub. A full breakfast is served each morning. Also available is a separate cottage with full kitchen for $120 for families (no breakfast).

Also recommended is **Robin's Nest B&B** (1508 Alger Ave., 307/527-7208 or 866/723-7797, www.robinsnestcody.com, $135–145 d). On a quiet street just a few blocks from the heart of town, this 1928 brick and frame home features a relaxing and shady backyard, a large living room, and four guest rooms with private baths, plus a guest computer and Wi-Fi. Unique is the tree-house suite, situated on an upstairs porch. A full breakfast is served each morning, and well-behaved kids are accepted. The owners have two Labrador retrievers and pets are sometimes accepted, but call ahead.

Built in 1914, **Salsbury Avenue Inn B&B** (1226 Salsbury Ave., 307/587-1226, www .salsburyavenueinn.com, $75–95 d) is a reasonably priced option close to downtown. Four guest rooms share an upstairs bath (hence the low rates), but two more are available downstairs. The home has Wi-Fi and a full breakfast is served. Kids welcome.

Angel's Keep B&B (1241 Wyoming Ave., 307/587-6205 or 877/320-2800, www.angels keep.com) is housed within a restored 1930s Assembly of God church and has three rooms with queen beds and a filling country breakfast, evening snacks, and Wi-Fi for $99–145 d. A gift shop here offers locally made items.

(**K3 Guest Ranch** (33 Nielsen Trail, 307/587-2080 or 888/587-2080, www.k3 guestranch.com) sits on 33 acres of land along the outskirts of Cody. The modern home has three Western-themed guest rooms ($199 for up to three), all with private baths and windows facing the hayfield. Add $19 for additional guests (max of six). The most unique spot is an old sheepherder wagon ($159) from the 1890s with air conditioning (!) and its own bath. The ultra-friendly owners Jerry and Bette Kinkade cook a big ranch breakfast over an open fire each morning and also offer a day ranch for wanna-be cowboys.

A rambling 8,000-square-foot home eight miles southwest of town near Buffalo Bill Reservoir, **Southfork Bed and Breakfast** (797 Southfork Rd., 307/587-8311, www .southforkbb.com) has two guest rooms ($125 d) with private baths and entrances. Guests are served a full breakfast by the owner who is also a professional chef. A third room ($65 extra) can be combined with the others for families. Other amenities at include a home theater, full bar, outdoor pool, indoor lap pool and hot tub, and spacious great room with a stone fireplace. Horse lodging is available, or you can just visit with the owner's (formerly) wild mustangs.

CAMPING

The closest public campground ($12 for non-residents, or $6 for Wyoming residents) is 11 miles west in **Buffalo Bill State Park.** Make campsite reservations ($9 fee) at 877/996-7275, http://wyoparks.state.wy.us). Find many more campgrounds ($10–15) in Shoshone National Forest; the nearest is 28 miles west of Cody in the upper North Fork.

Cody's finest RV park is **Ponderosa Campground** (1815 8th St., 307/587-9203, www.codyponderosa.com, open mid-Apr.– mid-Oct.), with attractive, shady sites ($20 tents or $39 RVs) along with tepees ($22) and simple cabins ($38 for four people).

Cody KOA (two miles east on U.S. Hwy. 14/16/20, 307/587-2369 or 800/562-8507, www.codykoa.com) opened in 1964 as the first franchised KOA. Rates are $31 for tents and $57 for RVs, and $57–146 for simple cabins. Open May–October, with a large heated outdoor pool, wading pool, hot tub, playground, Wi-Fi, $2 pancake breakfasts, and a rodeo shuttle.

Other good places are **Gateway Motel and RV Park** (203 W. Yellowstone Ave., 307/587-2561, www.gatewaycamp.qwest office.net, $31 RVs, $10.50 per person for tents, open May–Sept.) and **Absaroka Bay RV Park** (U.S. Hwy. 14/16/20 S., 307/527-7440 or 800/557-7440, www.cody-wy.com, $28 RVs, $20 tents). You can also park RVs at several of

the Wapiti Valley lodges including **Green Creek Inn and RV Park** and **Yellowstone Valley Inn.** Noncampers can take showers at Gateway Campground or Ponderosa Campground.

FOOD

Because Cody is a tourist town, it's no surprise to find many fine places to eat, covering the spectrum from buffalo burgers to sushi. All Cody restaurants are entirely non-smoking.

Breakfast and Lunch

Although **Peter's Café Bakery** (1219 Sheridan Ave., 307/527-5040, www.peters-cafe.com, daily 6:45 A.M.–10 P.M.) is open for dinner, the main attractions come earlier, with inexpensive breakfasts (two eggs, two pancakes, and bacon for $6) and lunchtime subs ($7–8) on freshly baked breads, plus home-made soups, buffalo burgers, and 32-plus flavors of ice cream. Banana splits, smoothies, and malts are big draws on hot summer afternoons. Heading into the park? Let Peter's pack you a peck of picnic lunches.

The Beta Coffeehouse (1132 12th St., 307/587-7707, Mon.–Fri. 7 A.M.–6 P.M., Sat.– Sun. 7 A.M.–4 P.M.) is the best local espresso joint, with a hip setting, fruit smoothies, iced coffees, homemade pastries (cinnamon rolls, scones, and muffins), and free Wi-Fi.

Charming **Willow Fence Tea Room** (1913 Stampede Ave., 307/587-0888, Wed.–Sat. 11 A.M.–3 P.M.) serves steaming pots of tea, along with homemade soups, sandwiches, and desserts.

For something quick that's always a hit with kids, head to **Nate's Hot Dog Stand** (1276 Sheridan Ave., 307/527-4147).

All-American Dinners

Proud Cut Saloon (1227 Sheridan Ave., 307/587-7343, Mon.–Sat. 11 A.M.–11 P.M., Sun. noon–10 P.M.) is a fine Wyoming bar and restaurant offering unusual lunchtime sandwiches and burgers (try the jalapeño burger) and out-standing steak and prime rib for dinner, or as the saloon calls it, "kick ass cowboy cuisine." It's the real thing, with a rustic and woodsy

Old West decor. Most dinners are $16–23, but burgers and sandwiches cost $7–12.

It's dark inside Buffalo Bill's old-time **Irma Hotel** (1192 Sheridan Ave., 307/587-4221, www.irmahotel.com, daily 6 A.M.–10 P.M. in summer, reduced winter hours), an old favorite for lunch and dinner. You can order à la carte with such dinner choices as chicken teriyaki, baby back ribs, or buffalo-sausage spaghetti for $15–26, but the Irma's sprawling buffets are a far better deal: $9 for breakfast, $12 for lunch, or $23 for a slow-roasted prime rib dinner buffet; kid rates are $5, $7, and $10 respectively. These all-you-can-eat affairs are great for families with picky eaters.

Sandwiched between a saddle shop and a tuxedo rental place on the north edge of town, **Suzette's Delicious Delectables** (513 16th St., 307/587-9999, Tues.–Sat. 11:30 A.M.–2 P.M. and 5–9 P.M., $12–16 lunches, $17–24 dinners) is a small upscale place that's a favorite munch-and-gab place for locals and the occasional tourist. Owner, chef, and bottle-washer Suzette Fontz serves a range of international fare with an oft-changing menu from Greek gyros to garam marsala chicken. All meals come with soup, salad, and homemade bread. There's a patio out back and homemade baklava for dessert. Reservations recommended for dinner.

Besides these dinner options, several Wapiti Valley/North Fork lodges serve outstanding meals and attract both locals and tourists. **Absaroka Mountain Lodge** (307/587-3963, www.absarokamtlodge.com) has Wednesday outdoor ribs BBQ ($16) and Saturday night all-you-can-eat Dutch oven beef stew ($13) feasts. Both take place outdoors under the trees at this historic old lodge. Another mountain lodge (38 miles west of Cody) is **Elephant Head Lodge** (307/587-3980, www.elephantheadlodge.com), with fine steaks in a rustic setting; reservations recommended.

Fine Dining

Close to the Cody Chamber of Commerce visitor center, ◖ **Wyoming Rib and Chop House** (937 Sheridan Ave., 307/587-7731, www.ribandchophouse.com, Mon.–Fri. 11 A.M.–10:30 P.M., Sat.–Sun. 4–10:30 P.M.) specializes in buffalo ribeye steaks, jambalaya, fresh seafood, and award-winning babyback pork ribs. The atmosphere is upscale and romantic; entrées cost $15–30, but you can also get buffalo burgers and other munchies for $7 and up. Definitely recommended.

Also of particular note is **The Mayor's Inn** (1413 Rumsey Ave., 307/587-0887 or 888/217-3001, www.mayorsinndinnerhouse.com), where gourmet dinners are served Thursday–Saturday evenings (starting at 6 P.M., with the last seating at 8 P.M.) in a quaint Victorian setting. The limited menu changes every couple of weeks but always includes Wyoming lamb, buffalo, and beef, along with other regional fare. Prices are reasonable, with most entrees at $16–26. Open May–October only. Reservations recommended.

International

For decent Chinese food—including a lunch buffet and family-style dinners—visit **Hong Kong Restaurant** (1201 17th St., 307/587-6420).

Shiki Restaurant (1420 Sheridan Ave., 307/527-7116, Mon.–Sat. 11 A.M.–2 P.M. and 4–9 P.M.) has a fresh sushi bar, plus elevated booths for an authentically Japanese experience. Lunch specials start at $7, with dinners (including vegetarian specials) for $15–26.

Adriano's Italian Restaurant (1244 Sheridan Ave., 307/527-7320, Mon.–Thurs. 11 A.M.–9 P.M., Fri.–Sat. 11 A.M.–10 P.M., closed Sun.) may not have the fastest service, but this is the real thing, with a big menu that features veal marsala, scampi, chicken Florentine, and pizzas; try the white pizza. Most dinners are $17–19. The $8 lunch pasta and salad buffet is also popular.

For Mexican meals, **La Comida** (1385 Sheridan Ave., 307/587-9556, www.lacomidacody.com, daily 11 A.M.–10 P.M., $8–18 entrées), has a front patio and house specialties that include pechuga over rice—chicken baked in cream with green chilies and Swiss cheese.

Groceries and Specialty Foods

Cody's grocers include an **Albertson's** (on the south side of Cody at 1825 17th St., 307/527-7007) and a big **Wal-Mart SuperCenter** (321 Yellowstone Ave., 307/527-4673) on the west end. For natural foods and supplements, head to **Whole Foods Trading Co.** (1239 Rumsey, 307/587-3213). **Wyoming Buffalo Company** (1270 Sheridan Ave., 307/587-8708 or 800/453-0636, www .wyomingbuffalocompany.com) specializes in buffalo jerky, salami, sausage, and fresh meat, with a variety of gift packages. Stop in for a free sample.

INFORMATION AND SERVICES

Get local information and an armload of brochures from the always-helpful folks at **Cody Country Chamber of Commerce** (836 Sheridan Ave., 307/587-2777 or 800/393-2639, www.codychamber.org). Hours are Monday–Friday 8 A.M.–6 P.M., Saturday 9 A.M.–5 P.M., and Sunday 10 A.M.–3 P.M. Memorial Day–September, and Monday–Friday 8 A.M.–5 P.M. the rest of the year. This log building—on the National Register of Historic Places—housed the original Buffalo Bill Museum from 1927 to 1969 and was built as a replica of Cody's TE Ranch. A regional tourism organization, **Park County Travel Council** (307/587-2297 or 800/393-2639, www.yellowstonecountry .org) is also based here. Another useful Web source is **www.codywyomingnet.com.**

Government offices include the **BLM's Cody Field Office** (1002 Blackburn Ave., 307/578-5900, www.wy.blm.gov), **Shoshone National Forest Supervisor's Office** (808 Meadow Lane, 307/527-6241, www.fs.fed.us/r2/ shoshone), and the **North Zone Ranger District Office** (203 W. Yellowstone, 307/527-6921).

Just down from the rec center, and up the street from the post office, the new **Park County Library** (1500 Heart Mt. St., 307/527-8820, www.parkcountylibrary .org) has regional titles and computers for Internet access. Open Monday 9 A.M.–8 P.M., Tuesday–Friday 9 A.M.–5:30 P.M., and Saturday 9 A.M.–4 P.M.

Cody's **West Park Hospital** (707 Sheridan Ave., 307/527-7501 or 800/654-9447, www .westparkhospital.org) is the largest in Bighorn Basin and one of the finest in the state. The hospital's **Urgent Care Clinic** (702 Yellowstone Ave., 307/587-7207) is open daily, with no appointment needed.

Wash clothes at **Eastgate Laundry** (1813 17th St., 307/587-5355) next to Albertson's, or **Cody Laundromat** (1728 Beck Ave., 307/587-8500); the latter is open 24 hours.

GETTING THERE AND AROUND

Yellowstone Regional Airport (www.fly yra.com) is just east of town on U.S. Hwy. 14/16/20. **SkyWest/Delta** (307/587-9740 or 800/221-1212, www.delta.com) has daily flights to Salt Lake City, while **United Express** (307/587-9740 or 800/864-8331, www.united.com) has daily service to Denver. **Spirit Mountain Aviation** (307/587-6732) offers scenic flights and charter service.

Rent cars at the airport from **Avis** (307/587-4082 or 800-331-1212, www .avis.com), **Budget** (307/587-6066 or 800/527-0700, www.budget.com), **Dollar** (307/587/3608 or 800-800-4000, www.dollar .com), **Hertz** (307/587-2914 or 800/654-3131, www.hertz.com), or **Thrifty** (307/587-8855 or 800/847-4389, www.cody.thrifty.com).

Cody Over Land Transit (COLT, 307/527-2958) provides public bus service across town for just $2 adults or $5 per family for all day. Buses operate daily June–mid-September, coming by every 45 minutes or so 9 A.M.–5 P.M. Buses have bike racks and wheelchair lifts.

Unfortunately, there is **no bus service** to Cody, or from Cody into Yellowstone.

Tours

Cody Trolley Tours (307/527-7043, www .codytrolleytours.com) take you on a very informative hour-long cruise through town and up to Buffalo Bill Dam for $22 adults, $10 kids. A combo $32 ticket includes entrance into the Buffalo Bill Historical Center. Tours are offered several times daily June–September.

For a more personalized trip, call **Grub Steak Expeditions** (307/527-6316 or 800/527-6316, www.grubsteaktours.com). The company leads 12-hour auto tours of the park, along with visits to Sunlight Basin, Wapiti Valley, and the South Fork. One-day tours cost $490 for two people, plus $125 for each additional guest. These are popular with families looking for a unique perspective on the park, and some are led by co-owner Bob Richard, a retired Yellowstone park ranger.

Yellowstone tours are also available from **Wyoming Touring Adventures** (307/587-5136) and **Yellowstone Wildlife & Photo Tours** (307/587-6988 or 800/293-0148, http://cu.imt.net/~rodeo). **High Country Adventures** (307/587-7669, www.yellowstoneadventuretours.com) has winter tours into the park. **Phidippides Shuttle Service** (307/527-6789 or 866/527-6789, www.codyshuttle.com) provides shuttle service to the Billings airport, Yellowstone tours, and hiker drop-offs.

Dubois

Approaching Dubois (pop. 1,000, elev. 6,917 feet) from either direction, you drive through the extraordinary red, yellow, and gray badlands that set this country apart. The luxuriant Wind River winds its way down a narrow valley where horses graze in the irrigated pastures and old barns and newer log homes stand against the hills, while the tree-covered Absaroka and Wind River mountains ring distant views.

The town of Dubois consists of a long main street that makes an abrupt elbow turn and then points due west toward the mountains. The log buildings and snatches of wooden sidewalks give the place an authentic frontier feel. Locals live in cabins, trailer homes, and simple frame houses. Dubois weather is famously mild; warm Chinook winds often melt any snow that falls. Grand scenery reigns

badlands along the Wind River near Dubois

© DON PITCHER

DUBOIS AND VICINITY

← To Yellowstone and Jackson Hole

To Double Cabin Campground ↑

TOGWOTEE PASS

Brooks Lake

BROOKS LAKE

BROOKS LAKE LODGE

26
287

FALLS

Pinnacle Buttes

DU NOIR CREEK RD

Ramshorn Peak 11,635ft

HORSE CREEK

TIE HACK MEMORIAL

WARM SPRINGS RD

HORSE CREEK RD

Continental Divide

Wind River

SCENIC OVERLOOK

NATIONAL BIGHORN SHEEP CENTER

Bridger-Teton National Forest

Shoshone National Forest

Badlands

Dubois

To Lander and Riverton

26
287

HATCHERY

Union Pass 9,210ft

WHISKEY BASIN HABITAT AREA

Torrey Lake

Ring Lake

To Green River Lakes and Pinedale

Trail Lake

0   5 mi
0   5 km

© AVALON TRAVEL

in all directions. Snowmobilers, hunters, and anglers have discovered that Dubois provides a good place to relax in Wyoming's "banana belt" while remaining close to the more temperamental mountains. The area basks in an average of 300 days of sunshine each year. By the way, Dubois is pronounced "DU-boys"; other pronunciations will reveal your tenderfoot status. Locals sometimes jokingly call it "Dubious."

HISTORY

Dubois began in the 1880s when pioneer ranchers and more than a few rustlers, including Butch Cassidy, settled in the area, followed by Scandinavian hand-loggers who cut lodgepole for railroad ties. The town that grew up along the juncture of Horse Creek and the Wind River was first known as Never Sweat, but when citizens applied for a post office the Postal Service refused to allow the name and suggested Dubois instead—the name of an Idaho senator who just happened to be on the Senate committee that provided funding for the post office.

Like many edge-of-the-mountain towns, Dubois is in transition from a logging and ranching past to one more focused on tourism. The visitor-oriented economy certainly has its downside—elaborate "trophy" log summer homes are beginning to overrun lush pastures on both ends of town—but so far this pretty little place has been spared the onslaught of "industrial tourism." Still, old attitudes die hard, and you'll see pickup trucks with bumper stickers saying "Save Wyoming's wildlife."

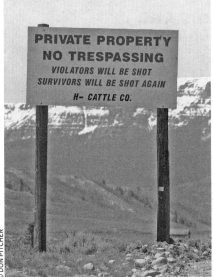

**PRIVATE PROPERTY
NO TRESPASSING**
VIOLATORS WILL BE SHOT
SURVIVORS WILL BE SHOT AGAIN
H— CATTLE CO.

© DON PITCHER

Be sure to obey this sign!

Shoot a tree hugger" or "Wolves—Government sponsored terrorists."

SIGHTS
Dubois Museum

The Dubois Museum (909 W. Ramshorn, 307/455-2284, www.duboismuseum.org, $2 adults, $1 kids, $5 for families) is open daily 9 A.M.–6 P.M. June–September and Tuesday–Saturday 10 A.M.–4 P.M. the rest of the year. The small museum houses a handful of exhibits on the Sheepeater Indians and their pictographs, with other displays on ranch life, geology, and wildlife. Surrounding the museum are 10 historic log cabins and other old structures, all containing interesting displays. Next to the museum is the **Headwaters Arts and Conference Center,** where an upstairs gallery (307/455-3404, www.wrvag.org) exhibits works by regional artists. It's open daily in the summer.

◖ National Bighorn Sheep Center

Just steps from the town museum, The National

Bighorn Sheep Interpretive Center (907 W. Ramshorn, 307/455-3429 or 888/209-2795, www.bighorn.org, $2.50 adults, $.75 kids under 12, or $10 families) houses a small collection of displays on desert bighorn, Rocky Mountain bighorn, stone sheep, and Dall sheep. The museum details how the population was brought back from the brink of extinction, and it includes hands-on exhibits and interactive displays on the lives of bighorns. Also here is a diorama of a Sheepeater Indian trap and mounted specimens around a 16-foot-high central "mountain." A small theater shows an 18-minute video on bighorn sheep biology and behavior, while a gift shop sells books and other items. The center is open daily 9 A.M.–8 P.M. Memorial Day–Labor Day, and Tuesday–Saturday 9 A.M.–5 P.M. the rest of the year (winter hours may vary).

The center offers wildlife tours of the Whiskey Basin Habitat Area just west of town November–March (details below). These four-hour van-and-hiking trips cost $25 per person and include binoculars and spotting scopes to view the animals. Reservations are required at least 24 hours in advance. The center also has an excellent brochure describing self-guided tours of Whiskey Basin.

Whiskey Basin

Approximately five miles east of Dubois, a sign points the way to Whiskey Basin. Follow the gravel road two miles to the **Dubois State Fish Hatchery,** (307/455-2431, open daily 8 A.M.–5 >P.M.) where rainbow, cutthroat, golden, brook, and brown trout as well as grayling are raised. The bucolic setting is hard to beat: a tree-lined creek surrounded by sage, mountains, and badlands.

A short distance up the road is a wildlife-viewing kiosk for the **Whiskey Basin Wildlife Habitat Area.** During winter the valley is home to the largest population of **Rocky Mountain bighorn sheep** anywhere on earth. Some 650 sheep congregate here because of the mild winters and the shallow snow. Although you're likely to find sheep all winter, the best time to photograph them is in the breeding

© DON PITCHER

male bighorn sheep in Whiskey Basin Wildlife Habitat Area

season, from late-November–December. During this period you'll see rams charging head-first into each other over the chance to mate. It's enough to give you a headache. The lambs are born in late May and early June high up on rocky slopes. Bighorn sheep are also sometimes seen in the meadows along the highway or in the hills just above Dubois. The National Bighorn Sheep Interpretive Center in Dubois leads wildlife tours of Whiskey Basin.

Beyond the wildlife-viewing kiosk, the road follows Torrey Creek up past a string of three small bodies of water: Torrey, Ring, and Trail Lakes. These were created by retreating glaciers centuries ago, but low dams have enlarged them. State Game and Fish **campsites** (free) are located along Ring and Trail Lakes. **Ring Lake Ranch** (307/455-2663 or 888/458-5253, www .ringlake.org) houses an ecumenical religious facility used for a variety of retreats, seminars, and other activities throughout the summer.

You'll discover quite a few **Indian pictographs** on large boulders in the Trail Lake vicinity; look for them along the hillside between Trail Lake and the south end of Ring Lake. (Unmarked wooden posts are near some of them). These figures—some four feet tall— are elaborate otherworldly creations with horns and headdresses, and are believed to represent shamans performing ceremonies under altered states of consciousness. While their age is unknown, they are probably at least 2,000 years old and of Athapaskan (a Canadian tribe) rather than Shoshonean origin. This is some of the oldest rock art in Wyoming. Do not touch, make rubbings, or put anything in contact with the pictographs since it could cause damage to these irreplaceable symbols from the past.

Badlands

Just west of Dubois is a signed turnoff to a **scenic overlook.** The gravel road climbs sharply (no RVs) for approximately one mile to the viewpoint, where displays note the surrounding peaks. Enjoy marvelous views of 11,635-foot Ramshorn Peak from here. **Rocky Mountain bighorn sheep** crowd the Dubois area in the winter. Many are visible on the hills just south

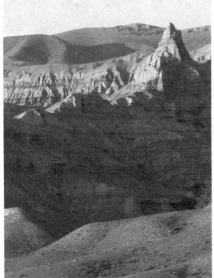

badlands near Dubois

riding the wild Jackalope

of town, with hundreds more gathered in the Whiskey Basin Habitat Area, five miles east.

The magnificent badlands on both sides of Dubois, but especially to the east, are well worth exploring. The fascinating **Badlands Interpretive Trail** heads up Mason Draw, 2.4 miles northeast of town. Pick up a booklet describing the trail (not well maintained) at the chamber of commerce office.

Rock hounds will find all sorts of petrified wood, agates, and other colorful rocks up the Wiggins Fork and Horse Creek drainages; ask at the chamber of commerce for directions.

Other Sights

One thing you certainly would not expect to find in Dubois is a training center for lawyers, but famed Wyoming attorney Gerry Spence has one on his Thunderhead Ranch east of town. His nonprofit (!) **Trial Lawyers College** (760/322-3783 or 800/688-1611, www.trial lawyerscollege.com) puts about 50 lawyers through an intense four-week session each summer, with mock trials and professional actors. Watch your step with all these lawyers around Dubois.

It's hard to miss the **Country Store Exxon** station (404 W. Ramshorn, 307/455-2677) on the west side of town with the **Jackalope** out front. Head inside for ice cream or slice of pie and the chance to plunk your kid on the giant Jackalope inside for a goofy photo. Only in Wyoming.

Horse drawn wagons known as the **Dubois Express** roll through town every half-hour all summer, departing from the KOA (225 W. Welty, 307/455-2238 or 800/562-0806, www .koa.com, $5).

RECREATION

Dubois sits at the confluence of the Wind River and Horse Creek, and both streams provide good trout fishing right in town. Hot springs keep the Wind River flowing all year. Directly behind the National Bighorn Sheep Center is a shady riverside **town park** with picnic tables, a playground, tennis courts, and a skatepark. The visitor center has descriptions of local fishing holes and brochures from local outfitters who offer pack trips and horseback rides.

Sixteen miles west of Dubois is **Mackenzie Highland Ranch** (307/455-3415, www.mac kenziehighlandranch.com) with horseback rides and ATV rentals in the summer. Rent mountain bikes from **Bob's Bike Corral** (307/455-2453, www.bobsbikecorral.com).

The nine-hole **Antelope Hills Golf Course** (307/455-2888) is on the western end of Dubois.

Winter Play

The Absarokas and Wind River Mountains around Dubois are crowded with **snowmobilers** during winter, and several places rent "sleds" in town and nearby. Don't expect peace and quiet with all of these machines roaring through the backcountry! More than 300 miles of trails head out in all directions, with the Union Pass area a particular focus.

For something quieter, **cross-country skiers** will find trails near Falls Campground and Brooks Lake (both 23 miles west of town) and Togwotee Mountain Lodge (40 miles west)

and in backcountry wilderness areas off-limits to snowmobiles.

Triangle C Ranch (307/455-2225 or 800/661-4928, www.trianglec.com) provides all-day snowcoach trips in a converted Ford Excursion from Dubois into Yellowstone. These head to either Old Faithful or Canyon for the day, departing at 7 A.M. and returning by 6 P.M. The cost is $250 per person including breakfast and lunch.

ENTERTAINMENT AND EVENTS

Find country-and-western bands at **Rustic Pine Tavern** (119 E. Ramshorn, 307/455-2430, www.rusticpinetavern.com), a classic Western bar with elk and moose heads, plenty of old wood, and a pool table. Check out the ashtrays, which note, "God spends his vacation here." Bring your dance boots for Tuesday-night square dance sessions all summer.

Whiskey Creek Saloon (204 W. Ramshorn, 307/455-2387) has a DJ or live music on Saturday nights, along with pool tables and dart boards.

TIE HACKS

Many of the trees cut in Wyoming's forests between 1870 and 1940 went to supply railroad ties for an ever-expanding network of rails throughout the Rockies. The men who cut these ties – tie hacks – spent long, hard months in the mountains, working through the winter. Most the woodsmen were emigrants from Sweden, Norway, Finland, Austria, and Italy. Tie hacks first felled a suitable lodgepole pine using a bucksaw, then limbed the tree and used a broadax to hew the tie into shape, finally peeling the remaining bark from the sides and cutting it to length. Hundreds of thousands of ties – each eight feet long and at least five inches on each side – were produced annually by tie hacks. Horses dragged the ties down to a creek bank or flume to await high spring flows, when thousands of ties could be sent downriver at once. The enormous log jams that resulted sometimes required dyna-

mite to loosen. Downstream booms caught the logs, where they could be hauled up and loaded onto railway cars.

Tie hacks found work in many parts of Wyoming, but especially in the Medicine Bow Mountains, Laramie Mountains, Sierra Madre, Big Horn Mountains, and Wind River Mountains, where major streams provided a way for the ties to reach the railheads. In the upper Wind River country, the industry spanned three decades, from 1914 to 1946. During this time, more than 10 million ties were cut and floated downstream to Riverton, where the Chicago and Northwestern Railroad used them. A stone monument to the tie hacks stands along U.S. Hwy. 26/287 approximately 18 miles west of Dubois. The visitor center in Dubois has a handout that provides a self-guided tour of historical sights associated with the tie hacks.

Events

The first weekend of February brings **Winterfest** with sled dog and skijoring races (cross-country skiing while being pulled by a dog). In mid-May **Dubois Antler Rendezvous** has five days of elk antler–sales in Dubois's town park. The **Swedish Smorgasbord** in June celebrates the Scandinavian tie hacks (men who cut railroad ties between 1870 and 1940) with a big dinner of Scandinavian favorites.

The town's biggest festivities take place over **Fourth of July** weekend, with a parade, ice-cream social, rodeo, games, Western barbecue, fireworks, and rubber-ducky races down the river. In mid-July, **Dubois Museum Day** is a folk art festival with Indian dancing, frontier crafts demonstrations, and lectures.

A **National Art Show** comes to town on the last week of July, attracting both professionals and amateurs. It's been going on for more than 50 years. Also don't miss the always popular Dubois firefighters' **Buffalo Barbecue,** held the second Saturday of August. A big quilt festival takes place that same weekend. Get specifics on these and other events from the Dubois Chamber of Commerce, 307/455-2556.

On Friday evenings mid-June–mid-August, you'll find **rodeos** at the town arena. **Archaeology Days** in August features guest lectures and workshops at the Dubois Museum.

SHOPPING

Drop by **Wind River Gear** (19 N. 1st St., 307/455-3468, www.windrivergearshop.com) for quality outdoor clothing and backpacking gear. Find traditional Western wear head at the old-time **Welty's General Store** (113 W. Ramshorn, 307/455-2377), and fishing supplies at **Whiskey Mountain Tackle** (1428 Warm Springs Dr., 307/455-2587).

Two Ocean Books (128 E. Ramshorn, 307/455-3554, www.cowboybookseller.com) is a fine local bookshop, though **Water Wheel Gift Shop** (113 E. Ramshorn, 307/455-2112) also carries a selection of regional titles.

Galleries

Several downtown galleries are worth a visit. **Trapline Gallery** (120 E. Ramshorn,

Dubois

© DON PITCHER

GATEWAYS TO YELLOWSTONE

307/455-2800) sells Indian-crafted beadwork, jewelry, and artwork. **Tukadeka Traders/ Horse Creek Gallery** (104 E. Ramshorn, 307/455-3345) has an impressive collection of antique trade beads, along with tacky antler carvings and Indian trinkets. Find works by a dozen local and Wyoming artists at **Silver Sage Gallery** (124 E. Ramshorn, 307/455-3002, www.silversagegallery.com). On the north side of town, **Antler Workshop and Gallery** (1404 Warm Springs Dr., 307/455-2204, www .antlergallery.com) has a big wagon filled with elk antlers out front and an unusual variety of antler furniture, chandeliers, and lamps inside, all crafted by Kurt Gordon.

ACCOMMODATIONS

Dubois makes an excellent stopping point on the way to Yellowstone and Grand Teton national parks, with lodging prices well below those in Jackson Hole. All places are open year-round unless noted otherwise.

Wind River Motel (519 W. Ramshorn, 307/455-2611 or 877/455-2621, www.dteworld .com/windriver, $40–80 s or $55–85 d) has a mix of rustic cabin-style units with microwaves and fridges, motel rooms (some with kitchenettes), and four-person suites. The cabins are basic but clean, with aging shag carpet and sloping floors, while motel rooms are somewhat nicer. There's a relaxing riverside deck in the back (a quiet escape from the noise of town). Most units contain fridges and microwaves; open May–October. No air conditioning, phones, or Wi-Fi. It's centrally located, with the donut shop right next door.

Branding Iron Inn (401 Ramshorn, 307/455-2893 or 888/651-9378, www.brand ingironinn.com, $55–75 d) features cozy, well-maintained duplex log cabins that were built in the 1940s. They've been substantially updated with standard rooms for $55–75 and kitchenette units for $100. Folks traveling with horses will appreciate the adjacent corral. No air conditioning, but some units contain ceiling fans and the thick log walls help keep the heat out.

Three miles east of town, **Longhorn RV and Motel** (307/455-2337, www.longhornrvand motel.com) has two-dozen newly completed motel rooms ($69–74 d), all with fridges, microwaves, and Wi-Fi.

Located on attractive grounds, **Trail's End Motel** (511 Ramshorn, 307/455-2540 or 888/455-6660, www.trailsendmotel.com) gets high marks from travelers. Clean, remodeled rooms start for $74 d, and the nicest ones ($129 d) include decks facing the Wind River along with in-room fridges and microwaves. Also available are two-room family units that sleep eight for $139. Free Wi-Fi too.

For historic rooms, stay at ◖ **Twin Pines Lodge and Cabins** (218 Ramshorn, 307/455-2600 or 800/550-6332, www.twin pineslodge.com). Built in 1934 and on the National Register of Historic Places, the lodge has both modern and rustic cabins. Rates are $90–100 d in cabins or rooms in the main lodge, or $117–123 d for two larger suites in the lodge, both with jetted tubs. Twin Pines amenities include a filling breakfast, fridges, Wi-Fi, and VCRs with hundreds of videos to borrow. Everything is immaculate in this place that gracefully blends old and new.

Find attractive accommodations at the largest motel in town, **Stagecoach Motor Inn** (103 Ramshorn, 307/455-2303 or 800/455-5090, www.stagecoachmotel-dubois.com). Rates are $75–79 d, six-person kitchenettes cost $110, and king suites run $90 d. Wi-Fi is available throughout the motel, and families appreciate the seasonal heated outdoor pool, year-round hot tub, and shady backyard playground.

A half-mile east of Dubois, **Chinook Winds Mountain Lodge** (307/455-2987 or 877/455-2987, www.chinookwindsmountain lodge.com) has motel units for $65–75 d and two cabins containing full kitchens and jetted tubs for $95–125 d. The Wind River is right out the back door, and pets are welcome ($5 extra).

On the west end of town, **Super 8 Motel** (1412 Warm Springs Dr., 307/445-3694 or 800/800-8000, www.super8.com) has predictable chain-motel rooms for $95–125, including a small indoor pool and hot tub, light breakfast, and Wi-Fi. Pets allowed.

Bed-and-Breakfast

Constructed from red clay blocks in the 1940s, **The Stone House B&B** (207 S. 1st St., 307/455-2555, www.duboisbnb.com) contains a variety of lodging choices just two blocks from downtown Dubois. Inside this stately home two upstairs guest rooms ($65–75 d) share a bath, and a two-room basement suite ($80 d 120 four) has its own bath. Adjacent is a small guest cottage with two bedrooms, each with a queen bed; $90 d or $130 d for four people. A full breakfast is served each morning, and the sitting room faces Whiskey Mountain, a good place to watch for bighorn sheep. Open May–October. No Wi-Fi.

Vacation Rentals

For a beautiful in-town option, stay at **Cabin on the Wind** (615 W. Ramshorn, 307/455-3472, www.vrbo.com/98864), a lovingly refurbished cabin with a deck overlooking the Wind River. Inside are three bedrooms with queen beds, a full kitchen and living room, log furnishings, hardwood floors, washer, dryer, and Wi-Fi. It rents for $145 with a three-night minimum stay.

Next door is **Flying W Vacation Rental** (307/455-2278, www.vrbo.com/99558), a simple but comfy riverside place with four bedrooms. It sleeps eight for $200 nightly with a three-night minimum. Both of these cabins are open year-round.

Mountain Pinnacle Properties (307/455-3735 or 866/738-4814, www.mountainpinnacleproperties.com) has additional vacation homes in the Dubois area.

Dude Ranches and Mountain Lodges

Quite a few dude ranches/mountain lodges are found around Dubois, including the country west of here on the way to Togwotee Pass.

Ten miles out East Fork Road, **Lazy L&B Ranch** (307/455-2839 or 800/453-9488, www.lazylb.com) is a century-old ranch offering creekside log cabins, horseback riding, an outdoor swimming pool and hot tub, stocked fishing ponds, kids' programs, volleyball, fly-fishing, and a rifle range. The ranch's horseback-riding program is excellent, and guests can choose trips through the badlands or high into the mountains. Lazy L&B is open late May–mid-September, with all-inclusive weekly rates of $2,800 for two people; adults only after Labor Day. The ranch also operates **Bear Basin Wilderness Camp** (www.bearbasincamp.com, $225 daily per person), a wonderful base from which to explore the Washakie Wilderness on horseback. A maximum of eight guests stay in wall tents during these backcountry trips.

Located 16 miles up East Fork Road, **Bitterroot Ranch** (307/455-2778 or 800/545-0019, www.bitterrootranch.com) emphasizes horseback riding for riders at all levels of ability; each guest gets to ride several different horses. The owners breed Arabian horses and offer centered riding clinics, a cross-country jumping course, pack trips, cattle drives, and fly-fishing. Both French and German are spoken here, attracting an international clientele. The ranch is open June–September and has space for 32 guests in a dozen cabins. All-inclusive weekly rates are $3,900 for two people. The owners also run Equitors (www.equitours.com), a travel agency specializing in horseback rides all over the globe.

South of Dubois in beautiful Jakeys Fork Canyon, **CM Ranch** (307/455-2331 or 800/455-0721, www.cmranch.com) is one of Wyoming's oldest dude ranches; it's been here since 1927. The ranch offers dramatic badlands topography and a variety of fossils, making it a favorite of geologists (and amateur rock hounds). Trails lead into the adjacent Fitzpatrick Wilderness, a destination for horseback trips. Fishing is another popular activity, and a fishing guide is available. The immaculate lodge buildings have space for 55 guests, and kids love the big outdoor pool and a hot tub. All-inclusive weekly rates at this delightful old-time ranch are $3,120–3,250 for two people. The ranch is owned by the Kemmerer family, whose ancestors founded the town of Kemmerer, Wyoming. The Kemmerers also own Jackson Hole Mountain Resort.

Operating as a dude ranch since 1920, **T-Cross Ranch** (307/455-2206 or 877/827-6770, www.tcross.com) is 15 miles north of Dubois near Horse Creek and is open mid-June–mid-September. Surrounded by the Shoshone National Forest, this remote ranch has weekly accommodations at $2,790 for two people, including horseback riding, all meals, activities for kids, trout fishing, and a hot tub. Backcountry pack trips and other activities are also available. Lodging is in eight comfortable log cabins, and the main lodge has a massive stone fireplace and spacious front porch.

Ramshorn Guest Ranch (307/455-3921 in summer or 307/333-4430 in winter, www.ramshornguestranch.com) has three cabins on a 250-acre ranch bordered on three sides by Forest Service land. Nearby trails lead into the Washakie Wilderness, making this a fine base for hikers and backpackers. Ignore "guest ranch" in the name; no horses or dudes here, just comfortable cabins with private baths and full kitchens and baths for $60–80 nightly with a three night minimum. Tent sites are $12 (shower house nearby), RV hookups cost $20, and a couple of bring-your-sleeping-bag tepees take you back in time for $25. Ramshorn is nine miles west of Dubois on U.S. 26/287, and another six miles up a dirt road. No phones, TVs, or Wi-Fi, but you don't need them up here in God's Country. Open mid-June–mid-August.

Sixteen miles west of Dubois is **Mackenzie Highland Ranch** (307/455-3415, www.mackenziehighlandranch.com), where accommodations are offered in a variety of cabins and other rustic buildings. The simplest cabins share a bathhouse and cost $55 for up to four people. Considerably nicer are the two-bedroom cabins with space for seven, full kitchens, baths, and living rooms that sleep up to four for $245. The finest is a modern four-bedroom home (it sleeps 10) with two baths and a full kitchen for $275. There's a three-night minimum for most cabins. RVs can park for $45 per night with full hookups, and limited Wi-Fi is available. This isn't an all-inclusive dude ranch, so meals aren't available, but trail rides, ATV

rentals, and guided fishing trips are offered in the summer. The ranch becomes a base for snowmobilers, cross-country skiers, and hunters at other times of the year.

Right along Highway 26/268 and 18 miles west of Dubois, **Triangle C Ranch** (307/455-2225 or 800/661-4928, www.trianglec.com) was established as the first tie-hack camp in the region. It now operates as a guest ranch where the main emphasis is horseback riding, but guests will also enjoy fishing, hiking, activities for kids and teens, wagon rides, and evening entertainment, plus the outdoor pool and hot tub. Weekly rates are $4,500 for two people. The ranch is open Memorial Day–mid-October. In winter, Triangle C leads snowcoach day trips from Dubois or Jackson into Yellowstone.

Twenty miles west of Dubois, **Lava Mountain Lodge** (307/455-2506 or 800/919-9570, www.lavamountainlodg.com) has motel rooms for $88 d, and a large rental house that sleeps up to 10 for $325. You'll also find a restaurant with home-cooked meals three times a day, along with camping spaces ($10 tents, $35 RVs), basic camper cabins ($40 d, bring sleeping bags, shower house close by), plus a convenience store, bar, and laundromat with coin-op showers. Open year-round, with a corral in the back for folks traveling with horses.

(See *Mountain Resorts* in the *Jackson Hole* chapter for information on Brooks Lake Lodge—on the lake of the same name—and Togwotee Mountain Lodge—a few miles west of Togwotee Pass.)

CAMPING

The closest public camping spot is **Horse Creek Campground** (open late May–Sept., $10), 12 miles north of Dubois on Horse Creek Road.

Dubois Wind River KOA (225 W. Welty, 307/455-2238 or 800/562-0806, www.koa.com, open May–Sept., $22 tents, $43 RVs, $46–56 cabins) is one of Wyoming's better private campgrounds, with an indoor pool, playground, game room, Wi-Fi, and a riverside location, plus chuckwagon dinner shows (described below) on Monday and Thursday evenings. Showers for noncampers are $6.

Three miles east of town, **Longhorn RV and Motel** (307/455-2337, www.longhornrvand motel.com, open May–mid-Oct.) has full hookup sites along the river for $40 and tent spaces for $20, including Wi-Fi.

FOOD
Breakfast and Lunch
Popular with both locals and tourists, **Cowboy Café** (115 E. Ramshorn, 307/455-2595, daily 6:30 A.M.–9 P.M., closed Wed. in winter) has good home-style breakfasts with big helpings of biscuits and gravy, and delicious homemade soups and pies for lunch. Dinners are $9–19.

Hang out with the locals at **Village Café/Daylight Donuts** (515 W. Ramshorn, 307/455-2122, daily 6 A.M.–9 P.M.), where homemade doughnuts, coffee, and conversation are the morning attractions. Also popular are burgers and sandwiches for lunch along with so-so pizzas (frozen crust) and ground-steak burgers for dinner.

Kathy's Koffee (306 W. Ramshorn, 307/455-3862, Sun. 7 A.M.–1 P.M., Mon.–Fri. 7 A.M.–3 P.M., Sat. 7 A.M.–2 P.M.) operates from a little log cabin with a deck and picnic tables in the back, and a light menu of salads, sandwiches, wraps, smoothies, shakes, espresso (including iced lattes), and bagels. This is where the fishing outfitters hold court. Free Wi-Fi for customers.

American
Rustic Pine Steakhouse (119 E. Ramshorn, 307/455-2772, www.rusticpinetavern.com, daily 5–10 P.M.) is a carnivore's delight, with steaks, London broil, chicken Dijon, and big salads; entrées run $16–29.

For an old-West treat head over to **Circle Up Chuckwagon Dinner Shows** at Dubois Wind River KOA (225 W. Welty, 307/455-2238 or 800/562-0806, www.circleupchuckwagon dinnershow.com, Mon. and Thurs. 6:30–9:30 P.M. late June–late Aug.). You'll find filling Dutch oven meals (BBQ brisket,

baked potato, coleslaw, baked beans, and cobbler), plus twangy cowboy music for $22 adults or $6 kids.

Fine Dining
For fine dining in rustic Dubois, you won't go wrong at ◖ **The Sundance Café** (106 E. Ramshorn, 307/455-3989, Tues.–Sat. 11:30 A.M.–2 P.M. and 5:30–9 P.M. year-round). The little log cabin has a shady wrap-around deck right on Horse Creek, perfect for a sunny afternoon. Everything is fresh and made to order; no deep fryer here! Try the chicken salad sandwich for lunch (with cranberries, pecans, red onions, and celery). Dinner faves include spicy plum shrimp kabobs and delicious rack of lamb in Middle Eastern spices. Entrées are $19–30. There's wine, beer, and a full bar, plus acoustic guitar music on Thursday evenings.

Two places are fine-dining destinations near the top of Union Pass, 13 scenic miles west of Dubois: **Line Shack Lodge** (307/455-3232, www.lineshack.com) and **The Sawmill Lodge** (307/455-2171 or 866472-9645, www.the sawmill.org). Both are open for three meals a day; Sawmill is probably a better bet.

Groceries and Sweets
Get groceries at **Dubois Super Foods** (610 W. Ramshorn, 307/455-2402). If kids are begging for a cone, take them to the **Country Store Exxon** (404 W. Ramshorn, 307/455-2677) for ice cream or slice of pie and a Jackalope ride.

Get malts and sundaes from the old-time soda fountain inside the **Dubois Drug Store** (126 E. Ramshorn, 307/455-2300, Sun. 9 A.M.–5 P.M., Mon.–Sat. 8:30 A.M.–6 P.M.).

INFORMATION AND SERVICES
The **Dubois Chamber of Commerce** (616 W. Ramshorn, 307/455-2556 or 888/518-0502, www.duboiswyoming.org) is—theoretically— open daily 8 A.M.–6 P.M. mid-May–mid-August, and Monday–Friday 10 A.M.–2 P.M. the rest of the year, but it's run by volunteers, so you may well find nobody home even during these hours.

Stop by the Shoshone National Forest

Wind River Ranger District office (1403 W. Ramshorn, 307/455-2466, www.fs.fed.us/r2/shoshone, Mon.–Fri. 8 A.M.–4:30 P.M.) one mile west of town for maps of Shoshone and Bridger-Teton national forests and information on local trails. It also has a listing of local horsepacking outfitters.

Open weekdays, the **Dubois Medical Clinic** (307/455-2516), just east of town on Hwy. 26, has a part-time doctor and nurse practitioners. Wash clothes at the **Laundromat** at 408 W. Ramshorn (across from Branding Iron Motel).

Check your email or surf the Web for free at the lovely new **Dubois Library** (202 N. 1st St., 307/455-2992, www.fremontcountylibraries.org, Mon.–Thurs. 11 A.M.–7 P.M., Wed. till 8 P.M., Fri.–Sat. 11 A.M.–3 P.M., closed Sun.), or for a fee ($2.50 for 10 minutes) at **Cyber Café** (308 W. Ramshorn, 307/455-4011).

DUBOIS VICINITY

Anyone who loves the outdoors will discover an abundance of pleasures around Dubois. There's good fishing for rainbow, cutthroat, brown, and brook trout in Wind River and for rainbow, brook, and Mackinaw trout in the many alpine lakes. You'll also see lots of deer, elk, and bighorn sheep. Hikers and horsepackers will find hundreds of miles of Forest Service trails in the area. Photographers love the brilliantly colored badlands that frame Dubois on both the east and west sides. Each winter, hundreds of snowmobilers climb on their "sleds" and cross-country skiers strap on their boards to enter the world of deep powder in the Absarokas.

Horse Creek Area

Horse Creek Road heads north from Dubois, with scenic views of the Absarokas and nearby badland country. Several dude ranches are in the area. **Horse Creek Campground** (open late May–Sept., $10) is 12 miles north. Forest Road 504 continues another five miles, providing access to the Washakie Wilderness via Horse Creek Trail. Forest Road 508 splits off near Horse Creek Campground and leads another 17 miles to **Double Cabin Campground** (open June–Sept., $10). Several trails head

into the wilderness from here; the most popular are Frontier Creek Trail and the Wiggins Fork Trail. You'll find remnants of a petrified forest six miles up the Frontier Creek Trail, but they have been rather picked over by illegal collectors. (It's unlawful to remove petrified wood from a wilderness area. Please leave pieces where you find them.) For other Washakie Wilderness trails information, ask at the Dubois Ranger Station.

Union Pass

The first road across the Absarokas headed through Union Pass southwest of Dubois. The pass forms a divide between the waters of the Columbia, Colorado, and Mississippi rivers and marks the boundary of the Absaroka, Wind River, and Gros Ventre mountain ranges. Near the pass are an interpretive sign and a nature trail through a flower-filled meadow. Union Pass Road (gravel) leaves U.S. Hwy. 26/287 eight miles northwest of Dubois and climbs across to connect with Hwy. 352 north of Pinedale. A major reconstruction project has dramatically improved the road in recent years, providing a beautiful over-the-mountains connection between Pinedale and Dubois in the summer. The road isn't plowed in winter, but it is popular with snowmobilers.

A scenic 20-mile side road begins a few miles up Union Pass Road, heads along Warm Springs Creek, and eventually reconnects with U.S. Hwy. 26/287. Find fantastic views of the Absaroka and Wind River ranges along this route. The remains of an old tie-hack logging flume are visible, and a warm spring (85°F) flows into the creek.

The Union Pass area is popular with mountain-bikers, cross-country skiers, and hordes of wintertime snowmobilers. Five miles up the road near the 8,600-foot summit, **Line Shack Lodge** (307/455-3232, www.lineshack.com) has a wonderful setting, an inviting interior with tall windows facing the mountains. Closed in summer, but open for winter snowmobilers.

One-quarter mile downhill from Line Shack is **The Sawmill Lodge** (307/455-2171 or 866/472-9645, www.thesawmill.org) with attractive condo-style rooms ($90–110 d) and two-level suites ($135 d). A restaurant and bar are on the premises. Closed May and November.

WestView Mountain Log Home (715/825-2560, www.vrbo.com/42587) is a large log home close to Line Shack. It has space for seven guests at $250 nightly in the summer or $330 in winter. A four-person cabin is also available here: $125 nightly. There's a six-night minimum stay in the main house, or four nights in the cabin.

The nonprofit **Teton Valley Ranch Camp** (307/733-2958, www.tvrcamp.org) provides a summertime Western experience for boys and girls. Formerly in Jackson Hole, the ranch moved to a 2,300-acre spread 10 miles west of Dubois in 2005.

◖ TOGWOTEE PASS

The enjoyable drive west from Dubois first cuts through the colorful badlands, playing tag with the Wind River as it begins a long ascent to 9,658-foot Togwotee Pass (TOE-go-tee). The pass is named for a subchief under Chief Washakie. Togwotee was one of the last independent Sheepeater Indians—a branch of the Shoshones—and the man who led a U.S. government exploratory expedition over this pass in 1873. He even guided President Chester Arthur on his month-long visit to Yellowstone in 1883.

Togwotee Pass (877/996-8724, www.go togwoteetrail.com) is one of the most scenic drives imaginable, with Ramshorn Peak peeking down from the north for several miles until the road plunges into dense lodgepole forests (Shoshone National Forest) with lingering glimpses of the Pinnacle Buttes. At the crest it emerges into grass-, willow-, and flower-bedecked meadows with Blackrock Creek winding through. Whitebark pine and Engelmann spruce trees cover the nearby slopes. As the highway drops down the western side into the Bridger-Teton National Forest, another marvelous mountain range—the Tetons—dominates the horizon in dramatic fashion. Snow lies along the roadsides until early July; notice the

high posts along the road used by snowplows. Togwotee Pass is a complete shock after all the miles of sagebrush and grassland that control the heartland of Wyoming. It's like entering another world—one of cool, forested mountains and lofty peaks instead of the arid land with horizon-wide vistas.

The highway over Togwotee Pass has been undergoing reconstruction in a process that will not be completed until 2012. New sections of the road have better shoulders and more passing lanes, but expect 15-minute delays somewhere along your route.

Pinnacle Buttes and Brooks Lake

Dominating the view along U.S. Hwy. 26/287 for perhaps 15 miles are the castlelike Pinnacle Buttes. Twenty-three miles west of Dubois, you'll come to the turnoff to Brooks Lake, elevation 9,100 feet. Take it, even if you don't plan on camping here. A five-mile gravel road leads to the cliff-rimmed lake, and a clear creek flows east and south from here. The Forest Service's excellent **Pinnacles** and **Brooks Lake** campgrounds are along the lakeshore and cost $10–15 per night; open mid-June–mid-September. Facing the lake is historic Brooks Lake Lodge (see *Mountain Resorts* under *Accommodations* in the *Jackson Hole* chapter).

Back on the main highway, you'll want to stop at **Falls Campground** (open June–mid-Sept., $15). Here, Brooks Creek tumbles into a deep canyon. Catch impressive views of **Brooks Creek Falls** along the short trail beginning from the parking lot. In winter, cross-country skiers will find an easy but ungroomed ski trail that heads out two miles from here. **Wind River Lake** is another five miles up the hill, just below the pass. It's a gorgeous place for picnics and fishing, with deep blue water and the sharp cliffs of Pinnacle Buttes behind. There's even a wheelchair-accessible float for anglers.

Continuing west over the pass the vista abruptly opens up, with magnificent Teton vistas from a pullout. A half-mile down the road is the popular **Togwotee Mountain Lodge** (307/543-2847 or 800/543-2847, www .togwoteelodge.com).

BACKGROUND

The Land

The term Greater Yellowstone Ecosystem is broadly applied to the high plateau and mountain ranges inside and surrounding Yellowstone National Park. Covering approximately 19 million acres, this high-elevation country includes two national parks—Yellowstone and Grand Teton—along with sections of six surrounding national forests—Beaverhead-Deerlodge, Bridger-Teton, Caribou-Targhee, Custer, Gallatin, and Shoshone—plus other public lands managed by the Bureau of Land Management (BLM) and national wildlife refuges managed by the U.S. Fish and Wildlife Service. This vast landscape centers on the northwest corner of Wyoming but also includes parts of Montana and Idaho. All together, this is one of the largest relatively intact temperate-zone ecosystems on the planet.

The official websites for Yellowstone (www.nps.gov/yell) and Grand Teton (www.nps.gov/grte) national parks are both packed with detailed information about plants, animals, geology, and other aspects of the Greater Yellowstone Ecosystem.

GEOGRAPHY

The Greater Yellowstone Ecosystem is a mountainous region, with several peaks topping

© DON PITCHER

13,000 feet. The nation's Continental Divide cuts diagonally across the region from the southeast to the northwest. Wyoming's highest summit, 13,804-foot Gannet Peak, is on the southern margin of the ecosystem in the Wind River Mountains, and the second-highest peak, Grand Teton (13,770 feet), forms the crown of the Tetons. Montana's tallest summit is 12,799-foot Granite Peak in the Absaroka-Beartooth Wilderness just northeast of Yellowstone. The little burgs of Cooke City and Silver Gate are not far away.

The heart of Yellowstone National Park is a high and rolling plateau that averages around 8,000 feet in elevation, but the eastern and northern sections of the park are considerably more rugged. The park's highest mountain is 11,358-foot Eagle Peak, on the southeastern border, and the lowest point (5,300 feet) is on the northwest corner near Gardiner,

Montana. The eastern and northern borders of Yellowstone National Park front on the Absaroka Range, which contains many peaks topping 12,000 feet. To the west and northwest of the park are the lower-elevation Gallatin, Madison, and Centennial ranges and the town of West Yellowstone, while the Caribou Range lies to the southwest. The Yellowstone gateway town of Cody sits at the eastern margin of the Absarokas within Bighorn Basin, and another gateway town, Dubois, occupies the upper end of protected Wind River Valley.

Grand Teton National Park and Jackson Hole lie just south of Yellowstone. The Teton Range creates an incredible western skyline, and the less grandiose, but still impressive, Gros Ventre Range is to the east. Jackson Hole is a relatively flat intermountain basin through which the Snake River flows, with the town of Jackson on its southern end. South of Jackson

Hole are the Wyoming and Salt River ranges, while to the west of the Tetons lies Teton Valley, Idaho. The massive Wind River Mountains have many peaks over 13,000 feet and reach southeastward from Union Pass to South Pass, a distance of 100 miles. Areas south of Jackson Hole, including the Wind River Mountains, are beyond the scope of this book; for details see Don Pitcher's *Moon Wyoming* (www.donpitcher.com).

CLIMATE

The complex and mountainous nature of the Greater Yellowstone Ecosystem creates widely varying microclimatic conditions. It may be a beautiful, sunny summer day in the town of Jackson, while backpackers 2,000 feet higher in the Tetons are getting drenched in a long and lightning-filled storm just a few miles away. The following overall weather description applies to Jackson Hole and the Yellowstone plateau (including the Old Faithful area). Temperatures may be a bit cooler along Yellowstone and Jackson lakes and are often warmer in the lower-elevation towns of Gardiner, Cody, and Dubois. Killing frosts are possible in any month of the year; I've awakened to new snow on the ground in late June! Total precipitation also varies across the region, from a low of just 11 inches annually at Gardiner to an estimated 70 inches or more in the Lewis Lake area of Yellowstone National Park. Most of the precipitation falls in the winter as snow; summers are relatively dry. (The exceptions to this are low-elevation areas on the north side of Yellowstone, where spring and early summer rains are more important.)

Get detailed climate data on the Web at www.wrcc.dri.edu/summary/climsmwy.html. For daily weather forecasts, head to the National Weather Service's site for western and central Wyoming, www.crh.noaa.gov/riw. Most visitor centers inside and outside the parks have updated forecasts.

Summer

In general, summers are short but pleasant throughout the region, with warm, sunny days and cool nights. Lower-elevation hiking trails are usually free of snow mid-June–mid-October, but some high areas may not melt until late July. You may need both shorts and a light jacket in the same day. Midsummer daytime temperatures in Jackson Hole are typically in the upper 70s or low 80s F, with nighttime lows around 40°F. It's several degrees warmer in low-elevation places such as Gardiner, and 5–10 degrees cooler in many road-accessible parts of Yellowstone. The warmest temperature recorded was 101°F for Jackson in 1934, and 103°F for Gardiner in 1960. Cody gets even hotter, and summer days over 90°F hit several times per month.

The air is generally dry, and most summer rain falls during afternoon thundershowers, when the rain can come down in torrents for brief periods, particularly in the mountains. Average rainfall for July and August in Jackson Hole is just one inch each month. All of this sunshine and showers makes for an abundance of rainbows. I've seen many days where a late-afternoon storm over the Tetons tapers off to a glorious display of colors arching into the sky.

Fall

Autumn provides a beautiful transition period from the warm summer days to the surprisingly cold winters. Nights are crisp and chilly, sending many folks scurrying for warmer climes. In Jackson Hole during September you can expect daytime highs around 55–65°F and nighttime lows around 25–30°F. Temperatures are 5–10 degrees cooler in the central sections of Yellowstone, where nighttime lows may reach into the single digits by late fall.

The peak of fall colors takes place around the first week of October in Jackson Hole and Grand Teton National Park, where aspens and cottonwoods turn a bright yellow (with a few orange trees). Although most of Yellowstone is covered with evergreen trees, you will find colorful deciduous stands in some areas, primarily on the north side of the park. You can expect to find snow on the ground anytime after late October and earlier at high elevations.

TROPICAL WYOMING

Sometimes I wish that Wyoming had more vegetation and less catarrh, more bloom and summer and fragrance and less Christmas and New Year's through the summer. I like the clear, bracing air of 7,500 feet above the civilized world, but I get weary of putting on and taking off my buffalo overcoat for meals all through dog days. I yearn for a land where a man can take off his ulster and overshoes while he delivers a Fourth of July oration, without flying into the face of Providence and dying of pneumonia.... As I write these lines I look out across the wide sweep of brownish gray plains dotted here and there with ranches and defunct buffalo craniums, and I see shutting down over the sides of the abrupt mountains, and meeting the foothills, a white mist which melts into the gray sky. It is a snow storm in the mountains.

I saw this with wonder and admiration for the first two or three million times. When it became a matter of daily occurrence as a wonder or curiosity, it was below mediocrity. Last July a snow storm gathered one afternoon and fell among the foothills and whitened the whole line to within four or five miles of town, and it certainly was a peculiar freak of nature, but it convinced me that whatever enterprises I might launch into here I would not try to raise oranges and figs until the isothermal lines should meet with a change of heart.

19th-century humorist Bill Nye

Winter

Winter brings snow and cold weather throughout the Greater Yellowstone Ecosystem, although again, local microclimatic conditions vary widely. You'll face the coldest conditions in January, when a typical Jackson Hole day is in the 20s, with nights dropping to around 0–5°F. When the sky is clear, conditions can sometimes turn severely cold, with temperatures below zero for days at a time; the record low was recorded at West Yellowstone in 1933: -66°F. Fortunately, the relative humidity is quite low, making these temperatures easier to tolerate and creating fluffy powder snow conditions. The town of Jackson receives less summertime rain and wintertime snow than the nearby mountains. In a typical January you'll find a foot of snow on the ground, but nearby Jackson Hole Mountain Resort gets 38 feet of snow annually. Even more impressive is Grand Targhee Ski Resort on the west side of the Tetons, which gets an average of 42 feet of snow per year!

At Old Faithful in Yellowstone the snow is typically around 30–40 inches deep in midwinter, but in Mammoth Hot Springs (park headquarters) you're likely to see just 6–9 inches on the ground and much milder temperatures. At the other extreme, the Lewis Lake area may see 50 feet of snow in a typical winter. Temperatures at Old Faithful average in the 20s in the day but often drop well below zero at night. At Mammoth Hot Springs, day temperatures approach 30°F, with nights dropping to around 10°F.

One surprising winter feature is the presence of temperature inversions in intermountain valleys such as Jackson Hole. These often occur on cold, clear nights when the cold air sinks into the valley floors. Skiers who leave the lodge bundled in down parkas and polypro long johns are often surprised to find temperatures 20 degrees warmer at the top of the mountain.

Spring

Spring in the Greater Yellowstone Ecosystem is a transitional period as the snow gradually melts and the plants reappear after a long winter. For many locals this is the time to escape mud season for a week or two in southern Utah. Snow often remains on the ground until late April in Jackson Hole and doesn't melt from the higher mountains until late July. In addition, a few snowfields and glaciers remain year-round in the highest and most protected areas. Spring is when you'll meet the fewest travelers because the roads may not be plowed yet, snow blocks hiking trails, skiing gets worse by the day, and many summertime recreation operations haven't yet opened. Expect daytime temperatures in the 40s and 50s in early May, but warming up rapidly as the long days of June appear.

Flora

Several vegetation types predominate in the Greater Yellowstone Ecosystem. Within Grand Teton National Park, sagebrush flats cover the valley floor, with riparian corridors and wetlands lining the Snake River and smaller creeks. Northern Yellowstone National Park also has sagebrush-dominated areas, but much of Yellowstone and the surrounding mountain country is covered with forests dominated by lodgepole pine. Other common trees within the Greater Yellowstone Ecosystem include quaking aspens, whitebark and limber pine, Engelmann spruce, Douglas fir, and subalpine fir. The tree line is approximately 10,000 feet, and above this point, low-growing alpine species survive the harsh conditions and brief summers.

Yellowstone National Park is primarily a series of high plateaus ranging 7,500–8,500 feet in elevation. Surrounding this gently rolling expanse are the Absaroka Mountains along the east and north sides and the Gallatin Range in the northwestern corner. Elevations are lowest along the northern end of the park, where the Yellowstone River and other rivers cut through, and highest on the eastern and northwestern margins. The plants that carpet Yellowstone are predominantly determined by the amount of precipitation and the type of soils in which they grow: Areas underlain by Absaroka volcanic bedrock have more nutrient-rich soils than areas with Yellowstone rhyolites. Vegetation types within the park include sagebrush-steppe, lodgepole pine forests, spruce-fir forests, and subalpine areas.

SAGEBRUSH-STEPPE

These habitats dominate dry areas of the region. Here the precipitation totals less than 20 inches annually, and one finds open country with sagebrush, grasses, and shrubs, along with pockets of aspen and Douglas fir. A dry sagebrush-steppe vegetation type can be seen in the Gardiner area, where you'll even find prickly pear cactus.

LODGEPOLE PINE

Forests of lodgepole pine cover much of the region. In these forests lodgepoles dominate, although you may find a sprinkling of whitebark pine, spruce, and fir trees. Lodgepole forests are mostly even-aged, having been established after a forest fire that destroyed the previous generation of trees. Some lodgepole cones are serotinous, meaning that they can hang on the tree for years, only opening to release the seeds when a fire melts the gluelike material holding them shut. After a fire, the seedlings grow rapidly if conditions are right. Young trees established after the 1988 fires are dense in many areas, with some already topping 20 feet. Lodgepole roots are shallow, making them susceptible to being blown over in windstorms.

SPRUCE-FIR

Higher elevations have cooler temperatures and forests dominated by Englemann spruce and subalpine fir. These sites get more precipitation than lodgepole forests and are underlain by better soils.

SUBALPINE

On mountain slopes between 8,000 and 10,000 feet you'll find whitebark pine trees. Although these trees seldom top 40 feet, their seeds are an important food source for red squirrels, Clark's nutcrackers, and more surprisingly, grizzlies. Above timberline (approximately 10,000 feet), even these trees give way, and only low-growing forbs, grasses, and shrubs survive. Mount Washburn is a good place to find an easily accessible subalpine area.

OTHER HABITAT TYPES

Several other types of vegetation exist in the Yellowstone Ecosystem, including areas dominated by Douglas fir trees within the sagebrush-steppe. Stands of aspen (beautiful in the fall) are present throughout Grand Teton, on the north end of Yellowstone, in the Bechler region, and near the Snake River. Both Yellowstone and Grand Teton contain extensive areas of wet meadows and willow flats where the water table is high and cottonwood-lined riparian areas along creeks and rivers. Yellowstone's geyser basins have given rise to plants that are specially adapted to heat and disturbance, including a species of grass (Ross' bentgrass) that grows where the temperature is 100°F just an inch below the surface.

Fauna

The Greater Yellowstone Ecosystem is famous as a place to view wildlife, particularly elk, bison, wolves, moose, and grizzlies. Because of its abundant animal populations, you'll sometimes hear the term "America's Serengeti" applied to Yellowstone, home to the largest concentration of large mammals in the Lower 48.

In summer, the best times to see wildlife are from sunrise to early morning or from late afternoon to early evening. At other times of the year they tend to be equally visible in the middle of the day. Bring a pair of binoculars for a close-up view, but make sure your behavior isn't disturbing the animal or causing it to move away. This is particularly true in midwinter when any unnecessary movements lessen their chance for survival. Always stay at least 25 yards from wildlife and 100 yards from bears. Park visitor centers have handouts showing where you're most likely to see wildlife in Yellowstone and Grand Teton.

Yellowstone National Park contains about 60 species of resident mammals, varying from shrews and bats to bison and grizzlies. In addition, 309 species of birds have been recorded, along with 18 species of fish (five of which are nonnative), four amphibians, and six reptiles. The only poisonous animal is the prairie rattlesnake, found at low elevations in the northern end of Yellowstone. Oh yes, countless insect species live here, too. Some Yellowstone critters are friendlier than others, most notably the mosquitoes that show up in large numbers early in the summer. By mid-August they're much less of a hassle, and winter visitors will have no problems at all.

BEARS

During Yellowstone's early years, bears were commonly viewed as either pets or nuisances. Cubs were tethered to poles in front of the hotels, and other bears fed on the garbage piles that grew up around the camps and hotels. Older folks still recall the bear-feeding grounds at the garbage dumps, where visitors might see 50 bears pawing through the refuse. The feeding shows continued until 1941, but it wasn't until 1970 that the park's open-pit dumps were finally sealed off and the garbage cans bear-proofed. Closure of the dumps helped create confrontations between "garbage bears" and humans; the bears nearly always lost. Between 1970 and 1972, dozens of grizzlies died in showdowns with humans in the park or surrounding areas. Fortunately, careful management in the intervening years has helped the population rebound. Today there are believed to be at least 400 grizzlies in the Greater Yellowstone Ecosystem, and their numbers have been increasing fairly steadily since the 1980s. (Some scientists believe there are more than 600 grizzlies.)

One unusual aspect of the Yellowstone grizzlies was just discovered in recent years: the importance of moths as a food source in the grizzly diet. Millions of army cutworm moths congregate on Yellowstone's high alpine slopes during summer, where they feed on nectar from the abundant flowers. Bears are attracted to this food source because of the insect's abundance and high fat content. Researchers have sometimes seen two dozen bears feeding on a single slope!

Old-timers joke that bears are easy to differentiate: A black bear climbs up the tree after you, whereas a grizzly snaps the tree off at the base. Black bears live in forested areas throughout Wyoming, but grizzlies exist mainly in the northwest corner of the state, primarily within and around Yellowstone National Park. Both grizzlies and black bears pose potential threats to backcountry travelers, although you are considerably more likely to be involved in a car accident while driving to a wilderness area than to be attacked by a bear once you arrive. (See *Health and Safety* for tips on safety around bears.)

Grizzlies once ranged across the entire Northern Hemisphere, from Europe across what is now Russia and through the western half of North America. When Europeans arrived, there were perhaps 50,000–100,000 grizzlies in what would become the Lower 48 states. Unfortunately, as white settlers moved in, they came to view these massive and powerful creatures (average adult males weigh 500 pounds) as a threat to themselves and their livestock. The scientific name, *Ursus arctos horribilis,* says much about human attitudes toward grizzlies.

Grizzlies still have healthy populations in Alaska and western Canada, but elsewhere they were shot, trapped, and poisoned nearly to the brink of extinction. In the Lower 48 states grizzlies survive in only a few of the most remote parts of Montana, Wyoming, Idaho, and Washington. By 1975, when the U.S. Fish and Wildlife Service listed them as threatened, fewer than 1,000 grizzlies survived south of Canada.

BIGHORN SHEEP

These stocky mountain dwellers are named for the massive curling horns of the males (rams). They have a tan-colored coat with a white rump patch. Bighorns were once abundant throughout the western United States, and early trappers in the mountains east of Yellowstone reported finding thousands of sheep in and around the present-day park. They were also an important source of food for the Sheepeater Indians who lived in Yellowstone before the arrival of whites. Bighorn sheep were virtually wiped out by hunters in the late 19th century, and domestic sheep overran their lands and brought deadly diseases. Within a few decades, the millions of sheep that had roamed the West were reduced to a few hundred survivors, though the population has since rebounded.

Both the rams and ewes (females) have horns that remain for life, but only the rams get the curl for which bighorn sheep are known. Rams are 125–275 pounds in size, with ewes 75–150 pounds. During the mating season in November and December you're likely to see the original head-bangers in action as rams clash to establish dominance. The clashes can be surprisingly violent, and to protect the brain, bighorns have a double cranium that absorbs much of the shock. Those with the larger horns are typically the dominant bighorns and the primary breeders. Lambs are born in May and June. In summer the sexes separate, with the ewes and lambs remaining lower while the bachelor herds climb higher into the mountains. Bighorns use their ability to climb steep and rocky terrain as protection from predators such as coyotes, wolves, and mountain lions. Winter often finds bighorns in mixed herds at lower elevations. Around 250 bighorns live within Yellowstone National

Park, with much larger populations in the surrounding national forests.

BISON

The bison is the definitive frontier animal and Wyoming's state mammal—its outline graces the state flag. Weighing up to 2,000 pounds, these are the largest land mammals in the New World. Bison live 45 years or more, with females bearing calves until they are in their 40s. The calves weigh 30–40 pounds at birth and within minutes are standing and able to graze. Two races of bison exist: the plains bison, primarily east of the Rockies, and the mountain bison (sometimes called wood bison) in the higher elevations. Technically, these huge, hairy beasts are bison—the only true buffalo are the water buffalo of Southeast Asia—but the name buffalo is commonly used.

With their massive heads, huge shoulder humps, heavy coats of fur, and small posteriors, buffalo are some of the strangest animals in North America. They look so front-heavy as to seem unstable, ready to topple forward onto their snouts at any time. Despite this impression, buffalo are remarkably well adapted to life on the plains. A bison will use its strong sense of smell to find grass buried in a deep snowdrift and then sweep the snow away with a sideways motion of its head. The animals are also surprisingly fleet-footed, as careless Yellowstone photographers have discovered. In addition, the buffalo is one very tough critter. In 1907, a buffalo was pitted against four of the meanest Mexican bulls at a bullring in Juárez, Mexico. After knocking heads several times with the buffalo, the bulls fled and were saved only when bullfighters opened the chute gates to let them escape.

Before their virtual annihilation in the 19th century, around 60 million bison were spread across America. When Yellowstone was established in 1872, hundreds of mountain bison (also called wood bison) still ranged across this high plateau. Sport and meat hunting—legal until 1894—and later poaching reduced the population so that by 1902 perhaps fewer

bison in Yellowstone National Park

© DON PITCHER

than 25 remained in the park. That year, 21 plains bison were brought in from private ranches in Montana and Texas to help restore the Yellowstone herd, and today there are more than 4,000 in the park, making this the largest free-ranging herd of bison anywhere on earth. Another 500 live in Grand Teton National Park. Unfortunately, interbreeding between the mountain and plains bison means that the animals in Yellowstone today are genetically different from the original inhabitants. In any case, the population has rebounded dramatically in the last century, and today 65,000 bison roam across America.

A favorite time to see bison in Yellowstone is late May, just after the new calves have been born. The calves' antics are always good for laughs. Be sure to use caution around bison; many people have been gored when they've come too close. Always stay at least 25 yards away, preferably farther. You'll find some entertaining (and simultaneously scary) wildlife safety videos of bison encounters with foolish tourists on the Yellowstone website (www .nps.gov/yell).

Cattle Versus Bison

Bison are carriers of brucellosis, a disease that causes cows to abort calves and is the source of undulant fever in humans. Brucellosis can be spread when other animals lick a contaminated fetus or birthing material, a situation that is unlikely given the timing of bison movements. In 1985, Yellowstone's bison began wandering north into the Gardiner area for the winter. Montana and Wyoming are certified as "brucellosis-free" states, and although there is no evidence that wild bison have ever transmitted the disease to cattle, ranchers feared that the bison might threaten Montana's brucellosis-free status. If cattle become infected, ranchers might be prohibited from shipping livestock out of state.

A highly controversial "hunt" during the late 1980s let hunters shoot bison when they wandered outside the park. After a public outcry, the job was turned over to the Montana state Division of Livestock (DOL), an agency accustomed to dealing with cattle, not wildlife. Ironically, Yellowstone's far more numerous elk also carry brucellosis, but you won't hear Montana authorities talking about slaughtering all of the elk that wander across the park's borders!

Today, the Park Service, Montana DOL, and U.S. Forest Service operate under a controversial bison-management plan that attempts to simultaneously maintain a free-ranging bison population while reducing the risk of transmission of brucellosis to cattle. Under this plan, some bison are tolerated on outside lands when cattle aren't present, and if the population continues to be high, others can be captured in pens and slaughtered when they wander outside the park, even if they haven't been tested for brucellosis. It's not a pleasant situation, especially for a national park that was established in part to help protect wild bison. Even a Yellowstone publication admits:

> Many park visitors are confused about why the National Park Service is a partner in a plan often results in killing bison, a natural resource the National Park Service goes to great lengths to protect within the boundaries of the park and an animal so representative of the agency's successful protection of wildlife that it is prominently featured on the National Park Service's familiar "arrowhead" logo.

In heavy snow winters (such as 2007–2008) fully a third of Yellowstone's bison can be sent to slaughter, leading to a widespread outcry from advocacy groups. Fortunately, the bison population rebounds, typically reaching the old level of 4,000 within eight years or so. You can find much more about this issue on the Yellowstone National Park website, www.nps .gov/yell, or in a variety of publications from the visitor centers.

Buffalo Field Campaign (www.buffalo fieldcampaign.org) is a West Yellowstone-based environmental group that has been at loggerheads with the Park Service and DOL over bison management for years.

COYOTES

Although wolves get the media attention, visitors to Yellowstone are probably more likely to see another native of the dog family: the coyote. Differentiating coyotes from wolves can be a bit tricky, especially from a distance without binoculars. Coyotes are considerably smaller animals; adult male coyotes weigh around 30 pounds, whereas wolves are far more massive, with many weighing 100 pounds or more. The wolf has a large head, short and rounded ears, and a broad and blocky muzzle, whereas the coyote has a small head, large and pointy ears, and a narrow, pointy nose. From a distance coyotes are more delicate in appearance, with smaller feet and thin legs.

The coyotes within Yellowstone generally live in packs containing 6–7 animals led by a dominant pair called the alpha male and female. Most packs have a long family lineage and a well-defined territory; some coyote packs have been using the same denning areas for at least 50 years! The average coyote lives about six years. The alphas mate in early February, and pups are born in early April. Other members of the pack guard the den from wolves and other predators and regurgitate food to feed the pups.

Top Dog No More

Before the reintroduction of wolves, coyotes were the big dogs (so to speak) in northern Yellowstone, and the primary predators of elk calves, killing about 1,200 each year. Wolves occupy a similar ecological niche as coyotes do, and their return has led to a 50 percent reduction in coyote numbers in northern Yellowstone. Some of this decrease comes from outright killing of coyotes by the far larger wolves, particularly alpha coyotes. The ever-resourceful coyotes have responded by banding together in larger packs, denning in rocky areas, becoming more wary, and staying on the margins of wolf territories. Despite competition, coyotes remain common and are certainly in no danger of being displaced from Yellowstone; after all, both species were here for thousands of years before the extermination of wolves in the 20th century.

DEER

Mule deer (also known as black-tailed deer) are common in many parts of Yellowstone during summer, but most migrate to lower elevations when winter comes. They are typically found in open areas containing sagebrush or grass. Mule deer are named for their long mulelike ears. They also have black-tipped tails and a peculiar way of pogoing away when frightened. Adult males (bucks) grow antlers each summer, and mating season arrives in November and December. Fawns are born in May or June.

The smaller **white-tailed deer** are occasionally seen within Yellowstone but are far less common. You are most likely to find them along rivers or in brushy areas at low elevations, such as around Mammoth Hot Springs or in Lamar Valley. Other places to watch for them are along Yellowstone Lake and in the Upper Geyser Basin.

ELK

A majestic member of the deer family, elk—some biologists prefer the term "wapiti"—are a favorite with both tourists and hunters. In summer nearly 100,000 elk can be found within the Greater Yellowstone Ecosystem. Bull elk can top 700 pounds, whereas the cows (females) weigh around 500–525 pounds, making elk the second-largest members of the deer family after moose.

Elk spend summers high in the mountains, feeding in alpine meadows and along forest edges. The young males and cows with their calves—generally born in late May and early June—group in large herds for protection. Meanwhile, the bachelor bulls hang out on their own, watching baseball games on TV while drinking Heineken (just kidding; they drink Teton Ale). Bulls grow massive antlers that can weigh 30 pounds or more, which prove useful in the fall mating season as bulls spar with each other.

When the fall rutting season arrives, bulls herd 25 or so cows and calves around, mating when cows come into estrus and defending their harem from other rivals. Approximately 90 percent of the elk cows become pregnant

© DON PITCHER

elk on the National Elk Refuge in Jackson

each year. During the fall, the bugling of bull elk is a common sound in the mountains (particularly noticeable at Mammoth Hot Springs), a challenge to any bull within earshot. It's a strange sound that starts out low, followed by a trumpetlike call and then a series of odd grunts. When a competitor appears, a dominance display often follows—complete with bugling, stomping, and thrashing of the ground—to show who is the baddest bull around. In a fight, bulls lock their massive antlers and try to push and twist until one finally gives in and retreats. These battles help ensure that the healthiest bulls produce the most offspring, although other bulls often wait in the wings for battles over harems, and then rush in to mate with the cows while the larger bulls are sparring. The mating season ends by mid- to late November, and the snows of late fall and winter push elk to lower elevations on the north side of Yellowstone or out of the park into surrounding areas, notably at the National Elk Refuge in Jackson Hole, where they are fed.

When spring comes, the bulls drop their antlers and immediately begin to grow new ones. The elk head back into the high country, following the melting snowline. Calves are born in late May or early June (sometimes during the migration) and weigh 25–40 pounds at birth. Elk—particularly young calves—are an important food source for predators in the Yellowstone ecosystem; almost one-third of the calves are killed each year by wolves, grizzly and black bears, coyotes, and golden eagles.

Elk and bison both can be infected with brucellosis, a bacterium causing spontaneous abortions. Brucellosis is transmitted to other animals by contact with the dead fetus or birthing material and can cause undulant fever in humans. Ranchers worry that brucellosis can spread from elk and bison to cattle, particularly around elk feeding grounds in western Wyoming. To lessen the incidence of brucellosis, state employees now routinely vaccinate elk at the feeding grounds, shooting them in the hindquarters with vaccine-loaded pellets.

MOOSE

The largest member of the deer family, moose are typically seen eating willow bushes in riparian areas. They are the loners of the deer world, and only during the fall mating season are you likely to see males (bulls) and females (cows) together or to see bulls jousting. Bulls can reach 1,300 pounds, while cows grow to 800 pounds and give birth to up to three calves. In addition to enormous racks, the bulls have a distinctive dewlap or "bell" that hangs below their throat but apparently serves no physical purpose. Both Yellowstone and Grand Teton support moose; look for them along streams, willow flats, and other wet places in the summer.

During winter, these moose migrate into high-elevation forests where the snow isn't as deep (tree branches hold the snow) or as crusty as in the open. In these forests they browse on subalpine fir and Douglas fir. The fires of 1988 burned through many of these forests, and the loss of cover has hurt the Yellowstone moose population.

PRONGHORN ANTELOPE

Antelope (biologists prefer the name pronghorn because they are not true antelopes) are sleek ungulates with beautiful reddish-brown coats accented by white throat patches and rumps. Antelope survive on grasses, forbs, and plants that other animals avoid, notably sagebrush—perhaps Wyoming's most abundant plant. They are almost never seen in wooded areas. Antelope are built for speed: Oversized lungs and windpipes give them the ability to run for miles at 30 mph, and they can accelerate up to 45 mph for short bursts. To watch for predators, they have the largest eyes by body weight of any mammal. Despite this speed, antelope have an innate inquisitiveness that makes them relatively easy to hunt, an attribute that nearly drove them to extinction by market hunting in the 20th century. One surprising trait in antelope is their inability to jump fences; instead they crawl under them. Fences that are too low will completely halt their migrations.

Both males and females grow horns, and those on the males typically have a prong (hence the name). Dominant males (bucks) gather harems of females (does) and fawns and fight off other bucks in the late-summer rutting season. In May or June does give birth to 1–2 fawns.

Antelope are abundant in many parts of Wyoming, and more than 400,000 of them live in the state. They are not nearly as common in the northwest corner, where the habitat is more marginal. You'll see small herds in open country within Grand Teton National Park and on the north side of Yellowstone National Park, from Lamar Valley to the Gardiner area.

Pronghorn antelope populations declined sharply in the 1990s within Yellowstone, where they now number around 200 animals. Coyotes and other predators take many newborn fawns each spring and may be a significant factor in the decline, combined with several other factors such as inbreeding caused by the small population; changes in vegetation; loss of habitat to development in their Paradise Valley wintering area north of the park; increasing numbers of fences across their range; and hunting.

WOLVES

Wolves are the largest members of the canids (dog family), with males averaging 70–120 pounds and stretching up to six feet long from head to tail. They are much more massive than coyotes, although the two are sometimes confused. Wolves live in packs of 2–8, led by an alpha male and female, and establish territories to exclude other wolf packs. Most pack members are from an extended family, but they may include outside members. The alphas are the only ones that generally mate, and a litter of six or so pups is born in early spring. Once they are weaned, the pack feeds pups regurgitated meat until they are large enough to join the hunt. Wolves hunt primarily in the evening and morning hours, when their prey—elk, deer, moose, bison, and pronghorn—are feeding.

The reintroduction of wolves to Yellowstone has brought back one of the park's top predators, and for many visitors, it's been a howling success. Today, Yellowstone is one of the few places in the Lower 48 where wolves can be viewed in the wild. Wolves once ranged across nearly all of North America, but white settlers regarded them—along with mountain lions, grizzly bears, and coyotes—as threats to livestock and unwanted predators on game animals. Even in Yellowstone, wolves were hunted and poisoned by both the army and the Park Service. By 1940, the wolf was probably gone from the park, although a few lone animals turned up briefly again in the early 1970s.

In the United States, until 1995, wolves could be found only in Alaska, in northern Minnesota, and in Isle Royale and Glacier national parks. With the more enlightened public attitude evident in recent years, ecologists and conservationists began pushing for the reintroduction of wolves to Yellowstone, considered one of the few remaining areas in the Lower 48 that could support a viable wolf population.

The proposal to return wolves to Yellowstone set off a firestorm from ranchers (with ardent support from Wyoming's Republican senators), who feared that the wolves would wander outside the park to destroy sheep and cattle. Opponents said hundreds of livestock would be killed each year around the park and that the reintroduction cost might reach $1.8 million per wolf, a figure that proved grossly inflated. Despite these dire predictions, the U.S.

Fish and Wildlife Service began reintroducing wolves to Yellowstone in 1995, initially releasing 14 gray wolves that had been captured in British Columbia. Additional wolves were set free the following spring. During subsequent years things have gone far better than anyone had predicted. By 2008, biologists estimated a population of 171 wolves inside Yellowstone National Park, spread across 11 different packs. Approximately 400 wolves inhabit the entire Greater Yellowstone Ecosystem from north and west of Yellowstone to the Pinedale area on the south, and eastward into Shoshone National Forest.

In 2008, the U.S. Fish & Wildlife Service (under the Bush administration) removed wolves from the Endangered Species list, but a court order later reinstated their protected status. If they are delisted, the states of Wyoming, Montana, and Idaho may allow the hunting of wolves to keep their numbers in check. For the latest on the ongoing saga, visit the **U.S. Fish and Wildlife Service's gray wolves homepage** (http://westerngraywolf.fws.gov). The Yellowstone website (www.nps.gov/yell) has additional details on wolves and tips for watching them, or for regional information updated weekly. For a different perspective, check out the Defenders of Wildlife website, www.defenders.org.

Environmental Issues

One of the largest intact temperate-zone ecosystems on the planet, Yellowstone was for decades viewed as an island of nature surrounded by a world of human development. Unfortunately, this attitude has led to a host of problems. Despite its size, Yellowstone alone is not large enough to support a viable population of all the animals that once existed within its borders, and developments outside the park pose threats within. In recent years, there have been increasing calls to treat the park as part of the larger Greater Yellowstone Ecosystem—18 million acres of land at the juncture of Wyoming,

Montana, and Idaho covering both public and private lands. With each year that passes it has become more obvious that Yellowstone can never be simply an island. Most of the issues that have made headlines in the last decade or so—from fisheries problems to snowmobile use—have been ones that spread beyond the artificial park boundaries.

Within surrounding lands, conflicts between development and preservation are even more obvious than within the park itself. Logging is one of the most apparent of these, and along the park's western border aerial photos reveal a perfectly straight line, with lodgepole pines on the park side and old clearcuts on the Forest Service side. One of these was the largest timber sale ever made outside of Alaska. Near the park boundaries, housing developments, the massive growth of the tourism industry, oil and gas drilling, mining, a grizzly bear and wolf theme park, and other activities all create potential problems within the park and for the Yellowstone ecosystem as a whole.

Controversy on the Northern Range

Wildlife has always been one of the big drawing cards at Yellowstone, and early on there were constant charges of mass slaughter by poachers and market hunters. It was not until 1894 that Congress passed the Lacey Act, finally making it illegal to hunt within the park. Unfortunately, predators such as wolves, coyotes, mountain lions, and wolverines were regarded as despoilers of the elk, deer, and moose and became fair targets for poisoning and shooting by early park managers. (This happened throughout the West, not just in the park.) The campaign proved all too successful, devastating the wolf and mountain lion populations. In recent years, wolves have returned in a spectacular way, although mountain lion numbers remain low.

A recurring area of strife in Yellowstone has been the suggestion that elk and bison are overgrazing and destroying the Lamar and Yellowstone river basins, an area known as the northern range. The issue periodically flares up, fed in part by the efforts of Montana ranchers and others who suffer from bison and elk that migrate out of Yellowstone onto their land each winter. They—and some researchers—believe that the Park Service has allowed too many animals to survive and that overgrazing is damaging the land. Most research, however, points in the opposite direction—that the land is not overgrazed, and that ecological processes are working fine in a system termed "natural regulation." The populations of elk and bison fluctuate through time; some years numbers are up, and other years they drop because of harsh winters, predation, hunting outside the park, or other factors.

Yellowstone National Park History

Yellowstone National Park has a rich and fascinating history that reaches back through thousands of years of settlement. The most thorough source for history is *The Yellowstone Story* (University Press of Colorado, www.up colorado.com), an excellent two-volume set by former park historian Aubrey L. Haines. For an engaging and personal journey through the past, read *Searching for Yellowstone* by Paul Schullery (Houghton Mifflin, www.hmco.com).

SHEEPEATER INDIANS

The last major glaciation ended around 15,000 years ago, and the first peoples may have reached Yellowstone while the ice was still retreating. There is good evidence that the country was occupied for at least 10,000 years, although the tribes apparently changed through time. By the mid-19th century, the country was surrounded by Blackfeet to the north, Crow to the east, and Shoshone and Bannock to the south and west. These tribes all traveled through and hunted in Yellowstone, building temporary shelters, called wickiups, made of aspen poles covered with pine boughs; a few of these still exist in the park. The primary inhabitants of this high plateau were the Sheepeater Indians, who may have been here for more than 2,000 years. Of Shoshone stock, the Sheepeaters hunted bighorn sheep (hence the name) and made bows from the sheep horns, but their diet also included other animals, fish, roots, and berries. Because they did not have horses, the Sheepeaters used dog-pulled travois to carry their few possessions from camp to camp. Summers were spent in high alpine meadows and along passes, where they hunted migrating game animals or gathered roots and berries. They wintered in protected canyons.

The Sheepeaters were smaller than other Indians and have achieved an aura of mystery because so little is known of their way of living. Yellowstone was at the heart of their territory, but with the arrival of whites came devastating diseases, particularly smallpox. The survivors joined their Shoshone brothers on the Wind River Reservation or the Bannock Reservation in Idaho. The last of the tribe left Yellowstone in the 1870s.

FUR TRAPPERS

The word "Yellowstone" appears to have come from the Minnetaree Indians, who called the river "Mi tsi a-da-zi," a word French-Canadian trappers translated into "Rive des Roche Jaunes"—literally, "River of Yellow Rock." The Indians apparently called it this because of the yellowish bluffs along the river near Billings, Montana (not because of the colorful Grand Canyon of the Yellowstone). The term "Yellow Stone" was first used on a map made in 1797. When the Lewis and Clark Expedition traveled through the country north of Yellowstone in 1805–1806, the Indians told them tales of this mysterious place: "There is frequently heard a loud noise like thunder, which makes the earth tremble, they state that they seldom go there because children Cannot sleep—and Conceive it possessed of spirits, who were adverse that men Should be near them." (This certainly was not the attitude of all the native peoples, for the park had long been inhabited.) The first white man to come through Yellowstone is believed to be John Colter, a former member of the Lewis and Clark Expedition who wandered through the region in the winter of 1807–1808. A map based on Colter's recollections shows Yellowstone Lake ("Eustis Lake"), along with an area of "Hot Spring Brimstone."

As fur trappers spread through the Rockies in the 1820s and 1830s, many discovered the geysers and hot springs of Yellowstone, and

stories quickly spread around the rendezvous fires. The word of the trappers was passed on to later settlers and explorers but not entirely believed. After all, mountain man Jim Bridger described not just petrified trees, but petrified birds singing petrified songs! His tales of a river that "ran so fast that it became hot on the bottom" could well have referred to the Firehole River. When Bridger tried to lead a party of military explorers into Yellowstone, they were stymied by deep snows. Still, word gradually got out that something very strange could be found in this part of the mountains. Little remains today from the mountain-man era, although in 1880 the letters "J.O.R. Aug. 19, 1819" were found carved in a tree near the Upper Falls of the Yellowstone, and later a cache of iron beaver traps similar to those used by the Hudson's Bay Company was discovered near Obsidian Cliff.

MOUNTAIN MEN

The era of the fur trapper is one of the most colorful slices of American history, a time when a rough and hardy breed of men took to the Rockies in search of furs and adventure. Romanticized in such films as *Jeremiah Johnson,* the trappers actually played but a brief role in history and numbered fewer than 1,000 individuals. Their real importance lay in acting as the opening wedge for the West, a vanguard for the settlers and gold miners who would follow their paths—often led by these same mountain men.

The Fur Business

Fashion sent men into the Rockies in the first place, since the waterproof underfur of a beaver could be used to create the beaver hat, which was all the rage in the early part of the 19th century. (It cost a month's wages for a man in England to buy a fine beaver hat in the 1820s!) Beavers in the eastern United States were soon trapped out, forcing trappers to head farther and farther west. Several companies competed for the lucrative fur market, but John Jacob Astor's American Fur Company proved the most successful. In 1811, Astor sent a party of men across the Rockies to the mouth of the Columbia to build a trading post and then set up a chain of posts across the West. The men—known as the Astorians—were probably the first whites to follow the route that would later become the Oregon Trail.

John Jacob Astor's trappers went head to head against the Rocky Mountain Fur Company, which was owned at various times by some of the most famous mountain men—Jedediah Smith, David Jackson, William and Milton Sublette, Jim Bridger, Thomas Fitzpatrick, and others. Competition for furs became so intense that Astor's men began following Jim Bridger and Tom Fitzpatrick to discover their trapping grounds. After trying unsuccessfully to shake the men tailing them, Bridger and Fitzpatrick deliberately headed into the heart of Blackfeet country, where Indians killed the leader of Astor's party and managed to leave Bridger with an arrowhead in his shoulder that was not removed until three years later.

A large number of Indians (particularly from the Flathead and Nez Perce tribes) were also involved in the fur trade, and a standard Indian trade value was 240 beaver pelts for a riding horse. In the mountains, anything from the world back east had considerable value: guns sold for $100 each, blankets for $40 apiece, tobacco for $3 per pound, and alcohol (often diluted) for up to $64 per gallon. After just two years of such trading, William Ashley retired with an $80,000 profit. Control of the fur market continued to change hands as the Rocky Mountain Fur Company and the American Fur Company competed with each other and with a mysterious company headed by Captain Benjamin Bonneville, which some believe was a front for the U.S. Army to explore the West.

Most of the men who trapped in the Rockies were hired and outfitted by the fur companies, but others worked under contract and traded furs for overpriced supplies. Many men found themselves in debt to the company at the end of a season. At the top of the heap were the free trappers, men who worked either alone or with others but who sold their furs to whoever offered the highest prices. Some men, primarily those who brought trade goods to the rendezvous, became rich in the process. Others, such as John Colter, Jim Bridger, James Beckwourth, Jedediah Smith, Thomas Fitzpatrick, and Kit Carson, would achieve fame for their rich knowledge of the land and their ability to survive against insurmountable odds. Many trappers married Indian women, learned sign language and various Indian tongues, and lived in tepees.

Trappers worked through the winter when the beaver pelts were their finest; most summers were spent hunting and fishing, or hanging out with fellow trappers or friendly Indians. A good trapper could take in more than 150 beaver in a year, worth $4–6 apiece. It was an arduous job, and the constant threat of attacks by the Blackfeet Indians made it even more difficult. The great letting-go came with the summer rendezvous, an event anticipated for months ahead of time.

The Rendezvous

William H. Ashley, founder of the Rocky Mountain Fur Company, was one of the most important figures in the fur trade. Ashley's company of men—along with $10,000 in supplies—made it up into the Yellowstone River country that summer, and the success of the trappers led to the first rendezvous in 1825 on the Henrys Fork near its confluence with the Green River, along the present-day Wyoming–Utah border. Thus began the first rendezvous. They would take place every summer until 1840. Ashley failed to bring booze that first summer, and the rendezvous lasted only two days. In future years, however, the whiskey flowed freely, and the festivities lasted for weeks.

The rendezvous—a French word meaning "appointed place of meeting"—was a time when both white and Indian trappers could sell their furs, trade for needed supplies and Indian women (who had little say in the matter), meet with old friends, get rip-roaring drunk, and engage in storytelling, gambling, gun duels, and contests of all sorts. Horse racing, wrestling bouts, and shooting contests were favorites— Kit Carson killed Shunar, a big French bully, in a duel during one of the Green River rendezvous. Debauchery reigned supreme in these three-week-long affairs, and by the time they were over, many of the trappers had lost their entire year's earnings.

During the heyday of the fur trade, a common saying was "all trails lead to the Seedskeedee [Green River]." Six rendezvous were held here in the 1830s, others were held in the Wind River/Popo Agie River area, on Ham's Fork of the Green River, and in Idaho and Utah. Sites were chosen where there was space for up to 500 mountain men and 3,000 Indians, plenty of game, ample grazing for the thousands of horses, and good water. Not coincidentally, all were held in Shoshone country rather than farther east or north, where the hostile Sioux, Blackfeet, and Crow held sway. Despite such precautions, more than half of Ashley's men were scalped by Indians.

Changing Times

The end of the rendezvous system—and most of the Rocky Mountain fur trapping—came about for a variety of reasons: overtrapping, the financial panic of 1837, and the growing use of other materials, particularly the South American nutria and Chinese silk, for hats. In addition, permanent trading posts such as Fort Laramie drew Indians away from the mountains to trade for buffalo robes instead of beaver furs. By 1840, when the last rendezvous was held on the banks of the Green River near present-day Pinedale, it was obvious there would be no more.

EXPEDITIONS

National attention finally came to Yellowstone with a series of three expeditions to check out the wild claims of local prospectors. In 1869, David E. Folsom, Charles W. Cook, and William Peterson headed south from Bozeman, finding the Grand Canyon, Yellowstone Lake, and the geyser basins. When a friend pressured them to submit a description of their travels for

publication, the *New York Tribune* refused to publish it, noting that the paper "had a reputation that they could not risk with such unreliable material."

The adventures of this first expedition led another group of explorers into Yellowstone the following year, but this time money was the motive. Jay Cooke's Northern Pacific Railroad needed investors for a planned route across Montana. A good public-relations campaign was the first step, and it happened to coincide with the visit of a former Montana tax collector named Nathaniel P. Langford, who had heard of the discoveries of Folsom, Cook, and Peterson. The party of 19 soldiers and civilians, including Langford, headed out in August of 1870 under General Henry D. Washburn. They were thrilled by what they discovered and proceeded to give the geysers names—Old Faithful, Castle, Giant, Grotto, Giantess—which became permanently attached to the features. The joy of the trip was marred when one man—Truman Everts— became separated from the others and then lost his horse. He was not found until 37 days later, by which time he weighed just 50 pounds. His rescuer did not even recognize him as human. Amazingly, Everts survived and recovered.

With the return of the Washburn Expedition, national newspapers and magazines finally began to pay attention to Yellowstone, and Langford began lecturing in the East on what they had found. One of those listening was Dr. Ferdinand V. Hayden, director of the U.S. Geological Survey. Hayden asked Congress to fund an official investigation. With the help of Representatives James G. Blaine (coincidentally a supporter of the Northern Pacific Railroad) and conservationist Henry M. Dawes, Congress appropriated $40,000 for an exploration of "the sources of the Missouri and Yellowstone Rivers." Thus began the most famous and influential trip into Yellowstone— the 1871 Hayden Expedition. The troop included 34 men, an escort of cavalry, painter Thomas Moran, and photographer William H. Jackson.

ESTABLISHING THE PARK

When Hayden returned to Washington to prepare his report, he found a letter from railroad promoter Jay Cooke. In the letter, Cooke proposed that "Congress pass a bill reserving the Great Geyser Basin as a public park forever—just as it has reserved that far inferior wonder the Yosemite valley and big trees." (Abraham Lincoln had established Yosemite earlier as a state park.) In an amazingly short time, a bill was introduced to set aside the land, and Hayden rushed to arrange a display in the Capitol rotunda of geological specimens, sketches by Moran, and photos by Jackson. The bill easily passed both houses of Congress and was signed into law on March 1, 1872, by President Ulysses S. Grant. The first national park had come into existence, a culmination not just of the discoveries in Yellowstone but also of a growing appreciation for preserving the wonders of the natural world.

Congress saw no need to set aside money for this new creation because it seemed to be doing fine already. Besides, it was thought that Jay Cooke's new railroad would soon arrive, making it easy for thousands of vacationers to explore Yellowstone. In turn, concessioners would build roads and hotels and pay the government franchise fees. The park was placed under the control of the Secretary of the Interior, with Nathaniel P. Langford as its unpaid superintendent. Meanwhile, the planned railroad fizzled when Jay Cooke and Co. declared bankruptcy, precipitating the panic of 1873.

THE NEZ PERCE WAR

One of the saddest episodes in the history of Yellowstone took place in 1877 and involved the Nez Perce Indians of Oregon's Wallowa Valley. When the government tried to force the people of Chief White Bird and Chief Joseph onto an Idaho reservation so that white ranchers could have their lands, the Indians stubbornly refused. A few drunken young Indians killed four whites, and subsequent raids led to the deaths of at least 14 more. The army retaliated but was turned back by the Nez Perce. Rather than face government reinforcements, more than 1,000 Nez Perce began an 1,800-mile flight in a desperate bid to reach Canada. A series of running battles followed as the Indians managed to confound the inept army using their geographic knowledge and battle skills. The Nez Perce entered Yellowstone from the west, and a few hotheads immediately attacked vacationing tourists and prospectors. Two whites were killed in the park, others were kidnapped, and another man nearly died from his wounds.

The Nez Perce exited Yellowstone two weeks after they arrived, narrowly missing an encounter with their implacable foe, General William T. Sherman, who just happened to be vacationing in Yellowstone at the time. East of the park, the Indians plotted a masterful escape from two columns of army forces, feinting a move down the Shoshone River and then heading north along a route that left their pursuers gasping in amazement – straight up the narrow Clarks Fork Canyon, "where rocks on each side came so near together that two horses abreast could hardly pass." Finally, less than 40 miles from the international border with Canada, the army caught up with the Nez Perce, and after a fierce battle the tribe was forced to surrender (although 300 did make good their escape).

Chief Joseph's haunting words still echo through the years: "Hear me, my chiefs, I am tired; my heart is sick and sad. From where the sun now stands, I will fight no more forever." Despite promises that they would be allowed to return home, the Nez Perce were hustled onto reservations in Oklahoma and Washington while whites remained on their ancestral lands. Chief Joseph spent the rest of his life on Washington's Colville Reservation and died in 1904, reportedly of a broken heart. Yellowstone's Nez Perce Creek, which feeds the Firehole River, is named for this desperate bid for freedom.

ROADS AND RAILROADS

Because of the difficult access, fewer than 500 people visited in each of Yellowstone's first few years as a park, most to soak in tubs at Mammoth Hot Springs. Not a few decided to take home souvenirs, bringing pickaxes and shovels for that purpose. Meanwhile, hunters—including some working for the Mammoth Hotel—began shooting the park's abundant game. Two brothers who had a ranch just north of the park killed 2,000 elk in a single year. Superintendent Langford did little to stop the slaughter and bothered to visit the park only twice. Finally, in 1877, the Secretary of the Interior fired him, putting Philetus W. Norris in charge instead. Norris proved a good choice, despite a knack for applying his name to everything in sight. (Most of his attempts at immortality have been replaced by other titles, but Norris Geyser Basin, Norris Road, and even the town of Norris, Michigan, remain.)

Norris oversaw construction of the first major road in Yellowstone, a rough 60-mile route built in just 30 days to connect Upper Geyser Basin with Mammoth and the western entrance. All of this was precipitated by the raids of the Nez Perce Indians earlier that summer and threats that the Bannock Indians would strike next. In addition, Norris began, but never completed, the Queen's Laundry, a bathhouse that is considered the first government building built for the public in any national park. The log walls are still visible in a meadow near Lower Geyser Basin.

By 1882, Norris had managed to alienate the company that helped found the park, the Northern Pacific Railroad. The company announced plans to build a railroad line to the geysers and construct a large hotel, "being assured by the Government of a monopoly therein." Norris's opposition led to his being fired and replaced by railroad man Patrick H. Conger. Soon, however, the scheme began to unravel. The Yellowstone Park Improvement Company—whose vice president happened to be construction superintendent for the Northern Pacific's branch line into Gardiner—had planned not just a lodging monopoly but also a monopoly on all transportation, timber rights, and ranching privileges in the park. Later it was discovered that the company had contracted for 20,000 pounds of venison (killed in the park) to feed the construction crews. As one newspaper writer commented, "It is a 'Park Improvement Company' doing this, and I suppose they consider it an improvement to rid the park, as far as possible, of game."

Finally, in 1884 Congress acted by limiting the land that could be leased—thus effectively ending the railroad's plans—and adding funding to hire 10 assistants to patrol Yellowstone. Unfortunately, it neglected to include any penalties for the poachers and despoilers other than expulsion, so even the few assistants who did decent work found the culprits quickly returning. The problems were myriad. Cooke City miners were fishing with spears, seine nets, and even dynamite. Guides were throwing rocks into the geysers, squatters had ensconced themselves on prime land in Lamar Valley, and visitors were leaving fires unattended and breaking off specimens from the geysers.

Superintendent Conger was later replaced by Robert E. Carpenter, a man about whom historian Hiram Chittenden noted, "In his opinion, the Park was created to be an instrument of profit to those who were shrewd enough to grasp the opportunity." Carpenter lobbied Congress to remove lands from the park so that the Northern Pacific could construct a railroad along the Yellowstone and Lamar rivers to Cooke City. In return, friends promised to locate claims in his name along the route so that he too might profit from the venture. The landgrab fell apart when the Senate vetoed the move, and Carpenter was summarily removed from office. Not long thereafter, Congress flatly refused to fund the civilian administration of Yellowstone, and the Secretary of the Interior was forced to request the aid of the military in 1886. It proved a fortuitous step.

THE ARMY YEARS

The U.S. Army finally brought a semblance of order to Yellowstone, eliminating the political appointees who viewed the park as a place to get rich. That first year, a temporary fort—Camp Sheridan—was thrown up and a troop of soldiers arrived, but it wasn't until 1891 that work began on a permanent Fort Yellowstone at Mammoth. By 1904, the fort consisted of some 26 buildings housing 120 men. The soldiers had clear objectives—protecting wildlife (or at least bison and elk) from poachers, fighting fires, stopping vandalism, and generally achieving order out of chaos. These goals were accomplished with a fervor that gained widespread respect, and in a way that would later influence the organization of the National Park Service. One of the major accomplishments of the soldiers was completion of the Grand Loop Road, which passes most of Yellowstone's attractions. The basic pattern was completed by 1905.

Fort Yellowstone was a favorite station for soldiers, and it was considered something of an honor to be sent to such a setting. The life of the soldiers was not always easy, however, and some died in the bitter winters or in accidents. A series of 16 soldier stations—actually little more than large cabins—was established around the park, and each was manned year-round, usually by four soldiers.

Before the arrival of cars, many visitors to Yellowstone were wealthy people from the East Coast or Europe intent on doing the grand tour of the West. The railroads (Northern Pacific to the north, Union Pacific to the west, and the Burlington to the east) deposited them near park borders, where they were met by carriages, Tallyhos (26-passenger stagecoaches), and surreys. In 1915, 3,000 horses were in use within the park! Most "dudes" paid approximately $50 for a six-day tour that included transportation, meals, and lodging at the hotels. They paid another $2.50 for the privilege of sailing across Yellowstone Lake on the steamship *Zillah*. By contrast, another group, the "sagebrushers," came to Yellowstone in smaller numbers, arriving in their own wagons or hiring a coach to transport them between the "Wylie Way" campgrounds. These seasonal tent camps were scattered around the park, providing an inexpensive way to see the sights—just $35 for a seven-day tour. Even as early as 1908, Yellowstone was being seen by 18,000 visitors per year.

The Northern Pacific was still intent on carving Yellowstone into a moneymaking resort, even going so far as to propose an electric railroad, to be powered by a dam at the falls of the Yellowstone River. Fortunately, equally powerful forces—notably General Philip Sheridan and naturalist Joseph Bird Grinnell—saw through their designs and thwarted each attempt to bring railroads into Yellowstone. Still, the Northern Pacific's interests were represented by its indirect control of many of Yellowstone's hotels, stagecoaches, wagons, and other vehicles used to transport tourists.

All of this changed when the first car was allowed through the gate on August 1, 1915. (Entrance fees were a surprisingly stiff $5 (around $100 in today's dollars) for single-seat vehicles and $7.50 for five-passenger cars.) Almost immediately, it became clear that horses and cars could not mix, and motor buses replaced the old coaches. From then on, the park would be increasingly a place for "autoists." Interestingly, within a year the park would come under the jurisdiction of the newly created National Park Service.

THE PARK SERVICE TAKES OVER

After years of army control, supporters of a separate National Park Service finally had their way in 1916. The congressional act created a dual role for the new park system: to "conserve the scenery" and to "provide for the enjoyment of the same," a contradictory mandate that would later lead to all sorts of conflicts. The first couple of years were tenuous, as management flip-flopped between the army and civilians; the final changeover came in 1918 and ended three decades of military supervision. The management of Yellowstone fell on the shoulders of two men, Horace M. Albright and his mentor, Stephen Mather, both of whom had been heavily involved in lobbying to create the new agency. Mather became the Park Service's first director, while Albright served as superintendent at Yellowstone and later stepped into Mather's shoes to head the agency.

Albright quickly upgraded facilities to meet the influx of motorists who demanded more camping facilities but also cabins, lodges, cafeterias, and bathhouses. Forty-six camps of one sort or another were constructed (only 12 survive today), fulfilling Albright's dream of "a motorist's paradise." The focus of the new Park Service was clearly visitation rather than preservation. Albright assembled a first-rate force of park rangers and instituted the environmental-education programs that have been the agency's hallmark ever since.

As the automobile took over Yellowstone, the railroads gradually lost their sway, and the final passenger train to the park's gateway towns stopped in 1960. In the 1950s, the Park Service initiated "Mission 66," a decade-long project to upgrade facilities and add lodging. By the late 1960s, a growing appreciation for the natural world was shifting public opinion away from such developments, and the 1973 master plan scaled back proposed developments. From day one, Yellowstone National Park had been set up for what Edward Abbey called "industrial tourism." The park had come into existence in part because of a railroad promoter who hoped to gain from its development, and it grew to maturity on a diet of roads, hotels, and curio shops. In recent years, Americans have taken a second look at this heritage and have begun to wonder which matters more: providing a public playground or preserving an area that is unique on this planet. The inherent conflict between the need for public facilities and services in Yellowstone and the survival of a functioning ecosystem will continue to create a tug-of-war between various factions.

Certainly the most famous recent event was the series of massive fires that swept across nearly half of Yellowstone in 1988. The land has recovered surprisingly well since then, and in recent years other issues came to the fore: wolf reintroduction, the killing of bison on the park boundaries, snowmobile and other winter use, and problems caused by exotic species and fish disease. There's always something stewing in the mud pots of Yellowstone! Some things have been improving in recent years, including efforts to repair aging roads and to replace outdated buildings in the park. Despite any problems and controversies, the park is just as fascinating as ever. The geysers never cease to amaze visitors, the scenery remains majestic, the Grand Canyon of the Yellowstone is still just as stunning, and the superb wildlife-viewing continues to make this the Serengeti of America.

THE YELLOWSTONE FIRES OF 1988

Many will long remember the summer of 1988 as the year that fires seared Yellowstone National Park. TV reporters flocked to the park, pronouncing the destruction of America's most famous national wonder as they stood before trees turned into towering torches and 27,000-foot-high clouds of black smoke. Newspaper headlines screamed, "Park Sizzles," "Winds Whip Fiery Frenzy Out of Control," and "Firestorms Blacken Yellowstone." Residents of nearby towns complained of lost tourism dollars, choking smoke, and intentionally lit backfires that threatened their homes and businesses; Wyoming politicians berated the Park Service's "Let Burn" policy; President Reagan expressed astonishment that fires were ever allowed to burn in the national parks, although the policy had been in place for 16 years. Perhaps the most enduring image is from a forest that had been blown down by tornado-force winds in 1984 and then burned by the wind-whipped fires of 1988. The media ate it up, with one headline reading, "Total Destruction: Intense Heat and Flames from the Fires in Yellowstone Left Nothing but Powdered Ash and Charcoal Near Norris Junction." Unfortunately, the real story behind the fires of '88 was lost in this media feeding frenzy.

A Century of Change

In reality, these fires were not unprecedented; we were just fortunate enough to witness a spectacle of nature that may not occur for another 300 years. When Yellowstone National Park was established in 1872, most of the land was carpeted with a mixture of variously aged stands of lodgepole pine established after a series of large fires. Fewer large fires, partly because of a fire-suppression policy in effect until 1972, meant that by the 1980s one-third of the park's lodgepole stands were more than 200 years old. Yellowstone was ripe to burn.

Since the early 1950s, Smokey the Bear had drummed an incessant message: "Only You Can Prevent Forest Fires." Forest fires were viewed as dangerous, destructive forces that had to be stopped to protect our valuable public lands. Unfortunately, this immensely effective and generally valid ad campaign convinced the public that *all* fires were bad. Ecological research has shown not only that this is wrong, but also that putting out all fires can sometimes create conditions far more dangerous than if fires had been allowed to burn in the first place. Fire, like the other processes that have affected Yellowstone—cataclysmic volcanic explosions, geothermal activity, and massive glaciation—is neither good nor evil. It is simply a part of the natural world that national parks are attempting to preserve. Unfortunately, national parks are no longer surrounded by similarly undeveloped land, so when fires burned in Yellowstone and on adjacent Forest Service lands, they also affected nearby towns and the people who made a living from tourism or logging.

Fire in Lodgepole Forests

Fire has played an important role in lodgepole pine forests for thousands if not millions of years, and as a result the trees have evolved an unusual adaptation. Some of the cones are sealed with a resin that melts in a fire, thus releasing the seeds. The parent trees are killed, but a new generation is guaranteed by the thousands of pine seeds released to the bare, nutrient-rich soil underneath the blackened overstory. Within five years the landscape is dotted with thousands of young pines, competing with a verdant cover of grasses and flowers.

Although some animals are killed in the

wildfires (including, in 1988, at least 269 of Yellowstone's 30,000 elk), and others, weakened by the lack of food available immediately after the fire, succumb to the rigors of the next succeeding winter, the early decades after major fires create conditions that are unusually rich for many animals. Wildlife diversity in lodgepole forests reaches a peak within the first 25 years after a fire as woodpeckers, mountain bluebirds, and other birds feed on insects in the dead trees, and elk and bears graze on the lush grasses.

As the forest ages, a dense thicket of trees develops, keeping light from reaching the forest floor and making it difficult for understory plants to survive. These trees are eventually thinned by disease and windthrow, creating openings in the forest, but after 200–300 years without fire, lodgepole forests become a tangle of fallen trees that are difficult to walk through, are of lesser value to many animals, and burn easily. They also become susceptible to attacks by bark beetles, such as those that killed thousands of acres of trees in Yellowstone starting in the 1960s and continuing through the 1980s. These beetle-killed trees added to the fuel available to burn once a fire started.

Yellowstone in 1988

Yellowstone's 1988 fires were caused by not just the heavy fuel loading from aging forests but also by weather conditions that were the driest and windiest on record. The winter of 1987–1988 had been a mild one, and by spring there was a moderate-to-severe drought in the park, lessened only by above-normal rainfall in April and May. Since 1972, when Yellowstone Park officials first began allowing certain lightning fires to burn in backcountry areas, the acreage burned had totaled less than 2 percent of the park. (Mistakenly called a "Let Burn" policy, the natural fire program actually involved close monitoring of these lightning-ignited fires to determine when and if a fire should be suppressed. All human-caused fires were immediately suppressed, as were any that threatened property or life.)

When the first lightning fires of the 1988

season began in late May, those in the back-country areas were allowed to burn, as fire management officials anticipated normal summer weather conditions. Many fires went out on their own, but when June and July came and the rains failed to materialize, the fires began to spread rapidly. Alarmed park officials declared them wildfires and sent crews to put them out. (Ironically, the largest fire, the North Fork/Wolf Lake Complex, was started by a logger outside the park who tossed a lit cigarette to the ground. Although firefighters immediately attacked the blaze, it consumed more than 500,000 acres.) As the summer progressed, more and more firefighters were called in, eventually totaling more than 25,000 personnel, at a cost exceeding $120 million. Firefighters managed to protect most park buildings but had little effect on the forest fires themselves. Experts say that conditions in summer 1988 were so severe that even if firefighters had immediately responded to all of the natural fires, it would likely have made little difference. Yellowstone has experienced these massive fires in the past and will again in the future, no matter what humans do.

Out of Control

August brought worsening conditions with each passing day. Winds blew steadily at 20–40 miles per hour, and gusts up to 70 mph threw firebrands two miles in beyond the firefront, across fire lines, roads, and even over the Lewis River Canyon. The amount of moisture in the large logs was less than that in kiln-dried wood. By mid-August, more than 25 fires were burning simultaneously across the park and in surrounding national forests, with many joining together to create massive complexes, such as the Clover-Mist Fire, the Snake River Complex, and the North Fork/Wolf Lake Complex. On a single day—September 7—more than 100,000 acres burned. Also torched that day were 20 cabins and outbuildings in the vicinity of Old Faithful (out of the more than 400 structures there). Fortunately, all of the major historical buildings were spared. The fires seemed poised to consume the remainder of Yellowstone, but

four days later the season's first snow carpeted the park. Within a few days firefighters had the upper hand.

A Transformed Landscape

The fires had burned nearly 800,000 acres—more than one-third of the park—plus another 600,000 acres on adjacent Forest Service lands. Of the park total, 41 percent was consumed in canopy fires in which all of the trees were killed, and another 35 percent burned in a mixture of ground fires and canopy fires. The remaining acreage suffered lighter burns. Less than one-tenth of 1 percent of the land was burned hot enough to sterilize the soil. The fires killed countless small mammals, along with at least 269 elk, nine bison, six black bears, four deer, and two moose. The drought of 1988 followed by the severe winter of 1988–1989 led to a large die-off of elk and bison, but their carcasses provided food for predators. Since then, wildlife populations have rebounded and may even exceed prefire levels.

It's been almost two decades since the massive fires were put out, and much has changed, including the park's natural-fire program. It was replaced by a somewhat more conservative version that requires managers to provide daily certifications that fires are controllable and that they will remain "in prescription" for another 24 hours. Visitors to Yellowstone today will find dense thickets of young lodgepole pines—some 20 feet tall—in many areas that burned, and other evergreen species are starting to emerge. In other places, grasses, colorful wildflowers, forbs, and other plants dominate. Not everything burned, of course, so you'll also see many green older forests next to burned stands, creating a complex mosaic of habitats that supports a high diversity of animal life. Once you grow accustomed to the burned areas and understand that they are a part of the natural process, they actually add interest to the park and help you appreciate Yellowstone as a functioning ecosystem rather than a static collection of plants and animals.

Take a hike through one of the burned areas to discover the wealth of new life within

Yellowstone. Vistas that were long blocked by forests are now more open and will gradually become more so; by the end of this decade most of the standing dead trees will have fallen. The Park Service has placed informative signboards at sites around Yellowstone describing the fires of 1988 and the changes they brought about. The **Grant Village Visitor Center** has an informative exhibit and film

about the fires. The fires of 1988 are, of course, not the last to strike these forests, and scientists warn that global warming may well lead to more intense fires in the future. Since 1988, thousands of acres have burned in a series of Yellowstone wildfires, and visitors will see evidence of these, especially on the east side of the park where fires in 2003 and 2007 burned almost 40,000 acres.

Grand Teton National Park History

Once the wonders of Yellowstone came to widespread public attention, it took only a few months for Congress to declare that area a national park. But the magnificent mountain range to the south proved an entirely different story. Early on, there were suggestions that Yellowstone be expanded to include the Tetons, but it would take decades of wrangling before Jackson Hole would finally be preserved.

"DAMNING" JACKSON LAKE

Jackson Lake represents one of the sadder chapters in the history of northwestern Wyoming. Jackson Lake Dam was built in the winter of 1910–1911 to supply water for Idaho potato and beet farmers. The town of Moran was built to house construction workers for Jackson Lake Dam and at one time included more than 100 ramshackle structures. Virtually nothing remains of the town. The 70-foot-tall dam increased the size of the natural lake, flooding out more than 7,200 acres of trees and creating a tangle of floating and submerged trunks and stumps. To some, the dam seemed like the serpent in the Garden of Eden, a symbol of the development that would destroy the valley if not stopped. The trees remained in Jackson Lake for many years, creating an eyesore until the Park Service and the CCC finally launched a massive cleanup project in the 1930s. The dam was completely rebuilt in 1988–1989, and while the lake now looks attractive, it remains yet another example of how Wyoming provides water for farmers in surrounding

states. Late in the fall, especially in dry years, the lake can drop to a large puddle with long stretches of exposed bottom at the upper end. Fortunately, Idaho irrigators did not succeed in their planned dams on Jenny, Leigh, and Taggart lakes in what is now Grand Teton National Park.

DUDES AND DEVELOPMENT

Because of the rocky soils and long winters, Jackson Hole has always been a marginal place for cattle ranching, and only in the southern end of the valley are the soils rich enough to support a decent crop of hay. This poor soil and harsh climate saved Jackson Hole from early development and forced the ranchers to bring in dudes to supplement their income. (One old-timer noted, "Dudes winter better than cattle.")

Louis Joy established the first Jackson Hole dude ranch, the JY, in 1908 along Phelps Lake. It was followed a few years later by the Bar BC Ranch of Struthers Burt, an acclaimed East Coast author who had come west as a dude but learned enough to go into the business for himself. The dude ranchers were some of the first to realize the value of Jackson Hole and to support its preservation. Burt proposed that the valley and mountains be saved not as a traditional park but as a "museum on the hoof," where ranching and tourism would join hands to stave off commercial developments. The roads would remain unpaved, all homes would be log, and Jackson would stay a frontier town. Needless to say, that didn't happen.

The movement to save Jackson Hole co-alesced in a 1923 meeting at the cabin of Maude Noble. Horace Albright, superintendent of Yellowstone National Park, was there, along with local dude ranchers, businessmen, and cattlemen who were eager to save the remote valley from exploitation. To accomplish this goal, they proposed finding a wealthy philan-thropist who might be willing to invest the $2 million that would be needed to buy the land. Fortunately, one of Struthers Burt's friends hap-pened to be Kenneth Chorley, an assistant to John D. Rockefeller Jr. Burt used this contact to get Rockefeller interested in the project.

ROCKY TO THE RESCUE
In 1926, Rockefeller traveled west for a 12-day trip to Yellowstone. Horace Albright used the chance to take him on a side trip into Jackson Hole and to proselytize for protection of the valley. What they saw portended badly for the future: the Jenny Lake dance hall, road-side tourist camps and hot dog stands, rusting abandoned cars, and a place that billboards pro-claimed "Home of the Hollywood Cowboy." Rockefeller was angered by the prospect of crass commercial developments blanketing Jackson Hole and quickly signed on to the idea of buy-ing the land and giving it to the Park Service.

To cover his tracks as he bought the land, Rockefeller formed the Snake River Land Company; if ranchers had known that the Rockefeller clan was behind the scheme, they would have either refused to sell or jacked up the price. Only a few residents—mostly sup-porters—knew of the plan. The local banker, Robert Miller, served as land-purchasing agent, although even he opposed letting the Park Service gain control of the valley. Miller used his position to buy out ranches with delinquent mortgages at his Jackson State Bank and then resigned, claiming the whole thing was part of a sinister plot to run the ranchers out and halt "progress." In 1929, Congress voted to estab-lish a small Grand Teton National Park that would encompass the mountains themselves, which stood little chance of development, but not much else. Conservationists knew that

without preservation of the valley below, the wonderful vistas would be lost.

A NATIONAL BATTLEGROUND
Rockefeller and Albright finally went public with their land-buying scheme in 1930, releas-ing a tidal wave of outrage. Antipark forces led by Senator Milward Simpson (father of recently retired Senator Alan Simpson) spent the next decade fighting the park tooth and nail, charging that it would destroy the econ-omy of Jackson Hole and that ranchers would lose their livelihoods. Rockefeller's agents were falsely accused of trying to intimidate holdouts with strong-arm tactics. Congress refused to accept Rockefeller's gift, and local opposition blocked the bill for more than a decade.

Finally, in 1943, President Roosevelt made an end run around the antipark forces; he accepted the 32,000 acres purchased by Rockefeller, added 130,000 acres of Forest Service land, and declared it the Jackson Hole National Monument. The move outraged those in the valley, prompting more hearings and bills to abolish the new national monument. Wyoming's politicians attacked Roosevelt's actions. A bill overturning the decision was pocket-vetoed by the president, but for the next several years, the Wyoming delegation kept re-introducing the measure.

Things came to a head when Wallace Beery—a Reaganesque Hollywood actor—threatened to "shoot to kill" park officials. Beery, who had to use a stepladder to climb on his horse, organized a cattle drive across the monument. Unable to find anyone to fire on in the new monument, his cadres sat on a creek bank and drank a case of beer, cuss-ing out the damn bureaucrats. So much for the Wild West.

By 1947, the tide had turned as increasing postwar tourism revitalized the local economy. Finally, in 1950, a compromise was reached, granting ranchers lifetime grazing rights and the right to trail their cattle across the park en route to summer grazing lands. The new-and-improved Grand Teton National Park had finally come to fruition.

POSTMORTEM

Some of the early fears that Rockefeller would use the new park for his own gain seemed partly justified. For many years his descendants owned the old JY Ranch and used Phelps Lake as something of a semiprivate playground, though it has now been generously donated to the Park Service. Rockefeller also built the enormous Grand Teton Lodge along Jackson Lake and facilities at Colter Bay Village and Jenny Lake, leading some to accuse the family of attempting to monopolize services within the park. The company, Grand Teton Lodge Company, is now owned by Vail Resorts, which manages Jackson Lake Lodge, Jenny Lake Lodge, and Colter Bay Village, along with Jackson Hole Golf and Tennis Club (near Jackson).

Looking back on the controversial creation of Grand Teton National Park, it's easy to see how wrong park opponents were. Teton County has Wyoming's most vibrant economy, and millions of people arrive each year to enjoy the beauty of the undeveloped Tetons. As writer Nathaniel Burt noted, "The old enemies of the park are riding the profitable bandwagon of unlimited tourism with high hearts and open palms." Park opponents' claims that the Park Service would "lock up" the land ring as hollow as similar anti-wilderness claims today by descendants of the same politicians who opposed Grand Teton National Park half a century ago. Without inclusion of the land purchased by Rockefeller, it is easy to imagine the valley covered with all sorts of summer-home developments, RV campgrounds, souvenir shops, motels, billboards, and neon signs. Take a look at the town of Jackson to see what might have been without Rockefeller's philanthropy.

ESSENTIALS

Getting There

Yellowstone National Park fills the north-west corner of Wyoming, with Grand Teton National Park and Jackson Hole immediately to the south. Although bus tours and limited public transportation are available, you will probably want a car to explore the Yellowstone area at your own pace. The vast majority of visitors arrive by car, either by driving their own vehicles or renting one at a regional airport. No interstates lead into this part of Wyoming, but year-round highways provide access from all directions. The closest interstates are I-80 across southern Wyoming, I-25 through eastern Wyoming, I-15 through Idaho, and I-94 across southern Montana.

BY AIR

Commercial airline service is available directly to three towns covered in this book: Cody, Jackson, and West Yellowstone (seasonal). The main regional hub is in Salt Lake City, but many travelers fly into closer airports in Billings and Bozeman, Montana, or Idaho Falls, Idaho. The regional carriers are: **American** (800/433-7300, www.aa.com), **Allegiant Air** (800/432-3810, www.allegiantair.com), **Delta/SkyWest**

(800/221-1212, www.deltaair.com), **Frontier Airlines** (800/432-1359, www.frontierairlines.com), **Northwest Airlines** (800/225-2525, www.nwa.com), and **United/United Express** (800/241-6522, www.unitedairlines.com).

Jackson Hole

A number of carriers provide nonstop service to Jackson Hole Airport (www.jacksonholeairport.com): Delta/SkyWest from Salt Lake City, with seasonal flights out of Atlanta and Cincinnati; American Airlines with summer and winter service from Dallas and Chicago; Northwest Airlines from Minneapolis/St. Paul; United/United Express from Denver year-round and seasonally from Los Angeles; and Frontier Airlines in summer from Denver. Many travelers opt to fly either to Salt Lake (275 miles away) or Idaho Falls (90 miles away) and pick up a rental car for the drive to Jackson.

Other Regional Airports

Delta/SkyWest has direct summer-only flights connecting Salt Lake City with **West Yellowstone, Montana.** Cody's **Yellowstone Regional Airport** (www.flyyra.com) is served by Delta/SkyWest from Salt Lake City and by United Express from Denver.

A 90-mile drive from Jackson, the airport at **Idaho Falls, Idaho** (www.ci.idaho-falls.id.us) is served by Horizon/Alaska from Seattle (via Boise), Delta/Sky West from Salt Lake City, Northwest Air from Minneapolis, and Allegiant Air from Las Vegas.

It's an 84-mile drive from **Bozeman, Montana** (www.gallatinfield.com) to Mammoth Hot Springs on the northwest corner of Yellowstone, or 225 miles from Bozeman to Jackson. Several airlines serve Bozeman: Allegiant Air from Las Vegas, Delta/Sky West from Salt Lake City, Horizon Air from Seattle, Northwest Airlines from Minneapolis, and United from Denver, Los Angeles, San Francisco, and Chicago.

Karst Stage (406/388-2293 or 800/287-4759, www.karststage.com) provides daily wintertime shuttles from the Bozeman airport to West Yellowstone, Mammoth Hot Springs, and Big Sky. No scheduled summertime shuttles, but Karst has custom service from Bozeman to Old Faithful, Mammoth Hot Springs, West Yellowstone, and Big Sky. For all Karst trips be sure to make reservations at least three days ahead.

BY BUS AND TRAIN

The closest **Greyhound** (800/231-2222, www.greyhound.com) stations are in Salt Lake City, Rock Springs, Bozeman, and Billings. Unfortunately, Greyhound does not serve Jackson, Cody, West Yellowstone, Idaho Falls, or other towns in the region. In fact, there is no bus service whatsoever into Cody. **Alltrans/Jackson Hole Express** (307/733-3135 or 800/443-6133, www.jacksonholealltrans.com) has daily shuttle vans to Jackson from Salt Lake City Airport, Idaho Falls, and Pocatello. A wide variety of park bus tours are available from surrounding towns; see the *Yellowstone National Park* and *Grand Teton National Park* chapters for details.

Amtrak's (800/872-7245, www.amtrak.com) California Zephyr runs between Chicago and Oakland but does not come close to Jackson Hole or Yellowstone. The nearest train station is in Salt Lake City, 275 miles from Jackson. Those traveling by train will need to take a bus, rental car, or plane from Salt Lake into Jackson.

FROM SALT LAKE CITY
Airport

Salt Lake City International Airport (www.slcairport.com) is served by most of the major national carriers and is a major hub for Delta/SkyWest, with hundreds of flights daily from around the country. Other large carriers include Southwest, United, Frontier, Continental, American, Northwest, Jet Blue, and US Airways. The airport is seven miles west of downtown and has two terminals and all the amenities travelers expect, including ATMs, Wi-Fi, and play areas for kids. The ground transportation desk is at the far end of baggage claim in both terminals.

Bus

Alltrans/Jackson Hole Express (307/733-3135

or 800/443-6133, www.jacksonholealltrans
.com) has daily buses between Jackson and Salt
Lake City Airport. **Greyhound** (800/231-2222,
www.greyhound.com) has a regional terminal
at 300 South 600 West in Salt Lake City, with
daily runs to San Francisco, Seattle, Denver, and
Los Angeles, but not to the Yellowstone area.

Car Rentals

All the major companies have rental counters
on the ground floor of the short-term parking garage, directly across from the terminal. These include **Advantage** (801/531-1199
or 800/777-5500, www.arac.com), **Alamo**
(801/575-2211 or 800/462-5266, www.alamo
.com), **Avis** (801/575-2847 or 800/230-4898,
www.avis.com), **Budget** (801/575-2821 or
800/527-0700, www.budget.com), **Dollar**
(801/575-2580 or 800/800-4000, www
.dollar.com), **Enterprise** (801/537-7433 or
800/261-7331, www.enterprise.com), **Hertz**
(801/575-2683 or 800/654-3131, www
.hertz.com), **National** (801/575-2277 or
800/227-7368, www.nationalcar.com), and
Thrifty (801/265-6677 or 800/847-4389, www
.thrifty.com).

RV Rentals

A number of companies rent recreation vehicles
in Salt Lake City, including **Access RV** (220 S.
Hwy. 89, 801/936-1200 or 800/327-6910, www
.accessrv.com), **Cruise America** (4125 S. State
St., 801/288-0930 or 800/671-8042, www
.cruiseamerica.com), **Hugh's RV** (250 S. Hwy.
89, 801/936-1010, www.myelmonterv.com),
Let's Go America RV Rentals (4221 S. 500
W., 801/263-3100), and **Pappy's Motorhome
Rentals** (8201 S. State St., 801/262-2100 or
800/888-2230, www.rentmotorhomes.com).

Accommodations

It's an all-day drive to Jackson Hole or West
Yellowstone from Salt Lake City, so if your flight
gets in late, find a room locally or in a town along
the way. Check the Salt Lake City Chamber of
Commerce website (www.saltlakechamber.org)
for an extensive listing of local lodging choices.
A number of comfortable mid-priced places are

close to the airport, including **Airport Quality
Inn** (1659 W. North Temple, 801/533-9000 or
877/424-6423, www.qualityinnairportutah
.com), **Airport Hilton** (5151 Wiley Post Way,
801/539-1515 or 800/999-3736, www.hilton
.com), and **La Quinta Inn and Suites** (1965
N. 1200 W., 801/776-6700 or 866/725-1661,
www.lq.com). All three of these have outdoor
pools, Wi-Fi, and hot tubs, and the La Quinta
also includes a breakfast.

Suggested Driving Routes

There are several ways to drive from Salt
Lake City to **Jackson,** but the shortest route
(via Evanston and Afton) is a rather circu-
itous 274-mile journey. Take I-80 east from
Salt Lake to Evanston, Wyoming (84 miles),
and turn north on Wyoming Hwy. 89, which
wanders back over the border as Utah Hwy.
16 before slicing back into Wyoming. Turn
north on U.S. Hwy. 30 shortly after crossing the Wyoming state line and follow it west
into Idaho, where you turn north again on
U.S. Hwy. 89 in the town of Montpelier. The
rest is pretty straightforward: drive U.S. Hwy.
89 through Star Valley and Alpine, along the
Snake River, through Hoback Junction, and
finally into Jackson.

An alternate—and slightly longer at 294
miles—route to Jackson follows the Green River
Valley, with the Wind River Mountains providing a snowcapped horizon. From Salt Lake
City, take I-80 east to Wyoming exit 18 (13
miles east of Evanston), and turn north on U.S.
Hwy. 189 through Kemmerer (stop to see Fossil
Butte National Monument) and Big Piney. You
may want a side trip to Pinedale before heading
into the mountains along the Hoback River to
Hoback Junction and Jackson.

The most direct route to **West Yellowstone**
is a relatively easy 319 miles. Follow I-84 north
to Tremonton, Utah, and turn onto I-15 to
Idaho Falls, where U.S. Hwy. 10 continues the
rest of the way to West Yellowstone.

FROM BILLINGS, MONTANA
Airport

Montana's largest airport, **Billings Logan**

International Airport (www.flybillings
.com) has daily nonstop flights by Frontier
from Denver, Delta/Sky West from Salt Lake
City, Horizon Air/Alaska Air from Seattle,
Northwest Airlines from Minneapolis, and
United from Denver and Chicago. The airport sits atop a local geological formation
called the Rim Rocks just north of town. The
airport houses a restaurant and bar, Montana-
made gift shop, and children's play area, with
Yellowstone County Museum directly across
the parking lot.

Bus and Shuttle

Greyhound (800/231-2222, www.greyhound
.com) has daily service connecting Billings
with points west all the way to Seattle. If you're
heading east to Fargo, North Dakota, take
Rimrock Stages Trailways (800/255-7566,
www.rimrocktrailways.com). Amtrak's nearest
train service goes through northern Montana.
Phidippides Shuttle Service (307/527-6789
or 866/527-6789, www.codyshuttle.com) provides shuttle vans to Cody, Wyoming.

Car Rentals

Most companies have counters inside the airport terminal, including **Alamo/National**
(406/252-7626 or 800/227-7368 www
.alamo.com), **Enterprise** (406/294-2930 or
800/261-7331, www.enterprise.com), **Hertz**
(406/248-9151 or 800/654-3131, www.hertz
.com), and **Thrifty/Dollar** (406/259-1025
or 800/847-4389, www.thrifty.com). **Avis**
(406/252-8007 or 800/230-4898, www.avis
.com) has a shuttle to its downtown location.

RV Rentals

Rent recreational vehicles locally from **Pierce
RV Center** (443 Zoo Dr., 406/655-8000 or
800/735-6342, www.pirecerv.com) or **Tour
America RV Center** (2220 Old Hardin Rd.,
406/248-7481 or 800/735-1330, www.tour
americarv.com).

Accommodations

A number of Billings places provide lodging if you want to overnight before starting
out for Yellowstone. The Billings Chamber
of Commerce website (www.billingschamber
.com) has a listing and Web links to many of
these. **Dude Rancher Lodge** (415 N. 29th St.,
406/259-5561 or 800/221-3302, www.dude
rancherlodge.com) is a good bargain place with
Old West styling and an attached restaurant.
The downtown **Riverstone Billings Inn** (880
N. 29th St., 406/252-6800 or 800/231-7782,
www.riverstone-inns.com) is a reasonably
priced place with big rooms, fridges and microwaves, and a continental breakfast. Just a
couple of minutes from the airport, **Country
Inn and Suites** (231 Main St., 406/245-9995
or 888/201-1746, www.countryinns.com) provides nice rooms, an indoor pool, continental
breakfast, and Wi-Fi.

Suggested Driving Routes

It's a 127-mile drive from Billings to the
**northeast corner of Yellowstone National
Park.** From Billings, take I-94 16 miles west
to Laurel, and turn south onto U.S. Hwy. 212,
which goes through the pretty mountain town
of Red Lodge before climbing over spectacular
Beartooth Pass (10,947 feet; closed Nov.–
May) and down to the tiny twin settlements of
Cooke City and Silver Gate, Montana, before
entering Yellowstone.

From Billings to **Cody,** the drive is 104 miles,
plus another 52 miles to the **Yellowstone's
east entrance.** From Billings, take I-94 west
to Laurel and turn south on U.S. Hwy. 310
to Bridger, where the road divides. Continue
south on Montana Hwy. 72 to Cody; the road
becomes Wyoming Hwy. 120 when you cross
the state line. Spend a couple of days seeing
the sights in Cody, and then turn west on U.S.
Hwy. 14/16/20 through pretty Wapiti Valley
to the east entrance of Yellowstone, a total distance of 156 miles from Billings.

The town of **Gardiner, Montana** can be
reached by driving west 125 miles on I-94
from Billings to Livingstone, and then south
on U.S. Hwy. 89 to Gardiner; stop at Chico
Hot Springs in appropriately named Paradise
Valley along the way. The total distance is 178
fairly easy miles.

Getting Around

BY CAR

Most summer travelers to the Yellowstone-Grand Teton area—and a substantial number of winter visitors—arrive by car. Some fly into Jackson Hole, Salt Lake City, or Idaho Falls and rent a vehicle, whereas others head out on a grand road trip from home. The northwest corner of Wyoming is accessible from all sides in the summer, but most roads inside Yellowstone National Park are closed when the snow flies.

Maps

Free state highway maps can be found at visitor centers in Wyoming, Montana, and Idaho, but map aficionados should also buy one of the excellent statewide topographic map books published by DeLorme Mapping (800/511-2459, www.delorme.com). These maps are indispensable for travelers heading off main routes and are sold in most local bookstores. National forest maps are also helpful for mountain driving in many parts of Wyoming; buy them in local Forest Service offices.

Car Rentals

You can rent cars, SUVs, and vans in all of the larger towns, and those with airports generally have Hertz, Avis, and other national chains. The best rental rates tend to be in the larger cities, where there's more competition. If you plan to rent a car for an extended period, check travel websites such as www.travelocity.com, www.expedia.com, or www.orbitz.com to see which company offers the best rates. Note, however, that these quotes may not include taxes, which can be substantial, especially if you rent from an airport office. Even if you've made a reservation, it pays to call around once more after you arrive. On one visit I saved hundreds of dollars by getting a last-minute quote. If you're visiting in the summer, try to get a light-colored car; dark ones can get incredibly hot.

Highway Conditions

The national phone number for up-to-date road and travel information is **511**. Dial this number almost anywhere and it will link to regional conditions. In addition, state highway departments provide detailed information on construction delays and current road conditions for Wyoming (888/996-7623, www.wyoroad.info), Montana (800/226-7623, www.mdt511.com), and Idaho (888/432-7623, www.511.idaho.gov). Extensive roadwork is also ongoing within Yellowstone National Park (307/344-7381, www.nps.gov/yell). Get today's regional **weather forecast** at www.crh.noaa.gov/cys.

Winter Closures

Jackson Hole remains accessible by highway year-round, but most roads in Yellowstone National Park close to cars when the first heavy snows block the passes. By the first of November, things are generally shut down all over except for the 56 miles between Gardiner and Cooke City. This is the only road within Yellowstone that remains open all year. The roads are groomed for snowcoaches

(a delightfully old-fashioned way to travel) and snowmobiles mid-December–mid-March. Plowing starts in March, but most park roads don't open for cars again until mid-May and sometimes not until early June. If you're planning a trip early or late in the season, contact the park (307/344-7381, www.nps.gov/yell) for current road conditions.

Within Grand Teton National Park (307/739-3399, www.nps.gov/grte), U.S. Hwy. 89/191/287 is plowed from Moran Junction to Flagg Ranch throughout the winter, providing a starting point for snowcoaches and guided snowmobiles heading into Yellowstone. Most other roads in Grand Teton are not plowed and are generally closed to cars November–April.

Outside the parks, most regional roads are plowed all winter, including Teton Pass (west of Jackson), Togwotee Pass (northeast of Jackson), and U.S. Hwy. 14/16/20 from Cody to Pahaska Tepee near the East Entrance to Yellowstone. Two roads that are not plowed are U.S. Hwy. 212 over Beartooth Pass (between Cooke City and Red Lodge, Montana), and an eight-mile stretch of Chief Joseph Scenic Highway east of Cooke City and northwest of Cody.

Winter Travel

Winter travelers need to take special precautions. Snow tires are a necessity, but you should also have emergency supplies, including tire chains, a shovel and bag of sand in case you get stuck, a first-aid kit, booster cables, signal flares, a flashlight with extra batteries, lighter and candle, transistor radio, nonperishable foods (granola bars, canned nuts, or dried fruit), a jug of water, ice scraper, winter clothes, blankets, a sleeping bag, ax, and tow strap. The most valuable tool may well be a cell phone to call for help—assuming you're in an area with reception.

If you become stranded in a blizzard, stay in your car. You're more likely to be found, and the vehicle provides shelter from the weather. Run the engine and heater sparingly, occasionally opening a downwind window for ventilation. Don't run the engine if the tailpipe is blocked by snow—you may risk carbon monoxide poisoning. For up-to-date road and travel conditions in Wyoming, call 307/772-0824 or 888/996-7623, or log onto www.wyoroad.info for updated information, webcams, and construction advisories. Get weather forecasts at www.crh.noaa.gov/cys.

BUSES AND TOURS

Greyhound (800/231-2222, www.greyhound .com) has buses to Salt Lake City and to the southern Wyoming cities of Rock Springs, Rawlins, and Laramie, but not to Jackson, West Yellowstone, or other cities in the region. **Alltrans/Jackson Hole Express** (307/733-3135 or 800/443-6133, www.jackson holealltrans.com) provides daily van connections between Salt Lake City and Jackson. (See the *Yellowstone National Park* and *Grand Teton National Park* chapters for details on park tours and shuttles.)

Recreation

Northwest Wyoming is famous for its year-round recreational opportunities. In the summertime, hiking, camping, horseback rides, river rafting, mountain biking, and other adventures top the charts, and winter brings out the skis, snowboards, skates, snowshoes, and snowmobiles. Each part of the region has its own attractions, from whitewater rafting through the Snake River Canyon, to mountain climbing within Grand Teton National Park, to family day hikes in Yellowstone. If outdoor adventure is what you crave, you've come to the right place!

FISHING

Outstanding fishing opportunities abound throughout the Greater Yellowstone Ecosystem, and several rivers have achieved an almost mythical status among fly fishers.

Fishing Licenses

Nonresident fishing permits cost $14 for one day or $92 for a season. Resident fishing licenses are $24 for the year. Nonresident youths (ages 14–17) pay $15 for the year ($3 for resident youths). With the exception of the one-day rate, you will also need to buy a $12.50 mandatory conservation stamp. Kids younger than 14 don't need a license if they're with an adult who has a valid fishing license. Buy permits at most sporting-goods stores or from Game and Fish offices. For detailed fishing information, contact the **Wyoming Game and Fish Department** (307/777-4600 or 800/548-9453, http://gf.state.wy.us).

Get Montana fishing information from the **Montana Fish, Wildlife and Parks Department** (406/444-2535, www.fwp.state.mt.us/fishing). Nonresident two-day licenses cost $15, and season licenses are $60; you're required to also have a conservation license ($10). No license is required for children younger than age 14 if accompanied by an adult with a Montana fishing license (but special restrictions apply).

In Idaho, nonresident fishing licenses are $11.50 for one day plus $5 per day for additional days, or $82 for an annual license. Kids ages 14–17 pay $13.75 annually. Get details from the **Idaho Department of Fish and Game** (208/334-3700 or 800/635-7820, www .fishandgame.idaho.gov).

Within Grand Teton National Park, a Wyoming fishing license is required, but separate regulations apply in Yellowstone National Park. Anglers don't need a state fishing license but must obtain a special **Yellowstone National Park permit,** available from visitor centers, ranger stations, and Yellowstone General Stores, plus fishing shops in surrounding towns. The adult fishing fee is $15 for a three-day permit, $20 for a seven-day permit, or $35 for a season permit. Kids under age 15 can get a free permit, or can fish without a permit under the supervision of an adult who has one. Park visitor centers and ranger stations have copies of current fishing regulations.

Fishing Information

Several good books provide detailed information for fishing enthusiasts. Try one of the following: *Bud Lilly's Guide to Fly Fishing the New West* by Bud Lilly and Paul Schullery (Frank Amato Publications), *Yellowstone Fishes: Ecology, History, and Angling in the Park* by John Varley and Paul Schullery (www .stackpolebooks.com), *Fishing Yellowstone* by Richard Parks (www.globepequot.com), or *Fishing the Beartooths* by Pat Marchuson (www .globepequot.com). For broader coverage, see *Fishing Wyoming* by Kenneth Graham (www .globepequot.com), or Ken Retallic's *Flyfisher's Guide to Wyoming* (Wilderness Adventures Press). Several other books detail the multitude of fishing options on surrounding lands in Montana and Idaho. In Jackson, stop by Jack Dennis' Outdoor Shop (50 E. Broadway, 307/733-3270 or 800/570-3270, www.jack dennis.com) to pick up a copy of its free *Western Fishing Newsletter,* with descriptions of regional fishing areas and which lures to try.

An exceptionally helpful online source for fishing information is the *Wyoming Fishing Network,* www.wyomingfishing.net. Here you'll find details on where to fish, lures, local guides, and up-to-date fishing reports for various rivers and lakes.

BOATING

Jackson Hole's most popular summertime recreational activity is floating Wyoming's largest river, the Snake. Almost 20 different rafting companies offer dozens of trips each day of the summer, and on a busy day you'll see several thousand folks floating the placid upper sections or blasting through the boiling rapids of Snake River Canyon. (See the *Jackson Hole* chapter for complete details on float trips and whitewater rafting.) Whitewater and float trips are also available from the towns of Cody, Gardiner, and West Yellowstone.

Two Jackson-based kayaking schools teach a full range of classes in river kayaking, sea kayaking, and canoeing. These and other companies also offer sea-kayak trips on Jackson Lake in Grand Teton National Park and Lake

rowing out of Bridge Bay Marina, Yellowstone National Park

Yellowstone within Yellowstone National Park. These are available in a variety of flavors, from quick half-day paddles to multi-night kayaking and camping trips. Motorboat rentals are also available on Lake Yellowstone and Jackson Lake.

HORSEBACK AND WAGON RIDES

Horseback day-rides are available throughout the region, including within both Yellowstone and Grand Teton national parks.

Two companies lead overnight wagon-train rides into the country around Jackson Hole: **Wagons West** (307/543-2418 or 800/447-4711, www.wagonswestwyo.com) and **Teton Wagon Train/Double H Bar** (307/734-6101 or 888/734-6101, www.tetonwagontrain.com).

In addition to these trips, very popular **chuckwagon cookouts** are offered in Jackson Hole and at Roosevelt Lodge within Yellowstone National Park. These outings combine a ride in a Conestoga-style wagon with a big Old West feast and cowboy entertainment.

BIKING

Bicycles are available for rent in Jackson, Cody, Moose (Grand Teton National Park), Gardiner, and West Yellowstone, and at Old Faithful inside Yellowstone National Park. Excellent paved paths can be found in Grand Teton National Park, around Jackson, and within Teton Valley, while hiking/mountain-biking trails and dirt roads crisscross the region, particularly on Forest Service lands. A few of these trails are described in this book; for others, contact local bike shops or get trail information from Forest Service or Park Service offices. Bikes are prohibited on backcountry trails in both Yellowstone and Grand Teton national parks but are allowed on most main roads and certain other paths.

Bike Touring

Many cyclists ride through this part of Wyoming, Montana, and Idaho, but conditions are not the safest, particularly within Yellowstone, where traffic is heavy and the roads are narrow and winding with little or

© DON PITCHER

Teton Valley Trail Rides, Jackson, Wyoming

no shoulders. During summer, the best times to ride are in the morning before traffic thickens or late in the afternoon before the light begins to fade and you become less visible to motorists. September and October are far less crowded than midsummer. (See the *Yellowstone National Park* chapter for details on riding in the park.)

Backroads (800/462-2848, www.back roads.com) leads six-day tours of the Greater Yellowstone area that include biking, hiking, rafting, and kayaking.

The Wyoming Department of Transportation publishes a useful *Bicycle Guidance Map*—on waterproof paper—showing the amount of traffic on each paved road, the width of paved shoulders, profiles of the steeper road grades, and general wind patterns. Anyone touring on a bike will find this map immensely valuable. Get a copy by calling the WYDOT Bicycle Coordinator at 307/777-4719, or on the Web at www.dot.state.wy.us.

INTO THE BACKCOUNTRY

To get a real feel for the Greater Yellowstone Ecosystem, you need to abandon your car, get away from the towns, and head out into the vast and undeveloped public lands. The region contains some of the most remote country in the Lower 48 and one of the largest intact temperate-zone ecosystems anywhere.

Many campers prefer to use horses for longer trips, but backpacking is popular on the shorter trails, especially in the national parks. Backcountry permits are required only within Yellowstone and Grand Teton national parks. It is, however, a good idea to check in at a local Forest Service ranger station to get a copy of the regulations because each place is different in such specifics as how far your tent must be from lakes and trails and whether wood fires are allowed. Be sure to take insect repellent along on any summertime trip because mosquitoes, deerflies, and horseflies can be thick, especially early in the summer.

Trail Information

This book describes several hiking trips, mostly two- or three-day hikes, for Yellowstone and Grand Teton national parks, along with nearby Forest Service wilderness areas. Recommended hiking guides for the Tetons and Jackson Hole are *Jackson Hole Hikes,* by Rebecca Woods (White Willow Publishing), and *Teton Trails* by Katy Duffy and Darwin Wile (www .grandtetonpark.org). For Yellowstone, there are two fine guidebooks: *Yellowstone Trails* by Mark Marschall (www.yellowstoneassociation .org), and *Hiking Yellowstone National Park* by Bill Schneider (www.globepequot.com). The National Park Service and the U.S. Forest Service can also provide specific trail information, and they post much of this information on their websites.

The **Continental Divide National Scenic Trail** (303/838-3760 or 888/909-2382, www .cdtrail.org) stretches for 3,100 miles from Mexico to Canada, including across the Teton Wilderness and Yellowstone National Park.

Horses

For many people, the highlight of a Western vacation is the chance to ride a horse into wild country. Although a few folks bring their own steeds, most visitors leave the driving to an expert local outfitter instead. (If you've ever worked around horses in the backcountry, you'll understand why.) Horsepacking is an entirely different experience from backpacking. The trade requires years of experience in learning how to properly load horses and mules with panniers (large baskets), which types of knots to use for different loads, how to keep the packstrings under control, which horses to picket and which to hobble, and how to awaken when the horses decide to head down the trail on hobbles at three in the morning. Add to this a knowledge of bear safety, an ability to keep guests entertained with campfire tales and ribald jokes, a complete vocabulary of horse-cussing terms, and a thorough knowledge of tobacco chewing, and you're still only about 10 percent of the way to becoming a packer.

Get a complete listing of local backcountry outfitters from the **Wyoming Outfitters and**

Guides Association (307/265-2376, www
.wyoga.org), **Montana Outfitters and Guides
Association** (406/449-3578, www.moga-
montana.org), or **Idaho Outfitters and Guides
Association** (208/342-1438 or 800/494-3246,
www.ioga.org). Not all of these guides and outfitters may be permitted in a given backcountry
area; contact the Park Service or Forest Service
to see which ones are licensed to use the place
you plan to visit.

Although horses are far more common,
llamas are used in some backcountry areas.
You can't ride them, but they're easier to control than horses and do not cause as much
damage to trails and backcountry meadows.
Llamas are perfect for folks who want to hike
while letting a pack llama carry most of the
weight. Contact local Forest Service and Park
Service offices for permitted llama-packers.

Trail Etiquette
Because horses are so commonly used in the
Yellowstone region, hikers should follow a
few rules of courtesy. Horses and mules are
not the brightest critters on this planet, and
they can spook at the most inane thing, even
a bush blowing in the breeze or a brightly colored hat. Hikers meeting a packstring should
move several feet off the trail and not speak
loudly or make any sudden moves. If you've
ever seen what happens when just one mule
in a string decides to act up, you'll appreciate
the chaos that can result from sudden noises or
movements. Anyone hiking with a dog should
keep it well away from the stock and not let
it bark. Last of all, never walk close behind a
horse, unless you don't mind spending time in
a hospital. Their kick is *definitely* worse than
their bite.

Backcountry Ethics
The wilderness areas of northwest Wyoming are
places to escape the crowds, enjoy the beauty
and peace of the countryside, and develop an
understanding of nature. Unfortunately, as
more and more people head into backcountry areas, these benefits are becoming endangered. To keep wild places wild, always practice

leave no trace principles when hiking and
camping:
- Use existing campsites and fire rings.
- Locate your campsite well away from trails and streams.
- Stay on designated trails; don't cut across switchbacks.
- Burn only dead and down wood.
- Extinguish all fires.
- Wash dishes 200 feet from lakes and creeks.
- Dig "cat holes" at least 200 feet from lakes or streams.
- Hang all food well above the reach of bears.
- Don't litter the ground with toilet paper; in-stead, bury it deep or burn it in your camp-fire. (Do not, however, try to burn toilet paper in the woods; more than one person has started a forest fire in this way.)

Your tent site should be 100 yards from the
food storage and cooking areas to reduce the
likelihood of bear problems. Wood fires are
not allowed in many areas, so be sure to bring
along a portable gas stove. And, of course, haul
your garbage out with you. Burning cans and
tinfoil in the fire lessens their weight (and the
odors that attract bears), but be sure to pick
them out of the fire pit before you depart. And
make sure that fire is completely out.

For detailed leave-no-trace brochures on
minimizing your impact and treating the land
with respect, contact the **Leave No Trace
Center** (800/332-4100, www.lnt.org).

WINTER SPORTS
Downhill Skiing and Snowboarding
Jackson Hole is the primary skiing and snowboarding area in Wyoming. This area includes
one of America's top winter destinations,
Jackson Hole Mountain Resort in Teton
Village, 12 miles from the town of Jackson. For
ease of access, it's hard to beat the smaller (but
surprisingly steep) **Snow King Resort,** just
seven blocks from Town Square. On the other

AVALANCHE SAFETY

Backcountry skiing is becoming increasingly popular in the mountains surrounding Jackson Hole. Unfortunately, many skiers fail to take the necessary precautions and more than a few have paid with their lives. Between 1995 and 2004, avalanches killed 29 people in Wyoming. Given the enormous snowfalls that occur, the steep slopes the snow piles up on, and the high winds that accompany many storms, it should come as no surprise that avalanches are a real danger.

Nearly all avalanches are triggered by the victims. If you really want to avoid avalanches, ski only on groomed ski trails or "bombproof" slopes that, because of aspect, shape, and slope angle, never seem to slide. Unfortunately, this isn't always possible, so an understanding of the conditions that lead to avalanches is imperative for backcountry skiers. The Forest Service produces a useful booklet called *Basic Guidelines for Winter Recreation,* available in many of its offices around Wyoming.

The best way to learn about backcountry safety is through an avalanche class. These are offered in the Jackson Hole area by **American Avalanche Institute** (307/733-3315, www.avalanchecourse.com), **Exum Mountain Guides** (307/733-2297, www.exumguides.com), and **Jackson Hole Mountain Guides** (307/733-4979 or 800/239-7642, www.jhmg.com). Failing that, you can help protect yourself by following these precautions when you head into the backcountry:

· Before leaving, get up-to-date avalanche information. Visit www.avalanche.org for links to avalanche forecasting sites throughout the western states. For the Jackson Hole area, check the Forest Service's 24-hour **Backcountry Avalanche Hazard and Weather Forecast** (307/733-2664, www.jhavalanche.org). For areas around Yellowstone – including West Yellowstone and Cooke City on the margins and the Washburn Range inside the park – contact the **Gallatin National Forest Avalanche Advisory Center** (406/587-6981, www.mtavalanche.com) in Bozeman. If the message says avalanche danger is high, ski on the flats instead. **Jackson Hole Snow Observations** (www.jhsnowobs.org) provides an online forum where backcountry users share observations on snowpack conditions and avalanche activity.

· Be sure to carry extra warm clothes, water,

---

side of Teton Pass—42 miles from Jackson—is **Grand Targhee Ski Resort,** famous for its deep powder skiing. **Sleeping Giant Ski Area** is a family area 50 miles west of Cody near Yellowstone. (See the appropriate chapters for descriptions of each of these places.) During winter, call the Wyoming Travel and Tourism Division at 800/225-5996 for the statewide ski report, or visit its website, www.wyomingtourism.org.

Many more ski resorts can be found in Montana, including ones at Red Lodge (northeast of Yellowstone) and Big Sky (south of Bozeman and west of Yellowstone).

Cross-Country Skiing

Skinny-skiers have an overwhelming choice of places to ski in the Yellowstone–Grand Teton–Jackson Hole area. Developed Nordic areas are in Jackson Hole, west of Cody, and at West Yellowstone, Montana. In addition, Yellowstone and Grand Teton national parks have cross-country skiing with views to die for, and some trails in Grand Teton are groomed. Adjacent Forest Service lands provide deep snow and inexhaustible opportunities for those with backcountry skiing experience. (See the sidebar *Avalanche Safety* for precautions to take while cross-country skiing in the backcountry.)

Snowmobiling

An extensive network of snowmobile trails leads through northwest Wyoming and high-energy snacks, a dual-frequency avalanche transceiver (make sure it's turned on and that you know how to use it!), a lightweight snow shovel (for digging snow pits or excavating avalanche victims), an emergency snow shelter, cell phone, first-aid supplies, a Swiss Army or Leatherman knife, a topographic map, an extra plastic ski tip, a flashlight, matches, and a compass or GPS unit. Many skiers also carry that cure-all, duct tape, wrapped around a ski pole. Let a responsible person know exactly where you are going and when you expect to return. It's also a good idea to carry special ski poles that extend into probes in case of an avalanche. Check with local ski shops or talk to Forest Service or Park Service folks for details on specific areas.

- Check the angle of an area before you ski through it. Slopes of 30–45 degrees are the most dangerous; lesser slopes do not slide as frequently.

- Watch the weather; winds over 15 mph can pile snow much more deeply on lee slopes, causing dangerous loading on the snowpack. Especially avoid skiing on or below cornices.

- Avoid the leeward side of ridges, where snow loading can be greatest.

- Be aware of gullies and bowls; they're more likely to slip than flat open slopes or ridgetops. Stay out of gullies at the bottom of wide bowls; these are natural avalanche chutes.

- Look out for cracks in the snow, and listen for hollow snow underfoot. These are strong signs of dangerous conditions.

- Look at the trees. Smaller trees may indicate that avalanches rip through an area frequently, knocking over the larger ones. Avalanches can, however, also run through forested areas.

- Know how much new snow has fallen recently. Heavy new snow over older weak snow layers is a sure sign of extreme danger on potential avalanche slopes. Most avalanches slip during or immediately after a storm.

- Learn how to dig a snow pit and how to read the various snow layers. Particularly important are the very weak layers of depth hoar or surface hoar that have been buried under heavy new snow.

nearby parts of Montana and Idaho, including the **Continental Divide Snowmobile Trail** (www.sledwyoming.com) in the Wind River Mountains. Yellowstone National Park is now open only to guided snowmobile tours; check with the Park Service for details.

Snowmobile trail maps and listings of snowmobile rental companies are available from local visitor centers. For trail conditions around Wyoming, call 307/777-7777 or 800/225-5996, and ask for the snowmobile hotline. Find detailed snowmobile information—and current trail reports—on the Web at http://wyotrails.state.wy.us/snow.

Snowcoaches

Yellowstone snowcoaches provide a fine alternative to snowmobiling through the park. These 10-passenger machines are old-fashioned and gawky, but they provide a delightful way to explore the sights. The Yellowstone concessioner (Xanterra) runs a wide variety of snowcoach trips, including ones that drop you off to cross-country ski or explore. Another company (Yellowstone Expeditions) leads snowcoach trips to a remote yurt near Grand Canyon of the Yellowstone. Here you stay overnight and can explore the winter wonderland at a slower pace.

Other Winter Activities

Several companies offer **dogsled** rides in the Greater Yellowstone area, including ones to delightful Granite Hot Springs and overnight trips to a remote yurt. You'll find them in Jackson, Grand Targhee, and West Yellowstone. **Sleigh rides** are also available in Jackson Hole and at Grand Targhee, and some are combined with a meal at a remote cabin. Unique sleigh rides take visitors among the elk on the National Elk Refuge.

Snowshoeing is popular and a good way to get to places others don't go. Guided snowshoe hikes are offered in both Grand Teton and Yellowstone national parks. You'll find **ice-skating rinks** at the three big Jackson Hole ski areas, in the towns of Jackson and Cody, and at Mammoth Hot Springs within Yellowstone.

Accommodations

Lodging in the Yellowstone and Jackson Hole area is generally at a premium during summer and the Christmas–New Year's holiday. During peak summer or winter seasons in Jackson Hole, you should expect to pay $100 for a decent room. Rates are somewhat lower in West Yellowstone, Gardiner, Cody, Driggs, Cooke City, and Dubois, but not nearly as cheap as in less-touristy towns in Wyoming, Montana, or Idaho.

Throughout this book I have typically listed only one price for most accommodations: double, or d for two people. Prices listed are the peak-season summertime rates, which are generally the highest of the year. These prices do not include state and local taxes, which typically run 4–8 percent. The prices are also, of course, not set in concrete and will certainly increase in time due to inflation.

If you're in doubt about where to stay, visit **Trip Advisor** (www.tripadvisor.com) or **Yahoo Travel** (www.travel.yahoo.com) to see what other travelers say, or see the annual *AAA TourBook* for Idaho, Montana, and Wyoming; it's free to AAA members (www.aaa.com), who often get discounted rates.

HOTELS AND MOTELS

The motel and hotel scene in the Greater Yellowstone area is geared to travelers with cash to spend, although there are inexpensive hostels in Jackson and West Yellowstone. If you are visiting the region and planning to save money by camping the entire time, *do* make one or two modifications to your plan by booking at least one night in Yellowstone's Old Faithful

Inn or Lake Yellowstone Hotel. Both of these are classics, and Old Faithful Inn occupies a league of its own. Rates are surprisingly reasonable if you're willing to walk down the hall for a shower. Call far ahead for reservations at these places.

BED-AND-BREAKFASTS

Wyoming Homestay and Outdoor Adventures (WHOA, www.wyomingbnb-ranchrec.com) produces a brochure listing most state B&Bs; get a copy from any visitor center. For Montana listings, contact the **Montana Bed and Breakfast Association** (www.mtbba.com). Find connections to Idaho B&Bs on the Web at www.visitid.org.

Favorites of 30- and 40-something professional couples, bed-and-breakfasts are a fine way to get acquainted with a new area. They're also a good choice if you're traveling alone because you'll have opportunities to meet fellow travelers in the library, over tea, and at breakfast. Note, however, that the single-person rate frequently differs little, if at all, from the price for couples.

One problem with B&Bs is that they sometimes get a bit too homey and lack the privacy afforded by motels. I've stayed at places where the owner sits by your table in the morning, feeling it is his duty to hold a conversation. This may be fine sometimes, especially if you want to learn more about the local area, but it's not so great if you're looking for a romantic place or you just want to read the newspaper in peace. In some places the intense personal attention and strict rules (no hard-soled shoes, no noise after 10 P.M., and so on) get to be a bit much, making you feel less a guest than an intruder. In others, hosts serve breakfast at precisely 8 A.M., and guests who sleep in miss out. Other B&Bs are more flexible, and some even offer separate cottages or suites for honeymooners seeking privacy.

Several regional B&Bs don't allow kids, and almost none allow pets or smoking inside. Most guest rooms have private baths, but if they don't, one is probably just a few steps away.

GUEST RANCHES

An old and respected Western tradition is the dude ranch, or guest ranch, which began as a sideline to the business of raising cattle. Friends from back east would remember old Jake out there in wild Wyoming, where the buffalo roam and the antelope play, and would decide it was time for a visit. So off they would head, living in the rancher's outbuildings and helping with the chores. The "dudes," as they became known, soon told their friends, and Jake found his ranch inundated. After a couple of years of this arrangement, the next step was obvious: Get those eastern scoundrels to fork over some cash for the privilege of visiting. Pretty soon the dude-ranching business was born. At its peak in the 1920s, dude ranching spread throughout much of the West. Dude ranching saved many cattle ranches from extinction by providing a second source of income and simultaneously brought these magnificent lands to the attention of people who had the money to prevent their development (most notably John D. Rockefeller Jr. in Grand Teton National Park).

At the older ranches, generations of families have returned year after year for a relaxing and rejuvenating vacation in the "Wild West." Many dude ranches now call themselves guest ranches, a term that reflects both the suspicious way people view the word "dude" and the changing nature of the business. Most city folks today lack the desire or skill to actually saddle up their own horses, much less push cattle between pastures. As a result,

guest/dude ranches tend to emphasize grand scenery, horseback riding—the centerpiece of nearly every ranch—campfires, hiking, fishing, hearty meals, chuckwagon cookouts, singalongs, and evenings around the fireplace. A few ranches still offer the chance to join in on such activities as cattle drives, branding, pregnancy testing, shot-giving, calving, and roundups. For some folks it's a great chance to learn about the real West; others view it as paying good money (sometimes a lot of good money!) to work as a cowhand.

Practicalities

Dude-ranch stays generally cost around $3,500 for two people per week, with lower rates for kids and surcharges for those staying by themselves. The price includes all meals, lodging, and horseback rides, but you'll usually pay more for features such as airport shuttles, rafting trips, guided fishing, beer and wine, or backcountry pack trips, not to mention local taxes and tips. The fanciest resort, Lost Creek Ranch in Jackson Hole, will set you back more than $15,000 for two people per week! Many guest ranches offer discounted rates in early June and late September and for repeat guests. A few also have special adults-only weeks. Most require that you stay a week, or at least three nights, although a few places offer overnight accommodations. To really get into the comfortably slow pace of ranch life, try to set aside at least a week.

Ask plenty of questions before you visit, such as what activities are available, what to bring in the way of clothing, what sort of meals to expect (vegetarians may have a hard time on some ranches), whether there are additional charges, whether it accepts credit cards (many don't), what the living accommodations are like, and how many other guests will likely be there at the same time—some house up to 125, others fewer than a dozen. Also note that some places provide six nights lodging, while others include seven nights in their weekly stays. Upon request, all ranches will provide lists of references from previous clients. Note that it is considered proper to tip the ranch hands, kitchen help, and others who work hard to keep the ranch running. The standard gratuity is 15 percent of your bill, and many ranches add this automatically to the total. For many workers, this is a way to fund their college education (or a big vacation in New Zealand).

Finding a Ranch

An outstanding source for detailed information about guest ranches in Wyoming (and elsewhere) is *Gene Kilgore's Ranch Vacations,* by Eugene Kilgore (www.ranchweb.com).

The **Wyoming Dude Rancher's Association** (307/455-2084, www.wyomingdra.com) has a useful website with links to more than 30 dude ranches in the state. Other useful sources are the national **Dude Ranchers' Association** (307/587-2339 or 866/399-2339, www.dude ranch.org), along with www.guestranches.com and www.duderanches.com. Nearly all dude ranches have their own websites, filled with beautiful photos of their ranch, glowing reports from past clients, and details on the packages available and their costs.

CAMPING

The Greater Yellowstone Ecosystem is dotted with several dozen Forest Service and Park Service campgrounds. Most of these have drinking water, garbage pickup, and outhouses, but they generally do not have showers.

The fee is typically $10–15 per night, with a 14-day limit on camping at any one location. It's generally legal to camp for free on undeveloped Forest Service land throughout the region, but check with local ranger district offices for any restrictions. Dispersed camping is not allowed in the Snake River Canyon south of Jackson or the North Fork of the Shoshone River west of Cody.

Campsite reservations are available for some Yellowstone National Park sites, but all of those within Grand Teton National Park are on a first-come basis. In addition, several Forest Service campgrounds in the area are on a reservation system; for an extra service charge of $10 you can reserve a site up to six months in advance. Get details from **Recreation.gov** (518/885-3639 or 877/444-6777, www.recreation.gov).

RV PARKS

Every Yellowstone-area town of any size contains at least one private RV park and so-called campground. Most of these are little more than vacant lots with sewer and electrical hookups, showers, and toilet facilities, but a few are quite nice. These private campgrounds generally charge $5 for showers if you're not camping there. A better deal in many towns is to use the shower at the local public swimming pool, where you get a free swim thrown in for the entrance charge.

Tips for Travelers

TRAVELING BY RV

Yellowstone and Grand Teton national parks are very popular destinations for RVers. Surrounding towns all have private RV parks with all the amenities; some even have wireless Internet and cable TV hookups. Motor-home rentals are available in Jackson, Billings, and Idaho Falls.

Many Yellowstone roads are narrow and winding, making them a challenge for large RVs and a potential hazard for cyclists who risk getting hit by side mirrors. Owners of large

RVs should consider leaving their rigs at the campground and taking one of the park bus tours. A few roads are closed to RVs, including Terrace Drive and the Old Gardiner Road near Mammoth. In Grand Teton National Park, RVs and trailers are not allowed on Signal Mountain Road or the Moose-Wilson Road.

Motor homes are prohibited from Jenny Lake Campground in Grand Teton, and some other park campgrounds have a 30-foot size limit. Conversely, only hard-sided campers and RVs are allowed at Yellowstone's Fishing Bridge

RV Park. Check with each park for regulations on generator use in the campgrounds.

TRAVELING WITH CHILDREN

Yellowstone is a major family destination in summer, and visiting the park has become something of a rite of passage for middle-class Americans (along with thousands of European and Japanese families). Families will especially appreciate the woodsy campgrounds, inexpensive cabins, stagecoach and horseback rides, and the reasonable cafeteria meals. Most lodges and hotels have cribs for those traveling with infants. Of special interest to kids ages 5–12 is the **Junior Ranger Program,** in which children attend a nature program, hike a trail, and complete other activities. They're rewarded with an official Junior Ranger patch and are sworn in. It's always a big hit, but your kids may later try to arrest you if you get too close to an elk.

The **Teton County Parks and Recreation Department** (155 E. Gill St., 307/739-9025, www.tetonwyo.org/parks) has a summertime day camp for children entering 1st through 8th grades; $30 per day. Also check out the excellent natural-history programs through **Teton Science Schools** (307/733-4765, www.teton science.org), and the family-friendly Lodging and Learning packages offered by **Yellowstone Association Institute** (307/344-2294, www .yellowstoneassociation.org).

The Yellowstone Association's four-day **Yellowstone for Families** program includes a mix of activities for both kids and parents. Yellowstone National Park's **Windows into Wonderland** (www.windowsintowonderland .org) is a great online source for kid-friendly park information, with details on wildlife, art, fires, history, geology, microorganisms, and more.

(See the *Jackson Hole* chapter for details on special kid-friendly activities in Jackson.)

TRAVELING WITH PETS

Pets must be leashed and are not allowed on trails or hydrothermal basins in Yellowstone and Grand Teton National Parks. They can't be more than 50 feet from roadways in Grand Teton or 100 feet from Yellowstone roads or parking areas. In Grand Teton, you cannot take pets on Snake River boats, inside visitor centers, or on ranger-led activities. Don't think of leaving a dog in your car or RV within Yellowstone; it's illegal. In other words, leave your dog at home or at one of the Jackson kennels. Some regional motels and hotels (but very few B&Bs) allow pets; call ahead for specifics.

Several local kennels in Jackson will keep an eye on Fido for you. **Happy Tails Pet Resort/ Spring Creek Animal Hospital** (1035 W. Broadway, 307/733-1606, www.springcreek animalhospital.com) provides veterinary care and kennels. **Critter Camp/Jackson Hole Veterinary Clinic** (2950 Big Trail Dr., 307/733-4279) has a small pet boarding facility, and **Rally's Pet Garage** (520 S. Hwy. 89, 307/733-7704, www.rallyspetgarage.com) is a unique service with "doggie daycare," boarding, dog baths, and grooming.

SENIORS

An **Interagency Senior Pass** for all national parks is available to anyone over 62 for a one-time fee of $10. The card also provides for a 50 percent reduction in most camping fees. Many lodging places and attractions offer senior discounts. A variety of **Elderhostel** (www.elder hostel.com) programs are also offered throughout the year in the Yellowstone region.

ACCESSIBILITY

The Park Service's free **Interagency Access Pass** allows blind and people with permanent disabilities entrance to all national parks, historic sites, and recreation areas. The passport also provides a 50 percent discount for camping in the parks. Pick them up from any park visitor center or entrance station.

People with disabilities who are visiting Yellowstone will find that the park is making a concerted effort to provide accessible facilities, although it has a long way to go. Most of the major tourist areas, including Old Faithful, have at least some paths that are paved, and accessible accommodations can be found at Canyon, Grant Village, Old Faithful, and Lake.

Accessible campsites are also available throughout the park. For details, see the *Visitor Guide to Accessible Features in Yellowstone National Park* (307/344-2018, www.nps.gov/yell).

Grand Teton National Park has some accessible campsites, and all park lodging places provide accessible units. Some hiking trails are paved. Get the park's "Accessibility" handout for complete details, or find it on the Web at www.nps.gov/grte.

Many hotels and B&Bs in Jackson and other gateway towns have accessible rooms. Contact **Wheelchair Getaways of Montana** (406/227-6524 or 800/630-8267, www.wheelchairgetaways.com) for accessible van rentals in the Yellowstone area.

OPPORTUNITIES FOR STUDY AND EMPLOYMENT
Yellowstone National Park

During summer, both the National Park Service and private concessioners provide several thousand jobs in Yellowstone. These positions rarely last more than six months. You can find much more about Yellowstone jobs—both public and private—by heading to www.nps.gov/yell/parkmgmt/jobs.htm on the Web.

Yellowstone National Park hires more than 300 seasonal employees each year, but many more people apply, so the competition is stiff for new hires. Most seasonals start out as a park ranger (leading naturalist walks, working in entrance stations, etc.) or laborer (building trails, cleaning campgrounds and restrooms, etc.), but more specialized positions are available in the fields of natural resources or law enforcement. You must be a U.S. citizen to be employed by the Park Service.

Although there is a national register for seasonal rangers, specific vacancy announcements come out when jobs are available, and you will need to apply within the specified time frame and meet all qualifications. For details on seasonal park service jobs, call Yellowstone's human resources office (307/344-2052, www.usajobs.gov) for a listing of park jobs. The Department of the Interior's site, www.doi.gov/hrm/jobs.html, has additional employment information.

Unpaid volunteers do many jobs in Yellowstone and other national parks, and it isn't necessary to be a U.S. citizen to do volunteer work. The Park Service operates a **Volunteers in Parks (VIP)** program at Yellowstone that includes more than 300 people each year. To join the ranks of the employed but unpaid, call the park's VIP coordinator (307/344-2047, www.nps.gov/volunteer).

A national nonprofit organization, the **Student Conservation Association** or SCA (603/543-1700, www.thesca.org), provides workers for Yellowstone who do a wide variety of activities, from trail maintenance to answering visitors' questions. Volunteers get most expenses paid.

The park has two primary concessioners, Xanterra Parks and Resorts and Delaware North Parks and Resorts, along with the smaller Yellowstone Park Service Stations. Most employees of these companies are college students (who live in dorm-style accommodations), retired folks (who live in their RVs), or young people from other countries (including many from Eastern Europe, Russia, or China). Don't expect high pay; entry-level positions start at around $7.25 per hour, with meals and lodging deducted from this paltry sum. A good overall website for concessioner jobs inside Yellowstone is www.coolworks.com/yell.htm.

Xanterra Parks and Resorts (307/344-5324, www.yellowstonejobs.com) is in charge of lodging, restaurants, bus tours, boat rentals, horse rides, several campgrounds, and similar services within the park. It is also the largest park- and resort-management company in the nation, with operations in such diverse spots as Everglades National Park and Grand Canyon National Park. The company hires some 3,500 people each summer in Yellowstone. It's best to apply early for summer jobs. The more competitive winter positions often go to those with previous work experience in the park.

The 12 Yellowstone General Stores are operated by **Delaware North Parks and Resorts,** (www.delawarenorth.com) with a regional office in Bozeman, Montana. The company employs about 800 folks seasonally in Yellowstone, with a handful more as year-round managers. Many of the seasonals are retirees who bring their RVs along for private accommodations. If you can start in April or May, you're considerably more likely to be hired. Employment details and applications are available from Yellowstone General Stores (406/586-7593, www.visit yellowstonepark.com).

The third concessioner is **Yellowstone Park Service Stations** (406/848-7333, www.ypss .com), the folks who pump Conoco gas and wash your windshield at seven stations in the park. A few higher-level positions are available for auto repair or towing operations.

Jackson Hole

Jackson Hole is an increasingly popular place to live and work—a fact that angers many longtime residents who came here to escape crowds elsewhere. The surrounding country is grand, with many things to do and places to explore, the weather is delightful, and you're likely to meet others with similar interests, not to mention all the good-looking young people. Jobs such as waiting tables, operating ski lifts, driving tour buses, cleaning hotels and condos, and doing construction work are plentiful. The unemployment rate generally hovers around 2 percent, and housing is so scarce—and jobs so plentiful—that the local rescue mission kicks folks out after a week if they don't find work. Wages are not high but have improved with the rising demand for workers. Get to Jackson in mid-May and you'll find the papers filled with half a dozen pages of employment ads and Help Wanted signs at virtually every shop. Even in midsummer, many places are looking for workers.

The best jobs are those that either offer such perks as housing or free ski passes or give you lots of free time to explore the area. To get an idea of available jobs, check local classified ads (www.jacksonholenewsandguide .com) or stop by the **Wyoming Workforce Center** (155 W. Gill, 307/733-4091, www .wyomingworkforce.org).

Because of Jackson Hole's popularity, finding a place to live is extremely difficult, especially during the peak summer and winter tourist seasons. As the moneyed class has moved in, those who work in service jobs find it tougher and tougher to obtain affordable housing. Many Jackson workers now suffer long commutes from Victor or Driggs in Idaho, or from the Wyoming towns of Alpine or Afton. Land prices (and consequently housing costs) have been rising an average of 15 percent per year for the past decade or so, and because of this, the median home price is more than twice what the median household income will buy! Two-bedroom furnished apartments often rent for $1,800 or more per month. The median single-family home in Jackson costs $1.1 million, and the median home in the area sells for a cool $1.9 million. More prestigious local homes sell for $3 million, and the very finest log mansions ("log cabins on steroids") can fetch more than $6 million. The inflation of real estate has attracted the major players: both Christie's and Sotheby's (the auction folks) have offices in Jackson. As a side note, Teton County is the wealthiest county in America, with the nation's highest average taxable income. (These figures are, of course, skewed by a relatively small number of ultra-rich individuals; you'll find many folks working at $10-an-hour jobs.)

Because of the extreme difficulty in finding rental housing, many Jackson-area businesses include this perk as a way to lure workers. In 2008, the county imposed a moratorium on new commercial developments that don't provide worker housing. Those workers who are not so lucky are often forced to jam into too-small apartments or to join the commuters from Driggs. The best times to look for a place to live are in April and October. Check the local newspapers (or their online versions if you haven't yet arrived in the area), Craig's List (www.craigslist.com), as well as local coin laundry and grocery-store bulletin boards for apartments or cabins. The *Trash and Treasure* morning program on radio station KMTN (96.9 FM, www.kmtnthemountain.com) is another place to try.

Health and Safety

Medical clinics can be found in most towns in the Yellowstone region, with good hospitals in Jackson and Cody, plus a smaller hospital in Driggs, Idaho. A summertime hospital is near Lake Yellowstone Hotel within Yellowstone, with clinics at Old Faithful and Mammoth. Inside Grand Teton National Park there's a summertime clinic near Jackson Lake Lodge. Both West Yellowstone and Dubois have medical clinics.

A common annoyance for travelers is insects, especially mosquitoes and blackflies. These pests are most prevalent in early summer in the mountains; by late August mosquito populations thin considerably. Use insect repellents containing DEET to help keep them away or wear a head net.

Beaver Fever

Although the lakes and streams of the Greater Yellowstone Ecosystem may appear clean, you could be risking a debilitating sickness by drinking the water without treating it first. The protozoan *Giardia lamblia* is found throughout the state, spread by both humans and animals (including beaver). The disease is curable with drugs, but it's always best to carry safe drinking water on any trip or to boil any water taken from creeks or lakes. Bringing water to a full boil for one minute is sufficient to kill *Giardia* and other harmful organisms. Another option—the one I much prefer—is to use one of the water filters sold in camping-goods stores. Make sure you buy one that filters out organisms such as *Campylobactor jejuni*, bacteria that are just 0.2 microns in size. Chlorine and iodine are not always reliable, taste foul, and can be unhealthy. The MSR Miox (www.msrcorp .com, $140) purifier uses an oxidant—not filtration—to clean water with little aftertaste.

Hypothermia

Anyone who has spent much time in the outdoors will discover the dangers of exposure to cold, wet, and windy conditions. Even at temperatures well above freezing, hypothermia—the reduction of the body's inner core temperature—can prove fatal.

In the early stages, hypothermia causes uncontrollable shivering, followed by a loss of coordination, slurred speech, and then a rapid descent into unconsciousness and death. Always travel prepared for sudden changes in the weather. Wear clothing that insulates well and that holds its heat when wet. Wool and polypro are far better than cotton, and clothes should be worn in layers to provide better trapping of heat and a chance to adjust to conditions more easily. Always carry a wool hat because your head loses more heat than any other part of the body. Bring a waterproof shell to cut the wind. Put on rain gear *before* it starts raining; head back or set up camp when the weather looks threatening, and eat candy bars, keep active, or snuggle with a friend in a down bag to generate warmth.

If someone in your party begins to show signs of hypothermia, don't take any chances, even if the person denies needing help. Get the victim out of the wind, strip off his clothes, and put him in a dry sleeping bag on an insulating pad. Skin-to-skin contact is the best way to warm a hypothermic person, and that means you'll also need to strip and climb in the sleeping bag. If you weren't friends before, this should heat up the relationship! Do not give the victim alcohol or hot drinks, and do not try to warm the person too quickly because it could lead to heart failure. Once the victim has recovered, get medical help as soon as possible. Actually, you're far better off keeping close tabs on everyone in the group and seeking shelter *before* exhaustion and hypothermia set in.

West Nile Encephalitis

Most people who are infected with West Nile encephalitis show mild (or no) symptoms, but the disease can be fatal. The virus is transmitted through mosquito bites, and it can infect not just humans, but also horses, many species of birds, and other animals—with potentially devastating impacts on horse and wildlife populations. At least 15 Wyoming residents have died from West Nile infections in the last decade. Reduce your chance of infection by applying insect repellents containing DEET. (A higher concentration lasts longer, but there's no benefit in using DEET in concentrations over 50 percent.) You can also spray your clothing with the repellent, wear long-sleeved shirts and long pants, and stay indoors at dusk and dawn, when the mosquitoes are their most active. The Wyoming Department of Health (877/996-2483, www.badskeeter.org) has details on the virus.

Hantavirus

This potentially fatal respiratory disease is spread by rodents, particularly deer mice. Contact with them or their droppings can lead to such symptoms as fever, muscle aches, coughing, and difficulty breathing resulting from fluid buildup in the lungs within 1–5 weeks. Once the symptoms appear, the disease progresses quickly, leading to hospitalization within 24 hours. Almost half of those who come down with hantavirus die, and in the last decade, it has killed at least three Wyoming residents. Avoid contact with rodents and their feces or urine to minimize your chances of infection. Campers should never sleep on bare ground and avoid cabins if you find signs of rodents. Fortunately, the disease is not contagious from person to person. For additional information, visit the Wyoming Department of Health website, http://wdh.state.wy.us.

Ticks

Ticks can be a bother in brushy and grassy areas in the spring and early summer. They drop onto unsuspecting humans and other animals to suck blood and can spread several potentially devastating diseases, including Rocky Mountain spotted fever, Ehrlichiosis, and Lyme disease. A few cases of these diseases have been reported in the Greater Yellowstone Ecosystem, but they are not common.

Avoid ticks by tucking pant legs into boots and shirts into pants, using insect repellents containing DEET, and carefully inspecting your clothes while outside. Light-colored clothing and socks are less attractive to ticks and make it easier for you to see them, while broad hats keep them out of your hair. Check your body while hiking and immediately after the trip. If possible, remove ticks before they become embedded in your skin. If one does become attached, use tweezers to remove the tick, making sure to get the head. Apply a triple-antibiotic ointment such as Neosporin to the area, and monitor the bite area for two weeks.

Lyme disease typically shows up as a large red spot with a lighter bull's-eye center and often causes muscle aches, fatigue, headache, and fever. Get medical help immediately if you show these symptoms after a tick bite. Fortunately, the disease can usually be treated with antibiotics. If untreated, it can cause a facial nerve palsy, memory loss, arthritis, heart damage, and other problems. A relatively effective vaccine has been developed for Lyme disease, but it requires a one-year regimen of doses and is expensive; check with your doctor for specifics. In northwest Wyoming, where the disease is relatively uncommon, the vaccine is probably not warranted, and it may give a false sense of security because ticks can still spread other—and more dangerous—diseases. No vaccinations are available against either Rocky Mountain spotted fever or Erlichia, both of which sometimes kill people. The best action is to prevent tick bites in the first place. For more on tick-borne diseases, see the Harvard Medical School's website at www.intelihealth.com.

SAFETY IN BEAR COUNTRY

Bears seem to bring out conflicting emotions in people. The first is an almost gut reaction of fear and trepidation: What if the bear attacks me? But then comes that other urge: What will my friends say when they see these *incredible* bear photos? Both of these reactions can lead to problems in bear country. "Bearanoia" is a justifiable fear but can easily be taken to such an extreme that one avoids going outdoors at all for fear of running into a bear. The "I want to get close-up shots of that bear and her cubs" attitude can lead to a bear attack. The middle ground incorporates a knowledge of and respect for bears with a sense of caution that keeps you alert for danger without letting fear rule your wilderness travels. Nothing is ever completely safe in this world, but with care you can avoid most of the common pitfalls that lead to bear encounters.

Avoiding Bear Hugs

Surprise bear encounters are rare but frightening experiences. There were just 32 bear-caused injuries in Yellowstone National Park between 1980 and 2002—one injury for every 1.9 million visitors. Avoid unexpected encounters with bears by letting them know you're there. Most bears hear or smell you long before you realize their presence, and they hightail it away. Surprising a bear, especially a sow with cubs, is the last thing you want to do in the backcountry. Before heading out, check at a local ranger station to see whether there have been recent bear encounters. If you discover an animal carcass, be extremely alert because a bear may be nearby and may attack anything that appears to threaten its food. Get away from such areas. Do not hike at night or dusk, when bears can be especially active. Safety is also in numbers: The more of you hiking together, the more likely a bear is to sense you and stay away.

Make noise in areas of dense cover or when coming around blind spots on trails. If you're unable to see everything around you for at least 50 yards, warn any hidden animals by talking, singing, clapping your hands, tapping a cup, or rattling a can of pebbles. Some people tie bells to their packs for this purpose, but others regard this as an annoyance to fellow hikers. In general, bells are probably of little value because the sound does not carry far, and they might actually attract bears. If bears can't hear you coming, don't be shy—make a lot of noise! It might seem a bit foolish, but loud voices may prevent an encounter of the furry kind. Unfortunately, it will probably scare off other animals, so you're not likely to see many critters, and other hikers may not appreciate the

noise. Personally, I reserve yelling "Hey Bear!" for situations where I'm walking in brushy bear country with low visibility and have to contend with other noises such as a nearby creek. I wouldn't recommend doing so while walking the paved path around Old Faithful Geyser; you might get carried off in a straitjacket.

Hunters and photographers are the main recipients of bear-hugs. Never under any circumstances approach a bear, even if it appears to be asleep. Move away if you see bear cubs, especially if one comes toward you, because mom is almost always close by. Dogs create dangerous situations by barking and exciting bears—leave yours at home (dogs are not allowed in the backcountry in national parks). Never leave food around for bears. Not only is this illegal, but it also trains the bears to associate people with free food. Fed bears become garbage bears, and that almost inevitably means that the bear gets killed. Remember, bears are dangerous wild animals. This is *their* country, not a zoo. By going in you accept the risk—and thrill—of meeting a bear.

At the Campsite

Before camping, take a look around the area to see if there are recent bear tracks or scat and to make sure you're not on a game trail. Bears are attracted to odors of all sorts, including food, horse feed, soap, toothpaste, perfume, and deodorants. Your cooking, eating, and food storage area should be at least 50 yards away from your tent. Keep your campsite clean and avoid such smelly items as tuna, ham, sausage, and bacon; freeze-dried food is light and relatively odorless (although also relatively tasteless). Store food away from your sleeping area in airtight containers or several layers of plastic bags, and be sure to hang all food and other items that bears may smell at least 12 feet off the ground and four feet from tree trunks. Bring 50 feet of rope for this purpose. Tie two cups or pots to it so you will hear if it's moved. Some Forest Service and Park Service wilderness areas provide food storage poles at campsites. In Grand Teton National Park backcountry campers must carry bearproof containers. In

Sleeping Area

100 yards

Cooking and Eating Area

Hang at least 10' from the ground and 4' from the top and side supports

BOB RACE

the Teton and Bridger wilderness areas, you can also rent bear-resistant backpacker food tubes or horse panniers from Forest Service offices. Camping stores in Jackson, Cody, and elsewhere sell similar containers.

Researchers have reported no evidence that either sexual activity or menstrual odors precipitate bear attacks. It is, however, wise for menstruating women to use tampons instead of pads and to store soiled tampons in double ziplock bags above the reach of bears.

Encounters of the Furry Kind

If you do happen to suddenly encounter a bear and it sees you, try to stay calm and not make any sudden moves. Do not run because you could not possibly outrun a bear; they can exceed 40 mph for short distances. Bear researchers now suggest that quickly climbing a tree is also not a wise way to escape bears and may actually incite an attack. Instead, make yourself visible by moving into the open so the bear will (you hope) identify you as a human and not something to eat. Never stare directly at a bear. Sometimes dropping an item such as a hat or jacket will distract the bear, and talking

calmly (easier said than done) also seems to have some value in convincing bears that you're a human. If the bear sniffs the air or stands on its hind legs it is probably trying to identify you. When it does, it will usually run away. If a bear woofs and postures, don't imitate— this is a challenge. Keep retreating. Most bear charges are also bluffs; the bear will often stop short and amble off.

If a **grizzly bear** actually attacks, hold your ground and freeze. It may well be a bluff charge, with the bear halting at the last second. If the bear does not stop its attack, curl up face-down on the ground in a fetal position with your hands wrapped behind your neck and your elbows tucked over your face. Your backpack may help protect you somewhat. Remain still even if you are attacked because sudden movements may incite further attacks. It takes an enormous amount of courage to do this, but often a bear will only sniff or nip you and leave. The injury you might sustain would be far less than if you tried to resist. After the attack, prevent further attacks by staying down on the ground until the grizzly has left the area.

Bear authorities now recommend against

dropping to the ground if you are attacked by a **black bear** because they tend to be more aggressive in such situations and are more likely to prey on humans. If a black bear attacks, fight back with whatever weapons are at hand; large rocks and branches can be surprisingly effective deterrents, as can yelling and shouting. (This, of course, assumes you can tell black bears from brown bears. If you can't, have someone who knows—such as a park ranger—explain the differences before you head into the backcountry.)

In the rare event of a **nighttime bear attack** in your tent, defend yourself *very* aggressively. Never play dead under such circumstances because the bear probably views you as prey and may give up if you make it a fight. Before going to bed, try to plan escape routes should you be attacked in the night, and be sure to have a flashlight and pepper spray handy. Keeping your sleeping bag partly unzipped also allows the chance to escape should a bear attempt to drag you away. If someone is attacked in a tent near you, yelling and throwing rocks or sticks may drive the bear away.

Protecting Yourself

Cayenne pepper sprays (sold in camping goods stores) have sometimes proven useful in fending off bear attacks. Note, however, that these "bear mace" sprays are effective only at close range (10–30 feet). This is particularly true in open country, where winds quickly disperse the mist or may blow it back in your own face.

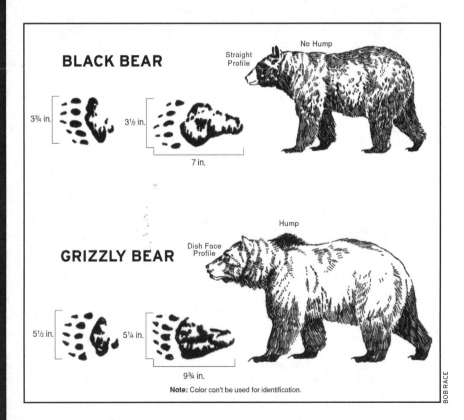

BLACK BEAR

Straight Profile

No Hump

3¾ in.   3½ in.

7 in.

GRIZZLY BEAR

Dish Face Profile

Hump

5½ in.   5¼ in.

9¾ in.

Note: Color can't be used for identification.

BOB RACE

Another problem with bear mace is that you cannot carry it aboard commercial jets because of the obvious dangers if a canister explodes. If you do carry a pepper spray, make sure it is readily available by carrying it in a holster on your belt or across your chest. Also be sure to test-fire it to see how the spray carries. Although they *are* better than nothing, pepper sprays are not a cure-all or a replacement for caution in bear country. It's far better to avoid bear confrontations in the first place.

The latest development for campers in bear country is the use of portable **electric fences** made by Electro Bear Guard (907/232-9758, www.electrobearguard.com) to surround your campsite; a backpacker unit runs on two AA batteries, weighs just two pounds, and costs $330.

A good source for up-to-date bear safety information is the Yellowstone National Park website, www.nps.gov/yell. Two recommended safety books are *Bear Attacks: Their Causes and Avoidance* by Stephen Herrero (www.lyonspress.com), and *Bear Aware: Hiking and Camping in Bear Country* by Bill Schneider, www.globepequot.com).

BACKCOUNTRY SAFETY TIPS

The most important part of enjoying—and surviving—the backcountry is to be prepared. Know where you're going; get maps, camping information, weather forecasts, and trail conditions from a ranger before setting out. Although I have often hiked alone, single hikers are at a greater risk of getting into trouble than those trekking with companions. Two are better than one, and three are better than two; if one gets hurt, one person can stay with the injured party and one can go for help. Bring more than enough food so hunger won't cause you to continue when weather conditions say stop. Tell a responsible person where you're going and when you'll be back.

Always carry the **10 essentials:** map, compass, water bottle, first-aid kit, flashlight, matches (or lighter) and fire starter, knife, extra clothing (a full set, in case you fall in a stream) including rain gear, extra food, and sunglasses—especially if you're hiking on snow. To this list, you might want to add a cell phone. Most backcountry areas have no service, but in an emergency you might be able to find a high point where the phone can hit an antenna. GPS units have become much cheaper and easier to use in recent years, making them an excellent option.

Check your ego at the trailhead; stop for the night when the weather gets bad, even if it's 2 P.M., or head back. And don't press on when you're exhausted; tired hikers are sloppy hikers, and even a small injury can be disastrous in the woods.

Information and Services

TOURIST INFORMATION

Chambers of commerce information centers are described for each town in this book. Both parks have visitor centers, and the large Jackson Hole and Greater Yellowstone Visitor Center is in Jackson. You'll find chambers of commerce offices in even the tiniest towns in the Yellowstone area.

Wyoming: For a helpful overall guide to Wyoming, along with a listing of events, chamber of commerce offices, and lodging and camping places, request a copy of the free *Wyoming Travelers Journal* from the Wyoming Travel and Tourism Division (307/777-7777 or 800/225-5996, www.wyomingtourism.org). The agency also has free state maps, or pick them up at any regional visitor center.

For additional information, head to the Wyoming state homepage: www.wyoming.gov. See Don Pitcher's *Moon Wyoming* (www.donpitcher.com) for the full story on the Cowboy State.

Montana: For Montana travel information, check out the fat *Montana Vacation Planner*

(406/841-2870 or 800/847-4868, www.visitmt .com). The maps in this publication are particularly revealing, showing Yellowstone as a brown appendage to Montana, even though virtually all the park lies within Wyoming! Request a free *Yellowstone Country Travel Guide* (406/556-8680 or 800/736-5276, www.yellowstonecountry .net). The state of Montana's homepage is www .mt.gov. The most complete travel guide for the state is *Moon Montana* (www.moon.com) by W. C. McRae and Judy Jewell.

Idaho: Contact the Idaho Department of Commerce Tourism Division (208/334-2470 or 800/847-4743, www.visitid.org) for the official *Idaho Travel Guide* and a state map. For Eastern Idaho info, request a free *Yellowstone Teton Territory* booklet (800/634-3246, www .yellowstoneteton.com). The state of Idaho's homepage is www.idaho.gov. Find comprehensive Idaho coverage in *Moon Idaho* (www .moon.com) by Don Root.

Land Management Agencies

The following phone numbers and websites provide contact information for major public land-management agencies in the Greater Yellowstone Ecosystem:

Grand Teton National Park, Moose, 307/739-3399, www.nps.gov/grte

Yellowstone National Park, Mammoth, 307/344-7381, www.nps.gov/yell

National Elk Refuge, Jackson, 307/733-9212, www.fws.gov/nationalelkrefuge

Bridger-Teton National Forest, Jackson, 307/739-5500, www.fs.fed.us/r4/btnf

Shoshone National Forest, Cody, 307/527-6241, www.fs.fed.us/r2/shoshone

Caribou-Targhee National Forest, Idaho Falls, Idaho, 208/524-7500, www.fs.fed.us/ r4/caribou-targhee

Gallatin National Forest, West Yellowstone, Montana, 406/823-6961, or Gardiner, Montana, 406/848-7375, www.fs.fed.us/r1/gallatin

Beaverhead-Deerlodge National Forest, Dillon, Montana, 406/683-3900, www.fs.fed .us/r1/bdnf

Custer National Forest, Red Lodge, Montana, 406/446-2103, www.fs.fed.us/r1/custer

COMMUNICATIONS AND MEDIA
Newspapers and Radio

Jackson's outstanding tabloid newspaper—the *Jackson Hole News and Guide* (307/733-2047, www.jhnewsandguide.com)—publishes a weekly edition with local news, along with freebie versions Monday–Saturday.

Wyoming's only statewide paper, the *Casper Star-Tribune* (www.casperstartribune.net) is ubiquitous throughout the area. Another paper you'll see in local racks (particularly within Yellowstone) is the *Billings Gazette* (www .billingsgazette.com).

Jackson, Cody, and other towns in the region have local radio stations of varying quality, offering the standard mix of top-40, rock, and country. For a bit more class, turn your dial to one of the **National Public Radio** stations that provide in-depth news, insightful call-in shows, and comedic relief. In Jackson, the local Wyoming Public Radio station is KUWJ 90.3 FM (www.wyomingpublicradio .net). In the Yellowstone area and Cody, you're also likely to hear "Yellowstone Radio" out of Bozeman, KBMC 102.1 FM. In Idaho's Teton Valley, listen to NPR on KRIC-FM 100.5 from Rexburg, Idaho.

On the Web

Internet addresses are listed in the text for local chamber of commerce offices and a multitude of businesses. Excellent places to begin your virtual voyage are the state tourism sites and land-management agencies. See specific town descriptions for listings of chambers of commerce websites.

Two particularly useful websites with abundant links to local businesses are the Jackson Hole Chamber of Commerce's site, www .jacksonholechamber.com, and the Cody-based Park County Travel Council, www.yellow stonecountry.org. Other websites worth browsing include www.jacksonholetraveler.com, www.jacksonholenet.com, www.westyellow stonechamber.com, www.westyellowstone traveler.com, and www.westyellowstonenet.com.

Looking for **Web cameras** to see the

Yellowstone-Grand Teton region in real time? The Wyoming Department of Transportation (www.wyoroad.info) has webcams for Teton Pass, Alpine, and Pinedale, while www.jackson holenet.com/webcams shows more than two dozen webcams scattered around Jackson Hole and Yellowstone (including Old Faithful).

All local libraries have computers with free Internet access, although you may need to sign up for a terminal. Find a listing of Wyoming libraries and links to their homepages at www.publiclibraries.com/wyoming .htm. In addition, the towns of Jackson, Cody, Gardiner, Cooke City, Dubois, and West Yellowstone all have Internet cafés or businesses with computers for rent by the hour. Most motels and many coffee shops also now provide **wireless Internet (Wi-Fi)** access for those with laptop computers.

MONEY

Travelers checks (in U.S. dollars) are accepted without charge at most stores and businesses throughout the Yellowstone region. It's not a good idea to travel with travelers checks in non-U.S. currency; they are accepted only at certain banks in Wyoming and are a time-consuming hassle. If you do arrive with pounds, yen, or Euros, several banks in Jackson, along with the park hotels inside Yellowstone, will exchange foreign currency for greenbacks.

Tipping is expected for many services, with 15 percent or more for wait staff at restaurants. In addition, tips are appreciated for other personal services, including river-rafting guides, taxi drivers, dude-ranch employees, and hotel maids. The amount varies widely, but it is common for a wildlife tour guide to receive a $20 tip at the end of a day's assistance.

RESOURCES

Suggested Reading

Note: A few of the following books are now out of print. You can find many of them in regional libraries, or check the Web for special orders or rare book auctions. Websites like www.amazon.com, www.barnesandnoble.com, and others will search used bookstores for out-of-print titles.

REGIONAL TITLES

Birkby, Jeff. *Touring Montana and Wyoming Hot Springs.* Guilford, CT: Globe Pequot Press, www.globepequot.com, 1999.

Blackstone, D. L., Jr. *Traveler's Guide to the Geology of Wyoming.* Laramie, WY: Geological Survey of Wyoming, www.wsgsweb.uwyo.edu, 1988. An excellent overview of Wyoming's geological history and how to see it in today's landscapes.

Graham, Kenneth L. *Camping Wyoming and the Black Hills.* Guilford, CT: Globe Pequot Press, www.globepequot.com, 2001.

Graham, Kenneth Lee. *Fishing Wyoming.* Guilford, CT: Globe Pequot Press, www.globepequot.com, 1998. A 300-page tome that goes far beyond the standard coverage of Yellowstone and Jackson Hole.

Herrero, Stephen. *Bear Attacks: Their Causes and Avoidance.* Guilford, CT: The Lyons Press, www.lyonspress.com, 2002. An authoritative volume on the lives of bears and staying safe in their country.

Kilgore, Gene. *Gene Kilgore's Ranch Vacations.* Berkeley, CA: Avalon Travel Publishing, www.avalontravelbooks.com, 2004. The definitive guide to dude and guest ranches in Wyoming and the rest of North America. Includes detailed, up-to-date descriptions of the best places to be a city-slicker cowboy.

Largeson, David R., and Darwin R. Spearing. *Roadside Geology of Wyoming.* Missoula, MT: Mountain Press Publishing Co., www.mountain-press.com, 1988. Wyoming is perhaps the most geologically interesting of all the states. This is an invaluable road guide for anyone wanting to know more about geology without resorting to dense textbooks.

Phillips, Wayne. *Central Rocky Mountain Wildflowers: Including the Greater Yellowstone Ecosystem.* Guilford, CT: Globe Pequot Press, www.globepequot.com, 1999.

Retallic, Ken. *Flyfisher's Guide to Wyoming.* Gallatin Gateway, MT: Wilderness Adventures Press, 2005. An excellent guide; particularly helpful for anglers headed to Yellowstone.

Schneider, Bill. *Bear Aware.* Guilford, CT: Globe Pequot Press, www.globepequot.com, 2004. A handy pocket-size book that is easy to read and up to date.

Travsky, Amber. *Mountain Biking Wyoming.* Guilford, CT: Globe Pequot Press, www.globepequot.com, 1999.

ONWARD TRAVEL

The following is a shameless promotion for other Moon books (www.moon.com) covering the region. All of these are authoritative guides for their respective states or regions.

Knopper, Steve. *Moon Colorado*. Berkeley, CA: Avalon Travel Publishing, 2006.

McRae, W. C., and Judy Jewell. *Moon Montana*. Berkeley, CA: Avalon Travel Publishing, 2005.

McRae, W. C., and Judy Jewell. *Moon Utah*. Berkeley, CA: Avalon Travel Publishing, 2008.

Pitcher, Don. *Moon Wyoming*. Berkeley, CA: Avalon Travel Publishing, 2006.

Root, Don. *Moon Idaho*. Berkeley, CA: Avalon Travel Publishing, 2004.

JACKSON HOLE AND GRAND TETON NATIONAL PARK

Good, John M., and Kenneth L. Pierce. *Interpreting the Landscape: Recent and Ongoing Geology of Grand Teton and Yellowstone National Parks*. Moose, WY: Grand Teton Association, www.grandteton-park.org, 1996. This attractive book has the latest geologic research on the parks and presents it in an understandable format with excellent illustrations.

Love, David D., John C. Reed, Jr., and Kenneth L. Pierce. *Creation of the Teton Landscape: the Geologic Story of Grand Teton National Park*. Moose, WY: Grand Teton Association, www.grandtetonpark.org, 2003. A small but authoritatively detailed guide to the geology of Jackson Hole and the Tetons.

History

Betts, Robert B. *Along the Ramparts of the Tetons: The Saga of Jackson Hole, Wyoming*. Boulder, CO: University Press of Colorado,

www.upcolorado.com, 1978. A substantial, detailed, and beautifully written book about the history of Jackson Hole.

Burt, Nathaniel. *Jackson Hole Journal*. Norman, OK: University of Oklahoma Press, www.oupress.com, 1983. Tales of growing up as a dude in Jackson Hole. Contains some very amusing stories.

Hayden, Elizabeth Wied, and Cynthia Nielsen. *Origins, A Guide to the Place Names of Grand Teton National Park and the Surrounding Area*. Moose, WY: Grand Teton Association, www.grandtetonpark.org, 1988. A guide to the obscure sources for place names in Grand Teton.

Huidekoper, Virginia. *The Early Days in Jackson Hole*. Moose, WY: Grand Teton Association, www.grandtetonpark.org, 1996. Filled with more than 100 photos from old-time Jackson Hole.

Righter, Robert W. *Crucible for Conservation: The Creation of Grand Teton National Park*. Boulder, CO: University Press of Colorado, www.upcolorado.com, 1982. The story of how the Tetons were spared through a half-century battle.

Thompson, Edith M., and William Leigh Thompson. *Beaver Dick: The Honor and the Heartbreak*. Laramie, WY: Jelm Mountain Press, 1982. A touching historical biography of Beaver Dick Leigh, one of the first white men to settle in Jackson Hole. Out of print.

Natural History

Carrighar, Sally. *One Day at Teton Marsh*. Lincoln, NE: University of Nebraska Press, www.unp.unl.edu, 1979. A classic natural history of life in a Jackson Hole marsh. Made into a movie by Walt Disney. Out of print.

Murie, Margaret, and Olaus Murie. *Wapiti Wilderness*. Boulder, CO: University Press of Colorado, www.upcolorado.com, 1986. The lives of two of America's most-loved conservationists in Jackson Hole and their work with elk.

Shaw, Richard J. *Plants of Grand Teton and Yellowstone National Parks*. Salt Lake City, UT: Wheelwright Press, 1981. Photos and descriptions of the most commonly found plants in the parks.

Vizgirdas, Ray S. *A Guide to Plants of Yellowstone and Grand Teton National Parks* Salt Lake City, UT: University of Utah Press, www.uofupress.com, 2007. The definitive guide to regional plants.

Travsky, Amber. *Mountain Biking Jackson Hole*. Guilford, CT: Globe Pequot Press, www .globepequot.com, 2001. Thirty-one rides in Jackson Hole, Grand Teton National Park, and surrounding areas.

Recreation

Craighead, Charles. *Day Hikes and Short Walks of Grand Teton National Park*. Moose, WY: Grand Teton Association, www .grandtetonpark.org, 2005. A handy little guide with up-to-date trail information and plenty of photos.

Dufy, Katy, and Darwin Wile. *Teton Trails*. Moose, WY: Grand Teton Association, www .grandtetonpark.org, 1995. A useful guide to more than 200 miles of trails in the park.

Jackson, Reynold G. *A Climber's Guide to the Teton Range*. Seattle, WA: Mountaineers Books, www.mountaineerbooks.org, 1996. The definitive (415 pages!) climbing guide for the Tetons.

Prax, Brian, and Mark Schultheis. *The Book: Guide to Mountain Biking in the Jackson Hole Area*. Jackson, WY: Prax Photography and Productions, 2001. This spiral-bound book is the most complete guide to local cycling options, and includes coverage on Teton Valley.

Rossiter, Richard. *Teton Classics: 50 Selected Climbs in Grand Teton National Park*.

Guilford, CT: Globe Pequot Press, www.globe pequot.com, 1994. A small and nicely illustrated guide to 50 climbing routes in the Tetons.

Schneider, Bill. *Best Easy Day Hikes Grand Teton*. Guilford, CT: Globe Pequot Press, www.globepequot.com, 2005.

Schneider, Bill. *Hiking Grand Teton National Park*. Guilford, CT: Globe Pequot Press, www.globepequot.com, 2005.

Stone, Robert. *Day Hikes in Grand Teton National Park and Jackson Hole*. Guilford, CT: Globe Pequot Press, www.globepequot .com, 2004.

Watters, Ron. *Winter Tales and Trails: Skiing, Snowshoeing and Snowboarding in Idaho, the Grand Tetons and Yellowstone National Park*. Pocatello, ID: Great Rift Press, 1997. A book that combines lucid writing on the area's rich history with guides to winter trails. More than 350 pages of details from an expert in the field. Out-of-date, but still useful.

Woods, Rebecca. *Jackson Hole Hikes*. Jackson, WY: White Willow Publishing, 1999. An excellent guide that includes trails in Grand Teton National Park and surrounding national forest areas. Easy to use and informative.

YELLOWSTONE NATIONAL PARK

Note: Several natural history and geology books encompass both Yellowstone and Grand Teton National Parks. See the preceding section on Jackson Hole and Grand Teton National Park for additional titles with overlapping coverage.

Geology

Bryan, Scott T. *The Geysers of Yellowstone*. Boulder, CO: University Press of Colorado, www.upcolorado.com, 2008. The definitive guide to more than 400 geysers and other geothermal features in Yellowstone.

Fritz, William J. *Roadside Geology of the Yellowstone Country*. Missoula, MT: Mountain Press Publishing Co., www.mountain-press .com, 1986. All of the park roads are covered in this easy-to-follow Yellowstone geology primer.

History

Bartlett, Richard A. *Yellowstone: A Wilderness Besieged*. Tucson, AZ: University of Arizona Press, www.uapress.arizona.edu, 1989. The history of Yellowstone and the fight to prevent its destruction by railroad magnates, concessioners, and others.

Haines, Aubrey L. *The Yellowstone Story: A History of Our First National Park*. Boulder, CO: University Press of Colorado, www.up colorado.com, 1996. A definitive two-volume history of the park. Volume one (history up to the park's establishment) is the most interesting.

Janetski, Joel C. *Indians of Yellowstone Park*. Salt Lake City, UT: University of Utah Press, www.upress.utah.edu, 1987. A general overview of the earliest settlers in Yellowstone and later conflicts with incoming whites.

Milstein, Michael. *Yellowstone Album: 125 Years of America's Best Idea*. Billings, MT: The Billings Gazette, www.billingsgazette.com, 1996. A delightful book filled with historical photographs, along with photos of postcards, souvenirs, and other tourist artifacts.

Schreier, Carl (ed.). *Yellowstone: Selected Photographs 1870–1960*. Moose, WY: Homestead Publishing, 1989. An outstanding collection of historical photographs from the park. Now out of print.

Whittlesey, Lee H. *Yellowstone Place Names: Mirrors of History*. Helena, MT: Montana State Historical Press, www.montana historicalsociety.org, 2006. For the Trivial Pursuit enthusiast; 290 pages of detailed descriptions with every possible name from every obscure corner of Yellowstone.

Natural History

Craighead, Frank J. *Track of the Grizzly*. San Francisco, CA: Sierra Club Books, www .sierraclub.org, 1982. The life of grizzlies in Yellowstone, by one of the most famous bear researchers. Dated, but still a classic.

Halfpenny, James C. *Yellowstone Wolves in the Wild*. Helena, MT: Riverbend Publishing, www.riverbendpublishing.com, 2003. An excellent look at the reintroduction of wolves and their lives. It's scientific in scope and nicely illustrated with photos.

Krakell, Dean, II. *Downriver: A Yellowstone Journey*. San Francisco, CA: Sierra Club Books, www.sierraclub.org, 1987. An extraordinarily moving journey down the magnificent Yellowstone River.

McEneaney, Terry. *Birds of Yellowstone*. Boulder, CO: Roberts Rinehart, www.roberts-rinehart.com, 1988. A guide to Yellowstone birds and where to find them.

Reese, Rick and Terry Tempest Williams. *Greater Yellowstone: The National Park and Adjacent Wildlands*. Helena, MT: American Geographic Publishing, 1991. An attractive book with considerable information on ecological conditions in one of the Lower 48's largest intact ecosystems. Out of print.

Schullery, Paul (ed.). *Yellowstone Bear Tales*. Boulder, CO: Roberts Rinehart Publishers, www.roberts-rinehart.com, 2001. First-person stories of bear encounters from a range of travelers—including President Theodore Roosevelt—between 1880 and 1950.

Schullery, Paul. *Searching for Yellowstone*. New York: Houghton Mifflin Co., www.hmco .com, 1997. An eloquently written book by a longtime park ranger whose knowledge of the park goes far beyond the hype. Must-reading for anyone who cares about Yellowstone.

Shaw, Richard J. *Wildflowers of Yellowstone and Grand Teton National Parks*. Salt Lake

City, UT: Wheelwright Press, 1992. Color photos and short descriptions of more than 100 wildflowers in the Greater Yellowstone Ecosystem.

Smith, Douglas W. and Gary Ferguson. *Decade of the Wolf: Returning the Wild to Yellowstone.* Guilford, CT: The Lyons Press, www.lyons press.com, 2005. The story of how wolves were reintroduced to Yellowstone and how it changed the park, as told by a naturalist at the center of the project.

Wuerthner, George. *Yellowstone: A Visitor's Companion.* Mechanicsburg, PA: Stackpole Books, www.stackpolebooks.com, 1992. A detailed natural history of Yellowstone.

Recreation

Anderson, Roger and Carol Shively Anderson. *A Ranger's Guide to Yellowstone Day Hikes.* Helena, MT: *Montana Magazine,* www .montanamagazine.com, 2000. One of the best books for short park hikes.

Bach, Orville E., Jr. *Hiking the Yellowstone Backcountry.* San Francisco, CA: Sierra Club Books, www.sierraclub.org, 1998. A pocket-size guide to hiking, canoeing, biking, and skiing in the park.

Butler, Susan Springer. *Scenic Driving Yellowstone and Grand Teton National Parks.* Guilford, CT: Globe Pequot Press, www .globepequot.com, 2006.

Carter, Tom. *Day Hiking Yellowstone.* Garland, TX: Dayhiking Press, 1991. A pocket-size guide to 20 day-treks, coordinated with the Trails Illustrated topographic maps.

Henry, Jeff. *Yellowstone Winter Guide.* Boulder, CO: Roberts Rinehart Publishers, www .roberts-rinehart.com, 1998. A detailed guide to visiting Yellowstone in the winter; especially good for cross-country skiers.

Lilly, Bud, and Paul Schullery. *Bud Lilly's Guide to Fly Fishing the New West.* Portland, OR: Frank Amato Publications, 2000. The authoritative fishing source from the father of Western trout fishing.

Marschall, Mark C. *Yellowstone Trails: A Hiking Guide.* Yellowstone National Park, WY: The Yellowstone Association, www.yellow stoneassociation.org, 1999. An excellent, detailed guidebook to the park's 1,000 miles of hiking trails.

Nelson, Don. *Paddling Yellowstone and Grand Teton National Parks.* Guilford, CT: Globe Pequot Press, www.globepequot.com, 1999.

Parks, Richard. *Fishing Yellowstone National Park.* Guilford, CT: Globe Pequot Press, www.globepequot.com, 2007. One of several authoritative guides, this one provides details on fly- and lure fishing, along with descriptions of more than 100 sites.

Schneider, Bill. *Hiking Yellowstone National Park.* Guilford, CT: Globe Pequot Press, www.globepequot.com, 2003. Clear maps and helpful trail profiles make this the most useful book for anyone heading out on Yellowstone hiking routes. Contains descriptions of more than 100 trails.

Stone, Robert. *Day Hikes in Yellowstone National Park and Jackson Hole.* Guilford, CT: Globe Pequot Press, www.globepequot.com, 2005.

Varley, John D., and Paul D. Schullery. *Yellowstone Fishes: Ecology, History, and Angling in the Park.* Mechanicsburg, PA: Stackpole Books, www.stackpolebooks.com, 1998. The comprehensive guide to the fish of Yellowstone, written by two authorities in the field.

CODY AND SHOSHONE NATIONAL FOREST

Cook, Jeannie (ed.). *Buffalo Bill's Town in the Rockies: A Pictorial History of Cody, Wyoming.* Cody, WY: Park County Historical Society, 1996. A photographic visit to Cody's interesting past.

Rosa, Joseph G., and Robin May. *Buffalo Bill and His Wild West.* Lawrence, KS: University Press of Kansas, www.kansaspress.ku.edu, 1989. One of the newer books on Buffalo Bill, with a somewhat revisionist take on his life and times. Rich in detail on Cody's Wild West show.

Russell, Don. *The Lives and Legends of Buffalo Bill.* Norman, OK: University of Oklahoma Press, www.oupress.com, 1979. The most complete biography on the life of Buffalo Bill Cody.

Stone, Robert. *Day Hikes in the Beartooth Mountains.* Guilford, CT: Globe Pequot Press, www.globepequot.com, 2006.

Internet Resources

Yellowstone National Park
www.nps.gov/yell
A fine starting point for any exploration of the Yellowstone area.

Grand Teton National Park
www.nps.gov/grte
This official Park Service site has an abundance of background information about Grand Teton.

National Elk Refuge
www.fws.gov/nationalelkrefuge
This website details Jackson Hole's famous refuge with its picturesque sleigh rides among the elk.

U.S. Forest Service
www.fs.fed.us
This federal agency manages land within several national forests in the Greater Yellowstone Ecosystem. These include Bridger-Teton National Forest, www.fs.fed.us/r4/btnf, Shoshone National Forest, www.fs.fed.us/r2/shoshone, Caribou-Targhee National Forest, www.fs.fed.us/r4/caribou-targhee, Gallatin National Forest, www.fs.fed.us/r1/gallatin, Beaverhead-Deerlodge National Forest, www.fs.fed.us/r1/bdnf, and Custer National Forest, www.fs.fed.us/r1/custer.

Recreation.gov
www.recreation.gov
Head here to book reservations at regional Forest Service campgrounds.

Wyoming Travel & Tourism Division
www.wyomingtourism.org
The state's tourism site has everything you'd expect in the way of an interactive visitor center and much more.

Wyoming Department of Transportation
www.wyoroad.info
This website has updated road conditions, webcams, and details on road construction projects; call 511 for the phone version.

Wyoming Public Radio
www.wyomingpublicradio.net
A good starting place for information on public radio around Wyoming.

Wyoming Homestay & Outdoor Adventures
www.wyomingbnb-ranchrec.com
Better known as WHOA, this organization maintains links to several dozen bed-and-breakfasts, dude ranches, guest cabins, and other distinctive lodging options.

Wyoming Game and Fish Department
http://gf.state.wy.us
Head to this website for details on fishing licenses and seasons, along with current issues affecting fish. You can even download application forms.

Wyoming Fishing Network
www.wyomingfishing.net
An exceptionally useful online source for Wyoming anglers.

Wyoming Outfitters and Guides Association
www.wyoga.org
Interested in a backcountry pack trip? Visit this website to find outfitters for the area you plan to visit.

Wyoming Dude Rancher's Association
www.wyomingdra.com
This statewide organization's homepage has links to the websites of 30 different Wyoming guest ranches.

National Museum of Wildlife Art
www.wildlifeart.org
This large Jackson museum exhibits the works of many internationally recognized artists.

Jackson Hole Chamber of Commerce
www.jacksonholechamber.com
This website is a fine starting point for travel to Jackson, with a multitude of weblinks to local businesses.

Grand Targhee Ski Resort
www.grandtarghee.com
This resort on the west side of the Tetons is a favorite of powderhounds.

Jackson Hole Gallery Association
www.jacksonholegalleries.com
A fine Web source for more than 30 Jackson art galleries.

Jackson Hole Mountain Resort
www.jacksonhole.com
The big one, this is the primary ski and snowboard destination in Jackson Hole.

Snow King Resort
www.snowking.com
Jackson's town hill, this small ski area is accessible and surprisingly challenging.

Jackson Hole Traveler
www.jacksonholetraveler.com
This private website is nicely designed and packed with useful information and links.

West Yellowstone Chamber of Commerce
www.westyellowstonechamber.com
The most complete Web source for West Yellowstone, Montana.

Gardiner Chamber of Commerce
www.gardinerchamber.com
Details on the little edge-of-Yellowstone town of Gardiner, Montana.

Buffalo Bill Historical Center
www.bbhc.org
Cody's famous museum now covers an incredible 300,000 square feet, making it easily the most impressive museum in the region.

Park County Travel Council
www.yellowstonecountry.org
This regional tourism agency has a great website for travelers heading into Cody.

Dubois Chamber of Commerce
www.duboiswyoming.org
This is the best Web source for information on the Dubois area.

Cooke City, Colter Pass, and Silver Gate Chamber of Commerce
www.cookecitychamber.org
Head here for details on these rustic and remote Montana towns on the northeast corner of Yellowstone National Park.

Webcams
www.jacksonholenet.com/webcams
Check out the current activity at Old Faithful, Jackson's Town Square, and a multitude of other places with live webcams.

Don Pitcher
www.donpitcher.com
Author Don Pitcher's website provides details on all his books and photographic projects, plus Web links to many of the places listed in this book.

Index

List of Maps

Acknowledgments

For Aziza Bali
Who still loves cats, hamsters, and Jumping Horse stories
May you always chase snowflakes, hockey pucks, and dreams
May you never lose your sense of wonder

It would be impossible to thank all those who helped me with this fourth edition of *Moon Yellowstone & Grand Teton,* but a number of individuals deserve a round of applause. A big thank you goes to the following chambers of commerce people and federal employees who helped open doors to their hometowns or reviewed the manuscript for errors: Heather Faulk and Niki Panos in Jackson, Lee Anne Ackerman and Claudia Wade in Cody, Jackie Skaggs in Grand Teton National Park, Keren Walters in Gardiner, Stacy Simonet and Heather Kopf in Driggs, Julie Kosmata Elliott in Dubois, Donna Rowland in Cooke City, and Lee Haines at Buffalo Bill Historical Center.

I also wish to thank the owners of Cody Legacy Inn, Angler's Inn (Jackson), and Elk Country Inn (Jackson) for their generous assistance with lodging. A special thanks goes to Tom and Mona Mesereau of Mesereau Communications for providing Yellowstone accommodations.

This book was shepherded through the production process by my helpful editor, Michelle Cadden. Thanks to her and everyone else at Avalon Travel for getting this book into your hands.

I offer special gratitude to my wife, Karen Shemet, and our children, Aziza and Rio, for keeping me grounded while I researched and wrote this edition. It's even more fun visiting Yellowstone with wide-eyed kids, even if they find bugs and frogs more interesting than wolves!

www.moon.com

DESTINATIONS | ACTIVITIES | BLOGS | MAPS | BOOKS

MOON.COM is ready to help plan your next trip! Filled with fresh trip ideas and strategies, author interviews, informative travel blogs, a detailed map library, and descriptions of all the Moon guidebooks, Moon.com is all you need to get out and explore the world—or even places in your own backyard. While at Moon.com, sign up for our monthly e-newsletter for updates on new releases, travel tips, and expert advice from our on-the-go Moon authors. As always, when you travel with Moon, expect an experience that is uncommon and truly unique.

MAP SYMBOLS

▦ Expressway	**(** Highlight	✗ Airfield	⚓ Golf Course
Primary Road	○ City/Town	✈ Airport	**P** Parking Area
Secondary Road	◉ State Capital	▲ Mountain	⬭ Archaeological Site
Unpaved Road	⊛ National Capital	✚ Unique Natural Feature	
Trail	★ Point of Interest		⛪ Church
Ferry	• Accommodation	🌿 Waterfall	🔲 Gas Station
Railroad	▾ Restaurant/Bar	▲ Park	Glacier
Pedestrian Walkway	▪ Other Location	**T** Trailhead	Mangrove
Stairs	⋀ Campground	🎿 Skiing Area	Reef
			Swamp

CONVERSION TABLES

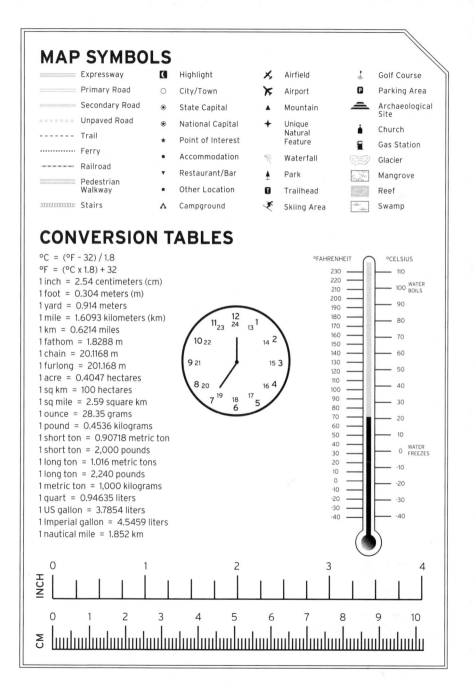

°C = (°F - 32) / 1.8
°F = (°C x 1.8) + 32
1 inch = 2.54 centimeters (cm)
1 foot = 0.304 meters (m)
1 yard = 0.914 meters
1 mile = 1.6093 kilometers (km)
1 km = 0.6214 miles
1 fathom = 1.8288 m
1 chain = 20.1168 m
1 furlong = 201.168 m
1 acre = 0.4047 hectares
1 sq km = 100 hectares
1 sq mile = 2.59 square km
1 ounce = 28.35 grams
1 pound = 0.4536 kilograms
1 short ton = 0.90718 metric ton
1 short ton = 2,000 pounds
1 long ton = 1.016 metric tons
1 long ton = 2,240 pounds
1 metric ton = 1,000 kilograms
1 quart = 0.94635 liters
1 US gallon = 3.7854 liters
1 Imperial gallon = 4.5459 liters
1 nautical mile = 1.852 km

**MOON YELLOWSTONE
& GRAND TETON**

Avalon Travel
a member of the Perseus Books Group
1700 Fourth Street
Berkeley, CA 94710, USA
www.moon.com

Editor: Michelle Cadden
Series Manager: Sabrina Young
Copy Editor: NaNa' Stoelzle
Graphics Coordinator: Elizabeth Jang
Production Coordinator: Elizabeth Jang
Cover Designer: Elizabeth Jang
Map Editor: Kevin Anglin
Cartographers: Kat Bennett, Chris Markiewicz,
    Jon Niemczyk
Director of Cartography: Mike Morgenfeld
Indexer: Rachel Kuhn

ISBN-13: 978-1-59880-160-6
ISSN: 1542-8850

Printing History
1st Edition – April 2000
4th Edition – May 2009
5 4 3

KEEPING CURRENT

If you have a favorite gem you'd like to see included in the next edition, or see anything
that needs updating, clarification, or correction, please drop us a line. Send your
comments via email to feedback@moon.com, or use the address above.